GATE PREP SERIES

GATE

Graduate Aptitude Test in Engineering

2022

D1753442

22 Years

Chapter-Wise Solved Papers

(2000-2021)

Mathematics

G. K. PUBLICATIONS (P) LTD.

Title : GATE 2022 - Mathematics - 22 Years Chapter-wise Solved Papers 2000-2021

Language : English

Editor's Name : Vinit Garg

Typeset & Published by :

Career Launcher Infrastructure (P) Ltd.

A-45, Mohan Cooperative Industrial Area, Near Mohan Estate Metro Station, New Delhi - 110044

Marketed by :

G.K. Publications (P) Ltd.

Plot No. 9A, Sector-27A, Mathura Road, Faridabad, Haryana-121003

ISBN : **978-93-91061-22-7**

Printer's Details : Made in India, New Delhi.

GATE
Mathematics

Contents

Solved Papers (Chapter-Wise)

Verbal Ability

Numerical Ability

5.	**Permutations and Combinations & Probability**	**5.1 - 5.4**	5. **Algebra**	**5.1 - 5.14**
	MCQ Type Questions	5.1	*Answers*	5.7
	Numerical Type Questions	5.2	*Explanations*	5.8
	– *Answers*	5.2	6. **Functional Analysis**	**6.1 - 6.14**
	– *Explanations*	5.3	*Answers*	6.9
6.	**Miscellaneous**	**6.1 - 6.6**	*Explanations*	6.9
	MCQ Type Questions	6.1	7. **Numerical Analysis**	**7.1 - 7.22**
	Numerical Type Questions	6.3	*Answers*	7.9
	– *Answers*	6.4	*Explanations*	7.10
	– *Explanations*	6.4	8. **Partial Differential Equations**	**8.1 - 8.18**

Mathematics

			Answers	8.9
			Explanations	8.9
1.	**Linear Algebra**	**1.1 - 1.28**	9. **Topology**	**9.1 - 9.9**
	~~*Answers*~~	1.12	*Answers*	9.6
	Explanations	1.13	*Explanations*	9.7
2.	**Complex Analysis**	**2.1 - 2.22**	10. **Probability & Statistics**	**10.1 - 10.18**
	Answers	2.9	*Answers*	10.13
	Explanations	2.10	*Explanations*	10.13
3.	**Real Analysis**	**3.1 - 3.28**	11. **Linear Programming**	**11.1 - 11.17**
	Answers	3.15	*Answers*	11.10
	Explanations	3.16	*Explanations*	11.11
4.	**Ordinary Differential Equations**	**4.1-4.22**	● **Solved Paper 2017**	**1 – 15**
	Answers	4.9	● **Solved Paper 2018**	**1 – 15**
	Explanations	4.10	● **Solved Paper 2019**	**1 – 16**
			● **Solved Paper 2020**	**1 – 18**
			● **Solved Paper 2021**	**1 – 21**

GATE

Graduate Aptitude Test in Engineering

IIT Institutes

GATE 2021 conducted by
Indian Institute of Technology, Mumbai

GATE 2022 will be conducted by
Indian Institute of Technology, Kharagpur

Indian Institute of Technology, Delhi

Indian Institute of Technology, Chennai

Indian Institute of Technology, Guwahati

Indian Institute of Technology, Roorkee

Indian Institute of Technology, Kanpur

Preface

The Graduate Aptitude Test in Engineering (GATE) is an online exam conducted by the IITs for admissions to PG courses in IITs, IISc Bangalore, NITs and many state run universities as well as private universities. Also there are more than 37 PSUs that use GATE score for recruitments. A large number of corporates are also using GATE score as a tool to screen students for placements.

GK Publications is well known as the "publisher of choice" to students preparing for GATE and other technical examinations in the country. We published the first set of books in 1994 when GATE exam, both objective and conventional, was conducted in the paper and pencil environment, and used as a check point for entry to post graduate courses in IITs and IISCs. At that time, students had little access to technology and relied mainly on instructor led learning followed by practice with books available for these examinations.

A lot has changed since then!

Today, GATE is conducted in an online only mode with multiple choice and numerical based questions. The score is valid for three years and is used not only for post graduate courses but is also used by major PSUs for recruitment. Today's students have easy access to technology and the concept of a monologue within the classroom has changed to dialogue where students come prepared with concepts and then discuss topics. They learn a lot of things on the go with their mobile devices and practice for mock tests online.

We, as a leading publisher of GATE books, have also embraced change. Today, our books are no more guides and papers only but come with a fully supported mobile app and a web portal. The mobile app provides access to video lectures, short tests and regular updates about the exam. The web portal in additional to what is available on the app provides full length mock tests to mimic the actual exam and help you gauge your level of preparedness. The combination of practice content in print, video lectures, and short and full length tests on mobile and web makes this product a complete courseware for GATE preparation.

This book includes previous years GATE questions along with detailed solution of each question for better understanding. It will help the GATE aspirants to know an idea about the pattern of questions asked in GATE examination.

We also know that improvement is a never ending process and hence we welcome your suggestions and feedback or spelling and technical errors if any. Please write to us at gkp@gkpublications.com

We hope that our small effort will help you prepare well for the examination.

We wish you all the best!

GK Publications Pvt. Ltd.

About GATE

The Graduate Aptitude Test in Engineering (GATE) conducted by IISc and IITs has emerged as one of the bench mark tests for engineering and science aptitude in facilitating admissions for higher education (M.Tech./Ph.D.) in IITs, IISc and various other Institutes/Universities/Laboratories in India. With the standard and high quality of the GATE examination in 27 disciplines of engineering and science, Humanities and Social Sciences subjects, it identifies the candidate's understanding of a subject and aptitude and eligibility for higher studies. During the last few years, GATE score is also being used as one of the criteria for recruitment in Government Organizations such as Cabinet Secretariat, and National/State Public Sector Undertakings in India. Because of the importance of the GATE examination, the number of candidates taking up GATE exams has increased tremendously. GATE exams are conducted by the IITs and IISc as a computer based test having multiple choice questions and numerical answer type questions. The questions are mostly fundamental, concept based and thought provoking. From 2017 onwards GATE Exam is being held in Bangladesh, Ethiopia, Nepal, Singapore, Sri Lanka and United Arab Emirates. An Institute with various nationalities in its campus widens the horizons of an academic environment. A foreign student brings with him/her a great diversity, culture and wisdom to share. Many GATE qualified candidates are paid scholarships/assistantship, especially funded by Ministry of Human Resources Development, Government of India and by other Ministries. IIT, Kharagpur is the Organizing Institute for GATE 2022.

Why GATE?

Admission to Post Graduate and Doctoral Programmes

Admission to postgraduate programmes with MHRD and some other government scholarships/ assistantships in engineering colleges/institutes is open to those who qualify through GATE. GATE qualified candidates with Bachelor's degree in Engineering/Technology/Architecture or Master's degree in any branch of Science/Mathematics/Statistics/Computer Applications are eligible for admission to Master/Doctoral programmes in Engineering/Technology/Architecture as well as for Doctoral programmes in relevant branches of Science with MHRD or other government scholarships/ assistantships. Candidates with Master's degree in Engineering/Technology/Architecture may seek admission to relevant Ph.D programmes with scholarship/assistantship without appearing in the GATE examination.

Financial Assistance

A valid GATE score is essential for obtaining financial assistance during Master's programs and direct Doctoral programs in Engineering/Technology/Architecture, and Doctoral programs in relevant branches of Science in Institutes supported by the MHRD or other Government agencies. As per the directives of the MHRD, the following procedure is to be adopted for admission to the post-graduate programs (Master's and Doctoral) with MHRD scholarship/assistantship. Depending upon the norms adopted by a specific institute or department of the Institute, a candidate may be admitted directly into a course based on his/her performance in GATE only **or** based on his/her performance in GATE **and** an admission test/interview conducted by the department to which he/she has applied **and/or** the candidate's academic record. If the candidate is to be selected through test/interview for post-graduate programs, a minimum of 70% weightage will be given to the performance in GATE and the remaining 30% weightage will be given to the candidate's performance in test/interview and/or academic record, as per MHRD guidelines. The admitting institutes could however prescribe a minimum passing percentage of marks in the test/interview. Some colleges/institutes specify GATE qualification as the mandatory requirement even for admission without MHRD scholarship/assistantship.

To avail of the financial assistance (scholarship), the candidate must first secure admission to a program in these Institutes, by a procedure that could vary from institute to institute. Qualification in GATE is also a minimum requirement to apply for various fellowships awarded by many Government organizations. Candidates are advised to seek complete details of admission procedures and availability of MHRD scholarship/assistantship from the concerned admitting institution. The criteria for postgraduate admission with scholarship/assistantship could be different for different institutions. The management of the post-graduate scholarship/assistantship is also the responsibility of the admitting institution. Similarly, reservation of seats under different categories is as per the policies and norms prevailing at the admitting institution and Government of India rules. *GATE offices will usually not entertain any enquiry about admission, reservation of seats and / or award of scholarship / assistantship.*

PSU Recruitments

As many as 37 PSUs are using GATE score for recruitment. It is likely that more number of PSUs may start doing so by next year. Below is the list of PSUs:

MDL, BPCL, GAIL, NLC LTD, CEL, Indian Oil, HPCL, NBPC, NECC, BHEL, WBSEDCL, NTPC, ONGC, Oil India, Power Grid, Cabinet Secretariat, Govt. of India, BAARC, NFL, IPR, PSPCL, PSTCL, DRDO, OPGC Ltd., THDC India Ltd., BBNL, RITES, IRCON, GHECL, NHAI, KRIBHCO, Mumbai Railway Vikas Corporation Ltd. (MRVC Ltd.), National Textile Corporation, Coal India Ltd., BNPM, AAI, NALCO, EdCIL India.

Important :

1. Admissions in IITs/IISc or other Institutes for M.Tech./Ph.D. through GATE scores shall be advertised separately by the Institutes and GATE does not take the responsibility of admissions.
2. Cabinet Secretariat has decided to recruit officers for the post of Senior Field Officer (Tele) (From GATE papers of EC, CS, PH), Senior Research Officer (Crypto) (From GATE papers of EC, CS, MA), Senior Research Officer (S&T) (From GATE papers EC, CS, CY, PH, AE, BT) in the Telecommunication Cadre, Cryptographic Cadre and Science & Technology Unit respectively of Cabinet Secretariat. The details of the scheme of recruitment shall be published in National Newspaper/Employment News by the concerned authority.
3. Some PSUs in India have expressed their interest to utilize GATE scores for their recruitment purpose. The Organizations who intend to utilize GATE scores shall make separate advertisement for this purpose in Newspapers etc.

Who Can Appear for GATE?

Eligibility for GATE

Before starting the application process, the candidate must ensure that he/she meets the eligibility criteria of GATE given in Table.

Eligibility Criteria for GATE 2022

Degree/Program	Qualifying Degree/Examination	Description of Eligible Candidates	Expected Year of Completion
B.E. / B.Tech. / B.Pharm.	Bachelor's degree in Engineering / Technology (4 years after 10+2 or 3 years after B.Sc. / Diploma in Engineering / Technology)	Currently in the 3rd year or higher grade or already completed	2022
B. Arch.	Bachelor's degree of Architecture (5- year course) / Naval Architecture (4- year course) / Planning (4- year course)	Currently in the 3rd year or higher grade or already completed	2023 (for 5-year program), 2022 (for 4-year program)
B.Sc. (Research) / B.S.	Bachelor's degree in Science (Post-Diploma/4 years after 10+2)	Currently in the 3rd year or higher grade or already completed	2022
Pharm. D. (after 10+2)	6 years degree program, consisting of internship or residency training, during third year onwards	Currently in the 3rd/4th/5th/6th year or already completed	2024
M.B.B.S.	Degree holders of M.B.B.S. and those who are in the 5th/6th/7th semester or higher semester of such programme.	5th, 6th, 7th or higher semester or already completed	2022
M. Sc. / M.A. / MCA or equivalent	Master's degree in any branch of Arts/Science/Mathematics/Statistics/ Computer Applications or equivalent	Currently in the first year or higher or already Completed	2022
Int. M.E./ M.Tech. (Post-B.Sc.)	Post-B.Sc Integrated Master's degree programs in Engineering/ Technology (4-year program)	Currently in the 1st / 2nd/3rd/4th year or already completed	2024
Int. M.E./ M.Tech. or Dual Degree (after Diploma or 10+2)	Integrated Master's degree program or Dual Degree program in Engineering/Technology (5-year program)	Currently in the 3rd /4th/5th year or alreadycompleted	2023
B.Sc. / B.A. / B.Com.	Bachelor degree in any branch of Science / Arts / Commerce (3 years program)	Currently in the 3rd year or already completed	2021
Int. M.Sc. / Int. B.S. / M.S.	Integrated M.Sc. or 5-year integrated B.S.-M.S. program	Currently in the 3rd year or higher or already completed	2022
Professional Society Examinations (equivalent to B.E. / B.Tech. / B.Arch.)	B.E./B.Tech./B.Arch. equivalent examinations of Professional Societies, recognized by MoE/UPSC/AICTE (e.g. AMIE by Institution of Engineers-India, AMICE by the Institute of Civil Engineers-India and so on)	Completed Section A or equivalent of such professional courses	NA

In case a candidate has passed one of the qualifying examinations as mentioned above in 2020 or earlier, the candidate has to submit the degree certificate / provisional certificate / course completion certificate / professional certificate / membership certificate issued by the society or institute. In case, the candidate is expected to complete one of the qualifying criteria in 2022 or later as mentioned above, he/she has to submit a certificate from Principal or a copy of marks card for section A of AMIE.

Certificate From Principal

Candidates who have to submit a certificate from their college Principal have to obtain one from his/ her institution beforehand and upload the same during the online submission of the application form.

Candidates With Backlogs

Candidates, who have appeared in the final semester/year exam in 2022, but with a backlog (arrears/ failed subjects) in any of the papers in their qualifying degree should upload a copy of any one of the mark sheets of the final year,

OR

obtain a declaration from their Principal along with the signature and seal beforehand and upload the same during the online submission of the application form.

GATE Structure

Structure of GATE

GATE 2022 will be conducted on 27 subjects (papers). Table below shows the list of papers and paper codes for GATE 2022. A candidate is allowed to appear in ANY ONE or UP TO TWO papers of the GATE examination. However, note that the combination of TWO papers in which a candidate can appear MUST be from the pre-defined list as given in Table. Also note that for a paper running in multiple sessions, a candidate will be mapped to appear for the examination in one of the sessions ONLY.

List of GATE Papers and Corresponding Codes

GATE Paper	Code	GATE Paper	Code
Aerospace Engineering	AE	Instrumentation Engineering	IN
Agricultural Engineering	AG	Mathematics	MA
Architecture and Planning	AR	Mechanical Engineering	ME
Bio-medical Engineering	BM	Mining Engineering	MN
Biotechnology	BT	Metallurgical Engineering	MT
Civil Engineering	CE	Petroleum Engineering	PE
Chemical Engineering	CH	Physics	PH
Computer Science and Information Technology	CS	Production and Industrial Engineering	PI
Chemistry	CY	Statistics	ST
Electronics and Communication Engineering	EC	Textile Engineering and Fibre Science	TF
Electrical Engineering	EE	Engineering Sciences	XE*
Environmental Science & Engineering	ES	Humanities & Social Sciences	XH**
Ecology and Evolution	EY	Life Sciences	XL***
Geology and Geophysics	GG		

Note: *Environmental Science and Engineering (ES) and Humanities and Social Sciences (XH) are two new papers introduced in GATE 2022.*

*XE Paper Sections	Code	**XH Paper Sections	Code	***XL Paper Sections	Code
Engineering Mathematics (Compulsory) (15 marks)	A	Reasoning and Comprehension (Compulsory) (25 marks)	B1	Chemistry (Compulsory) (25 marks)	P
Any TWO optional Sections (2x35 = 70 marks)		Any ONE optional Section (60 marks)		Any TWO optional Sections (2x30 = 60 marks)	
Fluid Mechanics	B	Economics	C1	Biochemistry	Q
Materials Science	C	English	C2	Botany	R
Solid Mechanics	D	Linguistics	C3	Microbiology	S
Thermodynamics	E	Philosophy	C4	Zoology	T
Polymer Science and Engineering	F	Psychology	C5	Food Technology	U
Food Technology	G	Sociology	C6		
Atmospheric and Oceanic Sciences	H				

*XE (Engineering Sciences), **XH (Humanities & Social Sciences), ***XL (Life Sciences), papers are of general nature and will be comprised of Sections listed in the above table

Note: *Each subject/paper is of total 100 marks. General Aptitude (GA) section of 15 marks is common for all papers. Hence remaining 85 marks are for the respective subject/paper code.*

Combination of Two Papers Allowed to Appear in GATE 2022 (subject to availability of infrastructure and schedule)

Code of The First (Primary) Paper	Codes of Papers Allowed as The Second Paper
AE	XE
AG	ES
AR	CE
BM	BT / XL
BT	BM / XL
CE	AR / ES
CH	CY / PE / XE
CS	MA
CY	CH / XL
EC	IN / PH
EE	IN
ES	AG / CE
EY	XL
GG	MN / PE / PH
IN	EC / EE / PH
MA	CS / PH / ST
ME	XE
MN	GG / XE
MT	PH / XE
PE	CH / GG / XE
PH	EC / GG / IN / MA / MT / ST
PI	XE
ST	MA / PH
TF	XE
XE	AE / CH / ME / MN / MT / PE / PI / TF
XH	----
XL	BM / BT / CY / EY

General Aptitude Questions

All the papers will have a few questions that test the General Aptitude (Language and Analytical Skills), apart from the core subject of the paper.

Duration and Examination Type

All the papers of the GATE 2022 examination will be for 3 hours duration and they consist of 65 questions for a total of 100 marks. Since the examination is an ONLINE computer based test (CBT), at the end of the stipulated time (3-hours), the computer screen will automatically close the examination inhibiting any further action.

Candidates will be permitted to occupy their allotted seats 40 minutes before the scheduled start of the examination. Candidates can login and start reading the instructions 20 minutes before the start of examination. The late login time (if any) recorded by the computer system MUST NOT be beyond 30 minutes from the actual starting time of the examination. Under NO circumstances, will a candidate be permitted to login after 30 minutes from the actual examination starting time. Candidates will NOT be permitted to leave the examination hall before the end of the examination.

Pattern of Question Papers

GATE 2022 may contain questions of THREE different types in all the papers:

(i) **Multiple Choice Questions (MCQ)** carrying 1 or 2 marks each, in all the papers and sections. These questions are objective in nature, and each will have choice of four answers, out of which ONLY ONE choice is correct.

Negative Marking for Wrong Answers: For a wrong answer chosen in a MCQ, there will be negative marking. For 1-mark MCQ, 1/3 mark will be deducted for a wrong answer. Likewise, for 2-mark MCQ, 2/3 mark will be deducted for a wrong answer.

(ii) **Multiple Select Questions (MSQ)** carrying 1 or 2 marks each in all the papers and sections. These questions are objective in nature, and each will have choice of four answers, out of which ONE or MORE than ONE choice(s) is / are correct.

Note: There is NO negative marking for a wrong answer in MSQ questions. However, there is NO partial credit for choosing partially correct combinations of choices or any single wrong choice.

(iii) **Numerical Answer Type (NAT)** Questions carrying 1 or 2 marks each in most of the papers and sections. For these questions, the answer is a signed real number, which needs to be entered by the candidate using the virtual numeric keypad on the monitor (keyboard of the computer will be disabled). No choices will be shown for these types of questions. The answer can be a number such as 10 or –10 (an integer only). The answer may be in decimals as well, for example, 10.1 (one decimal) or 10.01 (two decimals) or –10.001 (three decimals). These questions will be mentioned with, up to which decimal places, the candidates need to present the answer. Also, for some NAT type problems an appropriate range will be considered while evaluating these questions so that the candidate is not unduly penalized due to the usual round-off errors. Candidates are advised to do the rounding off at the end of the calculation (not in between steps). Wherever required and possible, it is better to give NAT answer up to a maximum of three decimal places.

Note: *There is NO negative marking for a wrong answer in NAT questions.*
Also, there is NO partial credit in NAT questions.

Marking Scheme – Distribution of Marks and Questions

General Aptitude (GA) Questions

In all papers, GA questions carry a total of 15 marks. The GA section includes 5 questions carrying 1-mark each (sub-total 5 marks) and 5 questions carrying 2-marks each (sub-total 10 marks).

Question Papers other than GG, XE, XH and XL

These papers would contain 25 questions carrying 1-mark each (sub-total 25 marks) and 30 questions carrying 2-marks each (sub-total 60 marks) consisting of some MCQ type questions, while the remaining may be MSQ and / or NAT questions.

GG (Geology and Geophysics) Paper

Apart from the General Aptitude (GA) section, the GG question paper consists of two parts: Part A and Part B. Part A is compulsory for all the candidates. Part B contains two sections: Section 1 (Geology) and Section 2 (Geophysics). Candidates will have to attempt questions in Part A and questions in either Section 1 or Section 2 of Part B. The choice of Section 1 OR Section 2 of Part B has to be made at the time of online registration in GOAPS. At the examination hall, candidate cannot request for change of section.

Part A consists of 25 questions carrying 1-mark each (sub-total 25 marks and some of these will be MSQ and/or numerical answer type questions while remaining questions will be MCQ type). Either section of Part B (Section 1 and Section 2) consists of 30 questions carrying 2-marks each (sub-total 60 marks and some of these will be MSQ and/or numerical answer type questions while remaining questions will be MCQ type).

XE Paper (Engineering Sciences)

A candidate appearing in the XE paper has to answer the following:

- GA – General Aptitude carrying a total of 15 marks.
- Section A – Engineering Mathematics (Compulsory): This section contains 11 questions carrying a total of 15 marks: 7 questions carrying 1-mark each (sub-total 7 marks), and 4 questions carrying 2-marks each (sub-total 8 marks). Some questions will be of numerical answer type while remaining questions will be MCQ type.
- Any two of XE Sections B to H: The choice of two sections from B to H can be made during the examination after viewing the questions. Only TWO optional sections can be answered at a time. A candidate wishing to change midway of the examination to another optional section must first choose to deselect one of the previously chosen optional sections (B to H). Each of the optional sections of the XE paper (Sections B through H) contains 22 questions carrying a total of 35 marks: 9 questions carrying 1-mark each (sub-total 9 marks) and 13 questions carrying 2-marks each (sub-total 26 marks). Some questions will be of MSQ and/or numerical answer type while remaining questions will be MCQ type.

XH Paper (Humanities and Social Sciences)

A candidate appearing in the XH paper has to answer the following:

- **GA – General Aptitude** carrying a total of 15 marks.
- **Section B1 – Reasoning and Comprehension (Compulsory):** This section contains 15 questions carrying a total of 25 marks: 5 questions carrying 1-mark each (sub-total 5 marks) and 10 questions carrying 2-marks each (sub-total 20 marks). Some questions will be of MSQ and/or numerical answer type while remaining questions will be MCQ type.
- **Any ONE of XH Sections C1 to C6:** The ONE choice of section from C1 to C6 has to be made at the time of online registration in GOAPS. At the examination hall, candidate cannot request for change of section. Each of the optional sections of the XH paper (Sections C1 through C6) contains 40 questions carrying a total of 60 marks: 20 questions carrying 1-mark each (sub-total 20 marks) and 20 questions carrying 2-marks each (sub-total 40 marks). Some questions will be of MSQ and/or numerical answer type while remaining questions will be MCQ type.

XL Paper (Life Sciences)

A candidate appearing in the XL paper has to answer the following:

- **GA – General Aptitude** carrying a total of 15 marks.
- **Section P–Chemistry (Compulsory):** This section contains 15 questions carrying a total of 25 marks: 5 questions carrying 1-mark each (sub-total 5 marks) and 10 questions carrying 2-marks each (sub-total 20 marks). Some questions will be of MSQ and/or numerical answer type while remaining questions will be MCQ type.
- **Any two of XL Sections Q to U:** The choice of two sections from Q to U can be made during the examination after viewing the questions. Only TWO optional sections can be answered at a time. A candidate wishing to change midway of the examination to another optional section must first choose to deselect one of the previously chosen optional sections (Q to U). Each of the optional sections of the XL paper (Sections Q through U) contains 20 questions carrying a total of 30 marks: 10 questions carrying 1-mark each (sub-total 10 marks) and 10 questions carrying 2-marks each (sub-total 20 marks). Some questions will be of MSQ and/or numerical answer type while remaining questions will be MCQ type.

GATE Score

After the evaluation of the answers, the actual (raw) marks obtained by a candidate will be considered for computing the GATE Score. For multi-session papers (subjects), raw marks obtained by the candidates in different sessions will be converted to Normalized marks for that particular subject. Thus, raw marks (for single session papers) or normalized marks (for multi-session papers) will be used for computing the GATE Score, based on the qualifying marks.

Calculation of Normalized Marks for Multi-Session Papers

In GATE 2022 examination, some papers may be conducted in multi-sessions. Hence, for these papers, a suitable normalization is applied to take into account any variation in the difficulty levels of the question papers across different sessions. The normalization is done based on the fundamental assumption that "in all multi-session GATE papers, the distribution of abilities of candidates is the same across all the sessions". This assumption is justified since the number of candidates appearing in multi-session papers in GATE 2022 is large and the procedure for allocation of session to candidates is random. Further, it is also ensured that for the same multi-session paper, the number of candidates allotted in each session is of the same order of magnitude.

Based on the above, and considering various normalization methods, the committee arrived at the following formula for calculating the normalized marks for the multi-session papers.

Nsormalization mark of jth candidate in the ith session $\widehat{M_{ij}}$ is given by

$$\widehat{M_{ij}} = \frac{\bar{M}_t^g - M_q^g}{\bar{M}_{ti} - M_{iq}}(M_{ij} - M_{iq}) + M_q^g$$

where

M_{ij} : is the actual marks obtained by the jth candidate in i^{th} session

$\bar{M}_t^g$: is the average marks of the top 0.1% of the candidates considering all sessions

M_q^g : is the sum of mean and standard deviation marks of the candidates in the paper considering all sessions

$\bar{M}_{ti}$: is the average marks of the top 0.1% of the candidates in the ith session

M_{iq} : is the sum of the mean marks and standard deviation of the ith session

Calculation of GATE Score for All Papers

For all papers for which there is only one session, actual marks obtained by the candidates will be used for calculating the GATE 2022 Score. For papers in multi-sessions, normalized marks will be calculated corresponding to the raw marks obtained by a candidate and the GATE 2022 Score will be calculated based on the normalized marks.

The GATE 2022 score will be computed using the formula given below.

$$\text{GATE Score} = S_q + (S_t - S_q)\frac{(M - M_q)}{(\bar{M}_t - M_q)}$$

where

M : marks obtained by the candidate (actual marks for single session papers and normalized marks for multi-session papers)

M_q : is the qualifying marks for general category candidate in the paper

$\bar{M}_t$: is the mean of marks of top 0.1% or top 10 (whichever is larger) of the candidates who appeared in the paper (in case of multi-session papers including all sessions)

S_q : 350, is the score assigned to M_q

S_t : 900, is the score assigned to $\bar{M}_t$

In the GATE 2022 the qualifying marks (M_q) for general category student in each subject will be 25 marks (out of 100) or $\mu + \sigma$, whichever is larger. Here μ is the mean and σ is the standard deviation of marks of all the candidates who appeared in the paper.

After the declaration of results, GATE Scorecards can be downloaded by the GATE qualified candidates ONLY.

The GATE 2022 Committee has the authority to decide the qualifying mark/score for each GATE paper. In case of any claim or dispute with respect to GATE 2022 examination or score, the Courts and Tribunals in Mumbai alone will have the exclusive jurisdiction to entertain and settle them.

GATE Syllabus

Calculus: Functions of two or more variables, continuity, directional derivatives, partial derivatives, total derivative, maxima and minima, saddle point, method of Lagrange's multipliers; Double and Triple integrals and their applications to area, volume and surface area; Vector Calculus: gradient, divergence and curl, Line integrals and Surface integrals, Green's theorem, Stokes' theorem, and Gauss divergence theorem.

Linear Algebra: Finite dimensional vector spaces over real or complex fields; Linear transformations and their matrix representations, rank and nullity; systems of linear equations, characteristic polynomial, eigenvalues and eigenvectors, diagonalization, minimal polynomial, Cayley-Hamilton Theorem, Finite dimensional inner product spaces, Gram-Schmidt orthonormalization process, symmetric, skew-symmetric, Hermitian, skew-Hermitian, normal, orthogonal and unitary matrices; diagonalization by a unitary matrix, Jordan canonical form; bilinear and quadratic forms.

Real Analysis: Metric spaces, connectedness, compactness, completeness; Sequences and series of functions, uniform convergence, Ascoli-Arzela theorem; Weierstrass approximation theorem; contraction mapping principle, Power series; Differentiation of functions of several variables, Inverse and Implicit function theorems; Lebesgue measure on the real line, measurable functions; Lebesgue integral, Fatou's lemma, monotone convergence theorem, dominated convergence theorem.

Complex Analysis: Functions of a complex variable: continuity, differentiability, analytic functions, harmonic functions; Complex integration: Cauchy's integral theorem and formula; Liouville's theorem, maximum modulus principle, Morera's theorem; zeros and singularities; Power series, radius of convergence, Taylor's series and Laurent's series; Residue theorem and applications for evaluating real integrals; Rouche's theorem, Argument principle, Schwarz lemma; Conformal mappings, Mobius transformations.

Ordinary Differential Equations: First order ordinary differential equations, existence and uniqueness theorems for initial value problems, linear ordinary differential equations of higher order with constant coefficients; Second order linear ordinary differential equations with variable coefficients; Cauchy-Euler equation, method of Laplace transforms for solving ordinary differential equations, series solutions (power series, Frobenius method); Legendre and Bessel functions and their orthogonal properties; Systems of linear first order ordinary differential equations, Sturm's oscillation and separation theorems, Sturm-Liouville eigenvalue problems, Planar autonomous systems of ordinary differential equations: Stability of stationary points for linear systems with constant coefficients, Linearized stability, Lyapunov functions.

Algebra: Groups, subgroups, normal subgroups, quotient groups, homomorphisms, automorphisms; cyclic groups, permutation groups, Group action, Sylow's theorems and their applications; Rings, ideals, prime and maximal ideals, quotient rings, unique factorization domains, Principle ideal domains, Euclidean domains, polynomial rings, Eisenstein's irreducibility criterion; Fields, finite fields, field extensions, algebraic extensions, algebraically closed fields

Functional Analysis: Normed linear spaces, Banach spaces, Hahn-Banach theorem, open mapping and closed graph theorems, principle of uniform boundedness; Inner-product spaces, Hilbert spaces, orthonormal bases, projection theorem, Riesz representation theorem, spectral theorem for compact self-adjoint operators.

Numerical Analysis: Systems of linear equations: Direct methods (Gaussian elimination, LU decomposition, Cholesky factorization), Iterative methods (Gauss-Seidel and Jacobi) and their convergence for diagonally dominant coefficient matrices; Numerical solutions of nonlinear equations: bisection method, secant method, Newton-Raphson method, fixed point iteration; Interpolation: Lagrange and Newton forms of interpolating polynomial, Error in polynomial interpolation of a function; Numerical differentiation and error, Numerical integration: Trapezoidal and Simpson rules, Newton-Cotes integration formulas, composite rules, mathematical errors involved in numerical integration formulae; Numerical solution of initial value problems for ordinary differential equations: Methods of Euler, Runge-Kutta method of order 2.

Partial Differential Equations: Method of characteristics for first order linear and quasilinear partial differential equations; Second order partial differential equations in two independent variables: classification and canonical forms, method of separation of variables for Laplace equation in Cartesian and polar coordinates, heat and wave equations in one space variable; Wave equation: Cauchy problem and d'Alembert formula, domains of dependence and influence, non-homogeneous wave equation; Heat equation: Cauchy problem; Laplace and Fourier transform methods.

Topology: Basic concepts of topology, bases, subbases, subspace topology, order topology, product topology, quotient topology, metric topology, connectedness, compactness, countability and separation axioms, Urysohn's Lemma.

Linear Programming: Linear programming models, convex sets, extreme points; Basic feasible solution, graphical method, simplex method, two phase methods, revised simplex method ; Infeasible and unbounded linear programming models, alternate optima; Duality theory, weak duality and strong duality; Balanced and unbalanced transportation problems, Initial basic feasible solution of balanced transportation problems (least cost method, north-west corner rule, Vogel's approximation method); Optimal solution, modified distribution method; Solving assignment problems, Hungarian method.

Verbal Ability

CHAPTER 1

English Grammar

MCQ TYPE QUESTIONS

2016

1. Computers were invented for performing only high-end useful computations. However, it is no understatement that they have taken over our world today. The internet, for example, is ubiquitous. Many believe that the internet itself is an unintended consequence of the original invention. With the advent of mobile computing on our phones, a whole new dimension is now enabled. One is left wondering if all these developments are good or, more importantly, required.

   Which of the statement(s) below is/are logically valid and can be inferred from the above paragraph?

   (*i*) The author believes that computers are not good for us.

   (*ii*) Mobile computers and the internet are both intended inventions

   (*a*) (*i*) only (*b*) (*ii*) only
   (*c*) both (*i*) and (*ii*) (*d*) neither (*i*) nor (*ii*)

2. All hill-stations have a lake. Ooty has two lakes.

   Which of the statement(s) below is/are logically valid and can be inferred from the above sentences?

   (*i*) Ooty is not a hill-station.

   (*ii*) No hill-station can have more than one lake.

   (*a*) (*i*) only (*b*) (*ii*) only
   (*c*) both (*i*) and (*ii*) (*d*) neither (*i*) nor (*ii*)

3. Identify the correct spelling out of the given options :

   (*a*) Managable (*b*) Manageable
   (*c*) Mangaeble (*d*) Managible

4. Choose the statement(s) where the underlined word is used correctly :

   (*i*) A <u>prone</u> is a dried plum.

   (*ii*) He was lying <u>prone</u> on the floor.

   (*iii*) People who eat a lot of fat are <u>prone</u> to heart disease.

   (*a*) (*i*) and (*iii*) only (*b*) (*iii*) only
   (*c*) (*i*) and (*ii*) only (*d*) (*ii*) and (*iii*) only

5. The policeman asked the victim of a theft, "What did you ?"

   (*a*) loose (*b*) lose
   (*c*) loss (*d*) louse

6. In a world filled with uncertainty, he was glad to have many good friends. He had always assisted them in times of need and was confident that they would reciprocate. However, the events of the last week proved him wrong.

   Which of the following inference(s) is/are logically valid and can be inferred from the above passage?

   (*i*) His friends were always asking him to help them.

   (*ii*) He felt that when in need of help, his friends would let him down.

   (*iii*) He was sure that his friends would help him when in need.

   (*iv*) His friends did not help him last week.

   (*a*) (*i*) and (*ii*) (*b*) (*iii*) and (*iv*)
   (*c*) (*iii*) only (*d*) (*iv*) only

7. An apple costs Rs. 10. An onion costs Rs. 8.

   Select the most suitable sentence with respect to grammar and usage.

   (*a*) The price of an apple is greater than an onion.

   (*b*) The price of an apple is more than onion.

   (*c*) The price of an apple is greater than that of an onion.

   (*d*) Apples are more costlier than onions.

8. He <u>turned a deaf ear</u> to my request. What does the underlined phrasal verb mean?

   (*a*) ignored (*b*) appreciated
   (*c*) twisted (*d*) returned

2015

9. Choose the statement where underlined word is used correctly

   (*a*) The minister <u>insured</u> the victims that everything would be all right.

   (*b*) He <u>ensured</u> that the company will not have to bear any loss.

   (*c*) The actor got himself <u>ensured</u> against any accident.

   (*d*) The teacher <u>insured</u> students of good results

10. The following question presents a sentence, part of which is underlined. Beneath the sentence you find four ways of phrasing the underline part. Following the requirements of the standard written English, select the answer that produces the most effective sentence.

Tuberculosis, together with its effects, ranks one of the leading causes of death in India.

(*a*) ranks as one of the leading causes of death
(*b*) rank as one of the leading causes of death
(*c*) has the rank of one of the leading causes of death
(*d*) are one of the leading causes of death

11. Choose the statement where underlined word is used correctly.

(*a*) When the teacher eludes to different authors, he is being elusive
(*b*) When the thief keeps eluding the police, he is being elusive
(*c*) Matters that are difficult to understand, identify or remember are allusive
(*d*) Mirages can be allusive, but a better way to express them is illusory

12. Fill in the blank with the correct idiom/phrase.

That boy from the town was a ________ in the sleepy village.

(*a*) Dog out of herd (*b*) Sheep from the heap
(*c*) Fish out of water (*d*) Bird from the flock

13. Select the appropriate option in place of underlined part of the sentence.

Increased productivity necessary reflects greater efforts made by the employees.

(*a*) Increase in productivity necessary
(*b*) Increase productivity is necessary
(*c*) Increase in productivity necessarily
(*d*) No improvement required

14. Ram and Shyam shared a secret and promised to each other that it would remain between them. Ram expressed himself in one of the following ways as given in the choices below. Identify the correct way as per standard English.

(*a*) It would remain between you and me
(*b*) It would remain between me and you
(*c*) It would remain between you and I
(*d*) It would remain with me

15. What is the adverb for the given word below? Misogynous

(*a*) Misogynousness (*b*) Misogynity
(*c*) Misogynously (*d*) Misogynous

16. In the following sentence certain parts are underlined and marked P, Q and R. One of the parts may contain certain error or may not be acceptable in standard written communication. Select the part containing an error. Choose D as your Answer: if there is no error.

The student corrected all the errors (P) that the instructor marked (Q) on the answer book (R)

(*a*) P (*b*) Q
(*c*) R (*d*) No Error

17. Choose the statement where underlined word is used correctly.

(*a*) The industrialist had a personnel jet.
(*b*) I write my experience in my personnel diary.
(*c*) All personnel are being given the day off.
(*d*) Being religious is a personnel aspect.

18. Out of the following four sentences, select the most suitable sentence with respect to grammer and usage:

(*a*) Since the report lacked needed information, it was of no use to them.
(*b*) The report was useless to them because there were no needed information in it.
(*c*) Since the report did not contain the needed information, it was not real useful to them.
(*d*) Since the report lacked needed information, it would not had been useful to them.

19. Select the alternative meaning of the underlined part of the sentence.

The chain snatchers took to their heels when the police party arrived.

(*a*) took shelter in a thick jungle
(*b*) open indiscriminate fire
(*c*) took to flight
(*d*) unconditionally surrendered

2014

20. Which of the following options is the closest in meaning to the word underlined in the sentence below?

In a democracy, everybody has the freedom to disagree with the government.

(*a*) dissent (*b*) descent
(*c*) decent (*d*) decadent

21. 'Advice' is ________.

(*a*) a verb (*b*) a noun
(*c*) an adjective (*d*) both a verb and a noun

22. Which of the options given below best completes the following sentence?

She will feel much better if she ________.

(*a*) will get some rest
(*b*) gets some rest
(*c*) will be getting some rest
(*d*) is getting some rest

23. <u>While trying to collect</u> (I) an envelope <u>from under the table,</u> (II) <u>Mr. X fell down</u> (III) and <u>was losing consciousness.</u> (IV)

Which one of the above underlined parts of the sentence is NOT appropriate?

(*a*) I (*b*) II
(*c*) III (*d*) IV

24. Which of the following options is the closest in meaning to the phrase underlined in the sentence below?

It is fascinating to see life forms <u>cope with</u> varied environmental conditions.

(*a*) Adopt to (*b*) Adapt to
(*c*) Adept in (*d*) Accept with

25. In a press meet on the recent scam, the minister said, "The buck stops here". What did the minister convey by the statement?

(*a*) He wants all the money
(*b*) He will return the money
(*c*) He will assume final responsibility
(*d*) He will resist all enquiries

2013

26. <u>The professor</u> (I) <u>ordered to</u> (II) <u>the students to go</u> (III) <u>out of the class.</u> (IV)

Which of the above underlined parts of the sentence is grammatically incorrect?

(*a*) I (*b*) II
(*c*) III (*d*) IV

27. Choose the grammatically INCORRECT sentence:

(*a*) He is of Asian origin.
(*b*) They belonged to Africa.
(*c*) She is an European.
(*d*) They migrated from India to Australia.

28. Choose the grammatically CORRECT sentence:

(*a*) Two and two add four.
(*b*) Two and two become four.
(*c*) Two and two are four.
(*d*) Two and two make four.

29. <u>All engineering students</u> (I) <u>should learn mechanics,</u> (II) <u>mathematics and</u> (III) <u>how to do computation.</u> (IV)

Which of the above underlined parts of the sentence is not appropriate?

(*a*) I (*b*) II
(*c*) III (*d*) IV

2012

30. Choose the most appropriate alternative from the options given below to complete the following sentence :

Suresh's dog is the one ______ was hurt in the stampede.

(*a*) that (*b*) which
(*c*) who (*d*) whom

31. Choose the grammatically **INCORRECT** sentence :

(*a*) They gave us the money back less the service charges of Three Hundred rupees.
(*b*) This country's expenditure is not less than that of Bangladesh.
(*c*) The committee initially asked for a funding of Fifty Lakh rupeesr, but later settled for a lesser sum.
(*d*) This country's expenditure on educational reforms is very less.

32. One of the parts (A, B, C, D) in the sentence given below contains an ERROR. Which one of the following is **INCORRECT** ?

I requested that he should be given the driving test today instead of tomorrow.

(*a*) requested that
(*b*) should be given
(*c*) the driving test
(*d*) instead of tomorrow

ANSWERS

MCQ Type Questions

1. (*d*)	**2.** (*d*)	**3.** (*b*)	**4.** (*d*)	**5.** (*b*)	**6.** (*b*)	**7.** (*c*)	**8.** (*a*)	**9.** (*b*)	**10.** (*a*)
11. (*b*)	**12.** (*c*)	**13.** (*c*)	**14.** (*a*)	**15.** (*c*)	**16.** (*b*)	**17.** (*c*)	**18.** (*a*)	**19.** (*c*)	**20.** (*a*)
21. (*b*)	**22.** (*b*)	**23.** (*d*)	**24.** (*b*)	**25.** (*c*)	**26.** (*b*)	**27.** (*c*)	**28.** (*d*)	**29.** (*d*)	**30.** (*a*)
31. (*d*)	**32.** (*b*)								

EXPLANATIONS

MCQ TYPE QUESTIONS

4. 'lying prone' means lie down flat. 'Prone to' means vulnerable to.

5. Lose (verb)

9. *Insured*–the person, group, or organization whose life or property is covered by an <u>insurance</u> policy.

Ensured–to secure or guarantee

11. Elusive: Difficult to answer.

12. From the statement, it appears that boy found it tough to adapt to a very different situation.

16. The is not required in 'Q'.

30. The correct answer is 'that'. In the given sentence 'was hurt in the stampede' determines which dog belongs to Suresh.

■■

2 CHAPTER Sentence Completion

MCQ TYPE QUESTIONS

2016

1. The man who is now Municipal Commissioner worked as ___________________.
   (*a*) the security guard at a university
   (*b*) a security guard at the university
   (*c*) a security guard at university
   (*d*) the security guard at the university
2. Nobody knows how the Indian cricket team is going to <u>cope with</u> the difficult and seamer-friendly wickets in Australia.
   Choose the option which is closest in meaning to the underlined phrase in the above sentence.
   (*a*) put up with (*b*) put in with
   (*c*) put down to (*d*) put up against
3. The chairman requested the aggrieved shareholders to ________ him.
   (*a*) bare with (*b*) bore with
   (*c*) bear with (*d*) bare
4. The unruly crowd demanded that the accused be ____________ without trial.
   (*a*) hanged (*b*) hanging
   (*c*) hankering (*d*) hung
5. Which of the following is CORRECT with respect to grammar and usage?
   Mount Everest is ___________.
   (*a*) the highest peak in the world
   (*b*) highest peak in the world
   (*c*) one of highest peak in the world
   (*d*) one of the highest peak in the world
6. Despite the new medicine's ______________ in treating diabetes, it is not ______________widely.
   (*a*) effectiveness --- prescribed
   (*b*) availability --- used
   (*c*) prescription --- available
   (*d*) acceptance --- proscribed
7. The students _____ the teacher on teachers' day for twenty years of dedicated teaching.
   (*a*) facilitated (*b*) felicitated
   (*c*) fantasized (*d*) facillitated
8. After India's cricket world cup victory in 1985, Shrotria who was playing both tennis and cricket till then, decided to concentrate only on cricket. And <u>the rest is history</u>.
   What does the underlined phrase mean in this context?
   (*a*) history will rest in peace
   (*b*) rest is recorded in history books
   (*c*) rest is well known
   (*d*) rest is archaic
9. If I were you, I _________ that laptop. It's much too expensive.
   (*a*) won't buy (*b*) shan't buy
   (*c*) wouldn't buy (*d*) would buy
10. Choose the most appropriate set of words from the options given below to complete the following sentence.
    _____ ________ is a will, ________ is a way.
    (*a*) Wear, there, their (*b*) Were, their, there
    (*c*) Where, there, there (*d*) Where, their, their

2015

11. Choose the most appropriate word from the options given below to complete the following sentence. The official answered _________ that the complaints of the citizen would be looked into.
    (*a*) respectably (*b*) respectfully
    (*c*) reputably (*d*) respectively
12. Choose the most appropriate word from the options given below to complete the following sentence.
    The principal presented the chief guest with a ____________, as token of appreciation.
    (*a*) momento (*b*) memento
    (*c*) momentum (*d*) moment
13. Choose the appropriate word/phrase, out of the four options given below, to complete the following sentence : Frogs ________.
    (*a*) Croak (*b*) Roar
    (*c*) Hiss (*d*) Patter
14. Extreme focus on syllabus and studying for tests has become such a dominant concern of Indian students that they close their minds to anything ______ to the requirements of the exam
    (*a*) related (*b*) extraneous
    (*c*) outside (*d*) useful

15. The Tamil version of _____ John Abraham-starrer Madras café _____ cleared by the Censor Board with no cuts last week but the film's distributors _____ no takers among the exhibitors for a release in Tamil Nadu _____ this Friday.

(*a*) Mr., was, found, on (*b*) a, was, found, at

(*c*) the, was, found, on (*d*) a, being, find at

16. Choose the appropriate word/phase, out of the four options given below, to complete the following sentence:

Apparent lifelessness ______ dormant life.

(*a*) harbours (*b*) lead to

(*c*) supports (*d*) affects

17. Choose the correct verb to fill in the blank below :

Let us ____________.

(*a*) Introvert (*b*) Alternate

(*c*) Atheist (*d*) Altruist

18. Choose the most appropriate word from the options given below to complete the following sentence :

If the Athlete had wanted to come first in the race, he __________ several hours everyday

(*a*) should practice (*b*) should have practiced

(*c*) practiced (*d*) should be practicing

19. Choose the appropriate word/phrase, out of the four options given below, to complete the following sentence:

Dhoni, as well as the other team members of Indian team, _____ present on the occasion.

(*a*) were (*b*) was

(*c*) has (*d*) have

20. We ________ our friend's birthday and we _______ how to make it up to him.

(*a*) completely forgot — don't just known

(*b*) forget completely — don't just know

(*c*) completely forget —just don't know

(*d*) forgot completely —just don't know

21. Which of the following options is the closest in meaning to the sentence below?

She enjoyed herself immensely at the party.

(*a*) She had a terrible time at the party

(*b*) She had a horrible time at the party

(*c*) She had a terrific time at the party

(*d*) She had a terrifying time at the party

22. Didn't you buy _______ when you went shopping?

(*a*) any paper

(*b*) much paper

(*c*) no paper

(*d*) a few paper

2014

23. Choose the most appropriate word from the options given below to complete the following sentence:

A person suffering from Alzheimer's disease _________ short-term memory loss.

(*a*) experienced (*b*) has experienced

(*c*) is experiencing (*d*) experiences

24. Choose the most appropriate word from the options given below to complete the following sentence:

_________ is the key to their happiness; they are satisfied with what they have.

(*a*) Contentment (*b*) Ambition

(*c*) Perseverance (*d*) Hunger

25. Choose the most appropriate word from the options given below to complete the following sentence:

One of his biggest _____ was his ability to forgive.

(*a*) vice (*b*) virtues

(*c*) choices (*d*) strength

26. After the discussion, Tom said to me, 'Please revert!' He expects me to ________.

(*a*) retract (*b*) get back to him

(*c*) move in reverse (*d*) retreat

27. The value of one U.S. Dollar is 65 Indian Rupees today, compared to 60 last year. The Indian Rupee has ________.

(*a*) Depressed (*b*) Depreciated

(*c*) Appreciated (*d*) Stabilized

28. Choose the most appropriate word from the options given below to complete the following sentence:

Communication and interpersonal skills are ________ important in their own ways.

(*a*) each (*b*) both

(*c*) all (*d*) either

29. Choose the most appropriate pair of words from the options given below to complete the following sentence:

She could not ________ the thought of ________ the election to her bitter rival.

(*a*) bear, loosing (*b*) bare, loosing

(*c*) bear, losing (*d*) bare, losing

30. Choose the most appropriate phrase from the options given below to complete the following sentence:

The aircraft _________ take off as soon as its flight plan was filed.

(*a*) is allowed to (*b*) will be allowed to

(*c*) was allowed to (*d*) has been allowed to

31. Choose the most appropriate word from the options given below to complete the following sentence:

Many ancient cultures attributed disease to supernatural causes. However, modern science has largely helped ______ such notions.

(*a*) impel (*b*) dispel
(*c*) propel (*d*) repel

32. If she __________ how to calibrate the instrument, she ________ done the experiment.

(*a*) knows, will have
(*b*) knew, had
(*c*) had known, could have
(*d*) should have known, would have

33. Who _______ was coming to see us this evening?

(*a*) you said (*b*) did you say
(*c*) did you say that (*d*) had you said

34. Choose the most appropriate word from the options given below to complete the following sentence:

He could not understand the judges awarding her the first prize, because he thought that her performance was quite ________________.

(*a*) Superb (*b*) Medium
(*c*) Mediocre (*d*) Exhilarating

2013

35. Friendship, no matter how ________ it is, has its limitations.

(*a*) cordial (*b*) intimate
(*c*) secret (*d*) pleasant

36. Were you a bird, you_____ in the sky.

(*a*) would fly (*b*) shall fly
(*c*) should fly (*d*) shall have flown

37. Complete the sentence:

Dare _________ mistakes.

(*a*) commit (*b*) to commit
(*c*) committed (*d*) committing

38. The Headmaster ______ to speak to you.

Which of the following options is incorrect to complete the above sentence?

(*a*) is wanting (*b*) wants
(*c*) want (*d*) was wanting

2012

39. Choose the most appropriate alternative from the options given below to complete the following sentence :

Despite several ______ the mission succeeded in its attempt to resolve the conflict.

(*a*) attempts (*b*) setbacks
(*c*) meetings (*d*) delegations

40. Choose the most appropriate alternative from the options given below to complete the following sentence :

If the tired soldier wanted to lie down, he ___ the mattress out on the balcony.

(*a*) should take (*b*) shall take
(*c*) should have taken (*d*) will have taken

41. Choose the most appropriate word from the options given below to complete the following sentence :

Given the seriousness of the situation that he had to face, his ___ was impressive.

(*a*) beggary (*b*) nomenclature
(*c*) jealousy (*d*) nonchalance

2011

42. Choose the most appropriate word from the options given below to complete the following sentence:

If you are trying to make a strong impression on your audience, you cannot do so by being understated, tentative or _______ .

(*a*) hyperbolic (*b*) restrained
(*c*) argumentative (*d*) indifferent

43. Choose the most appropriate word(s) from the options given below to complete the following sentence.

I contemplated ______ Singapore for my vacation but decided against it.

(*a*) to visit (*b*) having to visit
(*c*) visiting (*d*) for a visit

44. Choose the most appropriate word from the options given below to complete the following sentence:

Under ethical guidelines recently adopted by the Indian Medical Association, human genes are to be manipulated only to correct diseases for which_______treatments are unsatisfactory.

(*a*) similar (*b*) most
(*c*) uncommon (*d*) available

45. Choose the most appropriate word from the options given below to complete the following sentence:

It was her view that the country's problems had been_________by foreign technocrats, so that to invite them to come back would be counter-productive.

(*a*) identified
(*b*) ascertained
(*c*) exacerbated
(*d*) analysed

2010

46. Choose the most appropriate word from the options given below to complete the following sentence:

If we manage to ________ our natural resources, we would leave a better planet for our children.

(*a*) uphold (*b*) restrain
(*c*) cherish (*d*) conserve

47. Choose the most appropriate word from the options given below to complete the following sentence:

His rather casual remarks on politics ________ his lack of seriousness about the subject.

(*a*) masked (*b*) belied
(*c*) betrayed (*d*) suppressed

ANSWERS

MCQ Type Questions

1. (*b*)	**2.** (*a*)	**3.** (*c*)	**4.** (*a*)	**5.** (*a*)	**6.** (*a*)	**7.** (*b*)	**8.** (*c*)	**9.** (*c*)	**10.** (*c*)
11. (*b*)	**12.** (*b*)	**13.** (*a*)	**14.** (*b*)	**15.** (*c*)	**16.** (*a*)	**17.** (*b*)	**18.** (*b*)	**19.** (*b*)	**20.** (*c*)
21. (*c*)	**22.** (*a*)	**23.** (*d*)	**24.** (*a*)	**25.** (*b*)	**26.** (*b*)	**27.** (*b*)	**28.** (*b*)	**29.** (*c*)	**30.** (*c*)
31. (*b*)	**32.** (*c*)	**33.** (*b*)	**34.** (*c*)	**35.** (*b*)	**36.** (*a*)	**37.** (*b*)	**38.** (*c*)	**39.** (*b*)	**40.** (*a*)
41. (*d*)	**42.** (*b*)	**43.** (*c*)	**44.** (*d*)	**45.** (*c*)	**46.** (*a*)	**47.** (*c*)			

EXPLANATIONS

MCQ TYPE QUESTIONS

2. From the given underlined phrase <u>copewith</u> means put up with.

4. 'hanged' means death by hanging 'hung' is used only with things and not with people.

6. Here 'effectiveness' is noun and 'prescribed' is verb. So these words are apt and befitting with the given word 'medicine'.

12. The principal presented the chief guest with a memento, as token of appreciation.

13. Frogs make 'croak' sound.

14. Extraneous -irrelevant or unrelated to the subject being dealt with.

15. John-Abraham starrer Madras Cafe talks about the movie not the person, so Mr. is ruled out.

'Find no takers' is not the correct phrase. At this Friday is incorrect.

So, option (*c*) is correct.

16. Apparent: looks like; dormant: hidden
Harbour: give shelter; Effect (verb): results in

18. For condition regarding something which already happened, should have practiced is the correct choice.

23. The correct word to fill in the blank is experiences. This is because the sentence is in present tense and the sense is in present indefinite.

24. Contentment is the right word which is appropriate to the meaning of the sentence. Contentment is the sign of true happiness as it gives a sense of fulfillment.

39. The word despite tells us that mission succeeded even though there were problems. Hence the correct answer is Setbacks.

42. Tone of the sentence clearly indicates a word that is similar to understated is needed for the blank. Alternatively, word should be antonym of strong (fail to make strong impression). Therefore, best choice is restrained which means controlled / reserved / timid.

43. Contemplate is a transitive verb and hence is followed by a gerund Hence the correct usage of contemplate is verb + ing form.

44. The context seeks to take a deviation only when existing / present / current / alternative treatments are unsatisfactory. So word for the blank should be a close synonym of existing / present / current / alternative. Available is the closest of all.

45. Clues: foreign technocrats did something negatively to the problems – so it is counter-productive to invite them. All other options are non-negative. Best choice is exacerbated which means aggravated or worsened.

47. Betrayed, **means** 'showed' or revealed.

■■

3 CHAPTER

Synonyms

MCQ TYPE QUESTIONS

2016

1. The Buddha said, "Holding on to anger is like grasping a hot coal with the intent of throwing it at someone else; you are the one who gets burnt."

Select the word below which is closest in meaning to the word underlined above.

(*a*) burning (*b*) igniting
(*c*) clutching (*d*) flinging

2015

2. The word similar in meaning to 'dreary' is

(*a*) cheerful (*b*) dreamy
(*c*) hard (*d*) dismal

3. Choose the word most similar in meaning to the given word :

Educe

(*a*) Exert (*b*) Educate
(*c*) Extract (*d*) Extend

4. Choose the most suitable one word substitute for the following expression

Connotation of a road or way

(*a*) Pertinacious (*b*) Viaticum
(*c*) Clandestine (*d*) Ravenous

5. Choose the word most similar in meaning to the given word:

Awkward

(*a*) Inept (*b*) Graceful
(*c*) Suitable (*d*) Dreadful

6. A generic term that includes various items of clothing such as a skirt, a pair of trousers and a shirt as

(*a*) fabric
(*b*) textile
(*c*) fibre
(*d*) apparel

7. Which of the following combinations is incorrect?

(*a*) Acquiescence – Submission
(*b*) Wheedle – Roundabout
(*c*) Flippancy – Lightness
(*d*) Profligate – Extravagant

2014

8. A student is required to demonstrate a high level of comprehension of the subject, especially in the social sciences.

The word closest in meaning to comprehension is

(*a*) understanding (*b*) meaning
(*c*) concentration (*d*) stability

9. While receiving the award, the scientist said, "I feel vindicated". Which of the following is closest in meaning to the word 'vindicated'?

(*a*) punished (*b*) substantiated
(*c*) appreciated (*d*) chastened

10. Choose the word that is opposite in meaning to the word "coherent".

(*a*) sticky (*b*) well-connected
(*c*) rambling (*d*) friendly

11. Match the columns:

Column-1	Column-2
1. eradicate	P. misrepresent
2. distort	Q. soak completely
3. saturate	R. use
4. utilize	S. destroy utterly

(*a*) 1 : S, 2 : P, 3 : Q, 4 : R
(*b*) 1 : P, 2 : Q, 3 : R, 4 : S
(*c*) 1 : Q, 2 : R, 3 : S, 4 : P
(*d*) 1 : S, 2 : P, 3 : R, 4 : Q

2013

12. Which of the following options is the closest in meaning to the word given below:

Primeval

(*a*) Modern (*b*) Historic
(*c*) Primitive (*d*) Antique

13. Which one of the following options is the closest in meaning to the word given below?

Nadir

(*a*) Highest (*b*) Lowest
(*c*) Medium (*d*) Integration

14. They were requested not to **quarrel** with others.

Which one of the following options is the closest in meaning to the word **quarrel**?

(*a*) make out (*b*) call out
(*c*) dig out (*d*) fall out

2012

15. Which one of the following options is the closest in meaning to the word given below?

Mitigate

(*a*) Diminish (*b*) Divulge
(*c*) Dedicate (*d*) Denote

16. Which one of the following options is the closest in meaning to the word given below ?

Latitude

(*a*) Eligibility (*b*) Freedom
(*c*) Coercion (*d*) Meticulousness

2011

17. Which of the following options is the closest in the meaning to the word below :

Inexplicable

(*a*) Incomprehensible (*b*) Indelible
(*c*) Inextricable (*d*) Infallible

2010

18. Which of the following options is the closest in meaning to the word below:

Circuitous

(*a*) cyclic (*b*) indirect
(*c*) confusing (*d*) crooked

ANSWERS

MCQ Type Questions

1. (*c*)	**2.** (*d*)	**3.** (*c*)	**4.** (*b*)	**5.** (*a*)	**6.** (*d*)	**7.** (*b*)	**8.** (*a*)	**9.** (*b*)	**10.** (*c*)
11. (*a*)	**12.** (*c*)	**13.** (*b*)	**14.** (*b*)	**15.** (*a*)	**16.** (*b*)	**17.** (*a*)	**18.** (*b*)		

EXPLANATIONS

MCQ TYPE QUESTIONS

1. The meaning of underlined word grasping means clutching (or holding something tightly).

2. *dreary* - depressingly dull and bleak or repetitive.

3. The word similar in meaning to Educe is Extract.

13. Given: A word "Nadir"

To find: Closest meaning word to 'Nadir' in the given options.

Analysis: The dictionary meaning of 'Nadir' is 'Lowest' which is potion (*b*)

Source: Google

Given: A sequence 44, 42, 40,......

To find: Maximum sum of the sequence

Analysis: To find the maximum sum, we have to ignore all the negative terms (they will only decrease the sum). Hence, we terminate the sequence at 0.

Now, the sequence is 44, 42,......,2, 0.

This sequence is an Arithmetic progression with common difference –2. Now, the problem reduces to finding the sum of this A.P.

To find the sum of A.P., we have to find the number of terms in A.P.

Let n be the number of terms

a be the first term

l be the last term

d be the common difference.

$n = ?$

$a = 44, \quad l = 0, \quad d = -2$

Now, $l = a + (n - 1)d$

15. 'Mitigate' means to make something less harmful, serious, intense etc. Hence correct answer is 'Diminis'

17. Inexplicable means not explicable; that cannot be explained, understood, or accounted for. So the best synonym here is incomprehensible.

18. Circuitous means round about or not direct

So circuitous : indirect.

■■

4
CHAPTER

Antonyms

MCQ TYPE QUESTIONS

2015

1. Which word is not a synonym for the word *vernacular*?

(*a*) regional

(*b*) indigeneous

(*c*) indigent

(*d*) colloquial

2011

2. Choose the word from the options given below that is most nearly opposite in meaning to the given word:

Amalgamate

(*a*) merge

(*b*) split

(*c*) collect

(*d*) separate

3. Choose the word from the options given below that is most nearly **opposite** in meaning to the given word :

Frequency

(*a*) periodicity

(*b*) rarity

(*c*) gradualness

(*d*) persistency

ANSWERS

MCQ Type Questions

1. (*c*) **2.** (*b*) **3.** (*b*)

EXPLANATIONS

MCQ TYPE QUESTIONS

1. *Vernacular* - expressed or written in the native language of a place

   Indigent - deficient in what is requisite

2. Amalgamate means combine or unite to form one organization or structure. So the best option here is split. Separate on the other hand, although a close synonym, it is too general to be the best antonym in the given question while Merge is the synonym; Collect is not related.

3. Best antonym is rarity which means shortage or scarcity.

■■

5 CHAPTER

Reasoning Ability

MCQ TYPE QUESTIONS

2016

1. Find the odd one in the following group of words.

mock, deride, praise, jeer

(*a*) mock (*b*) deride
(*c*) praise (*d*) jeer

2. Pick the odd one from the following options.

(*a*) CADBE (*b*) JHKIL
(*c*) XVYWZ (*d*) ONPMQ

3. Pick the odd one out in the following :

13, 23, 33, 43, 53

(*a*) 23 (*b*) 33
(*c*) 43 (*d*) 53

4. R2D2 is a robot. R2D2 can repair aeroplanes. No other robot can repair aeroplanes. Which of the following can be logically inferred from the above statements?

(*a*) R2D2 is a robot which can only repair aeroplanes.
(*b*) R2D2 is the only robot which can repair aeroplanes.
(*c*) R2D2 is a robot which can repair only aeroplanes.
(*d*) Only R2D2 is a robot.

5. A poll of students appearing for masters in engineering indicated that 60% of the students believed that mechanical engineering is a profession unsuitable for women. A research study on women with masters or higher degrees in mechanical engineering found that 99% of such women were successful in their professions.

Which of the following can be logically inferred from the above paragraph?

(*a*) Many students have misconceptions regarding various engineering disciplines.
(*b*) Men with advanced degrees in mechanical engineering believe women are well suited to be mechanical engineers.
(*c*) Mechanical engineering is a profession well suited for women with masters or higher degrees in mechanical engineering.
(*d*) The number of women pursuing higher degrees in mechanical engineering is small.

6. Sourya committee had proposed the establishment of Sourya Institutes of Technology (SITs) in line with Indian Institutes of Technology (IITs) to cater to the technological and industrial needs of a developing country.

Which of the following can be logically inferred from the above sentence?

Based on the proposal,

(*i*) In the initial years, SIT students will get degrees from IIT.
(*ii*) SITs will have a distinct national objective.
(*iii*) SIT like institutions can only be established in consulation with IIT.
(*iv*) SITs will serve technological needs of a developing country.

(*a*) (*iii*) and (*iv*) only (*b*) (*i*) and (*iv*) only
(*c*) (*ii*) and (*iv*) only (*d*) (*ii*) and (*iii*) only

7. **Fact :** If it rains, then the field is wet.

Read the following statements:

(*i*) It rains (*ii*) The field is not wet
(*iii*) The field is wet (*iv*) It did not rain

Which one of the options given below is NOT logically possible, based on the given fact?

(*a*) If (*iii*), then (*iv*) (*b*) If (*i*), then (*iii*)
(*c*) If (*i*), then (*ii*) (*d*) If (*ii*), then (*iv*)

8. Students taking an exam are divided into two groups, **P** and **Q** such that each group has the same number of students. The performance of each of the students in a test was evaluated out of 200 marks. It was observed that the mean of group **P** was 105, while that of group **Q** was 85. The standard deviation of group **P** was 25, while that of group **Q** was 5. Assuming that the marks were distributed on a normal distribution, which of the following statements will have the highest probability of being **TRUE**?

(*a*) No student in group **Q** scored less marks than any student in group **P**.
(*b*) No student in group **P** scored less marks than any student in group **Q**.
(*c*) Most students of group **Q** scored marks in a narrower range than students in group **P**.
(*d*) The median of the marks of group **P** is 100.

9. A smart city integrates all modes of transport, uses clean energy and promotes sustainable use of resources. It also uses technology to ensure safety and security of the city, something which critics argue, will lead to a surveillance state.

Which of the following can be logically inferred from the above paragraph?

(*i*) All smart cities encourage the formation of surveillance states.

(*ii*) Surveillance is an integral part of a smart city.

(*iii*) Sustainability and surveillance go hand in hand in a smart city.

(*iv*) There is a perception that smart cities promote surveillance.

(*a*) (*i*) and (*iv*) only (*b*) (*ii*) and (*iii*) only

(*c*) (*iv*) only (*d*) (*i*) only

10. Find the missing sequence in the letter series.

B, FH, LNP, _ _ _ _.

(*a*) SUWY (*b*) TUVW

(*c*) TVXZ (*d*) TWXZ

11. Michael lives 10 km away from where I live. Ahmed lives 5 km away and Susan lives 7 km away from where I live. Arun is farther away than Ahmed but closer than Susan from where I live. From the information provided here, what is one possible distance (in km) at which I live from Arun's place?

(*a*) 3.00 (*b*) 4.99

(*c*) 6.02 (*d*) 7.01

12. Leela is older than her cousin Pavithra. Pavithra's brother Shiva is older than Leela. When Pavithra and Shiva are visiting Leela, all three like to play chess. Pavithra wins more often than Leela does.

Which one of the following statements must be TRUE based on the above?

(*a*) When Shiva plays chess with Leela and Pavithra, he often loses.

(*b*) Leela is the oldest of the three.

(*c*) Shiva is a better chess player than Pavithra.

(*d*) Pavithra is the youngest of the three.

13. Based on the given statements, select the appropriate option with respect to grammar and usage.

Statements :

I. The height of Mr. X is 6 feet.

II. The height of Mr. Y is 5 feet.

(*a*) Mr. X is longer than Mr. Y.

(*b*) Mr. X is more elongated than Mr. Y

(*c*) Mr. X is taller than Mr. Y

(*d*) Mr. X is lengthier than Mr. Y

14. Social science disciplines were in existence in an amorphous form until the colonial period when they were institutionalized. In varying degrees, they were intended to further the colonial interest. In the time of globalization and the economic rise of postcolonial countries like India, conventional ways of knowledge production have become obsolete.

Which of the following can be logically inferred from the above statements?

I. Social science disciplines have become obsolete.

II. Social science disciplines had a pre-colonial origin.

III. Social science disciplines always promote colonialism.

IV. Social science must maintain disciplinary boundaries.

(*a*) II only (*b*) I and III only

(*c*) II and IV only (*d*) III and IV only

15. Two and a quarter hours back, when seen in a mirror, the reflection of a wall clock without number markings seemed to show 1 : 30. What is the actual current time shown by the clock?

(*a*) 8:15 (*b*) 11:15

(*c*) 12:15 (*d*) 12:45

16. M and N start from the same location. M travels 10 km East and then 10 km North-East. N travels 5 km South and then 4 km South-East. What is the shortest distance (in km) between M and N at the end of their travel?

(*a*) 18.60 (*b*) 22.50

(*c*) 20.61 (*d*) 25.00

17. M has a son Q and a daughter R. He has no other children. E is the mother of P and daughter-inlaw of M. How is P related to M?

(*a*) P is the son-in-law of M.

(*b*) P is the grandchild of M.

(*c*) P is the daughter-in-law of M.

(*d*) P is the grandfather of M.

18. The number that least fits this set: (324, 441, 97 and 64) is ________.

(*a*) 324

(*b*) 441

(*c*) 97

(*d*) 64

19. The overwhelming number of people infected with rabies in India has been flagged by the World Health Organization as a source of concern. It is estimated that inoculating 70% of pets and stray dogs against rabies can lead to a significant reduction in the number of people infected with rabies.

Which of the following can be logically inferred from the above sentences ?

(*a*) The number of people in India infected with rabies is high

(*b*) The number of people in other parts of the world who are infected with rabies is low

(*c*) Rabies can be eradicated in India by vaccinating 70% of stray dogs

(d) Stray dogs are the main source of rabies worldwide

20. A flat is shared by four first year undergraduate students. They agreed to allow the oldest of them to enjoy some extra space in the flat. Manu is two months older than Sravan, who is three months younger than Trideep. Pavan is one month older than Sravan. Who should occupy the extra space in the flat ?

(*a*) Manu (*b*) Sravan

(*c*) Trideep (*d*) Pavan

21. Today, we consider Ashoka as a great ruler because of the copious evidence he left behind in the form of stone carved edicts. Historians tend to correlate greatness of a king at his time with the availability of evidence today. Which of the following can be logically inferred from the above sentences?

(*a*) Emperors who do not leave significant sculpted evidence are completely forgotten.

(*b*) Ashoka produced stone carved edicts to ensure that later historians will respect him.

(*c*) Statues of kings are a reminder of their greatness.

(*d*) A king's greatness, as we know him today, is interpreted by historians.

22. **Fact 1 :** Humans are mammals.

Fact 2 : Some humans are engineers.

Fact 3 : Engineers build houses.

If the above statements are facts, which of the following can be logically inferred ?

I. All mammals build houses.

II. Engineers are mammals.

III. Some humans are not engineers.

(*a*) II only (*b*) III only

(*c*) I, II and III (*d*) I only

2015

23. Mr. Vivek walks 6 meters North-East, then turns and walks 6 meters South- East, both at 60 degrees to East. He further moves 2 meters South and 4 meters West. What is the straight distance in meters between the point he started from and the point he finally reached?

(*a*) $2\sqrt{2}$ (*b*) 2

(*c*) $\sqrt{2}$ (*d*) $1/\sqrt{2}$

24. There are 16 teachers who can teach Thermodynamics (TD), 11 who can teach Electrical Sciences (ES), and 5 who can teach both TD and Engineering Mechanics (EM). There are a total of 40 teachers, 6 cannot teach any of the three subjects, i.e. EM, ES or TD. 6 can teach only ES. 4 can teach all three subjects, i.e. EM, ES and TD. 4 can teach ES and TD. How many can teach both ES and EM but not TD?

(*a*) 1 (*b*) 2

(*c*) 3 (*d*) 4

25. The given question is followed by two statements: select the most appropriate option that solves the question

Capacity of a solution tank A is 70% of the capacity of tank B. How many gallons of solution are in tank A and tank B?

Statements:

I. Tank A is 80% full and tank B is 40% full

II. Tank A if full contains 14,000 gallons of solution

(*a*) Statement I alone is sufficient

(*b*) Statement II alone is sufficient

(*c*) Either statement I or II alone is sufficient

(*d*) Both the statements I and II together are sufficient

26. Operators $\square, \diamond$ and $\to$ are defined by

$$a \square b = \frac{a-b}{a+b};\ a \diamond b = \frac{a+b}{a-b};\ a \to b = ab.$$

Find the value $(66 \square 6) \to (66 \diamond 6)$

(*a*) –2 (*b*) –1

(*c*) 1 (*d*) 2

27. Humpty Dumpty sits on a wall every day while having lunch. The wall sometimes breaks. A person sitting on the wall falls if the wall breaks.

Which one of the statements below is logically valid and can be inferred from the above sentences?

(*a*) Humpty Dumpty always falls while having lunch

(*b*) Humpty Dumpty does not fall sometimes while having lunch

(*c*) Humpty Dumpty never falls during dinner

(*d*) When Humpty Dumpty does not sit on the wall, the wall does not break

28. If ROAD is written as URDG, then SWAN should be written as :

(*a*) VXDQ (*b*) VZDQ

(*c*) VZDP (*d*) UXDQ

29. Select the pair that best expresses a relationship similar to that expressed in the pair :

Children : Pediatrician

(*a*) Adult : Orthopaedist

(*b*) Females : Gynaecologist

(*c*) Kidney : Nephrologist

(*d*) Skin : Dermatologist

30. The head of a newly formed government desires to appoint five of the six selected members P,Q,R,S,T and U to portfolios of Home, Power, Defense, Telecom, and Finance. U does not want any portfolio if S gets one of the five. R wants either Home or Finance or no portfolio. Q says that if S gets either Power or Telecom, then she must get the other one. T insists on a portfolio if P gets one.

Which is the valid distribution of portfolios?

(*a*) P-Home, Q-Power, R-Defense, S-Telecom, T-Finance

(*b*) R-Home, S-Power, P-Defense, Q-Telecom, T-Finance

(*c*) P-Home, Q-Power, T-Defense, S-Telecom, U-Finance

(*d*) Q-Home, U-Power, T-Defense, R-Telecom, P-Finance

31. Most experts feel that in spite of possessing all the technical skills required to be a batsman of the highest order, he is unlikely to be so due to lack of requisite temperament. He was guilty of throwing away his wicket several times after working hard to lay a strong foundation. His critics pointed out that until he addressed this problem success at the highest level will continue to elude him.

Which of the statement (s) below is/are logically valid and can be inferred from the above passage?

(*i*) He was already a successful batsman at the highest level

(*ii*) He has to improve his temperament in order to become a great batsman

(*iii*) He failed to make many of his good starts count

(*iv*) Improving his technical skills will guarantee success

(*a*) (*iii*) and (*iv*) (*b*) (*ii*) and (*iii*)

(*c*) (*i*), (*ii*) and (*iii*) (*d*) (*ii*) only

32. Alexander turned his attention towards India, since he had conquered Persia.

Which one of the statements below is logically valid and can inferred from the above sentence?

(*a*) Alexander would not have turned his attention towards India had he not conquered Persia.

(*b*) Alexander was not ready to rest on his laurels, and wanted to march to India

(*c*) Alexander was completely in control of his army and could command it to move towards India

(*d*) Since Alexander's kingdom extended to Indian borders after the conquest of Persia, he was keen to move further

33. Tanya is older than Enc.

Cliff is older than Tanya.

Eric is older than Cliff.

If the first two statements are true, then the third statement is

(*a*) True (*b*) False

(*c*) Uncertain (*d*) Data insufficient

34. Given below are two statements followed by two conclusions. Assuming these statements to be true, decide which one logically follows:

Statements:

I. No manager is a leader.

II. All leaders are executive.

Conclusions:

I. No manager is a executive.

II. All executive is a manager.

(*a*) Only conclusion I follows.

(*b*) Only conclusion II follows.

(*c*) Neither conclusion I nor II follows.

(*d*) Both conclusion I and II follow.

35. Find the missing sequence in the letter series below :

A, CD, GHI, _?___, UVWXY

(*a*) LMN (*b*) MNO

(*c*) MNOP (*d*) NOPQ

36. Ms. X will be in Bagdogra from 1/5/14 to 20/5/14 and from 22/5/14 to 31/5/14. On the morning of 21/5/14, she will reach Kochi via Mumbai.

Which one of the statements below is logically valid and can be inferred from the above sentences?

(*a*) Ms. X will be in Kochi for only one day only in May

(*b*) Ms. X will be in Kochi for only one day in May

(*c*) Ms. X will be only in Kochi for one day in May

(*d*) Only Ms. X will be in Kochi for one day in May

37. Given below are two statements followed by two conclusions. Assuming these statements to be true, decide which one logically follows.

Statement:

I. All film stars are playback singers.

II. All film directors are film stars.

Conclusions:

I. All film directors are playback singers.

II. Some film stars are film directors.

(*a*) Only conclusion I follows

(*b*) Only conclusion II follows

(*c*) Neither conclusion I nor II follows

(*d*) Both conclusions I and II follow

38. Lamenting the gradual sidelining of the arts in school curricula, a group of prominent artists wrote to the Chief Minister last year, asking him to allocate more funds to support arts education in schools. However, no such increase has been announced in this year's Budget. The artists expressed their deep anguish at their request not being approved, but many of them remain optimistic about funding in the future.

Which of the statement(*s*) below is/are logically valid and can be inferred from the above statements?

i. The artists expected funding for the arts to increase this year.

ii. The Chief Minister was receptive to the idea of increasing funding for the arts.

iii. The Chief Minister is a prominent artist.

iv. Schools are giving less importance to arts education nowadays.

(*a*) *iii* and *iv* (*b*) *i* and *iv*

(*c*) *i*, *ii* and *iv* (*d*) *i* and *iii*

39. Four branches of a company are located at M, N, O, and P. M is north of N at a distance of 4 km; P is south of O at a distance of 2 km; N is southeast of O by 1 km. What is the distance between M and P in km?

(*a*) 5.34 (*b*) 6.74

(*c*) 28.5 (*d*) 45.49

40. The given statement is followed by some courses of action. Assuming the statement to be true, decide the correct option.

Statement:

There has been a significant drop in the water level in the lakes supplying water to the city.

Course of action:

I. The water supply authority should impose a partial cut in supply to tackle the situation.

II. The government should appeal to all the residents through mass media for minimal use of water.

III. The government should ban the water supply in lower areas.

(*a*) Statements I and II follow.

(*b*) Statements I and III follow.

(*c*) Statements II and III follow.

(*d*) All statements follow.

2014

41. In a group of four children, Som is younger to Riaz. Shiv is elder to Ansu. Ansu is youngest in the group. Which of the following statements is/are required to find the eldest child in the group?

Statements

1. Shiv is younger to Riaz.

2. Shiv is elder to Som.

(*a*) Statement 1 by itself determines the eldest child.

(*b*) Statement 2 by itself determines the eldest child.

(*c*) Statements 1 and 2 are both required to determine the eldest child.

(*d*) Statements 1 and 2 are not sufficient to determine the eldest child.

42. X is 1 km northeast of Y. Y is 1 km southeast of Z. W is 1 km west of Z. P is 1 km south of W. Q is 1 km east of P. What is the distance between X and Q in km?

(*a*) 1 (*b*) $\sqrt{2}$

(*c*) $\sqrt{3}$ (*d*) 2

43. Rajan was not happy that Sajan decided to do the project on his own. On observing his unhappiness, Sajan explained to Rajan that he preferred to work independently.

Which one of the statements below is logically valid and can be inferred from the above sentences?

(*a*) Rajan has decided to work only in a group.

(*b*) Rajan and Sajan were formed into a group against their wishes.

(*c*) Sajan had decided to give in to Rajan's request to work with him.

(*d*) Rajan had believed that Sajan and he would be working together.

44. Find the odd one in the following group: ALRVX, EPVZB, ITZDF, OYEIK

(*a*) ALRVX

(*b*) EPVZB

(*c*) ITZDF

(*d*) OYEIK

45. Anuj, Bhola, Chandan, Dilip, Eswar and Faisal live on different floors in a six-storeyed building (the ground floor is numbered 1, the floor above it 2, and so on). Anuj lives on an even-numbered floor. Bhola does not live on an odd numbered floor. Chandan does not live on any of the floors below Faisal's floor. Dilip does not live on floor number 2. Eswar does not live on a floor immediately above or immediately below Bhola. Faisal lives three floors above Dilip. Which of the following floor-person combinations is correct?

	Anuj	*Bhola*	*Chandan*	*Dilip*	*Eswar*	*Faisal*
(*a*)	6	2	5	1	3	4
(*b*)	2	6	5	1	3	4
(*c*)	4	2	6	3	1	5
(*d*)	2	4	6	1	3	5

46. Find the next term in the sequence: 13M, 17Q, 19S, ________

(*a*) 21W (*b*) 21V
(*c*) 23W (*d*) 23V

47. If 'KCLFTSB' stands for 'best of luck' and 'SHSWDG' stands for 'good wishes', which of the following indicates 'ace the exam'?

(*a*) MCHTX (*b*) MXHTC
(*c*) XMHCT (*d*) XMHTC

48. "India is a country of rich heritage and cultural diversity."

Which one of the following facts best supports the claim made in the above sentence?

(*a*) India is a union of 28 states and 7 union territories.

(*b*) India has a population of over 1.1 billion.

(*c*) India is home to 22 official languages and thousands of dialects.

(*d*) The Indian cricket team draws players from over ten states.

49. In which of the following options will the expression P < M be definitely true?

(*a*) M < R > P > S (*b*) M > S < P < F
(*c*) Q < M < F = P (*d*) P = A < R < M

50. Find the next term in the sequence:

7G, 11K, 13M, ________

(*a*) 15Q
(*b*) 17Q
(*c*) 15P
(*d*) 17P

51. The multi-level hierarchical pie chart shows the population of animals in a reserve forest. The correct conclusions from this information are:

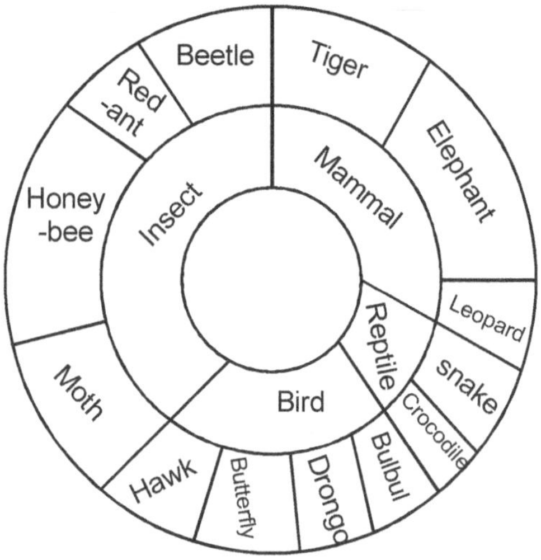

(*i*) Butterflies are birds

(*ii*) There are more tigers in this forest than red ants

(*iii*) All reptiles in this forest are either snakes or crocodiles

(*iv*) Elephants are the largest mammals in this forest

(*a*) (*i*) and (*ii*) only
(*b*) (*i*), (*ii*), (*iii*) and (*iv*)
(*c*) (*i*), (*iii*) and (*iv*) only
(*d*) (*i*), (*ii*) and (*iii*) only

52. Find the odd one in the following group

Q,W,Z,B B,H,K,M W,C,G,J M,S,V,X

(*a*) Q, W, Z, B (*b*) B, H, K, M
(*c*) W, C, G, J (*d*) M, S, V, X

53. Lights of four colors (red, blue, green, yellow) are hung on a ladder. On every step of the ladder there are two lights. If one of the lights is red, the other light on that step will always be blue. If one of the lights on a step is green, the other light on that step will always be yellow. Which of the following statements is not necessarily correct?

(*a*) The number of red lights is equal to the number of blue lights

(*b*) The number of green lights is equal to the number of yellow lights

(*c*) The sum of the red and green lights is equal to the sum of the yellow and blue lights

(*d*) The sum of the red and blue lights is equal to the sum of the green and yellow lights

54. Read the statements:

All women are entrepreneurs.

Some women are doctors.

Which of the following conclusions can be logically inferred from the above statements?

(*a*) All women are doctors

(*b*) All doctors are entrepreneurs

(*c*) All entrepreneurs are women

(*d*) Some entrepreneurs are doctors

55. Find the odd one from the following group:

(*a*) W,E,K,O (*b*) I,Q,W,A

(*c*) F,N,T,X, (*d*) N,V,B,D

56. For submitting tax returns, all resident males with annual income below ₹ 10 lakh should fill up Form P and all resident females with income below ₹ 8 lakh should fill up Form Q. All people with incomes above ₹ 10 lakh should fill up Form R, except non residents with income above ₹ 15 lakhs, who should fill up Form S. All others should fill Form T. An example of a person who should fill Form T is

(*a*) a resident male with annual income ₹ 9 lakh

(*b*) a resident female with annual income ₹ 9 lakh

(*c*) a non-resident male with annual income ₹ 16 lakh

(*d*) a non-resident female with annual income ₹ 16 lakh

57. Which number does not belong in the series below?

2, 5, 10, 17, 26, 37, 50, 64

(*a*) 17 (*b*) 37

(*c*) 64 (*d*) 26

58. A dance programme is scheduled for 10.00 a.m. Some students are participating in the programme and they need to come an hour earlier than the start of the event. These students should be accompanied by a parent. Other students and parents should come in time for the programme. The instruction you think that is appropriate for this is

(*a*) Students should come at 9.00 a.m. and parents should come at 10.00 a.m.

(*b*) Participating students should come at 9.00 a.m. accompanied by a parent, and other parents and students should come by 10.00 a.m.

(*c*) Students who are not participating should come by 10.00 a.m. and they should not bring their parents. Participating students should come at 9.00 a.m.

(*d*) Participating students should come before 9.00 a.m. Parents who accompany them should come at 9.00 a.m. All others should come at 10.00 a.m.

59. The number of people diagnosed with dengue fever (contracted from the bite of a mosquito) in north India is twice the number diagnosed last year. Municipal authorities have concluded that measures to control the mosquito population have failed in this region.

Which one of the following statements, if true, does not contradict this conclusion?

(*a*) A high proportion of the affected population has returned from neighbouring countries where dengue is prevalent

(*b*) More cases of dengue are now reported because of an increase in the Municipal Office's administrative efficiency

(*c*) Many more cases of dengue are being diagnosed this year since the introduction of a new and effective diagnostic test

(*d*) The number of people with malarial fever (also contracted from mosquito bites) has increased this year

60. Geneticists say that they are very close to confirming the genetic roots of psychiatric illnesses such as depression and schizophrenia, and consequently, that doctors will be able to eradicate these diseases through early identification and gene therapy.

On which of the following assumptions does the statement above rely?

(*a*) Strategies are now available for eliminating psychiatric illnesses

(*b*) Certain psychiatric illnesses have a genetic basis

(*c*) All human diseases can be traced back to genes and how they are expressed

(*d*) In the future, genetics will become the only relevant field for identifying psychiatric illnesses

2013

61. Select the pair that best expresses a relationship similar to that expressed in the pair:

Medicine: Health

(*a*) Science : Experiment

(*b*) Wealth : Peace

(*c*) Education : Knowledge

(*d*) Money : Happiness

62. Abhishek is elder to Savar.

Savar is younger to Anshul.

Which of the given conclusions is logically valid and is inferred from the above statements?

(*a*) Abhishek is elder to Anshul

(*b*) Anshul is elder to Abhishek

(*c*) Abhishek and Anshul are of the same age

(*d*) No conclusion follows

63. Complete the sentence:

Universalism is to particularism as diffuseness is to _____

(*a*) specificity

(*b*) neutrality

(*c*) generality

(*d*) adaptation

64. After several defeats in wars, Robert Bruce went in exile and wanted to commit suicide. Just before committing suicide, he came across a spider attempting tirelessly to have its net. Time and again, the spider failed but that did not deter it to retrain from making attempts. Such attempts by the spider made Bruce curious. Thus, Bruce started observing the near-impossible goal of the spider to have the net. Ultimately, the spider succeeded in having its net despite several failures. Such act of the spider encouraged Bruce not to commit suicide. And then, Bruce went back again and won many a battle, and the rest is history.

Which one of the following assertions is best supported by the above information?

(*a*) Failure is the pillar of success.

(*b*) Honesty is the best policy.

(*c*) Life begins and ends with adventures.

(*d*) No adversity justifies giving up hope.

65. Statement: You can always give me a ring whenever you need.

Which one of the following is the best inference from the above statement?

(*a*) Because I have a nice caller tune.

(*b*) Because I have a better telephone facility.

(*c*) Because a friend in need is a friend indeed.

(*d*) Because you need not pay towards the telephone bills when you give me a ring.

66. Statement: There were different streams of freedom movements in colonial India carried out by the moderates, liberals, radicals, socialists, and so on.

Which one of the following is the best inference from the above statement?

(*a*) The emergence of nationalism in colonial India led to our Independence.

(*b*) Nationalism in India emerged in the context of colonialism.

(*c*) Nationalism in India is homogeneous.

(*d*) Nationalism in India is heterogeneous.

67. Select the pair that best expresses a relationship similar to that expressed in the pair :

water : pipe : :

(*a*) cart : road

(*b*) electricity : wire

(*c*) sea : beach

(*d*) music: instrument

68. All professors are researchers

Some scientists are professors

Which of the given conclusions is logically valid and is inferred from the above arguments :

(*a*) All scientists are researchers

(*b*) All professors are scientists

(*c*) Some researchers are scientists

(*d*) No conclusion follows

2012

69. Wanted Temporary, Part-time persons for the post of Field Interviewer to conduct personal interviews to collect and collate economic data. Requirements: High School-pass, must be available for Day, Evening and Saturday work. Transportation paid, expenses reimbursed.

Which one of the following is the best inference from the above advertisement?

(*a*) Gender-discriminatory

(*b*) Xenophobic

(*c*) Not designed to make the post attractive

(*d*) Not gender-discriminatory

70. Given the sequence of terms, AD CG FK JP, the next term is

(*a*) OV (*b*) OW

(*c*) PV (*d*) PW

2011

71. A transporter receives the same number of orders each day. Currently, he has some pending orders (backlog) to be shipped. If he uses 7 trucks, then at the end of the 4th day he can clear all the orders. Alternatively, if he uses only 3 trucks, then all the orders are cleared at the end of the 10th day. What is the minimum number of trucks required so that there will be no pending order at the end of the 5th day?

(*a*) 4

(*b*) 5

(*c*) 6

(*d*) 7

72. Few school curricula include a unit on how to deal with bereavement and grief, and yet all students at some point in their lives suffer from losses through death and parting.

Based on the above passage which topic would not be included in a unit on bereavement?

(*a*) How to write a letter of condolence

(*b*) What emotional stages are passed through in the healing process

(*c*) What the leading causes of death are

(*d*) How to give support to a grieving friend

73. The question below consists of a pair of related words followed by four pairs of words. Select the pair that best expresses the relation in the original pair :

Gladiator : Arena

(*a*) dancer : stage

(*b*) commuter : train

(*c*) teacher : classroom

(*d*) lawyer : courtroom

74. The horse has played a little known but very important role in the field of medicine. Horses were injected with toxins of diseases until their blood built up immunities. Then a serum was made from their blood. Serums to fight with diphtheria and tetanus were developed this way.

It can be inferred from the passage, that horses were

(*a*) given immunity of diseases

(*b*) generally quite immune to diseases

(*c*) given medicines to fight toxins

(*d*) given diphtheria and tetanus serums

2010

75. The question below consists of a pair of related words followed by four pairs of words. Select the pair that best expresses the relation in the original pair.

Unemployed : Worker

(*a*) fallow : land (*b*) unaware : sleeper

(*c*) wit : jester (*d*) renovated : house

76. Hari (H), Gita (G), Irfan (I) and Saira (S) are siblings (i.e. brothers and sisters). All were born on 1st January. The age difference between any two successive siblings (that is born one after another) is less than 3 years. Given the following facts:

I. Hari's age + Gita age > Irfan's age + Saira's age

II. The age difference between Gita and Saira is 1 year. However, Gita is not the oldest and Saira is not the youngest.

III. There are no twins.

In what order were they born (oldest first)?

(*a*) HSIG

(*b*) SGHI

(*c*) IGSH

(*d*) IHSG

77. Modern warfare has changed from large scale clashes of armies to suppression of civilian populations. Chemical agents that do their work silently appear to be suited to such warfare; and regretfully, there exist people in military establishments who think that chemical agents are useful tools for their cause.

Which of the following statements best sums up the meaning of the above passage:

(*a*) Modern warfare has resulted in civil strife

(*b*) Chemical agents are useful in modern warfare

(*c*) Use of chemical agents in warfare would be undesirable

(*d*) People in military establishments like to use chemical agents in war

78. If 137 + 276 = 435 how much is 731 + 672?

(*a*) 534 (*b*) 1403

(*c*) 1623 (*d*) 1513

NUMERICAL TYPE QUESTIONS

2015

1. Fill in the missing value

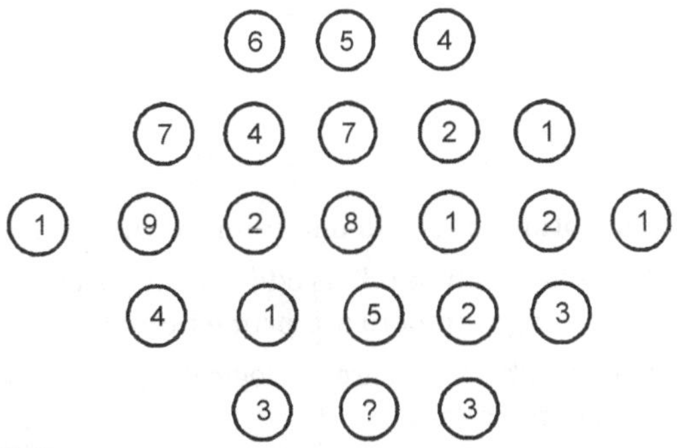

2014

2. The next term in the series 81, 54, 36, 24,.... is ________

3. Fill in the missing number in the series.

2 3 6 15 ___ 157.5 630

4. What is the next number in the series?

12 35 81 173 357 ____

ANSWERS

MCQ Type Questions

1. (*c*)	**2.** (*d*)	**3.** (*b*)	**4.** (*b*)	**5.** (*a*)	**6.** (*c*)	**7.** (*c*)	**8.** (*c*)	**9.** (*b*)	**10.** (*c*)
11. (*c*)	**12.** (*d*)	**13.** (*c*)	**14.** (*a*)	**15.** (*d*)	**16.** (*c*)	**17.** (*b*)	**18.** (*c*)	**19.** (*a*)	**20.** (*c*)
21. (*d*)	**22.** (*b*)	**23.** (*a*)	**24.** (*a*)	**25.** (*d*)	**26.** (*c*)	**27.** (*b*)	**28.** (*b*)	**29.** (*b*)	**30.** (*b*)
31. (*b*)	**32.** (*a*)	**33.** (*b*)	**34.** (*c*)	**35.** (*c*)	**36.** (*b*)	**37.** (*d*)	**38.** (*b*)	**39.** (*a*)	**40.** (*a*)
41. (*a*)	**42.** (*c*)	**43.** (*d*)	**44.** (*d*)	**45.** (*b*)	**46.** (*c*)	**47.** (*b*)	**48.** (*c*)	**49.** (*d*)	**50.** (*b*)
51. (*d*)	**52.** (*c*)	**53.** (*d*)	**54.** (*d*)	**55.** (*d*)	**56.** (*b*)	**57.** (*c*)	**58.** (*b*)	**59.** (*d*)	**60.** (*b*)
61. (*c*)	**62.** (*d*)	**63.** (*a*)	**64.** (*d*)	**65.** (*c*)	**66.** (*d*)	**67.** (*b*)	**68.** (*c*)	**69.** (*d*)	**70.** (*a*)
71. (*c*)	**72.** (*c*)	**73.** (*d*)	**74.** (*b*)	**75.** (*d*)	**76.** (*b*)	**77.** (*c*)	**78.** (*c*)		

Numerical Type Questions

1. (3) **2.** (16) **3.** (45) **4.** (725 to 725)

EXPLANATIONS

MCQ TYPE QUESTIONS

1. Given words 'mock, deride and jeer' are synonyms which means mockery. So, the given word praise is odd one.

2.

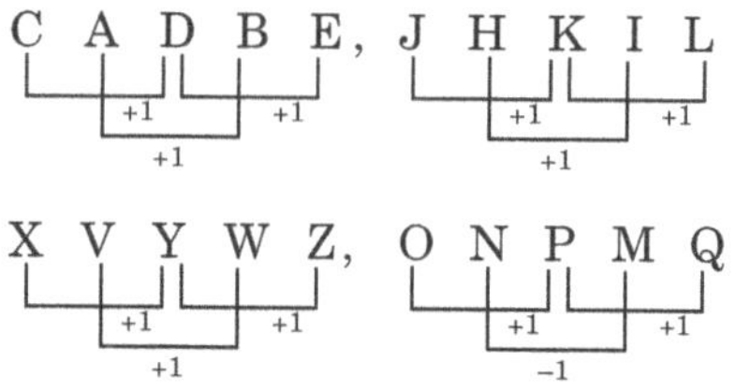

So, option (d) is odd one from the given group.

3. The given number 33 is odd one out, because the remaining numbers are prime number.

7. Statements i and ii are not logically possible based on the given fact.

8. Group 'P'

Mean (μ) = 105

Standard deviation (σ_1) = 25

$\Pr(\mu - \sigma \le x \le \mu + \sigma) \approx 0.6827$

$\therefore$ 68% within one standard deviation

$$\mu_1 - \sigma_1 = 105 - 25 = 80$$

$$\mu_1 + \sigma_1 = 105 + 25 = 130$$

$\therefore$ range = 80 to 130

Distribution of P:

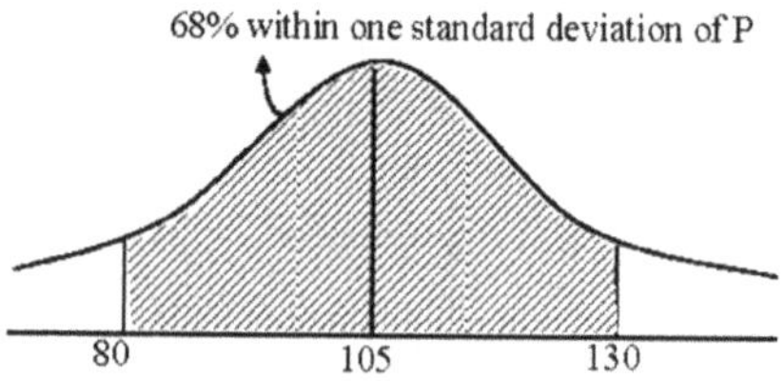

Group 'Q'

Mean (μ_2) = 85

Standard deviation (σ_2) = 5

$\Pr(\mu - \sigma \le x \le \mu + \sigma) \approx 0.6827$

$\therefore$ 68% within one standard deviation

$$\mu_2 - \sigma_2 = 85 - 5 = 80$$

$$\mu_2 + \sigma_2 = 85 + 5 = 90$$

$\therefore$ Range of Q in one standard deviation is 80 to 90

Distribution of 'Q'

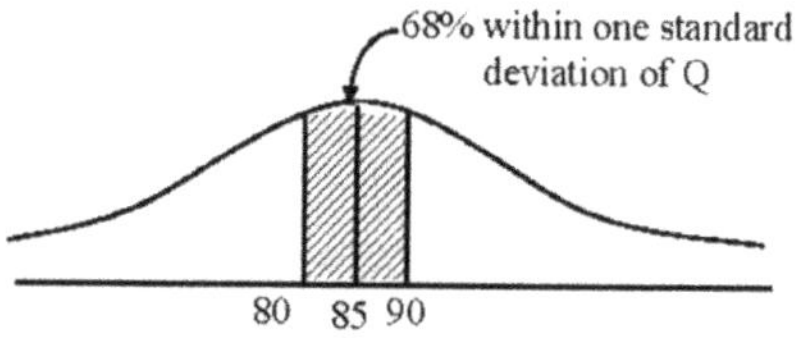

68% within one standard deviation of Q is narrower

$\therefore$ 68% within one standard deviation of Q means most students of group Q.

$\therefore$ Most students of group 'Q' scored marks in a narrower range than students in group 'P'

10. The following letter series is in the order of even letters series

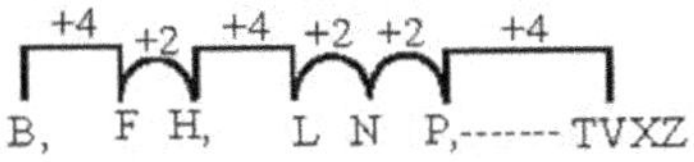

11. From given data, the following diagram can be possible.

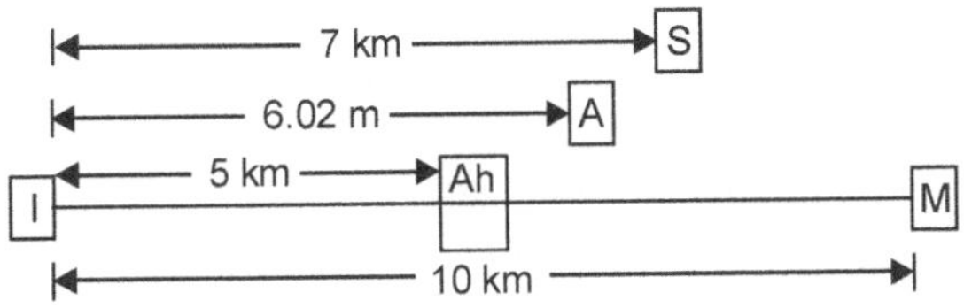

Here S → Susan

A → Arun

Ah → Ahmed

M → Michael

From the above diagram, Arun lives farthest away than Ahmed means more than 5 km but closer than Susan means less than 7 km, from the given alternatives.

So, only option 'c' is possible.

12. From the given question two statements will be followed.

For statment I

Arrange the given data according to their ages

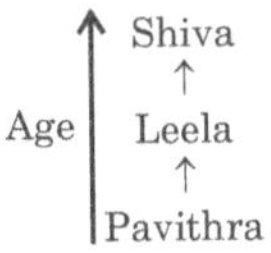

For statement II

Arrange the given data according to their winning

So, from statement I and II, it is clear that only option (*d*) is possible (i.e., statement I).

13.

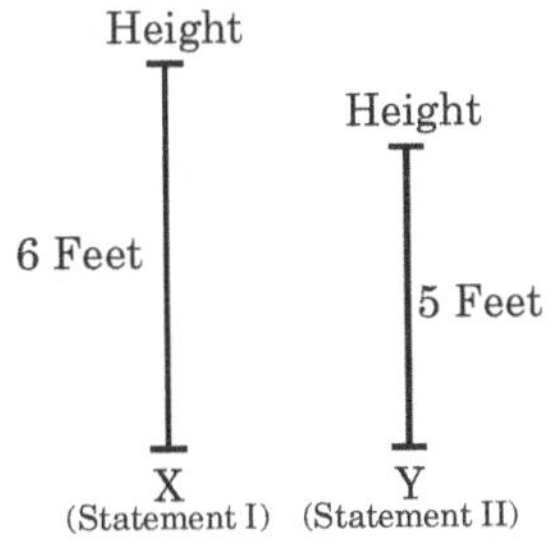

Hence from the given figure Mr. X is taller than Mr. Y by 1 foot.

14. Social science disciplines had a pre-colonial origin.

15.

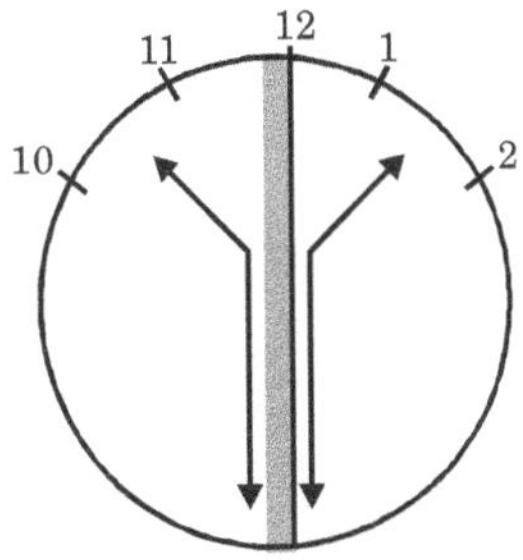

Mirror image of 1 : 20 is 10 : 30

10 : 30 was the time two and quarter hour back so time now will be 12 : 45

16.

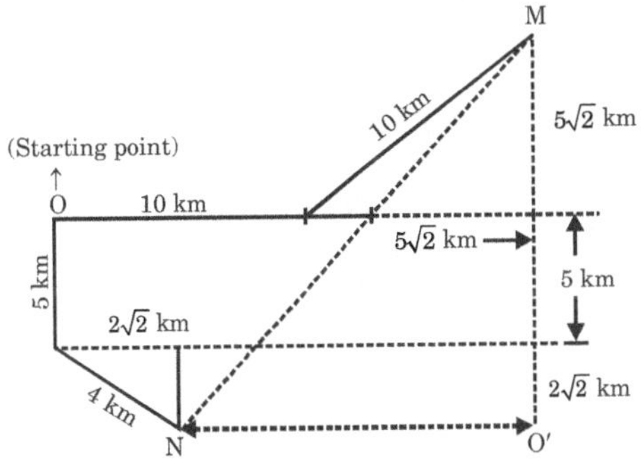

From the given figure

$$MN = \sqrt{(O'M)^2 + (O'N)^2}$$

$$O'M = 5\sqrt{2} + 5 + 2\sqrt{2} = 5 + 7\sqrt{2}$$

$$O'N = 10 + 5\sqrt{2} - 2\sqrt{2} = 10 + 3\sqrt{2}$$

$$MN = \sqrt{(5 + 7\sqrt{2})^2 + (10 + 3\sqrt{2})^2}$$

$$= \sqrt{25 + 98 + 70\sqrt{2} + 100 + 18 + 60\sqrt{2})}$$

$$\approx 20.61 \text{ km}$$

17.

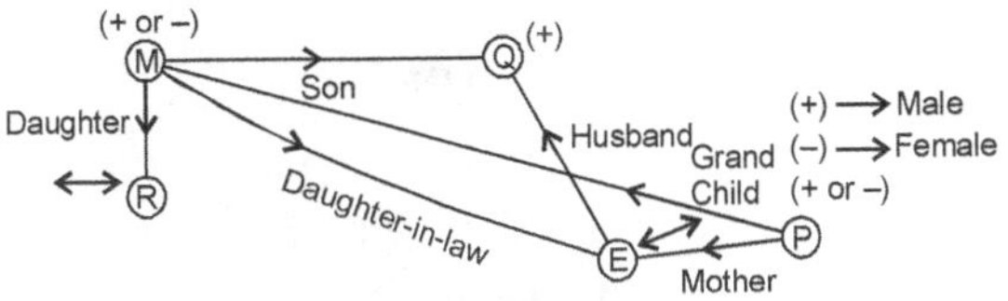

So, from the above relation diagram it is clear that P is the grandchild of M.

20. Manu age = sravan age + 2 months

Manu age = Trideep age – 3 months

Pavan age = Sravan's age + 1 month

From the above statement

Trideep age > Man > Pavan > Sravan

Hence, Trideep can occupy the extra space in the flat.

24.

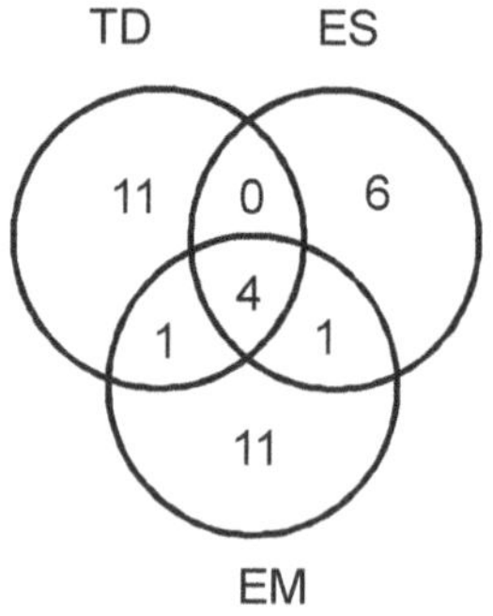

25. Statement-I can be used to solve the question if capacity of both tanks is already known

Statement-II can be used if it is known what quantity of each tank is full/empty.

Therefore, by using both statements

Let capacity of tank B is x

$$\frac{70}{100}x = 14000$$

$$\Rightarrow \quad x = 20000 \text{ gallons}$$

$$\text{Solution in tank A} = \frac{80}{100} \times 14000 = 11200 \text{ gallons}$$

$$\text{Solution in tank B} = \frac{40}{100} \times 20000 = 8000 \text{ gallons}$$

$\therefore$ Total solution = 11200 + 8000 = 19200 gallons

26. $$66\square 6 = \frac{66-6}{66+6} = \frac{60}{72} = \frac{5}{6}$$

$$66\diamond 6 = \frac{66+6}{66-6} = \frac{72}{60} = \frac{6}{5}$$

$$(66\square 6) \rightarrow (66\diamond 6) = \frac{5}{6} \times \frac{6}{5} = 1$$

28. R + 3 = U, O + 3 = R,

A + 3 = D, D + 3 = G;

S + 3 = V, W + 3 = Z,

A + 3 = D, N + 3 = Q

29. Community of people : Doctor

30. Since U does not want any portfolio, (*c*) and (*d*) are ruled out. R wants Home, or Finance or No portfolio, (*a*) is not valid.

Hence option (*b*) is correct.

34. S + 1: S + 2 :

Therefore concluding diagram can be

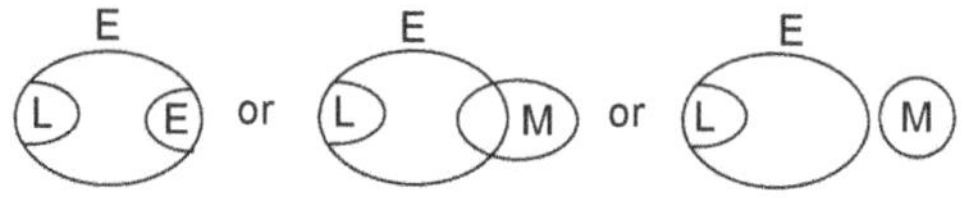

35.

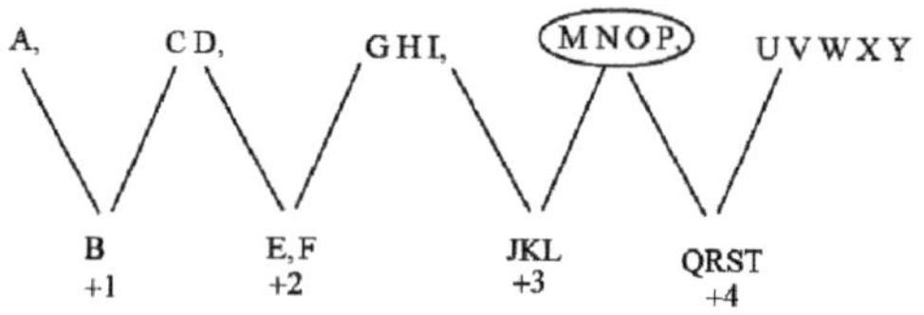

36. Second sentence says that Ms. X reaches Kochi on 21/05/2014. Also she has to be in Bagdogora on 22/05/2014.

$\therefore$ She stays in Kochi for only one day in may.

39.

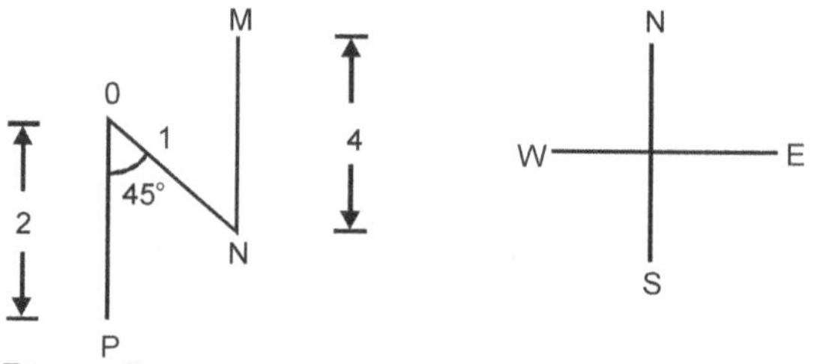

41. Riaz > Som ...(*i*)

Shiv > Ansu ...(*ii*)

Ansu is youngest in the group

$\therefore$ From equations (*i*) and (*ii*)

$\therefore$ Riaz > Som > Shiv > Ansu

42.

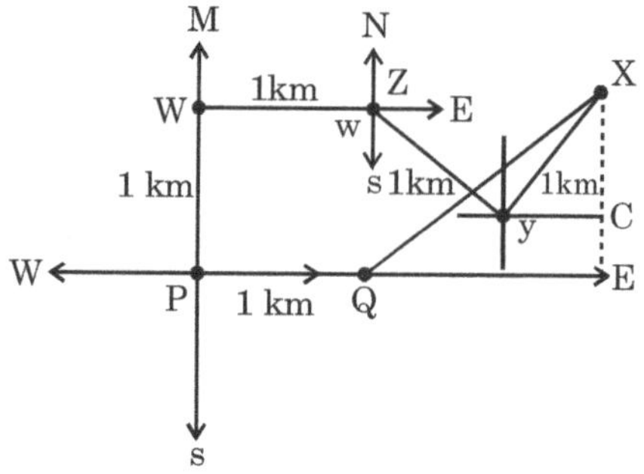

Here XE = 1 km

$$QE = \frac{2}{\sqrt{2}} = \sqrt{2}$$

$\therefore$ using Pythagoras theorem,

$$XQ = \sqrt{(QE)^2 + (XE)^2}$$

$$= \sqrt{2+1} = \sqrt{3} \text{ km}$$

$\therefore$ Statement I itself determines the eldest child which statement 2 is incorrect as Ansu is youngest in the group is not satisfied by statement 2

Hence option (*a*) is correct

44. ALRVX → only one vowel
EPVZB → only one vowel
ITZDF → only one vowel
OYEIK → three vowels

45. (*a*) Anuj: Even numbered floor (2, 4, 6)
(*b*) Bhola: Even numbered floor (2, 4, 6)
(*c*) Chandan lives on the floor above that of Faisal.
(*d*) Dilip: not on 2nd floor.
(*e*) Eswar: does not live immediately above or immediately below Bhola
From the options its clear, that only option (*b*) satisfies condition (*e*).
So, correct Ans is (*b*).

47. KCLFTSB: BST-Best, F-Of, LCK-Luck (Reverse order)
SHSWDG: GD-Good, WSHS-Wishes (Reverse order)
Similarly "ace the Exam'- C-Ace, T-The, XM-Exam

48. Diversity is shown in terms of difference language.

51. It is not mentioned that elephant is the largest animal.

52.

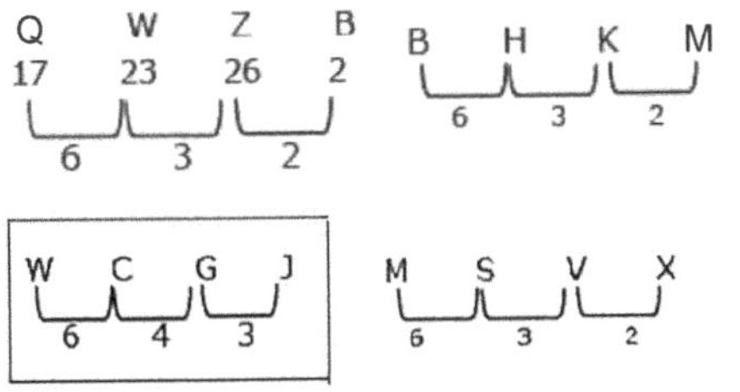

55.

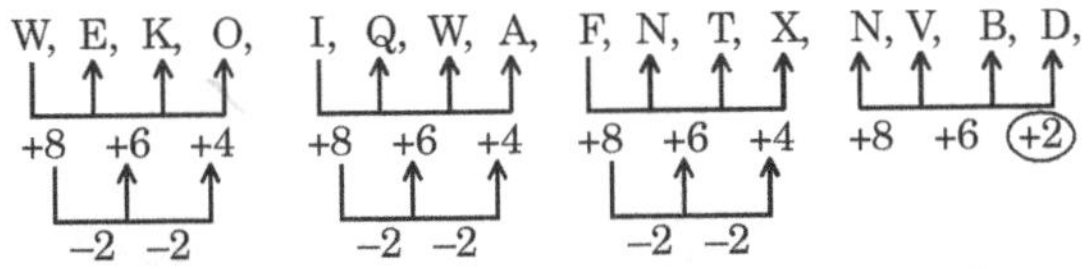

Hence the odd one from the following group is N, V, B, D.

56. By reading the instructions, it is clear that person who fills form T is a resident female with annual income of ₹ 9 Lakh.

59. Among given option, option (*d*) *i.e.* the number of people with malarial fever has increased this year do not contradic the conclusion.

70.

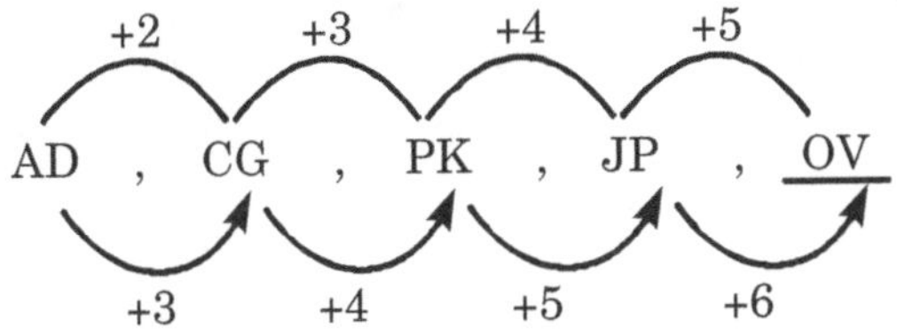

71. Let each truck carry 100 units.

$$2800 = 4n + e$$

where n = normal

$$3000 = 10n + e$$

where e = excess/pending

$$\therefore \quad n = \frac{100}{3}, \quad e = \frac{8000}{3}$$

$$5 \text{ days} \Rightarrow 500\,x = \frac{5100}{3} + \frac{8000}{3}$$

$$\Rightarrow \quad 500x = \frac{8500}{3} = 17$$

$$\Rightarrow \quad x > 5$$

Minimum possible = 6

72. The given passage clearly deals with how to deal with bereavement and grief and so after the tragedy occurs and not about precautions. Therefore, irrespective of the causes of death, a school student rarely gets into details of causes—which is beyond the scope of the context. Rest all are important in dealing with grief.

73. Given relationship is worker: workplace. A gladiator is
(*i*) a person, usually a professional combatant trained to entertain the public by engaging in mortal combat with another person or a wild.
(*ii*) A person engaged in a controversy or debate, especially in public.

74. From the passage it cannot be inferred that horses are given immunity as in option (*a*), since the aim is to develop medicine and in turn immunize humans. Option (*b*) is correct since it is given that horses develop immunity after some time. Refer "until their blood built up immunities". Even option(*c*) is invalid since medicine is not built till immunity is developed in the horses. Option (*d*) is incorrect since specific examples are cited to illustrate and this cannot capture the essence.

76. $H + G > I + S$ ...(1)
and $G - S = 1$ ...(2)
G is not oldest, S is not youngest
$\therefore \quad H + 1 > I$
Irfan older than Hari
Gita older than Sarita
From given option SGHI

77. Use of chemical agents in warfare would be undesirable

78.

$$\begin{array}{rl} 137- & \overline{001}\;\;\overline{011}\;\;\overline{111} \\ +276- & 010\;\;111\;\;110 \\ \hline & 100\;\;011\;\;101 = 435 \end{array}$$

Octal number system

$$\therefore \begin{array}{rl} 731- & 111\;\;011\;\;001 \\ 672- & 110\;\;111\;\;110 \\ \hline & 100\;\;010\;\;011 \end{array}$$

Hence 1623

NUMERICAL TYPE QUESTIONS

1. Middle number is the average of number on both sides

$\therefore$ Average of 3 and 3 is $\frac{3+3}{2} = \frac{6}{2} = 3$

2. $81 - 54 = 27; 27 \times \frac{2}{3} = 18$

$54 - 36 = 18; 18 \times \frac{2}{3} = 12$

$36 - 24 = 12; 12 \times \frac{2}{3} = 8$

$\therefore \quad 24 - 8 = 16$

3. 2 3 6 15 [45] 157.5 630

1.5 2 2.5 3 3.5 4

$\frac{\text{2nd number}}{\text{1st number}}$ is in increasing order as shown above

4. The given series is

12, 35, 81, 173, 357, ...

The given series follows the following pattern

$12 \times 2 + 11 = 35$

$35 \times 2 + 11 = 81$

$81 \times 2 + 11 = 173$

$173 \times 2 + 11 = 357$

$357 \times 2 + 11 = 725$

■■

Numerical Ability

1 CHAPTER

Numbers and Algebra

MCQ TYPE QUESTIONS

2016

1. In a quadratic function, the value of the product of the roots (α, β) is 4. Find the value of

$$\frac{\alpha^n + \beta^n}{\alpha^{-n} + \beta^{-n}}$$

(a) n^4 (b) 4^n
(c) 2^{2n-1} (d) 4^{n-1}

2. Among 150 faculty members in an institute, 55 are connected with each other through Facebook® and 85 are connected through WhatsApp®. 30 faculty members do not have Facebook® or WhatsApp® accounts. The number of faculty members connected only through Facebook® accounts is ____________.

(a) 35 (b) 45
(c) 65 (d) 90

3. If $|9y - 6| = 3$, then $y^2 - \frac{4y}{3}$ is ________.

(a) 0 (b) $+\frac{1}{3}$
(c) $-\frac{1}{3}$ (d) Undefined

4. If $q^{-a} = \frac{1}{r}$ and $r^{-b} = \frac{1}{s}$ and $s^{-c} = \frac{1}{q}$, the value of abc is .

(a) $(rqs)^{-1}$ (b) 0
(c) 1 (d) $r^{+}q^{+}s$

5. The sum of the digits of a two digit number is 12. If the new number formed by reversing the digits is greater than the original number by 54, find the original number.

(a) 39 (b) 57
(c) 66 (d) 93

6. Two finance companies, P and Q, declared fixed annual rates of interest on the amounts invested with them. The rates of interest offered by these companies may differ from year to year. Year-wise annual rates of interest offered by these companies are shown by the line graph provided below.

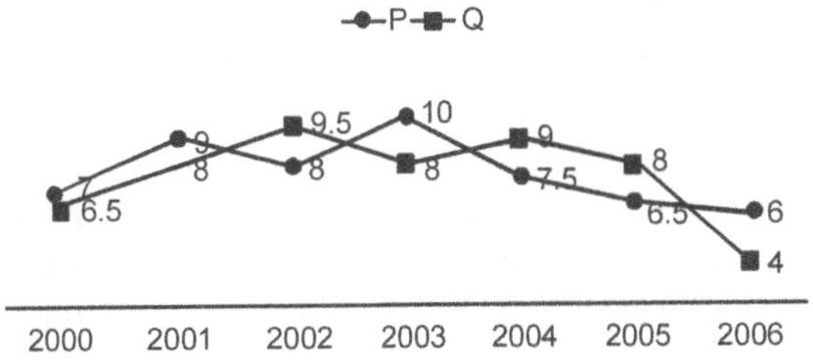

If the amounts invested in the companies, P and Q, in 2006 are in the ratio 8 : 9, then the amounts received after one year as interests from companies P and Q would be in the ratio:

(a) 2 : 3 (b) 3 : 4
(c) 6 : 7 (d) 4 : 3

2015

7. Read the following table giving sales data of five types of batteries for years 2006 to 2012

Year	Type I	Type I	Type I	Type I	Type I
2006	75	144	114	102	108
2007	90	126	102	84	126
2008	96	114	75	105	135
2009	105	90	150	90	75
2010	90	75	135	75	90
2011	105	60	165	45	120
2012	115	85	160	100	145

Out of the following, which type of battery achieved highest growth between the years 2006 and 2012?

(a) Type V (b) Type III
(c) Type II (d) Type I

8. If $a^2 + b^2 + c^2 = 1$, then $ab + bc + ac$ lies in the interval

(a) $\left[1, \frac{2}{3}\right]$

(b) $\left[\frac{-1}{2}, 1\right]$

(c) $\left[-1, \frac{1}{2}\right]$

(d) [2,–4]

9. If the list of letters, P, R, S, T, U is an arithmetic sequence, which of the following are also in arithmetic sequence?

I. 2P, 2R, 2S, 2T, 2U

II. P–3, R–3, S–3, T–3, U–3

III. P^2, R^2, S^2, T^2, U^2

(*a*) I only (*b*) I and II

(*c*) II and III (*d*) I and III

10. The number of students in a class who have answered correctly, wrongly, or not attempted each question in an exam, are listed in the table below. The marks for each question are also listed. There is no negative or partial marking.

Q. No.	Marks	Answered Correctly	Answered Wrongly	Not Attempted
1	2	21	17	6
2	3	15	27	2
3	1	11	29	4
4	2	23	18	3
5	5	31	12	1

What is the average of the marks obtained by the class in the examination?

(*a*) 2.290 (*b*) 2.970

(*c*) 6.795 (*d*) 8.795

2014

11. The monthly rainfall chart on 50 years of rainfall in Agra is shown in the following figure. Which of the following are true? (k percentile is the value such that k percent of the data fall below that value)

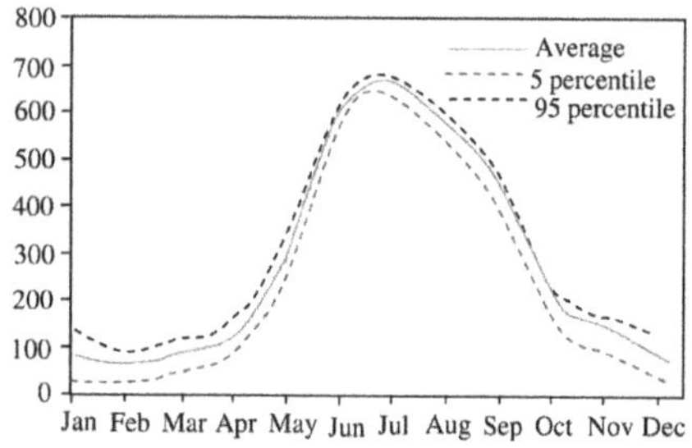

(*i*) On average, it rains more in July than in December

(*ii*) Every year, the amount of rainfall in August is more than that in January

(*iii*) July rainfall can be estimated with better confidence than February rainfall

(*iv*) In August, there is at least 500 mm of rainfall

(*a*) (*i*) and (*ii*)

(*b*) (*i*) and (*iii*)

(*c*) (*ii*) and (*iii*)

(*d*) (*iii*) and (*iv*)

12. The total exports and revenues from the exports of a country are given in the two charts shown below. The pie chart for exports shows the quantity of each item exported as a percentage of the total quantity of exports. The pie chart for the revenues shows the percentage of the total revenue generated through export of each item. The total quantity of exports of all the items is 500 thousand tonnes and the total revenues are 250 crore rupees. Which item among the following has generated the maximum revenue per kg?

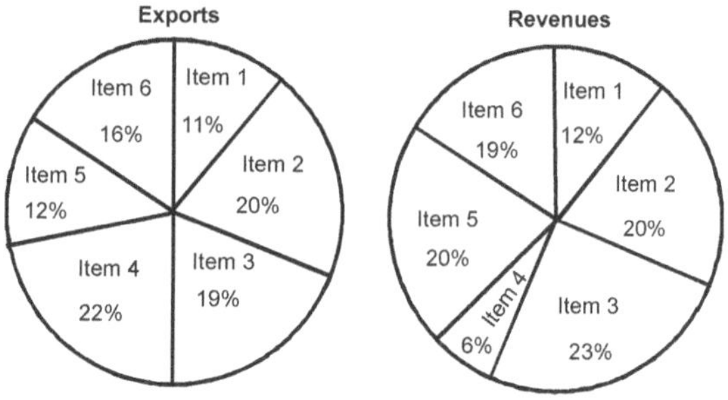

(*a*) Item 2 (*b*) Item 3

(*c*) Item 6 (*d*) Item 5

13. The statistics of runs scored in a series by four batsmen are provided in the following table. Who is the most <u>consistent</u> batsman of these four?

Batsman	Average	Standard deviation
K	31.2	5.21
L	46.0	6.35
M	54.4	6.22
N	17.9	5.90

(*a*) K (*b*) L

(*c*) M (*d*) N

14. The exports and imports (in crores of ₹) of a country from 2000 to 2007 are given in the following bar chart. If the trade deficit is defined as excess of imports over exports, in which year is the trade deficit 1/5th of the exports?

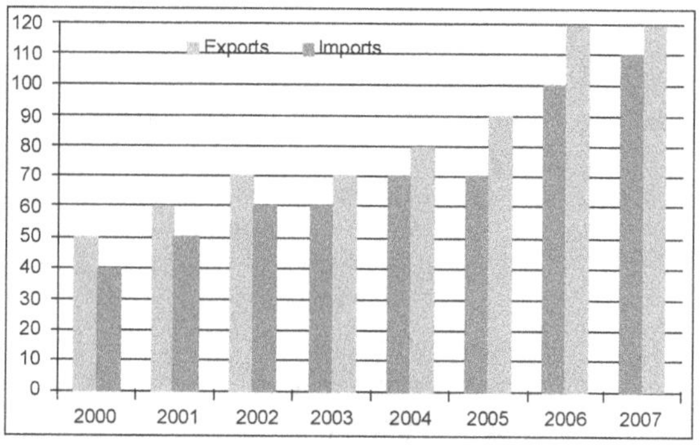

(*a*) 2005

(*b*) 2004

(*c*) 2007

(*d*) 2006

15. The table below has question-wise data on the performance of students in an examination. The marks for each question are also listed. There is no negative or partial marking in the examination.

Q.No.	Marks	Answered Correctly	Answered Wrongly	Not Attempted
1	2	21	17	6
2	3	15	27	2
3	2	23	18	3

What is the average of the marks obtained by the class in the examination?

(*a*) 1.34 (*b*) 1.74

(*c*) 3.02 (*d*) 3.91

16. The ratio of male to female students in a college for five years is plotted in the following line graph. If the number of female students in 2011 and 2012 is equal, what is the ratio of male students in 2012 to male students in 2011?

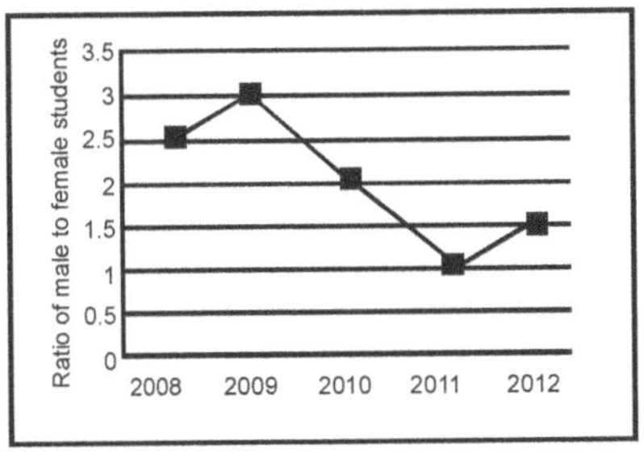

(*a*) 1 : 1 (*b*) 2 : 1

(*c*) 1.5 : 1 (*d*) 2.5 : 1

17. What is the average of all multiples of 10 from 2 to 198?

(*a*) 90 (*b*) 100

(*c*) 110 (*d*) 120

18. The value of $\sqrt{12+\sqrt{12+\sqrt{12+\ldots}}}$ is

(*a*) 3.464 (*b*) 3.932

(*c*) 4.000 (*d*) 4.444

19. If x is real and $|x^2 - 2x + 3| = 11$, then possible values of $|-x^3 + x^2 - x|$ include

(*a*) 2, 4 (*b*) 2, 14

(*c*) 4, 52 (*d*) 14, 52

2013

20. A number is as much greater than 75 as it is smaller than 117. The number is

(*a*) 91

(*b*) 93

(*c*) 89

(*d*) 96

21. Following table provides figures (in rupees) on annual expenditure of a firm for two years - 2010 and 2011.

Category	2010	2011
Raw material	5200	6240
Power & fuel	7000	9450
Salary & wages	9000	12600
Plant & machinery	20000	25000
Advertising	15000	19500
Research & Development	22000	26400

In 2011, which of the following two categories have registered increase by same percentage?

(*a*) Raw material and Salary & wages

(*b*) Salary & wages and Advertising

(*c*) Power & fuel and Advertising

(*d*) Raw material and Research & Development

22. What will be the maximum sum of 44, 42, 40,... ?

(*a*) 502 (*b*) 504

(*c*) 506 (*d*) 500

23. The current erection cost of a structure is ₹ 13,200. If the labour wages per day increase by 1/5 of the current wages and the working hours decrease by 1/24 of the current period, then the new cost of erection in ₹ is

(*a*) 16,500 (*b*) 15,180

(*c*) 11,000 (*d*) 10,120

24. Find the sum of the expression

$$\frac{1}{\sqrt{1}+\sqrt{2}}+\frac{1}{\sqrt{2}+\sqrt{3}}+\frac{1}{\sqrt{3}+\sqrt{4}}+\ldots\ldots+\frac{1}{\sqrt{80}+\sqrt{81}}$$

(*a*) 7 (*b*) 8

(*c*) 9 (*d*) 10

25. In the summer of 2012, in New Delhi, the mean temperature of Monday to Wednesday was 41°C and of Tuesday to Thursday was 43°C. If the temperature on Thursday was 15% higher than that of Monday, then the temperature in °C on Thursday was

(*a*) 40 (*b*) 43

(*c*) 46 (*d*) 49

26. The set of values of p for which the roots of the equation $3x^2 + 2x + p(p - 1) = 0$ are of opposite sign is

(*a*) $(-\infty, 0)$ (*b*) $(0, 1)$

(*c*) $(1, \infty)$ (*d*) $(0, \infty)$

27. Find the sum to n terms of the series 10 + 84 + 734 + ...

(*a*) $\frac{9(9^n+1)}{10}+1$ (*b*) $\frac{9(9^n-1)}{8}+1$

(*c*) $\frac{9(9^n-1)}{8}+n$ (*d*) $\frac{9(9^n-1)}{8}+n^2$

28. If $3 \le X \le 5$ and $8 \le Y \le 11$ then which of the following options is TRUE?

(*a*) $\frac{3}{5} \le \frac{X}{Y} \le \frac{8}{5}$ (*b*) $\frac{3}{11} \le \frac{X}{Y} \le \frac{5}{8}$

(*c*) $\frac{3}{11} \le \frac{X}{Y} \le \frac{8}{5}$ (*d*) $\frac{3}{5} \le \frac{X}{Y} \le \frac{8}{11}$

29. Following table gives data on tourists from different countries visiting India in the year 2011.

Country	Number of Tourists
USA	2000
England	3500
Germany	1200
Italy	1100
Japan	2400
Australia	2300
France	1000

Which two countries contributed to the one third of the total number of tourists who visited India in 2011?

(*a*) USA and Japan

(*b*) USA and Australia

(*c*) England and France

(*d*) Japan and Australia

2012

30. If $(1.001)^{1259} = 3.52$ and $(1.001)^{2062} = 7.85$, then $(1.001)^{3321} =$

(*a*) 2.23 (*b*) 4.33

(*c*) 11.37 (*d*) 27.64

31. Raju has 14 currency notes in his pocket consisting of only ₹ 20 notes and ₹ 10 notes. The total money value of the notes is ₹ 230. The number of ₹ 10 notes that Raju has is

(*a*) 5 (*b*) 6

(*c*) 9 (*d*) 10

32. The data given in the following table summarizes the monthly budget of an average household.

Category	**Amount (Rs.)**
Food	4000
Clothing	1200
Rent	2000
Savings	1500
Other expenses	1800

The approximate percentage of the monthly budget **NOT** spent on savings is

(*a*) 10% (*b*) 14%

(*c*) 81% (*d*) 86%

2011

33. P, Q, R and S are four types of dangerous microbes recently found in a human habitat. The area of each circle with its diameter printed in brackets represents the growth of a single microbe surviving human immunity system within 24 hours of entering the body. The danger to human beings varies proportionately with the toxicity, potency and growth attributed to a microbe shown in the figure below :

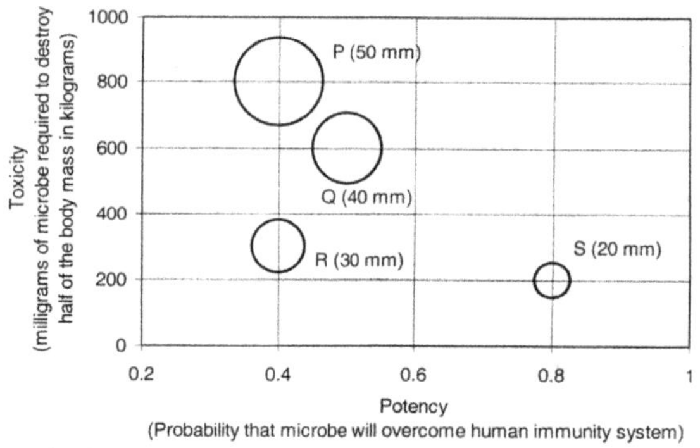

A pharmaceutical company is contemplating the development of a vaccine against the most dangerous microbe. Which microbe should the company target in its first attempt?

(*a*) P (*b*) Q

(*c*) R (*d*) S

34. The sum of n terms of the series 4 + 44 + 444 + ... is

(*a*) $(4/81)\,[10^{n+1} - 9n - 1]$

(*b*) $(4/81)\,[10^{n-1} - 9n - 1]$

(*c*) $(4/81)\,[10^{n+1} - 9n - 10]$

(*d*) $(4/81)\,[10^{n} - 9n - 10]$

35. Given that $f(y) = |y|/y$, and q is any non-zero real number, the value of $|f(q) - f(-q)|$ is

(*a*) 0 (*b*) –1

(*c*) 1 (*d*) 2

NUMERICAL TYPE QUESTIONS

2016

1. The following graph represents the installed capacity for cement production (in tonnes) and the actual production (in tonnes) of nine cement plants of a cement company. Capacity utilization of a plant is defined as ratio of actual production of cement to installed capacity. A plant with installed capacity of at least 200 tonnes is called a large plant and a plant with lesser capacity is called a small plant. The difference between total production of large plants and small plants, in tonnes is ________.

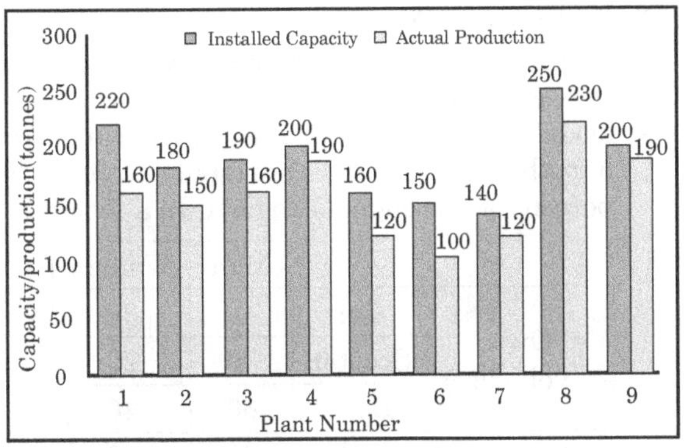

2. The numeral in the units position of

$211^{870} + 146^{127} \times 3^{424}$ is ________.

2015

3. The exports and imports (in crores of Rs.) of a country from the year 2000 to 2007 are given in the following bar chart. In which year is the combined percentage increase in imports and exports the highest ?

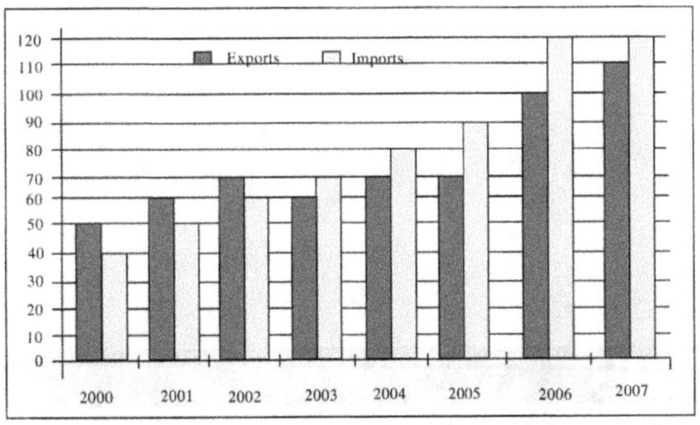

4. The pie chart below has the breakup of the number of students from different departments in an engineering college for the year 2012. The proportion of male to female students in each department is 5 : 4. There are 40 males in Electrical Engineering. What is the difference between numbers of female students in the Civil department and the female students in the Mechanical department?

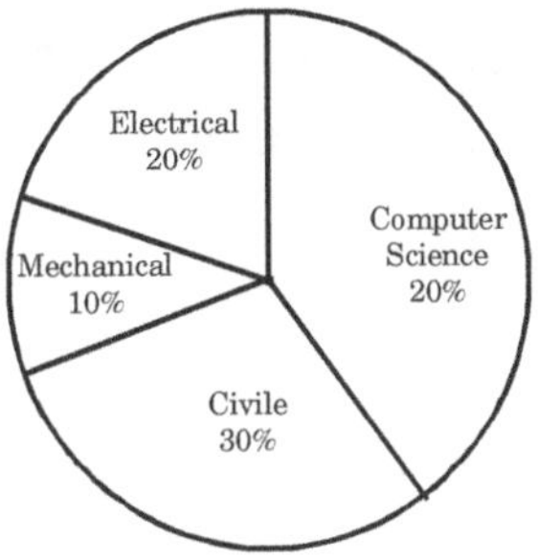

2014

5. A foundry has a fixed daily cost of ₹ 50,000 whenever it operates and variable cost of ₹ 800Q, where Q is the daily production in tonnes. What is the cost of production in ₹ per tonne for a daily production of 100 tonnes?

6. The smallest angle of a triangle is equal to two thirds of the smallest angle of a quadrilateral. The ratio between the angles of the quadrilateral is 3 : 4 : 5 : 6. The largest angle of the triangle is twice its smallest angle. What is the sum, in degrees, of the second largest angle of the triangle and the largest angle of the quadrilateral?

7. In a sequence of 12 consecutive odd numbers, the sum of the first 5 numbers is 425. What is the sum of the last 5 numbers in the sequence?

8. A firm producing air purifiers sold 200 units in 2012. The following pie chart presents the share of raw material, labour, energy, plant & machinery, and transportation costs in the total manufacturing cost of the firm in 2012. The expenditure on labour in 2012 is ₹ 4,50,000. In 2013, the raw material expenses increased by 30% and all other expenses increased by 20%. What is the percentage increase in total cost for the company in 2013?

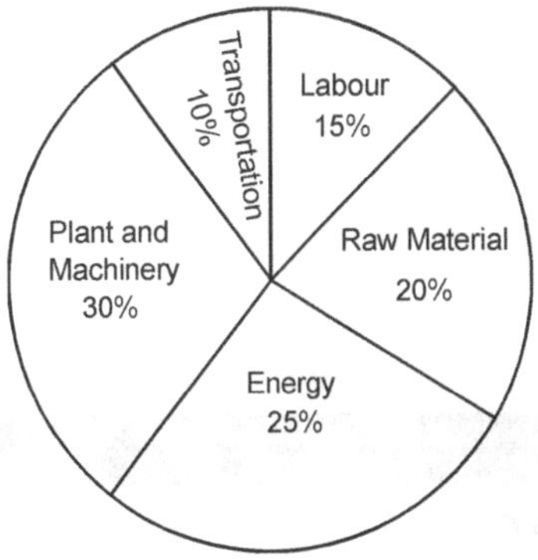

9. A firm producing air purifiers sold 200 units in 2012. The following pie chart presents the share of raw material, labour, energy, plant & machinery, and transportation costs in the total manufacturing cost of the firm in 2012. The expenditure on labour in 2012 is ₹ 4,50,000. In 2013, the raw material expenses increased by 30% and all other expenses increased by 20%. If the company registered a profit of ₹ 10 lakhs in 2012, at what price (in ₹) was each air purifier sold?

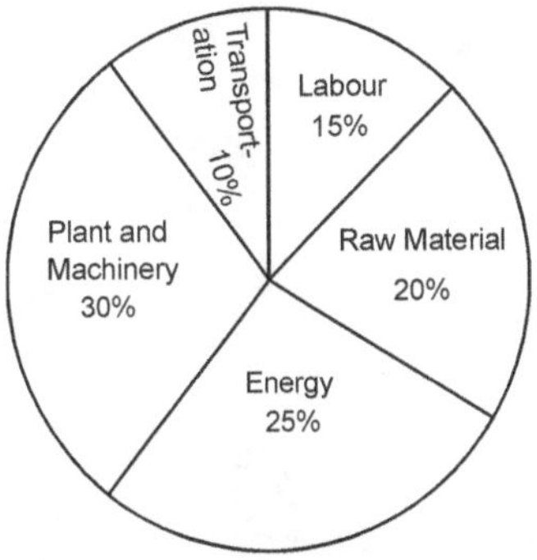

10. The sum of eight consecutive odd numbers is 656. The average of four consecutive even numbers is 87. What is the sum of the smallest odd number and second largest even number?

11. The ratio of male to female students in a college for five years is plotted in the following line graph. If the number of female students doubled in 2009, by what percent did the number of male students increase in 2009?

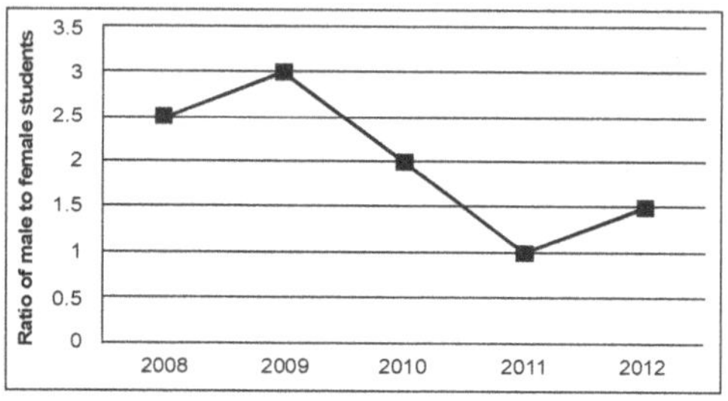

12. If $(z + 1/z)^2 = 98$, compute $(z^2 + 1/z^2)$

13. In a survey, 300 respondents were asked whether they own a vehicle or not. If yes, they were further asked to mention whether they own a car or scooter or both. Their responses are tabulated below. What percent of respondents do not own a scooter?

		Men	Women
Own vehicle	Car	40	34
	Scooter	30	20
	Both	60	46
Do not own vehicle		20	50

14. Round–trip tickets to a tourist destination are eligible for a discount of 10% on the total fare. In addition, groups of 4 or more get a discount of 5% on the total fare. If the one way single person fare is ₹ 100, a group of 5 tourists purchasing round–trip tickets will be charged ₹ ________.

ANSWERS

MCQ Type Questions

1. (*b*) **2.** (*a*) **3.** (*c*) **4.** (*c*) **5.** (*a*) **6.** (*d*) **7.** (*d*) **8.** (*b*) **9.** (*b*) **10.** (*c*)
11. (*b*) **12.** (*d*) **13.** (*a*) **14.** (*d*) **15.** (*c*) **16.** (*c*) **17.** (*b*) **18.** (*c*) **19.** (*d*) **20.** (*d*)
21. (*d*) **22.** (*c*) **23.** (*a*) **24.** (*b*) **25.** (*c*) **26.** (*b*) **27.** (*d*) **28.** (*b*) **29.** (*c*) **30.** (*d*)
31. (*a*) **32.** (*d*) **33.** (*d*) **34.** (*c*) **35.** (*d*)

Numerical Type Questions

1. (120) **2.** (7) **3.** (2006) **4.** (32) **5.** (1300 to 1300) **6.** (180 to 180) **7.** (495) **8.** (22)
9. (20,000) **10.** (163) **11.** (140 to 140) **12.** (96) **13.** (48) **14.** (850)

EXPLANATIONS

MCQ TYPE QUESTIONS

1. $\dfrac{\alpha^n+\beta^n}{\alpha^{-n}+\beta^{-n}} = \dfrac{\alpha^n+\beta^n}{\dfrac{1}{\alpha^n}+\dfrac{1}{\beta^n}} = \dfrac{\alpha^n+\beta^n}{\dfrac{\beta^n+\alpha^n}{\alpha^n\times\beta^n}} = \alpha^n\times\beta^n$

$\alpha^n \times \beta^n = (\alpha \times \beta)^n = (4)^n$

So, the value of $\dfrac{\alpha^n+\beta^n}{\alpha^{-n}+\beta^{-n}}$ is 4^n.

2. From question

Total number of faculty members = 150

The number of faculty members having facebook account = (FB) = 55

The number of faculty members having whatsapp = (W) = 85

The number of faculty members do not have face book or Whats App accounts = 30

The number of faculty members having any account = 150 – 30 = 120

The number of faculty members having both the accounts = (FB + W) – 120 = (55 + 85) – 120 = 20

∴ The number of faculty members connected only through Facebook accounts = 55 – 20 = 35

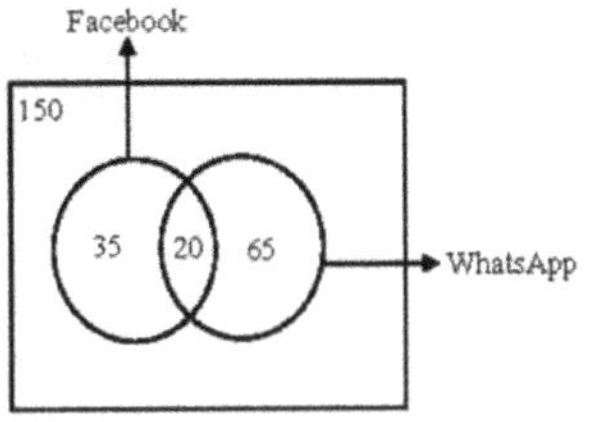

So the number of faculty members connected only through facebook accounts is 35.

3. Given, $|9y-6| = 3$

It has two values either

$(9y-6) = 3$ ...(*i*)

Or $-(9y-6) = 3$

$9y - 6 = -3$ ...(*ii*)

From equation (*i*),

$9y = 9$

∴ $y = 1$

Or from equation (*ii*),

$9y = 3$

∴ $y = \dfrac{1}{3}$

Now $y^2 = \dfrac{4y}{3}$

put $y = 1$,

we get $= 1-\dfrac{4}{3} = -\dfrac{1}{3}$

and also put $y = \dfrac{1}{3}$

we get, $\dfrac{1}{9}-\dfrac{4}{9} = \dfrac{-3}{9} = \dfrac{-1}{3}$

So, the required value is $\dfrac{-1}{3}$.

4. Given $q^{-a} = \dfrac{1}{r}$

⇒ $\dfrac{1}{q^a} = \dfrac{1}{r}$

⇒ $q^a = r$ ...(*i*)

$r^{-b} = \dfrac{1}{s}$

⇒ $\dfrac{1}{r^b} = \dfrac{1}{s}$

⇒ $s = r^b$ ...(*ii*)

$s^{-c} = \dfrac{1}{q}$

⇒ $\dfrac{1}{s^c} = \dfrac{1}{q}$

⇒ $s^c = q$ ...(*iii*)

From equation (*i*),

$q^a = r$

$(s^c)^a = r$ (from eq. (*iii*))

$S^{ac} = r$

$s^{ac} = (s)^{\frac{1}{b}}$ (from eq. (*ii*))

$s^{abc} = s = s^1$

∴ $abc = 1$

So the value of abc is 1

5. Let the two digit number be xy

Now sum of the digit of a two digit number is 12

∴ $x + y = 12$ ...(*i*)

Now according to question,

$(10y + x) - (10x + y) = 54$

∴ $9y - 9x = 54$

∴ $y - x = 6$ ...(*ii*)

Now solving equation (*i*) and (*ii*) we get,

$x = 3$ and $y = 9$

Hence the original number is 39.

∴ Option (*a*) is correct.

6. Amount invested by Company P in 2006 = ₹ 8x

and amount invested by Company Q in 2006 = ₹ $9x$

Interest from Company P

$$= \frac{\frac{₹\, 8x \times 6}{100}}{\frac{₹\, 9x \times 4}{100}}$$

$$= \frac{4}{3}$$

∴ Option (d) is correct.

7. Type-I achieved a growth of 53% in the period which is higher than any other type of battery

10. Total number of students in class = 44

Average of marks,

$$= \frac{(2\times 21)+(3\times 15)+(1\times 11)+(2\times 23)+(5\times 31)}{42}$$

$$= \frac{42+45+11+46+155}{44} = \frac{299}{44} = 6.795$$

∴ Option (c) is correct.

11. In the question the monthly average rainfall chart for 50 years has been given.

Let us check the options.

(i) On average, it rains more in July than in December ⇒ correct.

(ii) Every year, the amount of rainfall in August is more than that in January.

⇒ may not be correct because average rainfall is given in the question.

(iii) July rainfall can be estimated with better confidence than February rainfall.

⇒ From chart it is clear the gap between 5 percentile and 95 percentile from average is higher in February than that in July ⇒ correct.

(iv) In August at least 500 mm rainfall

⇒ May not be correct, because its 50 year average.

So correct option (b) (i) and (iii).

12. Item : 2

$$\frac{\frac{20}{100}\times 250\times 10^7}{\frac{20}{100}\times 500\times 10^3}$$

$0.5\times 10^4 = 5\times 10^3$ $\boxed{1}$ = Item 2

Item : 3

$$\frac{23\times 250\times 10^7}{19\times 500\times 10^3}$$

1.2 = Item 3

Item : 6

$\frac{19}{16} = 1.18 =$ Item 6

Item : 5

$\frac{20}{12} = \frac{5}{3} = 1.6 \Rightarrow$ $\boxed{1.6 = \text{Item 5}}$

14. For 2005,

trade defict = (90 – 70) crores = 20 crores

Now $\frac{1}{5}^{th}$ of export = $\frac{1}{5}(70)$ crores

= 14 crores ≠ 20 crores.

Hence option (a) is wrong.

For 2004,

Trade defict =(80 – 70) crores = 10 crores

Now $\frac{1}{5}^{th}$ of export = $\frac{1}{5}(70)$ crores

= 14 crores ≠ 20 crores.

Hence option (b) is wrong.

For 2007

Trade defict = (120 – 110) crores

= 10 crores

Now $\frac{1}{5}^{th}$ of export = $\frac{1}{5}(110)$ crores

= 22 crores ≠ 10 crores.

Hence option (c) is wrong.

For 2006,

Trade defict = (120 – 100) crores

= 20 crores

Now $\frac{1}{5}^{th}$ of export = $\frac{1}{5}(100)$ crores

= 20 crores = Trade deficts

Hence option (d) is correct.

15. Total question

44 × 2 = 88

44 × 3 = 132

$$\frac{144}{132} = \frac{88}{308}$$

Total marks obtained = (21×2) + (15×3) + (23×2)

= 133

Total Number of students = 44

$$\text{Average} = \frac{133}{44} = 3.02$$

16. Take number of female students in 2011 = 100

$\therefore$ Number of male in 2011 = 100

No. of female in 2012 = 100

No. of male in 2012 = 150

$$\text{Ratio} = \frac{150}{100}$$

17. All multiples of 10 from 2 to 198

= 10, 20,............190

Now $a_n = a + (n-1)d$

$190 = 10 + (n-1) \times 10$

$180 = (n-1) \times 10$

$18 = n - 1$

$\therefore$ $n = 19$

Hence total number of multiples are 19.

Now $S_n = \frac{n}{2}[2a + (n-1)d]$

$= \frac{19}{2}[20 + (18)(10)]$

$= \frac{19}{2}[20 + 180] = 1900$

Now average of all multiples of 10 from 2 to198

$= \frac{10 + 20 + \ldots + 190}{19}$

$\therefore$ $= \frac{1900}{19} = 100$

18. $\sqrt{12 + \sqrt{12 + \sqrt{12 + \ldots}}}$

For a particular type of question

i.e. $\sqrt{a + \sqrt{a + \sqrt{a + \ldots}}}$ we find a two consecutive number whose product is a. The greater number among the two consecutive number is the answer.

Here $a = 12$

i.e. $12 = 3 \times 4$
↓
greater number

Hence $\sqrt{12 + \sqrt{12 + \sqrt{12 + \ldots}}} = 4$

19. Here it is given that x is real

Now $|x^2 - 2x + 3| = 11$

$\Rightarrow$ $x^2 - 2x + 3 = 11$ or $x^2 - 2x + 3 = -11$

For $x^2 - 2x + 3 = 11 \Rightarrow x^2 - 2x - 8 = 0$

$b^2 - 4ac = 4 - 4(1)(-8) = 36 > 0$

Hence roots are real.

and for $x^2 - 2x + 14 = 0$

$b^2 - 4ac = 4 - 4(1)(14) < 0$

Hence roots are imaginary

$\therefore$ The value of x is the root of $x^2 - 2x - 8 = 0$

Now $x = \frac{+2 \pm \sqrt{4 - 4(1)(-8)}}{2}$

$= \frac{2 \pm \sqrt{36}}{2}$

$= \frac{2 \pm 6}{2}$

$\therefore$ $x = 4, -2.$

Now for $x = 4$,

$|-x^3 + x^2 - x| = |-64 + 16 - 4| = 52.$

and for $x = -2$

$|-x^3 + x^2 - x| = |+8 + 4 + 2| = 14$

Hence possible values of $|-x^3 + x^2 - x| = 14, 52$

22. $0 = 44 + (n-1)(-2)$

$n - 1 = 22$

$n = 23$

Sum $= \frac{n}{2}(a + l)$

$= \frac{23}{2}(44 + 0)$

$= 23 \times 22 = 506$

Hence (c) is the answer

23. Let 'd' be the # of days required

Let 'h' be the daily working hours.

$\therefore$ dh can be taken as a measure of the total work be done in order to erect the structure.

Now working hours per day $h' = \frac{23}{24}h$

$\therefore$ # of days $d' = \frac{dh}{h'} = \frac{dh}{\left(\frac{23}{24}h\right)} = \frac{24}{23}d$

Let c = daily wages earlier

$\therefore$ $c = \frac{13,200}{d}$

Now daily wages $c' = \frac{6}{5}c$

$\therefore$ Total new cost = $c' \times d'$

$= \frac{6}{5} \times \frac{13200}{d} \times \frac{24}{23}d \approx 16,500$

24. Given: The expression

$$S = \frac{1}{\sqrt{1}+\sqrt{2}} + \frac{1}{\sqrt{2}+\sqrt{3}} + \ldots\ldots + \frac{1}{\sqrt{80}+\sqrt{81}}$$

To find: Sum of the expression.

Analysis: Each term of the expression is having irrational denominator. One can also see, that both the elements in the denominator of a term differ by only 1.

This gives an idea that on rationalising the denominator, each denominator will become 1, so the sum will be easier than earlier.

Rationalising the denominator,

$$S = \frac{\sqrt{2}-\sqrt{1}}{(\sqrt{2})^2-(\sqrt{1})^2} + \frac{\sqrt{3}-\sqrt{2}}{(\sqrt{3})^2-(\sqrt{2})^2} + \ldots + \frac{\sqrt{81}-\sqrt{80}}{(\sqrt{81})^2-(\sqrt{80})^2}$$

$$= \frac{\sqrt{2}-\sqrt{1}}{1} + \frac{\sqrt{3}-\sqrt{2}}{3-2} + \ldots. + \frac{\sqrt{81}-\sqrt{80}}{81-80}$$

$$= \sqrt{2}-\sqrt{1}+\sqrt{3}-\sqrt{2}+\ldots.+81-\sqrt{80}$$

Now, one can see that the terms will cancel out.

Each term except $\sqrt{1}$ & $\sqrt{81}$

Occurs twice, once as positive and once a negative. So, after cancelling out, we are left with the following:

$$S = \sqrt{81}-\sqrt{1} = 9-1 = 8$$

So, the answer is (*b*).

25. $\frac{\text{Mon + Tues + Wed.}}{3} = 41$

Mon + Tues + Wed. = 123 ...(1)

$\frac{\text{Tues + Wed + Thurs.}}{3} = 43°$

Tue + Wed + Thu. = 129° ...(2)

(2) – (1)

Tues + Wed + Thu – (Mon + Tues. + Wed.)

= 129 – 123 = 6°

Thu. – Mon. = 6° ⇒ $\frac{115x}{100} - x = 6°$

Thus. = Mon × $\frac{115}{100}$ = $\frac{15x}{100}$ = 6°

Mon = x x = 40°

Thurs = $\frac{115x}{100}$

∴ Thurs = $\frac{115 \times 40}{100}$ = 46°

30. Let $1.001 = x$

$x^{1259} = 3.52$, and $x^{2062} = 7.85$

∴ $x^{3321} = x^{1259} . x^{2062}$

$= 3.52 \times 7.85$

$= 27.64$

31. Let number of ₹ 20 notes be x and ₹ 10 notes be y

∴ $20x + 10y = 230$ ...(1)

and $x + y = 14$ ...(2)

Solving equations (1) and (2), we have

$x = 9$ and $y = 5$

Hence numbers of 10 rupee notes are 5.

32. Total budget = 10,500

Expenditure other than savings = 9000

Hence approximate percentage of monthly budget

$$= \frac{9000}{10500} = 86\%$$

33. By observation of the table, we can say S

	P	Q	R	S
Requirement	800	600	300	200
Potency	0.4	0.5	0.4	0.8

34. Let S = 4 (1 + 11 + 111 + ...)

$$= \frac{4}{9}(9 + 99 + 999 + \ldots)$$

$$= \frac{4}{9}\{(10-1) + (10^2-1) + (10^3-1) + \ldots\ldots\ldots\}$$

$$= \frac{4}{9}\{(10 + 10^2 + \ldots.+ 10^n) - n\}$$

$$= \frac{4}{9}\left\{10\frac{(10^n-1)}{9} - n\right\}$$

$$= \frac{4}{81}\{10^{n+1} - 9n - 10\}$$

35. Given : $f(y) = \frac{|y|}{y}$

$$\Rightarrow \quad f(q) = \frac{|q|}{q}$$

$$f(-q) = \frac{|-q|}{-q}$$

$$= \frac{-|q|}{q}$$

$$|f(q) - f(q)| = \frac{|q|}{q} + \frac{|q|}{q}$$

$$= \frac{2|q|}{q} = 2$$

NUMERICAL TYPE QUESTIONS

1. From the given graph large plants which are having installed capacity of at least 200 tonnes are 1, 4, 8 and 9.

So, the total production of large plants

$= 160 + 190 + 230 + 190$

$= 770$

Now the remaining plants with installed capacity is less then 200 tonnes are 2, 3, 5, 6 and 7.

So, total production of small plants

$= 150 + 160 + 120 + 100 + 120$

$= 650$

Then difference $= 770 - 650$

$= 120$

2. Unit digit of $211^{870} + 146^{127} \times 3^{424}$ is $1 + 6 \times 1 = 7$

3. Increase in exports in 2006

$$= \frac{100-70}{70} = 42.8\%$$

Increase in imports in 2006

$$= \frac{120-90}{90} = 33.3\%$$

which is more than any other year.

4. According to question,

There are 40 males in Electrical Engg.

∴ Total number of females in Electrical Engg.

$= 72 - 40 = 32$

∴ Total number of students in Electrical Engg. = 72

⇒ 20% = 72

∴ 30% = Total number of students in Civil Engg.

∴ Total number of students in Civil Engg.

$$= \frac{30 \times 72}{20} = 36 \times 3 = 108$$

∴ Number of female students in Civil Engg.

$$= \frac{4 \times 108}{9} = 4 \times 12 = 48$$

Now, total number of students in Mechanical Engg.

$$= \frac{10 \times 72}{20} = 36$$

∴ Number of female students in Mechanical Engg.

$$= \frac{4 \times 36}{9} = 16$$

∴ Difference between female students in Civil and Mechanical departments = 48 – 16 = 32

5. Fixed cost = ₹ 50,000

Variable cost = ₹ 800Q

Q = daily production in tones

For 100 tonnes of production daily, total cost of production = 50,000 + 800 × 100 = 130,000

So, cost of production per tonne of daily production

$$= \frac{130{,}000}{100} = ₹\ 1300.$$

6. Let the angles of quadrilateral are $3x$, $4x$, $5x$, $6x$

So, $3x + 4x + 5x + 6x = 360$

$x = 20$

Smallest angle of quadrilateral $= 3 \times 20 = 60°$

Smallest angle of triangle $= \frac{2}{3} \times 60° = 40°$

Largest angle of triangle $= 2 \times 40° = 60°$

Three angles of triangle are 40°, 60°, 80°

Largest angle of quadrilateral is 120°

Sum (2nd largest angle of triangle + largest angle of quadrilateral) = 60° + 120° =180°.

7. 8th observation is 7 × 2 = 14 more than 1st observation

9th observation is 14 more than 2nd observation

10th observation is 14 more than 3rd observation

11th observation is 14 more than 4th observation

12th observation is 14 more than 5th observation

Total 14 × 5 =70

Sum of the first five numbers = 425

Sum of last five numbers = 495

8.

	2012	2013
Transport (10%)	300,000	360,000
Labour (15%)	450,000	540,000
Raw material (20%)	750,000	780,000
Energy (25%)	750,000	900,000
Plant and Machinery (30%)	900,000	1,080,000
Total	**3,000,000**	**3,660,000**

Percentage increase in total cost = 22%

9. Total expenditure $= \frac{15}{100} x = 4{,}50{,}000$

$x = 3 \times 10^6$

Profit = 10 lakhs

So, total selling price = 40,00,000 ...(1)

Total purifies = 200 ...(2)

S.P. of each purifier = (1)/(2) = 20,000

10. Eight consecutive odd number = 656

$a - 6, a - 1, a - 2, a, a + 2, a + 4, a + 6$

$a + 8 = 656$

$a = 81$

Smallest $m = 75$ ...(1)

Average consecutive even numbers

$$\Rightarrow \frac{a-2+a+a+2+a+4}{4} = 87$$

$\Rightarrow a = 86$

Second largest number = 88 ...(2)

Adding equation (1) and (2),

$$75 + 88 = 163$$

11. Ratio of male to female student in 2008 = 5 : 2

In 2009, let the male student be $5x$ and female student be $2x$

Now if number of female students double in 2009

$\therefore$ Number of female student = $4x$

$\therefore$ Number of male student = $12x$

Gender	2008	2009
Male	$5x$	$12x$
Female	$2x$	$4x$

% of male student increase in 2009

$$= \left[\left(\frac{12x-5x}{5x}\right)\times 100\right]\%$$

$$= \left[\frac{7}{5}\times 100\right]\%$$

$$= 140\%$$

12. Expanding

$$\left(z+\frac{1}{z}\right)^2 = 98$$

$$\therefore \quad z^2+\frac{1}{z^2}+2(z)\left(\frac{1}{z}\right) = 98$$

$$\therefore \quad z^2+\frac{1}{z^2} = 96$$

13. Total respondents = 300

Now men respondents who do not have scooter

= 40 + 20 = 60

And women respondents who do not have scooter

= 34 + 50 = 84

$\therefore$ Total respondents who do not have scooter

= 60 + 84 = 144

$$\therefore \text{Required percent} = \left(\frac{144}{300}\times 100\right)\% = 48\%$$

14. One way single person fare = ₹ 100

$\therefore$ Two way fare for single person = ₹ 200

$\therefore$ For 5 persons two way fare = ₹ 1000

Now, total discount = (10 + 5)% = 15%

$$\text{Discount amount} = ₹\left[\frac{15}{100}\times 1000\right] = ₹\ 150$$

Amount to be paid = ₹(1000 – 150) = ₹ 850

2 CHAPTER

Percentage and Its Applications

MCQ TYPE QUESTIONS

2016

1. In a huge pile of apples and oranges, both ripe and unripe mixed together, 15% are unripe fruits. Of the unripe fruits, 45% are apples. Of the ripe ones, 66% are oranges. If the pile contains a total of 5692000 fruits, how many of them are apples?
   (*a*) 2029198 (*b*) 2467482
   (*c*) 2789080 (*d*) 3577422
2. A person moving through a tuberculosis prone zone has a 50% probability of becoming infected. However, only 30% of infected people develop the disease. What percentage of people moving through a tuberculosis prone zone remains infected but does not show symptoms of disease?
   (*a*) 15 (*b*) 33
   (*c*) 35 (*d*) 37
3. (*x* % of *y*) + (*y* % of *x*) is equivalent to ______.
   (*a*) 2 % of *xy* (*b*) 2 % of (*xy*/100)
   (*c*) *xy* % of 100 (*d*) 100 % of *xy*

2014

4. The population of a new city is 5 million and is growing at 20% annually. How many years would it take to double at this growth rate?
   (*a*) 3 – 4 years (*b*) 4 – 5 years
   (*c*) 5 – 6 years (*d*) 6 – 7 years
5. One percent of the people of country X are taller than 6 ft. Two percent of the people of country Y are taller than 6 ft. There are thrice as many people in country X as in country Y. Taking both countries together, what is the percentage of people taller than 6 ft?
   (*a*) 3.0 (*b*) 2.5
   (*c*) 1.5 (*d*) 1.25
6. Industrial consumption of power doubled from 2000-2001 to 2010-2011. Find the annual rate of increase in percent assuming it to be uniform over the years.
   (*a*) 5.6 (*b*) 7.2
   (*c*) 10.0 (*d*) 12.2
7. The Gross Domestic Product (GDP) in Rupees grew at 7% during 2012-2013. For international comparison, the GDP is compared in US Dollars (USD) after conversion based on the market exchange rate. During the period 2012-2013 the exchange rate for the USD increased from ₹ 50/ USD to ₹ 60/ USD. India's GDP in USD during the period 2012-2013
   (*a*) increased by 5% (*b*) decreased by 13%
   (*c*) decreased by 20% (*d*) decreased by 11%

2013

8. A firm is selling its product at ₹ 60 per unit. The total cost of production is ₹ 100 and firm is earning total profit of ₹ 500. Later, the total cost increased by 30%. By what percentage the price should be increased to maintained the same profit level.
   (*a*) 5 (*b*) 10
   (*c*) 15 (*d*) 30

2012

9. An automobile plant contracted to buy shock absorbers from two suppliers X and Y. X supplies 60% and Y supplies 40% of the shock absorbers. All shock absorbers are subjected to a quality test. The ones that pass the quality test are considered reliable. Of X's shock absorbers, 96% are reliable. Of Y's shock absorbers, 72% are reliable.
   The probability that a randomly chosen shock absorber, which is found to be reliable, is made by Y is
   (*a*) 0.288 (*b*) 0.334
   (*c*) 0.667 (*d*) 0.720

2011

10. There are two candidates P and Q in an election. During the campaign, 40% of the voters promised to vote for P, and rest for Q. However, on the day of election 15% of the voters went back on their promise to vote for P and instead voted for Q. 25% of the voters went back on their promise to vote for Q and instead voted for P. Suppose, P lost by 2 votes, then what was the total number of voters?
    (*a*) 100 (*b*) 110
    (*c*) 90 (*d*) 95

NUMERICAL TYPE QUESTION

2015

1. From a circular sheet of paper of radius 30 cm, a sector of 10% area is removed. If the remaining part is used to make a conical surface, then the ratio of the radius and height of the cone is ____.

ANSWERS

MCQ Type Questions

1. (*a*) **2.** (*c*) **3.** (*a*) **4.** (*a*) **5.** (*d*) **6.** (*b*) **7.** (*d*) **8.** (*a*) **9.** (*b*) **10.** (*a*)

Numerical Type Question

1. (2.06)

EXPLANATIONS

MCQ TYPE QUESTIONS

1. Given,

Total no. of fruits = 5692000

Unripe type of apples = 45% of 15% of 5692000

$$= \frac{45}{100} \times \frac{15}{100} \times 5692000$$
$$= 384210$$

Ripe type of apples $= (100 - 66)\% \times (100 - 15)\% \times 5692000$

$$= \frac{34}{100} \times \frac{85}{100} \times 5692000$$
$$= 1644988$$

$\therefore$ Total no. of apples = 384210 + 1644988

= 2029198

2. The percentage of people moving through a tuberculosis prone zone remains infected but does not show symptoms of disease.

$$= (100 - 30)\% \times 50\% = \frac{70}{100} \times \frac{50}{100} = \frac{35}{100} = 35\%$$

3. (x% of y) + (y% of x)

$$\frac{x}{100} \times y + \frac{y}{100} \times x = \frac{2xy}{100} = 2\% \text{ of } xy$$

$\therefore$ Option (*a*) is correct.

4.
$$A = P\left[1 + \frac{r}{100}\right]^t$$

$$10 \text{ million} = 5 \text{ million}\left[1 + \frac{20}{100}\right]^t$$

$$2 = \left[1 + \frac{1}{5}\right]^t$$

$$2 = \left(\frac{6}{5}\right)^t = \log 2 = t \log\left(\frac{6}{5}\right)$$

$$0.301 = t\ 0.0791$$

$$t = \frac{0.301}{0.0791} = 3.8 \text{ years}$$

$\therefore$ Hence around 3–4 years would it take to double the growth rate

5. Let number of people in country y = 100

So, number of people in country x = 300

Total number of people taller than 6ft in both the countries $= 300 \times \frac{1}{100} + 100 \times \frac{2}{100} = 5$

% of people taller than 6ft in both the countries

$$= \frac{5}{400} \times 100 = 1.25\%.$$

7. Per ₹ 100 final value ₹ 107

$\Rightarrow$ per $\frac{100}{50}$ Dollars final value $\frac{107}{60}$

for 100 dollars _____?

$$= \frac{100 \times 50}{100} \times \frac{107}{60} = 89.16$$

Descreased by 11%

9.

	X	Y
Supply	60%	40%
Reliable	96%	72%
Overall	0.576	0.288

$$\therefore \quad P(x) = \frac{0.288}{0.576 + 0.288} = 0.334$$

10.

P	Q
40%	60%
–6%	+6%
+15%	–15%
49%	51%

$\therefore$ 2% = 2 $\Rightarrow$ 100% = 100

NUMERICAL TYPE QUESTION

1. 90% of area of sheet = Cross sectional area of cone

$\Rightarrow 0.9 \times \pi \times 30 \times 30 = \pi \times r_1 \times 30$

($\because$ Slant height of cone (l) = 30)

$\Rightarrow$ 27 cm = r_1

$\therefore$ Height of the cone = $\sqrt{30^2 - 27^2}$ = 13.08 cm

Hence ratio of radius and height is 2.06.

3
CHAPTER

Time and Work

MCQ TYPE QUESTIONS

2016

1. P, Q, R and S are working on a project. Q can finish the task in 25 days, working alone for 12 hours a day. R can finish the task in 50 days, working alone for 12 hours per day. Q worked 12 hours a day but took sick leave in the beginning for two days. R worked 18 hours a day on all days. What is the ratio of work done by Q and R after 7 days from the start of the project?

(*a*) 10:11 (*b*) 11:10
(*c*) 20:21 (*d*) 21:20

2. S, M, E and F are working in shifts in a team to finish a project. M works with twice the efficiency of others but for half as many days as E worked. S and M have 6 hour shifts in a day whereas E and F have 12 hours shifts. What is the ratio of contribution of M to contribution of E in the project?

(*a*) 1 : 1 (*b*) 1 : 2
(*c*) 1 : 4 (*d*) 2 : 1

3. It takes 10 s and 15 s, respectively, for two trains travelling at different constant speeds to completely pass a telegraph post. The length of the first train is 120 m and that of the second train is 150 m. The magnitude of the difference in the speeds of the two trains (in m/s) is ______.

(*a*) 2.0 (*b*) 10.0
(*c*) 12.0 (*d*) 22.0

4. The velocity V of a vehicle along a straight line is measured in m/s and plotted as shown with respect to time in seconds. At the end of the 7 seconds, how much will the odometer reading increase by (in m) ?

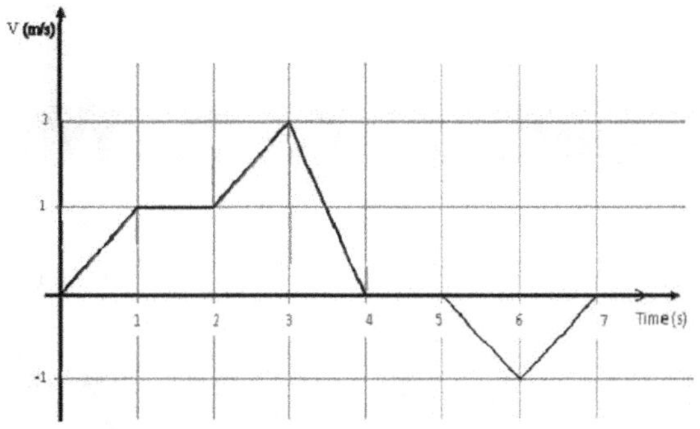

(*a*) 0 (*b*) 3
(*c*) 4 (*d*) 5

5. Ananth takes 6 hours and Bharath takes 4 hours to read a book. Both started reading copies of the book at the same time. After how many hours is the number of pages **to be** read by Ananth, twice that **to be** read by Bharath? Assume Ananth and Bharath read all the pages with constant pace.

(*a*) 1 (*b*) 2
(*c*) 3 (*d*) 4

2015

6. An electric bus has onboard instruments that report the total electricity consumed since the start of the trip as well as the total distance covered. During a single day of operation, the bus travels on stretches *M*, *N*, *O* and *P*, in that order. The cumulative distances travelled and the corresponding electricity consumption are shown in the table below.

Stretch	Comulative distance(km)	Electricity used (kWh)
M	20	12
N	45	25
O	75	45
P	100	57

The stretch where the electricity consumption per km is minimum is

(*a*) M
(*b*) N
(*c*) O
(*d*) P

2014

7. It takes 30 minutes to empty a half-full tank by draining it at a constant rate. It is decided to simultaneously pump water into the half-full tank while draining it. What is the rate at which water has to be pumped in so that it gets fully filled in 10 minutes?

(*a*) 4 times the draining rate
(*b*) 3 times the draining rate
(*c*) 2.5 times the draining rate
(*d*) 2 times the draining rate

2013

8. A tourist covers half of his journey by train at 60 km/h, half of the remainder by bus at 30 km/h and the rest by cycle at 10 km/h. The average speed of the tourist in km/h during his entire journey is

(*a*) 36 (*b*) 30
(*c*) 24 (*d*) 18

9. A car travels 8 km in the first quarter of an hour, 6 km in the second quarter and 16 km in the third quarter. The average speed of the car in km per hour over the entire journey is

(*a*) 30 (*b*) 36
(*c*) 40 (*d*) 24

2011

10. The fuel consumed by a motorcycle during a journey while traveling at various speeds is indicated in the graph below.

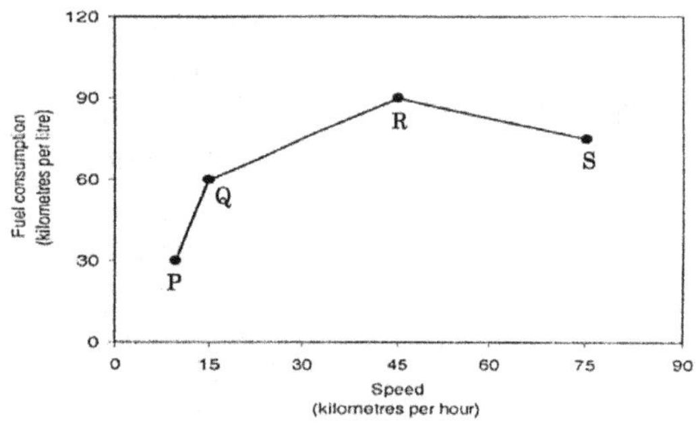

The distances covered during four laps of the journey are listed in the table below

Lap	Distance (kilometers)	Average speed (kilometers per hour)
P	15	15
Q	75	45
R	40	75
S	10	10

From the given data, we can conclude that the fuel consumed per kilometre was least during the lap

(*a*) P
(*b*) Q
(*c*) R
(*d*) S

2010

11. 5 skilled workers can build a wall in 20 days; 8 semi-skilled workers can build a wall in 25 days; 10 unskilled workers can build a wall in 30 days. If a team has 2 skilled, 6 semi-skilled and 5 unskilled workers, how long will it take to build the wall?

(*a*) 20 days
(*b*) 18 days
(*c*) 16 days
(*d*) 15 days

NUMERICAL TYPE QUESTIONS

2015

1. A tiger is 50 leaps of its own behind a deer. The tiger takes 5 leaps per minute to the deer's 4. If the tiger and the deer cover 8 metre and 5 metre per leap respectively, what distance in meters will the tiger have a run before it catches the deer?

2014

2. A man can row at 8 km per hour in still water. If it takes him thrice as long to row upstream, as to row downstream, then find the stream velocity in km per hour.

3. A train that is 280 metres long, travelling at a uniform speed, crosses a platform in 60 seconds and passes a man standing on the platform in 20 seconds. What is the length of the platform in metres?

ANSWERS

MCQ Type Questions

1. (*c*) **2.** (*b*) **3.** (*a*) **4.** (*d*) **5.** (*c*) **6.** (*b*) **7.** (*a*) **8.** (*c*) **9.** (*c*) **10.** (*a*)
11. (*d*)

Numerical Type Questions

1. (800) **2.** (4) **3.** (560 to 560)

EXPLANATIONS

MCQ TYPE QUESTIONS

1. Q can finish 1 day's 1 hour's work

$$= \frac{1}{25 \times 12} = \frac{1}{300}$$

R can finish 1 day's 1 hour's work

$$= \frac{1}{50 \times 12}$$

$$= \frac{1}{600}$$

Now Q working hours

$$= (7 - 2) \times 12$$

$$= 60 \text{ hr}$$

$\therefore$ R working hours = 7 × 18 = 126

After 7 days, the ratio of work done by Q & R is

$$Q : R$$

$$\frac{60}{300} : \frac{126}{600}$$

$$Q : R = 120 : 126$$

$$= 20 : 21$$

2. M is twice as efficient as E but worked for half as many days. So in this case they will do equal work if their shifts had same timings. But M's shift is for 6 hours, while E's shift for 12 hours. Hence, E will do twice the work as M.

Ratio of contribution of M : E in work is 1 : 2.

3. Here the speed of first train $(S_1) = \frac{120}{10} = 12$ m/s

and the speed of second train $(S_2) = \frac{150}{15} = 10$ m/s

$\therefore$ The magnitude of difference in the speeds of two trains = $(S_1 - S_2)$ = (12 – 10) m/s = 2 m/s

4. From the given figure.

The odometer reading increases from starting point to end point.

Odometer reading = Area of the given diagram

Area of the velocity and time graph per second

1st sec $\Rightarrow$ triangle

$$= \frac{1}{2} \times 1 \times 1 = \frac{1}{2}$$

2nd sec $\Rightarrow$ square

$$= 1 \times 1 = 1$$

3rd sec $\Rightarrow$ square + triangle

$$= 1 \times 1 + \frac{1}{2} \times 1 \times 1 = 1\frac{1}{2}$$

4th sec $\Rightarrow$ triangle

$$= \frac{1}{2} \times 1 \times 2 = 1$$

5th sec $\Rightarrow$ straight line

$$= 0$$

6th sec $\Rightarrow$ triangle

$$= \frac{1}{2} \times 1 \times 1 = \frac{1}{2}$$

7th sec $\Rightarrow$ triangle

$$= \frac{1}{2} \times 1 \times 1 = \frac{1}{2}$$

Total Odometer reading at 7 seconds

$$= \left(\frac{1}{2} + 1 + 1\frac{1}{2} + 1 + 0 + \frac{1}{2} + \frac{1}{2}\right) \text{m}$$

$$= 5 \text{ m}$$

So, the odometer reading is increased by 5 m.

6. For $M \Rightarrow \frac{12}{20} = 0.6$

$$N \Rightarrow \frac{25}{45} = 0.55$$

$$O \Rightarrow \frac{45}{75} = 0.6$$

$$P \Rightarrow \frac{57}{100} = 0.57$$

7. $V_{half} = 30(s)$ drawing rate = s

Total volume = 60 S tank

$(s^1)(10) - (s)10 = 30s$

$s^1(s) - s = 3s$

$s1 = 4s$

$s^1 = 4$ drawing rate

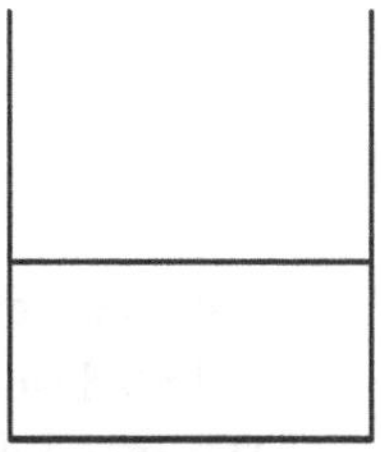

8. **Given:** A tourist covers half the journey at 60 km/h, one fourth at 30 km/h and the remaining one fourth at 10 km/h

To find: Avearge speed of the whole journey.

Analysis: One approach to this is to find individual time consumed in each of the three parts and use that value to get total time, and find average speed.

So,

Lets assume total length of journey = x km

$\therefore$ First phase at 60 km/h

$$\text{Time } t_1 = \frac{\text{Distance}}{\text{Speed}} = \frac{x}{2}\frac{1}{60} = \frac{x}{120}h$$

Second phase at 30 km/h

$$\text{Distance} = \frac{x}{4}\text{km}$$

$$\text{Time } t_2 = \frac{x}{4.30} = \frac{x}{120}$$

Third phase at 10 km/h

$$\text{Distance} = \frac{x}{4}\text{ km}$$

$$\text{Time } t_3 = \frac{x}{4.10} = \frac{x}{40}h$$

$$\therefore \quad \text{Total time} = \frac{x}{120}+\frac{x}{120}+\frac{x}{40} = \frac{x}{40}\left(\frac{1}{3}+\frac{1}{3}+1\right)$$

$$= \frac{x}{40}\frac{(1+1+3)}{3} = \frac{5x}{120}$$

$$\therefore \text{Average speed} = \frac{\text{Total Distance}}{\text{Total time}}$$

$$= \frac{x \cdot 120}{5x} = 24 \text{ km}/h$$

Hence, the answer is (c)

9. Average Speed = $\dfrac{\text{Total distance}}{\text{total time taken}}$

$$\text{Total Distance} = \frac{8+6+16}{15+15+15} = \frac{30 \times 60}{45}$$

= 40km/h.

10.

	Fuel consumption	Actual
P	60 km/l	$\frac{15}{60} = \frac{1}{4}l$
Q	90 km/l	$\frac{75}{90} = \frac{5}{6}l$
R	75 km/l	$\frac{40}{75} = \frac{8}{15}l$
S	30 km/l	$\frac{10}{30} = \frac{1}{3}l$

11. 5 skilled workers build wall in 20 days

1 skilled worker build wall in 20 × 5 days

Hence in 1 day, part of work done by skilled work

$$= \frac{1}{100}$$

Similarly in 1 day part of work done by semi-skilled workers

$$= \frac{1}{25 \times 8}$$

and in 1 day part of work done by un-skilled worker

$$= \frac{1}{30 \times 10}$$

So part of work done in 1 day by 2 skilled, 6 semi-skilled and 5 unskilled

$$= \frac{2}{100}+\frac{6}{200}+\frac{5}{300} = \frac{1}{15}$$

So work done by given workers in days = 15

NUMERICAL TYPE QUESTIONS

1. Tiger – 1 leap ⇒ 8 meter

Speed = 5 leap/hr = 40m/min

Deer → 1 leap = 5 meter

speed = 4hr = 20m/min

Let at time 't' the tiger catches the deer.

∴ Distance travelled by deer + initial distance between them

50 × 8 ⇒ 400m = distance covered by tiger.

⇒ 40 × t = 400 + 20t

$$\Rightarrow t = \frac{400}{200} = 20 \text{ min}$$

⇒ total distance ⇒ 400 + 20 × t = 800 m

2. Speed of man = 8;

Left distance = d

$$\text{Time taken} = \frac{d}{8}$$

Upstream: Speed of stream = s

⇒ speed upstream = S' = (8 – s)

$$t' = \left(\frac{d}{8-s}\right)$$

Downstream:

$$\text{Given speed downstream} = t'' = \frac{d}{8+s}$$

$$\Rightarrow 3t' = t'' \Rightarrow \frac{3d}{8-s} = \frac{d}{8+s}$$

$$\Rightarrow \quad \frac{3d}{8-s} = \frac{d}{8+s}$$

⇒ s = 4 km/hr

3. Let the length of platform = x.m

and train length = 280 m (given)

According to Question

$$\frac{x+280}{60} = \frac{280}{20}$$

$$\therefore \quad x = 560 \text{ m.}$$

4

CHAPTER

Ratio, Proportion and Mixtures

MCQ TYPE QUESTIONS

2015

1. A cube of side 3 units is formed using a set of smaller cubes of side 1 unit. Find the proportion of the number of faces of the smaller cubes visible to those which are NOT visible.

(*a*) 1 : 4

(*b*) 1 : 3

(*c*) 1 : 2

(*d*) 2 : 3

2011

2. A container originally contains 10 litres of pure spirit. From this container 1 litre of spirit is replaced with 1 litre of water. Subsequently, 1 litre of the mixture is again replaced with 1 litre of water and this process is repeated one more time. How much spirit is now left in the container?

(*a*) 7.58 litres

(*b*) 7.84 litres

(*c*) 7 litres

(*d*) 7.29 litres

ANSWERS

MCQ Type Questions

1. (*c*) **2.** (*d*)

EXPLANATIONS

MCQ TYPE QUESTIONS

1.

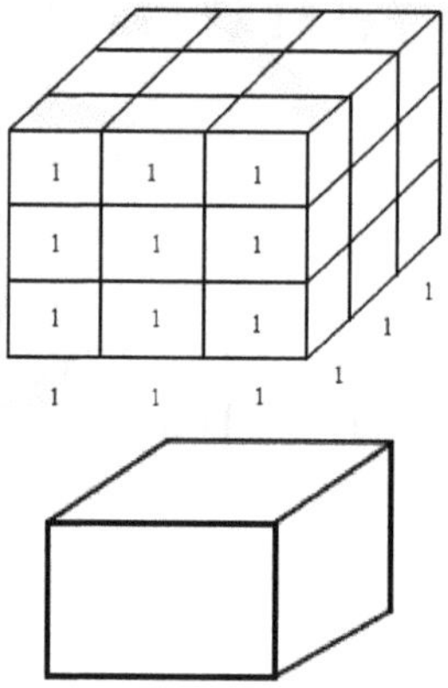

Number of faces per cube = 6

Total number of cubes = $9 \times 3 = 27$

$\therefore$ Total number of faces = $27 \times 6 = 162$

$\therefore$ Total number of non visible faces = $162 - 54 = 108$

$$\therefore \frac{\text{Number of visible faces}}{\text{Number of non visible faces}} = \frac{54}{108} = \frac{1}{2}$$

2. $10\left(\frac{10-1}{10}\right)^3 = 10\left(\frac{9}{10}\right)^3 = \frac{729}{1000}$

$$\therefore \frac{729}{1000} \times 1 = 7.29 \text{ litres}$$

5 CHAPTER

Permutations and Combinations & Probability

MCQ TYPE QUESTIONS

2016

1. Shaquille O' Neal is a 60% career free throw shooter, meaning that he successfully makes 60 free throws out of 100 attempts on average. What is the probability that he will successfully make exactly 6 free throws in 10 attempts?
   (*a*) 0.2508 (*b*) 0.2816
   (*c*) 0.2934 (*d*) 0.6000

2015

2. Four cards are randomly selected from a pack of 52 cards. If the first two cards are kings, what is the probability that the third card is a king?
   (*a*) 4/52 (*b*) 2/50
   (*c*) 1/52 × (1/52) (*d*) 1/52 × (1/52) × (1/50)
3. Five teams have to compete in a league, with every team playing every other team exactly once, before going to the next round. How many matches will have to be held complete the league round of matches?
   (*a*) 20 (*b*) 10
   (*c*) 8 (*d*) 5
4. Right triangle PQR is to be constructed in the xy – plane so that the right angle is at P and line PR is parallel to the-axis. The x and y coordinates of P, Q, and R are to be integers that satisfy the inequalities: $-4 \le x \le 5$ and $6 \le y \le 16$. How many different triangles could be constructed with these properties?
   (*a*) 110 (*b*) 1,100
   (*c*) 9,900 (*d*) 10,000
5. A coin is tossed thrice. Let X be the event that head occurs in each of the first two tosses. Let Y be the event that a tail occurs on the third toss. Let Z be the event that two tails occurs in three tosses. Based on the above information, which one of the following statements is TRUE?
   (*a*) X and Y are not independent
   (*b*) Y and Z are dependent
   (*c*) Y and Z are independent
   (*d*) X and Z independent
6. Ram and Ramesh appeared in an interview for two vacancies in the same department. The probability of Ram's selection is 1/6 and that of Ramesh is 1/8. What is the probability that only one of them will be selected?
   (*a*) $\frac{47}{48}$ (*b*) $\frac{1}{4}$
   (*c*) $\frac{13}{48}$ (*d*) $\frac{35}{48}$
7. Given set A = {2, 3, 4, 5} and Set B = {11, 12, 13, 14, 15}, two numbers are randomly selected, one from each set. What is probability that the sum of the two numbers equals 16 ?
   (*a*) 0.20 (*b*) 0.25
   (*c*) 0.30 (*d*) 0.33
8. The probabilities that a student passes in Mathematics, Physics and Chemistry are m, p and c respectively. Of these subjects, the student has 75% chance of passing in at least one, a 50% chance of passing in at least two and a 40% chance of passing in exactly two. Following relations are drawn in $m, p.c$:
   I. $p + m + c = \frac{27}{20}$ II. $p + m + c = \frac{13}{20}$
   III. $(p) \times (m) \times (c) = \frac{1}{10}$
   (*a*) Only relation I is true.
   (*b*) Only relation II is true.
   (*c*) Relations II and III are true.
   (*d*) Relations I and III are true.

2014

9. A five digit number is formed using the digits 1,3,5,7 and 9 without repeating any of them. What is the sum of all such possible five digit numbers?
   (*a*) 6666660 (*b*) 6666600
   (*c*) 6666666 (*d*) 6666606
10. You are given three coins: one has heads on both faces, the second has tails on both faces, and the third has a head on one face and a tail on the other. You choose a coin at random and toss it, and it comes up heads. The probability that the other face is tails is
    (*a*) 1/4 (*b*) 1/3
    (*c*) 1/2 (*d*) 2/3

2013

11. Out of all the 2-digit integers between 1 and 100, a 2-digit number has to be selected at random. What is the probability that the selected number is not divisible by 7?

(*a*) 13/90 (*b*) 12/90

(*c*) 78/90 (*d*) 77/90

12. What is the chance that a leap year, selected at random, will contain 53 Saturdays?

(*a*) 2/7 (*b*) 3/7

(*c*) 1/7 (*d*) 5/7

13. In a factory, two machines M1 and M2 manufacture 60% and 40% of the autocomponents respectively. Out of the total production, 2% of M1 and 3% of M2 are found to be defective. If a randomly drawn autocomponent from the combined lot is found defective, what is the probability that it was manufactured by M2?

(*a*) 0.35 (*b*) 0.45

(*c*) 0.5 (*d*) 0.4

2012

14. A and B are friends. They decide to meet between 1 PM and 2 PM on a given day. There is a condition that whoever arrives first will not wait for the other for more than 15 minutes. The probability that they will meet on that day is

(*a*) $\frac{1}{4}$ (*b*) $\frac{1}{16}$

(*c*) $\frac{7}{16}$ (*d*) $\frac{9}{16}$

2010

15. Given digits 2, 2, 3, 3, 3, 4, 4, 4, 4 how many distinct 4 digit numbers greater than 3000 can be formed?

(*a*) 50 (*b*) 51

(*c*) 52 (*d*) 54

NUMERICAL TYPE QUESTIONS

2015

1. How many four digit numbers can be formed with the 10 digits 0, 1, 2, ... 9 if no number can start with 0 and if repetitions are not allowed?

2014

2. In any given year, the probability of an earthquake greater than Magnitude 6 occurring in the Garhwal Himalayas is 0.04. The average time between successive occurrences of such earthquakes is _____ years.

3. 10% of the population in a town is HIV^+. A new diagnostic kit for HIV detection is available; this kit correctly identifies HIV^+ individuals 95% of the time, and HIV^- individuals 89% of the time. A particular patient is tested using this kit and is found to be positive. The probability that the individual is actually positive is ______

4. A batch of one hundred bulbs is inspected by testing four randomly chosen bulbs. The batch is rejected if even one of the bulbs is defective. A batch typically has five defective bulbs. The probability that the current batch is accepted is ________

ANSWERS

MCQ Type Questions

1. (*a*) **2.** (*b*) **3.** (*b*) **4.** (*c*) **5.** (*d*) **6.** (*b*) **7.** (*a*) **8.** (*d*) **9.** (*b*) **10.** (*b*)

11. (*d*) **12.** (*a*) **13.** (*c*) **14.** (*c*) **15.** (*b*)

Numerical Type Questions

1. 4536 **2.** (25 to 25) **3.** (0.47 to 0.48) **4.** (0.8145)

EXPLANATIONS

MCQ TYPE QUESTIONS

1. The question clearly explains that shaquille makes 60 free throws out of 100

Hence, Probability of free throw = $\frac{60}{100} = 0.6$

And probability of NOT free throw

$= 1 - 0.6 = 0.4$

So required probability of exactly 6 throws in 10 attempts will be given by

$^{10}C_6\, 0.6^6 \times 0.4^4 = 0.2508$

2. There are 4 kings in a pack of 52 cards.

If 2 cards are selected and both are kings, remaining cards will be 50 out of which 2 will be kings.

3. For a match to be played, we need 2 teams

No. of matches = No. of ways of selections 2 teams out of 5

$= {}^5C_2 = 10$

5. $x = \{HHT, HHH\}$

y depends on x

$z = \{TTH, TTT\}$

$\therefore$ '*d*' is the correct choice.

6. P (Ram) = 1/6; p(Ramesh) = 1/8

p(only at) = p (Ram) × p (not ramesh) + p(Ramesh) × p($n_0 \times R_{am}$)

$= \frac{1}{6} + \frac{7}{8} + \frac{1}{8} \times \frac{5}{6}$

$\Rightarrow \frac{12}{40} = \frac{1}{4}$

7. Here the given sets are

$A = \{2, 3, 4, 5\}$

and $B = \{11, 12, 13, 14, 15\}$

desired outcome = {(2, 14), (3, 13), (4, 12), (5, 11)}

$\therefore$ $n(E) = 4$

and total outcome = 4 × 5 = 20

$\therefore$ $n(s) = 20$

$\therefore$ Probability of an event

$= \frac{n(E)}{n(s)}$

$= \frac{4}{20} = \frac{1}{5} = 0.2$

9. The digit in unit place is selected in 4! Ways

The digit in tens place is selected in 4! Ways

The digit in hundreds place is selected in 4! Ways

The digit in thousands place is selected in 4! Ways

The digit in ten thousands place is selected in 4! Ways

Sum of all values for 1

$4! \times 1 \times (10^0 + 10^1 + 10^2 + 10^3 + 10^4)$

$= 4! \times 11111 \times 1$

Similarly for '3' $4! \times (11111) \times 3$

Similarly for '5' $4! \times (11111) \times 5$

Similarly for '7' $4! \times (11111) \times 7$

Similarly for '9' $4! \times (11111) \times 9$

$\therefore$ sum of all such numbers

$4! \times (11111) \times (1 + 3 + 5 + 7 + 9)$

$= 24 \times (11111) \times 25$

$= 6666600$

10. The probability that the other face is tail is $\frac{1}{3}$.

11. Given: All the 2-digit numbers

To find: Probability of selecting a number at random not divisible by 7

Analysis: Total number of 2-digit numbers

10, 11, ..., 99 → 90 numbers

Unfavourable numbers *i.e.* numbers divisible by 7 : 14, 21, ..., 98

Number of unfavourable numbers = 13

This can be hand counted or we can use the following properties:

Last term = First time + (no. – 1) Diff

$98 = 14 + (no. - 1)\, 7$

$\Rightarrow$ no. = 13

$\Rightarrow$ Probability = $\frac{\text{Total} - \text{unfavourable}}{\text{Total}}$

$= \frac{90 - 13}{90} = 77/90$

Hence, the solution is (*d*)

12. at a leap year

52 weeks, and 2 extra day they are (Mon, Tues) (Tues, Wed) (Wed Thu.) (Thus. Fri) (Fri. Sat) (Sat. Sun) (Sun Mond.)

$n(s) = 7$

$n(E) = 2$ $P(E) = \frac{2}{7}$

14.

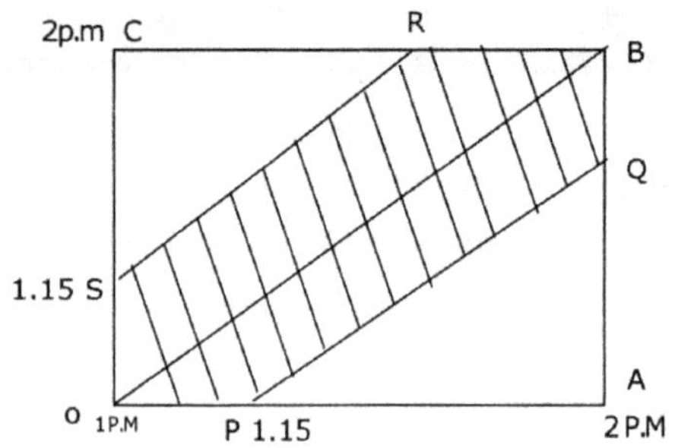

OB is the line when both A and B arrive at same time.

Total sample sapce = $60 \times 60 = 3600$

Favourable cases = Area of OABC – 2(Area of SRC)

$$= 3600 - 2 \times \left(\frac{1}{2} \times 45 \times 45\right)$$

$$= 1575$$

$\therefore$ Required probability $= \dfrac{1575}{3600} = \dfrac{7}{16}$

15. 2, 2, 3, 3, 4, 4, 4, 4 $\quad x > 3000$

322 — 3, 4	344 — 2, 3, 4
323 — 2, 3, 4	422 — 3, 4
324 — 2, 3, 4	423 — 2, 3, 4
332 — 2, 3, 4	424 — 2, 3, 4
333 — 2, 4	432 — 2, 3, 4
334 — 2, 3, 4	433 — 2, 3, 4
342 — 2, 3, 4	434 — 2, 3, 4
343 — 2, 3, 4	442 — 2, 3, 4
	443 — 2, 3, 4
	444 — 2, 3, 4

NUMERICAL TYPE QUESTIONS

1. In thousands place, 9 digits except 0 can be placed

In hundreds place, 9 digits can be placed (including 0, excluding the one used in thousands place)

In tens place, 8 digits can be placed (excluding the ones used in thousands and hundreds place)

In ones place, 7 digits can be placed (excluding the one used in thousands, hundreds and tens place)

Total number of combinations

$$= 9 \times 9 \times 8 \times 7 = 4536$$

2. Given, in one year, probability of an earthquake > 6 magnitude = 0.04

So, average time between successive earthquakes = 1/0.04 = 25 years

3. Given, 10% of the population is HIV^+, so probability = 0.1 for HIV^+ and 0.9 for HIV^-

The diagnostic kit identifies → 0.95 HIV^+ and 0.89 HIV^- correctly

So, the required probability that the person is actually HIV^+ = 0.95/2 = 0.475

4. Probability for one bulb to be non-defective is $\dfrac{95}{100}$

$\therefore$ Probabilities that none of the bulbs is defectives $\left(\dfrac{95}{100}\right)^4 = 0.8145$

■■

6 CHAPTER Miscellaneous

MCQ TYPE QUESTIONS

2016

1. In a 2×4 rectangle grid shown below, each cell is a rectangle. How many rectangles can be observed in the grid?

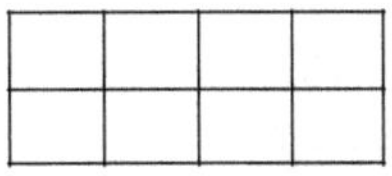

(*a*) 21 (*b*) 27

(*c*) 30 (*d*) 36

2.

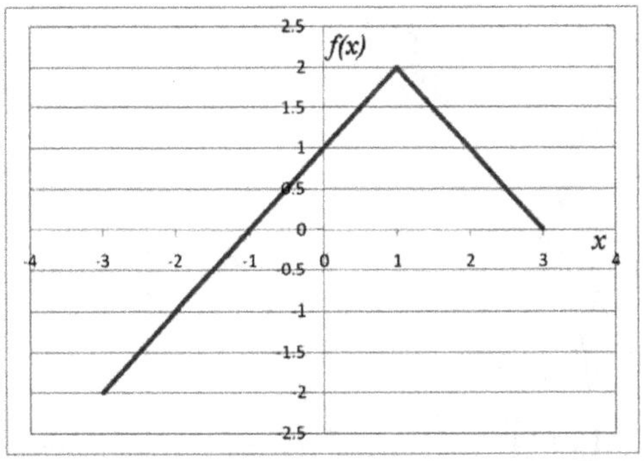

Choose the correct expression for $f(x)$ given in the graph.

(*a*) $f(x) = 1 - |x - 1|$ (*b*) $f(x) = 1 + |x - 1|$

(*c*) $f(x) = 2 - |x - 1|$ (*d*) $f(x) = 2 + |x - 1|$

3. The volume of a sphere of diameter 1 unit is ________ than the volume of a cube of side 1 unit.

(*a*) least (*b*) less

(*c*) lesser (*d*) low

4. A window is made up of a square portion and an equilateral triangle portion above it. The base of the triangular portion coincides with the upper side of the square. If the perimeter of the window is 6 m, the area of the window in m^2 is ________.

(*a*) 1.43 (*b*) 2.06

(*c*) 2.68 (*d*) 2.88

5. The binary operation $\square$ is defined as $a \square b = ab + (a + b)$, where a and b are any two real numbers. The value of the identity element of this operation, defined as the number x such that $a \square x = a$, for any a, is _______.

(*a*) 0 (*b*) 1

(*c*) 2 (*d*) 10

6. Which of the following curves represents the function $y = \ln\left(\left|e^{\left[\left|\sin(|x|)\right|\right]}\right|\right)$ for $|x| < 2\pi$?

Here, x represents the abscissa and y represents the ordinate.

(*a*)

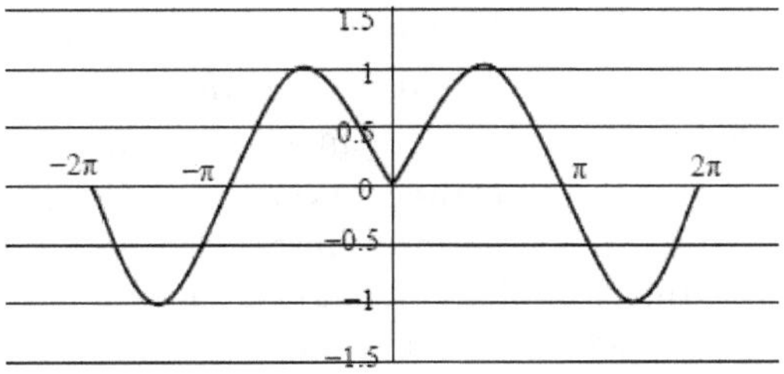

(*b*)

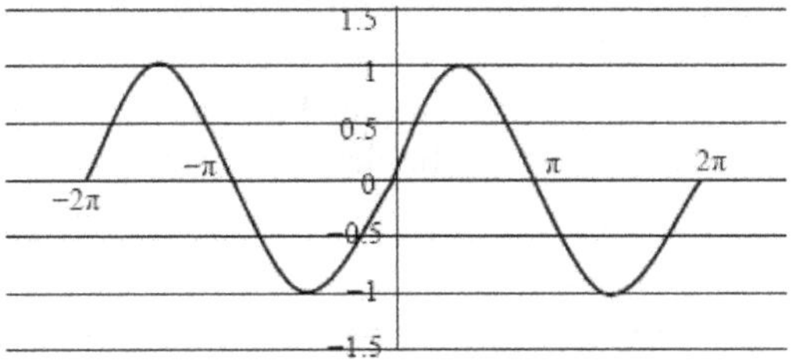

(*c*)

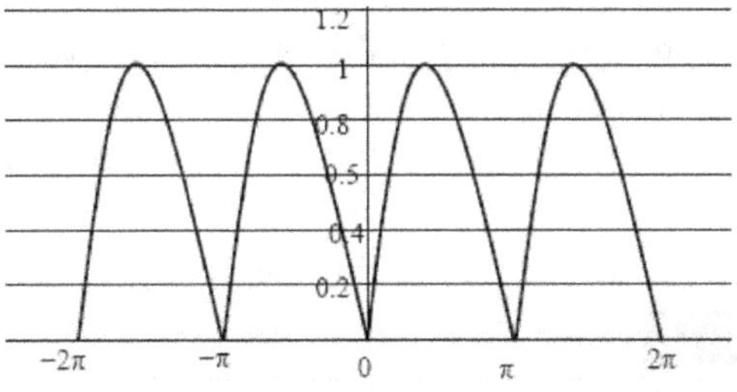

(*d*)

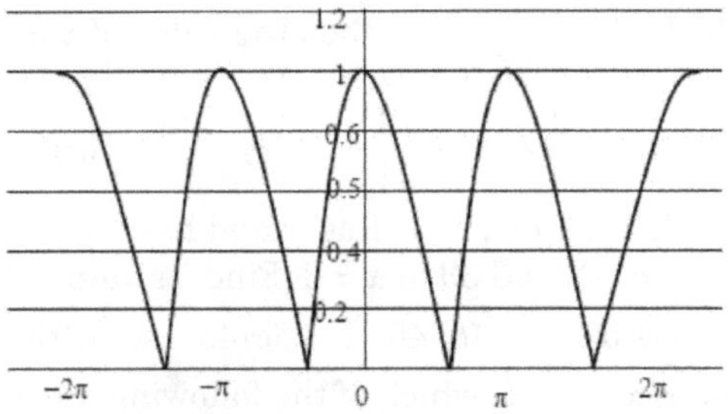

7. Given $(9 \text{ inches})^{1/2} = (0.25 \text{ yards})^{1/2}$, which one of the following statements is TRUE?

(*a*) 3 inches = 0.5 yards

(*b*) 9 inches = 1.5 yards

(*c*) 9 inches = 0.25 yards

(*d*) 81 inches = 0.0625 yards

8. The Venn diagram shows the preference of the student population for leisure activities.

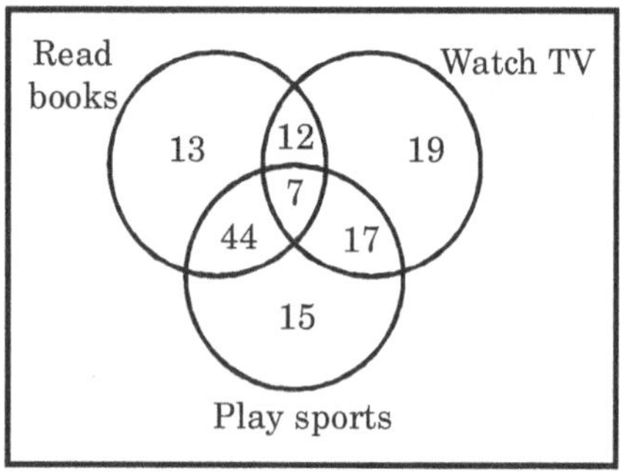

From the data given, the number of students who like to read books or play sports is ____.

(*a*) 44 (*b*) 51 (*c*) 79 (*d*) 108

9. A wire of length 340 mm is to be cut into two parts. One of the parts is to be made into a square and the other into a rectangle where sides are in the ratio of 1:2. What is the length of the side of the square (in mm) such that the combined area of the square and the rectangle is a MINIMUM?

(*a*) 30 (*b*) 40 (*c*) 120 (*d*) 180

10. Find the area bounded by the lines $3x + 2y = 14$, $2x - 3y = 5$ in the first quadrant

(*a*) 14.95 (*b*) 15.25 (*c*) 15.70 (*d*) 20.35

11. A straight line is fit to a data set ($\ln x, y$). This line intercepts the abscissa at $\ln x = 0.1$ and has a slope of -0.02. What is the value of y at $x = 5$ from the fit?

(*a*) –0.030 (*b*) –0.014 (*c*) 0.014 (*d*) 0.030

12. A square pyramid has a base perimeter x, and the slant height is half of the perimeter. What is the lateral surface area of the pyramid?

(*a*) x^2 (*b*) $0.75\,x^2$ (*c*) $0.50\,x^2$ (*d*) $0.25\,x^2$

2015

13. If $\log_x\left(\frac{5}{7}\right) = -\frac{1}{3}$, then the value of x is

(*a*) $\frac{343}{125}$ (*b*) $\frac{125}{343}$ (*c*) $-\frac{25}{49}$ (*d*) $-\frac{49}{25}$

14. A function $f(x)$ is linear and has a value of 29 at $x = -2$ and 39 at $x = 3$. Find its value at $x = 5$.

(*a*) 59 (*b*) 45 (*c*) 43 (*d*) 35

15. If $x > y > \mathrm{I}$, which of the following must be true?

(*i*) $\ln x > \ln y$ (*ii*) $e^x > e^y$

(*iii*) $y^x > x^y$ (*iv*) $\cos x > \cos y$

(*a*) *i* and *ii* (*b*) *i* and *iii*

(*c*) *iii* and *iv* (*d*) *ii* and *iv*

16. log tan1° + log tan2° +-------+ log tan89° is ____.

(*a*) 1 (*b*) $1/\sqrt{2}$ (*c*) 0 (*d*) –1

17. Based on the given statements, select the most appropriate option to solve the given question.

What will be the total weight of 10 poles each of same weight?

Statements:

(I) One fourth of the weight of a pole is 5 kg

(II) The total weight of these poles is 160 kg more than the total weight of two poles.

(*a*) Statement II alone is not sufficient

(*b*) Statement II alone is not sufficient

(*c*) Either I or II alone is sufficient

(*d*) Both statements I and II together are not sufficient.

18. Consider a function $f(x) = 1 - |x|$ on $-1 \le x \le 1$. The value of x at which the function attains a maximum, and the maximum value of function are:

(*a*) 0, –1 (*b*) –1, 0

(*c*) 0, 1 (*d*) –1, 2

19. In a triangle PQR, PS is the angle bisector of ∠QPR and ∠QPS = 60°. What is the length of PS?

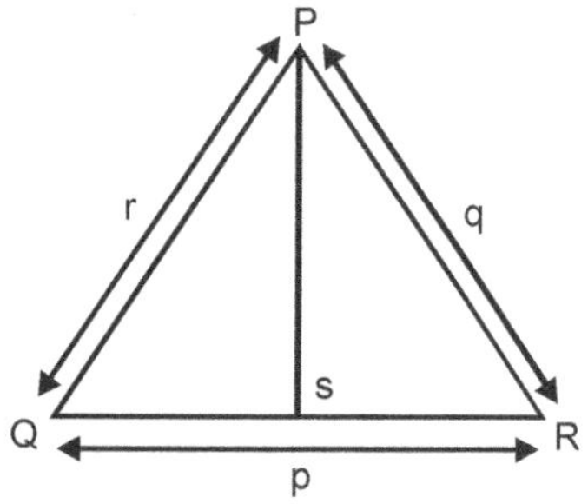

(*a*) $\frac{(q+r)}{qr}$

(*b*) $\frac{qr}{(q+r)}$

(*c*) $\sqrt{(q^2+r^2)}$

(*d*) $\frac{(q+r)^2}{qr}$

20. Based on the given statements, select the most appropriate option to solve the given question.

If two floors in a certain building are 9 feet apart, how many steps are there in a set of stairs that extends from the first floor to the second floor of the building?

Statements:

I. Each step is ¾ foot high.

II. Each step is 1 foot wide.

(*a*) Statement I alone is sufficient, but statement II alone is not sufficient.

(*b*) Statement II alone is sufficient, but statementI alone is not sufficient.

(*c*) Both statements together are sufficient, but neither statement alone is sufficient.

(*d*) Statement I and II together are not sufficient.

2014

21. If $y = 5x^2 + 3$, then the tangent at $x = 0, y = 3$

(*a*) passes through $x = 0, y = 0$

(*b*) has a slope of +1

(*c*) is parallel to the x-axis

(*d*) has a slope of –1

22. Let $f(x, y) = x^n y^m = P$. If x is doubled and y is halved, the new value of f is

(*a*) 2^{n-m} P (*b*) 2^{m-n} P
(*c*) $2(n - m)$ P (*d*) $2(m - n)$ P

23. A regular die has six sides with numbers 1 to 6 marked on its sides. If a very large number of throws show the following frequencies of occurrence: $1 \to 0.167$; $2 \to 0.167$; $3 \to 0.152$; $4 \to 0.166$; $5 \to 0.168$; $6 \to 0.180$. We call this die

(*a*) irregular (*b*) biased
(*c*) Gaussian (*d*) insufficient

24. Consider the equation : $(7526)_8 - (Y)_8 = (4364)_8$, where $(X)_N$ stands for X to the base N. Find Y.

(*a*) 1634 (*b*) 1737 (*c*) 3142 (*d*) 3162

25. At what time between 6 *a.m.* and 7 *a.m.* will the minute hand and hour hand of a clock make an angle closest to 60°?

(*a*) 6 : 22 *a.m.* (*b*) 6 : 27 *a.m.*
(*c*) 6 : 38 *a.m.* (*d*) 6 : 45 *a.m.*

26. The roots of $ax^2 + bx + c = 0$ are real and positive a, b and c are real. Then $ax^2 + b\,|x| + c = 0$ has

(*a*) No roots (*b*) 2 real roots
(*c*) 3 real roots (*d*) 4 real roots

2012

27. The cost function for a product in a firm is given by $5q^2$, where q is the amount of production. The firm can sell the product at a market price of ₹ 50 per unit. The number of units to be produced by the firm such that the profit is maximized is

(*a*) 5 (*b*) 10 (*c*) 15 (*d*) 25

28. Which of the following assertions are **CORRECT ?**

P : Adding 7 to each entry in a list adds 7 to the mean of the list

Q : Adding 7 to each entry in a list adds 7 to the standard deviation of the list

R : Doubling each entry in a list doubles the mean of the list

S : Doubling each entry in a list leaves the standard deviation of the list unchanged

(*a*) P, Q (*b*) Q, R (*c*) P, R (*d*) R, S

29. A political party orders an arch for the entrance to the ground in which the annual convention is being held. The profile of the arch follows the equation $y = 2x - 0.1x^2$ where y is the height of the arch in meters. The maximum possible height of the arch is

(*a*) 8 meters (*b*) 10 meters
(*c*) 12 meters (*d*) 14 meters

30. There are eight bags of rice looking alike, seven of which have equal weight and one is slightly heavier. The weighing balance is of unlimited capacity. Using this balance, the minimum number of weighings required to identify the heavier bag is

(*a*) 2 (*b*) 3 (*c*) 4 (*d*) 8

2011

31. If log (P) = (1/2) Log (Q) = (1/3) Log (R), then which of the following options is TRUE?

(*a*) $P^2 = Q^3 R^2$ (*b*) $Q^2 = PR$
(*c*) $Q^2 = R^3 P$ (*d*) $R = P^2 Q^2$

32. The variable cost (V) of manufacturing a product varies according to the equation V = 4q, where q is the quanity produced. The fixed cost (F) of production of same product reduces with q according to the equation $F = 100/q$. How many units should be produced to minimize the total cost (V + F)?

(*a*) 5 (*b*) 4 (*c*) 7 (*d*) 6

33. Three friends R, S and T shared toffee from a bowl. R took 1/3rd of the toffees, but returned four to the bowl. S took 1/4th of what was left but returned three toffees to the bowl. T took half of the remainder but returned two back into the bowl. If the bowl had 17 toffees left, how many toffees were originally there in the bowl?

(*a*) 38 (*b*) 31 (*c*) 48 (*d*) 41

NUMERICAL TYPE QUESTIONS

2015

1. In the given figure angle Q is a right angle, PS : QS = 3:1, RT : QT = 5:2 and PU : UR = 1:1. If area of triangle QTS is 20 cm², then the area of triangle PQR in cm² is ______.

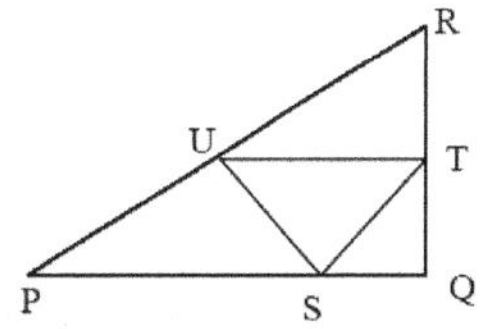

2. If p, q, r, s are distinct integers such that:

$f(p, q, r, s) = \max(p, q, r, s)$

$g(p, q, r, s) = \min(p, q, r, s)$

$h(p, q, r, s)$ = remainder of $(p \times q)/(r \times s)$ if $(p \times q) > (r \times s)$ or remainder of $(r \times s)/(p \times q)$ if $(r \times s) > (p \times q)$

Also a function $fgh(p, q, r, s) = f(p, q, r, s) \times g(p, q, r, s) \times h(p, q, r, s)$

Also the same operations are valid with two variable function of the form $f(p, q)$.

What is the value of $fg(h(2, 5, 7, 3), 4, 6, 8$

2014

3. When a point inside of a tetrahedron (a solid with four triangular surfaces) is connected by straight lines to its corners, how many (new) internal planes are created with these lines? ________.

ANSWERS

MCQ Type Questions

1. (*c*)	**2.** (*c*)	**3.** (*c*)	**4.** (*b*)	**5.** (*a*)	**6.** (*c*)	**7.** (*c*)	**8.** (*d*)	**9.** (*b*)	**10.** (*b*)
11. (*a*)	**12.** (*d*)	**13.** (*a*)	**14.** (*c*)	**15.** (*a*)	**16.** (*c*)	**17.** (*c*)	**18.** (*c*)	**19.** (*b*)	**20.** (*a*)
21. (*c*)	**22.** (*a*)	**23.** (*b*)	**24.** (*c*)	**25.** (*a*)	**26.** (*d*)	**27.** (*a*)	**28.** (*c*)	**29.** (*b*)	**30.** (*a*)
31. (*b*)	**32.** (*a*)	**33.** (*c*)							

Numerical Type Questions

1. 280	**2.** (8)	**3.** (6)

EXPLANATIONS

MCQ TYPE QUESTIONS

1. In the given 2×4 rectangle grid, the following type of rectangles are present.

One figured rectangles = 8

Two figured rectangles = 10

Three figured rectangles = 4

Four figured rectangles = 5

Six figured rectangles = 2

Eight figured rectangles = 1

$\therefore$ Total number of rectangles

$$= 8 + 10 + 4 + 5 + 2 + 1 = 30$$

So the number of rectangles observed in the given grid is 30.

2. From the given graph function $f(x)$ must be equals to zero at $x = 3$.

From Option A :

$$f(x) = 1 - |x - 1|$$

at $x = 3$

$$f(x) = 1 - |3 - 1| = 1 - 2 = -1$$

So, it is false

From Option B :

$$f(x) = 1 + |x - 1|$$

at $x = 3$

$$f(x) = 1 + |3 - 1| = 1 + 2 = 3$$

So, it is false

From Option C :

$$f(x) = 2 - |x - 1|$$

at $x = 3$

$$f(x) = 2 - |3 - 1| = 2 - 2 = 0$$

So, it is true.

From Option D :

$$f(x) = 2 + |x - 1|$$

at $x = 3$

$$f(x) = 2 - |3 - 1| = 2 + 2 = 4$$

So, it is false.

Hence the correct expression for $f(x)$ given in the graph is $2 - |x - 1|$.

3. 'Lesser than' is apt because the sentence should be in comparative degree.

4. The possible window will be as follows :

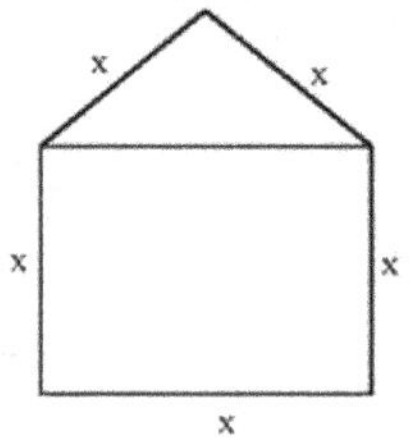

Perimeter of window = $5x$ = 6m

$$x = 1.2 \text{ m}$$

So area of window = Area of triangle + Area of square

$$= \frac{\sqrt{3}}{4}x^2 + x^2$$

$$= \frac{\sqrt{3}}{4}(1.2)^2 + (1.2)^2 = 2.06 \text{ m}^2$$

5. The binary operation $\square$ is defined

$\Rightarrow$ $a \square b = ab + (a + b)$

$a \square x = a$

$\therefore$ From the equation 'b' is the variable

Option A: $x = 0$

$a \square o = a \times 0 + (a + 0) = 0 + a = a$

Option B: $x = 1$

$a \square 1 = a \times 1 + (a + 1) = a + a + 1 = 2a + 1$

Option C: $x = 2$

$a \square 2 \Rightarrow a \times 2 + (a + 2) = 2a + a + 2 = 3a + 2$

Option D: $x = 10$

$a \square 10 \Rightarrow a \times 10 + (a + 10) = 10a + a + 10$

$= 11a + 10$

$\therefore$ Option 'A' only True.

7. $(9 \text{ inches})^{1/2} = (0.25 \text{ yards})^{1/2}$,

Solving we get 9 inch = 0.25 yards

(since 1 inch = 0.028 yard)

8. Given Venn diagram is

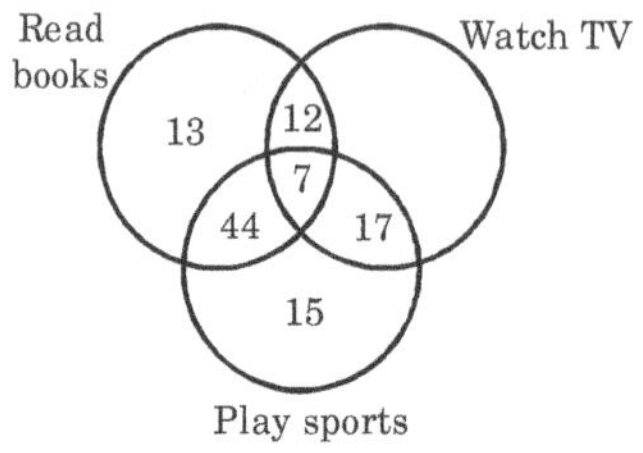

The number of students who like to read books or play sports

$= 13 + 12 + 44 + 7 + 15 + 17 = 108$

10. $A = \left[\frac{14}{3}, 0\right]$

$B = [0, 7]$,

$C = \left[\frac{5}{2}, 0\right]$

$D = \left[0, \frac{-5}{3}\right]$

$E = [4, 1]$,

$F = [0, 1]$

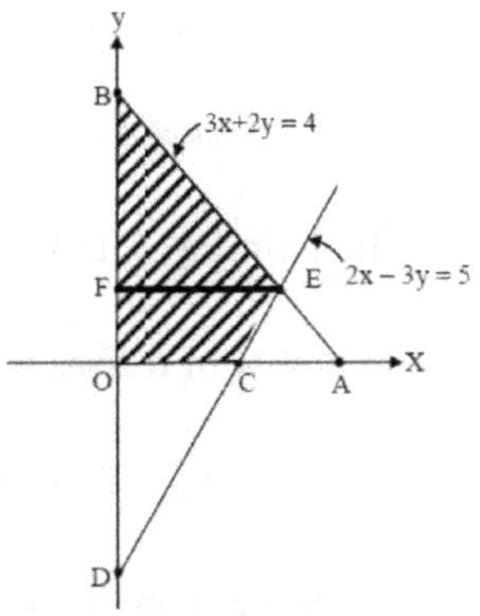

Required area = Area of Δ BFE + Area of quadrilateral FEOC

$= \frac{1}{2} \times 4 \times 6 + \frac{1}{2} \times (4 + 2.5) \times 1$

$= 2 \times 6 + \frac{1}{2} \times 6.5$

$= 12 + 3.25 = 15.25$ sq. units

So, the area bounded by the given lines is 15.25 sq. units.

11. The equation of a straight line is

$y = mx + c$

m = slope = – 0.02

set $(\log x, y)$

Now, the line intercepts the abscissa at

$\log x = 0.1$

So, at abscissa $y = 0$

$\therefore$ $y = mx + c$

$0 = -0.02 \times 0.1 + c$

$\therefore$ $c = 0.002$

$y = mx + c$

$y = -0.02 \times \log x + c$

At $x = 5$

$\therefore$ $y = -0.02 \times \log 5 + 0.002 = -0.030$

So, the value of y is – 0.030.

13. $\frac{5}{7} = x^{-1/3} \Rightarrow \frac{7}{5} = x^{1/3} \Rightarrow \left(\frac{7}{5}\right)^3 = x \Rightarrow x = \frac{343}{125}$

14. $f(x) = 2x + 33 = 2(5) + 33 = 43$

15. For whole numbers, greater the value greater will be its log.

Same logic for power of e.

16. $\log \tan 1° + \log \tan 89° = \log(\tan 1° \times \tan 89°)$

$= \log(\tan 1° \times \cot 1°)$

$= \log 1 = 0$

Using the same logic total sum is '0'.

18. The given function is

$f(x) = 1 - |x|$ on $-1 \le x \le 1$

In order to find maximum and minimum value of function in interval [–1, 1]

At $x = -1$, $f(-1) = 1 - |-1| = 1 - 1 = 0$

At $x = -0.5$, $f(-0.5) = 1 - |-0.5| = 1 - 0.5 = 0.5$

At $x = 0$, $f(0) = 1 - |0| = 1$

At $x = 0.5$, $f(0.5) = 1 - |0.5| = 0.5$

At $x = 1$, $f(1) = 1 - |1| = 1 - 1 = 0$

$\therefore$ Hence, maximum value occurs at $x = 0$ and its maximum value is 1.

$\therefore$ Option (c) is correct.

21. $y = 5x^2 + 3$, $\frac{dy}{dx} = 10x$

Slope of tangent $= \left(\frac{dy}{dx}\right)_{x=0, y=3} = 10 \times 0 = 0$

Slope = 0

$\Rightarrow$ tangent is parallel to x-axis.

22. $P' = 2^n X^n \left(\frac{1}{2}\right)^m y^m$

$= 2^{n-m} X^n Y^m = 2^{n-m} P$

23. For a very large number of throws, the frequency should be same for unbiased throw. As it not same, then the die is baised.

24. $(7526)_8 - (y)_8 = (4364)_8$

$\Rightarrow y_8 = (7526)_8 - (4364)_8$

$$\begin{array}{cccc} & 4 & \scriptstyle(8+2=10) & \\ 7 & \not{5} & 2 & 6 \\ 4 & 3 & 6 & 4 \\ \hline 3 & 1 & 4 & 2 \end{array}$$

When we have base 8, we borrow 8 instead of 10 as done in normal subtraction.

25.

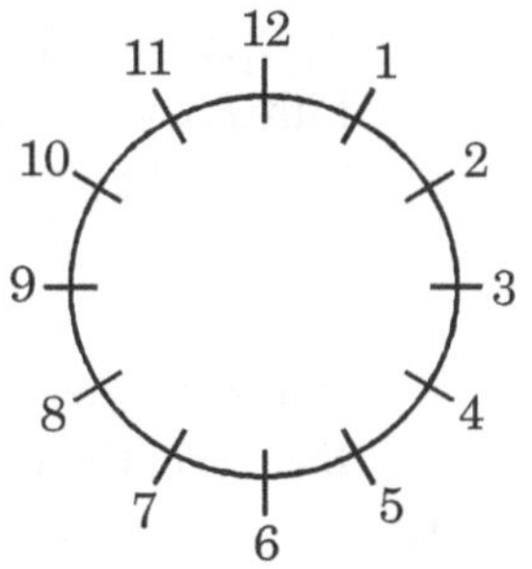

From option

At 6 a.m.

Both hand – 180° aparts,

At 6 : 20 a.m. – both hand apart

$\Rightarrow$ $180° + 10° - 120° = 70°$

At 6 : 22 a.m. – both hand apart

$\Rightarrow$ $180° + 12° - 132° = 60°$ (closest)

26. $ax^2 + bx + c = 0$

Roots are real and positive

$\therefore \quad b^2 - 4ac > 0$

By the above condition we get two positive real roots

Now, $ax^2 + b|x| + c = 0$

This can be written as;

$ax^2 + bx + c$

$\Delta = b^2 - 4ac > 0$

Now for $ax^2 - bx + c$

$(-b)^2 - 4ac$

$\Rightarrow \quad b^2 - 4ac$

Again $b^2 - 4ac > 0$

So again we get real roots

Thus we have 4 real roots of $ax^2 + b|x| + c = 0$

27. $P = 50q - 5q^2$

$\frac{dp}{dq} = 50 - 10q; \ \frac{d^2p}{dq^2} < 0$

$\therefore$ p is maximum at $50 - 10q = 0$ or, $q = 5$

Else check with options

28. P and R always holds true

Else consider a sample set {1, 2, 3, 4} and check accordingly

29. $y = 2x - 0.1x^2; \ \frac{dy}{dx} = 2 - 0.2x; \ \frac{d^2y}{dx^2} < 0$

$\therefore$ y maximises at $2 - 0.2x = 0$

$\Rightarrow x = 10$

$\therefore$ $y = 20 - 10 = 10$m

30. Let us categorize bags in three groups as

$A_1 A_2 A_3 \quad B_1 B_2 B_3 \quad C_1 C_2$

1st weighing A vs B

Case-1	**Case-2**
$A_1 A_2 A_3 = B_1 B_2 B_3$	$A_1 A_2 A_3 \neq B_1 B_2 B_3$
Then either C_1 or C_2 is heavier	Either A or B would be heavier (Say A > B)
2nd weighing	
C_1 vs C_2	A_1 vs A_2
If $C_1 > C_2$, then C_1	If $A_1 = A_2$, then A_3
If $C_1 < C_2$, then C_2	If $A_1 > A_2$, then A_1
	If $A_1 < A_2$, then A_2

31. $\log P = \frac{1}{2} \log Q$

$= \frac{1}{3} \log (R) = k$

$\therefore \quad P = b^k, Q = b^{2k}, R = b^{3k}$

Hence, $Q^2 = b^{4k} = b^{3k} \ b^k = PR$

32. Checking with all options in formula: $(4q+100/q)$ i.e. (V+F). Option (*a*) gives the minimum cost.

33. Let total number of toffees in bowl be x

R took $\frac{1}{3}$ of toffees and returned 4 to the bowl

$\therefore$ Number of toffees with R $= \frac{1}{3}x - 4$

Remaining of toffees in bowl $= \frac{2}{3}x + 4$

Number of toffees with S $= \frac{1}{4}\left(\frac{2}{3}x + 4\right) - 3$

Remaining toffees in bowl $= \frac{3}{4}\left(\frac{2}{3}x + 4\right) + 4$

Number of toffees with T $= \frac{1}{2}\left(\frac{3}{4}\left(\frac{2}{3}x + 4\right) + 4\right) + 2$

Remaining toffees in bowl

$= \frac{1}{2}\left[\frac{3}{4}\left(\frac{2}{3}x + 4\right) + 4\right] + 2$

Given : $\frac{1}{2}\left[\frac{3}{4}\left(\frac{2}{3}x + 4\right) + 4\right] + 2 = 17$

$\Rightarrow \quad \frac{3}{4}\left(\frac{2}{3}x + 4\right) = 27$

$\Rightarrow \quad x = 48$

NUMERICAL TYPE QUESTIONS

1. Let area of triangle PQR be 'A'

$\frac{SQ}{PQ} = \frac{1}{1+3} = \frac{1}{4}$

$\frac{QT}{QR} = \frac{2}{2+5} = \frac{2}{7}$

$\therefore$ Area of $\Delta QTS = \frac{1}{2} \times SQ \times QT$

$= \frac{1}{2} \times \left(\frac{1}{4}PQ\right) \times \left(\frac{2}{7}QR\right)$

$= \frac{1}{4} \times \frac{2}{7} \times \left(\frac{1}{2} \times PQ \times QR\right)$

$= \frac{1}{14} \times$ Area of ΔPQR

Given 20 cm^2 $= \frac{1}{14} \times A$

$\therefore \quad A = 14 \quad 20 = 280$ cm^2

2. $fg(h(2, 5, 7, 3), 4, 6, 8) = fg(1, 4, 6, 8)$

$= f(1, 4, 6, 8) \times g(1, 4, 6, 8)$

$= 8 \times 1 = 8$

Mathematics

1 CHAPTER

Linear Algebra

2016

1. Consider the following statements P and Q:

(P) : If $M = \begin{bmatrix} 1 & 1 & 1 \\ 1 & 2 & 4 \\ 1 & 3 & 9 \end{bmatrix}$, then M is singular.

(Q) : Let S be a diagonalizable matrix. If T is a matrix such that S + 5T = Id, then T is diagonalizable.

Which of the above statements hold TRUE?

(*a*) both P and Q (*b*) only P

(*c*) only Q (*d*) Neither P nor Q

2. Consider the following statements P and Q:

(P) : If M is an n n complex matrix, then $R(M) = (N(M^*))^{\perp}$.

(Q) : There exists a unitary matrix with an eigenvalues λ such that $|\lambda| < 1$.

Which of the above statements hold TRUE?

(*a*) both P and Q (*b*) only P

(*c*) only Q (*d*) Neither P nor Q

3. Consider a real vector space V of dimension n and a non-zero linear transformation $T : V \to V$. If dimension $(T(V)) < n$ and $T^2 = \lambda T$, for some $\lambda \in \mathbb{R} \setminus \{0\}$, then which of the following statements is TRUE?

(*a*) determinant(T) = $|\lambda|^n$

(*b*) There exists a non-trivial subspace V_1 of V such that T(X) = 0 for all $X \in V_1$

(*c*) T is invertible

(*d*) λ is the only eigenvalue of T

4. Let $M = \begin{bmatrix} a & b & c \\ b & d & e \\ c & e & f \end{bmatrix}$ be a real matrix with eigenvalues 1, 0 and 3. If the eigenvectors 1, 0 and 3. If the eigenvectors corresponding to 1 and 0 are $(1, 1, 1)^T$ and $(1, -1, 0)^T$ respectively, then the value of 3f is equal to __________.

5. Let $M = \begin{bmatrix} 1 & 1 & 0 \\ 0 & 1 & 1 \\ 0 & 0 & 1 \end{bmatrix}$ and $e^M = Id + M + \frac{1}{2!}M^2 + \frac{1}{3!}M^3 + ...$ If $e^M = [b_{ij}]$, then $\frac{1}{e}\sum_{i=1}^{3}\sum_{j=1}^{3} b_{ij}$ is equal to __________.

2015

6. Let M be a 3×3 singular matrix and suppose that 2 and 3 are eigenvalues of M. Then the number of linearly independent eigenvectors of $M^3 + 2M + I_3$ is equal to _____

7. Let M be a 3×3 matrix such that $M\begin{pmatrix} -2 \\ 1 \\ 0 \end{pmatrix} = \begin{pmatrix} 6 \\ -3 \\ 0 \end{pmatrix}$ and suppose that $M^3\begin{pmatrix} 1 \\ -1/2 \\ 0 \end{pmatrix} = \begin{pmatrix} \alpha \\ \beta \\ \gamma \end{pmatrix}$ for some $\alpha, \beta, \gamma \in \mathbb{R}$. Then $|\alpha|$ is equal to _____

8. Let $T : \mathbb{R}^4 \to \mathbb{R}^4$ be a linear map defined by
$T(x, y, z, w) = (x + z, 2x + y + 3z, 2y + 2z, w)$
Then the rank of T is equal to _______

9. Let M be *a* 3×3 matrix and suppose that 1, 2 and 3 are the eigenvalues of M. If

$$M^{-1} = \frac{M^2}{\alpha} - M - \frac{11}{\alpha} I_3$$

for some scalar $\alpha \neq 0$, then α is equal to _______

10. Let V be a closed subspace of $L^2[0, 1]$ and let $f, g \in L^2[0, 1]$ be given by $f(x) = x$ and $g(x) = x^2$. If $V^{\perp}$ = Span $\{f\}$ and Pg is the orthogonal projection of g on V, then $(g - Pg)(x)$, $x \in [0, 1]$, is

(*a*) $\frac{3}{4}x$ (*b*) $\frac{1}{4}x$

(*c*) $\frac{3}{4}x^2$ (*d*) $\frac{1}{4}x^2$

11. Let M be an invertible Hermitian matrix and let $x, y \in \mathbb{R}$ be such that $x^2 < 4y$. Then

(*a*) both $M^2 + x M + y I$ and $M^2 - x M + y I$ are singular

(*b*) $M^2 + x M + y I$ is singular but $M^2 - x M + y I$ is non-singular

(*c*) $M^2 + x M + y I$ is non-singular but $M^2 - x M + y I$ is singular

(*d*) both $M^2 + x M + y I$ and $M^2 - x M + y I$ are non-singular

12. Let $W = \text{Span}\left\{\frac{1}{\sqrt{2}}(0,0,1,1), \frac{1}{\sqrt{2}}(1,-1,0,0)\right\}$ be a subspace of the Euclidean space $\mathbb{R}^4$. Then the square of the distance from the point (1, 1, 1, 1) to the subspace W is equal to __________

13. Let $T : \mathbb{R}^4 \to \mathbb{R}^4$ be a linear map such that the null space of T is

$$\{(x, y, z, w)\} \in \mathbb{R}^4 : x + y + z + w = 0\}$$

and the rank of $(T - 4\, I_4)$ is 3. If the minimal polynomial of T is $x(x - 4)^{\alpha}$, then α is equal to ________.

2014

14. Consider the group homomorphism $\varphi: M_2(\mathbb{R}) \to \mathbb{R}$ given by $\varphi(A) = \text{trace}(A)$. The kernel of φ is isomorphic to which of the following groups?

(a) $M_2(\mathbb{R})/\{A \in M_2(\mathbb{R}): \varphi(A) = 0\}$

(b) $\mathbb{R}^2$

(c) $\mathbb{R}^3$

(d) $GL_2(\mathbb{R})$

15. Let $A \in M_3(\mathbb{R})$ be such that $\det(A - I) = 0$, where I denotes the $3 \;\; 3$ identity matrix If the trace(A) = 13 and $\det(A) = 32$, then the sum of squares of the eigenvalues of A is _______.

16. Let V denote the vector space $C^5[a, b]$ over $\mathbb{R}$ and

$$W = \left\{ f \in V : \frac{d^4 f}{dt^4} + 2\frac{d^2 f}{dt^2} - f = 0 \right\}. \text{ Then}$$

(a) $\dim(V) = \infty$ and $\dim(W) = \infty$

(b) $\dim(V) = \infty$ and $\dim(W) = 4$

(c) $\dim(V) = 6$ and $\dim(W) = 5$

(d) $\dim(V) = 5$ and $\dim(W) = 4$

17. Let V be a real inner product space of dimension 10. Let $x, y \in V$ be non-zero vectors such that $\langle x, y \rangle = 0$. Then the dimension of $\{x\}^{\perp} \cap \{y\}^{\perp}$ is _______

18. Consider the vector space $C[0, 1]$ over $\mathbb{R}$. Consider the following statements:

P: If the set $\{tf_1, t^2 f_2, t^3 f_3\}$ is linearly independent, then the set $\{f_1, f_2, f_3\}$ is linearly independent, where $f_1, f_2, f_3 \in C[0, 1]$ and t^n represents the polynomial function $t \mapsto t^n, n \in \mathbb{N}$

Q: If $F: C[0, 1] \to \mathbb{R}$ is given by

$$F(x) = \int_0^1 x(t^2)dt \text{ for each } x \in C[0, 1],$$

then F is a linear map.

Which of the above statements hold **TRUE**?

(a) Only **P**

(b) Only **Q**

(c) Both **P** and **Q**

(d) Neither **P** nor **Q**

19. Let $X = \begin{bmatrix} 2 & 0 & -3 \\ 3 & -1 & -3 \\ 0 & 0 & -1 \end{bmatrix}$. A matrix P such that $P^{-1}XP$ is a diagonal matrix, is

(a) $\begin{bmatrix} 1 & 1 & 1 \\ 0 & 1 & 1 \\ 1 & 1 & 0 \end{bmatrix}$ (b) $\begin{bmatrix} -1 & 1 & 1 \\ 0 & 1 & 1 \\ 1 & 1 & 0 \end{bmatrix}$

(c) $\begin{bmatrix} 1 & -1 & 1 \\ 0 & 1 & 1 \\ 1 & 1 & 0 \end{bmatrix}$ (d) $\begin{bmatrix} -1 & -1 & 1 \\ 0 & -1 & 1 \\ 1 & 1 & 0 \end{bmatrix}$

20. Let $T_1, T_2 : \mathbb{R}^5 \to \mathbb{R}^3$ be linear transformations such that $rank(T_1) = 3$ and $nullity(T_2) = 3$.

Let $T_3 : \mathbb{R}^3 \to \mathbb{R}^3$ be a linear transformation such that $T_3 \cdot T_1 = T_2$. Then $rank(T_3)$ is ____

21. Let $\mathbb{F}_3$ be the field of 3 elements and let $\mathbb{F}_3 \;\; \mathbb{F}_3$ be the vector space over $\mathbb{F}_3$. The number of distinct linearly dependent sets of the form $\{u, v\}$, where $u, v \in \mathbb{F}_3 \;\; \mathbb{F}_3 \setminus \{(0, 0)\}$ and $u \neq v$ is ______

2013

22. The possible set of eigen values of a 4×4 skew-symmetric orthogonal real matrix is

(a) $\{\pm i\}$ (b) $\{\pm i \pm 1\}$

(c) $\{\pm 1\}$ (d) $\{0, \pm i\}$

23. Let P be a 2×2 complex matrix such that trace(P) =1 and det(P) =–6. Then, trace$(P^4 - P^3)$ is ______

24. Let V be the real vector space of all polynomials in one variable with real coefficients and having degree at most 20. Define the subspaces

$$W_1 = \left\{p \in V : p(1) = 0,\ p\left(\frac{1}{2}\right) = 0,\ p(5) = 0,\ p(7) = 0\right\},$$

$$W_2 = \left\{p \in V : p\left(\frac{1}{2}\right) = 0,\ p(3) = 0, p(4) = 0,\ p(7) = 0\right\}.$$

Then the dimension of $W_1 \cap W_2$ is ______

25. Let M be the real vector space of 2×3 matrices with real entries. Let $T : M \to M$ be defined by

$$T\left(\begin{bmatrix} x_1 & x_2 & x_3 \\ x_4 & x_5 & x_6 \end{bmatrix}\right) = \begin{bmatrix} -x_6 & x_4 & x_1 \\ x_3 & x_5 & x_2 \end{bmatrix}.$$

The determinant of T is _______

26. The matrix $A = \begin{bmatrix} 1 & 2 & 0 \\ 1 & 3 & 1 \\ 0 & 1 & 3 \end{bmatrix}$ can be decomposed uniquely into the product A = LU, where $L = \begin{bmatrix} 1 & 0 & 0 \\ l_{21} & 1 & 0 \\ l_{31} & l_{32} & 1 \end{bmatrix}$ and $U = \begin{bmatrix} u_{11} & u_{12} & u_{13} \\ 0 & u_{22} & u_{23} \\ 0 & 0 & u_{33} \end{bmatrix}$.

The solution of the system LX = $[1\ 2\ 2]^t$ is

(a) $[1\ 1\ 1]^t$ (b) $[1\ 1\ 0]^t$

(c) $[0\ 1\ 1]^t$ (d) $[1\ 0\ 1]^t$

27. Let B be a real symmetric positive-definite $n \times n$ matrix. Consider the inner product on $\mathbb{R}^n$ defined by $\langle X, Y\rangle = Y^t BX$. Let A be an $n \times n$ real matrix and let $T: \mathbb{R}^n \to \mathbb{R}^n$ be the linear operator defined by $T(X) = AX$ for all $X \in \mathbb{R}^n$. If S is the adjoint of T, then $S(X) = CX$ for all $X \in \mathbb{R}^n$, where C is the matrix

(a) $B^{-1}A^tB$ (b) BA^tB^{-1}

(c) $B^{-1}AB$ (d) A^t

28. Let M be the space of all 4×3 matrices with entries in the finite field of three elements. Then the number of matrices of rank three in M is

(a) $(3^4-3)(3^4-3^2)(3^4-3^3)$

(b) $(3^4-1)(3^4-2)(3^4-3)$

(c) $(3^4-1)(3^4-3)(3^4-3^2)$

(d) $3^4(3^4-1)(3^4-2)$

29. Let V be a vector space of dimension $m \geq 2$. Let $T: V \to V$ be a linear transformation such that $T^{n+1} = 0$ and $T^n \neq 0$ for some $n \geq 1$. Then which of the following is necessarily **TRUE**?

(a) Rank $(T^n) \leq$ Nullity (T^n)

(b) trace $(T) \neq 0$

(c) T is diagonalizable

(d) $n = m$

COMMON DATA QUESTIONS

Common Data for Questions 30 and 31 :

Let C_{00} be the vector space of all complex sequences having finitely many non-zero terms. Equip C_{00} with the inner product $\langle x, y\rangle = \sum_{n=1}^{\infty} x_n \overline{y_n}$ for all $x = (x_n)$ and $y = (y_n)$ in C_{00}. Define $f: C_{00} \to \mathbb{C}$ by $f(x) = \sum_{n=1}^{\infty} \frac{x_n}{n}$. Let N be the kernel of f.

30. Which of the following is **FALSE**?

(a) f is a continuous linear functional

(b) $\|f\| \leq \frac{\pi}{\sqrt{6}}$

(c) There does not exist any $y \in C_{00}$ such that $f(x) = \langle x, y\rangle$ for all $x \in C_{00}$

(d) $N^{\perp} \neq \{0\}$

31. Which of the following is **FALSE**?

(a) $C_{00} \neq N$

(b) N is closed

(c) C_{00} is not a complete inner product space

(d) $C_{00} = N \oplus N^{\perp}$

2012

32. The straight lines $L_1 : x = 0$, $L_2 : y = 0$ and $L_3 : x + y = 1$ are mapped by the transformation $w = z^2$ into the curves C_1, C_2 and C_3 respectively. The angle of intersection between the curves at $w = 0$ is

(a) 0 (b) $\frac{\pi}{4}$

(c) $\frac{\pi}{2}$ (d) π

33. Let $\alpha = e^{2\pi i/5}$ and the matrix

$$M = \begin{bmatrix} 1 & \alpha & \alpha^2 & \alpha^3 & \alpha^4 \\ 0 & \alpha & \alpha^2 & \alpha^3 & \alpha^4 \\ 0 & 0 & \alpha^2 & \alpha^3 & \alpha^4 \\ 0 & 0 & 0 & \alpha^3 & \alpha^4 \\ 0 & 0 & 0 & 0 & \alpha^4 \end{bmatrix}$$

Then the trace of the matrix $I + M + M^2$ is

(a) –5 (b) 0

(c) 3 (d) 5

34. Let $V = \mathbb{C}^2$ be the vector space over the field of complex numbers and $B = \{(1, i), (i, 1)\}$ be a given ordered basis of V. Then for which of the following, $B^* = \{f_1, f_2\}$ is a dual basis of B over $\mathbb{C}$?

(a) $f_1(z_1, z_2) = \frac{1}{2}(z_1 - iz_2), f_2(z_1, z_2) = \frac{1}{2}(z_1 + iz_2)$

(b) $f_1(z_1, z_2) = \frac{1}{2}(z_1 + iz_2), f_2(z_1, z_2) = \frac{1}{2}(iz_1 + z_2)$

(c) $f_1(z_1, z_2) = \frac{1}{2}(z_1 - iz_2), f_2(z_1, z_2) = \frac{1}{2}(-iz_1 + z_2)$

(d) $f_1(z_1, z_2) = \frac{1}{2}(z_1 + iz_2), f_2(z_1, z_2) = \frac{1}{2}(-iz_1 - z_2)$

35. If $A = \begin{bmatrix} 1 & 0 & 0 \\ 1 & 0 & 1 \\ 0 & 1 & 0 \end{bmatrix}$, then A^{50}

(a) $\begin{bmatrix} 1 & 0 & 0 \\ 50 & 1 & 0 \\ 50 & 0 & 1 \end{bmatrix}$ (b) $\begin{bmatrix} 1 & 0 & 0 \\ 48 & 1 & 0 \\ 48 & 0 & 1 \end{bmatrix}$

(c) $\begin{bmatrix} 1 & 0 & 0 \\ 25 & 1 & 0 \\ 25 & 0 & 1 \end{bmatrix}$ (d) $\begin{bmatrix} 1 & 0 & 0 \\ 24 & 1 & 0 \\ 24 & 0 & 1 \end{bmatrix}$

36. Let the linear transformation $T : F^2 \to F^3$ be defined by $T(x_1, x_2) = (x_1, x_1 + x_2, x_2)$. Then the nullity of T is

(a) 0 (b) 1

(c) 2 (d) 3

37. The approximate eigenvalue of the matrix

$$A = \begin{bmatrix} -15 & 4 & 3 \\ 10 & -12 & 6 \\ 20 & -4 & 2 \end{bmatrix}$$

obtained after two iterations of Power method, with the initial vector $[1\ 1\ 1]^T$, is

(*a*) 7.768 (*b*) 9.468
(*c*) 10.548 (*d*) 19.468

38. For the matrix $M = \begin{bmatrix} 2 & 3+2i & -4 \\ 3-2i & 5 & 6i \\ -4 & -6i & 3 \end{bmatrix}$

which of the following statements are correct?

P : M is skew-Hermitian and iM is Hermitian

Q : M is Hermitian and iM is skew Hermitian

R : eigenvalues of M are real

S : eigenvalues of iM are real

(*a*) P and R only (*b*) Q and R only
(*c*) P and S only (*d*) Q and S only

39. Let $T : P_3 \to P_3$ be the map given by $T(p(x)) = \int_1^x p'(t)dt$. If the matrix of T relative to the standard bases $B_1 = B_2 = \{1, x, x^2, x^3\}$ is M and M^t denotes the transpose of the matrix M, then $M + M^t$ is

(*a*) $\begin{bmatrix} 0 & -1 & -1 & -1 \\ -1 & 2 & 0 & 0 \\ 0 & 0 & 2 & 0 \\ 0 & 0 & 0 & 2 \end{bmatrix}$ (*b*) $\begin{bmatrix} -1 & 0 & 0 & 2 \\ 0 & -1 & 1 & 0 \\ 0 & 1 & -1 & 0 \\ 2 & 0 & 2 & -1 \end{bmatrix}$

(*c*) $\begin{bmatrix} 2 & 0 & 0 & -1 \\ 0 & 2 & 1 & 0 \\ 0 & 1 & 2 & -1 \\ -1 & 0 & -1 & 0 \end{bmatrix}$ (*d*) $\begin{bmatrix} 0 & 2 & 2 & 2 \\ 2 & -1 & 0 & 0 \\ 2 & 0 & -1 & 0 \\ 2 & 0 & 0 & -1 \end{bmatrix}$

Common Data Questions

Common Data for Questions 40 and 41

The optimal table for the primal linear programming problem:

Maximize $Z = 6x_1 + 12x_2 + 12x_3 - 6x_4$

Subject to $x_1 + x_2 + x_3 = 4$

$x_1 + 4x_2 + x_4 = 8$

$x_1, x_2, x_3, x_4 \geq 0,$

is

Basic variables (x_B)	x_1	x_2	x_3	x_4	RHS Constants (b)
x_3	3/4	0	1	–1/4	2
x_2	1/4	1	0	1/4	3
$z_j - c_j$	6	0	0	6	$z = 48$

40. If y_1 and y_2 are the dual variables corresponding to the first and second primal constraints, then their values in the optimal solution of the dual problem are, respectively,

(*a*) 0 and 6 (*b*) 12 and 0
(*c*) 6 and 3 (*d*) 4 and 4

41. If the right hand side of the second constraint is changed from 8 to 20, then in the optimal solution of the primal problem, the basic variables will be

(*a*) x_1 and x_2 (*b*) x_1 and x_3
(*c*) x_2 and x_3 (*d*) x_2 and x_4

2011

42. The distinct eigenvalues of the matrix

$$\begin{bmatrix} 1 & 1 & 0 \\ 1 & 1 & 0 \\ 0 & 0 & 0 \end{bmatrix}$$

are

(*a*) 0 and 1 (*b*) 1 and – 1
(*c*) 1 and 2 (*d*) 0 and 2

43. The minimal polynomial of the matrix

$$\begin{bmatrix} 3 & 3 & 0 \\ 3 & 3 & 0 \\ 0 & 0 & 6 \end{bmatrix}$$

is

(*a*) $x(x-1)(x-6)$

(*b*) $x(x-3)$

(*c*) $(x-3)(x-6)$

(*d*) $x(x-6)$

44. The subspace $P = \{(x, y, z) \in R^3 : z = x^2 + y^2 + 1\}$ is

(*a*) compact and connected

(*b*) compact but not connected

(*c*) not compact but connected

(*d*) neither compact nor connected

45. The application of Gram-Schmidt process of orthonormalization to

$u_1 = (1, 1, 0), u_2 = (1, 0, 0), u_3 = (1, 1, 1)$ yields

(*a*) $\frac{1}{\sqrt{2}}(1, 1, 0), (1, 0, 0), (0, 0, 1)$

(*b*) $\frac{1}{\sqrt{2}}(1, 1, 0), \frac{1}{\sqrt{2}}(1, -1, 0), \frac{1}{\sqrt{2}}(1, 1, 1)$

(*c*) $(0, 1, 0), (1, 0, 0), (0, 0, 1)$

(*d*) $\frac{1}{\sqrt{2}}(1, 1, 0), \frac{1}{\sqrt{2}}(1, -1, 0), (0, 0, 1)$

46. Let T : $C^3 \to C^3$ be defined by

$$T\begin{pmatrix} z_1 \\ z_2 \\ z_3 \end{pmatrix} = \begin{pmatrix} z_1 - iz_2 \\ iz_1 + z_2 \\ z_1 + z_2 + iz_3 \end{pmatrix}.$$ Then, the adjoint T* of T is given by $T^*\begin{pmatrix} z_1 \\ z_2 \\ z_3 \end{pmatrix} =$

(a) $\begin{pmatrix} z_1 + iz_2 \\ -iz_1 + z_2 \\ z_1 + z_2 - iz_3 \end{pmatrix}$ (b) $\begin{pmatrix} z_1 - iz_2 + z_3 \\ -iz_1 + z_2 + z_3 \\ iz_3 \end{pmatrix}$

(c) $\begin{pmatrix} z_1 - iz_2 + z_3 \\ iz_1 + z_2 + z_3 \\ -iz_3 \end{pmatrix}$ (d) $\begin{pmatrix} iz_1 + z_2 \\ z_1 - iz_2 \\ z_1 - z_2 - iz_3 \end{pmatrix}$

47. Let T : $R^4 \to R^4$ be defined by $T(x, y, z, w) = (x + y + 5w, x + 2y + w, -z + 2w, 5x + y + 2z)$. The dimension of the eigenspace of T is

(a) 1 (b) 2

(c) 3 (d) 4

Statement for Linked Answer Questions 48 and 49:

The matrix $A = \begin{bmatrix} 1 & 1 & 1 \\ 2 & 1 & 2 \\ 1 & 3 & 2 \end{bmatrix}$ can be decomposed into the product of a lower triangular matrix L and an upper triangular matrix U as A = LU where

$$L = \begin{bmatrix} 1 & 0 & 0 \\ l_{21} & 1 & 0 \\ l_{31} & l_{32} & 1 \end{bmatrix} \text{ and } U = \begin{bmatrix} u_{11} & u_{12} & u_{13} \\ 0 & u_{22} & u_{23} \\ 0 & 0 & u_{33} \end{bmatrix}$$

Let $x, z \in R^3$ and $b = [1, 1, 1]^T$.

48. The solution $z = [z_1, z_2, z_3]^T$ of the system $Lz = b$ is

(a) $[-1, -1, -2]^T$ (b) $[1, -1, 2]^T$

(c) $[1, -1, -2]^T$ (d) $[-1, 1, 2]^T$

49. The solution $x = [x_1, x_2, x_3]^T$ of the system $Ux = z$ is

(a) $[2, 1, -2]^T$ (b) $[2, 1, 2]^T$

(c) $[-2, -1, -2]^T$ (d) $[-2, 1, -2]^T$

2010

50. If the nullity of the matrix $\begin{bmatrix} k & 1 & 2 \\ 1 & -1 & -2 \\ 1 & 1 & 4 \end{bmatrix}$ is 1, then the value of k is

(a) – 1 (b) 0

(c) 1 (d) 2

51. If a 3 × 3 real skew-symmetric matrix has an eigenvalue $2i$, then one of the remaining eigen values is

(a) $\frac{1}{2i}$ (b) $-\frac{1}{2i}$

(c) 0 (d) 1

52. Let T : $\mathbb{R}^3 \to \mathbb{R}^3$ be a linear transformation defined by $T(x, y, z) = (x + y, y + z, z - x)$. Then, an orthonormal basis for the range of T is

(a) $\left\{\left(\frac{1}{\sqrt{2}}, \frac{1}{\sqrt{2}}, 0\right), \left(\frac{1}{\sqrt{3}}, -\frac{1}{\sqrt{3}}, \frac{1}{\sqrt{3}}\right)\right\}$

(b) $\left\{\left(\frac{1}{\sqrt{2}}, -\frac{1}{\sqrt{2}}, 0\right), \left(\frac{1}{\sqrt{6}}, \frac{1}{\sqrt{6}}, \frac{2}{\sqrt{6}}\right)\right\}$

(c) $\left\{\left(\frac{1}{\sqrt{2}}, \frac{1}{\sqrt{2}}, 0\right), \left(\frac{1}{\sqrt{6}}, -\frac{1}{\sqrt{6}}, -\frac{2}{\sqrt{6}}\right)\right\}$

(d) $\left\{\left(\frac{1}{\sqrt{2}}, \frac{1}{\sqrt{2}}, 0\right), \left(\frac{1}{\sqrt{3}}, -\frac{1}{\sqrt{3}}, -\frac{1}{\sqrt{3}}\right)\right\}$

53. Let $T : P_3[0,1] \to P_2[0,1]$ be defined by $(Tp)(x) = p''(x) + p'(x)$. Then the matrix representation of T with respect to the bases $\{1, x, x^2, x^3\}$ and $\{1, x, x^2\}$ of $P_3[0,1]$ and $P_2[0,1]$ respectively is

(a) $\begin{bmatrix} 0 & 0 & 0 \\ 1 & 0 & 0 \\ 2 & 2 & 0 \\ 0 & 6 & 3 \end{bmatrix}$ (b) $\begin{bmatrix} 0 & 1 & 2 & 0 \\ 0 & 0 & 2 & 6 \\ 0 & 0 & 0 & 3 \end{bmatrix}$

(c) $\begin{bmatrix} 0 & 2 & 1 & 0 \\ 6 & 2 & 0 & 0 \\ 3 & 0 & 0 & 0 \end{bmatrix}$ (d) $\begin{bmatrix} 0 & 0 & 0 \\ 0 & 0 & 1 \\ 0 & 2 & 2 \\ 3 & 6 & 0 \end{bmatrix}$

54. Consider the basis $\{u_1, u_2, u_3\}$ of $\mathbb{R}^3$, where $u_1 = (1, 0, 0)$, $u_2 = (1, 1, 0)$, $u_3 = (1, 1, 1)$. Let $\{f_1, f_2, f_3\}$ be the dual basis of $\{u_1, u_2, u_3\}$ and f be a linear functional defined by $f(a, b, c) = a + b + c$, $(a, b, c) \in \mathbb{R}^3$. If $f = \alpha_1 f_1 + \alpha_2 f_2 + \alpha_3 f_3$, then $(\alpha_1, \alpha_2, \alpha_3)$ is

(a) (1, 2, 3) (b) (1, 3, 2)

(c) (2, 3, 1) (d) (3, 2, 1)

Statement for Linked Answer Q. (55 - 56)

Let X = C[0,1] with the inner product

$$\langle x, y \rangle = \int_0^1 x(t)\,\overline{y(t)}\,dt, \quad x, y \in C[0,1],$$

$X_0 = \left\{ x \in X : \int_0^1 t^2 x(t) dt = 0 \right\}$ and $X_0^{\perp}$ be the orthogonal complement of X_0.

55. Which one of the following statements is correct?

(*a*) Both X_0 and $X_0^\perp$ are complete

(*b*) Neither X_0 nor $X_0^\perp$ is complete

(*c*) X_0 is complete but $X_0^\perp$ is not complete

(*d*) $X_0^\perp$ is complete but X_0 is not complete

56. Let $y(t) = t^3$, $t \in [0,1]$ and $x_0 \in X_0^\perp$ be the approximation of y. Then $x_0(t)$, $t \in [0,1]$ is

(*a*) $\frac{4}{5}t^2$ (*b*) $\frac{5}{6}t^2$

(*c*) $\frac{6}{7}t^2$ (*d*) $\frac{7}{8}t^2$

2009

57. The dimension of the vector space $V = \{ A = (a_{ij})_{n \times n} : a_{ij} \in \mathbb{C}, a_{ij} = -a_{ji}\}$ over the field $\mathbb{R}$ is

(*a*) n^2 (*b*) $n^2 - 1$

(*c*) $n^2 - n$ (*d*) $\frac{n^2}{2}$

58. The minimal polynomial associated with the matrix $\begin{bmatrix} 0 & 0 & 3 \\ 1 & 0 & 2 \\ 0 & 1 & 1 \end{bmatrix}$ is

(*a*) $x^3 - x^2 - 2x - 3$ (*b*) $x^3 - x^2 + 2x - 3$

(*c*) $x^3 - x^2 - 3x - 3$ (*d*) $x^3 - x^2 + 3x - 3$

59. If

$$A = \begin{pmatrix} 1 & 0 & 0 \\ i & \frac{-1+i\sqrt{3}}{2} & 0 \\ 0 & 1+2i & \frac{-1-i\sqrt{3}}{2} \end{pmatrix}$$

then the trace of A^{102} is

(*a*) 0 (*b*) 1

(*c*) 2 (*d*) 3

60. Which of the following matrices is NOT diagonalizable?

(*a*) $\begin{pmatrix} 1 & 1 \\ 1 & 2 \end{pmatrix}$ (*b*) $\begin{pmatrix} 1 & 0 \\ 3 & 2 \end{pmatrix}$

(*c*) $\begin{pmatrix} 0 & -1 \\ 1 & 0 \end{pmatrix}$ (*d*) $\begin{pmatrix} 1 & 1 \\ 0 & 1 \end{pmatrix}$

61. Let V be the column space of the matrix $A = \begin{pmatrix} 1 & -1 \\ 1 & 2 \\ 1 & -1 \end{pmatrix}$. Then the orthogonal projection of $\begin{pmatrix} 0 \\ 1 \\ 0 \end{pmatrix}$ on V is

(*a*) $\begin{pmatrix} 0 \\ 1 \\ 0 \end{pmatrix}$ (*b*) $\begin{pmatrix} 0 \\ 0 \\ 1 \end{pmatrix}$

(*c*) $\begin{pmatrix} 1 \\ 1 \\ 0 \end{pmatrix}$ (*d*) $\begin{pmatrix} 1 \\ 0 \\ 1 \end{pmatrix}$

Common Data Questions

Common Data for Questions 62–63

Let $T : \mathbb{R}^3 \to \mathbb{R}^3$ be the linear transformation defined by $T(x_1, x_2, x_3) = (x_1 + 3x_2 + 2x_3,\ 3x_1 + 4x_2 + x_3,\ 2x_1 + x_2 - x_3)$.

62. The dimension of the range space of T^2 is

(*a*) 0 (*b*) 1

(*c*) 2 (*d*) 3

63. The dimension of the null space of T^3 is

(*a*) 0 (*b*) 1

(*c*) 2 (*d*) 3

2008

64. Consider the subspace $W = \{[a_{ij}] : a_{ij} = 0$ if i is even$\}$ of all 10×10 real matrices. Then the dimension of W is

(*a*) 25 (*b*) 50

(*c*) 75 (*d*) 100

65. Let $T : R^4 \to R^4$ be the linear map satisfying $T(e_1) = e_2$, $T(e_2) = e_3$, $T(e_3) = 0$, $T(e_4) = e_3$, where $\{e_1, e_2, e_3, e_4\}$ is the standard basis of R^4. Then

(*a*) T is idempotent (*b*) T is invertible

(*c*) Rank T = 3 (*d*) T is nilpotent

66. Let $M = \begin{bmatrix} 1 & 1 & 2 \\ 0 & 1 & 1 \\ 0 & 1 & 1 \end{bmatrix}$ and $V = \{M x^t : x \in R^3\}$.

Then orthonormal basis for V is

(*a*) $\left\{(1,0,0)^t, \left(0, \frac{2}{\sqrt{5}}, \frac{1}{\sqrt{5}}\right)^t, \left(\frac{2}{\sqrt{6}}, \frac{1}{\sqrt{6}}, \frac{1}{\sqrt{6}}\right)^t\right\}$

(*b*) $\left\{(1,0,0)^t, \left(0, \frac{1}{\sqrt{2}}, \frac{1}{\sqrt{2}}\right)^t\right\}$

(*c*) $\left\{(1,0,0)^t, \left(0, \frac{1}{\sqrt{3}}, \frac{1}{\sqrt{3}}, \frac{1}{\sqrt{3}}\right)^t, \left(\frac{2}{\sqrt{6}}, \frac{1}{\sqrt{6}}, \frac{1}{\sqrt{6}}\right)^t\right\}$

(*d*) $\{(1, 0, 0)^t (0, 0, 1)^t\}$

67. For any $n \in N$, let P_n denote the vector space of all polynomials with real coefficients and of degree at most n. Define $T : P_n \to P_{n+1}$ by

$$T(p)(x) = p'(x) - \int_0^x p(t)dt$$

Then the dimension of the null space of T is

(a) 0 (b) 1

(c) n (d) $n + 1$

68. Let $M = \begin{bmatrix} 1 & 0 & 0 \\ 0 & \cos\theta & -\sin\theta \\ 0 & \sin\theta & \cos\theta \end{bmatrix}$ where $0 < \theta < \frac{\pi}{2}$.

Let $V = \{u \in R^3 : M u^t = u^t\}$. Then the dimension of V is

(a) 0 (b) 1

(c) 2 (d) 3

69. The number of linearly independent eigenvectors of the matrix $\begin{bmatrix} 2 & 2 & 0 & 0 \\ 2 & 1 & 0 & 0 \\ 0 & 0 & 3 & 0 \\ 0 & 0 & 1 & 4 \end{bmatrix}$ is

(a) 1 (b) 2

(c) 3 (d) 4

Statement for Linked Answer Questions 70 and 71:

Let $N = \begin{bmatrix} \frac{3}{5} & -\frac{4}{5} & 0 \\ \frac{4}{5} & \frac{3}{5} & 0 \\ 0 & 0 & 1 \end{bmatrix}$

70. Then N is

(a) non-invertible

(b) skew-symmetric

(c) symmetric

(d) orthogonal

71. If M is any 3×3 real matrix, then trace (NMN^t) is equal to

(a) $[\text{trace}(N)]^2\ \text{trace}(M)$

(b) $2\ \text{trace}(N) + \text{trace}(M)$

(c) $\text{trace}(M)$

(d) $[\text{trace}(N)]^2 + \text{trace}(M)$

2007

72. Consider the system of linear equations $x + y + z = 3$, $x - y - z = 4$, $x - 5y + kz = 6$.

Then the value of k for which this system has an infinite number of solutions is

(a) $k = -5$

(b) $k = 0$

(c) $k = 1$

(d) $k = 3$

73. Let $A = \begin{bmatrix} 1 & 1 & 1 \\ 2 & 2 & 3 \\ x & y & z \end{bmatrix}$ and let $V = \{(x, y, z) \in R^3 : \det(A) = 0\}$. Then the dimension of V equals

(a) 0 (b) 1

(c) 2 (d) 3

74. A basis of $V = \{(x, y, z, w) \in R^4 : x + y - z = 0, y + z + w = 0, 2x + y - 3z - w = 0\}$ is

(a) $\{(1, 1, -1, 0), (0, 1, 1, 1), (2, 1, --3, 1)\}$

(b) $\{(1, -1, 0, 1)\}$

(c) $\{(1, 0, 1, -1)\}$

(d) $\{(1, -1, 0, 1), (1, 0, 1, -1)\}$

75. Consider R^3 with the standard inner product. Let $S = \{(1, 1, 1), (2, -1, 2), (1, -2, 1)\}$.

For a subset W of R^3, let L(W) denote the linear span of W in R^3. Then an orthonormal set T with L(S) = L(T) is

(a) $\{\frac{1}{\sqrt{3}}(1,1,1), \frac{1}{\sqrt{6}}(1,-2,1)\}$

(b) $\{(1, 0, 0), (0, 1, 0), (0, 0, 1)\}$

(c) $\{\frac{1}{\sqrt{3}}(1, 1, 1), \frac{1}{\sqrt{2}}(1, -1, 0)\}$

(d) $\{\frac{1}{\sqrt{3}}(1, 1, 1), \frac{1}{\sqrt{2}}(0, 1, -1)\}$

76. Let A be a 3×3 matrix. Suppose that the eigenvalues of A are $-1, 0, 1$ with respective eigenvectors $(1, -1, 0)^t$, $(1, 1, -2)^t$ and $(1, 1, 1)^t$. Then 6A equals

(a) $\begin{bmatrix} -1 & 5 & 2 \\ 5 & -1 & 2 \\ 2 & 2 & 2 \end{bmatrix}$ (b) $\begin{bmatrix} 1 & 0 & 0 \\ 0 & -1 & 0 \\ 0 & 0 & 0 \end{bmatrix}$

(c) $\begin{bmatrix} 1 & 5 & 3 \\ 5 & 1 & 3 \\ 3 & 3 & 3 \end{bmatrix}$ (d) $\begin{bmatrix} -3 & 9 & 0 \\ 9 & -3 & 0 \\ 0 & 0 & 6 \end{bmatrix}$

77. Let $T : R^3 \to R^3$ be a linear transformation defined by

$T((x, y, z)) = (x + y - z, x + y + z, y - z)$.

Then the matrix of the linear transformation T with respect to the ordered basis $B = \{(0, 1, 0), (0, 0, 1), (1, 0, 0)\}$ of R^3 is 0

(a) $\begin{bmatrix} 1 & 1 & -1 \\ 1 & 1 & 1 \\ 0 & 1 & -1 \end{bmatrix}$ (b) $\begin{bmatrix} 1 & 1 & 0 \\ 1 & 1 & 1 \\ 1 & 0 & -1 \end{bmatrix}$

(c) $\begin{bmatrix} 1 & 1 & 1 \\ 1 & -1 & 0 \\ 1 & -1 & 1 \end{bmatrix}$ (d) $\begin{bmatrix} 1 & -1 & 1 \\ 1 & 1 & 1 \\ 1 & -1 & 0 \end{bmatrix}$

78. Suppose $y(x) = \lambda \int_0^{2\pi} y(t)\sin(x+t)dt, x \in [0, 2\pi]$ has eigenvalues $\lambda = \frac{1}{\pi}$ and $\lambda = -\frac{1}{\pi}$ with corresponding eigen functions $y_1(x) = \sin(x) + \cos(x)$ and $y_2(x) = \sin(x) - \cos(x)$, respectively. Then the integral equation

$$y(x) = f(x) + \frac{1}{\pi}\int_0^{2\pi} y(t)\sin(x+t)dt, x \in [0,2\pi]$$

has a solution when $f(x) =$

(a) 1 (b) $\cos(x)$
(c) $\sin(x)$ (d) $1 + \sin(x) + \cos(x)$

Statement for Linked Answer Questions 79 and 80

Let $A = \begin{bmatrix} 3 & 0 & 0 \\ 0 & 6 & 2 \\ 0 & 2 & 6 \end{bmatrix}$

and let $\lambda_1 \geq \lambda_2 \geq \lambda_3$ be the eigenvalues of A.

79. The triple $(\lambda_1, \lambda_2, \lambda_3)$ equals

(a) (9, 4, 2) (b) (8, 4, 3)
(c) (9, 3, 3) (d) (7, 5, 3)

80. The matrix P such that $P^t AP = \begin{bmatrix} \lambda_1 & 0 & 0 \\ 0 & \lambda_2 & 0 \\ 0 & 0 & \lambda_3 \end{bmatrix}$ is

(a) $\begin{bmatrix} \frac{1}{\sqrt{3}} & 0 & \frac{-2}{\sqrt{6}} \\ \frac{1}{\sqrt{3}} & \frac{1}{\sqrt{2}} & \frac{1}{\sqrt{6}} \\ \frac{1}{\sqrt{3}} & -\frac{1}{\sqrt{2}} & \frac{1}{\sqrt{6}} \end{bmatrix}$ (b) $\begin{bmatrix} \frac{1}{\sqrt{3}} & \frac{-2}{\sqrt{6}} & 0 \\ \frac{1}{\sqrt{3}} & \frac{1}{\sqrt{6}} & \frac{1}{\sqrt{2}} \\ \frac{1}{\sqrt{3}} & \frac{1}{\sqrt{6}} & -\frac{1}{\sqrt{2}} \end{bmatrix}$

(c) $\begin{bmatrix} 0 & 0 & 1 \\ \frac{1}{\sqrt{2}} & \frac{1}{\sqrt{2}} & 0 \\ \frac{1}{\sqrt{2}} & -\frac{1}{\sqrt{2}} & 0 \end{bmatrix}$ (d) $\begin{bmatrix} 0 & 1 & 0 \\ \frac{1}{\sqrt{2}} & 0 & \frac{1}{\sqrt{2}} \\ \frac{1}{\sqrt{2}} & 0 & \frac{1}{\sqrt{2}} \end{bmatrix}$

2006

81. The dimension of the subspace $\{(x_1, x_2, x_3, x_4, x_5) : 3x_1 - x_2 + x_3 = 0\}$ of R^5 is

(a) 1 (b) 2
(c) 3 (d) 4

82. Let the linear transformations S and $T : R^3 \to R^3$ be defined by

$S(x,y,z) = (2x, 4x - y, 2x + 3y - z)$

$T(x, y, z) = (x \cos\theta - y \sin\theta, \sin\theta + y \cos\theta, z)$

where $0 < \theta <, \pi/2$. Then,

(a) S is one to one but not T
(b) T is one to one but not S
(c) both S and T are one to one
(d) neither S nor T is one to one

83. Let V be the vector space of all real polynomials. Consider the subspace W spanned by

$t^2 + t + 2, t^2 + 2t + 5, 5t^2 + 3t + 4$ and $2t^2 + 2t + 4$.

Then, the dimension of W is

(a) 4 (b) 3
(c) 2 (d) 1

84. Let $M = \begin{pmatrix} 1 & a & b \\ 0 & 2 & c \\ 0 & 0 & 1 \end{pmatrix}, a, b, c \in R$.

Then, M is diagonalizable, if and only if

(a) $a = bc$ (b) $b = ac$
(c) $c = ab$ (d) $a = b = c$

85. Let M be the real 5×5 matrix having all of its entries equal to 1. Then,

(a) M is not diagonalizable
(b) M is idempotent
(c) M is nilpotent
(d) the minimal polynomial and the characteristic polynomial of M are not equal

86. Let $\{v_1, v_2, .v_{16}\}$ be an ordered basis for $V = C^{16}$. If T is a linear transformation on V defined by

$T(v_i) = v_i+1$ for $1 \leq i \leq 15$ and $T(v_{16}) = -(v_1 + v_2 + ... + v_{16})$.

Then,

(a) T is singular with rational eigen values
(b) T is singular but has no rational eigen values
(c) T is regular (invertible) with rational eigen values
(d) T is regular but has no rational eigen values

Statement for Linked Answer Questions 87 & 88:

Let $T: C^3 \to C^3$ be defined by $T(x_1, x_2, x_3) = (x_1 + x_2 + x_3, - x_1 - x_2, - x_1 - x_3)$ and M be its matrix with respect to the standard ordered basis.

87. The eigenvalues of M are

(a) $-1, i, -i$ (b) $1, i, -i$
(c) $1, i, i$ (d) $-1, -i, -i$

88. The matrix M is similar to a matrix which is

(a) unitary (b) Hermitian
(c) skew Hermitian (d) having trace 0

2005

89. The set of all $x \in R$ for which the vectors$(1, x, 0)$, $(0, x^2, 1)$ and $(0, 1, x)$ are linearly independent in R^3 is

(a) $\{x \in R : x = 0\}$ (b) $\{x \in R : x \neq 0\}$

(c) $\{x \in R : x \neq 1\}$ (d) $\{x \in R : x \neq -1\}$

90. Consider the vector space $R^3$and the maps f, g : $R^3 \to R^3$ defined by $f(x, y, z) = (x, |y|, z)$ and $g(x, y, z) = (x + 1, y - 1, z)$. Then

(a) both f and g are linear

(b) neither f nor g is linear

(c) g is linear but not f

(d) f is linear but not g

91. Let $M = \begin{pmatrix} 1 & 3 & 3 \\ 0 & 4 & 5 \\ 0 & 0 & 9 \end{pmatrix}$. Then

(a) M is diagonalizable but not M^2

(b) M^2 is diagonalizable but not M

(c) both M and $M^2$are diagonalizable

(d) neither M nor M^2 is diagonalizable

92. Let M be a skew symmetric, orthogonal real matrix, The only possible eigenvalues are

(a) –1, 1 (b) $-i, i$

(c) 0 (d) $1, i$

93. Let S and T be two linear operators on R^3 defined by $S(x, y, z,) = (x, x + y, x - y - z)$ $T(x, y, z) = (x + 2z, y - z, x + y + z)$. Then

(a) S is invertible but not T

(b) T is invertible but not S

(c) both S and T are invertible

(d) neither S nor T is invertible

94. Let V, W and X be three finite dimensional vector spaces such that dim V = dim X. Suppose S : $V \to W$ and T : $W \to X$ are two linear maps such that T o S :$V \to X$ is injective. Then

(a) S and T are surjective

(b) S is surjective and T is injective

(c) S and T are injective

(d) S is injective and T is surjective

95. If a square matrix of order 10 has exactly 4 distinct eigenvalues , then the degree of its minimal polynomial is

(a) at least 4

(b) at most 4

(c) at least 6

(d) at most 6

96. Consider the matrix $M = \begin{pmatrix} 0 & 1 & 2 & 0 \\ 1 & 0 & 1 & 0 \\ 2 & 1 & 0 & 2 \\ 0 & 0 & 2 & 0 \end{pmatrix}$. Then

(a) M has no real eigenvalues

(b) all real eigenvalues of M are positive

(c) all real eigenvalues of M are negative

(d) M has both positive and negative real eigenvalues

97. Consider the real inner product space P[0,1] of all polynomials with the inner product $\langle f,g \rangle = \int_0^1 f(x)\, g(x)\, dx$. Let M = span {1}.The orthogonal projection of x^2onto M is

(a) 1 (b) $\frac{1}{2}$

(c) $\frac{1}{3}$ (d) $\frac{1}{4}$

Statement for Linked Answer Questions 98 and 99:

Let V be the vector space of real polynomials of degree at most 2. Define a linear operator

$T : V \to V$ by

$$T(x^i) = \sum_{j=0}^{i} x^j, i = 0,1,2$$

98. The matrix of T^{-1} with respect to the basis $\{1, x, x^2\}$ is

(a) $\begin{pmatrix} 1 & 1 & 1 \\ 1 & 1 & 0 \\ 1 & 0 & 0 \end{pmatrix}$ (b) $\begin{pmatrix} 1 & -1 & 0 \\ 0 & 1 & -1 \\ 0 & 0 & 1 \end{pmatrix}$

(c) $\begin{pmatrix} 1 & 1 & 1 \\ 0 & 1 & 1 \\ 0 & 0 & 1 \end{pmatrix}$ (d) $\begin{pmatrix} 1 & 0 & 0 \\ -1 & 1 & 0 \\ 0 & -1 & 1 \end{pmatrix}$

99. The dimension of the eigenspace of T^{-1} corresponding to the eigenvalue 1 is

(a) 4 (b) 3

(c) 2 (d) 1

2004

100. Let S and T be two subspaces of R^{24} such that dim (S) =19 and dim (T) = 17. Then, the

(a) smallest possible value of dim $(S \cap T)$ is 2

(b) largest possible value of dim $(S \cap T)$ is 18

(c) smallest possible value of dim (S + T) is 19

(d) largest possible value of dim (S + T) is 22

101. Let $v_1 = (1,2,0,3,0)$, $v_2 = (1,2,-1,-1,0)$, $v_3 = (0,0,1,4,0)$, $v_4 = (2,4,1,10,1)$, and $v_5 = (0, 0, 0, 0, 1)$. The dimension of the linear span of $(v_1, v_2, v_3, v_4, v_5)$ is

(*a*) 2 (*b*) 3

(*d*) 4 (*d*) 5

102. The set $V = \{(x, y) \in R^2 : xy \geq 0\}$ is

(*a*) a vector subspace of $\mathbf{R}^2$

(*b*) not a vector subspace of R^2 since every element does not have an inverse in V

(*c*) not a vector subspace of $\mathbf{R}^2$ since it is not closed under scalar multiplication

(*d*) not a vector subspace of $\mathbf{R}^2$ since it is not closed under vector addition

103. Let $f : R^4 \to R$ be a linear functional defined by $f(x_1, x_2, x_3, x_4) = -x_2$. If $\langle . , . \rangle$ denotes the standard inner product on R^4, then the unique vector $v \in R^4$ such that $f(w) = (v, w)$ for all $W \in R^4$, is

(*a*) $(0, -1, 0, 0)$ (*b*) $(-1, 0, -1, 1)$

(*c*) $(0, 1, 0, 0)$ (*d*) $(1, 0, 1, -1)$

104. Let V be the subspace of R^3 spanned by $u = (1, 1, 1)$ and $v = (1, 1, -1)$. The orthonormal basis of V obtained by the Gram-Schmidt process on the ordered basis (u, v) of V is

(*a*) $\left\{\left(\frac{1}{\sqrt{3}}, \frac{1}{\sqrt{3}}, \frac{1}{\sqrt{3}}\right), \left(\frac{2}{3}, \frac{2}{3}, -\frac{4}{3}\right)\right\}$

(*b*) $\{(1, 1, 0), (1, 0, 1)\}$

(*c*) $\left\{\left(\frac{1}{\sqrt{3}}, \frac{1}{\sqrt{3}}, \frac{1}{\sqrt{3}}\right), \left(\frac{1}{\sqrt{6}}, \frac{1}{\sqrt{6}}, -\frac{2}{\sqrt{6}}\right)\right\}$

(*d*) $\left\{\left(\frac{1}{\sqrt{3}}, \frac{1}{\sqrt{3}}, \frac{1}{\sqrt{3}}\right), \left(\frac{2}{\sqrt{6}}, \frac{1}{\sqrt{6}}, -\frac{1}{\sqrt{6}}\right)\right\}$

105. In R^2, $\langle (x_1, y_1), (x_2, y_2) \rangle = x_1 x_2 - \alpha(x_2 y_1 + x_1 y_2) + y_1 y_2$ is an inner product

(*a*) for all $\alpha \in \mathbf{R}$ (*b*) if and only if $\alpha = 0$

(*c*) if and only if $\alpha < 1$ (*d*) if and only if $|\alpha| < 1$

106. Let $(v_1, v_2, v_3\ v_4)$ be a basis of R^4 and $v = a_1 v_1 + a_2 v_2 + a_3 v_3 + a_4 v_4$, where $a_i \in R$, $i = 1, 2, 3, 4$. Then $(v_1 - v, v_2 - v, v_3 - v, v_4 - v)$ is a basis of R^4 if and only if

(*a*) $a_1 = a_2 = a_3 = a_4$ (*b*) $a_1 a_2 a_3 a_4 = -1$

(*c*) $a_1 + a_2 + a_3 + a_4 \neq 0$ (*d*) $a_1 + a_2 + a_3 + a_4 \neq 0$

107. Let $R^{2\times 2}$ be the real vector space of all 2×2 real matrices. For $Q = \begin{pmatrix} 1 & -2 \\ -2 & 4 \end{pmatrix}$, define a linear transformation T on $R^{2\times 2}$ as $T(P) = QP$. Then the rank of T is

(*a*) 1 (*b*) 2

(*c*) 3 (*d*) 4

108. Let P be a $n \times n$ matrix with integral entries and $Q = P + \frac{1}{2} I$, where I denotes the $n \times n$ identity matrix. Then Q is

(*a*) idempotent, i.e. $Q^2 = Q$

(*b*) invertible

(*c*) nilpotent

(*d*) unipotent, i.e., $Q - I$ is nilpotent

109. Let M be a square matrix of order, 2 such that rank of M is 1. Then M is

(*a*) diagonalizable and nonsingular

(*b*) diagonalizable and nilpotent

(*c*) neither diagonalizable nor nilpotent

(*d*) either diagonalizable or nilpotent but not both

110. *If* M is a 7×5 matrix of rank 3 and N is a 5×7 matrix of rank 5, then rank (MN) is

(*a*) 5 (*b*) 3

(*c*) 2 (*d*) 1

2003

111. Let T be an arbitrary linear transformation from R^n to R^n which is not one-one. Then

(*a*) Rank $T > 0$ (*b*) Rank $T = n$

(*c*) Rank $T \leq n$ (*d*) Rank $T = n - 1$

112. Let T be a linear transformation from $R^3 \to R^2$ defined by $T(x, y, z) = (x + y, y - z)$. Then the matrix of T with respect to the ordered bases $\{(1, 1, 1), (1, -1, 0), (0, 1, 0)\}$ and $\{(1, 1), (1, 0)\}$ is

(*a*) $\begin{bmatrix} -2 & 0 & 1 \\ 1 & 1 & -1 \end{bmatrix}$ (*b*) $\begin{bmatrix} 0 & -1 & 1 \\ 2 & 1 & 0 \end{bmatrix}$

(*c*) $\begin{bmatrix} 2 & 1 \\ 0 & -1 \\ 1 & 1 \end{bmatrix}$ (*d*) $\begin{bmatrix} 0 & 2 \\ -1 & 1 \\ 1 & 0 \end{bmatrix}$

113. Let the characteristics equation of a matrix M be $\lambda^2 - \lambda - 1 = 0$, then

(*a*) M^{-1} does not exist

(*b*) M^{-1} exists but cannot be determined from the data

(*c*) $M^{-1} = M + 1$

(*d*) $M^{-1} = M - 1$

114. Consider the matrix $M = \begin{pmatrix} 1 & 0 & -1 \\ 0 & 1 & 0 \\ 1 & 1 & -1 \end{pmatrix}$ and let S_M be the set of 3×3 matrices N such that $MN = 0$. Then the dimension of the real vector space S_M is equal to

(*a*) 0 (*b*) 1

(*c*) 2 (*d*) 3

115. Choose the correct matching from a, b, c and d for the transformation T_1, T_2 and T_3 (mappings from R^2 to R^3) as defined in Group 1 with the statements given in Group 2.

Group 1

P. $T_1(x, y) = (x, x, 0)$

Q. $T_2(x, y) = (x, x + y, y)$

R. $T_3(x, y) = (x, x + 1, y)$

Group 2

1. Linear transformation of rank 2
2. Not a linear transformation
3. Linear transformation of rank 1

(a)	(b)	(c)	(d)
P – 3	P – 1	P – 3	P – 1
Q – 1	Q – 2	Q – 2	Q – 3
R – 2	R – 3	R – 1	R – 2

116. Let $M = \begin{pmatrix} 0 & 0 & -1 & 0 \\ 2 & 0 & 0 & 0 \\ 0 & 0 & 0 & 3 \\ 0 & -4 & 0 & 0 \end{pmatrix}$. Then

(a) $MM^T = I$ where M^T is the transpose of M and I is the identify matrix

(b) Column vectors of M form an orthogonal system of vectors

(c) Column vectors of M form an orthonormal system of vectors

(d) $(MX, MY) = (X, Y)$ for all X, Y in R^4 where (,) is the standard inner product on R^4

117. Let $M = \begin{pmatrix} 1 & 1+i & 2i & 9 \\ 1-i & 3 & 4 & 7-i \\ -2i & 4 & 5 & i \\ 9 & 7+i & -i & 7 \end{pmatrix}$. Then

(a) M has purely imaginary eigen values

(b) M is not diagonalizable

(c) M has eigen values which are neither real nor purely imaginary

(d) M has only real eigen values

118. Consider the matrix $M = \begin{pmatrix} a^2 & ab & ac \\ ab & b^2 & bc \\ ac & bc & c^2 \end{pmatrix}$

where a, b and c are non-zero real numbers. Then the matrix has

(a) three non-zero real eigen values

(b) complex eigen values

(c) two non-zero eigen value

(d) only one non-zero eigen value

119. The minimal polynomial of $\begin{pmatrix} 1 & 0 & 0 & 0 \\ 1 & 1 & 0 & 0 \\ 0 & 0 & 2 & 0 \\ 0 & 0 & 0 & 2 \end{pmatrix}$ is

(a) $(x - 1)^2 (x - 2)$ (b) $(x - 1)(x - 2)^2$

(c) $(x - 1)(x - 2)$ (d) $(x - 1)^2 (x - 2)^2$

2002

120. The dimension of the vector space of all 3×3 real symmetric matrices is:

(a) 3 (b) 9

(c) 6 (d) 4

121. Let A be a non-zero upper triangular matrix all of whose eigenvalues are 0. Then I + A is :

(a) invertible (b) singular

(c) idempotent (d) nilpotent

122. The eigenvalues of a skew-symmetric matrix are

(a) negative

(b) real

(c) of absolute value 1

(d) purely imaginary or zero

123. Let A be a 3×3 matrix with eigenvalues 1, – 1, 0. Then the determinant of $I + A^{100}$ is

(a) 6 (b) 4

(c) 9 (d) 100

124. Let A be a 2×2 orthogonal matrix of trace and determinant 1. Then the angle between Au and u ($u = [1\ 0]^t$) is

(a) 15° (b) 30°

(c) 45° (d) 60°

125. Let J_n be the $n \times n$ matrix each of whose entries equals 1. Find the nullity and the characteristic polynomial of J_n.

2001

126. The eigenvalues of a 3×3 real matrix P are 1, – 2, 3. Then

(a) $P^{-1} = \frac{1}{6}(5I + 2P - P^2)$ (b) $P^{-1} = \frac{1}{6}(5I - 2P + P^2)$

(c) $P^{-1} = \frac{1}{6}(5I - 2P - P^2)$ (d) $P^{-1} = \frac{1}{6}(5I + 2P + P^2)$

127. Let $T : C^n \to C^n$ be a linear operator having n distinct eigenvalues. Then

(a) T is invertible

(b) T is invertible as well as diagona-lizable

(c) T is not diagonalizable

(d) T is diagonalizable

128. Let U be a 3×3 complex Hermitian matrix which is Unitary. Then the distinct eigenvalues of U are

(*a*) $\pm i$ (*b*) $1 \pm i$

(*c*) ± 1 (*d*) $\frac{1}{2}(1 \pm i)$

129. Let A be an $n \times n$ complex matrix whose characteristic polynomial is given by

$f(t) = t^n + C_{n-1} t^{n-1} + ... + c_1 t + C_0$.

Then

(*a*) $\det(A) = c_{n-1}$ (*b*) $\det(A) = c_0$

(*c*) $\det(A) = (-1)^n c_{n-1}$ (*d*) $\det(A) = (-1)^n c_0$

130. Let A be any $n \times n$ non-singular complex matrix and let $B = (\bar{A})^t A$, where $(\bar{A})^t$ is the conjugate transpose of A. If λ is an eigenvalue of B, then

(*a*) λ is real and $\lambda < 0$ (*b*) λ is real and $\lambda \leq 0$

(*c*) λ is real and $\lambda \geq 0$ (*d*) λ is real and $\lambda > 0$

131. Let $T : C^n \to C^n$ be a linear operator of rank $n - 2$. Then

(*a*) 0 is not an eigenvalue of T

(*b*) 0 must be an eigenvalue of T

(*c*) 1 can never be an eigenvalue of T

(*d*) 1 must be an eigenvalue of T

132. Let $T : V \to V$ be a linear transformation on a vector space V over a field K satisfying the property $Tx = 0 \to x = 0$. If $x_1, x_2 ...., x_n$ are linearly independent

elements in V, show that $Tx_1, Tx_2, ..., Tx_n$ are also linearly independent.

133. Let $T : V \to V$ be a linear operator on a finite dimensional vector space V over a field K and let $p(t)$ be the minimal polynomial of T. If T is diagonalizable, show that $p(t) = (t - \lambda_1)(t - \lambda_2) ... (t - \lambda_r)$ for some distinct scalars $\lambda_1, \lambda_2, ..., \lambda_r$.

2000

134. Let W be the space spanned by $f = \sin x$ and $g = \cos x$. Then for any real value of θ, $f_1 = \sin(x + \theta)$ and $g_1 = \cos(x + \theta)$.

(*a*) are vectors in W

(*b*) are linearly independent

(*c*) do not form a basis for W

(*d*) form a basis for W

135. Consider the basis $S = \{v_1, v_2, v_3\}$ for R^3 where $v_1 = (1, 1, 1)$, $v_2 = (1, 1, 0)$ $v_3 = (1, 0, 0)$ and let $T : R^3 \to R^2$ be a linear transformation such that

$Tv_1 = (1, 0)$, $Tv_2 = (2, -1)$, $Tv_3 = (4, 3)$. Then $T(2, -3, 5)$ is

(*a*) $(-1, 5)$ (*b*) $(3, 4)$

(*c*) $(0, 0)$ (*d*) $(9, 23)$

136. For $0 < \theta < \pi$; the matrix $\begin{bmatrix} \cos\theta & -\sin\theta \\ \sin\theta & \cos\theta \end{bmatrix}$

(*a*) has no real eigenvalue

(*b*) is orthogonal

(*c*) is symmetric

(*d*) is skew symmetric

ANSWERS

1. (*c*)	**2.** (*b*)	**3.** (*b*)	**4.** (7)	**5.** (5.5)	**6.** (3)	**7.** (27)	**8.** (3)	**9.** (6)	**10.** (*a*)
11. (*d*)	**12.** (2)	**13.** (1)	**14.** (*c*)	**15.** (80.99 to 81.01)		**16.** (*b*)	**17.** (7.99 to 8.01)		**18.** (*b*)
19. (*a*)	**20.** (1.99 to 2.01)		**21.** (3.99 to 4.01)		**22.** (*a*)	**23.** (78)	**24.** (15)	**25.** (–1)	**26.** (*a*)
27. (*a*)	**28.** (*c*)	**29.** (*a*)	**30.** (*d*)	**31.** (*d*)	**32.** (*c*)	**33.** (*d*)	**34.** (*c*)	**35.** (*c*)	**36.** (*a*)
37. (*c*)	**38.** (*b*)	**39.** (*)	**40.** (*b*)	**41.** (*d*)	**42.** (*d*)	**43.** (*d*)	**44.** (*c*)	**45.** (*d*)	**46.** (*a*)
47. (*d*)	**48.** (*c*)	**49.** (*a*)	**50.** (*a*)	**51.** (*c*)	**52.** (*d*)	**53.** (*b*)	**54.** (*a*)	**55.** (*b*)	**56.** (*d*)
57. (*c*)	**58.** (*a*)	**59.** (*d*)	**60.** (*d*)	**61.** (*a*)	**62.** (*c*)	**63.** (*b*)	**64.** (*b*)	**65.** (*d*)	**66.** (*b*)
67. (*a*)	**68.** (*c*)	**69.** (*d*)	**70.** (*b*)	**71.** (*c*)	**72.** (*a*)	**73.** (*d*)	**74.** (*d*)	**75.** (*a*)	**76.** (*a*)
77. (*c*)	**78.** (*a*)	**79.** (*c*)	**80.** (*b*)	**81.** (*d*)	**82.** (*c*)	**83.** (*d*)	**84.** (*a*)	**85.** (*d*)	**86.** (*c*)
87. (*a*)	**88.** (*a*)	**89.** (*a*)	**90.** (*c*)	**91.** (*d*)	**92.** (*a*)	**93.** (*a*)	**94.** (*c*)	**95.** (*a*)	**96.** (*a*)
97. (*c*)	**98.** (*b*)	**99.** (*b*)	**100.** (*c*)	**101.** (*b*)	**102.** (*d*)	**103.** (*a*)	**104.** (*c*)	**105.** (*d*)	**106.** (*d*)
107. (*a*)	**108.** (*b*)	**109.** (*a*)	**110.** (*b*)	**111.** (*d*)	**112.** (*b*)	**113.** (*d*)	**114.** (*d*)	**115.** (*a*)	**116.** (*b*)
117. (*d*)	**118.** (*a*)	**119.** (*c*)	**120.** (*b*)	**121.** (*d*)	**122.** (*d*)	**123.** (*a*)	**124.** (*c*)	**125.** (*)	**126.** (*a*)
127. (*b*)	**128.** (*c*)	**129.** (*b*)	**130.** (*d*)	**131.** (*b*)	**132.** (*)	**133.** (*)	**134.** (*d*)	**135.** (*d*)	**136.** (*b*)

EXPLANATIONS

1. $M = \begin{bmatrix} 1 & 1 & 1 \\ 1 & 2 & 4 \\ 1 & 3 & 9 \end{bmatrix}$ $|M| \neq 0$, then M is singular

If S is diagonalizable matrix, then a non-singular matrix P s.t

$$D = P^{-1}SP = \text{diagonal}$$

If T is s.t $S + 5T = Id$

$$P^{-1}(S + 5T)P = P^{-1}(Id)P$$

$$P^{-1}SP + 5P^{-1}TP = Id$$

$$\Rightarrow \quad D + 5P^{-1}TP = Id$$

$$\Rightarrow \quad P^{-1}TP = \text{diagonal matrix}$$

$$= B \text{ (say)}$$

$\Rightarrow$ T is diagonalizable.

2. The characteristics roots of a unitary matrix are of unit modulus i.e. $|\lambda|^2 = 1.$ or $|\lambda| = \pm 1$

$$R(M) + N(M^*) = n$$

$$N(M^*) + (N(M^*))^{\perp} = n$$

$$\Rightarrow \quad R(M) = (N(M^*))^{\perp}$$

3. $T : V \to V$, $\dim(v) = n$

$\dim(T(V)) < n$ and $T^2 = \lambda T$, $(T - \lambda I)TX = 0$ for some $X \in V_1$ and $(T - \lambda I)X = 0$ or $TX = 0$

Nullity $(N(T)) > 0 \Rightarrow \in a \times$ s.t

$TX = 0$ for some non zero $X \in V$

$\Rightarrow$ There exists non-trivial subspace of V s.t. $T(X) = 0$ for $X \in V_1$

4. $A = \begin{bmatrix} a & b & c \\ b & d & e \\ c & e & f \end{bmatrix}$

Characteristic equation is

$$\Delta(t) = t^3 - tr(A)t^2 + (A_{11} + A_{22} + A_{33})t - |A|$$

$$= 0$$

$$= t^3 - (a + d + f)t^2$$

$$+ (df - e^2 + af - c^2 + ad - b^2)t = 0$$

If $\quad \lambda_1 = 1, 0$ and 3 Then

$$\Delta(t) = t^3 - 4t^2 + 3 = 0$$

$$\Rightarrow \quad a + \alpha + f = 4 \quad \text{...(1)}$$

Similarly using eigen vector for eigenvalues 1 and 0 are

$$a + b + c = 1$$

and $\quad a = b = d$ and $c = e$

$$b + d + e = 1$$

$$c + e + f = 1 \quad \text{...(2)}$$

using (1) and (2) we have

$$3f^2 - 10f + 7 = 0$$

$$\therefore \quad 3f = 7$$

5. If $M = \begin{bmatrix} 1 & 1 & 0 \\ 0 & 1 & 1 \\ 0 & 0 & 1 \end{bmatrix}$,

$$M^k = \begin{bmatrix} 1^k & (1^k)1^{k-1} & \binom{k}{2}1^{k-2} \\ 0 & 1^k & \binom{k}{1}1^{k-1} \\ 0 & 1 & 1^k \end{bmatrix}$$

Then $e^M = I + M + \frac{1}{2!}M^2 + ... + \frac{1}{K!}M^k + ...$

$$= \begin{bmatrix} e^1 & \frac{1}{1!}e^1 & \frac{1}{2!}e^1 \\ 0 & e^1 & e^1 \\ 0 & 0 & e^1 \end{bmatrix}$$

$$= \begin{bmatrix} e & e & \frac{e}{2} \\ 0 & e & e \\ 0 & 0 & e \end{bmatrix} = \begin{bmatrix} b_{11} & b_{12} & b_{13} \\ b_{21} & b_{22} & b_{23} \\ b_{31} & b_{32} & b_{33} \end{bmatrix}$$

$$\frac{1}{e}\sum_{i=1}^{3}\sum_{j=1}^{3} b_{ij} = \frac{1}{e}\left[\sum_{i=1}^{3}\{b_{i1} + b_{i2} + b_{i3}\}\right]$$

$$= \frac{1}{e}[(b_{11} + b_{12} + b_{13}) + (b_{21} + b_{22} + b_{23})$$

$$+ (b_{31} + b_{32} + b_{33})]$$

$$= \frac{1}{e}\left[\frac{5}{2}e + 2e + e\right] = \frac{1}{e} \times \frac{11}{2}e = \frac{11}{2} = 5.5$$

14. Given group homomorphism

$\phi : M_2(R) \to R$ such that $\phi(A) = \text{trace}(A)$

Kernel of ϕ is the collection of those matrices whose trace are zero.

Here dimension of domain space is 4 i.e. $\dim M_2(R) = 4$

Also, $\dim |\ker \phi| + \dim |\text{image } \phi| = \dim M_2(R)$

i.e, $\quad \eta + \rho = 4 \quad \text{...(i)}$

and dimension of co-domain space i.e. dim [Image ϕ]

i.e., $\quad$ Rank $(\rho) = 1$

$$\therefore \quad \eta + 1 = 4$$

$$\Rightarrow \quad \eta = 3$$

i.e. $\quad \dim(\ker \phi) = 3$

Hence $\quad \ker(\phi) \cong R^3$.

15. Let eigen values of $[A]_{3\times3}$ are $\lambda_1, \lambda_2, \lambda_3$ then given trace of $A = 13$

$\Rightarrow \quad \lambda_1+\lambda_2+\lambda_3 = 13 \quad ...(i)$

and $\quad \det(A) = 32$

$\Rightarrow \quad \lambda_1\lambda_2\lambda_3 = 32 \quad ...(ii)$

Also let eigen values of $(A-I)$ are $\lambda_1-1, \lambda_2-1, \lambda_3-1$.

where, $[I]_{3\times3}$ is identity matrix whose eigen values are 1, 1, 1

Given, det $(A - I) = 0$ which shows that atleast one eigen values of matrix $(A - I)$ is 0.

So, let $\quad \lambda_1 - 1 = 0$

$\Rightarrow \quad \lambda_1 = 1$

$\Rightarrow$ one eigen value of A is 1.

Then, from equation(i) and (ii) we get

$$\lambda_2+\lambda_3 = 13-1 = 12 \quad ...(iii)$$

$$\lambda_2\lambda_3 = 32$$

$$\Rightarrow \quad \lambda_2 = \frac{32}{\lambda_3}$$

On putting the value of λ_2 in (iii), we get

$$\frac{32}{\lambda_3}+\lambda_3 = 12$$

$\Rightarrow \quad \lambda_3^2 - 12\lambda_3 + 32 = 0$

$\Rightarrow \quad \lambda_3^2 - 8\lambda_3 - 4\lambda_3 + 32 = 0$

$\Rightarrow \quad (\lambda_3-8)(\lambda_3-4) = 0$

$\Rightarrow \quad \lambda_3 = 8$ or 4.

Then $\quad \lambda_2 = 4$ or 8.

So, eigen values of matrix $[A]_{3\times3}$ are $\lambda_1 = 1, \lambda_2 = 8$ or 4 and $\lambda_3 = 4$ or 8.

If we take, $\lambda_1 = 1, \lambda_2 = 8$ and $\lambda_3 = 4$,

then $\quad \lambda_1^2+\lambda_2^2+\lambda_3^2 = 1+64+16 = 81$

and if we take, $\lambda_1 = 1$, $\lambda_2 = 4$ and $\lambda_3 = 8$, then $\lambda_1^2+\lambda_2^2+\lambda_3^2 = 1+16+64 = 81$.

16. Given, V be the vector space $C^5[a, b]$ over R.

i.e. V be the set of all real valued, n times continuously differentiable functions on the real interval $[a, b]$

$\therefore \quad \dim(V) = \infty$

Let any finite set $S = \{f_1(t), f_2(t) \ .... \ f_m(t)\}$ of polynomials in V and let m denote the largest degree of polynomials. Then any polynomial $g(t)$ of degree exceeding m cannot be expressed as linear combination of elements of S. Thus S cannot be basis of V. It means dimension of V is infinite.

and $\quad W = \left\{f \in V : \frac{d^4f}{dt^4} + 2\frac{d^2f}{dt^2} - f = 0\right\}$

i.e., collection of all functions which satisfies 4th order homogeneous differential equation.

So, $\quad \dim(W) = 4$.

17. Given, V be a real inner product space of dimension 10. $x, y \in V$ and x, y are non-zero vectors such that, $\langle x, y \rangle = 0$

$\therefore$ Dimension of $\{x\}^\perp \cap \{y\}^\perp$ is 8.

18. Only statement Q is true.

19. Here, $\quad X = \begin{bmatrix} 2 & 0 & -3 \\ 3 & -1 & -3 \\ 0 & 0 & -1 \end{bmatrix}$

From option (a)

If $\quad P = \begin{bmatrix} 1 & 1 & 1 \\ 0 & 1 & 1 \\ 1 & 1 & 0 \end{bmatrix}$

then $\quad P^{-1} = \frac{1}{|P|}\text{adj}(P)$

$\therefore \quad P^{-1} = \begin{bmatrix} 1 & -1 & 0 \\ -1 & 1 & 1 \\ 1 & 0 & -1 \end{bmatrix}$

Now $P^{-1}XP$

$$= \begin{bmatrix} 1 & -1 & 0 \\ -1 & 1 & 1 \\ 1 & 0 & -1 \end{bmatrix}\begin{bmatrix} 2 & 0 & -3 \\ 3 & -1 & -3 \\ 0 & 0 & -1 \end{bmatrix}\begin{bmatrix} 1 & 1 & 1 \\ 0 & 1 & 1 \\ 1 & 1 & 0 \end{bmatrix}$$

$$= \begin{bmatrix} 1 & -1 & 0 \\ -1 & 1 & 1 \\ 1 & 0 & -1 \end{bmatrix}\begin{bmatrix} 2-3 & 2-3 & 2 \\ 3-3 & 3-1-3 & 3-1 \\ -1 & -1 & 0 \end{bmatrix}$$

$$\therefore \quad P^{-1}XP = \begin{bmatrix} 1 & -1 & 0 \\ -1 & 1 & 1 \\ 1 & 0 & -1 \end{bmatrix}\begin{bmatrix} -1 & -1 & 2 \\ 0 & -1 & 2 \\ -1 & -1 & 0 \end{bmatrix}$$

$$= \begin{bmatrix} -1 & -1+1 & 2-2 \\ 1-1 & 1-1-1 & -2+2 \\ -1+1 & -1+1 & 2 \end{bmatrix}$$

$$= \begin{bmatrix} -1 & 0 & 0 \\ 0 & -1 & 0 \\ 0 & 0 & 2 \end{bmatrix}$$

Hence $P^{-1}XP$ is a diagonal matrix

$\therefore$ option (a) is correct

20. Given $T_1 : R^5 \to R^3$ and $T_2 : R^5 \to R^3$ be linear transformation.

rank $(T_1) = 3$. Then nullity $(T_1) = 2$.

and given $\rightarrow$ nullity $(T_2) = 3$. then rank $(T_2) = 2$.

Also given $T_3 : R^3 \rightarrow R^3$ be linear transformation such that $T_3 . T_1 = T_2$

Here $T_1 : R^5 \rightarrow R^3$ and $T_3 : R^3 \rightarrow R^3$

$\Rightarrow$ $T_3 . T_1 : R^5 \rightarrow R^3$

or we can write $T_1 \cdot T_3 : R^5 \rightarrow R^3$ i.e. $[T_3 T_1]_{3\times5}$

By given condition

$$[T_3 T_1]_{3\times5} = [T_2]_{3\times5}$$

but $\rho(T_2)$ i.e. Rank $(T_2) = 2$

$\Rightarrow$ $\rho[T_3 T_1] = 2$

we know:

$$\text{Rank } [T_1 \cdot T_3] \le \max\{\text{Rank } T_1, \text{Rank } T_3\}$$

$$2 \le \max\{3, \text{Rank } (T_3)\} \quad ...(i)$$

Also, $\text{Rank } [T_1 T_3] \ge \text{Rank}[T_1] + \text{Rank}[T_3] - \text{Rank}[T_1 \cap T_3]$

$\Rightarrow$ $2 \ge 3 + \text{Rank}[T_3] - 3$

$\Rightarrow$ $2 \ge \text{Rank}[T_3] \quad ...(ii)$

From equation (i) and (ii), we get

$$\text{Rank } [T_3] = 2$$

21. $F_3 \times F_3$ be the vector space over F_3 and $F_3 = \{0, 1, 2\}$, where F_3 is field with three elements. Now to find the number of distinct linearly dependent sets of the form $\{u, v\}$ where $u, v \in F_3 \times F_3 \setminus \{(0, 0)\}$ and $u \ne v$

$\therefore$ $F_3 \times F_3 = \{0, 1, 2\} \times \{0, 1, 2\}$

$= \{(0, 0) (0, 1) (0, 2) (1, 0) (1, 1) (1, 2) (2, 0) (2, 1) (2, 2)\}$

By given condition,

$\{(0, 1), (0, 2)\}, \{(1, 0), (2, 0)\} \in F_3 \times F_3$

Also, $\{(0, 2), (0, 1)\}, \{(2, 0), (1, 0)\} \in F_3 \times F_3$

$\therefore$ Number of distinct linearly dependent set of the form $\{u, v\}$ where $u, v \in F_3 \times F_3 \setminus \{0, 0\}$ and $u \ne v$ is 4.

22. Skew symmetric matrix

$$A = A^T$$

Orthogonal matrix $= A^T = A^{-1}$

So for 4×4 skew symmetric orthogonal real matrix eigen values will be $\{\pm i\}$

23. trace (P) = 1

det (P) = – 6

Let matrix has 2 eigen values λ_1 & λ_2

$$\lambda_1 + \lambda_2 = 1$$

$$\lambda_1 \lambda_2 = -6$$

$$\lambda_1 = 3,$$

$$\lambda_2 = -2$$

From $tr(p^k) = \Sigma\lambda^k$;

So $tr(p^4 - p^3) = \left[(\lambda_1)^4 + (\lambda_2)^4\right] - \left[(\lambda_1)^3 + (\lambda_2)^3\right]$

$= 78$

26. $A = \begin{bmatrix} 1 & 2 & 0 \\ 1 & 3 & 1 \\ 0 & 1 & 3 \end{bmatrix}$

$A = LU \quad ...(1)$

$$L = \begin{bmatrix} 1 & 0 & 0 \\ l_{21} & 1 & 0 \\ l_{31} & l_{32} & 1 \end{bmatrix};$$

$$U = \begin{bmatrix} u_{11} & u_{12} & u_{13} \\ 0 & u_{22} & u_{23} \\ 0 & 0 & u_{33} \end{bmatrix}$$

Put values of L & U in equation (1) then by comparing

$$\begin{bmatrix} 1 & 0 & 0 \\ l_{21} & 1 & 0 \\ l_{31} & l_{32} & 1 \end{bmatrix}$$

$$\begin{bmatrix} u_{11} & u_{12} & u_{13} \\ 0 & u_{22} & u_{23} \\ 0 & 0 & u_{33} \end{bmatrix} = \begin{bmatrix} 1 & 2 & 0 \\ 1 & 3 & 1 \\ 0 & 1 & 3 \end{bmatrix}$$

$$\begin{bmatrix} u_{11} & u_{12} & u_{13} \\ l_{21}u_{11} & l_{21}u_{12} + u_{22} & l_{21}u_{13} + u_{23} \\ l_{31}u_{11} & l_{31}u_{12} + l_{32}u_{22} & l_{31}u_{13} + l_{32}u_{23} + u_{33} \end{bmatrix}$$

$u_{11} = 1;\ u_{12} = 2,\ u_{13} = 0$

$l_{21}\, u_{11} = 1;\ l_{21} = 1$

$l_{31}\, u_{11} = 0;\ l_{31} = 0$

$l_{21}\, u_{12} + u_{22} = 3$

$u_{22} = 1$

$l_{31}\, u_{12} + l_{32} + u_{22} = 1$

$l_{32} = 1$

$$L = \begin{bmatrix} 1 & 0 & 0 \\ 1 & 1 & 0 \\ 0 & 1 & 1 \end{bmatrix}$$

$LX = [1\,2\,2]^t$

$X = L^{-1}[1\,2\,2]^t$

$X = [1\,1\,1]^t$

28. The number of matrices of rank three in M will be $(3^4 - 1)(3^4 - 3)(3^4 - 3^2)$

29. Given V = Vector space of $m \ge 2$

$T^{n+1} = 0$

$T^n \ne 0$

Then Rank $(T^n) \le$ Nullity (T^n)

trace (T) = 0

T is not diagonalizable and $n \neq m$

32. Given lines are

$$L_1 : x = 0$$
$$L_2 : y = 0$$
$$L_3 : x + y = 1$$

and transformation is

$$w = z^2$$

Let $z = x + iy$

$\therefore$ $w = (x + iy)^2$

$\therefore$ $c_1 : w = -y^2$

$$c_2 : w = x^2$$
$$c_3 : w = [x + i(1 - x)]^2$$
$$= x^2 - (1 - x)^2 + 2ix(1 - x)$$
$$= -1 + 2x + 2ix(1 - x)$$

Now, the graph of c_1 and c_2 on w-plane is given below

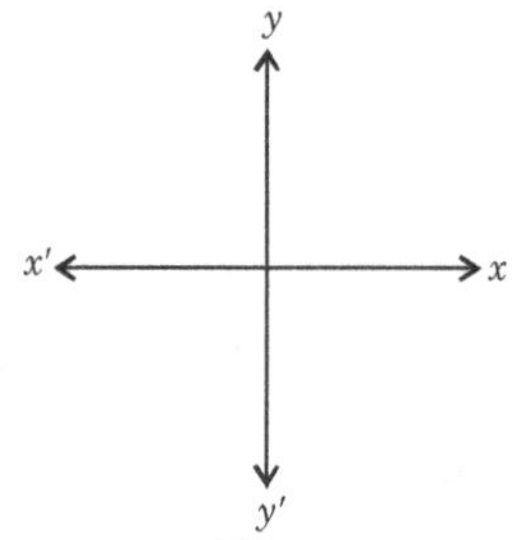

Fig.

$\therefore$ angle between curves at $w = 0$ is $\frac{\pi}{2}$

33. We have

$$\alpha = e^{\frac{2\pi i}{5}} = (-1)^{\frac{2}{5}} = 1^{\frac{1}{5}}$$
$$\alpha^5 = 1$$

i.e., α is fifth root of unity.

$\therefore$ $1 + \alpha + \alpha^2 + \alpha^3 + \alpha^4 = 0$ ...(1)

and $1.\ \alpha.\ \alpha^2.\ \alpha^3.\ \alpha^4 = 1$ ...(2)

$$\text{Now } M = \begin{bmatrix} 1 & \alpha & \alpha^2 & \alpha^3 & \alpha^4 \\ 0 & \alpha & \alpha^2 & \alpha^3 & \alpha^4 \\ 0 & 0 & \alpha^2 & \alpha^3 & \alpha^4 \\ 0 & 0 & 0 & \alpha^3 & \alpha^4 \\ 0 & 0 & 0 & 0 & \alpha^4 \end{bmatrix}$$

$\therefore$ Trace (M) = $1 + \alpha + \alpha^2 + \alpha^3 + \alpha^4 = 0$

$$M^2 = \begin{bmatrix} 1 & \alpha & \alpha^2 & \alpha^3 & \alpha^4 \\ 0 & \alpha & \alpha^2 & \alpha^3 & \alpha^4 \\ 0 & 0 & \alpha^2 & \alpha^3 & \alpha^4 \\ 0 & 0 & 0 & \alpha^3 & \alpha^4 \\ 0 & 0 & 0 & 0 & \alpha^4 \end{bmatrix} \begin{bmatrix} 1 & \alpha & \alpha^2 & \alpha^3 & \alpha^4 \\ 0 & \alpha & \alpha^2 & \alpha^3 & \alpha^4 \\ 0 & 0 & \alpha^2 & \alpha^3 & \alpha^4 \\ 0 & 0 & 0 & \alpha^3 & \alpha^4 \\ 0 & 0 & 0 & 0 & \alpha^4 \end{bmatrix}$$

$$M^2 = \begin{bmatrix} 1 & \alpha+\alpha^2 & \alpha^2+\alpha^3+\alpha^4 & \alpha^3+\alpha^4+\alpha^5+\alpha^6 & \alpha^4+\alpha^5+\alpha^6+\alpha^7+\alpha^8 \\ 0 & \alpha^2 & \alpha^3+\alpha^4 & \alpha^4+\alpha^5+\alpha^6 & \alpha^5+\alpha^6+\alpha^7+\alpha^8 \\ 0 & 0 & \alpha^4 & \alpha^5+\alpha^6 & \alpha^6+\alpha^7+\alpha^8 \\ 0 & 0 & 0 & \alpha^6 & \alpha^7+\alpha^8 \\ 0 & 0 & 0 & 0 & \alpha^8 \end{bmatrix}$$

$$\text{Trace}(M^2) = 1 + a^2 + a^4 + a^6 + a^8$$
$$= \frac{1[1 - (\alpha^2)^5]}{1 - \alpha^2}$$
$$= \frac{1 - e^{4\pi i}}{1 - e^{\frac{4\pi i}{5}}} \qquad \left(\because \alpha = e^{\frac{2\pi i}{5}}\right)$$
$$= \frac{1 - 1}{1 - e^{\frac{4\pi i}{5}}} = 0$$

Also $\text{Trace}(I)_{5\times5} = 5$

Hence Trace $(I + M + M^2)$

$$= \text{Trace}(I) + \text{Trace}(M) + \text{Trace}(M^2)$$
$$= 5 + 0 + 0 = 5$$

34. Given that $B = \{(1, i), (i, 1)\}$ be an ordered basis of vector space $\mathbb{C}^2$

Let $f_1(z_1, z_2) = a_1 z_1 + a_2 z_2$

$$f_2(z_1, z_2) = b_1 z_1 + b_2 z_2$$

where $a_i, b_i \in \mathbb{C}$ $(j = 1, 2)$ are to be determined

$$1 = f_1(1, i) = a_1 + a_2 i$$
$$0 = f_1(i, 1) = a_1 i + a_2$$

By solving, we get

$$a_1 = \frac{1}{2}, a_2 = \frac{1}{2i}$$
$$f_1(z_1, z_2) = \frac{1}{2}z_1 + \frac{1}{2i}z_2 = \frac{1}{2}(z_1 - iz_2)$$

Similarly $0 = f_2(1, i) = b_1 + b_2 i$

$$1 = f_2(i, 1) = b_1 i + b_2$$

By solving, we get

$$b_1 = \frac{1}{2i}, b_2 = \frac{1}{2}$$
$$f_2(z_1, z_2) = \frac{1}{2i}z_1 + \frac{1}{2}z_2 = \frac{1}{2}(-iz_1 + z_2)$$

Hence dual basis of

$$B = \{(1, i), (i, 1)\} \text{ is}$$
$$B^* = \{(f_1, f_2)\}$$

where $f_1(z_1, z_2) = \frac{1}{2}(z_1 - iz_2)$

and $f_2(z_1, z_2) = \frac{1}{2}(-iz_1 + z_2)$

35.

$$A = \begin{bmatrix} 1 & 0 & 0 \\ 1 & 0 & 1 \\ 0 & 1 & 0 \end{bmatrix}$$

$$A^2 = A.A = \begin{bmatrix} 1 & 0 & 0 \\ 1 & 0 & 1 \\ 0 & 1 & 0 \end{bmatrix}\begin{bmatrix} 1 & 0 & 0 \\ 1 & 0 & 1 \\ 0 & 1 & 0 \end{bmatrix} = \begin{bmatrix} 1 & 0 & 0 \\ 1 & 1 & 0 \\ 1 & 0 & 1 \end{bmatrix}$$

$$A^4 = A^2.A^2$$

$$= \begin{bmatrix} 1 & 0 & 0 \\ 1 & 1 & 0 \\ 1 & 0 & 1 \end{bmatrix}\begin{bmatrix} 1 & 0 & 0 \\ 1 & 1 & 0 \\ 1 & 0 & 1 \end{bmatrix} = \begin{bmatrix} 1 & 0 & 0 \\ 2 & 1 & 0 \\ 2 & 0 & 1 \end{bmatrix}$$

$$A^8 = A^4.A^4$$

$$= \begin{bmatrix} 1 & 0 & 0 \\ 2 & 1 & 0 \\ 2 & 0 & 1 \end{bmatrix}\begin{bmatrix} 1 & 0 & 0 \\ 2 & 1 & 0 \\ 2 & 0 & 1 \end{bmatrix} = \begin{bmatrix} 1 & 0 & 0 \\ 4 & 1 & 0 \\ 4 & 0 & 1 \end{bmatrix}$$

$$A^{16} = A^8.\,A^8$$

$$= \begin{bmatrix} 1 & 0 & 0 \\ 4 & 1 & 0 \\ 4 & 0 & 1 \end{bmatrix}\begin{bmatrix} 1 & 0 & 0 \\ 4 & 1 & 0 \\ 4 & 0 & 1 \end{bmatrix} = \begin{bmatrix} 1 & 0 & 0 \\ 8 & 1 & 0 \\ 8 & 0 & 1 \end{bmatrix}$$

$$A^{32} = A^{16}.\,A^{16}$$

$$= \begin{bmatrix} 1 & 0 & 0 \\ 8 & 1 & 0 \\ 8 & 0 & 1 \end{bmatrix}\begin{bmatrix} 1 & 0 & 0 \\ 8 & 1 & 0 \\ 8 & 0 & 1 \end{bmatrix} = \begin{bmatrix} 1 & 0 & 0 \\ 16 & 1 & 0 \\ 16 & 0 & 1 \end{bmatrix}$$

$$A^{48} = A^{32}.A^{16}$$

$$= \begin{bmatrix} 1 & 0 & 0 \\ 16 & 1 & 0 \\ 16 & 0 & 1 \end{bmatrix}\begin{bmatrix} 1 & 0 & 0 \\ 16 & 1 & 0 \\ 16 & 0 & 1 \end{bmatrix}$$

$$= \begin{bmatrix} 1 & 0 & 0 \\ 24 & 1 & 0 \\ 24 & 0 & 1 \end{bmatrix}$$

$$A^{50} = A^{48}.A^2$$

$$= \begin{bmatrix} 1 & 0 & 0 \\ 24 & 1 & 0 \\ 24 & 0 & 1 \end{bmatrix}\begin{bmatrix} 1 & 0 & 0 \\ 1 & 1 & 0 \\ 1 & 0 & 1 \end{bmatrix}$$

$$= \begin{bmatrix} 1 & 0 & 0 \\ 25 & 1 & 0 \\ 25 & 0 & 1 \end{bmatrix}$$

36. Given linear transformation

$$T = F^2 \to F^3 \text{ is defined by}$$

$$T(x_1, x_2) = (x_1, x_1 + x_2, x_2)$$

Let $(x_1, x_2) \in \ker T$

$$T(x_1, x_2) = (0, 0, 0)$$

$$(x_1, x_1 + x_2, x_2) = (0, 0, 0)$$

$$x_1 = 0, x_1 + x_2 = 0, x_2 = 0$$

$$x_1 = x_2 = 0$$

$$\ker T = \{(0, 0)\}$$

Nullity of $T = \dim \ker T = 0$

37. Start the iteration using the unit vector as the initial vector

$$V_0 = [1, 1, 1]^T$$

$$y_1 = [-8, 4, 18]^T,$$

$$V = \left[-\frac{4}{9}, \frac{2}{9}, 1\right]^T$$

$$y_2 = [10.5555, -1.1111, -7.7777]$$

$$v_2 = [1, -0.1052, -0.7368]$$

Hence approximate eigen value after two iteration by power method is 10.548

38.

$$M = \begin{bmatrix} 2 & 3+2i & -4 \\ 3-2i & 5 & 6i \\ -4 & -6i & 3 \end{bmatrix}$$

$$\overline{M} = \begin{bmatrix} 2 & 3-2i & -4 \\ 3+2i & 5 & -6i \\ -4 & 6i & 3 \end{bmatrix}$$

$$\therefore \quad M^{\ominus} = (\overline{M})^T$$

$$= \begin{bmatrix} 2 & 3+2i & -4 \\ 3-2i & 5 & 6i \\ -4 & -6i & 3 \end{bmatrix} = M$$

Hence M is a Hermitian Matrix

Now

$$iM = \begin{bmatrix} 2i & -2+3i & -4i \\ 2+3i & 5i & -6 \\ -4i & 6 & 3i \end{bmatrix}$$

$$(\overline{iM}) = \begin{bmatrix} -2i & -2-3i & 4i \\ 2-3i & -5i & -6 \\ 4i & 6 & -3i \end{bmatrix}$$

$$(iM)^{\ominus} = (\overline{iM})^T$$

$$= \begin{bmatrix} -2i & 2+3i & 4i \\ -2-3i & -5i & 6 \\ 4i & -6 & -3i \end{bmatrix}$$

$$= -\begin{bmatrix} 2i & -2-3i & -4i \\ 2+3i & 5i & -6 \\ -4i & 6 & 3i \end{bmatrix}$$

$$= -(iM)$$

Hence iM is Skew-Hermition matrix. We know that a complex Hermition Matrix has real eigen values. Hence Eigen vlaues of M are real.

39. Given linear operator $T : P_3 \to P_3$ be defined by

$$T[P(x)] = \int_1^x P'(t)dt$$

Let $B_1 = B_2 = \{1, x, x^2, x^3\}$

be ordered basis of P_3, then

$$T(1) = \int_1^x 0dt = 0$$

$$T(x) = \int_1^x 1dt = x$$

$$T(x^2) = \int_1^x 2t\,dt = x^2$$

$$T(x^3) = \int_1^x 3t^2\,dt = x^3$$

Hence $$M = \begin{bmatrix} 0 & 0 & 0 & 0 \\ 0 & 1 & 0 & 0 \\ 0 & 0 & 1 & 0 \\ 0 & 0 & 0 & 1 \end{bmatrix}$$

$$M' = \begin{bmatrix} 0 & 0 & 0 & 0 \\ 0 & 1 & 0 & 0 \\ 0 & 0 & 1 & 0 \\ 0 & 0 & 0 & 1 \end{bmatrix}$$

$$M + M' = \begin{bmatrix} 0 & 0 & 0 & 0 \\ 0 & 1 & 0 & 0 \\ 0 & 0 & 1 & 0 \\ 0 & 0 & 0 & 1 \end{bmatrix} + \begin{bmatrix} 0 & 0 & 0 & 0 \\ 0 & 1 & 0 & 0 \\ 0 & 0 & 1 & 0 \\ 0 & 0 & 0 & 1 \end{bmatrix}$$

$$= \begin{bmatrix} 0 & 0 & 0 & 0 \\ 0 & 2 & 0 & 0 \\ 0 & 0 & 2 & 0 \\ 0 & 0 & 0 & 2 \end{bmatrix}$$

No option Matches.

42. Given Matrix

$$A = \begin{bmatrix} 1 & 1 & 0 \\ 1 & 1 & 0 \\ 0 & 0 & 0 \end{bmatrix}$$

The characteristic equation of matrix A is

$$\begin{vmatrix} 1-\lambda & 1 & 0 \\ 1 & 1-\lambda & 0 \\ 0 & 0 & -\lambda \end{vmatrix} = 0$$

$$\lambda^2(2-\lambda) = 0$$
$$\lambda = 0, 2$$

Eigen value of matrix A are 0 and 2.

43. Given matrix is

$$A = \begin{bmatrix} 3 & 3 & 0 \\ 3 & 3 & 0 \\ 0 & 0 & 6 \end{bmatrix}$$

The characterstics equation of matrix A is

$$|A - xI| = 0$$

$$\begin{vmatrix} 3-x & 3 & 0 \\ 3 & 3-x & 0 \\ 0 & 0 & 6-x \end{vmatrix} = 0$$

$$x(6-x)^2 = 0$$
$$x(x-6)^2 = 0$$

Therefore minimal polynomial of A is either $x(x-6)$ or $x(x-6)^2$ but $A(A-6I) = 0$

Hence minimal polynomial is $x(x-6) = 0$

45. $u_1 = (1, 1, 0)$
$u_2 = (1, 0, 0)$
$u_3 = (1, 1, 1)$

Then By Gram Schmidt process of orthonormalization

$$v_1 = \frac{u_1}{\|u_1\|} = \frac{(1,1,0)}{\sqrt{2}} = \left(\frac{1}{\sqrt{2}}, \frac{1}{\sqrt{2}}, 0\right)$$

$$w_2 = u_2 - \langle u_2, v_1\rangle v_1$$
$$= (1,0,0) - \frac{1}{\sqrt{2}}\left(\frac{1}{\sqrt{2}}, \frac{1}{\sqrt{2}}, 0\right)$$
$$= \left[+\frac{1}{\sqrt{2}}, -\frac{1}{\sqrt{2}}, 0\right]$$

$$v_2 = \frac{w_2}{\|w_2\|} = \left(\frac{1}{\sqrt{2}}, \frac{1}{\sqrt{2}}, 0\right)$$

$$w_3 = u_3 - \langle u_3, v_1\rangle v_1 - \langle u_3, v_2\rangle v_2$$
$$= (1,1,1) - \frac{2}{\sqrt{2}}\left(\frac{1}{\sqrt{2}}, \frac{1}{\sqrt{2}}, 0\right)$$
$$-0\left(\frac{1}{\sqrt{2}}, \frac{1}{\sqrt{2}}, 0\right)$$
$$= (1, 1, 1) - (1, 1, 0) = (0, 0, 1)$$

so $\left(\frac{1}{\sqrt{2}}, \frac{1}{\sqrt{2}}, 0\right), \left(\frac{1}{\sqrt{2}}, -\frac{1}{\sqrt{2}}, 0\right), (0,0,1)$

$$= \left\{\frac{1}{\sqrt{2}}(1,1,0), \frac{1}{\sqrt{2}}(1,-1,0), (0,0,1)\right\}$$

46. Given that $T : \mathbb{C}^3 \to \mathbb{C}^3$

$$T\begin{bmatrix} z_1 \\ z_2 \\ z_3 \end{bmatrix} = \begin{bmatrix} z_1 - iz_2 \\ iz_1 + z_2 \\ z_1 + z_2 + iz_3 \end{bmatrix}$$

Let B = {(1, 0, 0), (0, 1, 0), (0, 0, 1)} be standard basic of $\mathbb{C}^3$ (C) then

$$T\begin{bmatrix} 1 \\ 0 \\ 0 \end{bmatrix} = \begin{bmatrix} 1 \\ i \\ 1 \end{bmatrix} = 1\begin{bmatrix} 1 \\ 0 \\ 0 \end{bmatrix} + i\begin{bmatrix} 0 \\ 1 \\ 0 \end{bmatrix} + 1\begin{bmatrix} 0 \\ 0 \\ 1 \end{bmatrix}$$

$$T\begin{bmatrix} 0 \\ 1 \\ 0 \end{bmatrix} = \begin{bmatrix} -i \\ 1 \\ 1 \end{bmatrix} = -i\begin{bmatrix} 1 \\ 0 \\ 0 \end{bmatrix} + 1\begin{bmatrix} 0 \\ 1 \\ 0 \end{bmatrix} + 1\begin{bmatrix} 0 \\ 0 \\ 1 \end{bmatrix}$$

$$T\begin{bmatrix} 0 \\ 0 \\ 1 \end{bmatrix} = \begin{bmatrix} 0 \\ 0 \\ i \end{bmatrix} = 0\begin{bmatrix} 1 \\ 0 \\ 0 \end{bmatrix} + 0\begin{bmatrix} 0 \\ 1 \\ 0 \end{bmatrix} + i\begin{bmatrix} 0 \\ 0 \\ 1 \end{bmatrix}$$

Hence the matrix of T corresponding to B is

$$A = \begin{bmatrix} 1 & i & 1 \\ -i & 1 & 1 \\ 0 & 0 & i \end{bmatrix}$$

Now the matrix corresponding to T* is defined as

$$A^{\ominus} = \begin{bmatrix} 1 & i & 0 \\ -i & 1 & 0 \\ 1 & 1 & -i \end{bmatrix}$$

$$T^*\begin{bmatrix} z_1 \\ z_2 \\ z_3 \end{bmatrix} = A^{-}\begin{bmatrix} z_1 \\ z_2 \\ z_3 \end{bmatrix} = \begin{bmatrix} 1 & i & 0 \\ -i & 1 & 0 \\ 1 & 1 & -i \end{bmatrix}\begin{bmatrix} z_1 \\ z_2 \\ z_3 \end{bmatrix}$$

$$= \begin{bmatrix} z_1 + iz_2 \\ -iz_1 + z_2 \\ z_1 + z_2 - iz_3 \end{bmatrix}$$

47. We have $T : R^4 \to R^4$ defined by

$T(x, y, z, w) = (x + y + 5w, x + 2y + w - z + 2w, 5x + y + 2z)$

Let B = {(1, 0, 0, 0)(, (0, 1, 0, 0), (0, 0, 1, 0), (0, 0, 0, 1)} be the standard basis of R^4.

Then

$$\begin{aligned} T(1, 0, 0, 0) &= (1, 1, 0, 5) \\ &= 1(1, 0, 0, 0) + 1(0, 1, 0, 0) + 0(0, 0, 1, 0) + 5(0, 0, 0, 1) \\ T(0, 1, 0, 0) &= (1, 2, 0, 1) \\ &= 1(1, 0, 0, 0) + 2(0, 1, 0, 0) + 0(0, 0, 1, 0) + 1(0, 0, 0, 1) \\ T(0, 0, 1, 0) &= (0, 0, -1, 2) \\ &= 0(1, 0, 0, 0) + 0(0, 1, 0, 0) - 1(0, 0, 1, 0) + 2(0, 0, 0, 1) \\ T(0, 0, 0, 1) &= (5, 1, 2, 0) \\ &= 5(1, 0, 0, 0) + 1(0, 1, 0, 0) + 2(0, 0, 1, 0) + 0(0, 0, 0, 1) \end{aligned}$$

Hence matrix of T corresponding to B is

$$\begin{bmatrix} 1 & 1 & 0 & 5 \\ 1 & 2 & 0 & 1 \\ 0 & 0 & -1 & 2 \\ 5 & 1 & 2 & 0 \end{bmatrix}$$

Which is a symmetric matrix and hence diagonalizable therefore dimension of eigen space is 4.

48. $z = [z_1\, z_2\, z_3]^T$

$b = [1\ 1\ 1]^T$

$$LZ = b$$

$$\begin{bmatrix} 1 & 0 & 0 \\ 2 & 1 & 0 \\ 1 & -2 & 1 \end{bmatrix}\begin{bmatrix} z_1 \\ z_2 \\ z_3 \end{bmatrix} = \begin{bmatrix} 1 \\ 1 \\ 1 \end{bmatrix}$$

$$\begin{aligned} z_1 &= 1 \\ 2z_1 + z_2 &= 1 \\ z_1 - 2z_2 + z_3 &= 1 \\ z_1 &= 1 \\ z_2 &= -1 \\ z_3 &= -2 \\ z &= [z_1\, z_2\, z_3]^T = [1\ -1\ -2]^T \end{aligned}$$

49. We have $x = [x_1\, x_2\, x_3]^T$

$$Ux = z$$

$$\begin{bmatrix} 1 & 1 & 1 \\ 0 & -1 & 0 \\ 0 & 0 & 1 \end{bmatrix}\begin{bmatrix} x_1 \\ x_2 \\ x_3 \end{bmatrix} = \begin{bmatrix} 1 \\ -1 \\ 2 \end{bmatrix}$$

$$\begin{aligned} x_1 + x_2 + x_3 &= 1 \\ -x_2 &= -1 \Rightarrow x_2 = 1 \\ x_3 &= -2 \\ x_1 &= 2\,;\ x_2 = 1, x_3 = -2 \\ x &= [x_1\, x_2\, x_3]^T = [2\ 1\ -2]^T \end{aligned}$$

50.

$$A = \begin{bmatrix} k & 1 & 2 \\ 1 & -1 & -2 \\ 1 & 1 & 4 \end{bmatrix}$$

and Nullity of A, $n(A) = 1$

then rank nullity theorem implies that

$$P(A) = 3 - 1 = 2$$

$$|A| = 0 \Rightarrow \begin{vmatrix} k & 1 & 2 \\ 1 & -1 & -2 \\ 1 & 1 & 4 \end{vmatrix} = 0$$

$$\begin{aligned} 2k + 6 - 4 &= 0 \\ k &= -1 \end{aligned}$$

51. Since $A = \left[a_{ij}\right]_{3\times 3}$ is real skew-symmetric matrix *i.e.* skew hermitian matrix. So its eigen values are either zero or purely imaginary. If one is 2i then other two are $-2i$, 0

52.

$$T(x,y, z) = [x + y, y + z, z + x]$$

$$[T] = \begin{bmatrix} 1 & 1 & 0 \\ 0 & 1 & 1 \\ -1 & 0 & 1 \end{bmatrix}$$

$$R_2 \to R_3 + R_1 = \begin{bmatrix} 1 & 1 & 0 \\ 0 & 1 & 1 \\ 0 & 1 & 1 \end{bmatrix}$$

$$R_3 \to R_3 - R_2 = \begin{bmatrix} 1 & 1 & 0 \\ 0 & 1 & 1 \\ 0 & 0 & 0 \end{bmatrix}$$

So Range space is {(1, 1, 0), (0, 1, 1)}

Let $u_1 = (1, 1, 0)$ and $u_2 = (0, 1, 1)$

$$v_1 = \frac{u_1}{\|u_1\|} = \left(\frac{1}{\sqrt{2}}, \frac{1}{\sqrt{2}}, 0\right)$$

$$w_2 = u_2 - \langle u_2, v_1\rangle\, v_1$$

$= (0, 1, 1) - \frac{1}{\sqrt{2}}\left(\frac{1}{\sqrt{2}}, \frac{1}{\sqrt{2}}, 0\right) = \left(-\frac{1}{2}, \frac{1}{2}, 1\right)$

$v_2 = \frac{w_2}{\|w_2\|} = \frac{\left(-\frac{1}{2}, \frac{1}{2}, 1\right)}{\sqrt{3}/\sqrt{2}}$

$v_2 = \left(-\frac{\sqrt{2}}{2\sqrt{3}}, \frac{\sqrt{2}}{2\sqrt{3}}, \frac{\sqrt{2}}{\sqrt{3}}\right) = \left[-\frac{1}{\sqrt{6}}, \frac{1}{\sqrt{6}}, \frac{2}{\sqrt{6}}\right]$

$\left\{\left(\frac{1}{\sqrt{2}}, \frac{1}{\sqrt{2}}, 0\right)\left(-\frac{1}{\sqrt{6}}, \frac{1}{\sqrt{6}}, \frac{2}{\sqrt{6}}\right)\right\}$

be the orthonormal basis. No option match

53. $T : P_3[0, 1] \to P_2[0, 1]$ defined by

$T_P(x) = P''(x) + P'(x)$

$P(x) = a + bx + cx^2 + dx^3$

$P'(x) = b + 2cx + 3dx^2$

$P''(x) = 2c + 6dx$

$T_P(x) = (b + 2c) + (2c + 6d)x + 3dx^2$

$$T\begin{bmatrix} a \\ b \\ c \\ d \end{bmatrix} = \begin{bmatrix} 0 & 1 & 2 & 0 \\ 0 & 0 & 2 & 6 \\ 0 & 0 & 0 & 3 \end{bmatrix}\begin{bmatrix} a \\ b \\ c \\ d \end{bmatrix}$$

$$T = \begin{bmatrix} 0 & 1 & 2 & 0 \\ 0 & 0 & 2 & 6 \\ 0 & 0 & 0 & 3 \end{bmatrix}$$

54. Let $\{u_1, u_2, u_3\} = \{(1, 0, 0), (1, 1, 0), (1, 1, 1)\}$ be the basis of $\mathbb{R}^3$ and $\{f_1, f_2, f_3\}$ be the dual basis of $\{u_1, u_2, u_3\}$ and f is linear functional defined by

$f(a, b, c) = a + b + c(a, b, c) \in \mathbb{R}^3$

If $f = \alpha_1 f_1 + \alpha_2 f_2 + \alpha_3 f_3$

then $(\alpha_1, \alpha_2, \alpha_3)$ is (1, 2, 3)

since dual basis of (u_1, u_2, u_3) is

$f_1(u_1) = 1 \quad f_1(u_2) = 0 \quad f_1(u_3) = 0$

$f_2(u_1) = 0 \quad f_2(u_2) = 1 \quad f_2(u_3) = 0$

$f_3(u_1) = 0 \quad f_3(u_2) = 0 \quad f_3(u_3) = 1$

$(a, b, c) = x4_1 + y4_2 + z4_3 \quad \dots (1)$

$f_1(a, b, c) = x$

$f_2(a, b, c) = y$

$f_3(a, b, c) = z$

from equation (1) $\Rightarrow a = x + y + z$

$b = y + z$

$c = z$

$x = a - b, y = b - c, z = c$

so dual basis is $(a - b, b - c, c)$

Now $f = \alpha_1 f_1 + \alpha_2 f_2 + \alpha_3 f_3$

$f(a, b, c) = \alpha_1 f_1(a, b, c) + \alpha_2 f_2(a, b, c) + \alpha_3 f_3(a, b, c)$

$\Rightarrow \quad a + b + c = \alpha_1(a - b) + \alpha_2(b - c) + \alpha_2 c$

$a(\alpha_1 - 1) + b(\alpha_2 - \alpha_1 - 1) + c(\alpha_3 - \alpha_2 - 1) = 0$

$\alpha_1 = 1, \alpha_2 = 2\ \alpha_3 = 3$

57. $V = \{A = (a_{ij})_{n\times n} : a_{ij} \in \not\subset a_{ij} = -a_{ji}\}$

i.e., v is collection of all skew-symmetric matrix.

Hence $\dim(v) = \frac{n^2 - n}{2}$

No option matches.

58. Minimal polynomial of $A = \begin{bmatrix} 0 & 0 & 3 \\ 1 & 0 & 2 \\ 0 & 1 & 1 \end{bmatrix}$

is $x^3 - x^2 - 2x - 3 = 0$

which is same as characteristic polynomial, since its eigen values are distinct.

59. $A = \begin{bmatrix} 1 & 0 & 0 \\ i & \frac{-1 + i\sqrt{3}}{2} & 0 \\ 0 & 1 + 2i & \frac{-1 - i\sqrt{3}}{2} \end{bmatrix}$

$\lambda = 1, \frac{-1 + i\sqrt{3}}{2}, \frac{-1 - i\sqrt{3}}{2},$

i.e., $\lambda = 1, \omega, \omega^2$ are eigen values of A.

Then trace (A^{102}) is

$= 1^{102} + (\omega)^{102} + (\omega^2)^{102}$

$= 1 + (\omega^3)^{34} + (\omega^3)^{68}$

$= 1 + 1 + 1 = 3$

60. $A = \begin{bmatrix} 1 & 1 \\ 0 & 1 \end{bmatrix}$

is not diagonalizable since for $\lambda = 1$

AM (Algebraic multiplicity) = 2

GM (Geometric multiplicity) = 1

so AM $\neq$ GM

61. $V = \{(1, 1, 1), (-1, 2, -1)\}$

Let $W_1 = (1, 1, 1),$

$W_2 = (-1, 2, -1)$

$V = \begin{bmatrix} 0 \\ 1 \\ 0 \end{bmatrix} \in V$ (Given)

then orthogonal projection of

$V = \begin{bmatrix} 0 \\ 1 \\ 0 \end{bmatrix}$ on V is

$= \frac{< v, w_1 >}{< w_1, w_1 >} w_1 + \frac{< v_1, w_2 >}{< w_2, w_2 >} w_2$

$$= \frac{1}{3}(1,1,1) + \frac{2}{6}(-1,2,-1)$$

$$= \left(\frac{1}{3},\frac{1}{3},\frac{1}{3}\right) + \left(\frac{-1}{3},\frac{2}{3},\frac{-1}{3}\right) = (0, 1, 0)$$

62. $T(x_1, x_2, x_3) = (x_1 + 3x_2 + 2x_3, 3x_1 + 4x_2 + x_3, 2x_1 + x_2 - x_3)$

$$T = \begin{bmatrix} 1 & 3 & 2 \\ 3 & 4 & 1 \\ 2 & 1 & -1 \end{bmatrix}$$

$$[T^2] = \begin{bmatrix} 14 & 17 & 3 \\ 17 & 26 & 9 \\ 3 & 9 & 6 \end{bmatrix}$$

$r(T^2) = 2$

63. $$[T^3] = \begin{bmatrix} 71 & 113 & 42 \\ 113 & 164 & 51 \\ 42 & 51 & 9 \end{bmatrix}$$

$n[T^3] = 1$

64. $W = \{[a_{ij}] : a_{ij} = 0 \text{ if i is even}\}$ is the set of all 10×10 matrices then $\dim(W) = 50$

65. $T(e_1) = e_2$
$T(e_2) = e_3$
$T(e_3) = 0$
$T(e_4) = e_3$
where $\{e_1, e_2, e_3, e_4\}$ is standard basis of $\mathbb{R}^4$

Let $(a, b, c, d) = x(1, 0, 0, 0) + y(0, 1, 0, 0) + z(0, 0, 1, 0) + w(0, 0, 0, 1)$ ... (1)

$T(a, b, c, d) = xT(1, 0, 0, 0) + yT(0, 1, 0, 0) + zT(0, 0, 1, 0) + wT(0, 0, 0, 1)$
$= x(0, 1, 0, 0) + y(0, 0, 1, 0) + z(0, 0, 0, 0) + w(0, 0, 1, 0)$

$T(a, b, c, d) = (0, x, y + w, 0)$ ... (2)

Now equation (2), we get $T(a, b, c, d) = (0, a, b + d, 0)$

So $$T\begin{bmatrix} a \\ b \\ c \\ d \end{bmatrix} = \begin{bmatrix} 0 & 0 & 0 & 0 \\ 1 & 0 & 0 & 0 \\ 0 & 1 & 0 & 1 \\ 0 & 0 & 0 & 0 \end{bmatrix}\begin{bmatrix} a \\ b \\ c \\ d \end{bmatrix}$$

$r(T) = 2$ and $T^3 = 0$ *i.e.*, nippotent

66. $$M = \begin{bmatrix} 1 & 1 & 2 \\ 0 & 1 & 1 \\ 0 & 1 & 1 \end{bmatrix}$$

and $V = \{Mx : x \in R^3\}$

i.e. $$V = \left\{\begin{bmatrix} 1 & 1 & 2 \\ 0 & 1 & 1 \\ 0 & 1 & 1 \end{bmatrix}\begin{bmatrix} x_1 \\ x_2 \\ x_3 \end{bmatrix} : (x_1, x_2, x_3) \in \mathbb{R}^3\right\}$$

$= \{(x_1 + x_2 + 2x_3 + x_2 + x_3, x_2 + x_3); (x_1, x_2, x_3) \in R^3\}$

i.e., $\{(1, 0, 0), (1, 1, 1), (2, 1, 1)\}$ generates V

$\Rightarrow \{(1, 0, 0), (1, 1, 1)\}$ is basis of V

$\quad\quad || \quad\quad\quad ||$

$\quad\quad u_1 \quad\quad u_2$

Then by Gram-schmidt process of orthonormalization

$$V_1 = \frac{u_1}{||u_1||} = \frac{(1,0,0)}{\sqrt{1^2+0+0}} = (1, 0, 0)$$

$w_2 = u_2 - \langle u_2, v_1 \rangle v_1$
$= (1, 1, 1) - (1, 0, 0) = (0, 1, 1)$

$$V_2 = \frac{w_2}{||w_2||} = \left(0, \frac{1}{\sqrt{2}}, \frac{1}{\sqrt{2}}\right)$$

so $\{V_1, V_2\}$ is orthonormal basis.

67. For any $n \in N$. Let P_n denotes the vector space all polynomials with real coefficients and of degree atmost n.

Let $T : P_n \to P_n + 1$

by $T(p)(x) = P^1(x) - \int_0^x P(t)dt$

Let $P(x) = a_0 + a_1x + a_2x^2 \ldots + a_nx^n$

$T(P)(x) = a_1 + 2a_2x + 3a_3x^2 + \ldots + na_nx^{n-1}$
$$-\left(a_0x + a_1\frac{x^2}{2} + a_2\frac{x^3}{3} + \ldots + \frac{a_nx^{n+1}}{n+1}\right)$$

$$= a_1 + (2a_2 - a_0)x + \left(3a_3 - \frac{a_1}{2}\right)x^2$$

$$+\left(4a_4 - \frac{a_2}{3}\right)x^3 + \ldots + \left(na_n - \frac{a_{n-2}}{n-1}\right)x^{n-1}$$

$$+\frac{a_{n-1}}{n}x^n + \frac{a_n}{n+1}x^{n+1}$$

Transformation matrix of T is

$$[T] = \begin{bmatrix} 0 & 1 & 0 & 0 & \ldots & 0 \\ -1 & 0 & 2 & 0 & \ldots & 0 \\ 0 & -\frac{1}{2} & 0 & 3 & \ldots & 0 \\ 0 & 0 & -\frac{1}{3} & 0 & \ldots & 0 \\ \ldots & \ldots & \ldots & \ldots & \ldots & \ldots \\ 0 & 0 & 0 & 0 & \ldots & \frac{1}{n+1} \end{bmatrix}$$

Rank (T) $= n$

so by Sylvester law

$$r(t) + n(\mathrm{T}) = \dim(\mathrm{T})$$
$$n + n\,(\mathrm{T}) = n$$
$$n(\mathrm{T}) = 0 = \text{nullity of T}$$

68. Given that $M = \begin{bmatrix} 1 & 0 & 0 \\ 0 & \cos\theta & -\sin\theta \\ 0 & \sin\theta & \cos\theta \end{bmatrix}$

$$0 < \theta < \frac{\pi}{2}$$

and $\quad V = \{4 \in \mathbb{R}^3 : M_4 = u\}$

$$= \left\{ u \in \mathbb{R} : \begin{bmatrix} 1 & 0 & 0 \\ 0 & \cos\theta & -\sin\theta \\ 0 & \sin\theta & \cos\theta \end{bmatrix} \begin{bmatrix} u_1 \\ u_2 \\ u_3 \end{bmatrix} = \begin{bmatrix} u_1 \\ u_2 \\ u_3 \end{bmatrix} \right.$$

$$= \left\{ u \in \mathbb{R} : \begin{bmatrix} 0 & 0 & 0 \\ 0 & \cos\theta - 1 & -\sin\theta \\ 0 & \sin\theta & \cos\theta - 1 \end{bmatrix} \begin{bmatrix} u_1 \\ u_2 \\ u_3 \end{bmatrix} = \begin{bmatrix} 0 \\ 0 \\ 0 \end{bmatrix} \right.$$

i.e. $\lambda = 1$ is an eigen value of M. Then the collection of eigen vectors with respect to $\lambda = 1$ generates the vector space V *i.e.,* they form the basis of V.

So number of eigen vectors corresponding to $\lambda = 1$ is equal to dimension of vector space V.

So for $\quad \lambda = 1$

$$\begin{bmatrix} 0 & 0 & 0 \\ 0 & \cos\theta - 1 & -\sin\theta \\ 0 & \sin\theta & \cos\theta - 1 \end{bmatrix} \begin{bmatrix} u_1 \\ u_2 \\ u_3 \end{bmatrix} = \begin{bmatrix} 0 \\ 0 \\ 0 \end{bmatrix}$$

$(\cos\theta - 1)\, u_2 - \sin\theta\, u_3 = 0$

$\sin\theta\, u_2 + (\cos\theta - 1)\, u_3 = 0$

$$u_2 = \frac{-u_3}{\sqrt{3}}$$

$\left[\text{as } \cos\theta = \frac{1}{2} \because 0 < \theta < \frac{\pi}{2}\right]$

$\{(u_1, u_2, -u_2\sqrt{3}) : u_1, u_2 \in \mathrm{R}\} = V$

$\dim V = 2$

69. Given that $A = \begin{bmatrix} 2 & 2 & 0 & 0 \\ 2 & 1 & 0 & 0 \\ 0 & 0 & 3 & 0 \\ 0 & 0 & 1 & 4 \end{bmatrix}$

then the linearly independent eigen vectors are 4 as its characterstic equation is

$$c(\lambda) = (3 - \lambda)(4 - \lambda)(\lambda^2 - 3\lambda - 2)$$

i.e., all eigen value are distinct.

So $\exists$ unique eigen vector corresponding to every eigen value. Since, the eigen vector corresponding to distinct eigen values are lineraly independent.

73. Given matrix is

$$A = \begin{bmatrix} 1 & 1 & 0 \\ 1 & 1 & 0 \\ 0 & 0 & 0 \end{bmatrix}$$

The characteristics equation of matrix A is

$$\begin{bmatrix} 1-\lambda & 1 & 0 \\ 1 & 1-\lambda & 0 \\ 0 & 0 & -\lambda \end{bmatrix} = 0$$

$$(1-\lambda)\begin{vmatrix} 1-\lambda & 0 \\ 0 & -\lambda \end{vmatrix} - 1\begin{vmatrix} 1 & 0 \\ 0 & -\lambda \end{vmatrix} + 0\begin{vmatrix} 1 & 1-\lambda \\ 0 & 0 \end{vmatrix} = 0$$

$$= 0$$

$$\Rightarrow (1-\lambda)^2(-\lambda) + \lambda = 0$$
$$\lambda[1 - 1 - \lambda^2 + 2\lambda] = 0$$
$$\lambda\{\lambda(2-\lambda)\} = 0$$
$$\lambda^2(2-\lambda) = 0$$
$$\lambda = 0, 2$$

Hence eigen values of matrix A are 0 and 2.

74. We have

$$V = \{(x, y, z, w) \in \mathrm{R}^4 : x + y - z = 0,$$
$$y + z + w = 0,\ 2x + y - 3z - w = 0\}$$

then basis of v is

$x + y - z = 0$

$y + z + w = 0$

$2x + y - 3z - w = 0$

$$\begin{bmatrix} 1 & 1 & -1 & 0 \\ 0 & 1 & 1 & 1 \\ 2 & 1 & -3 & -1 \end{bmatrix} \begin{bmatrix} x \\ y \\ z \\ w \end{bmatrix} = \begin{bmatrix} 0 \\ 0 \\ 0 \end{bmatrix} [R_3 \to R_3 - 2R_1]$$

$$\begin{bmatrix} 1 & 1 & -1 & 0 \\ 0 & 1 & 1 & 1 \\ 0 & -1 & -1 & -1 \end{bmatrix} \begin{bmatrix} x \\ y \\ z \\ w \end{bmatrix} = \begin{bmatrix} 0 \\ 0 \\ 0 \end{bmatrix} [R_3 \to R_3 + R_1]$$

$$\begin{bmatrix} 1 & 1 & -1 & 0 \\ 0 & 1 & 1 & 1 \\ 0 & 0 & 0 & 0 \end{bmatrix} \begin{bmatrix} x \\ y \\ z \\ w \end{bmatrix} = \begin{bmatrix} 0 \\ 0 \\ 0 \end{bmatrix}$$

$$\Rightarrow \quad x + y - z = 0$$
$$y + z + w = 0$$
$$x - z - z - w = 0$$
$$x = 2z + w \text{ and}$$
$$y = -z - w$$

$V = \{(\in 2z + w_1 - z - w, z, w) : z_1\, w, \in \mathrm{R}\}$

i.e. $\dim(v) = 2$

so (1, –1, 0, 1)(1, 0, 1, –1) be the basic of V both taking $z = 0$ $w = 1$ $z = 1$ $w = -1$, respectively.

77. Let $T : R^3 \to R^3$ be a linear transformation defined by

$T(x, y, z) = (x + y - z, x + y + z, y - z)$

Then, the matrix of the linear trans-formation T with respect to the ordered basis

$B = \{(0, 1, 0), (0, 0, 1),(1, 0, 0)\}$ of R^3 is '0'

$$T(0, 1, 0) = (1, 1, 1)$$
$$= 1(0, 1, 0) + 1(0, 0, 1) + 1 (1, 0, 0)$$
$$T(0, 0, 1) = (-1, 1, -1)$$
$$= 1(0, 1, 0) -1(0, 0, 1) -1(1, 0, 0)$$
$$T(1, 0, 0) = (1, 1, 0)$$
$$= 1(0, 1, 0) + 0(0, 0, 1) + 1(1, 0, 0)$$

$$(T)_B = \begin{bmatrix} 1 & 1 & 1 \\ 1 & -1 & 0 \\ 1 & -1 & 1 \end{bmatrix}$$

78. The eigen values and eigen functions of the internal equation

$$y(x) = \lambda\int_0^{2\pi} y(t)\sin(x+t)dt, x \in (0,2\pi) are$$

$$\lambda_1 = \frac{1}{\pi}, \lambda_2 = -\frac{1}{\pi}$$

and corresponding eigen functions $y_1(x) = \sin x + \cos x$, $y_2(x) = \sin x - \cos x$

The normalized eigen function corres-ponding to the eigen function $y_1(x)$ is

$$\phi 1(x) = \frac{y_1(x)}{\left[\int_0^{2\pi} (y_1(x))^2 dx\right]^{\frac{1}{2}}}$$

$$\left(\because \int_0^{2\pi} \sin x dx = 0 \text{ and } \int_0^{2\pi} \cos x dx = 0\right)$$

Since $\lambda = \frac{1}{\pi} = \lambda_1$ and $f_1 = 0$, therefore inifinitely many solution exists.

81. Let $w = \{x_1, x_2, x_3, x_4, x_5\} : 3x_1 - x_2 + x_3 = 0\}$ be the subspace of R^5

Now by putting $x_1 = c_1$

and $x_2 = c_2$

(any two of three) arbitery we determine

$$x_3 = C_2 - 3C_1$$
$$\dim (w) = 4$$

Alternative method

$\dim w$ = number of variable – No. of Restriction

$= 5 - 1 = 4$

82. Let the linear transformations S and $T : R^3 \to R^3$ be defined by

$$S(x, y, z) = (2x, 4x - y, 2x + 3y - z)$$

and $T(x, y, z) = (x \cos\theta - y \sin\theta, x \sin\theta + y \cos\theta, z)$

where $0 < \theta < \frac{\pi}{2}$

Then both transformations S & T are non-regular *i.e.* invertible, since their matrices are

$$\begin{pmatrix} 2 & 0 & 0 \\ 4 & -1 & 0 \\ 2 & 3 & -1 \end{pmatrix} \text{ and } \begin{pmatrix} \cos\theta & -\sin\theta & 0 \\ \sin\theta & \cos\theta & 0 \\ 0 & 0 & 1 \end{pmatrix}$$

respectively with non-zero determinant so both S and T are invertible *i.e.* one to one.

Alternative Method

We have the linear transformations S and T: $R^3 \to R^3$ defined by

$$S(x, y, z) = (2x, 4x - y, 2x + 3y - z)$$

and $T(x, y, z) = (x \cos\theta - y \sin\theta; x \sin\theta + y \cos\theta, z)$

Let $(x, y, z) \in \ker S$

$\Rightarrow S(x, y, z) = (0, 0, 0)$

$\Rightarrow (2x, 4x - y, 2x + 3\underline{y} - z) = 0$

$\Rightarrow x = 0 \; y = 0 \; z = 0$

$\ker S = \{(0, 0, 0)\}$

$\Rightarrow$ S is one-one

Next, let $(x, y, z) \in \ker T$

$T(x, y, z) = (0, 0, 0)$

$\Rightarrow (x \cos\theta - y \sin\theta, x \sin\theta + y \cos\theta, z) = (0, 0, 0)$

$\Rightarrow x \cos\theta - y \sin\theta = 0$ ...(*i*)

$x \sin\theta + y \cos\theta = 0$ ...(*ii*)

$z = 0$ ...(*iii*)

Now multipling eqn.(i) by $\cos\theta$ and eqn. (*ii*) by $\sin\theta$ and adding, we get

$y \cos^2\theta + y \sin^2\theta = 0$

$\Rightarrow y(\cos^2\theta + \sin^2\theta) = 0$

$y.1 = 0$

$y = 0$

hence $\ker T = \{(0, 0, 0)\}$

$\Rightarrow$ T is one to one

83. $w = L[(t^2 + t + 2),(t^2 + 2t + 5), (5t^2 + 3t + 4) (2t^2 + 2t + 4)]$

dim w = no. of linearly independent vectors spamed w.

Let $a_1(t^2 + t + 2) + a_2(t^2 + 2t + 5)$

$+ a_3(5t^2 + 3t + 4) + a_4(2t^2 + 2t + 4)$

$= 0t^2 + 0t + 0$

$\Rightarrow \quad a_1 + a_2 + 5a_3 + 2a_4 = 0$

$a_1 + 2a_2 + 3a_3 + 2a_4 = 0$

$2a_1 + 5a_2 + 4a_3 + 4a_4 = 0$

$$= \begin{bmatrix} 1 & 1 & 5 & 2 \\ 1 & 2 & 3 & 2 \\ 2 & 5 & 4 & 4 \end{bmatrix} \begin{bmatrix} a_1 \\ a_2 \\ a_3 \\ a_4 \end{bmatrix} = \begin{bmatrix} 0 \\ 0 \\ 0 \end{bmatrix}$$

$$= \begin{bmatrix} 1 & 1 & 5 & 2 \\ 0 & 1 & -2 & 0 \\ 0 & 3 & -6 & 0 \end{bmatrix} \begin{bmatrix} a_1 \\ a_2 \\ a_3 \\ a_4 \end{bmatrix} = \begin{bmatrix} 0 \\ 0 \\ 0 \end{bmatrix}$$

$$\Rightarrow \begin{bmatrix} 1 & 1 & 5 & 2 \\ 0 & 1 & -2 & 0 \\ 0 & 0 & 0 & 0 \end{bmatrix} \begin{bmatrix} a_1 \\ a_2 \\ a_3 \\ a_4 \end{bmatrix} = \begin{bmatrix} 0 \\ 0 \\ 0 \end{bmatrix}$$

as $r(A) < 3$ so $a_1, a_2, a_3, a_4 \neq 0$

since only one vector is sufficient to span w_1 so dim $w = 1$

86. $[V_1, V_2, .,. V_{16}]$ be an ordered baris of $V = e^{16}$. if T is a linear transformation on V such that

$$T(V_i) = V_{i+2}, \quad \forall\ 1 \le i \le 15$$

and $\quad T(V_{16}) = V_1 + V_2 + ..+ V_{16}$

so the matrix

$$(T)_B = \begin{bmatrix} 0 & 1 & 0 & 0 & \dots & 0 \\ 0 & 0 & 1 & 0 & \dots & 0 \\ 0 & 0 & 0 & 1 & \dots & 0 \\ \hline 1 & 1 & 1 & 1 & 1 & 1 \end{bmatrix}$$

Then, T is regular (invertible) and it has rational eigen values.

87. Its eigen values are –1, i, –i

88. It is similar to unitary matrix,

Since, eigen values are of unit modulus.

89. $a_1 (1, x, 0) + a_2 (0, x^2, 1) + a_3 (0, 1, x) = 0$

This is for linearly independence

On comparing, we get

$a_1 = 0 \quad ...(i)$

$a_1x + a_2x^2 + a_3 = 0$

$\Rightarrow \quad a_2x^2 + a_3 = 0 \quad ...(ii)$

$a_2 + a_3x = 0 \quad ...(iii)$

From equations (*i*), (*ii*), (*iii*),

$a_1 = a_2 = a_3 = 0$ for linear independent

This is true only for $x = 0$

90. Let $\quad f = a_1 x + a_2 |y| + a_3 z$

Here f are two functions one for y and other for $-y$

$f' = a_1 x + a_2 y + a_3 z$

and $\quad f'' = a_1 x - a_2 y + a_3 z$

Now $\quad g = a_1(x + 1) + a_2(y - 1) + a_3 z$

$= a_1 x + a_2 y + a_3 z + (a_1 - a_2)$

$= f' + (a_1 - a_2)$

i.e., g is linear but not f.

91.
$$M^T = \begin{bmatrix} 1 & 3 & 3 \\ 0 & 4 & 5 \\ 0 & 0 & 9 \end{bmatrix}$$

$$\text{Then, } MM^T = \begin{bmatrix} 1 & 0 & 0 \\ 3 & 4 & 0 \\ 3 & 5 & 9 \end{bmatrix}$$

$\Rightarrow \quad M^2M^{T2} \neq I$

$$\text{Now} \quad M^2 = \begin{bmatrix} 1 & 3 & 3 \\ 0 & 4 & 5 \\ 0 & 0 & 9 \end{bmatrix} \begin{bmatrix} 1 & 3 & 3 \\ 0 & 4 & 5 \\ 0 & 0 & 9 \end{bmatrix}$$

$$= \begin{bmatrix} 1 & 15 & 45 \\ 0 & 16 & 45 \\ 0 & 0 & 81 \end{bmatrix}$$

$M^2 M'^2 \neq I$

Hence neither M nor M^2 is diagonalizable.

92. Let
$$M = \begin{bmatrix} a_1 & a_2 & a_3 \\ b_1 & b_2 & b_3 \\ c_1 & c_2 & c_3 \end{bmatrix}$$

But M is skew symmetric matrix

i.e. $\quad M^T = -M$

$$\Rightarrow \begin{bmatrix} a_1 & a_2 & a_3 \\ b_1 & b_2 & b_3 \\ c_1 & c_2 & c_3 \end{bmatrix} = \begin{bmatrix} -a_1 & -a_2 & -a_3 \\ -b_1 & -b_2 & -b_3 \\ -c_1 & -c_2 & -c_3 \end{bmatrix}$$

On comparing, we get

$a_1 = -a_1$

$\Rightarrow \quad a_1 = 0$

$a_2 = -b_1$ and so on

$$\text{Then} \quad M = \begin{bmatrix} 0 & -b_1 & -c_1 \\ -a_2 & 0 & -c_2 \\ -a_3 & -b_3 & 0 \end{bmatrix}$$

But M is also orthogonal real matrix.

i.e. $M M^T = I$

$$\Rightarrow \begin{bmatrix} b_1^2+c_1^2 & c_1c_2 & b_1b_3 \\ c_1c_2 & a_2^2+c_2^2 & a_2a_3 \\ b_1b_3 & a_2a_3 & a_3^2+b_3^2 \end{bmatrix} = \begin{bmatrix} 1 & 0 & 0 \\ 0 & 1 & 0 \\ 0 & 0 & 1 \end{bmatrix}$$

On comparing, we get

$$M = \begin{bmatrix} b_1^2+c_1^2 & 0 & 0 \\ 0 & a_2^2+c_2^2 & a_2a_3 \\ b_1b_3 & a_1a_3 & a_3^2+b_3^2 \end{bmatrix}$$

For eigen values, $|M - \lambda I| = 0$

Hence, $\lambda = -1, 1$

93. Let $\alpha = (a_1, b_1, c_1)$, $\beta = (a_2, b_2, c_2)$

Then$S(\alpha) = S(\beta)$

$\Rightarrow (a_1, a_1 + b_1, a_1 - b_1 - c_1)$

$= (a_2, a_2 + b_2, a_2 - b_2 - c_2)$

$\Rightarrow a_1 = a_2, a_1 + b_1 = a_2 + b_2, a_1 - b_1 - c_1$

$= a_2 - b_2 - c_2$

$\Rightarrow a_1 = a_2, b_1 = b_2, c_1 = c_2$

Hence, S is one-one.

Therefore S must be onto also and thus S is invertible.

Similarly, $T(\alpha) = T(\beta)$

$\Rightarrow (a_1 + 2c_1, b_1 - c_1, a_1 + b_1 + c_1)$

$= (a_2 + 2c_2, b_2 - c_2, a_2 + b_2 + c_2)$

$\Rightarrow a_1 \neq a_2, b_1 \neq b_2, c_1 \neq c_2$

$\therefore$ T is not one-one.

Hence, T is not onto and thus T is not invertible.

94. $\dim V = \dim X$

where V, W and X be three finite dimensional vector spaces.

$S : V \to W$

$T : W \to X$

Such that $T \circ S : V \to X$ is one-one

Hence, S and T both are injective.

95. A square matrix of order 10 has exactly 4 distinct eigenvalues, then the degree of its minimal polynomials must be at least 4.

96. $$|M - \lambda I| = \begin{vmatrix} -\lambda & 1 & 2 & 0 \\ 1 & -\lambda & 1 & 0 \\ 2 & 1 & -\lambda & 2 \\ 0 & 0 & 2 & -\lambda \end{vmatrix}$$

on expanding

$$= -\lambda \begin{vmatrix} -\lambda & 1 & 0 \\ 1 & -\lambda & 2 \\ 0 & 2 & -\lambda \end{vmatrix} - 1 \begin{vmatrix} 1 & 1 & 0 \\ 2 & -\lambda & 2 \\ 0 & 2 & -\lambda \end{vmatrix} + 2 \begin{vmatrix} 1 & -\lambda & 0 \\ 2 & 1 & 2 \\ 0 & 0 & -\lambda \end{vmatrix}$$

$= -\lambda^4 - 9\lambda^2 - 2\lambda + 4$

$\Rightarrow |M - \lambda I| = 0$

$\Rightarrow \lambda^4 + 9\lambda^2 + 2\lambda - 4 = 0$

$\Rightarrow$ M has no real eigenvalues.

98. $T(x_0, x_1, x_2) = (x_0, x_0 + x_1, x_0 + x_1 + x_2)$

Let basis are $(1, 0, 0)$, $(0, x, 0)$, and $(0, 0, x^2)$

Then $T(1, 0, 0) = (1, 1, 1)$

$T(0, x, 0) = (0, x, x)$

$T(0, 0, x^2) = (0, 0, x^2)$

$$\Rightarrow T = \begin{bmatrix} 1 & 1 & 1 \\ 0 & x & x \\ 0 & 0 & x^2 \end{bmatrix}$$

$|T| = 1(x^3) = x^3$

At $x = 1$, $T = \begin{bmatrix} 1 & 1 & 1 \\ 0 & 1 & 1 \\ 0 & 0 & 1 \end{bmatrix}$ and $|T| = 1$

Cofactors of T

$T_{11} = 1$ $T_{12} = 0$ $T_{13} = 0$

$T_{21} = -1$ $T_{22} = 1$ $T_{23} = 0$

$T_{31} = 0$ $T_{32} = -1$ $T_{33} = 1$

$\therefore$ adj. T = Transpose of co-factors matrix

$$= \begin{bmatrix} 1 & -1 & 0 \\ 0 & 1 & -1 \\ 0 & 0 & 1 \end{bmatrix}$$

Hence $$T^{-1} = \frac{1}{|T|} \text{adj. } T = \begin{bmatrix} 1 & -1 & 0 \\ 0 & 1 & -1 \\ 0 & 0 & 1 \end{bmatrix}$$

99. $$|T^{-1} - \lambda I| = \begin{bmatrix} 1-\lambda & -1 & 0 \\ 0 & 1-\lambda & -1 \\ 0 & 0 & 1-\lambda \end{bmatrix}$$

$= (1 - \lambda)^3$

Hence, dimension of eigenspace of T^{-1} is 3.

100. Let S and T be two subspaces of R^{24} such that $\dim(S) = 19$, $\dim(T) = 17$

Then, the smallest possible value of $\dim(S \cap T)$ is 12.

i.e. $\dim(S \cap T) = \dim(S) + \dim(T) - \dim(S \cup T)$

$= 19 + 17 - 24$

$= 12$

and the smallest possible value of $\dim(S + T)$

$\dim(S + T) = \dim(S) + \dim(T) - \dim(S \cap T)$

$= 19 + 17 - 17$

$= 19$

101. We have $V_1 = (1, 2, 0, 3, 0)$
$V_2 = (1, 2, -1, -1, 0)$
$V_3 = (0, 0, 1, 4, 0)$
$V_4 = (2, 4, 1, 10, 1)$
$V_5 = (0, 0, 0, 0, 1)$

The dimension of the linear span of $(V_1, V_2, V_3, V_4, V_5)$ is $L[V_1, V_2, V_3, V_4, V_5]$

$= [a1, 2, 0, 3, 0] + b\,[1, 2, -1, -1, 0] + c\,[0, 0, 1, 1, 4, 0] + d\,[2, 4, 1, 10, 1] + e\,[0, 0, 0, 0, 1]$

$= [a + b + 2d,\ 2a + 2b + d,\ - b + c + d,\ 3a - b + 4c + 10d + d + e, \forall\, a, b, c, d, e \in R]$

$$= \left\{\begin{bmatrix} 1 & 1 & 0 & 2 & 0 \\ 2 & 2 & 0 & 4 & 0 \\ 0 & -1 & 1 & 1 & 0 \\ 3 & -1 & 4 & 10 & 0 \\ 0 & 0 & 0 & 1 & 1 \end{bmatrix}\begin{bmatrix} a \\ b \\ c \\ d \\ e \end{bmatrix} \forall a,b,c,d,e \in R\right\}$$

(by $R_2 \to R_2 - 2R_1$)
(by $R_4 \to R_4 - 3R_1$)

$$\left\{\begin{bmatrix} 1 & 1 & 0 & 2 & 0 \\ 0 & 0 & 0 & 0 & 0 \\ 0 & -1 & 1 & 1 & 0 \\ 0 & -4 & 4 & 4 & 0 \\ 0 & 0 & 0 & 1 & 1 \end{bmatrix}\begin{bmatrix} a \\ b \\ c \\ d \\ e \end{bmatrix}, \forall\, a,b,c,d,e \in R\right\}$$

(by $R_4 \to R_4 - R_3$)

$$\left\{\begin{bmatrix} 1 & 1 & 0 & 2 & 0 \\ 0 & 0 & 0 & 0 & 0 \\ 0 & -1 & 1 & 1 & 0 \\ 0 & 0 & 0 & 0 & 0 \\ 0 & 0 & 0 & 1 & 1 \end{bmatrix}\begin{bmatrix} a \\ b \\ c \\ d \\ e \end{bmatrix}, \forall\, a,b,c,d,e \in R\right\}$$

dim $[L(V_1, V_2, V_3 .. V_5)$ is rank of coefficient matrix i.e., 3]

102. $V = \{(x, y) \in R^2 : xy \geq 0\}$

is not a vector subspace of R^2, since it is not closed under vector addition. Because let $(-1, -4)(2, 3) \in V$ but $(-1, -4) + (2, 3)$

$= (1, -1) \notin V$

or $1.(-1) \ngeq 0$

103. $f : R^4 \to R$ be a linear functional defined by $f(x_1, x_2, x_3, x_4) = -x_2$

Then $V \in R^4$ such that

$f(W) = \langle V, W \rangle$, $v - W \in R^4 = -x_2$

where $W = (x_1, x_2, x_3, x_4)$

$V = (0, -1, 0, 0)$

104. $u_1 = u = (1, 1, 1)$,
$V = (1, 1, -1) = u_2$

$$V_1 = \frac{u_1}{\|u_1\|} = \frac{(1,1,1)}{\sqrt{3}}$$

$w_2 = u_2 - \langle u_2, V_1 \rangle V_1$

$$= u_2 - \frac{1}{\sqrt{3}}\frac{(1,1,1)}{\sqrt{3}} = (1, 1, -1)$$

$= (1/3, 1/3, 1/3) = (2/3, 2/3, -4/3)$

$$V_2 = \frac{w_2}{\|w_2\|} = \frac{(2/3, 2/3, -4/3)}{\sqrt{4/9 + 4/9 + 16/9}}$$

$$= \frac{(2, 2, -4)}{\sqrt{24}} = \frac{(1, 1, -2)}{\sqrt{6}}$$

so, $[v_1\ v_2]$

i.e., $\left(\frac{1}{\sqrt{3}}, \frac{1}{\sqrt{3}}, \frac{1}{\sqrt{3}}\right)\left(\frac{1}{\sqrt{6}}, \frac{1}{\sqrt{6}}, \frac{-2}{\sqrt{6}}\right)$

be the orthonormal basis.

105. In R^2, $(x_1, y_1), (x_2, y_2)$

$= x_1, x_2 - \alpha(x_2y_1 + x_1y_2) + y_1y_2$ is an inner product, if

(*i*) $(au_1 + bu_2, v)$

$= a\langle u, v\rangle + b\,\langle u_2, v\rangle + (1 - a_3)\, v_3 - a_4v_4) + d\,(-a_1v_1 - a_2v_2 - a_3v_3) + (1 - a_4)\, v_4 = 0$

$\Rightarrow a(1 - a_1) - ba_1 - ca_1 - da_1 = 0$

$-aa_2 + (1 - a_2)b - ca_2 - da_2 = 0$

$-aa_3 - a_3b + (1 - a_3)\,c - a_3d = 0$

$-aa_4 - a_4b - a_4c + (1 - a_4)d = 0$

$$\Rightarrow \begin{bmatrix} 1-a_1 & -a_1 & -a_1 & -a_1 \\ -a_2 & 1-a_2 & -a_2 & -a_2 \\ -a_3 & -a_3 & 1-a_3 & -a_3 \\ -a_4 & -a_4 & -a_4 & 1-a_4 \end{bmatrix}\begin{bmatrix} a \\ b \\ c \\ d \end{bmatrix} = \begin{bmatrix} 0 \\ 0 \\ 0 \\ 0 \end{bmatrix}$$

$$\Rightarrow = \begin{vmatrix} 1-a_1 & -a_1 & -a_1 & -a_1 \\ -a_2 & 1-a_2 & -a_2 & -a_2 \\ -a_3 & -a_3 & 1-a_3 & -a_3 \\ -a_4 & -a_4 & -a_4 & 1-a_4 \end{vmatrix} \neq 0$$

For $a = 0 = b = c = d$ (as by equation (*i*)

$$\Rightarrow = \begin{bmatrix} 1-a_1 & -1 & -1 & -1 \\ -a_2 & 1 & 0 & 0 \\ -a_3 & 0 & 1 & 0 \\ -a_4 & 0 & 0 & 1 \end{bmatrix} \neq 0$$

$$= -a_4 \begin{vmatrix} -1 & -1 & -1 \\ 1 & 0 & 0 \\ 0 & 1 & 0 \end{vmatrix} + 1 \begin{vmatrix} 1-a_1 & -1 & -1 \\ -a_2 & 1 & 0 \\ -a_3 & 0 & 1 \end{vmatrix} \neq 0$$

$\Rightarrow -a_4 + (1 - a_1) - a_2 - a_3 \neq 0$

$\Rightarrow a_1 + a_2 + a_3 + a_4 \neq 1$

Now $[a(x_1, y_1) + b\,(x'_1, + y'_1), (x_2, y_2)]$

$= [(ax_1 + bx'_1, ay_1 + by'_1), (x_2, y_2)]$

$= (ax_1 + bx'_1)\,x_2 - \alpha\,[x_2\,(ay_1 + by'_1) +$

$(ax_1 + bx'_1)y_2] + (ay_1 + by'_2)\,y_2$

$= a[x_1x_2 - \alpha\,(x_2y_1 + x_1y_2) + y_1y_2] + b\,[x_1, x_2$

$- \alpha\,(x_2y'\,x'_1\,y_2) + y'_1y_2]$

$= a(x_1, y_1)\,(x_2, y_2) + b\,(x_1', y_1')(x_2\,, y_2)$

(*ii*) $<u_1\, v> = <v, u>$

(*iii*) $<u_1\, v> \geq 0$ if $v = (x_1y_1)$

$\Rightarrow x_1^2 - \alpha(x_1y_1 + x_1y_1) + y_1^2 \geq 0$

$\Rightarrow x_1^2 + y_1^2 - 2\alpha x_1y_1 \geq 0$

i.e., $|\alpha| < 1$

106. $\{v_1, v_2, v_3, v_4\}$ is a basis of R^4

and $v = a_1v_1 + a_2v_2 + a_3v_3 + a_4v_4$

Then $\{v_1 - v, v_2 - v, v_3 - v, v_4 - v\}$

is a basis of R^4 ...(*i*)

Now, $a(v_1 - v) + b\,(v_2 - v) + c\,(v_3 - v) + d\,(v_4 - v) = 0$

$\Rightarrow a(1 - a_1v_1 - a_2v_2 - a_3v_3 - a_4v_4) + b\,(-a_1v_1 + 1 - a_2)$
$v_2 - a_3v_3 - a_4v_4) + c\,(-a_1v_1 - a_2v_2 +)$

107. We have $Q = \begin{pmatrix} 1 & -2 \\ -2 & 4 \end{pmatrix}$

$T(P) = QP$

is with rank 1 as Rank (Q) = 1

108. $P = (Q_{ij})\; n \times n\; j\; P_{ij} \in z$

$$Q = P + \frac{1}{2}\ell$$

Then, Q is invertible since for and one

$$P = \begin{pmatrix} a & b \\ c & d \end{pmatrix}$$

$|Q| = ad + 1/4 + (a + d)\,1/2 - bc$

$$= ab - bc + \frac{(a+d)}{2} + \frac{1}{4} \neq 0$$

112. $f_1 = (1, 1, 1), f_2 = (1, -1, 0),$

$f_3 = (0, 1, 0)$

$g_1 = (1, 1),$

$g_2 = (1, 0).$

$\therefore\quad (a, b) = xg_1 + yg_2 = x(1, 1) + y\,(1, 0)$

$= (x + y, x + 0.y)$

$\therefore\quad x + y = a$

$x + 0.y = b$

$\Rightarrow\quad x = b$ and $y = a - b.$

$\therefore\quad (a, b) = bg_1\,(a - b)g_2$

$\therefore$ $T\,(x, y, z) = (x + y, y - z).$

$F(f_1) = F(1, 1, 1) = (2, 0) = 0.g_1 + 2g_2$

$F(f_2) = F(1, -1, 0) = (0, -1) = -g_1 + g_2$

$F(f_3) = F(0, 1, 0) = (1, 1) = g_1 + 0.g_2$

$$[F]_f^g = \begin{bmatrix} 0 & -1 & 1 \\ 2 & 1 & 0 \end{bmatrix}$$

113. Characteristic equation is, $\lambda^2 - \lambda - 1 = 0$

$\Rightarrow\quad 1 = \lambda^2 - \lambda$

$\Rightarrow\quad \lambda^{-1} = \lambda - 1$

$\Rightarrow\quad M^{-1} = M - I$

115. $P : T = \begin{pmatrix} 1 & 0 \\ 1 & 0 \\ 0 & 0 \end{pmatrix}$

$\Rightarrow$ Rank = 1

$Q : T_2\,(x, y) = (x, x + y, y)$

Linear transformation of rank 2.

116. Let A_1 and A_2 be two complex n-vectors, then A_1 is said to be orthogonal to A_2,

if $(A_1, A_2) = 0$, i.e. $A_1^T A_2 = 0$

Here, $A_1 = \begin{bmatrix} 0 \\ 2 \\ 0 \\ 0 \end{bmatrix}$; $A_2 = \begin{bmatrix} 0 \\ 0 \\ 0 \\ -4 \end{bmatrix}$

$A_1^T = [0, 2, 0, 0]$

$$\therefore (A_1\,A_2) = [0\;2\;0\;0] \begin{bmatrix} 0 \\ 0 \\ 0 \\ -4 \end{bmatrix} = 0$$

Similary $(A_2\,A_3) = (A_3\,A_4) = 0$

Thus column vectors form the orthogonal set of system.

117. Since M is Hermitian matrix, so it will have only real eigen values.

119. The monic polynomial of lowest degree that arihilates a matrix A is called the minimal polynomial of A.

Here

$$|A - \lambda I| = \begin{vmatrix} 1-\lambda & 0 & 0 & 0 \\ 1 & 1-\lambda & 0 & 0 \\ 0 & 0 & 2-\lambda & 0 \\ 0 & 0 & 0 & 2-\lambda \end{vmatrix}$$

$= (1-\lambda)^2 (2-\lambda)^2$

$\therefore$ Roots of equation $|A - \lambda I| = 0$ are 1, 1, 2, 2.

Each characteristic root of A is also a root of minimal polynomial. If $m(x)$ is the minimal polynomial of A, then both $(x-1)$ and $(x-2)$ are factors of $m(x)$.

121. Let

$$A = \begin{bmatrix} 2 & 3 & 4 \\ 0 & 1 & 2 \\ 0 & 0 & 5 \end{bmatrix}$$

Then $$A + I = \begin{bmatrix} 2 & 3 & 4 \\ 0 & 1 & 2 \\ 0 & 0 & 5 \end{bmatrix} + \begin{bmatrix} 1 & 0 & 0 \\ 0 & 1 & 0 \\ 0 & 0 & 1 \end{bmatrix}$$

$$= \begin{bmatrix} 3 & 3 & 4 \\ 0 & 2 & 2 \\ 0 & 0 & 6 \end{bmatrix}$$

It is also non-zero upper triangular matrix.

Since each eigen value of A = 0

$\Rightarrow$ Characteristics equation of A is, $\lambda^n = 0$

$\Rightarrow$ A is nilopotent because a non-zero matrix A is said to be nilopotent if for some +ve integer r, $A^r = 0$.

122. Suppose A is a skew-Hermitian matrix. Then iA is Hermitian.

Let λ, be a characteristic root of A.

Then $\quad AX = XX$

$(iA)X = (i\lambda,)X$

From this it follows that $i\lambda$ is a characteristic root of A. which is Hermitian.

Hence $i\lambda$, is real, Therefore either λ must be zero or pure imaginary.

123. (None of these)

Characteristic equation is

$\lambda(\lambda-1)(\lambda+1) = 0$

$\Rightarrow \quad \lambda(\lambda^2-1) = 0$

$\Rightarrow \quad \lambda^3 - 1 = 0$

$\Rightarrow \quad A^3 - A = 0$

$\Rightarrow \quad A^3 = A$

So $\quad A^{100} = A^{99}.A = (A^3)^{33}A$

$= A^{33}.A = (A^3)^{11}.A$

$= A^{11}.A = A^{12}$

$= (A^3)^4 = A^4$

$= A^3.A = A^2$

Now $\quad A^3 = A$

$A^2 = I$

So $\quad A^{100} = A^2 = I$

So $\quad I + I = 2I$

$\therefore \quad |2I| = 8$

132. Given

x_1, x_2, x_n are linearly independent. So,

$a_1x_1 + a_2x_2 + ... + a_n x_n = 0$

Using given property

$$T(a_1x_1 + a_2x_2 + ... + a_n x_n) = T(0) = 0$$

i.e. T is one to one.

$\therefore \quad a_1 T(x_1) + a_2 T(x_2) + ... + a_n T(x_n) = 0.$

$\Rightarrow \quad c_1 Tx_1 + a_2 Tx_2 + ... + a_n Tx_n = 0.$

For $a_1 = a_2 = ... = a_n = 0$.

Hence $Tx_1, Tx_2, ... = Tx_n$ are also linearly independent.

■■

2 CHAPTER

Complex Analysis

2016

1. Let $a_1 = 1$ and $a_n = a_{n-1} + 4$, $n \geq 2$. Then,

$$\lim_{n\to\infty}\left[\frac{1}{a_1a_2}+\frac{1}{a_2a_3}+....+\frac{1}{a_{n-1}a_n}\right]$$ is equal to _____.

2. Let, a, b, c, d $\in \mathbb{R}$ such that $c^2 + d^2 \neq 0$. Then, the Cauchy problem

$a\,u_x + b\,u_y = e^{x+y}$, $x, y \in \mathbb{R}$,

$u(x, y) = 0$ on $c\,x + d\,y = 0$

has a unique solution if

(*a*) $a\,c + b\,d \neq 0$ (*b*) $a\,d - b\,c \neq 0$

(*c*) $a\,c - b\,d \neq 0$ (*d*) $a\,d + b\,c \neq 0$

3. Let $S_n = \sum_{k=1}^{n}\frac{1}{k}$ and $I_n = \int_1^n \frac{x-[x]}{x^2}dx$. Then, $S_{10} + I_{10}$ is equal to

(*a*) $\ln 10 + 1$ (*b*) $\ln 10 - 1$

(*c*) $\ln 10 - \frac{1}{10}$ (*d*) $\ln 10 + \frac{1}{10}$

2015

4. Let $C = \{z \in \mathbb{C} : |z - i| = 2\}$. Then $\frac{1}{2\pi}\oint_C \frac{z^2-4}{z^2+4}dz$ is equal to _____

5. Consider the power series $\sum_{n=0}^{\infty} a_n z^n$, where $a_n = \begin{cases}\frac{1}{3^n} & \text{if } n \text{ is even}\\ \frac{1}{5^n} & \text{if } n \text{ is odd.}\end{cases}$

The radius of convergence of the series is equal to _______

6. Let $D = \{z \in \mathbb{C} : |z| < 1\}$. Then there exists a non-constant analytic function *f* on D such that for all $n = 2, 3, 4, ...$

(*a*) $f\left(\frac{\sqrt{-1}}{n}\right) = 0$ (*b*) $f\left(\frac{1}{n}\right) = 0$

(*c*) $f\left(1-\frac{1}{n}\right) = 0$ (*d*) $f\left(\frac{1}{2}-\frac{1}{n}\right) = 0$

7. Let $\sum_{n=-\infty}^{\infty} a_n z^n$ be the Laurent series expansion of $f(z) = \frac{1}{2z^2 - 13z + 15}$ in the annulus $\frac{3}{2} < |z| < 5$.

Then $\frac{a_1}{a_2}$ is equal to__________.

8. The value of $\frac{i}{4-\pi}\int_{|z|=4}\frac{dz}{z\cos(z)}$ is equal to________.

2014

9. The function $f(z) = |z|^2 + i\bar{z} + 1$ is differentiable at

(*a*) i (*b*) 1

(*c*) $-i$ (*d*) no point in $\mathbb{C}$

10. The radius of convergence of the power series $\sum_{n=0}^{\infty} 4^{(-1)^n n} Z^{2n}$ is ______

11. The maximum modulus of e^{z^2} on the set $S = \{z \in \mathbb{C} : 0 \leq Re(z) \leq 1, 0 \leq Im(z) \leq 1\}$ is

(*a*) $2/e$ (*b*) e

(*c*) $e + 1$ (*d*) e^2

12. Let $\Omega = \{z \in \mathbb{C} : Im(z) > 0\}$ and let C be a smooth curve lying in Ω with initial point $-1 + 2i$ and final point $1 + 2i$. The value of $\int_C \frac{1+2z}{1+z}dz$ is

(*a*) $4 - \frac{1}{2}\ln 2 + i\frac{\pi}{4}$ (*b*) $-4 + \frac{1}{2}\ln 2 + i\frac{\pi}{4}$

(*c*) $4 + \frac{1}{2}\ln 2 - i\frac{\pi}{4}$ (*d*) $4 - \frac{1}{2}\ln 2 + i\frac{\pi}{2}$

13. If $a \in \mathbb{C}$ with $|a| < 1$, then the value of

$$\frac{(1-|a|^2)}{\pi}\int_{\Gamma}\frac{|dz|}{|z+a|^2},$$

where Γ is the simple closed curve $|z| = 1$ taken with the positive orientation, is ______.

14. If the power series $\sum_{n=0}^{\infty} a_n (z+3-i)^n$ converges at $5i$ and diverges at $-3i$, then the power series

(*a*) converges at $-2 + 5i$ and diverges at $2 - 3i$

(*b*) converges at $2 - 3i$ and diverges at $-2 + 5i$

(*c*) converges at both $2 - 3i$ and $-2 + 5i$

(*d*) diverges at both $2 - 3i$ and $-2 + 5i$

2013

15. The coefficient of $(z - \pi)^2$ in the Taylor series expansion of $f(z) = \begin{cases}\frac{\sin z}{z-\pi} & if\ z \neq \pi\\ -1 & if\ z = \pi\end{cases}$ around π is

(*a*) $\frac{1}{2}$ (*b*) $-\frac{1}{2}$

(*c*) $\frac{1}{6}$ (*d*) $-\frac{1}{6}$

16. Let f be an entire function on $\mathbb{C}$ such that $|f(z)| \leq' 100 \log |z|$ for each z with $|z| \geq 2$. If $f(i) = 2i$, then $f(1)$

(a) must be 2

(b) must be $2i$

(c) must be i

(d) cannot be determined from the given data

17. Let C be the contour $|z| = 2$ oriented in the anti-clockwise direction. The value of the integral $\oint_C ze^{3/z}dz$ is

(a) $3\pi i$ (b) $5\pi i$

(c) $7\pi i$ (d) $9\pi i$

18. Let f be an analytic function on $\overline{D} = \{z \in \mathbb{C} : |z| \leq 1\}$. Assume that $|f(z)| \leq 1$ for each $z \in \overline{D}$. Then, which of the following is **NOT** a possible value of $(e^f)''(0)$?

(a) 2 (b) 6

(c) $\frac{7}{9}e^{1/9}$ (d) $\sqrt{2} + i\sqrt{2}$

19. Let $f : \mathbb{C} \setminus \{3i\} \to \mathbb{C}$ be defined by $f(z) = \frac{z - i}{iz + 3}$.

Which of the following statements about f is **FALSE?**

(a) f is conformal on $\mathbb{C} \setminus \{3i\}$

(b) f maps circles in $\mathbb{C} \setminus \{3i\}$ onto circles in $\mathbb{C}$

(c) All the fixed points of f are in the region $\{z \in \mathbb{C} : \text{Im}(z) > 0\}$

(d) There is no straight line in $\mathbb{C} \setminus \{3i\}$ which is mapped onto a straight line in $\mathbb{C}$ by f

20. The image of the region $\{z \in \mathbb{C} : \text{Re}(z) > \text{Im}(z) > 0\}$ under the mapping $z \mapsto e^{z^2}$ is

(a) $\{w \in \mathbb{C} : \text{Re}(w) > 0, \text{Im}(w) > 0\}$

(b) $\{w \in \mathbb{C} : \text{Re}(w) > 0, \text{Im}(w) > 0, |w| > 1\}$

(c) $\{w \in \mathbb{C} : |w| > 1\}$

(d) $\{w \in \mathbb{C} : \text{Im}(w) > 0, |w| > 1\}$

21. Let u be a real valued harmonic function on $\mathbb{C}$ Let $g : \mathbb{R}^2 \to \mathbb{R}$ be defined by

$$g(x, y) = \int_0^{2\pi} u(e^{i\theta}(x + iy)) \sin\theta \, d\theta.$$

Which of the following statements is **TRUE?**

(a) g is a harmonic polynomial

(b) g is a polynomial but not harmonic

(c) g is harmonic but not a polynomial

(d) g is neither harmonic nor a polynomial

22. Let $S = \{z \in \mathbb{C} : |z| = 1\}$ with the induced topology from $\mathbb{C}$ and let $f : [0, 2] \to S$ be defined as $f(t) = e^{2\pi it}$. Then, which of the following is TRUE?

(a) K is closed in $[0,2] \Rightarrow f(K)$ is closed in S

(b) U is open in $[0,2] \Rightarrow f(U)$ is open in S

(c) $f(X)$ is closed in S $\Rightarrow$ X is closed in $[0,2]$

(d) $f(Y)$ is open in S $\Rightarrow$ Y is open in $[0,2]$

2012

23. Let $\int_C \left[\frac{1}{(z-2)^4} - \frac{(a-2)^2}{z} + 4\right] dz = 4\pi$, where the close curve C is the triangle having vertices at i, $\left(\frac{-1-i}{\sqrt{2}}\right)$ and $\left(\frac{1-i}{\sqrt{2}}\right)$, the integral being taken in anti-clockwise direction. Then one value of a is

(a) $1 + i$ (b) $2 + i$

(c) $3 + i$ (d) $4 + i$

Statement for Linked Answer Questions 24 – 25:

Consider the functions $f(z) = \frac{z^2 + az}{(z+1)^2}$ and $g(z) = \sin h\,(z - \frac{\pi}{2\alpha})$, $\alpha \neq 0$.

24. The residue of $f(z)$ at its pole is equal to 1. Then the value of α is

(a) –1 (b) 1

(c) 2 (d) 3

25. For the value of α obtained in Q.54, the function $g(z)$ is not conformal at a point

(a) $\frac{\pi(1+3i)}{6}$ (b) $\frac{\pi(3+i)}{6}$

(c) $\frac{2\pi}{3}$ (d) $\frac{i\pi}{2}$

2011

26. Which of the following is the imaginary part of a possible value of $(\sqrt{i})$?

(a) π (b) $\frac{\pi}{2}$

(c) $\frac{\pi}{4}$ (d) $\frac{\pi}{8}$

27. Let $f : C \to C$ be analytic except for a simple pole at $z = 0$ and let g $C \to C$ be analytic. Then, the value of $\frac{\operatorname{Res}_{z=0}\{f(z)g(z)\}}{\operatorname{Res}_{z=0} f(z)}$ is

(a) $g(0)$ (b) $g'(0)$

(c) $\lim_{z\to 0} z f(z)$ (d) $\lim_{z\to 0} z f(z) g(z)$

28. Let $f(z)$ be an entire function such that

$|f(z)| \leq K|z|, \forall z \in C$, for some $K > 0$. If $f(1) = i$, the value of $f(i)$ is

(a) 1 (b) – 1

(c) i (d) $-i$

Common Data for Questions 29 and 30:

Let $f(z) = \dfrac{z}{8-z^3}$, $z = x + iy$

29. $\underset{z=2}{\text{Res}} f(z)$ is

(a) $-\dfrac{1}{8}$ (b) $\dfrac{1}{8}$

(c) $-\dfrac{1}{6}$ (d) $\dfrac{1}{6}$

30. The Cauchy principal value of $\int_{-\infty}^{\infty} f(x)dx$

(a) $-\dfrac{\pi}{6}\sqrt{3}$ (b) $-\dfrac{\pi}{8}\sqrt{3}$

(c) $\pi\sqrt{3}$ (d) $-\pi\sqrt{3}$

2010

31. Let $u(x, y) = 2x(1 - y)$ for all real x and y. Then a function $v(x, y)$, so that $f(z) = u(x, y) + i\, v(x, y)$ is analytic, is

(a) $x^2 - (y-1)^2$ (b) $(x-1)^2 - y^2$

(c) $(x-1)^2 + y^2$ (d) $x^2 + (y-1)^2$

32. Let $f(z)$ be analytic on $D = \{z \in \mathbb{C} : |z-1| < 1\}$ such that $f(1) = 1$. If $f(z) = f(z^2)$ for all $z \in D$, then which one of the following statements is **NOT** correct?

(a) $f(z) = [f(z)]^2$ for all $z \in D$

(b) $f\left(\dfrac{z}{2}\right) = \dfrac{1}{2}f(z)$ for all $z \in D$

(c) $f(z^3) = [f(z)]^3$ for all $z \in D$

(d) $f'(1) = 0$

33. Let $I = \int_C \dfrac{f(z)}{(z-1)(z-2)}dz$, where $f(z) = \sin\dfrac{\pi z}{2} + \cos\dfrac{\pi z}{2}$ and C is the curve $|z| = 3$ oriented anti-clockwise. Then the value of I is

(a) $4\pi i$

(b) 0

(c) $-2\pi i$

(d) $-4\pi i$

34. Let $\sum_{n=-\infty}^{\infty} b_n z^n$ be the Laurent series expansion of the function $\dfrac{1}{z\sinh z}$, $0 < |z| < \pi$. Then which one of the following is correct?

(a) $b_{-2} = 1, b_0 = -\dfrac{1}{6}, b_2 = \dfrac{7}{360}$.

(b) $b_{-3} = 1, b_{-1} = -\dfrac{1}{6}, b_1 = \dfrac{7}{360}$.

(c) $b_{-2} = 0, b_0 = -\dfrac{1}{6}, b_2 = \dfrac{7}{360}$.

(d) $b_0 = 1, b_2 = -\dfrac{1}{6}, b_4 = \dfrac{7}{360}$.

35. Under the transformation $w = \sqrt{\dfrac{1-iz}{z-i}}$, the region $D = \{z \in \mathbb{C} : |z| < 1\}$ is transformed to

(a) $\{z \in \mathbb{C} : 0 < \arg z < \pi\}$

(b) $\{z \in \mathbb{C} : -\pi < \arg z < 0\}$

(c) $\{z \in \mathbb{C} : 0 < \arg z < \dfrac{\pi}{2}$ or $< \arg z < \dfrac{3\pi}{2}\}$

(d) $\{z \in \mathbb{C} : \dfrac{\pi}{2} < \arg z < \pi$ or $\dfrac{3\pi}{2} < \arg z < 2\pi\}$

2009

36. For the function $f(z) = \sin\left(\dfrac{1}{\cos(1/z)}\right)$, the point $z = 0$ is

(a) a removable singularity

(b) a pole

(c) an essential singularity

(d) a non-isolated singularity

37. Let $f(z) = \sum_{n=0}^{15} z^n$ for $z \in \mathbb{C}$. If $C : |z - i| = 2$ then $\oint_C \dfrac{f(z)dz}{(z-i)^{15}} =$

(a) $2\pi i(1+15i)$ (b) $2\pi i(1-15i)$

(c) $4\pi i(1+15i)$ (d) $2\pi i$

38. Let $\sum_{n=-\infty}^{\infty} a_n(z+1)^n$ be the Laurent series expansion of $f(z) = \sin\left(\dfrac{z}{z+1}\right)$. Then $a_{-2} =$

(a) 1 (b) 0

(c) $\cos(1)$ (d) $\dfrac{-1}{2}\sin(1)$

39. Let $u(x, y)$ be the real part of an entire function $f(z) = u(x, y) + iv(x, y)$ for $z = x + iy \in \mathbb{C}$. If C is the positively oriented boundary of a rectangular region R in $\mathbb{R}^2$, then $\oint_C \left[\dfrac{\partial u}{\partial y}dx - \dfrac{\partial u}{\partial x}dy\right] =$

(a) 1 (b) 0

(c) 2π (d) π

Linked Answer Questions

Statement for Linked Answer Q. 40 – 41

Consider the function $f(z) = \dfrac{e^{iz}}{z(z^2+1)}$

40. The residue of f at the isolated singular point in the upper half plane $\{z = x + iy \in \mathbb{C} : y > 0\}$ is

(a) $\dfrac{-1}{2e}$ (b) $\dfrac{-1}{e}$

(c) $\dfrac{e}{2}$ (d) 1

41. The Cauchy Principal Value of the integral $\int_{-\infty}^{\infty} \dfrac{\sin x\, dx}{x(x^2+1)}$ is

(a) $-2\pi(1+2e^{-1})$ (b) $\pi(1-e^{-1})$

(c) $2\pi(1+e)$ (d) $-\pi(1+e^{-1})$

2008

42. Let S be the open unit disk and $f : S \to C$ be a real-valued analytic function with $f(0) = 1$. Then the set $\{z \in S : f(z) \neq 1\}$ is

(a) empty (b) nonempty finite

(c) countably infinite (d) uncountable

43. Let f be a bilinear transformation that maps -1 to 1, i to ∞ and $-i$ to 0. Then $f(1)$ is equal to

(a) -2 (b) -1

(c) i (d) $-i$

44. Let S be the positively oriented circle given by $|z - 3i| = 2$. Then the value of $\int_S \dfrac{dz}{z^2+4}$ is

(a) $\dfrac{-\pi}{2}$ (b) $\dfrac{\pi}{2}$

(c) $\dfrac{-i\pi}{2}$ (d) $\dfrac{i\pi}{2}$

45. Let T be the closed unit disk and ∂T be the unit circle. Then which one of the following holds for every analytic function $f : T \to C$.

(a) $|f|$ attains its minimum and its maximum of ∂T

(b) $|f|$ attains its minimum of ∂T but need not attain its maximum on ∂T

(c) $|f|$ attains its maximum on ∂T but need not attain its minimum on ∂T

(d) $|f|$ need not attain its maximum on ∂T and also it need not attain its minimum on ∂T

46. Let S be the disk $|z| < 3$ in the complex plane and let $f : S \to C$ be an analytic function such that $f\left(1+\dfrac{\sqrt{2}}{n}i\right) = -\dfrac{2}{n^2}$ for each natural number n. Then $f(\sqrt{2})$ is equal to

(a) $3-2\sqrt{2}$ (b) $3+2\sqrt{2}$

(c) $2-3\sqrt{2}$ (d) $2+3\sqrt{2}$

Statement for Linked Answer Questions 47 and 48:

Let $f(z) = \cos z - \dfrac{\sin z}{z}$ for non-zero $z \in C$ and $f(0) = 0$. Also, let $g(z) = \sinh z$ for $z \in C$.

47. Then $f(z)$ has a zero at $z = 0$ of order

(a) 0 (b) 1

(c) 2 (d) greater than 2

48. Then $\dfrac{g(z)}{zf(z)}$ has a pole at $z = 0$ of order

(a) 1 (b) 2

(c) 3 (d) greater than 3

2007

49. Let $S = \{0\} \cup \left\{\dfrac{1}{4n+7} : n = 1, 2, \ldots\right\}$. Then the number of analytic functions which vanish only on S is

(a) infinite (b) 0

(c) 1 (d) 2

50. It is given that $\sum_{n-0}^{\infty} a_n z^n$ converges at $z = 3 + i4$. Then the radius of convergence of the power series $\sum_{n-0}^{\infty} a_n z^n$ is

(a) ≤ 5 (b) ≥ 5

(c) < 5 (d) > 5.

51. Let $f(z)$ be an analytic function. Then the value of $\int_0^{2\pi} f(e^{it})\cos(t)\,dt$ equals

(a) 0 (b) $2\pi f(0)$

(c) $2\pi f'(0)$ (d) $\pi f(0)$

52. Let G_1 and G_2 be the images of the disc $\{z \in C : |z+1| < 1\}$ under the transformations

$$w = \frac{(1-i)z+2}{(1+i)z+2} \text{ and } w = \frac{(1+i)z+2}{(1-i)z+2}$$

respectively.

Then

(a) $G_1 = \{w \in C : Im(w) < 0\}$ and $G_2 = \{w \in C : Im(w) > 0\}$

(b) $G_1 = \{w \in C : Im(w) > 0\}$ and $G_2 = \{w \in C : Im(w) < 0\}$

(c) $G_1 = \{w \in C : |w| > 2\}$ and $G_2 = \{w \in C: |w| < 2\}$

(d) $G_1 = \{w \in C : |w| < 2\}$ and $G_2 = \{w \in C: |w| > 2\}$

53. Let $f(z) = 2z^2 - 1$. Then the maximum value of $|f(z)|$ on the unit disc $D = \{z \in C : |z| \le 1)$ equals

(a) 1 (b) 2

(c) 3 (d) 4

54. Let $f(z) = \dfrac{1}{z^2 - 3z + 2}$

Then the coefficient of $\dfrac{1}{z^3}$ in the Laurent series expansion of $f(z)$ for $|z| > 2$ is

(a) 0 (b) 1

(c) 3 (d) 5

55. Let $f : C \to C$ be an arbitrary analytic function satisfying $f(0) = 0$ and $f(1) = 2$. Then

(a) there exists a sequence $\{z_n\}$ such that $|z_n| > n$ and $f(z_n)| > n$

(b) there exists a sequence $\{z_n\}$ such that $|z_n| > n$ and $f(z_n) < n$

(c) there exists a bounded sequence $\{z_n\}$ such that $|f(z_n) > n$

(d) there exists a sequence $\{z_n\}$ such that $z_n \to 0$ and $f(z_n) \to 2$

56. Define $f : C \to C$ by

$$f(z) = \begin{cases} 0, & \text{if } \operatorname{Re}(z) = 0 \text{ or } \operatorname{Im}(z = 0) \\ z, & \text{otherwise.} \end{cases}$$

Then the set of points where f is analytic is

(a) $\{z : \operatorname{Re}(z) \ne 0$ and $\operatorname{Im}(z) \ne 0\}$

(b) $\{z : \operatorname{Re}(z) \ne 0\}$

(c) $\{z: \operatorname{Re}(z) \ne 0$ or $\operatorname{Im}(z) \ne 0\}$

(d) $\{z : \operatorname{Im}(z) \ne 0\}$

2006

57. The value of $\int_0^{2\pi} \exp(e^{i\theta} - i\theta)d\theta$ equals

(a) $2\pi i$ (b) 2π

(c) π (d) $i\pi$

58. The sum of the residues at all the poles of $f(z) = \dfrac{\cot \pi z}{(z+a)^2}$, where a is a constant, $(a \ne 0, \pm 1, \pm 2, ...)$ is

(a) $\dfrac{1}{\pi}\sum_{n=-\infty}^{\infty} \dfrac{1}{(n+a)^2} - \pi \operatorname{cosec}^2 \pi a$

(b) $-\dfrac{1}{\pi}\sum_{n=-\infty}^{\infty} \dfrac{1}{(n+a)^2} + \pi \operatorname{cosec}^2 \pi a$

(c) $-\dfrac{1}{\pi}\sum_{n=-\infty}^{\infty} \dfrac{1}{(n+a)^2} - \pi \operatorname{cosec}^2 \pi a$

(d) $\dfrac{1}{\pi}\sum_{n=-\infty}^{\infty} \dfrac{1}{(n+a)^2} + \pi \operatorname{cosec}^2 \pi a$

59. Let $f(z)$ be an entire function such that for some constant

$\alpha, |f(z)| \le \alpha |z|^3$ for $|z| \ge 1$ and $f(z) = f(iz)$ for all $z \in C$. Then

(a) $f(z) = \alpha z^3$ for all $z \in C$

(b) $f(z)$ is a constant

(c) $f(z)$ is a quadratic polynomial

(d) no such $f(z)$ exists

60. Which of the following is not the real part of an analytic function?

(a) $x^2 - y^2$ (b) $\dfrac{1}{1+x^2+y^2}$

(c) $\cos x \cos y$ (d) $x + \dfrac{x}{x^2+y^2}$

61. The radius of convergence of $\sum_{n=0}^{\infty} \dfrac{\left(1+\frac{1}{n}\right)^{n^2}}{n^3} z^n$ is

(a) e (b) $1/e$

(c) 1 (d) ∞

2005

62. The principal value of $\log\left(i^{\frac{1}{4}}\right)$ is

(a) $i\pi$ (b) $\dfrac{i\pi}{2}$

(c) $\dfrac{i\pi}{4}$ (d) $\dfrac{i\pi}{8}$

63. Consider the functions $f(z) = x^2 + iy^2$ and $g(z) = x^2 + y^2 + ixy$. At $z = 0$,

(a) f is analytic but not g

(b) g is analytic but not f

(c) both f and g are analytic

(d) neither f nor g is analytic

64. The coeffecient of $\dfrac{1}{z}$ in the expansion of Log $\left(\dfrac{z}{z-1}\right)$, valid in $|z|>1$, is

(a) –1 (b) 1

(c) $-\dfrac{1}{2}$ (d) $\dfrac{1}{2}$

65. Let γ be a simple closed curve in the complex. Then the set of all possible values of

$$\oint_\gamma \frac{dz}{z(1-z^2)} \text{ is}$$

(a) $\{0, \pm\pi i\}$ (b) $\{0, \pi i, 2\pi i\}$

(c) $\{0, \pm\pi i, \pm 2\pi i\}$ (d) $\{0\}$

66. The principal value of the improper integral

$$\int_{-\infty}^{\infty} \frac{\cos x}{1+x^2} dx \text{ is}$$

(a) $\frac{\pi}{e}$ (b) πe

(c) $\pi + e$ (d) $\pi - e$

67. The number of roots of the equation $z^5 - 12z^2 + 14 = 0$ that lie in the region $\{z \in C : 2 \le |z| < \frac{5}{2}\}$ is

(a) 2 (b) 3

(c) 4 (d) 5

68. Let $f : (0, 2) \to R$ be defined by

$$f(x) = \begin{cases} x^2 & \text{if } x \text{ is rational} \\ 2x-1 & \text{if } x \text{ is irrational} \end{cases}$$

Then

(a) f is differentiable exactly at one point

(b) f is differentiable exactly at two points

(c) f is not differentiable at any point in (0, 2)

(d) f is differentiable at every point in (0, 2)

69. Let $f : R^2 \to R$ be defined by

$$f(x, y) = \begin{cases} x^2 + y^2 & \text{if } x \text{ and } y \text{ are rational} \\ 0 & \text{otherwise} \end{cases}$$

Then

(a) f is not continuous at (0,0)

(b) f is continuous at (0,0) but not differentiable at (0,0)

(c) f is differentiable only at (0,0)

(d) f is differentiable everywhere

70. Let $f, g : R^2 \to R$ be defined by $f(x, y) = x^4 + y^2$; $g(x, y) = x^4 + y^2 - 10x^2y$.

Then at (0, 0)

(a) f has a local minimum but not g

(b) g has a local minimum but not f

(c) both f and g have a local minimum

(d) neither f nor g has a local minimum

71. Suppose C_1 is the boundary of $\{(x, y) \in R^2 : 0 \le x \le 1, 0 \le y \le 1\}$ and C_2 is the boundary of $\{(x, y) \in R^2 : -1 \le x \le 0, -1 \le y \le 0\}$. Let

$$\alpha_i = \int_{C_i} xy^2 dx + (x^2y + 2x) dy, \; i = 1, 2$$

be evaluated in the counterclockwise direction. Then

(a) $\alpha_1 = 1, \alpha_2 = -1$ (b) $\alpha_1 = \alpha_2 = 1$

(c) $\alpha_1 = 2, \alpha_2 = -2$ (d) $\alpha_1 = \alpha_2 = 2$

72. Consider R^2 with the usual metric and the functions $f : [0, (2\pi) \to R^2$ and $g : [0, 2\pi] \to R^2$ defined by defined by $f(t) = (\cos t, \sin t), 0 \le t < 2\pi$ and $g(t) = (\cos t, \sin t), 0 \le t \le 2\pi$.

Then on the respective domains

(a) f is uniformly continuous but not g

(b) g is uniformly continuous but not f

(c) both f and g are uniformly continuous

(d) neither f nor g is uniformly continuous

73. Let $f : R \to R$ be a nonzero function such that $|f(x)| \le \frac{1}{1+2x^2}$ for all $x \in R$. Define real valued functions f_n on R for all $n \in N$ by $f_n(x) = f(x + n)$.

Then the series $\sum_{n=1}^{\infty} f_n(x)$ converges uniformly

(a) on [0, 1] but not on [–1, 0]

(b) on [–1, 0] but not on [0, 1]

(c) on both [–1, 0] and [0, 1]

(d) neither on [–1, 0] nor on [0, 1]

74. Let E be a nonmeasurable subset of (0, 1). Define two functions f_1 and f_2 on (0,1) as follows :

$$f_1(x) = \begin{cases} 1/x & \text{if } x \in E \\ 0 & \text{if } x \notin E \end{cases} \Big/ \text{ and}$$

$$f_2(x) = \begin{cases} 0 & \text{if } x \in E \\ 1/x & \text{if } x \notin E \end{cases}$$

Then

(a) f_1 is measurable but not f_2

(b) f_2 is measurable but not f_1

(c) both f_1 and f_2 are measurable

(d) neither f_1 nor f_2 is measurable

75. Consider the following improper integrals :

$$I_1 = \int_1^{\infty} \frac{dx}{(1+x^2)^{1/2}} \text{ and } I_2 = \int_1^{\infty} \frac{dx}{(1+x^2)^{3/2}} \text{ Then}$$

(a) I_1 converges but not I_2

(b) I_2 converges but not I_1

(c) both I_1 and I_2 converge

(d) neither I_1 nor I_2 converges

2004

76. If D is the open unit disk in C and $f : C \to D$ is analytic with $f(10) = , \frac{1}{2}$ then $f(10 + i)$ is

(a) $\frac{1+i}{2}$ (b) $\frac{1-i}{2}$

(c) $\frac{1}{2}$ (d) $\frac{i}{2}$

77. The real part of the principal value of 4^{4-i} is

(*a*) 256 cos (In 4) (*b*) 64 cos (In 4)

(*c*) 16 cos (In 4) (*d*) 4 cos (In 4)

78. If $\sin z = \sum_{n=0}^{\infty} a_n \left(z - \frac{\pi}{4}\right)^n$ then a_6 equals

(*a*) 0 (*b*) $\frac{1}{720}$

(*c*) $\frac{1}{(720\sqrt{2})}$ (*d*) $\frac{-1}{(720\sqrt{2})}$

79. The equation $x^6 - x - 1 = 0$ has

(*a*) no positive real roots

(*b*) exactly one positive real root

(*c*) exactly two positive real roots

(*d*) all positive real roots

80. In the Laurent series expansion of $f(z) = \frac{1}{z-1} - \frac{1}{z-2}$ valid in the region $|z| > 2$, the coefficient of $\frac{1}{z^2}$ is

(*a*) – 1 (*b*) 0

(*c*) 1 (*d*) 2

81. Let $w = f(z)$ be the bilinear transformation that maps –1, 0 and 1 to $-i$, 1 and i respectively. Then $f(1-i)$ equals

(*a*) $-1 + 2i$ (*b*) $2i$

(*c*) $-2 + i$, (*d*) $-1 + i$

82. For the positively oriented unit circle,

$$\oint_{|z|=1} \frac{2\text{Re}(z)}{z+2} dz =$$

(*a*) 0 (*b*) πi

(*c*) $2\pi i$ (*d*) $4\pi i$

83. The number of zeroes, counting multiplicities, of the polynomial $z^5 + 3z^3 + z^2 + 1$ inside the circle $|z| = 2$ is

(*a*) 0 (*b*) 2

(*c*) 3 (*d*) 5

84. Let $f = u + iv$ and $g = v + iu$ be non-zero analytic functions on $|z| < 1$. Then it follows that

(*a*) $f' \equiv 0$

(*b*) f is conformal on $|z| < 1$

(*c*) $f \equiv kg$ for some real k

(*d*) f is one to one

2003

85. Consider a function $f(z) = u + iv$ defined on $|z - i| < 1$ where u, v are real valued functions of x, y. Then $f(z)$ is analytic for u equals to

(*a*) $x^2 + y^2$ (*b*) $ln\ (x^2 + y^2)$

(*c*) e^{xy} (*d*) $e^{x^2} - y^2$

86. At $z = 0$, the function $f(z) = z^2\bar{z}$

(*a*) does not satisfy Cauchy – Reimann equations

(*b*) satisfies Cauchy – Reimann equations but is not differentiable

(*c*) is differentiable

(*d*) is analytic

87. The bilinear transformation w, which maps the points 0, 1, ∞ in the z-plane onto the points $-i$, ∞, 1 in the w-plane is

(*a*) $\frac{z-1}{z+i}$ (*b*) $\frac{z-i}{z+1}$

(*c*) $\frac{z+i}{z-1}$ (*d*) $\frac{z+1}{z-i}$

88. Let γ be the curve : $r = 2 + 4\cos\theta$, $(0 \le \theta \le 2\pi)$. If $I_1 = \int_\gamma \frac{dz}{z-1}$ and $I_2 = \int_\gamma \frac{dz}{z-3}$ then

(*a*) $I_1 = 2I_2$ (*b*) $I_1 = I_2$

(*c*) $2I_1 = I_2$ (*d*) $I_1 = 0, I_2 \neq 0$

89. Let $f(z)$ be defined on the domain $E: |z - 2i| < 3$ and on its boundary ∂E. Then which of the following statements is always true :

(*a*) if $f(z)$ is analytic on E and $f(z) \neq 0$ for any z in E, then $|f|$ attains its maximum on ∂E

(*b*) if $f(z)$ is analytic on $E \cup \partial E$, then $|f|$ attains its minimum on ∂E

(*c*) if $f(z)$ is analytic on E and continuous on $E \cup \partial E$, then $|f|$ attains its maximum and minimum on ∂E

(*d*) if $f(z)$ is analytic on $E \cup \partial E$ and $f(z) \neq 0$ for any z in $E \cup \partial E$, then $|f|$ attains its minimum on ∂E

90. Let $f(z)$ be an analytic function with a simple pole at $z = 1$ and a double pole at $z = 2$ with residues 1 and – 2 respectively. Further if $f(0) = 0$, $f(3) = -\frac{3}{4}$ and f is bounded as $z - \infty$, then $f(z)$ must be

(*a*) $z(z-3) - \frac{1}{4} + \frac{1}{z-1} - \frac{2}{z-1} + \frac{1}{(z-2)^2}$

(*b*) $-\frac{1}{4} + \frac{1}{z-1} - \frac{2}{z-2} + \frac{1}{(z-2)^2}$

(*c*) $\frac{1}{z-1} - \frac{2}{z-2} + \frac{5}{(z-2)^2}$

(*d*) $\frac{15}{4} + \frac{1}{z-1} + \frac{2}{z-2} - \frac{7}{(z-2)^2}$

91. An example of a function with a non-isolated essential singularity at $z = 2$ is

(*a*) $\tan\frac{1}{z-2}$ (*b*) $\sin\frac{1}{z-2}$

(*c*) $e^{-(z-2)}$ (*d*) $\tan\frac{z-2}{z}$

2.8 Complex Analysis

92. Let $f(z) = u(x, y) + iv(x, y)$ be an entire function having Taylor's Series expansion as $\sum_{n=0}^{\infty} a_n z^n$. If $f(x) = u(x, 0)$ and $f(iy) = iv(0, y)$ then

(a) $a_{2n} = 0$ for all n

(b) $a_0 = a_1 = a_2 = a_3 = 0, a_4 \neq 0$

(c) $a_{2n+1} = 0$ for all n

(d) $a_0 \neq 0$ but $a_2 = 0$

93. Let $I = \int_C \frac{\cot(\pi z)}{(z-i)^2} dz$, where C is the contour $4x^2 + y^2 = 2$ (counter clock-wise). Then I is equal to

(a) 0 (b) $-2\pi i$

(c) $2\pi i\left(\frac{\pi}{\sin h^2 \pi} - \frac{1}{\pi}\right)$ (d) $-\frac{2\pi^2 i}{\sin h^2 \pi}$

2002

94. The function $f(z) = z^2$ maps the first quadrant onto

(a) itself (b) upper half plane

(c) third quadrant (d) right half plane

95. The radius of convergence of the power series of the function $f(z) = \frac{1}{1-z}$ about $z = \frac{1}{4}$ is

(a) 1 (b) $\frac{1}{4}$

(c) $\frac{3}{4}$ (d) 0

96. Let T be any circle enclosing the origin and oriented counter-clockwise. Then the value of the integral $\int_\Gamma \frac{\cos z}{z^2} dz$ is

(a) $2\pi i$ (b) 0

(c) $-2\pi i$ (d) undefined

97. Let $w(z) = \frac{az+b}{cz+d}$ and $f(z) = \frac{\alpha z+\beta}{\gamma z+\delta}$ be bilinear (Mobius) transformations. Then the following is also a bilinear transformation

(a) $f(z)w(z)$ (b) $f(w(z))$

(c) $f(z) + w(z)$ (d) $f(z)+\frac{1}{w(z)}$

98. For the function $f(z) = \sin\frac{1}{z}$, $z = 0$ is a

(a) removable singularity

(b) simple pole

(c) branch point

(d) essential singularity

99. Evaluate the integral

$$\int_{-\infty}^{\infty} \frac{dx}{\left(x^2 + a^2\right)^2}, a > 0$$

by the method of residue calculus.

2001

100. The function $\sin z$ is analytic in

(a) $C \cup \{\infty\}$

(b) C except on the negative real axis

(c) $C - \{0\}$

(d) C

101. The series $\sum_{n=1}^{\infty} \frac{z^n}{n\sqrt{n+1}}$, $|z| \leq 1$ is

(a) uniformly but not absolutely convergent

(b) uniformly and absolutely convergent

(c) absolutely convergent but not uniformly convergent

(d) convergent but not uniformly convergent

102. If $f(z) = z^3$ then it

(a) has an essential singularity at $z = \infty$

(b) has a pole of order 3 at $z = \infty$

(c) has a pole of order 3 at $z = 0$

(d) is analytic at $z = \infty$

103. The fixed Points of $f(z) = \frac{2iz+5}{z-2i}$ are

(a) $1 \pm i$ (b) $1 \pm 2i$

(c) $2i \pm 1$ (d) $i \pm 1$

104. The function $f(z) = |z|^2$ is

(a) differentiable everywhere

(b) differentiable only at the origin

(c) not differentiable anywhere

(d) differentiable on real x-axis

105. Suppose $z = a$ is an isolated singularity of $f(z)$. Prove that $f(z)$ cannot be bounded in a neighbourhood of $z = a$.

106. Evaluate

$$\int_{-\infty}^{\infty} \frac{x \sin \pi x}{x^2 + 2x + 5} dx$$

using the method of residues.

2000

107. For the function $f(z) = \frac{1-e^{-z}}{z}$, the point $z = 0$ is

(a) an essential singularity

(b) a pole of order zero

(c) a pole of order one

(d) a removable singularity

108. The transformation $w = e^{i\theta}\left(\dfrac{z-p}{\bar{p}z-1}\right)$ where p is a constant, maps $|z| < 1$ onto

(*a*) $|w| < 1$ if $|p| < 1$ (*b*) $|w| > 1$ if $|p| > 1$

(*c*) $|w| = 1$ if $|p| = 1$ (*d*) $|w| = 3$ if $p = 0$

109. The value of the integral

$$\oint_c \frac{dz}{z^2-1}, C : |z| = 4$$

is equal to

(*a*) πi (*b*) 0

(*c*) $-\pi i$ (*d*) $2\pi i$

110. Expand the function $f(z) = \dfrac{1}{3-2z}$ in powers of $(z-3)$ and find the radius of convergence of the series so obtained.

111. Evaluate the integral $\int_C \dfrac{e^{1/z^2}}{z^2+1}dz$; $C : |z-i| = \dfrac{7}{2}$, where integration is to be taken counterclockwise. [5]

112. (*a*) Construct an analytic function $f(z)$ of which the real part is [5]

$$u(x, y) = 2xy + \cosh x \sin y,$$

given that $f(0) = 0$

(*b*) Determine all harmonic functions of the form $u = f\left(\dfrac{x^2+y^2}{x}\right)$ that are not constant. [3]

ANSWERS

1. (0.25) **2.** (*a*) **3.** (*a*) **4.** (–2) **5.** (3) **6.** (*c*) **7.** (5) **8.** (2) **9.** (*c*)
10. (0.49 to 0.51) **11.** (*b*) **12.** (*a*) **13.** (1.99 to 2.01) **14.** (*a*) **15.** (*c*) **16.** (*b*) **17.** (*d*)
18. (*b*) **19.** (*c*) **20.** (*c*) **21.** (*a*) **22.** (*a*) **23.** (*c*) **24.** (*d*) **25.** (*a*) **26.** (*c*) **27.** (*a*)
28. (*b*) **29.** (*c*) **30.** (*a*) **31.** (*a*) **32.** (*a*) **33.** (*d*) **34.** (*a*) **35.** (*d*) **36.** (*c*) **37.** (*a*)
38. (*b*) **39.** (*b*) **40.** (*a*) **41.** (*b*) **42.** (*a*) **43.** (*b*) **44.** (*b*) **45.** (*c*) **46.** (*b*) **47.** (*c*)
48. (*b*) **49.** (*a*) **50.** (*b*) **51.** (*c*) **52.** (*b*) **53.** (*c*) **54.** (*c*) **55.** (*c*) **56.** (*a*) **57.** (*b*)
58. (*a*) **59.** (*b*) **60.** (*b*) **61.** (*b*) **62.** (*b*) **63.** (*c*) **64.** (*a*) **65.** (*a*) **66.** (*a*) **67.** (*b*)
68. (*a*) **69.** (*b*) **70.** (*d*) **71.** (*a*) **72.** (*b*) **73.** (*d*) **74.** (*a*) **75.** (*c*) **76.** (*c*) **77.** (*a*)
78. (*d*) **79.** (*c*) **80.** (*a*) **81.** (*c*) **82.** (*a*) **83.** (*d*) **84.** (*a*) **85.** (*b*) **86.** (*d*) **87.** (*c*)
88. (*b*) **89.** (*d*) **90.** (*b*) **91.** (*a*) **92.** (*b*) **93.** (*d*) **94.** (*b*) **95.** (*a*) **96.** (*b*) **97.** (*b*)
98. (*d*) **99.** (*) **100.** (*d*) **101.** (*b*) **102.** (*b*) **103.** (*c*) **104.** (*c*) **105.** (*) **106.** (*) **107.** (*d*)
108. (*a*) **109.** (*b*) **110.** (*) **111.** (*) **112.** (*)

EXPLANATIONS

1. $\lim_{n\to\infty}\left[\frac{1}{a_1a_2}+\frac{1}{a_2a_3}+....+\frac{1}{a_{n-1}a_n}\right]$

$$=\lim_{n\to\infty}\frac{1}{4}\left[\frac{1}{a_1}-\frac{1}{a_n}\right]$$

$$=\lim_{n\to\infty}\left[\frac{1}{4}\left(1-\frac{1}{4n-3}\right)\right]=0.25$$

2. Auxiliary equation is

$$\frac{dx}{a}=\frac{dy}{b}=\frac{du}{e^{x+y}}$$

After Simplification, we have two independent solutions as

$$bx-ay=c_1$$

$$u-\frac{1}{a+b}e^{x+y}=c_2$$

The general solution is

$$u-\frac{1}{a+b}e^{x+y}=\phi(bx-ay)$$

on curve C : cx + dy = 0

$$0-\frac{1}{a+b}e^{\left(\frac{d-c}{d}\right)x}=\phi\left(\frac{ca+bd}{d}x\right)$$

Arbitrary function have unique representation if

$$ca+bd\neq 0$$

3.
$$S_{10}=\frac{7381}{2520}\ \&$$

$$I_{10}=\int_1^{10}\frac{x-[x]}{x^2}dx$$

$$=-\frac{4861}{2520}+\ln 10$$

$$S_{10}+I_{10}=\ln 10+1$$

9. Given, $f(z)=|z|^2+i\bar{z}+1$

$$\Rightarrow\quad f(z)=z\bar{z}+i\bar{z}+1\ [\because |z|^2=z\bar{z}]\quad ...(i)$$

$f(z)$ will be differentiable on those points at which

$$\frac{\partial f}{\partial \bar{z}}=0$$

On differentiating partially,

equation (i) w.r.t. $\bar{z}$, we get

$$\frac{\partial f}{\partial \bar{z}}=z+i$$

Now, put $\frac{\partial f}{\partial \bar{z}}=0$

$$\Rightarrow\quad z+i=0$$

$$\Rightarrow\quad z=-i$$

Hence, $f(z)$ is differentiable at $z=-i$.

10. Given power series is

$$\sum_{n=0}^{\infty}4^{(-1)^n n}z^{2n}=1+4^{-1}z^2+4^2z^4+4^{-3}z^6$$
$$+4^4z^8+4^{-5}z^{10}\ ...(i)$$

Now $\frac{1}{R}=\lim_{n\to\infty}\sup|a_n|^{1/n}$

$$=\sup\{(4^{-1})^{1/1},(4^2)^{1/2},(4^{-3})^{1/3},(4^4)^{1/4}....\}$$

$$=\sup\left\{\frac{1}{4},4,\frac{1}{4},4,\frac{1}{4},4...\right\}$$

$$\Rightarrow\quad \frac{1}{R}=4$$

$$\Rightarrow\quad R=\frac{1}{4}$$

Thus $|z|^2\leq\frac{1}{4}\Rightarrow|z|\leq\frac{1}{2}\Rightarrow|z|\leq 0.50$

Hence radius of convergence of this series is 0.50.

11. Given, set

$$S=\{z\in c:0\leq Re(z)\leq 1,\ 0\leq I_m(z)\leq 1\}$$

i.e., $0\leq x\leq 1,\ 0\leq y\leq 1$

Now, $e^{z^2}=e^{(x+iy)^2}$

$$=e^{x^2-y^2+2i\,xy}$$

$$\therefore\quad \left|e^{z^2}\right|=e^{x^2+y^2}$$

for maximum modulus of x^2 put

$$x=1,$$
$$y=1$$

we get $\max\left|e^{z^2}\right|=e^{1+1}=e^2$

12. Let $\Omega=\{z\in C: Im(z)>0\}$

Parametric equation of line segment joining the point $-1+2i$ to $1+2i$

$$r(t):[0,1]\to C$$

such that

$$r(t)=-1+2i+t[(1+2i)-(-1+2i)].$$

$$r(t)=-1+2(i+t),\ r'(t)=2$$

Now $\int_c f(z)dz=\int_0^1 f(r(t))r'(t)dt$

using

$$\int_c \frac{1+2z}{1+z}dz = \int_0^1 \frac{1+2\{-1+2(i+t)\}}{1-1+2(i+t)}.2dt$$

$$= \int_0^1 \frac{-1+4(i+t)}{(i+t)}dt$$

$$= \int_0^1 \left(4-\frac{1}{i+t}\right)dt$$

$$= [4t - \log(i+t)]_0^1$$

$$= 4 - \{\log(1+i) - \log i\}$$

$$= 4 - \left\{\log\left(\frac{1+i}{i}\right)\right\}$$

$$= 4 - [\log(1-i)]$$

$$= 4 - \left[\frac{1}{2}\log 2 + i\tan^{-1}(-1)\right]$$

$$= 4 - \left[\frac{1}{2}\log 2 - i\tan^{-1}(1)\right]$$

$$= 4 - \frac{1}{2}\log 2 + i\frac{\pi}{4}$$

13. Γ is the simple closed curve $|z| = 1$ taken with the positive orientation.

$|z| = 1$

$\Rightarrow \quad z = e^{i\theta}$

and $\quad |z|^2 = 1$

$\Rightarrow \quad z\bar{z} = 1$

now $\quad dz = ie^{i\theta}\, d\theta$

$\Rightarrow \quad dz = iz\, d\theta$

$\Rightarrow \quad \frac{dz}{iz} = d\theta$

$|dz| = d\theta$

Now, $\frac{(1-|a|^2)}{\pi}\int_\Gamma \frac{|dz|}{|z+a|^2}$

$$= \frac{1-|a|^2}{\pi}\int_0^{2\pi} \frac{d\theta}{(z+a)\overline{(z+a)}}$$

$$= \frac{1-|a|^2}{\pi}\int_0^{2\pi} \frac{d\theta}{(z+a)(\bar{z}+a)}$$

$$= \frac{1-|a|^2}{\pi}\cdot\frac{2\pi}{1-|a|^2} = 2$$

14. Given Power series

$$\sum_{n=0}^{\infty} a_n(z+3-i)^n \text{ i.e. } \sum_{n=0}^{\infty} a_n[z-(-3+i)]^n$$

is Converges at $z_1 = 5i$

Then this powers series converges at all the points in the disk

$\Delta[(-3+i), |5i-(-3+i)|]$

i.e. $\Delta[(-3+i), |3+4i|]$

i.e. $\Delta[(-3+i), 5]$

i.e. in the disk whose centre at (–3, 1) and radius of convergen is 5.

Again, this series diverges at $z_2 = -3i$

Then given power series diverges for all z with

$|z-(-3+i)| > |-3i-(-3+i)|$

i.e. $|z+3-i| > |-4i+3|$

$|z+3-i| > 5$

Hence the power series $\Sigma a_n(z+3-i)^n$ is converges at $-2+5i$

as $\Delta[(-3+i), |-2+5i+3-i|]$

$\Delta[(-3+i), 5]$

i.e. $-2+5i$ lies in this disk.

and the power series $\Sigma a_n(z+3-i)^n$ is diverges at $2-3i$

as $|2-3i+3-i| > 5$

i.e. $|5-4i| = \sqrt{41} > 5$

Hence this power series is converges at $-2+5i$ and diverges at $2-3i$.

15. Taylor series of $f(x)$ is

$$f(x) = f(a) + \frac{f'(x)}{11}(x-a) + \frac{f''(a)}{2!} + \frac{f^{(3)}(a)}{3!}(x-a)^3 + \ldots$$

So, for $f(z) = \frac{\sin z}{z-\pi}$ $z \neq \pi$

For coefficient of $(z-\pi)^2$

$$f(z) = \frac{f^{(3)}(a)}{3!}(z-a)^3$$

$$\text{Coefficient} \pm \frac{1}{3!} = \frac{1}{6}$$

16. $|f(z)| \leq 100 \log |z|$ for each z $z \geq 2$

$f(i) = 2i$

then $\quad f(1) = 2i$

17. $|z| = 2$ in anticlockwise direction

$$\oint_c ze^{3/z}dz = \int \frac{ze^{3/z}}{z-2}dz$$
$$= 9\pi i$$

19. $f: \mathbb{C}/\{3i\} \to \mathbb{C}$

$$f(z) = \frac{z-i}{iz+3}$$

f is conformal on $\mathbb{C}/\{3i\}$

f maps circles is $\mathbb{C}/\{3i\}$ onto circles in $\mathbb{C}$.

There is no straight line in $\mathbb{C}/3i$ which mapped onto a straight line in $\mathbb{C}$ by f.

20. $\{z\in\mathbb{C} : \text{Re}(z) > \text{Im}(z) > 0\}$

Mapping $z \to e^{z^2}$

Image of the region is $\{w\in\mathbb{C} : |w|>1\}$

23. $$\int_C \left[\frac{1}{(z-2)^4} - \frac{(a-2)^2}{z} + 4\right]dz = 4\pi \quad ...(1)$$

where C is triangle having vertices at i,

$$\frac{-1-i}{\sqrt{2}} \text{ and } \frac{1-i}{\sqrt{2}}$$

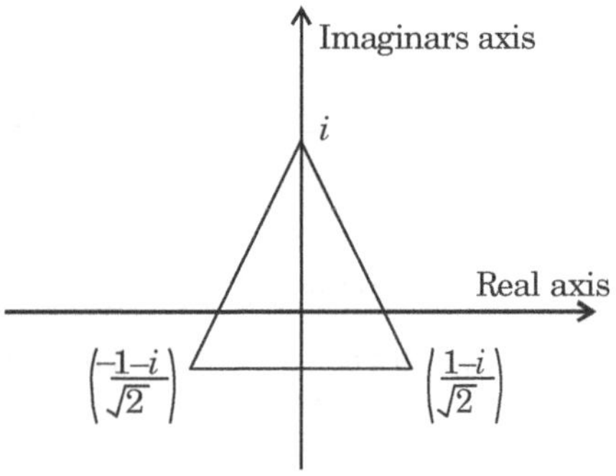

Fig.

By Cauchy's integral formula.

$$\int_C \frac{1}{(z-2)^4}dz = 0$$

$$\int_C \frac{(a-z)^2}{z}dz = 2\pi i(a-2)^2$$

and $$\int_C 4dz = 0$$

Hence from Eqn (1), we get

$0 - 2\pi i(a-2)^2 + 0 = 4\pi$

$(a-2)^2 = 2i$

Put $a = 3 + i$

L.H.S. $(a-2)^2 = (3+i-2)^2$

$= (1+i)^2$

$= 1 + i^2 + 2i$

$= 2i$ = R.H.S.

Hence $a = 3 + i$

24. Residue of $f(z)$ at $(z = -1)$

$$= \frac{1}{(z-1)!}\lim_{z\to-1}\left[\frac{d}{dz}\{(z+1)^2 f(z)\}\right]$$

$$= \lim_{z\to-1}\left[\frac{d}{dz}(z+1)^2 \frac{z^2+\alpha z}{(z+1)^2}\right]$$

$$= \lim_{z\to-1}\left[\frac{d}{dz}(z^2+\alpha z)\right]$$

$$= \lim_{z\to-1} 2z+\alpha$$

$= -2 + \alpha$

But residue of $f(z)$ at $(z = -1)$ is 1

$-2 + \alpha = 1$

$\alpha = 3$

25. $g(z) = \sinh\left(z - \frac{\pi}{2\alpha}\right) \quad \alpha \neq 0$

for $\alpha = 3$

$$g(z) = \sinh\left(z - \frac{\pi}{6}\right)$$

Now $g(z)$ is not conformal, if

$$g'(z) = 0$$

$$\cosh\left(z - \frac{\pi}{6}\right) = 0$$

$$\cos i\left(z - \frac{\pi}{6}\right) = 0$$

$$i\left(z - \frac{\pi}{6}\right) = -\frac{\pi}{2}$$

$$z = \frac{\pi(1+3i)}{6}$$

26. Let $y = \sqrt{i}$

$y^2 = i = e^{i\pi/2}$

$y = e^{i\pi/4}$

so imaginary part is $\pi/4$

27. Let $f : \mathbb{C} \to \mathbb{C}$ be analytic except for a simple pole at $z = 0$ and $g : \mathbb{C} \to \mathbb{C}$ be analytic. Then the value of

$$\frac{\underset{z\to0}{\text{Res}}\{f(z)g(z)\}}{\underset{z\to0}{\text{Res}}\, f(z)} = \frac{\lim_{z\to0} zf(z).g(z)}{\lim_{z\to0} zf(z)}$$

$$= g(0)\frac{\lim_{z\to0} zf(z)}{\lim_{z\to0} zf(z)} = g(0)$$

28. Let $f(z)$ is an entire function such that

$$|f(z)| \leq K|z|, \ \forall z \in \mathbb{C}$$

for some $K > 0$

If $f(1) = i$ then $f(i) = -1$

Since Let $f(z) = kz$

as $f(1) = i = K \Rightarrow K = i$

and $f(z) = iz$

so $f(i) = i \times i = -1$

29. $f(z) = \dfrac{Z}{8-z^3}$, $Z = x + iy$

$$\operatorname*{Res}_{z=2} f(z) = \lim_{z\to 2}(z-2)\frac{z}{(8-z^3)}$$

$$= \lim_{z\to 2}\frac{Z}{-(z^2+2^2+2z)}$$

$$= -\frac{2}{12} = -\frac{1}{6}$$

30. $\displaystyle\int_{-\infty}^{\infty}\frac{x}{8-x^3}dx$

$$f(z) = \frac{z}{8-z^3}$$

for poles $8 - z^3 = 0$

$(z-2)(z^2 + 2z + 4) = 0$

$z = 2,\ z = -1 \pm \sqrt{3}i$

$z = 2$ lies on Real line and $z = -1\pm\sqrt{3}i$ lies on upper half plane.

so $$\int_C f(z)dz = \int_{2+r}^{R} f(z)dz \int_T f(z)dz$$

$$+\int_{-R}^{2-r} f(z)dz + \int_y f(z)dz$$

$$= \operatorname*{Res}_{z\to -1+\sqrt{3}i} f(z)\times 2\pi i$$

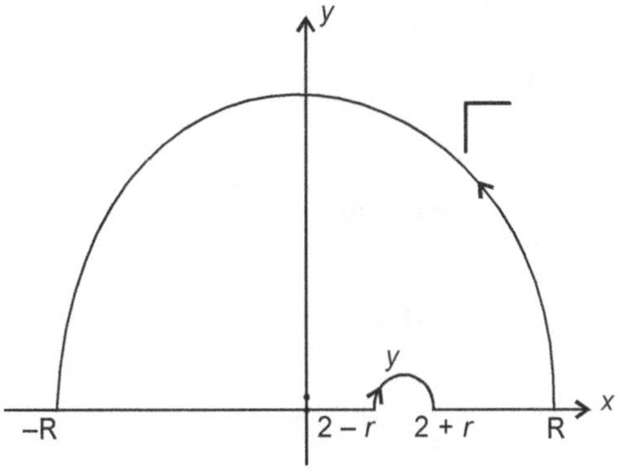

Fig.

$$= \lim_{z\to -1+\sqrt{3}i}\frac{z}{(z-2)(z+1+\sqrt{3}i)}\times 2\pi i$$

$$= \frac{(-1+\sqrt{3}i)(2\pi i)}{(-3+\sqrt{3}i)(2\sqrt{3}i)}$$

$$= \frac{(-i-\sqrt{3})(-3-\sqrt{3}i)2\pi i}{2\sqrt{3}(-3-9)}$$

$$= \frac{3i-\sqrt{3}+3\sqrt{3}+3i}{-24\sqrt{3}}\times 2\pi i$$

$$= -2\pi i\frac{(\sqrt{3}+3i)}{12\sqrt{3}}$$

Now by Jorden's lema as $y \to 0$ and $R \to \infty$

$$\int_0^{\infty} f(x)dx + \int_{-\infty}^{\infty} f(x)dx - \frac{i\pi}{6}$$

$$= \frac{-\pi(\sqrt{3}i-3)}{6\sqrt{3}}$$

as $$\lim_{z\to 2}(z-2)f(z) = \lim_{z\to 2}\frac{z(z-2)}{z^3-8}$$

$$= \lim_{z\to 2}\frac{z}{z^2+2z+4}$$

$$= \frac{2}{4+8} = \frac{1}{6}$$

so $$\int_y f(z)dz = \frac{i(0-\pi)}{6} = \frac{-i\pi}{6}$$

$$\int_{-\infty}^{\infty} f(x)dx = \frac{+3\pi}{6\sqrt{3}} = \frac{\pi}{2\sqrt{3}} = \frac{-\sqrt{3}\pi}{6}$$

31. Let $u(x, u) = 2x(1-y);\ \forall x, y \in \mathrm{I}\mathbb{R}$

$u_x = 2(1-y) = Vy$

$V = 2(y - y^2/2) + f(x)$

$Vx = f'(x) = -uy$

$f'(x) = 2x$

$f(x) = x^2 + c$

so $f(z) = u + iv$

$= (2x - 2xy) + i(2y - y^2) + x^2 + c$

Let $c = -1$

then $V = -(1-y)^2 + x^2$

$V = x^2 - (y-1)^2$

32. Let $f(z)$ be analytic on

$$D = \{z \in c : |z-1| c\}$$

such that $f(1) = 1$

if $f(z) = f(z^2),\ \forall z \in D$

then $f(z) = [f(z)]^2$ for $z \in D$

33. Let $I = \int_C \frac{f(z)dz}{(z-1)(z-2)}$

where $f(z) = \sin\frac{\pi z}{2} + \cos\frac{\pi z}{2}$

where C: $|z| = 3$ oriented anti clockwise

then $I = \oint_z \frac{f(z)/(z-2)}{(z-1)}dz + \oint_z \frac{f(z)/(z-1)}{(z-2)}dz$

$$= 2\pi i\left[\lim_{z\to 1}\frac{\sin\frac{\pi z}{2}+\cos\frac{\pi z}{2}}{(z-2)} + \lim_{z\to 2}\frac{\sin\frac{\pi z}{2}+\cos\frac{\pi z}{2}}{(z-1)}\right]$$

$$= 2\pi i\,[-1+(-1)] = -4\pi i$$

34. Let $\sum_{n=-\infty}^{\infty} b_n z^n = \frac{1}{z\sin nz}$, $0 < |z| < \pi$

$$= \frac{2}{z(e^z - e^{-z})}$$

$$= \frac{2}{z\left[\left(1+z+\frac{z^2}{2!}+\ldots\right)-\left[1-z+\frac{z^2}{2!}\ldots\right]\right]}$$

$$= \frac{2}{2z\left[z+\frac{z^3}{3!}+\frac{z^5}{5!}+\ldots\right]}$$

$$= \frac{1}{z^2}\left[1+\left[\frac{z^2}{3!}+\frac{z^4}{5!}+\ldots\right]^{-1}\right]$$

$$= \frac{1}{z^2}\left[1-\left(\frac{z^2}{3!}+\frac{z^4}{4!}+\ldots\right)+\left(\frac{z^2}{3!}+\frac{z^4}{4!}+\ldots\right)^2\ldots\right]$$

So $b_{-2} = 1$, $b_0 = -1/6$, $b_2 = 7/360$

35. Under the transformation

$$w = \sqrt{\frac{1-iz}{z-i}}$$

$$D = \{z \in ¢ : |z| < 1\}$$

is transformed to $\left\{z \in ¢ : \frac{\pi}{2} < \arg(z) < \pi \right.$

or $\left.\frac{3\pi}{2} < \arg(z) < 2\pi\right\}$

36. $f(z) = \sin\left(\frac{1}{\cos(1/z)}\right)$

Now for zero's of $\sin\left(\frac{1}{\cos\frac{1}{z}}\right)$ are

$$\left(\frac{1}{\cos\frac{1}{z}}\right) = n\pi$$

$$\cos\frac{1}{z} = \frac{1}{n\pi}$$

$$n \in z$$

as $n \to \infty$

$$\cos\frac{1}{z} = 0$$

$\Rightarrow$ $z = \frac{2}{(2n+1)\pi}$,

$n \in z$

so $z = 0$ as $n \to \infty$

Hence $z = 0$ is an essential singularity.

37. Let $f(z) = \sum_{n=0}^{15} z^n$ for $z \in ⊂$

If C : $|z - i| = 2$

then $\oint_c \frac{f(z)dz}{(z-i)^{15}} = 2\pi i \operatorname{Res}_{z=1} f(z)$

as $f(z) = 1 + z + z^2 + \ldots + z^{15}$

$$\operatorname{Res}_{z=1} f(z) = \frac{f^{(14)}(i)}{14!} = \frac{14!+15!i}{14!}$$

$$= 1 + 15i$$

so $\oint_c \frac{f(z)dz}{(z-i)^{15}} = 2\pi i(1+15i)$

38. Let $\sum_{n=-\infty}^{\infty} a_n(z+1)^n = \sin\left(\frac{z}{z+1}\right)$

$$a_{-z} = \frac{1}{2\pi i}\oint_c (z+1)\sin\left(\frac{z}{z+1}\right)dz$$

$$= \frac{1}{2\pi i}.0 = 0$$

39. $\oint_c\left(\frac{\partial u}{\partial y}dx - \frac{\partial u}{\partial x}dy\right)$

$$= \iint_R\left(\frac{\partial^2 u}{\partial x\partial y} - \frac{\partial^2 u}{\partial y\partial x}\right)dxdy = 0$$

40. $f(z) = \dfrac{e^{iz}}{z(z^2+1)}$ has poles at $z = 0, z = \pm i$

only $z = i$ lies on upper half plane.

so $\quad \underset{z=i}{\text{Res}}\, f(z) = \lim\limits_{z \to i} \dfrac{e^{iz}}{z(z+i)}$

$$= \frac{e^{-1}}{i(zi)} = \frac{-e^{-1}}{2} = -\frac{1}{2e}$$

41. $\int\limits_{-\infty}^{\infty} f(x)dx = \dfrac{\pi}{a^2}(1-e^{-a}) \; a > 0$

i.e., $\quad \int\limits_{-\infty}^{\infty} \dfrac{\sin x dx}{x(x^2+a^2)} = \dfrac{\pi}{a^2}(1-e^{-a})$

here $a = 1$

$$\int\limits_{-\infty}^{\infty} \frac{\sin x dx}{x(x^2+a^2)} = \pi(1-e^{-1})$$

42. Let s be the open unit desk and $f: s \to c$ be a real valued analytic function with $f(0) = 1$ then set $\{z \in s : f(z) \neq 1\}$ is empty set.

Since no real valued function can be analytic it will be analytic. If it is constant.

So $f(z) = 1, \forall\, z \in s$.

43. $\dfrac{(z-z_1)(z_2-z_3)}{(z_1-z_2)(z_3-z)} = \dfrac{(w-w_1)(w_2-w_3)}{(w_1-w_2)(w_3-w)}$

$$\frac{(z+1)(i+1)}{(-1-i)(-i-z)} = \frac{(w-1)(\infty-0)}{(1-\infty)(0-w)}$$

$$\left(\frac{\infty}{1-\infty}\right)\left(\frac{w-1}{0-w}\right) = \frac{2i(z+1)}{(1+i)(z+i)}$$

$$\frac{w-1}{w} = \frac{2i(z+1)}{(z+i)(1+i)}$$

$$\frac{1}{w} = 1 - \frac{2i(z+1)}{(z+i)(1+i)}$$

$$= \frac{(z+i)(1+i) - 2i(z+1)}{(z+i)(1+i)}$$

$$= \frac{z+iz+i-1-2iz-2i}{z+i+iz-1}$$

$$= \frac{z-iz-i-1}{z+iz+i-1}$$

$$\frac{1}{w} = \frac{z(1-i)-(i+1)}{z(1+i)+(i-1)}$$

$$w = \frac{z(1+i)+(i-1)}{z(1-i)-(i+1)} = f(z)$$

$$f(1) = \frac{1+i+i-1}{1-i-i-1} = -1$$

44. $\oint \dfrac{dz}{z^2+4}$ has poles at $z = \pm 2i$

$|z - 3i| = 2$

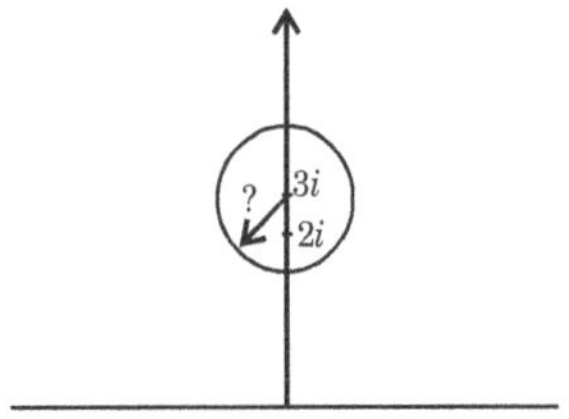

Fig.

$$\oint\limits_{|z-3i|=2} \frac{dz}{z^2+4} = 2\pi i \times \lim_{z \to 2i}(z-2i)\frac{1}{z^2+4}$$

$$= 2\pi i \times \frac{1}{4i} = \frac{\pi}{2}$$

45. Let T be the closed unit desk and ∂T be the unit circle. Then for every analytic funtion $f: \mathrm{T} \to \mathbb{C}$, $|f|$ attains its maximum on ∂T but need not attain its minimum on ∂T.

46. Let $\{z : |z| < 3\} = \mathrm{S}$ and $f: \mathrm{S} \to \mathbb{C}$ be an analytic function such that

$$f\left(1+\frac{\sqrt{2}}{n}i\right) = \frac{-2}{n^2}, \forall\, n \in \mathrm{N}$$

Then $f(\sqrt{2}) = 3 + 2\sqrt{2}$

47. $f(z) = \cos z - \dfrac{\sin z}{z}, \; \forall\; z \in \mathbb{C}$

and $\quad f(0) = 0$

$\quad g(z) = \sin h\, z$ for $z \in \mathbb{C}$

$$\lim_{z \to 0} \frac{\dfrac{z\cos z - \sin z}{z}}{z^m} = \lim_{z \to 0} \frac{z\cos z - \sin z}{z^{m+1}}$$

$$= \lim_{z \to 0} - \frac{z\sin z + \cos z - \cos z}{(m+1)z^m}$$

$$= \lim_{z \to 0} \frac{\sin z}{(m+1)z^{m-1}}$$

$$= -\frac{1}{3} \text{ for } m = 2$$

$f(2)$ has zero of order z.

48. $\dfrac{g(z)}{zf'(z)} = \dfrac{\sin h z}{z\cos z - \sin z} = f(z)$

$$\lim_{z \to 0} \frac{z^2 \sin h z}{z\cos z - \sin z} = \lim_{z \to 0} \frac{2z \sin h z + z^2 \cos h z}{-z\sin z + \cos z - \cos z}$$

$$= \lim_{z \to 0} \frac{2\sin h z + z\cos h z}{-\sin z}$$

$$= \lim_{z\to 0} \frac{2\cosh z + \cosh z + 2\sinh z}{-\cos z}$$

$$= -3 \neq 0$$

$\Rightarrow$ pole of order 2.

49. Let $s = \{0\} \cup \left[\frac{1}{4n+7} : n \in N\right]$

Now the s consists the limit point of set s.

i.e., $\bar{s} = s$, so s is closed.

Now if $f(z)$ if analytic function and its zero's are at $\left[\frac{1}{4n+7} : n \in N\right]$ then, limit point of zero's is isolated essential singularity so '0' is an isolated essential singularity so '0' can't be zero of $f(z)$. Hence there is no such analytic function which vanish only on S.

50. Let s be the open unit disk and $f : s \to \mathbb{C}$ be a real-valued analytic function with f(0) = 1. Then set $\{z \in s : f(z) \neq 1\}$ is empty set. Since, no real valued function can be analytic will be analytic if it is constant. So, $f(z) = 1 \; \forall z \in s$

51. $\int_0^{2\pi} f(e^{it})\cos + dt$

Let $e^{it} = z \quad \Rightarrow \quad ie^{it}\, dt = dz$

$$= \oint_{|z|=1} f(z)\cos\left(\frac{\log z}{i}\right) dz / iz$$

$$= 2\pi f'(0)$$

52. G_1 and G_2 are the images of disc $\{z \in \mathbb{C} : |z+1| < 1\}$ under the transfor-mations

$$w = \frac{(1-i)z+2}{(1+i)z+2}$$

and $$w = \frac{(1+i)z+2}{(1-i)z+2}$$

then, $G_1 = \{w \in \mathbb{C} : Im(w) > 0\}$

$G_2 = \{w \in \mathbb{C} : Im\,(w) < 0\}$

53. $f(z) = 2z^2 - 1$

Then max $|f(z)| = 2|z^2| + 1 = 3$

on the boundary

54. $f(z) = \frac{1}{(z^2 - 3z + 2)} = \frac{1}{(z^2 - 2z - z + 2)}$

$$= \frac{1}{(z-2)(z-1)}$$

Now for $|z| > 2$ and $|z| > 1$

$$\Rightarrow \frac{2}{|z|} < 1 \text{ and } \frac{1}{|z|} < 1$$

$$f(z) = -\frac{1}{(z-1)} + \frac{1}{(z-2)}$$

$$= -\frac{1}{z\left(1-\frac{1}{z}\right)} + \frac{1}{z\left(1-\frac{2}{z}\right)}$$

$$= \frac{1}{z}\left[\left(1-\frac{2}{z}\right)^{-1} - \left(1-\frac{1}{z}\right)^{-1}\right]$$

$$= \frac{1}{z}\left[\left(1+\frac{2}{z}+\frac{4}{z^2}+\ldots\right) - \left(1+\frac{1}{z}+\frac{1}{z^2}+\ldots\right)\right]$$

$$= \frac{1}{z}\left[\frac{1}{z}+\frac{3}{z^2}+\ldots\right]$$

$$= \frac{1}{z^2}+\frac{3}{z^3}+\ldots$$

So coefficient of $\frac{1}{z^3} = 3$

55. Let $f : \mathbb{C} \to \mathbb{C}$ be an arbitary analytic function such that $f(0) = 0$ and $f(1) = 2$ then $\exists$ a bounded sequence $[z_n]$ such that $|f(z_n)| > n$.

56. $f : \mathbb{C} \to \mathbb{C}$

such that

$$f(z) = \begin{cases} 0, & if\, Re(z) = 0 \text{ or } Im(z) = 0 \\ z, & \text{otherwise} \end{cases}$$

Then, the set of points, where f is analytic is $s = \{z : Re(z) \neq 0$ and $Im(z) \neq 0\}$

57. $\int_0^{2\pi} e^{(ei\theta - i\theta)} d\theta$

Let $e^{i\theta} = z$

$\Rightarrow$ $ie^{i\theta} = dz$

$$= \frac{1}{i}\oint_c \frac{e^z}{z^2} dz = 2\pi$$

58. $$f(z) = \frac{\cot \pi z}{(z+a)^2}$$

where "a" is a constant (a ≠ 0, ±1, ±2, .).

Then poles of $f(z)$ at $z = -a$ (pole of orders) and at $z = n, n \in z$ (simple poles)

Res $z = -a$ $f(z) = -\pi \operatorname{cosec}^2 \pi a$ and

$$\operatorname*{Res}_{z=n} f(z) = \lim_{z\to n}(z-n)\frac{\cos \pi z}{\sin \pi z\left(z+a^2\right)}$$

$$= \frac{1}{\pi}\frac{i}{(n+a)^2}$$

so sum of residues of $\frac{\cot \pi z}{(z+a)^2}$ at

$$\text{poles} = \frac{1}{\pi}\sum_{n=-\infty}^{\infty}\frac{1}{(n+a)^2} - \pi \operatorname{cosec}^2 \pi a$$

59. Let $f(z)$ be an entire function such that for some constant α, $|f(z)| \le \alpha |z|^3$ for $|z| \ge 1$ and $f(z) = f(iz)\ \forall z \in c$

Then

$$f(z) = a_0 + a_1 z + a_2 z^2 + a_3 z^3$$

$$f(z) = f(iz)$$

$$\Rightarrow a_0 + a_1 z + a_2 z^2 + a_3 z^3$$

$$= a_0 + a_1 iz - a_2 z^2 - a_3 iz^3$$

$$\Rightarrow a_1(1-i)z + 2a_2 z^2 + (1-i)\,a_3 z^3 = 0$$

$$\Rightarrow \quad a_1 = 0 \qquad [\because 1 \neq i]$$

$$a_3 = 0 \qquad [\because 1 \neq i]$$

$$a_2 = 0$$

so $f(z) = a_0$ i.e. constant

60.

$$u = x + \frac{x}{x^2 + y^2}$$

$$\frac{\partial u}{\partial x} = 1 + \frac{1}{x^2+y^2} - \frac{2x^2}{\left(x^2+y^2\right)^2}$$

$$= \frac{1 + y^2 - x^2}{\left(x^2+y^2\right)^2}$$

$$\frac{\partial^2 u}{\partial x^2} = \frac{-2x}{\left(x^2+y^2\right)^2} - \frac{\left(y^2-x^2\right).2.2x}{\left(x^2+y^2\right)^3}$$

$$= \frac{-2x\left(x^2+y^2\right) - 4x\left(y^2-x^2\right)}{\left(x^2+y^2\right)^3}$$

$$= \frac{-2x^3 - 2xy^2 - 4xy^2 + 4x^3}{\left(x^2+y^2\right)^3}$$

$$= \frac{2x^3 - 6xy^2}{\left(x^2+y^2\right)^3}$$

$$\frac{\partial u}{\partial y} = -\frac{x.2y}{\left(x^2+y^2\right)^2}$$

$$\frac{\partial^2 u}{\partial y^2} = \frac{-2x}{\left(x^2+y^2\right)} + \frac{4xy.2y}{\left(x^2+y^2\right)^3}$$

$$= \frac{-2x^3 - 2xy^2 + 8xy^2}{\left(x^2+y^2\right)^3}$$

$$= \frac{6xy^2 - 2x^3}{\left(x^2+y^2\right)^3}$$

so $\dfrac{\partial^2 u}{\partial x^2} + \dfrac{\partial^2 u}{\partial y^2} = 0$

so $u = \dfrac{1}{\left(1 + x^2 + y^2\right)}$

be not a harmonic function so not a real part of $f(z)$

61.

$$\frac{1}{R} = \lim_{n\to\infty}\left(\frac{\left(1+\frac{1}{n}\right)^{n^2}}{n^3}\right)^{1/n}$$

$$= \lim_{n\to\infty}\frac{\left(1+\frac{1}{n}\right)^{n}}{\left(n^{1/n}\right)^3} = e/1$$

$$\Rightarrow \quad R = 1/e$$

62. Let $z = \log i^{1/4}$

$$\Rightarrow \quad z = \frac{1}{4}\log i$$

But $i = e^{i\pi/2}$

$$\Rightarrow \quad z = \frac{1}{4}\log e^{i\pi/2}$$

Hence principal value is $\dfrac{i\pi}{2}$

63.

$$f(z) = x^2 + iy^2$$

$$g(z) = x^2 + y^2 + ixy$$

$$u = x^2,\ v = y^2$$

$$u = x^2 + y^2 \quad v = xy$$

For analytic

$$\frac{\partial u}{\partial x} = 2x, \quad \frac{\partial v}{\partial y} = x$$

$$\frac{\partial u}{\partial x} = \frac{\partial v}{\partial y}$$

But at $z = 0$ *i.e.,* $x = 0, y = 0$

Hence, f is analytic $\dfrac{\partial u}{\partial x} = \dfrac{\partial v}{\partial y}$

Hence, g is also analytic

64.

$$\log\left(\frac{z}{z-1}\right) = -\log\left(\frac{z-1}{z}\right)$$

$$= -\log\left(1 - \frac{1}{z}\right)$$

$$= -\frac{1}{z} - \frac{1}{2z^2} - \ldots\ldots\ldots$$

Hence, coefficient of $\dfrac{1}{z}$ is –1.

66. $I \int_{-\infty}^{\infty} \frac{\cos x}{1+x^2} = dx$

$$= 2\int_0^{\infty} \frac{\cos x}{1+x^2}\, dx \qquad ...(i)$$

$$\left[\because \frac{\cos x}{1+x^2} \text{ is even function}\right]$$

Let $\quad I_1 \int_0^{\infty} \frac{\cos x}{1+x^2} = dx$

Let suppose $\int_0^{\infty} 2z \exp\{-(a^2+x^2)z^2\}dz = \frac{1}{a^2+x^2}$

If $a = 1$, then $\int_0^{\infty} 2z \exp\{-(1+x^2)z^2\}dz = \frac{1}{1+x^2}$

Now multiplying both sides by $\cos x$ and integrating from 0 to ∞ with respect to x, we have

$$I_1 = \int_0^{\infty} \frac{\cos x}{1+x^2} dx$$

$$= \int_0^{\infty}\int_0^{\infty} \cos x \times 2z \exp[-(1+x^2)z^2]dz\, dx$$

$$= \int_0^{\infty} 2ze^{-z^2}\left[\int_0^{\infty} e^{-x^2z^2} \cos x\, dy\right] dz$$

$$= \int_0^{\infty} 2ze^{-z^2} \frac{\sqrt{\pi}}{2z} \exp\left(-\frac{1}{4z^2}\right) dz$$

$$= \sqrt{\pi} \int_0^{\infty} \exp\left(-z^2 - \frac{1}{4z^2}\right) dz$$

$$= \sqrt{\pi} \int_0^{\infty} \exp\left(-a^2\left(z^2 + \frac{1}{4z^2}\right)\right) dz$$

$$= \sqrt{\pi}\, \frac{\sqrt{\pi}}{2} \exp\left(-2\frac{1}{2}\cdot 1\right) = \frac{\pi}{2e}$$

$$\Rightarrow I = 2I_1 = 2.\frac{\pi}{2e} = \frac{\pi}{e}$$

68. $f : (0, 2) \to R$

$$f(x) = \begin{cases} x^2 & \text{if } x \text{ is rational} \\ 2x-1 & \text{if } x \text{ is irrational} \end{cases}$$

$$f'(x) = \begin{cases} 2x & \text{if } x \text{ is rational} \\ 2 & \text{if } x \text{ is irrational} \end{cases}$$

$\Rightarrow$ $f(x)$ is differentiable only when $x = 1$

i.e., $f(x)$ is differentiable exactly at one point.

69. $f(x, y) = \begin{cases} x^2+y^2 & \text{if } x \text{ and } y \text{ are rational} \\ 0 & \text{otherwise} \end{cases}$

It shows $f(x, y)$ is continuous at (0, 0)

But it is not differentiable at (0, 0)

70. $\quad f(x, y) = x^4 + y^2$

$$\frac{\partial f}{\partial x} = 4x^3$$

$$\Rightarrow \quad r = \frac{\partial^2 f}{\partial x^2} = 12x^2$$

$$\frac{\partial f}{\partial y} = 2y$$

$$\Rightarrow \quad t = \frac{\partial^2 f}{\partial y^2} = 2$$

$$s = \frac{\partial^2 f}{\partial x \partial y} = 0$$

$\Rightarrow \quad rt - s^2 = 0 \quad \Rightarrow$ not a local minimum at (0, 0)

$\Rightarrow \quad g(x, y) = x^4 + y^2 - 10\, x^2y$

$$\frac{\partial g}{\partial x} = 4x^3 - 20xy$$

$$\Rightarrow \quad r = \frac{\partial^2 g}{\partial x^2} = 12x^2 - 20y$$

$$\Rightarrow \quad \frac{\partial g}{\partial y} = 2y - 10\, x^2,$$

$$t = \frac{\partial^2 g}{\partial y^2} = 2$$

$$s = \frac{\partial^2 g}{\partial x \partial y} = 0$$

$\Rightarrow \quad rt - s^2 = (12x^2 - 20)\, 2y - 0 = 0$ at (0, 0) not a local minimum at (0, 0)

Hence neither f nor g has a local minimum.

71.

$$\alpha_1 = \int_0^1 xy^2dx + \int_0^1 (x^2y + 2x)\, dy$$

$$= \left[\frac{x^2y^2}{2}\right]_0^1 + \left[\frac{x^2y^2}{2} + 2xy\right]_0^1$$

$$= \frac{y^2}{2} + \frac{x^2}{2} + 2x$$

$$\alpha_2 = \int_{-1}^0 xy^2dx + \int_{-1}^0 (x^2y + 2x)\, dy$$

$$= \left[\frac{x^2y^2}{2}\right]_{-1}^0 + \left[\frac{x^2y^2}{2} + 2xy\right]_{-1}^0$$

$$= -\frac{y^2}{2} - \frac{x^2}{2} + 2x$$

72. $f:(0, 2\pi) \to R^2$

$f(t) = (\cos t, \sin t), \quad 0 \le t < 2\pi$

This function is not continuous in its domain

Similarly, $g(t) = (\cos t, \sin t), 0 \le t < 2\pi$

$g : [0, 2\pi] \to R^2$

This is continuous in its domain

Hence g is uniformly continuous but not f.

74. E is a nonmeasurable subset of (0, 1)

$$f_1(x) = \begin{cases} 1/x & \text{if } x \in E \\ 0 & \text{if } x \notin E \end{cases} \quad ...(i)$$

$$f_2(x) = \begin{cases} 0 & \text{if } x \in E \\ 1/x & \text{if } x \notin E \end{cases} \quad ...(ii)$$

By these two equations, f_1 is measurable but not f_2.

75.
$$I_1 = \int_1^\infty \frac{dx}{(1+x^2)^{1/2}},$$

Here $\phi(x) = \dfrac{1}{(1+x^2)^{1/2}}$

Let $f(x) = \dfrac{1}{x}$

Now for $x \ge 1$, $\left|\dfrac{1}{(1+x^2)^{1/2}}\right| < \dfrac{1}{x}$,

i.e. $|\phi(x)| < f(x)$

But $\displaystyle\int_1^\infty \frac{dx}{x}$ is divergent

Hence by comparison test it follows that $\displaystyle\int_1^\infty \frac{dx}{(1+x^2)^{1/2}}$ is convergent.

Similarly, $I_2 = \displaystyle\int_1^\infty \frac{dx}{(1+x^2)^{3/2}}$,

Here $\phi(x) = \dfrac{1}{(1+x^2)^{3/2}}$

Let $f(x) = \dfrac{1}{x^3}$

i.e., $x > 1$ and $\left|\dfrac{1}{(1+x^2)^{3/2}}\right| < \dfrac{1}{x^3}$

So $\displaystyle\int_1^\infty \frac{dx}{x^3}$ is convergent

Hence by comparison test, $\displaystyle\int_1^\infty \frac{dx}{(1+x^2)^{3/2}}$ is convergent.

76. If D is an open unit disk in C and $f: C \to D$ with $f(10) = 1/2$ then, $f(10 + i) = 1/2$.

Since every entire and bounded function is constant (by Liouville's Theorem)

77. Let $Z = 4^{4-i} = e^{(4-i)\log 4}$

$= e^{4\log 4} . e^{-i\log 4}$

$= e^{\log 256} (\cos(\ln 4) + i \sin(\ln 4))$

so $\text{Re}(z) = 256 \cos(\ln 4)$

78. The Taylor's series expansion of $f(z)$ about $z = z_0$ is given by

$$f(z) = \sum_{n=0}^{\infty} a_n (z - z_0)^n$$

where $a_n = \dfrac{1}{2\pi i}\displaystyle\int_C \frac{f(z)}{(z-z_0)^{n+1}} dZ$

$= \dfrac{f^n(z_0)}{nl_0}$

Here $f(z) = \sin z, z_0 = \pi/4$

$a_6 = \dfrac{f^{v1}(z_0)}{61} = \dfrac{f^{v1}(\pi/4)}{720}$

$\Rightarrow \dfrac{\left[\dfrac{d_6}{dz^6}(\sin z)\right] = \pi 4}{720}$

$= \dfrac{[\sin(z + 6.\pi/2)]_z = \pi 4}{720}$

$\left[\because D^n \sin z = \sin\left(z + \dfrac{n\pi}{2}\right)\right]$

$= \dfrac{[\sin(3\pi + z)]_z = \pi/4}{720}$

$= \dfrac{[\sin^2]_z = \pi/4}{720} = \dfrac{1}{720.\sqrt{2}}$

80. $f(z) = \dfrac{1}{z-1} - \dfrac{1}{z-2} \ : |z| > 2$

$= \dfrac{1}{2}\left[\left(1 - \dfrac{1}{z}\right) - \left(1 - \dfrac{2}{z}\right)^{-1}\right]$

$= \dfrac{1}{2}\left[\left(1 - \dfrac{1}{z}\right) - \left(1 - \dfrac{2}{z}\right)^{-1}\right]$

$= \dfrac{1}{2}\left[1 + \dfrac{1}{z} + \dfrac{1}{z^2} + \ldots\right] - \left[1 + \dfrac{2}{z} + \left(\dfrac{2}{z}\right)^2 + \ldots\right]$

$= \dfrac{1}{z}\left[-\dfrac{1}{z} - \dfrac{3}{z^2}\ldots\right] = \left[-\dfrac{1}{z^2} - \dfrac{3}{z^3}\ldots\right] = -\dfrac{1}{z^2} - \dfrac{3}{z^3}\ldots$

Coefficient of $\dfrac{1}{z^2} = -1$

81. $\dfrac{(w-w_1)(w_2-w_3)}{(w_1-w_2)(w_3-w)} = \dfrac{(z-z_1)(z_2-z_3)}{(z_1-z_2)(z_3-z)}$

$\Rightarrow \dfrac{(w+i)(1-i)}{(-i-1)(i-w)} = \dfrac{(z+1)(0-1)}{(-1-0)(1-z)}$

$\Rightarrow \dfrac{[f(1-i)+i(1-i)]}{-(i+1)(i-f(1-i))} = \dfrac{(1-i+1)(-1)}{(-1)(1-1+i)}$

$= \dfrac{(2-i)}{i}\dfrac{(i+1)}{(i-1)}$

$\Rightarrow f(1-i) = -2+i$

82. $\displaystyle\oint_{|z|=1} \frac{2\,\mathrm{Re}(z)}{z+2}dz = \int_0^{2\pi} \frac{\sin\theta d\theta i.e^{i\theta}}{e^{i\theta}}$

$\displaystyle = i\int_0^{2\pi} \sin\theta d\theta = 0$

83. $z^5 + 3z^3 + z^2 + 1 = f(z)$ be the complex polynomial and the circle is $|z| = 2$ then zero's inside the circle one defined by

$f(z) \neq g(z) = f(z),$

where $g(z) = z^5$, $f(z) = 3z^3 + z^2 + 1$

$\left|\dfrac{f(z)}{g(z)}\right| \leq \dfrac{3.2+z^2+1}{25}$

$= \dfrac{24+4+1}{32} = \dfrac{29}{32} < 1$

$\Rightarrow \quad |f(z)| < |g(2)|$

$\Rightarrow f(z)$ has all five zero's in $|z| = 2$

84. $f = u + iv$ ...(*i*)

$g = v + iu$ ...(*ii*)

be non-zero analytic function on $|z| < 1$

Then, if follows that

$u_x = v_y$ and $v_x = -u_y$ from equation ...(*i*)

$v_x = u_y$ and $u_x = -v_y$ from equation ...(*ii*)

$u_n = 0\ v_y$ and $v_n = 0\ v_y$

$u = c_1$ and $v = c_1$

$\Rightarrow f$ is constant fuction

$\phi_0 \qquad f^1 \equiv 0$

85. $f(z) = (z^2 z) = (x+iy)^2(x-iy)$

$= (x^2+y^2)(x+iy)$

$= x(x^2+y^2) + iy(x^2+y^2)$

$= w + iv$

Since, $\quad u_x = v_y = 0,\ u_y = -u_x = 0$

Thus, $f(z)$ satisfies C – R equations and also $f(z)$ is a polynomial, so $f(z)$ is analytic.

86. Required transformation is

$(w, w_1, w_2, w_3) = (z, z_1, z_2, z_3)$

or $\quad (w, 0, 1, \infty) = (z, -i, \infty. 1)$

or $\quad \dfrac{(w-0)(1-\infty)}{(0-1)(\infty-w)} = \dfrac{(z+i)(\infty-1)}{(-i-\infty)(1-z)}$

or $\quad \dfrac{w(-\infty)}{(w-\infty)} = \dfrac{(z+i)(\infty)}{(-\infty)(1-z)}$

or $\quad w = \dfrac{z+i}{z-1}$

88. Both singularities are within the curve and are equal. So by Cavely Residue theorem

$I_1 = I_2.$

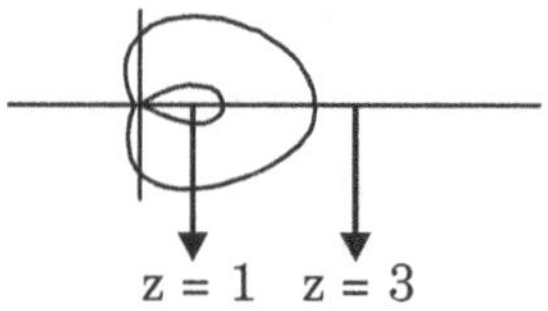

89. By minimum modulus theorem : Let $f(z)$ be analytic inside and on a simple closed curve c. If $f(z) = 0$ inside c; then $|f(z)|$ must assume its minimum value on *c*.

90. $f(z)$ has a simple pole at $z = 1$ with residue 1. Therefore the principal part of $f(z)$

must contain the term $\dfrac{1}{z-1}$.

Again $z = 2$ is a double pole with residue – 2, so that the principal part of $f(z)$ must contain the term $\dfrac{-2}{z-2} + \dfrac{b}{(z-2)^2}$.

Hence $f(z) = a_0 + a_1 z + a_2 z^2 + \dots + \dfrac{1}{z-1} + \dfrac{-2}{z-2} + \dfrac{b}{(z-2)^2}$ ...(*i*)

Given, as $z \to \infty$, $f(z)$ is bounded so that there are no singularities at $z = \infty$. It means that $f\left(\dfrac{1}{t}\right)$ has no singularity at $t = 0$.

Hence principal part of $f\left(\dfrac{1}{t}\right)$ should not contain any term.

$$f\left(\frac{1}{t}\right) = a_0 + \frac{a_1}{t} + \frac{a_2}{t^2} + \dots + \frac{t}{1-t} + \frac{-2t}{1-2t} + \frac{bt^2}{(1-t)^2}$$

The principal part of $f\left(\dfrac{1}{t}\right)$ is $\dfrac{a_1}{t} + \dfrac{a_2}{t^2} + \dots$

The above can be zero if $a_1 = 0$, $a_2 = 0$, $a_m = 0$.

$\therefore\ f(z) = a_0 + \dfrac{1}{z-1} + \dfrac{-2}{z-2} + \dfrac{b}{(z-2)^2}$ ...(*ii*)

$$f(0) = a_0 - 1 + 1 + \frac{b}{4}$$

$$= a_0 + \frac{b}{4} = 0 \qquad ...(iii)$$

and $$f(3) = a_0 + \frac{1}{2} - 2 + \frac{b}{1} = a_0 + b - \frac{3}{2}$$

$$= -\frac{3}{4}$$

$$\Rightarrow \quad a_0 + b = +\frac{3}{2} - \frac{3}{4}$$

$$= \frac{3}{4}$$

From equation (*iii*),

$$4a_0 + b = 0$$

$$\Rightarrow \quad b = -4a_0$$

$$\therefore \quad -4a_0 + a_0 = \frac{3}{4}$$

$$\Rightarrow \quad a_0 = -\frac{1}{4}$$

$$b = 1$$

$$\therefore \quad f(z) = -\frac{1}{4} + \frac{1}{z-1} + \frac{-2}{z-2} + \frac{1}{(z-2)^2}$$

91. $$\tan\frac{1}{z-2} = \frac{\sin\frac{1}{z-2}}{\cos\frac{1}{z-2}}$$

For singularities,

$$\cos\frac{1}{z-2} = 0$$

$$\Rightarrow \quad \frac{1}{z-2} = (2n+1)\frac{\pi}{2}$$

$$z - 2 = \frac{2}{\pi(2n+1)}$$

Hence, $z = 2$ is non-isolated essential singularity.

92. $$\text{Residue} = \underset{z\to i}{\text{Lt}} \frac{d}{dt}\cot \pi z$$

$$= -\frac{\pi}{\sin h^2 \pi}$$

From Cauchy residue theorem,

$$\text{I} = 2\pi \text{ i (R)}$$

$$= 2\pi i \times \frac{-\pi}{\sin h^2\pi}$$

$$= -\frac{2\pi^2 i}{\sin h^2 \pi}$$

95. $$f(z) = \frac{1}{1-z}$$

$$= (1-z)^{-1}$$

$$= 1 + z + z^2 + ...$$

Radius of Convergence,

$$\text{R} = \underset{n\to\infty}{\text{Lt}}\left|\frac{a_n}{a_{n+1}}\right|$$

$$= \underset{n\to\infty}{\text{Lt}}\left(\frac{1}{1}\right) = 1$$

96. $$\text{I} = \int_{\Gamma} \frac{\cos z}{z^2} dz$$

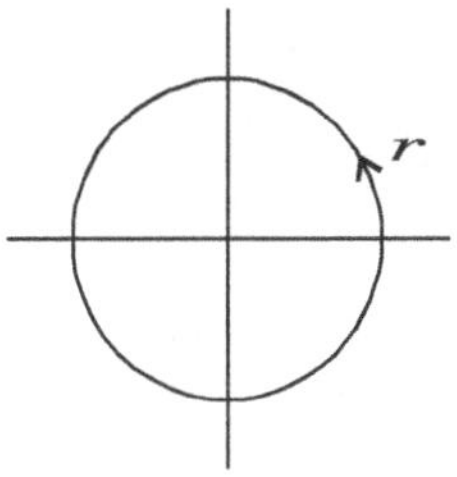

Residue at origin,

$$\text{R} = \underset{z\to 0}{\text{Lt}} \frac{d'}{dz'}(\cos z)$$

$$= \underset{z\to 0}{\text{Lt}}(-\sin z)$$

$$\therefore \quad \text{I} = 2\pi i, \text{R} = 0$$

98. Given, $$f(z) = \sin\frac{1}{z}$$

zeros of $f(z)$ are givn by

$$\sin\frac{1}{z} = 0$$

$$\therefore \quad \frac{1}{z} = \pi x$$

$$\Rightarrow \quad z = \frac{1}{n\pi};$$

where $n = 0, \pm 1, \pm 2, ...$

Clearly limit point of above sequence of zeros is given by $z = 0$, which therefore is an isolated essential singularity.

105. Given $z = a$ is an isolated singularity of $f(z)$. By the definition of isolated singularity there exist a circle which has no other singularity. That gives us $f(z)$ cannot be bounded in a neighbourhood of isolated singularity $z = a$ (using the definition of neighbourhood of $z = a$).

110. We have

$$f(z) = \frac{1}{3-2z}$$

$$= \frac{1}{2\left[\frac{3}{2} - z\right]}$$

$$= \frac{1}{2\left[\frac{3}{2} - 3 - (z-3)\right]}$$

$$= \frac{1}{2\left[\frac{3-6}{2} - (z-3)\right]}$$

$$= \frac{1}{2\left[-\frac{3}{2} - (z-3)\right]}$$

$$= \frac{1}{2.\left(-\frac{3}{2}\right)\left[1 + \frac{2}{3}(z-3)\right]}$$

$$= -\frac{1}{3}\left[1 + \frac{2}{3}(z-3)\right]^{-1}$$

$$= -\frac{1}{3}\left[1 - \frac{2}{3}(z-3) + \frac{4}{9}(z-3)^2 - .....\right]$$

and the region of convergence is

$$|z-3| < \frac{3}{2}$$

111. Let $\quad I = \int_C \frac{e^{1/z^2}}{z^2+1} dz;$

$$|z-i| = \frac{7}{2}$$

Here the singular points are

$$z = \pm i.$$

$$\therefore \int_c \frac{e^{1/z^2}}{(z+i)(z-i)} dx$$

$$= \frac{1}{2i}\int_c e^{1/z^2}\left[\frac{1}{z-i} - \frac{1}{z+i}\right] dz$$

$$= \frac{1}{2i}\int_c \frac{e^{1/z^2}}{z-i} dz - \frac{1}{2i}\int_c \frac{e^{1/z^2}}{z+i} dz$$

$$= \frac{1}{2i} 2\pi i\, e^{1/(i)^2} - \frac{1}{2i} 2\pi i\, e^{1/(-i)^2}$$

$$= 0$$

112. Let $\quad w = f(z)$

$$= u(x, y) + iv(x, y)$$

$$\therefore \quad f'(z) = \frac{\partial u}{\partial x} + i\frac{\partial u}{\partial x}$$

$$= \frac{\partial u}{\partial x} - i\frac{\partial u}{\partial y}$$

[Using Cauchy Riemann equation]

Given :

$$u(x, y) = 2xy + \cosh x.\ \sin y$$

and $\quad f(0) = 0$

$$\therefore \quad \frac{\partial u}{\partial x} = 2y - \sinh x \sin y$$

and $\quad \frac{\partial u}{\partial y} = 2x + \cosh x \cos y.$

Thus, $\quad f'(z) = 2y - \sinh x \sin y - i\,[2x + \cosh x \cos y]$

Using Milne's Thomson method

$$f'(z) = 2(0) - \sinh z \sin(0) - i[2z + \cosh(z)\cos 0]$$

$$= -i[2z + \cosh z]$$

Integrating with respect to z, we get

$$f(z) = -i\left[\frac{2z^2}{2} + \sin hz\right] + c$$

Using $\quad f(0) = 0$, we get $c = 0$

$$\therefore \quad f(z) = -[z^2 + \sin hz]$$

This is required analytic function.

where $\quad z = x + iy,$

■■

3 CHAPTER

Real Analysis

2016

1. Let $S = [0, 1) \cup [2, 3]$ and $f : S \to \mathbb{R}$ be a strictly increasing function such that f(S) is connected. Which of the following statements is TRUE?

   (a) f has exactly one discontinuity

   (b) f has exactly two discontinuities

   (c) f has infinitely many discontinuities

   (d) f is continuous

2. Maximum $\{x + y : (x, y) \in \overline{B(0,1)}\}$ is equal to ______.

3. Let u(x, t) be the d'Alembert's solution of the initial value problem for the wave equation

   $u_{tt} - c^2 u_{xx} = 0$

   $u(x, 0) = f(x),\ u_t(x, 0) = g(x),$

   where c is a positive real number and f, g are smooth odd functions. Then, u(0, 1) is equal to ________.

4. Let $P_n(x)$ be the Legendre polynomial of degree n and $I = \int_{-1}^{1} x^k P_n(x)dx$, where k is a non-negative integer. Consider the following statements P and Q:

   (P) : $I = 0$ if $k < n$.

   (Q) : $I = 0$ if $n - k$ is an odd integer.

   Which of the above statements hold TRUE?

   (a) both P and Q (b) only P

   (c) only Q (d) Neither P nor Q

5. Let $c_0 = \{(x_n) : x_n \in \mathbb{R}, x_n \to 0\}$ and $M = \{(x_n) \in c_0 : x_1 + x_2 + ... + x_{10} = 0\}$.
   Then, dimension (C_0/M) is equal to _______.

6. Consider $(\mathbb{R}^2, \|\cdot\|_\infty)$, where $\|(x, y)\|_\infty =$ maximum $\{|x|, |y|\}$. Let $f: \mathbb{R}^2 \to \mathbb{R}$ be defined by $f(x, y) = \dfrac{x+y}{2}$ and f the norm preserving linear extension of f to $(\mathbb{R}^3, \|\cdot\|_\infty)$. Then, f(1, 1, 1) is equal to __________.

7. Let $\gamma = \{z \in \mathbb{C} : |z| = 2\}$ be oriented in the counter-clockwise direction. Let

   $$I = \frac{1}{2\pi i}\oint_\gamma z^7 \cos\left(\frac{1}{z^2}\right)dz.$$

8. Let γ be the triangular path connecting the points (0, 0), (2, 2) and (0, 2) in the counter- clockwise direction in $\mathbb{R}^2$. Then

   $$I = \oint_\gamma \sin(x^3)dx + 6xy\,dy$$

   is equal to ________.

9. For any $(x, y) \in \mathbb{R}^2 \setminus \overline{B(0,1)}$, let

   $f(x, y) = \text{distance}\left((x,y), \overline{B(0,1)}\right) = \text{infimum}$

   $\left\{\sqrt{(x-x_1)^2 + (y-y_1)^2} : (x_1, y_1) \in \overline{B(0,1)}\right\}.$

   Then, $\|\nabla f(3, 4)\|$ is equal to _______.

10. Let $f(x) = \left(\int_0^x e^{-t^2}dt\right)^2$ and $g(x) = \int_0^1 \dfrac{e^{-x^2(1+t^2)}}{1+t^2}dt.$

    Then $f'(\sqrt{\pi}) + g'(\sqrt{\pi})$ is equal to ______.

11. Minimize $w = x + 2y$ subject to

    $2x + y \ge 3$

    $x + y \ge 2$

    $x \ge 0, y \ge 0.$

    Then, the minimum value of w is equal to ______.

12. Maximize $w = 11x - z$ subject to

    $10x + y - z \le 1$

    $2x - 2y + z \le 2$

    $x, y, z \ge 0.$

    Then, the maximum value of w is equal to _____.

2015

13. Let d_1 and d_2 denote the usual metric and the discrete metric on $\mathbb{R}$, respectively.

    Let $f : (\mathbb{R}, d_1) \to (\mathbb{R}, d_2)$ be defined by $f(x) = x, x \in \mathbb{R}$. Then

    (a) f is continuous but f^{-1} is NOT continuous

    (b) f^{-1} is continuous but f is NOT continuous

    (c) both f and f^{-1} are continuous

    (d) neither f nor f^{-1} is continuous

14. Let $f : [0, \infty) \to \mathbb{R}$ be defined by

    $$f(x) = \int_0^x \sin^2(t^2)dt$$

Then the function f is

(*a*) uniformly continuous on $[0, 1)$ but NOT on $(0, \infty)$

(*b*) uniformly continuous on $(0, \infty)$ but NOT on $[0, 1)$

(*c*) uniformly continuous on both $[0, 1)$ and $(0, \infty)$

(*d*) neither uniformly continuous on $[0, 1)$ nor uniformly continuous on $(0, \infty)$

15. Consider the unit sphere $S = \{(x, y, z) \in \mathbb{R}^3 : x^2 + y^2 + z^2 = 1\}$ and the unit normal vector $\hat{n} = (x, y, z)$ at each point (x, y, z) on S. The value of the surface integral

$$\iint_S \left\{\left(\frac{2x}{\pi} + \sin\left(y^2\right)\right)x + \left(e^z - \frac{y}{\pi}\right)y + \left(\frac{2z}{\pi} + \sin^2 y\right)z\right\}d\sigma$$

is equal to __________

16. Let $S = \left\{\left(x, \sin\frac{1}{x}\right) : 0 < x \leq 1\right\}$ and $T = S \cup \{(0, 0)\}$. Under the susal metric on $\mathbb{R}^2$.

(*a*) S is closed but T is NOT closed

(*b*) T is closed but S is NOT closed

(*c*) both S and T are closed

(*d*) Neither S nor T is closed

17. Let $D = \{(x, y) \in \mathbb{R}^2 : 1 \leq x \leq 1000, 1 \leq y \leq 1000\}$. Define

$$f(x, y) = \frac{xy}{2} + \frac{500}{x} + \frac{500}{y}.$$

Then the minimum value of f on D is equal to ____.

18. Define $f_1, f_2 : [0, 1] \to \mathbb{R}$ by

$$f_1(x) = \sum_{n=i}^{\infty} \frac{x\sin(n^2x)}{n^2}$$

and $f_2(x) = \sum_{n=i}^{\infty} x^2(1 - x^2)^{n-1}$.

Then

(*a*) f_1 is continuous but f_2 is NOT continuous

(*b*) f_2 is continuous but f_1 is NOT continuous

(*c*) both f_1 and f_2 are continuous

(*d*) neither f_1 nor f_2 is continuous

19. Suppose that among all continuously differentiable functions $y(x)$, $x \in \mathbb{R}$, with $y(0) = 0$ and $y(1) = \frac{1}{2}$, the function $y_0(x)$ minimizes the functional

$$\int_0^1 (e^{-(y'-x)} + (1 + y)y')dx.$$

Then $y_0\left(\frac{1}{2}\right)$ is equal to

(*a*) 0 (*b*) $\frac{1}{8}$

(*c*) $\frac{1}{4}$ (*d*) $\frac{1}{2}$

20. Let $y(t)$ be a continuous function on $[0, \infty)$ whose Laplace transform exists. If $y(t)$ satisfies

$$\int_0^t (1 - \cos(t - \tau))y(\tau)d\tau = t^4.$$

then $y(1)$ is equal to ___________.

21. Consider the initial value problem

$$x^2y'' - 6y = 0, y(1) = \alpha, y'(1) = 6.$$

If $y(x) \to 0$ as $x \to 0^+$, then α is equal to_____.

2014

22. Let

$$f(x) := \begin{cases} -3\pi & \text{if} \quad -\pi < x \leq 0 \\ 3\pi & \text{if} \quad 0 < x < \pi \end{cases}$$

be a periodic function of period 2π. The coefficient of $\sin 3x$ in the Fourier series expansion of $f(x)$ on the interval $[-\pi, \pi]$ is _________

23. For the sequence of functions

$$f_n(x) = \frac{1}{x^2}\sin\left(\frac{1}{nx}\right), \quad x \in [1, \infty),$$

consider the following quantities expressed in terms of Lebesgue integrals

I. $\lim_{n\to\infty} \int_1^{\infty} f_n(x)dx$

II. $\int_1^{\infty} \lim_{n\to\infty} f_n(x)dx$.

Which of the following is **TRUE**?

(*a*) The limit in I does not exist

(*b*) The integrand in II is not integrable on $[1, \infty)$

(*c*) Quantities I and II are well-defined, but I $\neq$ II

(*d*) Quantities I and II are well-defined and I = II

24. Let d_1, d_2 and d_3 be metrics on a set X with at least two elements. Which of the following is **NOT** a metric on X?

(*a*) $\min\{d_1, 2\}$ (*b*) $\max(d_2, 2)$

(*c*) $\frac{d_3}{1 + d_3}$ (*d*) $\frac{d_1 + d_2 + d_3}{3}$

25. Let $X = [0, 1) \cup (1, 2)$ be the subspace of $\mathbb{R}$, Where $\mathbb{R}$ is equipped with the usual topology. Which of the following is **FALSE**?

(*a*) There exists a non-constant continuous function $f: X \to \mathbb{Q}$

(*b*) X is homeomorphic to $(-\infty, -3) \cup [0, \infty)$

(*c*) There exists an onto continuous function $f: [0, 1] \to \bar{X}$, where $\bar{X}$ is the closure of X in $\mathbb{R}$

(*d*) There exists an onto continuous function $f: [0, 1] \to X$

26. Let $\vec{F}$ be a vector field defined on $\mathbb{R}^2 \setminus \{(0, 0)\}$ by

$$\vec{F}(x, y) = \frac{y}{x^2+y^2}\hat{i} - \frac{x}{x^2+y^2}\hat{j}.$$

Let $\gamma, \alpha : [0, 1] \to \mathbb{R}^2$ be defined by

$\gamma(t) = (8 \cos 2\pi t, 17 \sin 2\pi t)$ and $\alpha(t) = (26 \cos 2\pi t, -10 \sin 2\pi t)$.

If $3\int_\alpha \vec{F}\cdot d\vec{r} - 4\int_\gamma \vec{F}\cdot d\vec{r} = 2m\pi$, then m is __

27. Let g: $\mathbb{R}^3 \to \mathbb{R}^3$ be defined by $g(x, y, z) = (3y + 4z, 2x - 3z, x + 3y)$ and let

$S = \{(x, y, z) \in \mathbb{R}^3 :$

$0 \le x \le 1,\ 0 \le y \le 1, 0 \le z \le 1\}$.

If $\iiint_{g(S)} (2x + y - 2z) dx\,dy\,dz = \alpha \iiint_S z\,dx\,dy\,dz$,

then α is ________

28. The value of $\iint_R xy\,dx\,dy$, where R is the region in the first quadrant bounded by the curves $y = x^2$, $y + x = 2$ and $x = 0$ is ________

29. Consider the partial order in $\mathbb{R}^2$ given by the relation $(x_1, y_1) < (x_2, y_2)$ EITHER if $x_1 < x_2$ OR if $x_1 = x_2$ and $y_1 < y_2$. Then in the order topology on $\mathbb{R}^2$ defined by the above order

(*a*) $[0, 1] \times \{1\}$ is compact but $[0, 1] \times [0, 1]$ is NOT compact

(*b*) $[0, 1] \times [0, 1]$ is compact but $[0, 1] \times \{1\}$ is NOT compact

(*c*) both $[0, 1] \times [0, 1]$ and $[0, 1] \times \{1\}$ are compact

(*d*) both $[0, 1] \times [0, 1]$ and $[0, 1] \times \{1\}$ are NOT compact

2013

30. Let $f : \mathbb{R} \to \mathbb{R}$ be a continuous function with $f(1) = 5$ and $f(3) = 11$. If $g(x) = \int_1^3 f(x+t)dt$ then $g'(0)$ is equal to ______

31. The value of the integral $\int_0^\infty \int_x^\infty \left(\frac{1}{y}\right) e^{-y/2} dy dx$ is__________

32. Let $f(x) = \sum_{n=1}^{\infty} \frac{\sin(nx)}{n^2}$. Then

(*a*) $\lim_{x\to 0} f(x) = 0$

(*b*) $\lim_{x\to 0} f(x) = 1$

(*c*) $\lim_{x\to 0} f(x) = \pi^2/6$

(*d*) $\lim_{x\to 0} f(x)$ does not exist

33. Let $f : \mathbb{R}^2 \to \mathbb{R}^2$ be defined by $f(x, y) = (e^{x+y}, e^{x-y})$. The area of the image of the region $\{(x, y) \in \mathbb{R}^2 : 0 < x, y < 1\}$ under the mapping f is

(*a*) 1 (*b*) $e - 1$

(*c*) e^2 (*d*) $e^2 - 1$

34. Let $\{a_n\}$ be the sequence of consecutive positive solutions of the equation $\tan x = x$ and let $\{b_n\}$ be the sequence of consecutive positive solutions of the equation $\tan \sqrt{x} = x$. Then

(*a*) $\sum_{n=1}^{\infty} \frac{1}{a_n}$ convergebut $\sum_{n=1}^{\infty} \frac{1}{b_n}$ diverges

(*b*) $\sum_{n=1}^{\infty} \frac{1}{a_n}$ diverges but $\sum_{n=1}^{\infty} \frac{1}{b_n}$ converges

(*c*) Both $\sum_{n=1}^{\infty} \frac{1}{a_n}$ and $\sum_{n=1}^{\infty} \frac{1}{b_n}$ converge

(*d*) Both $\sum_{n=1}^{\infty} \frac{1}{a_n}$ and $\sum_{n=1}^{\infty} \frac{1}{b_n}$ diverge

35. Let $f, g : [0, 1] \to \mathbb{R}$ be defined by

and $f(x) = \begin{cases} x & \text{if } x' = \frac{1}{n} \text{ for } n \in \mathbb{N} \\ 0 & \text{otherwise} \end{cases}$

Then $g(x) = \begin{cases} 1 & \text{if } x \in \mathbb{Q} \cap [0,1] \\ 0 & \text{otherwise} \end{cases}$

(*a*) Both f and g are Riemann integrable

(*b*) f is Riemann integrable and g is Lebesgue integrable

(*c*) g is Riemann integrable and f is Lebesgue integrable

(*d*) Neither f nor g is Riemann integrable

36. Suppose X is a real-valued random variable. Which of the following values **CANNOT** be attained by E[X] and E[X^2], respectively?

(*a*) 0 and 1 (*b*) 2 and 3

(*c*) $\frac{1}{2}$ and $\frac{1}{3}$ (*d*) 2 and 5

37. Which of the following subsets of $\mathbb{R}^2$ is **NOT** compact?

(*a*) $\{(x, y) \in \mathbb{R}^2 : -1 \le x \le 1,\ y = \sin x\}$

(b) $\{(x, y) \in \mathbb{R}^2 : -1 \le y \le 1,\ y = x^8 - x^3 - 1\}$

(c) $\{(x, y) \in \mathbb{R}^2 : y = 0,\ \sin(e^{-x}) = 0\}$

(d) $\{(x, y) \in \mathbb{R}^2 : x > 0,\ y = \sin\left(\frac{1}{x}\right)\} \cap \left\{(x, y) \in \mathbb{R}^2 : x > 0,\ y = \frac{1}{x}\right\}$

38. The value of the limit

$$\lim_{n\to\infty} \frac{2^{-n^2}}{\sum_{k=n+1}^{\infty} 2^{-k^2}} \text{ is}$$

(a) 0 (b) some $c \in (0, 1)$

(c) 1 (d) ∞

39. Let $S = \left\{x \in \mathbb{R} : x \ge 0, \sum_{n=1}^{\infty} x^{\sqrt{n}} < \infty\right\}$. Then the supremum of S is

(a) 1 (b) $\frac{1}{e}$

(c) 0 (d) ∞

40. Let X be a convex region in the plane bounded by straight lines. Let X have 7 vertices. Suppose $f(x, y) = ax + by + c$ has maximum value M and minimum value N on X and N < M. Let S = {P : P is a vertex of X and N < f (P) < M}. If S has n elements, then which of the following statements is **TRUE**?

(a) n cannot be 5 (b) n can be 2

(c) n cannot be 3 (d) n can be 4

41. Which of the following statements are **TRUE**?

P: If $f \in L^1(\mathbb{R})$, then f is continuous.

Q: If $f \in L^1(\mathbb{R})$ and $\lim_{|x|\to\infty} f(x)$ exists, then the limit is zero.

R: If $f \in L^1(\mathbb{R})$, then f is bounded.

S: If $f \in L^1(\mathbb{R})$ is uniformly continuous, then $\lim_{|x|\to\infty} f(x)$ exists and equals zero.

(a) Q and S only (b) P and R only

(c) P and Q only (d) R and S only

LINKED ANSWER QUESTIONS

Statement for Linked Answer Questions 42 & 43:

Let $X = \{(x,y) \in \mathbb{R}^2 : x^2 + y^2 = 1\} \cup [-1, 1] \times \{0\} \cup \{0\} \times [-1,1]$).

Let $n_0 = \max\{k : k < \infty$, there are k distinct points $p_1, \ldots, p_R \in X$ such that $X \setminus \{p_1, \ldots, p_R\}$ is connected}

42. The value of n_0 is ______

43. Let $q_1, \ldots, q_{n0+1}$ be $n_0 + 1$ distinct points and $Y = X \setminus \{q_1, \ldots, q_{n0+1}\}$. Let m be then umber of connected components of Y. The maximum possible value of m is ______

2012

44. The function $\phi(x)$ satisfying the integral equation

$$\int_0^x e^{x-\xi}\phi(\xi)\,d\xi = \frac{x^2}{2} \text{ is}$$

(a) $\frac{x^2}{2}$ (b) $x + \frac{x^2}{2}$

(c) $x - \frac{x^2}{2}$ (d) $1 + \frac{x^2}{2}$

45. The Lebesgue measure of the set

$$A = \left\{0 < x \le 1 : x\sin\left(\frac{\pi}{2x}\right) \ge 0\right\} \text{ is}$$

(a) 0 (b) 1

(c) In2 (d) $1 - \text{In}\sqrt{2}$

46. Which of the following statements are **TRUE**?

P : The set $\{x \in R : |\cos x| \le \frac{1}{2}\}$ is compact.

Q : The set $\{x \in R : \tan x$ is not differentiable$\}$ is complete.

R : The set $\left\{x \in R : \sum_{n=0}^{\infty} \frac{(-1)^n x^{2n+1}}{(2n+1)!}\right.$ is convergent} is bounded.

S : The set $\{x \in R : f(x) = \cos x$ has a local maxima$\}$ is closed.

(a) P and Q (b) R and S

(c) Q and S (d) P and S

47. The maximum value of the function $f(x, y, z) = xyz$ subject to the constraint $xy + yz + zx - a = 0$, $a > 0$ is

(a) $a^{\frac{3}{2}}$ (b) $\left(\frac{a}{3}\right)^{\frac{3}{2}}$

(c) $\left(\frac{3}{a}\right)^{\frac{3}{2}}$ (d) $\left(\frac{3a}{2}\right)^{\frac{3}{2}}$

48. The functional $\int_0^1 \left(y'^2 + 4y^2 + 8ye^x\right)dx$, $y(0) = -\frac{4}{3}$, $y(1) = -\frac{4e}{3}$ possesses :

(a) strong minima on $y = -\frac{1}{3}e^x$

(b) strong minima on $y = -\frac{4}{3}e^x$

(c) weak maxima on $y = -\frac{1}{3}e^x$

(d) strong maxima on $y = -\frac{4}{3}e^x$

Common Data for Questions 49 and 50 :

Consider the Fredholm integral equation

$$u(x) = x + \lambda \int_0^1 xe^t u(t)\,dt.$$

49. The resolvent kernel R(x, t; λ) for this integral equation is

(a) $\frac{xe^t}{1-\lambda}$ (b) $\frac{\lambda xe^t}{1+\lambda}$

(c) $\frac{xe^t}{1+\lambda^2}$ (d) $\frac{xe^t}{1-\lambda^2}$

50. The solution of this integral equation is

(a) $\frac{x+1}{1-\lambda}$ (b) $\frac{x^2}{1-\lambda^2}$

(c) $\frac{x}{1+\lambda^2}$ (d) $\frac{x}{1-\lambda}$

2011

51. Let I = $\oint_C (2x^2 + y^2)\,dx + ey\,dy$, where C is the boundary (oriented anticlockwise) of the region in the first quadrant bounded by $y = 0$, $x^2 + y^2 = 1$ and $x = 0$. The value of I is

(a) -1 (b) $-\frac{2}{3}$

(c) $\frac{2}{3}$ (d) 1

52. The series $\sum_{m=1}^{\infty} x^{\ln m}$, $x > 0$, is convergent on the interval

(a) $(0, 1/e)$ (b) $(1/e, e)$

(c) $(0, e)$ (d) $(1, e)$

53. The eigenvalue λ of the following Fredholm integral equation

$$y(x) = \lambda \int_0^1 x^2 t y(t)\,dt$$

is

(a) -2 (b) 2

(c) 4 (d) -4

54. For $0 \le x \le 1$, let

$$f_n(x) = \begin{cases} \frac{n}{1+n}, & \text{if } x \text{ is irrational} \\ 0, & \text{if } x \text{ is rational} \end{cases}$$

and $f(x) = \lim_{n\to\infty} f_n(x)$. Then, on the interval [0, 1]

(a) f is measurable and Riemann integrable

(b) f is measurable and Lebesgue integrable

(c) f is not measurable

(d) f is not Lebesgue integrable

55. If x, y and z are positive real numbers, then the minimum value of

$x^2 + 8y^2 + 27z^2$ where $\frac{1}{x} + \frac{1}{y} + \frac{1}{z} = 1$ is

(a) 108 (b) 216

(c) 405 (d) 1048

Linked Answer Questions

Statement for Linked Answer Questions 56 and 57:

Let $f_n(x) = \frac{x}{\{(n-1)x+1\}\{nx+1\}}$

and $s_n(x) = \sum_{j=1}^{n} f_j(x)$ for $x \in [0, 1]$.

56. The sequence $\{s_n\}$

(a) converges uniformly on [0, 1]

(b) converges pointwise on [0, 1] but not uniformly

(c) converges pointwise for $x = 0$ but not for $x \in (0, 1)$

(d) does not converge for $x \in [0, 1]$

57. $\lim_{n\to\infty} \int_0^1 s_n(x)\,dx = 1$

(a) by dominated convergence theorem

(b) by Fatou's lemma

(c) by the fact that $\{s_n\}$ converges uniformly on [0, 1]

(d) by the fact that $\{s_n\}$ converges pointwise on [0, 1]

2010

58. If $f : [1, 2] \to \mathbb{R}$ is a non-negative Riemann-integrable function such that $\int_1^2 \frac{f(x)}{\sqrt{x}}dx = k\int_1^2 f(x)\,dx \neq 0$, then k belongs to the interval

(a) $\left[0, \frac{1}{3}\right]$

(b) $\left[\frac{1}{3}, \frac{2}{3}\right]$

(c) $\left[\frac{2}{3}, 1\right]$

(d) $\left[1, \frac{4}{3}\right]$

59. The set X = $\mathbb{R}$ with metric $d(x, y) = \frac{|x-y|}{1+|x-y|}$ is

(a) bounded but not compact

(b) bounded but not complete

(c) complete but not bounded

(d) compact but not complete

60. Let $f(x, y) = \begin{cases} \dfrac{xy}{(x^2+y^2)^{5/2}}[1-\cos(x^2+y^2)], & (x,y) \neq (0,0) \\ k, & (x,y) = (0,0) \end{cases}$

Then the value of k for which $f(x, y)$ is continuous at (0, 0) is

(*a*) 0 (*b*) $\frac{1}{2}$

(*c*) 1 (*d*) $\frac{3}{2}$

61. Let A and B be disjoint subsets of $\mathbb{R}$ and let m^* denote the Lebesgue outer measure on $\mathbb{R}$. Consider the statements:

P : $m^*(A \cup B) = m^*(A) + m^*(B)$

Q : Both A and B are Lebesgue measureable

R : One of A and B is Lebesgue measureable

Which one of the following is correct?

(*a*) If P is true, then Q is true

(*b*) If P is NOT true, then R is true

(*c*) If R is true, then P is NOT true

(*d*) If R is true, then P is true

62. Let $f: \mathbb{R} \to [0, \infty)$ be a Lebesgue measurable function and E be Lebesgue measurable subset of $\mathbb{R}$ such that $\int_E f\, dm = 0$, where m is the Lebesgue measure on $\mathbb{R}$. Then

(*a*) $m(E) = 0$

(*b*) $\{x \in \mathbb{R} : f(x) = 0\} = E$

(*c*) $M(\{x \in E : f(x) \neq 0\}) = 0$

(*d*) $m(\{x \in E : f(x) = 0\}) = 0$

63. Let $I = \int_C \frac{e^y}{x} dx + (e^y \ln x + x) dy$, where C is the positively oriented boundary of the region enclosed by $y = 1 + x^2$, $y = 2$, $x = \frac{1}{2}$. Then the value of I is

(*a*) $\frac{1}{8}$ (*b*) $\frac{5}{24}$

(*c*) $\frac{7}{24}$ (*d*) $\frac{3}{8}$

64. Let $\{f_n\}$ be a sequence of real valued differentiable functions on $[a, b]$ such that $f_n(x) \to f(x)$ as $n \to \infty$ for every $x \in [a, b]$ and for some Riemann-integrable function $f : [a,b] \to R$. Consider the statements

P_1 : $\{f_n\}$ converges uniformly

P_2 : $\{f_n'\}$ converges uniformly

P_3 : $\int_a^b f_n(x)dx \to \int_a^b f(x)dx$

P_4 : f is differentiable

Then which one of the following need **NOT** be true

(*a*) P_1 implies P_3 (*b*) P_2 implies P_1

(*c*) P_2 implies P_4 (*d*) P_3 implies P_1

65. Let $f_n(x) = \frac{x^n}{1+x}$ and $g_n(x) = \frac{x^n}{1+nx}$ for $x \in [0,1]$ and $x \in \mathbb{N}$. Then on the interval [0,1],

(*a*) both $\{f_n\}$ and $\{g_n\}$ converge uniformly

(*b*) neither $\{f_n\}$ nor $\{g_n\}$ converges uniformly

(*c*) $\{f_n\}$ converges uniformly but $\{g_n\}$ does not converge uniformly

(*d*) $\{g_n\}$ converges uniformly but $\{f_n\}$ does not converge uniformly

66. Consider the power series $\sum_{n=1}^{\infty} \frac{x^n}{\sqrt{n}}$ and $\sum_{n=1}^{\infty} \frac{x^n}{n}$. Then

(*a*) both converge on (–1,1]

(*b*) both converge on [–1,1)

(*c*) exactly one of them converges on (–1,1]

(*d*) none of them converges on [–1,1)

67. For a continuous function $f(t)$, $0 \le t \le 1$, the integral equation $y(t) = f(t) + 3\int_0^1 ts\, y(s)\, ds$ has

(*a*) a unique solution if $\int_0^1 sf(s)\, ds \neq 0$

(*b*) no solution if $\int_0^1 sf(s)\, ds = 0$

(*c*) infinitely many solutions if $\int_0^1 sf(s)\, ds = 0$

(*d*) infinitely many solutions if $\int_0^1 sf(s)\, ds \neq 0$

2009

68. The resolvent kernel for the integral equation

$$u(x) = F(x) + \int_{\log 2}^{x} e^{(t-x)} u(t)\, dt \text{ is}$$

(*a*) $\cos(x - t)$ (*b*) 1

(*c*) e^{t-x} (*d*) $e^{2(t-x)}$

69. A function $f : \mathbb{R} \to \mathbb{R}$ need NOT be Lebesgue measurable if

(*a*) f is monotone

(*b*) $\{x \in \mathbb{R} : f(x) \geq \alpha\}$ is measurable for each $\alpha \in \mathbb{Q}$

(*c*) $\{x \in \mathbb{R} : f(x) = \alpha\}$ is measurable for each $\alpha \in \mathbb{R}$

(*d*) For each open set G in $\mathbb{R}$, $f^{-1}(G)$ is measurable

70. Which of the following sequence $\{f_n\}_{n=1}^{\infty}$ of functions does NOT converge uniformly on [0, 1]?

(a) $f_n(x) = \frac{e^{-x}}{n}$ (b) $f_n(x) = (1-x)^n$

(c) $f_n(x) = \frac{x^2 + nx}{n}$ (d) $f_n(x) = \frac{\sin(nx+n)}{n}$

71. Let E = $\{(x, y) \in \mathbb{R}^2 : 0 < x < y\}$. Then $\iint_E y e^{-(x+y)} dx\, dy =$

(a) $\frac{1}{4}$ (b) $\frac{3}{2}$

(c) $\frac{4}{3}$ (d) $\frac{3}{4}$

72. Let $f_n(x) = \frac{1}{n}\sum_{k=0}^{n}\sqrt{k(n-k)}\binom{n}{k}x^k(1-x)^{n-k}$ for $x \in [0, 1]$, $n = 1, 2, \ldots$. If $\lim_{n\to\infty} f_n(x) = f(x)$ for $x \in [0, 1]$, then the maximum value of $f(x)$ on [0, 1] is

(a) 1 (b) $\frac{1}{2}$

(c) $\frac{1}{3}$ (d) $\frac{1}{4}$

Statement for Linked Answer Q. 73 – 74

Let $f(x, y) = kxy - x^3y - xy^3$ for $(x, y) \in \mathbb{R}^2$, where k is a real constant. The directional derivative of f at the point (1, 2) in the direction of the unit vector $u = \left(\frac{-1}{\sqrt{2}}, \frac{-1}{\sqrt{2}}\right)$ is $\frac{15}{\sqrt{2}}$.

73. The value of k is

(a) 2 (b) 4

(c) 1 (d) –2

74. The value of f at a local minimum in the rectangular region

$$R = \left\{(x, y) \in \mathbb{R}^2 : |x| < \frac{3}{2}, |y| < \frac{3}{2}\right\} \text{ is}$$

(a) – 2 (b) – 3

(c) $\frac{-7}{8}$ (d) 0

2008

75. Let E = $\{(x,y) \in \mathbb{R}^2: 0 \le x \le 1, 0 \le y \le x\}$.

Then $\iint_E (x + y)dx\, dy$ is equal to

(a) – 1 (b) 0

(c) 1 (d) $\frac{1}{2}$

76. For $(x, y) \in \mathbb{R}^2$, let

$$f(x, y) = \begin{cases} \frac{2xy}{x^2+y^2} & \text{if } (x, y) \neq (0,0), \\ 0 & \text{if } (x, y) = (0, 0) \end{cases}$$

Then

(a) f_x and f_y exist at (0,0), and f is continuous at (0,0)

(b) f_x and f_y exist at (0,0), and f is discontinuous at (0,0)

(c) f_x and f_y do not exist at (0,0), and f is continuous at (0,0)

(d) f_x and f_y exist at (0,0), and f is discontinuous at (0,0)

77. Let E be a connected subset of R with at least two elements. Then the number of elements in E is

(a) exactly two

(b) more than two but finite

(c) countably infinite

(d) uncountable

78. Let $q_1, q_2, .., q_n$ be the generalized coordinates and $\dot{q}_1, \dot{q}_2, \ldots, \dot{q}_n$ be the generalized velocities in a conservative force field. If under a transformation φ, the new coordinate system has the generalized coordinates $Q_1, Q_2, \ldots, Q_n$ and velocities $\dot{Q}_1, \dot{Q}_2, \ldots \dot{Q}_n$. Then the equation $\frac{\partial L}{\partial q_k} = \frac{d}{dt}\left(\frac{\partial L}{\partial \dot{Q}_k}\right)$ takes the form

(a) $\frac{\partial L}{\partial Q_k} = \varphi\frac{d}{dt}\left(\frac{\partial L}{\partial \dot{Q}_k}\right)$

(b) $\varphi\frac{\partial L}{\partial Q_k} = \frac{d}{dt}\left(\frac{\partial L}{\partial \dot{Q}_k}\right)$

(c) $\frac{\partial L}{\partial Q_k} = -\varphi\frac{d}{dt}\left(\frac{\partial L}{\partial \dot{Q}_k}\right)$

(d) $\frac{\partial L}{\partial Q_k} = \frac{d}{dt}\left(\frac{\partial L}{\partial \dot{Q}_k}\right)$

79. Which one of the following does NOT hold for all continuous functions $f : [-\pi, \pi] \to C$?

(a) If $f(-t) = f(t)$ for each $t \in [-\pi, \pi]$, then $\int_{-\pi}^{\pi} f(t)dt = 2\int_0^{\pi} f(t)dt$

(b) If $f(-t) = -f(t)$ for each $t \in [-\pi, \pi]$, then $\int_{-\pi}^{\pi} f(t)dt = 0$

(c) $\int_{-\pi}^{\pi} f(-t)dt = -\int_{-\pi}^{\pi} f(t)dt$

(d) There is an α with $-\pi < \alpha < \pi$ such that $\int_{-\pi}^{\pi} f(t)dt = 2\pi f(\alpha)$

80. Which one of the following statements holds?

(a) The series $\sum_{n=0}^{\infty} x^n$ converges each $x \in [-1, 1]$

(b) The series $\sum_{n=0}^{\infty} x^n$ converges uniformly in $[-1, 1]$

(c) The series $\sum_{n=1}^{\infty} \frac{x^n}{n}$ converges each $x \in [-1, 1]$

(d) The series $\sum_{n=1}^{\infty} \frac{x^n}{n}$ converges uniformly in $[-1, 1]$

81. For $x \in [-\pi,\pi]$, let

$$f(x) = (\pi + x)(\pi - x)$$

and

$$g(x) = \begin{cases} \cos(1/x) & \text{if } x \neq 0, \\ 0 & \text{if } x = 0. \end{cases}$$

Consider the statements

P : The Fourier series of f converges uniformly to f on $[-\pi, \pi]$.

Q : The Fourier series of g converges uniformly to g on $[-\pi, \pi]$.

Then

(a) P and Q are true

(b) P is true but Q is false

(c) P is false but Q is true

(d) Both P and Q are false

82. Let $W = \{(x, y, z) \in R^3 : 1 \leq x^2 + y^2 + z^2 \leq 4\}$ and $F : W \to R^3$ be defined by

$$F(x, y, z) = \frac{(x, y, z)}{[x^2 + y^2 + z^2]^{3/2}} \text{ for } (x, y, z) \in W.$$

If ∂W denotes the boundary of W oriented by the outward normal n to W, then $\int\int_{\partial W} F.n\, ds$ is equal to

(a) 0 (b) 4π

(c) 8π (d) 12π

83. For each $n \in N$, let $f_n : [0, 1] \to R$ be a measurable function such that $|f_n(t)| \leq \frac{1}{\sqrt{t}}$ for all $t \in (0, 1)$. Let $F : [0, 1] \to R$ be defined by $f(t) = 1$ if t is irrational and $f(t) = -1$ if t is rational. Assume that $f_n(t) \to f(t)$ as $n \to \infty$ for all $t \in [0, 1]$. Then

(a) f is not measurable

(b) f is measurable and $\int_{[0,1]} f_n d\mu \to 1$ as $n \to \infty$

(c) f is measurable and $\int_{[0,1]} f_n d\mu \to 0$ as $n \to \infty$

(d) f is measurable and $\int_{[0,1]} f_n d\mu \to -1$ as $n \to \infty$

84. Which one of the following subsets of R (with the usual metric) is NOT complete?

(a) $[1, 2] \cup [3,4]$ (b) $[0, \infty]$

(c) $[0, 1]$ (d) $\{0\} \cup \left\{\frac{1}{n} : n \in N\right\}$

85. The possible values of α for which the variational problem

$J[y(x)] = \int_0^1 (3y^2 + 2x^3 y')dx, y(\alpha) = 1$ has extremals are

(a) $-1, 0$ (b) $0, 1$

(c) $-1,1$ (d) $-1, 0, 1$

2007

86. Define $f : R^2 \to R$ by $f(x; y) = \begin{cases} 1, & \text{if } xy = 0, \\ 2, & \text{otherwise} \end{cases}$

If $S = \{(x, y) : f \text{ is continuous at the point } (x, y)\}$, then

(a) S is open (b) S is connected

(c) $S = \phi$ (d) S is closed

87. Let $\{E_n : n = 1, 2, ...\}$ be a decreasing sequence of Lebesgue measurable sets on R and let F be a Lebesgue measurable set on R such that $E_1 \cap F = \phi$. Suppose that F has Lebesgue measure 2 and the Lebesgue measure of E_n equals $\frac{2n+2}{3n+1}$, $n = 1, 2, ...$ Then the Lebesgue measure of the set $\left(\bigcap_{n=1}^{\infty} E_n\right) \cup F$ equals

(a) $\frac{5}{3}$ (b) 2

(c) $\frac{7}{3}$ (d) $\frac{8}{3}$

88. The extremum for the variational problem

$$\int_0^{\frac{\pi}{8}} \left((y')^2 + 2yy' - 16y^2\right)dx, y(0) = 0, y\left(\frac{\pi}{8}\right) = 1,$$

occurs for the curve

(a) $y = \sin(4x)$ (b) $y = \sqrt{2}\sin(2x)$

(c) $y = 1 - \cos(4x)$ (d) $y = \dfrac{1-\cos(8x)}{2}$

89. Let (X, d) be a metric space. Consider the metric ρ on X defined by

$\rho(x, y) = \min\{\frac{1}{2}, d(x, y)\}\ x, y \in X.$

Suppose $\Im_1$ and $\Im_2$ are topologies on X defined by d and ρ, respectively. Then

(a) $\Im_1$ is a proper subset of $\Im_2$

(b) $\Im_2$ is a proper subset of $\Im_1$

(c) neither $\Im_1 \subseteq \Im_2$ nor $\Im_2 \subseteq \Im_1$

(d) $\Im_1 = \Im_2$

90. Let C be the boundary of the triangle formed by the points (1, 0, 0), (0, 1, 0), (0, 0, 1). Then the value of the line integral

$$\oint_C -2y\,dx + \left(3x - 4y^2\right)dy + \left(z^2 + 3y\right)dz \text{ is}$$

(a) 0 (b) 1

(c) 2 (d) 4

91. Let X be a complete metric space and let E ⊆ X. Consider the following statements

(S_1)E is compact,

(S_2)E is closed and bounded,

(S_3)E is closed and totally bounded,

(S_4)Every sequence in E has a subsequence converging in E.

Which one of the above statements does NOT imply all the other statements ?

(a) S_1 (b) S_2

(c) S_3 (d) S_4

92. Consider the series $\sum_{n=1}^{\infty} \frac{1}{n^{3/2}} \sin(nx)$

Then the series

(a) converges uniformly on R

(b) converges pointwise but NOT uniformly on R

(c) converges in L^1 norm to an integrable function on [0, 2π] but does NOT converge uniformly on R

(d) does NOT converge pointwise

93. The value of $\int_0^{\infty}\int_{1/y}^{\infty} x^4 e^{-x^3 y} dx\,dy$ equals

(a) $\frac{1}{4}$ (b) $\frac{1}{3}$

(c) $\frac{1}{2}$ (d) 1

94. $\lim_{n\to\infty}\left[(n+1)\int_0^1 x^n \ln(1+x)\,dx\right] =$

(a) 0 (b) In 2

(c) In 3 (d) ∞

95. Consider the function $f: R \to R$ defined by

$$f(x) = \begin{cases} x^4, & \text{if } x \text{ is rational.,} \\ 2x^2 - 1, & \text{if } x \text{ is irrational.} \end{cases}$$

Let S be the set of points where f is continuous. Then

(a) S = {1} (b) S = {–1}

(c) S = {–1, 1} (d) S = ϕ

96. For a positive real number p, let $\{f_n : n = 1, 2, ...)$ be a sequence of functions defined on [0,1] by

$$f_n(x) = \begin{cases} n^{p+1}x, & \text{if } 0 \le x \le \frac{1}{n} \\ \frac{1}{x^p}, & \text{if } \frac{1}{n} < x \le 1 \end{cases}$$

Let $f(x) = \lim_{n\to\infty} f_n(x)$, $x \in [0, 1]$. Then, on [0, 1],

(a) f is Riemann integrable

(b) the improper integral $\int_0^1 f(x)\,dx$ converges for $p \ge 1$

(c) the improper integral $\int_0^1 f(x)\,dx$ converges for $p < 1$

(d) f_n converges uniformly

97. Which of the following inequality is NOT true for $x \in \left(\frac{1}{4}, \frac{3}{4}\right)$.

(a) $e^{-x} > \sum_{j=0}^{2} \frac{(-x)^j}{j!}$ (b) $e^{-x} < \sum_{j=0}^{3} \frac{(-x)^j}{j!}$

(c) $e^{-x} > \sum_{j=0}^{4} \frac{(-x)^j}{j!}$ (d) $e^{-x} > \sum_{j=0}^{5} \frac{(-x)^j}{j!}$

98. The value of α for which the integral equation $u(x) = \alpha\int_0^1 e^{x-1}u(t)\,dx$, has a nontrivial solution is

(a) –2 (b) –1

(c) 1 (d) 2

Statement for Linked Answer Questions 99 and 100

Suppose $E = \{(x, y) : xy \neq 0\}$. Let $f : R^2 \to R$ be defined by

$$f(x, y) = \begin{cases} 0, & \text{if } xy = 0 \\ y\sin\left(\frac{1}{x}\right) + x\sin\left(\frac{1}{y}\right), & \text{otherwise.} \end{cases}$$

Let S_1 be the set of points in R^2 where f_x exists and S_2 be the set of points in R^2 where f_y exists. Also, let E_1 be the set of points where f_x is continuous and E_2 be the set of points where f_y is continuous.

99. S_1 and S_2 are given by

(*a*) $S_1 = E \cup (x, y) : y = 0\}$, $S_2 = E \cup [(x, y) : x = 0\}$

(*b*) $S_1 = E \cup \{x, y) : x = 0\}$, $S_2 = E \cup \{(x, y) : y = 0\}$

(*c*) $S_1 = S_2 = R^2$

(*d*) $S_1 = S_2 = E \cup ((0, 0)\}$

100. E_1 and E_2 are given by

(*a*) $E_1 = E_2 = S_1 \cap S_2$

(*b*) $E_1 = E_2 = S_1 \cap S_2 \setminus \{(0, 0)\}$

(*c*) $E_1 = S_1$, $E_2 = S_2$

(*d*) $E_1 = S_2$, $E_2 = S_1$

2006

101. Let E be a non-measurable subset of [0, 1]. If $f : [0,1] \to R$ is defined by

$$f(x) = \begin{cases} \frac{-1}{2}, & x \in E \\ 0, & \text{otherwise.} \end{cases}$$

Then,

(*a*) f is measurable but not $|f|$

(*b*) $|f|$ is measurable but not f

(*c*) both f and $|f|$ are measurable

(*d*) neither f nor $|f|$ is measurable

102. Let L^2 ([0, 1]) denote the space of all square integrable functions on [0, 1].

Define $f_1, f_2 : [0, 1] \to R$ by

$$f_1(t) = \begin{cases} t^{-1/3}, 0 < t \leq 1 \\ 0, \quad t = 0 \end{cases}$$

$$f_2(t) = \begin{cases} t^{-2/3}, 0 < t \leq 1 \\ 0, \quad t = 0 \end{cases}$$

Then,

(*a*) f_1 belongs to L^2 ([0,1]) but NOT f_2

(*b*) f_2 belongs to L^2 ([0,1]) but NOT f_1

(*c*) Both f_1 and f_2 belong to L^2 ([0,1])

(*d*) neither f_1 nor f_2 belongs to L^2 ([0,1])

103. Let, $S, T \subseteq R^2$ be given by

$$S = \left\{(x, \sin\frac{1}{x}) : 0 < x \leq 1\right\} \cup \{(0,0)\}$$

and $T = \left\{(x, x\sin\frac{1}{x}) : 0 < x \leq 1\right\} \cup \{(0, 0)\}$. Then, under the usual metric on R^2,

(*a*) S is compact but not T

(*b*) T is compact but not S

(*c*) both S and T are compact

(*d*) neither S nor T is compact

104. Let $S, T \subseteq R$ be given by

$$S = \left\{x \in R : 2x^2 \cos\frac{1}{x} = 1\right\}$$

and $T = \left\{x \in R : 2x^2 \cos\frac{1}{x} \leq 1\right\} \cup \{0\}$.

Then, under the usual metric on R,

(*a*) S is complete but not T

(*b*) T is complete but not S

(*c*) both S and T are complete

(*d*) neither S nor T is complete

105. Let $f : R \to R$ be defined by

$$f(x) = \begin{cases} n, \text{ if } x = n, x \in N \\ 0, \text{ otherwise} \end{cases}$$

and $T = N \cup \left\{n + \frac{1}{n} : n \in N\right\}$. Then, under the usual metric on R, f is uniformly continuous on

(*a*) N but not T (*b*) T but not N

(*c*) both N and T (*d*) neither N nor T

106. For each $n \in N$, and $n > 1$, define $f_n : [0, 1] \to R$ by

$$f_n(x) = \begin{cases} |nx - 1| & \text{for } 0 \leq x < \frac{2}{n} \\ 1 & \text{for } \frac{2}{n} \leq x \leq 1. \end{cases}$$

Let $g_1, g_2 : [0,1] \to R$ be defined by

$$g_1(x) = \begin{cases} 1 & \text{for } 0 < x \leq 1 \\ 0 & \text{for } x = 0 \end{cases}$$

and $g_2(x) = 1$ for $0 \leq x \leq 1$.

Then, on [0, 1],

(*a*) $f_n \to g_1$ pointwise but not uniformly

(*b*) $f_n \to g_2$ pointwise but not uniformly

(*c*) $f_n \to g_1$ uniformly

(*d*) $f_n \to g_2$ uniformly

107. Let $f_n\, g_n : [0,1] \to R$ be defined by

$$f_n(x) = x^2(1-x^2)^{n-1} \text{ and } g_n(x) = \frac{1}{n^2(1+x^2)} \text{ for } n \in N.$$

Then, on [0, 1],

(a) $\sum_{n=1}^{\infty} f_n(x)$ converges uniformly but not $\sum_{n=1}^{\infty} g_n(x)$

(b) $\sum_{n=1}^{\infty} g_n(x)$ converges uniformly but not $\sum_{n=1}^{\infty} f_n(x)$

(c) both $\sum_{n=1}^{\infty} f_n(x)$ and $\sum_{n=1}^{\infty} g_n(x)$ converges uniformly

(d) neither $\sum_{n=1}^{\infty} f_n(x)$ nor $\sum_{n=1}^{\infty} g_n(x)$ converges uniformly

108. The function $f : [0, \infty] \to R$ defined by

$$f(x) = \int_0^x (2\sin^4 t\cos^2 t)dt \text{ is}$$

(a) not continuous

(b) continuous but not uniformly

(c) uniformly continuous but not Lipschitz continuous

(d) Lipschitz continuous

109. Let S be a non-measurable subset of R and T be measurable subset of R such that $S \subset T$. Denote the outer measure of a set U by $m^*(U)$. Then,

(a) $m^*(T/S) = 0$ and $m^*(S) = 0$

(b) $m^*(T/S) > 0$ and $m^*(S) > 0$

(c) $m^*(T/S) > 0$ and $m^*(S) = 0$

(d) $m^*(T/S) = 0$ and $m^*(S) > 0$

110. Let $f : R^2 \to R$ be defined by

$$f(x, y) = \begin{cases} \dfrac{x^2 y}{x^4 + y^2} & \text{for } (x, y) \neq (0,0), \\ 0 & \text{for } (x, y) = (0,0) \end{cases}$$

Then, the directional derivative of f at (0, 0) in the direction of the vector $\left(\frac{1}{\sqrt{2}}, \frac{1}{\sqrt{2}}\right)$ is

(a) $\frac{1}{\sqrt{2}}$ (b) $\frac{1}{2}$

(c) $\frac{1}{2\sqrt{2}}$ (d) $\frac{1}{4\sqrt{2}}$

111. Consider the hemisphere $x^2 + y^2 + (z-2)^2 = 9$, $2 \le z \le 5$ and the vector field $\bar{F}(x, y, z) = x\vec{i} + y\vec{j} + (z-2)\vec{k}$. The surface integral $\iint (\vec{F}.\vec{n})d\sigma$, evaluated over the hemisphere with $\vec{n}$ denoting the unit outward normal, is

(a) 9π

(b) 27π

(c) 54π

(d) 162π

2005

112. Suppose E is a nonmeasurable subset of [0,1]. Let $P = E^\circ \cup \{\frac{1}{n} : n \in N\}$ and $Q = \bar{E} \cup \{\frac{1}{n} : n \in N\}$ where E° is the interior of E and $\bar{E}$ is the closure of E. Then

(a) P is measurable but not Q

(b) Q is measurable but not P

(c) both P and Q are measurable

(d) neither P nor Q is measurable

113. The value of $\int_0^\pi \int_x^\pi \int_0^2 \frac{\sin y}{y}$ dz dy dx is

(a) –2 (b) 2

(c) –4 (d) 4

114. Let $S = \left\{\frac{1}{n} : n \in N\right\} \cup \{0\}$ and $T = \left\{n + \frac{1}{n} : n \in N\right\}$ be the subsets of the metric space R with the usual metric. Then

(a) S is complete but not T

(b) T is complete but not S

(c) both T and S are complete

(d) neither T nor S is complete

2004

115. Let f, g: $(0, 1) \times (0, 1) \to R$ be two continuous functions defined by $f(x, y) = \frac{1}{1 + x(1-y)}$ and $g(x, y) = \frac{1}{1 + x(y-1)}$. Then, on $(0,1) \times (0,1)$,

(a) f and g are both uniformly continuous

(b) f is uniformly continuous but g is not

(c) g is uniformly continuous but f is not

(d) neither f nor g is uniformly continuous

116. Let S be the surface bounding the region $x^2 + y^2 \leq 1$, $x \geq 0$, $y \geq 0$ $|z| \leq 1$, and $\hat{n}$ be the unit outer normal to S. Then

$$\iint_S [(\sin^2 x)\hat{i} + 2y\hat{j} - z(1 + \sin 2x)\hat{k}] \cdot \hat{n} \quad dS$$

equals

(a) 1 (b) $\frac{\pi}{2}$

(c) π (d) 2π

117. Let $f : [0, \infty) \to R$ be defined by

$$f(x) = \begin{cases} \frac{1}{\sqrt{x}}, x \neq 0 \\ 0 \ , x = 0 \end{cases}$$

Consider the two improper integrals $I_1 = \int_0^1 f(x)dx$ and $I_2 = \int_1^\infty f(x)dx$. Then

(a) both I_1 and I_2 exist

(b) I_1 exists but I_2 does not

(c) I_1 does not exist but I_2 does

(d) neither I_1 nor I_2 exists

118. Suppose $X = (1, \infty)$ and $T : X \to X$ is such that $d(T_x, T_y) < d(x, y)$ for $x \neq y$. Then

(a) T has at most one fixed point

(b) T has a unique fixed point, by Banach Contraction Theorem

(c) T has infinitely many fixed points

(d) for every $x \in X$, $\{T^n(x)\}$ converges to a fixed point

119. If $f(x, y)$

$$= \begin{cases} \frac{x^3}{(x^2 + y^2)}, (x, y) \neq (0,0) \\ 0, \quad (x, y) = (0,0) \end{cases}, \text{then at}(0,0)$$

(a) f_x, f_y do not exist

(b) f_x, f_y exist and are equal

(c) the directional derivative exists along any straight line

(d) f is differentiable

120. Let $\sigma > 1$ and $g(x) = \sum_{n=1}^{\infty} \frac{1}{n^x}$, $\sigma \leq x < \infty$. Then $g(x)$ is

(a) not continuous

(b) continuous but not differentiable

(c) differentiable but not continuously differentiable

(d) continuously differentiable

121. The sequence of functions (f_n) on [0, 1] with Lebesgue measure, defined by

$$f_n(x) = \begin{cases} x, 0 \leq x < 1 - \frac{1}{n} \\ \sqrt{n}, 1 - \frac{1}{n} \leq x \leq 1 \end{cases}, \text{ converges}$$

(a) almost everywhere and as well as in L^1

(b) almost everywhere but not in L^1

(c) in L^1, but not almost everywhere

(d) neither almost everywhere nor in L^1

122. Consider two sequences $\{f_n\}$ and $\{g_n\}$ of functions where $f_n : [0, 1] \to R$ and $g_n : R \to R$ are defined by $f_n(x) = x^n$ and $g_n(x)$

$$= \begin{cases} \cos(x - n)^{\frac{\pi}{2}} \text{ if } x \in [n-1, n+1] \\ 0 \qquad \text{otherwise} \end{cases}. \text{Then}$$

(a) neither $\{f_n\}$ nor $\{g_n\}$ is uniformly convergent

(b) $\{f_n\}$ is not uniformly convergent but $\{g_n\}$ is

(c) $\{g_n\}$ is not uniformly convergent but $\{f_n\}$ is

(d) both $\{f_n\}$ and $\{g_n\}$ are uniformly convergent

123. Let $f : [0, 1] \to R$ and $g : [0, 1] \to R$ be two functions defined by

$$f(x) = \begin{cases} \frac{1}{n} \text{ if } x = \frac{1}{n}, n \in N \\ 0 \quad \text{otherwise} \end{cases} \text{ and}$$

$$g(x) = \begin{cases} n \text{ if } x = \frac{1}{n}, n \in N \\ 0 \quad \text{otherwise} \end{cases}. \text{ Then}$$

(a) both f and g are Riemann integrable

(b) f is Riemann integrable but g is not

(c) g is Riemann integrable but f is not

(d) neither f nor g is Riemann integrable

124. The set of all continuous functions $f : [0, 1] \to R$ satisfying

$$\int_0^1 t^n f(t)dt = 0, n = 0, 1, 2, ...$$

(a) is empty

(b) contains a single element

(c) is countably infinite

(d) is uncountably infinite

125. Let $f : R^3 \to R^3$ be defined by $f(x_1, x_2, x_3) = (x_2 + x_3, x_3 + x_1, x_1 + x_2)$. Then the first derivative off is

(a) not invertible anywhere

(b) invertible only at the origin

(c) invertible everywhere except at the origin

(d) invertible everywhere

2003

126. The continuous function $f : R \to R$ defined by $f(x) = (x^2 + 1)^{2003}$ is

(a) onto but not one-one

(b) one-one but not onto

(c) both one-one and onto

(d) neither one-one nor onto

127. Diameter of a set S in a metric space with metric d is defined by

diam (S) = 1. *u*. *b*. $\{d(x, y) \mid x, y \text{ in } S\}$

Thus, diameter of the cylinder $C = \{(x, y, z) \text{ in } R^3 \mid x^2 + y^2 = 1, -1 < z < 1\}$ in R^3 with standard metric, is

(a) 2 (b) $2\sqrt{2}$

(c) $\sqrt{2}$ (d) $\pi + 2$

128. Let $X = (0, 1) \cup (2, 3)$ be an open set in R. Let f be a continuous function on X such that the derivative $f'(x) = 0$ for all x. Then the range off has

(a) uncountable number of points

(b) countably infinite number of points

(c) at most 2 points

(d) at most 1 point

129. Let $X = \{x \text{ in } Q \mid 0 < x < 1\}$ be the metric space with standard metric from R. The completion of X is

(a) $\{x \text{ in } Q \mid 0 < x < 1\}$ (b) $\{x \text{ in } R \mid 0 < x < 1\}$

(c) $\{x \text{ in } Q \mid 0 \le x \le 1\}$ (d) $\{x \text{ in } R \mid 0 \le x \le 1\}$

130. The function $f(x, y) = (e^x \cos y, e^x \sin y)$ from R^2 to R^2 is

(a) one-one on all of R^2

(b) one-one on some neighbourhood of any point in R^2

(c) an onto map

(d) such that some neighbourhood of any point surjects onto R^2

131. Let E and E_i $(i = 1, 2,., \infty)$ be measurable subsets of the real line such that $E = \bigcup_{i=1}^{\infty} E_i$. Let f be a non-negative function such that f is integrable over E, then $\int_E f\,dx = \sum_{i=1}^{\infty} \int_{E_i} f\,dx$

(a) true as $\sum_{i=1}^{\infty} \int_{E_i} f\,dx$ is finite

(b) true by dominated convergence theorem

(c) true by Fatou's lemma

(d) not true because $E_i \cap E_j$ may not be empty for some $i \neq j$

132. In the inerval [–1, 1], the series

$$\sum_{n=1}^{\infty} (-1)^{n-1} \frac{x^2 + n^2}{n^3} \text{ is}$$

(a) uniformly and absolutely convergent

(b) absolutely convergent but not uniformly convergent

(c) neither uniformly nor absolutely convergent

(d) uniformly convergent but not absolutely convergent

133. The maximum magnitude of the directional derivative for the surface

$$x^2 + xy + yz = 9$$

at the point (1, 2, 3) is along the direction

(a) $\hat{i} + \hat{j} + \hat{k}$ (b) $2\hat{i} + 2\hat{j} + \hat{k}$

(c) $\hat{i} + 2\hat{j} + 3\hat{k}$ (d) $\hat{i} - 2\hat{j} + 3\hat{k}$

134. Let $B = \{(x, y, z) \mid x, y, z, \in R \text{ and } x^2 + y^2 + z^2 \le 4\}$. Let $v(x, y, z) = x\hat{i} + y\hat{j} + z\hat{k}$ be a vector-valued function defined on B. If $r^2 = x^2 + y^2 + z^2$, the value of the integral $\iiint_B \nabla.(r^2 v(x, y, z))dV$ is

(a) 16 π (b) 32 π

(c) 64 π (d) 128 π

2002

135. Let T be any circle enclosing the origin and oriented counter-clockwise. Then the value of the integral $\int_\Gamma \frac{\cos z}{z^2} dz$ is

(a) $2\pi i$

(b) 0

(c) $-2\pi i$

(d) undefined

136. Let $f: [0, 1] \to R$ be a bounded Riemann integrable function and let $g : R \to R$ be continuous. Then $g o f$ is:

(a) Riemann integrable

(b) continuous

(c) Lebesgue integrable, but not Riemann integrable

(d) not necessarily measurable

137. Let V be the volume of a region bounded by a smooth closed surface S. Let r denote the position vector and $\hat{n}$ denote the outward unit normal to S. Then the integral $\iint_S r.\hat{n}\ dS$ equals

(a) V (b) $\frac{V}{3}$

(c) 3V (d) 0

138. For a subset A of a metric space, which of the following implies the other three ?

(*a*) A is closed

(*b*) A is bounded

(*c*) Closure of B is compact for every $B \subseteq A$

(*d*) A is compact

139. Pick out the largest of the sets given below on which the sequence of functions $\left\{e^{-n\cos^2 x}\right\}_{n=1}^{\infty}$ converges uniformly

(*a*) $\left[0, \frac{9\pi}{20}) \cup (\frac{11\pi}{20}, \pi\right]$

(*b*) $\left[0, \frac{\pi}{2}) \cup (\frac{\pi}{2}, \pi\right]$

(*c*) $\left[0, \frac{\pi}{2} - \delta) \cup (\frac{\pi}{2} + \delta, \pi\right], 0 < \delta < \frac{\pi}{100}$

(*d*) $[0, \pi]$

140. Let $f : R^2 \to R$ be a smooth function with positive definite Hessian at every point. Let $(a, b) \in R^2$ be a critical point off. Then

(*a*) f has a global minimum at (a, b).

(*b*) f has a local, but not a global minimum at (a, b).

(*c*) f has a local, but not a global maximum at (a, b).

(*d*) f has a global maximum at (a, b).

141. If u is harmonic on $\{(x, y) / x^2 + y^2 \le 1\}$, then $\int_0^{2\pi} \frac{\partial u}{\partial n} d\theta$ equals

(where $\frac{\partial u}{\partial n}$ is the normal derivative of u on the boundary of the unit disc)

(*a*) 2π (*b*) 1

(*c*) π (*d*) 0

142. Let a, b be real numbers with $0 < a < b$. Define sequences $\{a_n\}$ and $\{b_n\}$ recursively by

$$a_{n+1} = \sqrt{a_n b_n}$$

and $$b_{n+1} = \frac{a_n + b_n}{2},$$

where $a_1 = a, b_1 = b$.

Show that $\{a_n\}$ is an increasing sequence, $\{b_n\}$ is a decreasing sequence, and both converge to the same limit.

143. Let $f(t)$ be a real-valued continuous function on $[0, 1]$ such that

$$\int_0^1 f(t) t^n dt = 0, \text{ for all } n = 0, 1, 2, \dots$$

Prove that $f(t)$ vanishes identically.

2001

144. A uniformly continuous function is

(*a*) measurable

(*b*) not measurable

(*c*) measurable and simple

(*d*) integrable and simple

145. The connected subsets of the real line with the usual topology are

(*a*) all intervals

(*b*) only bounded intervals

(*c*) only compact intervals

(*d*) only semi-infinite intervals

146. Let $f : [a, b] \to R$ be a bounded function where $-\infty < a < b < \infty$. Then f is Riemann integrable if and only if f is continuous everywhere on $[a, b]$ except on

(*a*) the empty set

(*b*) a set of measure zero

(*c*) a finite number of points

(*d*) a countably infinite number of points

147. The function f is defined on $[0, 1]$ as follows $f(x) = x \sin \frac{1}{x}, x \ne 0$

$f(0) = 0.$

Find the (Lebesgue) measure of the set $\{x \mid f(x) \ge 0\}$.

148. Consider two metric spaces (R, d_1), (R, d_2) where

$d_1(y, z) = |y - z|$ and

$$d_2(y, z) = \left|\frac{y}{1+|y|} - \frac{z}{1+|z|}\right|.$$

Let the functions $f, f_n : [0, \infty] \to R$ be defined by

$$f(x) = x, f_n(x) = x\left(1 + \frac{1}{n}\right), \text{ for } 0 \le x < \infty,$$

where $[0, \infty]$ is the subspace of (R, d_1). Show that f_n converges to f uniformly on $[0, \infty]$ when R has metric d_2 but f_n does not converge uniformly to f on $[0, \infty]$ when R has metric d_1.

2000

149. Let E be the set of all rationals p such that $2 < p^2 < 3$. Then E is

(*a*) compact in Q

(*b*) closed and bounded in Q

(*c*) not compact in Q

(*d*) closed and unbounded in Q

150. Let A be the set of points in the interval (0, 1)

representing the numbers whose expansion as infinite decimals do not contain the digit 7. Then the measure of A is

(a) 1 (b) 0

(c) $\frac{1}{2}$ (d) ∞

151. The Fourier expansion in the interval [– 4, 4] of the function

$f(x) = -x, -4 \le x \le 0, = x, 0 \le x \le 4$, has

(a) no cosine term

(b) no sine term

(c) both cosine and sine terms

(d) none of these

152. If A is the subspace of l^∞ consisting of all sequences of zeros and ones and d is the induced metric on A, then the rare sets in (A, d) are

(a) empty set

(b) all singleton subsets of A

(c) power set of A

(d) set A itself

153. Evaluate $\iint_S (curl\, v).n\, dS$

where $v = 2yi + 3xj - z^2 k$ and S is the upper half surface of the sphere $x^2 + y^2 + z^2 = 9$, n is a positive unit normal vector to S and C is its boundary.

154. (a) Examine the series $\sum_{n=1}^{\infty} \frac{nx}{n+x}, x \in [0, 1]$ as regards to its uniform convergence on the domain $0 \le x \le 1$.

(b) Prove that set of points on which a sequence of measurable functions (f_n) converges is measurable.

ANSWERS

1. (d)	**2.** (1.41)	**3.** (0)	**4.** (a)	**5.** (1)	**6.** (1)	**7.** (0.041)	**8.** (16)	**9.** (1)	**10.** (0)
11. (2)	**12.** (1.2)	**13.** (b)	**14.** (c)	**15.** (4)	**16.** (d)	**17.** (150)	**18.** (a)	**19.** (b)	**20.** (28)
21. (2)	**22.** (3.99 to 4.01)		**23.** (d)	**24.** (b)	**25.** (d)	**26.** (6.99 to 7.01)		**27.** (74.99 to 75.01)	
28. (0.36 to 0.38)		**29.** (d)	**30.** (6)	**31.** (2)	**32.** (a)	**33.** (d)	**34.** (b)	**35.** (b)	**36.** (b)
37. (c)	**38.** (d)	**39.** (a)	**40.** (d)	**41.** (a)	**42.** (4)	**43.** (8)	**44.** (c)	**45.** (d)	**46.** (c)
47. (b)	**48.** (b)	**49.** (a)	**50.** (d)	**51.** (b)	**52.** (a)	**53.** (c)	**54.** (b)	**55.** (b)	**56.** (b)
57. (a,b)	**58.** (c)	**59.** (a)	**60.** (a)	**61.** (c)	**62.** (c)	**63.** (b)	**64.** (c)	**65.** (d)	**66.** (b)
67. (c)	**68.** (b)	**69.** (a)	**70.** (c)	**71.** (d)	**72.** (c)	**73.** (a)	**74.** (c)	**75.** (d)	**76.** (b)
77. (d)	**78.** (d)	**79.** (c)	**80.** (c)	**81.** (b)	**82.** (a)	**83.** (b)	**84.** (d)	**85.** (c)	**86.** (a)
87. (a)	**88.** (a)	**89.** (d)	**90.** (a)	**91.** (c)	**92.** (a)	**93.** (d)	**94.** (b)	**95.** (c)	**96.** (b)
97. (d)	**98.** (c)	**99.** (a)	**100.** (b)	**101.** (c)	**102.** (a)	**103.** (c)	**104.** (a)	**105.** (c)	**106.** (b)
107. (a)	**108.** (d)	**109.** (c)	**110.** (a)	**111.** (c)	**112.** (a)	**113.** (c)	**114.** (c)	**115.** (a)	**116.** (d)
117. (b)	**118.** (b)	**119.** (c)	**120.** (d)	**121.** (c)	**122.** (a)	**123.** (a)	**124.** (b)	**125.** (d)	**126.** (d)
127. (c)	**128.** (d)	**129.** (c)	**130.** (a)	**131.** (b)	**132.** (a)	**133.** (b)	**134.** (d)	**135.** (b)	**136.** (b)
137. (b)	**138.** (d)	**139.** (a)	**140.** (c)	**141.** (d)	**142.** (*)	**143.** (*)	**144.** (d)	**145.** (a)	**146.** (b)
147. (*)	**148.** (*)	**149.** (a)	**150.** (b)	**151.** (b)	**152.** (a)	**153.** (*)	**154.** (*)		

EXPLANATIONS

1. Function f is continuous

2. Here $f(x, y) = x + y$

$$g(x, y) = x^2 + y^2$$

$$\nabla f = \lambda \nabla g$$

$$\Rightarrow \quad x = \frac{1}{2\lambda}, y = \frac{1}{2\lambda}$$

$(x, y) \in \overline{B(0,1)}$

$$\Rightarrow \lambda \le \pm\frac{1}{\sqrt{2}}, x \le \pm\frac{1}{\sqrt{2}} ey \le \pm\frac{1}{\sqrt{2}}$$

more $\{x + y : (x, y) \in \overline{B(0,1)}\} \le \sqrt{2} \approx 1.41$

3. d' Alembert's solution of the initial value problem for wave equation is

$$u(x, t) = \frac{1}{2}\left[f(x+ct)+f(x-ct)) + \frac{1}{2c}\int_{x-ct}^{x+ct} g(\tau)d\tau\right.$$

Because f, g are smooth and odd functions,

$$\text{Then } u(0, 1) = \frac{1}{2}[f(c)+f(-c))] + \frac{1}{2c}\int_{-c}^{c} g(\tau)d\tau$$

$$= \frac{1}{2}[f(c) - f(c)] + 0 = 0$$

4. By using Rodrigue's formula, we can write

$$\int_{-1}^{1} f(x)P_n(x)dx = \frac{(-1)^n}{2^n n!}\int_{-1}^{1} f^n(x).(x^2-1)^n dx$$

$$\frac{d^n f}{dx^n} = \frac{d^n(x^k)}{dx^n} = 0 \text{ if } k < n$$

$$I = \int_{-1}^{1} x^k P_n(x)dx = 0 \text{ if } k < n$$

If n – k is odd integer, then Integrand become odd function and value of integral equal to zero.

6. Since (1, 1, 1) is non-zero element in $\mathbb{R}^3$, so we can find a functional $\tilde{f}$ on $\mathbb{R}^3$ as

$$\tilde{f}(x) = ||x|| \ \& \ ||\tilde{f}|| \ne 0$$

(By Hahn–Banach's Theorem)

$$\tilde{f}(1, 1, 1) = ||(1, 1, 1)|| = 1.$$

and $\quad ||\tilde{f}|| = \sup\{|\tilde{f}(1,1,1)|\} = 1 \ne 0$

7. Let $\gamma = \{z \in \mathbb{C} \mid |z| = 2\}$ in +ve sense we know that

$$f(z) = z^7 \cos\left(\frac{1}{22}\right) = z^7\left\{1 - \frac{1}{2!z^4} + \frac{1}{4!z^8}\ldots\right\}$$

$$\text{coff of } \frac{1}{z} = \frac{1}{4!} = \operatorname*{Res}_{z=0} f(z)$$

Cauchy Residue's theorem, we have

$$\text{By } \oint_\gamma z^7 \cos\left(\frac{1}{z^2}\right)dz = 2\pi i\frac{1}{4!}$$

$$\Rightarrow \frac{1}{2\pi i}\oint_\gamma z^7 \cos\left(\frac{1}{z^2}\right)dz = \frac{1}{4!} = 0.041$$

8. $\oint_\gamma \sin x^3 dx + 6xy\,dy$ (using line integral)

$$= \int_0^2 \sin x^3 dx + \int_0^2 6x^2 dx + \int_2^0 \sin x^3 dx$$

$$= 16$$

9. $f(x, y) = (x - x_1)^2 + (y - y_1)^2$

Let, $g(x, y) = x^2 + y^2$

$$\nabla F(x, y) = \nabla g(x, y)$$

$$\Rightarrow \quad x_1 = y_1 = 0$$

$$f(x, y) = \sqrt{x^2 + y^2}$$

$$\nabla f = \frac{1}{2}(x^2 + y^2)^{-\frac{1}{2}} 2x\hat{i} + \frac{1}{2}(x^2 + y^2)^{-\frac{1}{2}} 2y\hat{j}$$

$$\nabla f(3, 4) = \frac{6}{10}\hat{i} + \frac{8}{10}\hat{j}$$

$$||\nabla f(3,4)|| = \frac{1}{10}\sqrt{6^2 + 8^2} = 1$$

10. $f(x) = \left(\int_0^x e^{-t^2} dt\right)^2$

and $g(x) = \int_0^1 \frac{e^{-x^2(1+t^2)}}{1+t^2} dt$

$$f'(x) = e^{-x^2}\sqrt{\pi}\, E_r\, f[x]$$

$$f'\sqrt{\pi} = e^{-\pi}\sqrt{\pi}\, E_r\, f[\sqrt{\pi}]$$

$$g'(x) = -e^{-\pi^2}\sqrt{\pi}\, E_r\, f[x]$$

$$g'\sqrt{\pi} = -e^{-\pi}\sqrt{\pi}\, E_r f[\sqrt{\pi}]$$

Then $f'(\sqrt{\pi}) + g'(\sqrt{\pi}) = 0$

11.

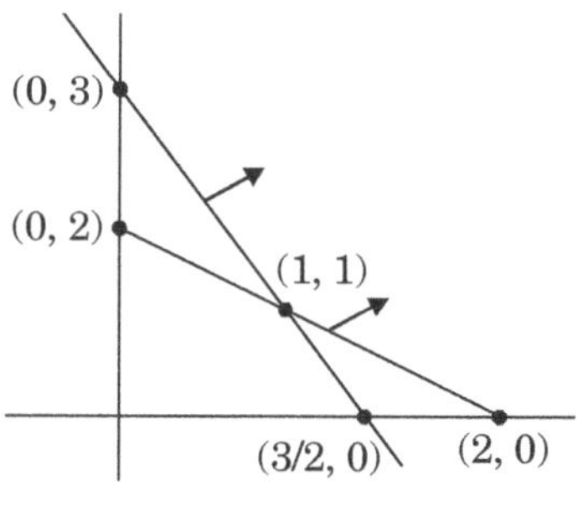

Minimize $w = x + 2y$

Subject $2x + y \geq 3$

$x + y \geq 2$

$x \geq 0, y \geq 0$

$(0, 3) \Rightarrow w = 6$

$(2, 0) \Rightarrow w = 2 \rightarrow$ minimize at (2, 0) with value $w = 2$

$(1, 1) = w = 3$

12. Using simplex method

	x	y	z	s_1	s_2	
	–11	0	1	0	0	0
s_1	$\boxed{10}$	1	–1	1	0	1
s_2	2	–2	1	0	1	2
	0	$\frac{11}{10}$	$-\frac{1}{10}$	$\frac{11}{10}$	0	$\frac{11}{10}$
x	1	$\frac{1}{10}$	$-\frac{1}{10}$	$\frac{1}{10}$	0	$\frac{1}{10}$
s_2	0	$-\frac{11}{5}$	$\frac{31}{5}$	$-\frac{1}{5}$	1	$\frac{9}{5}$
	0	$\frac{33}{31}$	0	$\frac{34}{31}$	$\frac{5}{31}$	$\frac{35}{31}$
x	1	–	0	–	–	$\frac{4}{31}$
z	0	–	1	–	–	$\frac{9}{31}$

all $z_j - c_j \geq 0$ with maximum value $= \frac{35}{31}$ $= 1.2$

and $x = \frac{4}{31}$, $y = 0$ and $z = \frac{9}{31}$

22. We know that fourier series is

$$f(x) = a_0 + \sum_{n=1}^{\infty} a_n \cos nx + \sum_{n=1}^{\infty} b_n \sin nx$$

where, coefficient of sin nx is

$$b_n = \frac{1}{\pi}\int_{-\pi}^{\pi} f(x) \sin nx \, dx$$

$\therefore$ coefficient of sin $3x$ is b_3.

$$\text{Now, } b_n = \frac{1}{\pi}\left[\int_{-\pi}^{0}(-3\pi)\sin nx\,dx + \int_{0}^{\pi}(3\pi)\sin nx\,dx\right]$$

$$= \frac{6}{n}[1-(-1)^n]$$

Put $n = 3$,

$$b_3 = \frac{6}{3}\left[1-(-1)^3\right] = 2.2 = 4$$

Hence, coefficient of sin $3x$ in fourier series expansion is 4.

23. Given sequence of functions,

$$f_n(x) = \frac{1}{x^2}\sin\left(\frac{1}{nx}\right), x \in [1, \infty]$$

$$\lim_{n\to\infty} f_n(x) = \lim_{n\to\infty} \frac{1}{x^2}\sin\left(\frac{1}{nx}\right)$$

$$= 0 = f(x)$$

Limiting function of this sequence of function $f_n(x)$ is 0

$\Rightarrow f_n(x)$ is bounded.

i.e., $|f_n(x)| \leq m \ \forall n \in N$ and $x \in [1, \infty]$

Hence by Lebesgue convergence theorem,

$$\lim_{n\to\infty}\int_1^{\infty} \sin x\, dx = \int_1^{\infty} \lim_{n\to\infty} f_n(x) dx$$

I. $$\lim_{n\to\infty}\int_1^{\infty}\frac{1}{x^2}\sin\left(\frac{1}{nx}\right)dx$$

$$= \lim_{n\to\infty}\left[-n\left\{-\cos\frac{1}{nx}\right\}_1^{\infty}\right]$$

$$= \lim_{n\to\infty}\left[n\left(\cos 0 - \cos\frac{1}{n}\right)\right]$$

$$= \lim_{n\to\infty} n\left[1-\left(1-\frac{1}{\lfloor 2 n^2}+\frac{1}{\lfloor 4 n^4}\cdots\right)\right]$$

$$= \lim_{n\to\infty} n\left(\frac{1}{\lfloor 2 n^2}+\frac{1}{\lfloor 4 n^4}+\ldots\right)$$

$$= 0$$

II. $$\int_1^{\infty}\lim_{n\to\infty} f_n(x)dx = \int_1^{\infty}\lim_{n\to\infty}\frac{1}{x^2}\sin\left(\frac{1}{nx}\right)dx$$

$$= \int_1^{\infty}\frac{1}{x^2}\sin 0\, dx$$

$$= 0$$

Hence quantities I and II are well defined and I = II.

24. We know that d will be metric on X if d satisfies following axioms.

(i) $d(x, y) \geq 0 \ \forall x, y \in X$

(ii) $d(x, y) = 0$ iff $x = y$

(iii) $d(x, y) = d(y, x) \ \forall x, y \in X$

(iv) $d(x, y) \leq d(x, z) + d(z, y) \ \forall x, y, z \in X$

Now, $D = \max\{d_2, 2\}$ is not metric on X because D does not satisfies IInd axiom $D(x, y) = 0$ iff $x = y$.

since, d_2 is metric then at $x = y$, $d_2(x, y) = 0$

$\therefore$ at $x = y$, max {0, 2} = 2

Thus at $x = y$, $D \neq 0$ i.e. $D(x, y) \neq 0$

Hence, $D(x, y)$ is not metric on X.

25. Given, $X = [0, 1) \cup (1, 2)$ be the subspace of R.

Then, there exist any onto continuous function $f : [0\ 1] \to X$.

28.

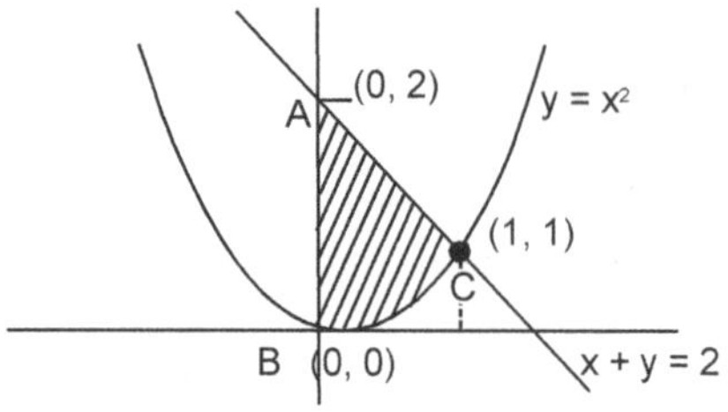

$$\iint_R xy\,dx\,dy = \int_{x=0}^{1}\int_{y=x^2}^{2-x} xy\,dx\,dy$$

$$= \int_{x=0}^{1}\left[\frac{y^2}{2}\right]_{x^2}^{2-x} x\,dx$$

$$= \int_0^1 \frac{1}{2}\left[(2-x)^2 - x^4\right]x\,dx$$

$$= \int_0^1 \frac{1}{2}\left[4x + x^3 - 4x^2 - x^5\right]dx$$

$$= \frac{1}{2}\left[2x^2 + \frac{x^4}{4} - \frac{4}{3}x^3 - \frac{x^6}{6}\right]_0^1$$

$$= \frac{9}{24} = \frac{3}{8} = 0.37$$

29. Given, partial order in R^2 such that

$(x_1, y_1) < (x_2, y_2)$ EITHER if $x_1 < x_2$ OR if $x_1 = x_2$ and $y_1 < y_2$.

Then $[0, 1] \times [0, 1]$ and $[0, 1] \times \{1\}$ both are not compact..

30. From
$$g(x) = \int_1^3 f(x+t)dt$$

$$g'(x) = f(x+t)\frac{d(x+t)}{dt}\Bigg|^3$$

$$= f(x + 3) - f(x + 1)$$

$$g'(0) = f(3) - f(1)$$

$$11 - 5 = 6$$

31.
$$I_1 = \int_0^{\infty}\int_x^{\infty}\left(\frac{1}{y}\right)e^{-y/2}dydx$$

Let
$$I = \int \frac{1}{y}e^{-y/2}dy$$

64 parts

$$I = \frac{-e^{-y/2}}{y^2} + \frac{1}{2}\int e^{-y/2}\frac{1}{y}dy$$

$$\frac{I}{2} = -\frac{e^{-y/2}}{y^2}$$

$$I = -\frac{2e^{-y/2}}{y^2}$$

Put limits

$$I = \frac{2e^{-x/2}}{x^2}$$

Now
$$I_1 = \int_0^{\infty} 2\frac{e^{-x/2}}{x^2}dx$$

Similarly $I_1 = ?$

32. $f(x) = \sum_{n=1}^{\infty}\frac{\sin nx}{n^2}$ $\lim_{x\to 0}\frac{\sin nx}{nx.n}\cdot x$

$$\lim_{x\to 0}\frac{x}{n} = 0$$

33.
$$f(x, y) = (e^{x+y}, e^{x-y})$$

The area of the image of the region for

$$x = 1, y = 1$$

$$e^{x+y} - e^{x-y}$$

$$= e^2 - e^0 = e^2 - 1$$

34.
$$\{a_n\} \to \tan x = x$$

$$\{b_n\} \to = \sqrt{x} = x$$

$$\sum_{n=1}^{\infty}\frac{1}{a_n},\ \lim_{n\to\infty}\frac{1}{a_n} \to \infty$$

So it diverges

$$\lim_{n\to\infty}\sum_{n=1}^{\infty}\frac{1}{b_n} \to 0$$

So it converges.

35.
$$f(x) = \begin{cases} x, & \text{if } x = \dfrac{1}{n} \quad \text{for } n \in \mathbb{N} \\ 0 & \text{otherwise} \end{cases}$$

function depends on x. f is Riemann integrable

$$g(x) = \begin{cases} 1 \text{ if } x \in \mathbb{Q} \cap [0, 1] \\ 0 \quad \text{otherwise} \end{cases}$$

Function does not depends on x, g is Lebesgue integrable.

36. X is a real values random variable

For expectation $E[x]$ and $E[x^2]$.2 and 3 value can not be attained.

38.
$$\lim_{n\to\infty}\frac{2^{-n^2}}{\sum_{k=n+1}^{\infty} 2^{-k^2}}$$

$$= \lim_{n\to\infty}\frac{2^{-n^2}}{2^{-(n+1)^2} + 2^{-(n+2)^2} + \ldots 2^{-\infty}}$$

$$= \infty$$

39. $S = \{x \in \mathbb{R} : x \geq 0, \sum_{n=1}^{\infty} x^{\sqrt{n}} < \infty\}$

Supremum of S is 1.

41. If $f \in L'(\mathbb{R})$ and $\lim_{|x| \to \infty} f(x)$ exists then limit is zero.

If $f \in L'(\mathbb{R})$ is uniformly continuous, then $\lim_{|x| \to \infty} f(x)$ exists and equals to zero.

48. Given functional is

$$\int_0^1 (y^2 + 4y^2 + 8ye^x)dx \quad \text{...(1)}$$

with $y(0) = -\frac{4}{3}, y(1) = -\frac{4e}{3}$

$$F(x, y, y') = y'^2 + 4y^2 + 8ye^x$$

$$\frac{\partial F}{\partial y} = 8y + 8e^x$$

$$\frac{\partial F}{\partial y'} = 2y'$$

$\therefore$ Euler's equation is

$$\frac{\partial F}{\partial y} - \frac{d}{dx}\left(\frac{\partial F}{\partial y'}\right) = 0 \quad \text{...(2)}$$

$$8y + 8e^x - \frac{d}{dx}(2y') = 0$$

$$2y'' - 8y = 8e^x$$

$$y'' - 4y = 4e^x \quad \text{...(3)}$$

which is non homogeneons ordinary differential equation of second order.

$\therefore$ Complementary function of equation (3) is

$$\text{C.F.} = c_1 e^{2x} + c_2 e^{-2x}$$

$$\text{P.I.} = \frac{1}{(D' - 4)} 4e^x$$

$$= \frac{1}{(1-4)}.4e^x = -\frac{4}{3}e^x$$

General solution of equation (3) is

$$y(x) = c_1 e^{2x} + c_2 e^{-2x} - \frac{4}{3}e^x \quad \text{...(4)}$$

$$y(0) = -\frac{4}{3}$$

$$-\frac{4}{3} = c_1 + c_2 - \frac{4}{3}$$

$$c_1 + c_2 = 0 \quad \text{...(5)}$$

$$y(1) = \frac{-4e}{3}$$

$$\frac{-4e}{3} = c_1 e^2 + c_2 e^{-2} - \frac{4e}{3}$$

$$C_1 e^2 + c_2 e^{-2} = 0 \quad \text{...(6)}$$

solve equation (5) and (6)

$$c_1 = c_2 = 0$$

Therefore from equation (4), we get

$$y(x) = -\frac{4}{3}e^x$$

$$P = -\frac{4}{3}e^x$$

Therefore Weierstrass function is.

$$\begin{aligned} F(x, y, P, y') &= F(x, y, y') - F(x, y, P) \\ &\quad - (y' - P) F_P(x, y, P) \\ &= y'^2 + 4y^2 + 8ye^x - P^2 \\ &\quad - 4y^2 - 8ye^x - (y' - P) zP \\ &= (y'^2 - P^2) - (y' - P) = P \\ &= y'^2 - P^2 - 2Py' + 2P^2 \\ &= y'^2 - 2y' P + P^2 \\ &= (y' - P)^2 \\ &\geq 0 \ \forall \ y' \end{aligned}$$

Therefore given function (1) posses strong minima on

Sol. (Q. 49 and 50)

Given Fredholm integral equation is

$$4(x) = x + \lambda \int_0^1 xe^t u(t)dt \quad \text{...(1)}$$

$$k(x, t) = xe^t$$

$$k_1(x, t) = k(x, t) = xe^t$$

$$k_2(x, t) = \int_0^1 k(x,z).k_1(z,t)dz$$

$$= \int_0^1 xe^z.ze^t dz$$

$$= xe^t \int_0^1 ze^z dz$$

$$= xe^t \left[e^z.z - e^z\right]_0^1$$

$$= xe^t[e - e - 0 + 1]$$

$$= xe^t$$

$$k_3(x, t) = \int_0^1 k(x,z)k_2(z,t)dz$$

$$= \int_0^1 xe^z.ze^t dz$$

$$= xe^t \int_0^1 ze^z dz$$

$$= xe^t \left[e^z.z - e^z\right]_0^1 = xe^t$$

Similarly $k_n(x, t) = xe^t$

49. Resolvent kernel is

$$R(x, t, d) = k_1(x, t) + \lambda k_2(x, t) + \lambda^2 k_3(x, t) + \ldots$$
$$= xe^t + \lambda xe^t + \lambda^2 xe^t + \ldots$$
$$= xe^t [1 + \lambda + \lambda^2 +] \ldots$$
$$= xe^t\left[\frac{1}{1-\lambda}\right]$$
$$= \frac{xe^t}{1-\lambda}$$

50. The solution of the integral equation is

$$y(x) = R(x) + \lambda\int_0^1 R(x,t,\lambda)F(t)dt$$
$$= x + \lambda\int_0^1 \frac{xe^t}{(1-\lambda)}t.dt$$
$$= x + \frac{\lambda x}{(1-\lambda)}\int_0^1 te^t dt$$
$$= x + \frac{\lambda x}{(1-\lambda)}[te^t - e^t]_0^1$$
$$= x + \frac{\lambda x}{1-\lambda}$$
$$= \frac{x}{1-\lambda}$$

51. By Greeh's Theorem

$$\oint_C (Mdx + Ndy) = \iint_R \left(\frac{\partial M}{\partial x} - \frac{\partial M}{\partial y}\right)dxdy$$
$$\therefore \oint_C \left[\left(2x^2 + y^2\right)dx + e^4 dy\right]$$
$$= \iint_R \left[\frac{\partial}{\partial x}(e^y) - \frac{\partial}{\partial y}\left(2x^2 + y^2\right)\right]dxdy$$
$$= \iint_R [0 - (0 + 2y)]dxdy$$
$$= -2\iint_R y\,dx\,dy$$

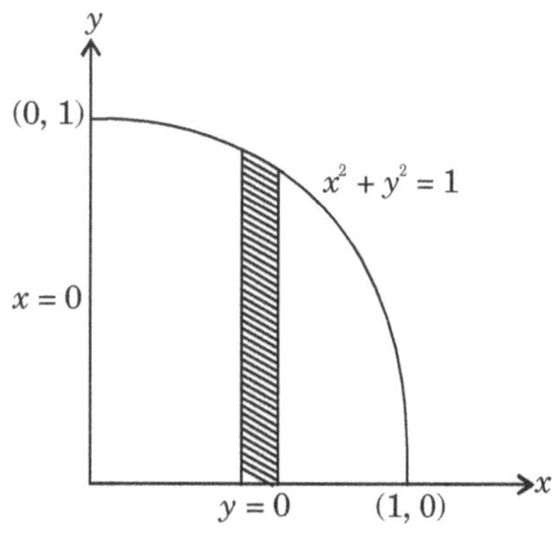

$$= -2\int_{x=0}^{1}\int_{y=0}^{\sqrt{1-x^2}} y\,dx\,dy = -2\int_{x=0}^{1}\left[\frac{y^2}{2}\right]_0^{\sqrt{1-x^2}} dx$$
$$= -2\int_{x=0}^{1}\frac{\left(1-x^2\right)}{2}dx = -\left[x - \frac{x^3}{3}\right]_0^1$$
$$= -\left[1 - \tfrac{1}{3}\right] = -2/3$$

53.
$$y(x) = \lambda\int_0^1 x^2 t\,y(t)dt$$
$$y(x) = \lambda x^2\int_0^1 t\,y(t)dt \quad \ldots (1)$$

Let
$$C = \int_0^1 t\,y(t)dt \quad \ldots (2)$$

Then equation (1) reduce to
$$y(x) = \lambda Cx^2 \quad \ldots (3)$$

from equation (3)
$$y(t) = \lambda Ct^2 \quad \ldots (4)$$

using equation (4) & (2)
$$C = \int_0^1 t\lambda Ct^2 dt$$
$$C = \lambda C\int_0^1 t^3 dt$$
$$C = \frac{\lambda C}{4}$$
$$\left[1 - \frac{\lambda}{4}\right]C = 0$$

If C = 0 then equation (4) gives $y(x) = 0$. we assume that for non-zero solution of equation (1). So $c \neq 0$

Then $1 - \frac{\lambda}{4} = 0 \Rightarrow \lambda = 4$

55. Let
$$f = x^2 + 8y^2 + 27z^2 \quad \ldots (1)$$
$$\phi = \frac{1}{x} + \frac{1}{y} + \frac{1}{z} - 1 = 0 \quad \ldots (2)$$

from equation (1) we have
$$\frac{\partial f}{\partial x} = 2x, \frac{\partial f}{\partial y} = 16y, \frac{\partial f}{\partial z} = 54z$$

from equation (2) we have
$$\frac{\partial \phi}{\partial x} = -\frac{1}{x^2}, \frac{\partial \phi}{\partial y} = -\frac{1}{y^2}, \frac{\partial \phi}{\partial z} = -\frac{1}{z^2}$$

By Lagrangis method of multiplies's

$$\frac{\partial f}{\partial x}+\lambda\frac{\partial \phi}{\partial x}=0$$

$$\Rightarrow \quad 2x-\frac{\lambda}{x^2}=0 \qquad \text{... (3)}$$

$$\frac{\partial f}{\partial y}+\lambda\frac{\partial \phi}{\partial y}=0$$

$$\Rightarrow \quad 16y-\frac{\lambda}{y^2}=0 \qquad \text{... (4)}$$

$$\frac{\partial f}{\partial z}+\lambda\frac{\partial \phi}{\partial z}=0$$

$$\Rightarrow \quad 54z-\frac{1}{z^2}=0 \qquad \text{... (5)}$$

from equation (3), we get

$$2x^3-\lambda=0$$

$$\Rightarrow \quad x=\frac{\lambda^{1/3}}{2^{1/3}} \qquad \text{... (6)}$$

from equation (4), we get

$$16y^3-\lambda=0$$

$$\Rightarrow \quad y=\frac{\lambda^{1/3}}{2.2^{1/3}} \qquad \text{... (7)}$$

from equation (5), we get

$$54z^3-\lambda=0$$

$$\Rightarrow \quad z=\frac{\lambda^{1/3}}{3.2^{1/3}} \qquad \text{... (8)}$$

using equation (6), (7) & (8) in equation (2), we get

$$\frac{3.2^{1/3}}{\lambda^{1/3}}+\frac{2.2^{1/3}}{\lambda^{1/3}}+\frac{2^{1/3}}{\lambda^{1/3}}=1$$

$$\frac{6.2^{1/3}}{\lambda^{1/3}}=1$$

$$\lambda^{1/3}=6.2^{1/3} \qquad \text{... (9)}$$

using equation (9) in equation (6), (7) & (8)

$$x=6, y=3, z=2$$

$$f=36+72+108$$

$$f=216$$

56. Given $f_n(x)=\dfrac{x}{[(n-1)x+1][nx+1]}$

$$=\frac{[nx+1]-[(n-1)x+x]}{[(n-1)x+1][nx+1]}$$

$$f_n(x)=\frac{1}{[(n-1)x+1]}-\frac{1}{[nx+1]}$$

Putting $n=1, 2, 3.....$

$$f_1(x)=1-\frac{1}{x+1}$$

$$f_2(x)=\frac{1}{x+1}-\frac{1}{2x+1}$$

$$f_3(x)=\frac{1}{2x+1}-\frac{1}{3x+1}$$

$$\vdots \qquad \vdots \qquad \vdots$$

$$f_{n-1}(x)=\frac{1}{(n-1)x+1}-\frac{1}{(x+1)}$$

$$f_n(x)=\frac{1}{(n-1)x+1}-\frac{1}{nx+1}$$

On adding all these

$$f_1(x)+f_2(x)+..+f_n(x)=1-\frac{1}{nx+1}$$

$$s_n(x)=\frac{nx}{nx+1}$$

Hence $\quad s(x)=\lim_{n\to\infty}s_n(x)$

$$=\begin{cases}0 & \text{when } x=0\\ 1 & \text{when } x\neq 0\end{cases}$$

we consider $x\neq 0$ we have

$Mn=\sup\{1S_n(x)-s(x)\mid : x\in R_0\}$

$$=\sup\left\{\frac{1}{1nx+1}: x\in R_0\right\}$$

$$\geq \frac{1}{\left(\frac{n.1}{n}+1\right)}=\frac{1}{2}\left[\text{taking } x=\frac{1}{n}\neq 0\right]$$

Hence M_n cannot tend to zero as $n\to\infty$ and consequently the sequence is not uniformly convergent by M_n test. Here 0 is a point of non-uniform convergence. Since $x\to 0$ as $x\to\infty$

58. We know that if $f(x)$ and $g(x)$ are continous on the interval $[a, b]$ and $f(t)>0$, $\forall\ t\in[a, b]$ then there exists $c\in[a, b]$ such that

$$\int_a^b f(x)g(x)dx=g(c)\int_a^b f(x)dx$$

in the given problem $f(x)$ is non negative

i.e. $f(t)>0\ \forall\ t\in[1, 2]$

and $\quad g(x)=\dfrac{1}{\sqrt{x}}$

$$g(x)\in\left[\frac{1}{\sqrt{2}},1\right],\forall x\in[1,2]$$

$$k\in\left[\frac{1}{\sqrt{2}},1\right]$$

$$\Rightarrow \quad k\in\left[\frac{2}{3},1\right]$$

59. Given that

$$d(x, y) = \frac{|x-y|}{1+|x-y|}$$

we know that

$$|x-y| < 1 + |x-y|$$

$$\frac{|x-y|}{1+|x-y|} < 1$$

$$d(x, y) < 1, \ \forall x, y \in R$$

$\Rightarrow d.(x_1, y)$ is bounded also it is not compact.

60. Given that

$$f(x, y) = \begin{cases} \frac{xy}{(x^2+y^2)^{3/2}}\left[1-\cos(x^2+y^2)\right], & (x, y) \neq (0,0) \\ k & (x, y) = (0,0) \end{cases}$$

Since F(x, y) is continous at (0, 0) therefore the limiting value of $f(x, y)$ at (0, 0) is equal to actual value of $f(x, y)$ at (0, 0)

i.e. $\lim_{(x,y)\to(0,0)} f(x,y) = f(0, 0)$

$$\lim_{(x,y)\to(0,0)} f(x,y) = k \quad \text{... } (i)$$

$$\lim_{(x,y)\to(0,0)} f(x,y)$$

$$= \lim_{(x,y)\to(0,0)} \left[\frac{xy}{(x^2+y^2)^{3/2}}\left[1-\cos(x^2+y^2)\right]\right]$$

We approach at (0, 0) along the x-axis i.e. $y = 0$ therefore $\lim_{(x,y)\to(0,0)} f(x,y) = \lim_{x\to 0}[0] = 0$

from equation (i) $k = 0$

63. $\int_C \frac{e^4}{x}dx + \left(e^4 \log x + x\right)dy$ ... (1)

The Green theorem we have

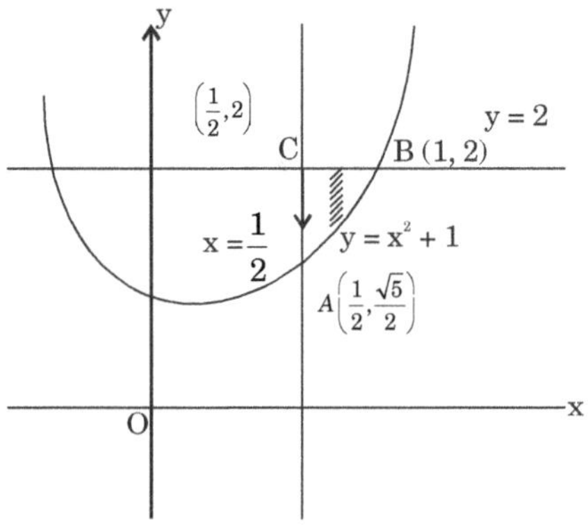

Fig.

$$\oint_C Mdx + Ndy = \iint R\left(\frac{\partial N}{\partial x} - \frac{\partial M}{\partial y}\right)dxdy \text{ ... (2)}$$

from equation (1) we have

$$M = \frac{e^4}{x}, \ N = e^4 \log x + x$$

$$\frac{\partial M}{\partial y} = \frac{e^4}{x}, \frac{\partial N}{\partial x} = \frac{e^4}{x} + 1 \text{ ... (3)}$$

$$\frac{\partial N}{\partial x} - \frac{\partial M}{\partial y} = 1 \quad \text{... (4)}$$

using equation (3) & (4) in equation (2)

$$\oint_C \frac{e^4}{x}dx + \left(e^4 \log x + x\right)dy = \iint_R dxdy$$

$$= \int_{x=1/2}^{1} \int_{y=1+x^2}^{2} dxdy = \int_{x=1/2}^{1} [y]_{1+x^2}^{2} dy$$

$$= \int_{x=1/2}^{1} \left(1-x^2\right)dy$$

$$= \left[x - \frac{x^3}{3}\right]_{1/2}^{1}$$

$$= \left[1-\frac{1}{3}\right] - \left(\frac{1}{2} - \frac{1}{24}\right) = 5/24$$

66. Let $\Sigma u_n = \sum \frac{x^n}{\sqrt{n}}$ and $\Sigma v_n = \sum \frac{x^n}{\sqrt{n}}$

clearly Σu_n and Σv_n both are converge on [–1, 1]

67. Given $y(t) = f(t) + 3\int_0^1 t\,s\,y(s)ds$

$$y(t) = f(t) + 3 + \int_0^1 s\,y(s)ds \text{ ... (1)}$$

Let $C = \int_0^1 S\,y(s)ds$ ... (2)

then equation (1) reduces to

$$y(t) = f(t) + 3tc \quad \text{... (3)}$$

from equation (3) $y(s) = f(s) + 3sc$ ... (4)

using (4) & (2) reduces to

$$C = \int_0^1 S\left[F(S) + 3sc\right]ds$$

$$C = \int_0^1 SF(s)ds + 3c\int_0^1 s^2 ds$$

$$C = \int_0^1 Sf(s)ds + C$$

if $\int_0^1 Sf(s)ds = 0$ then C = C since C is arbitary therefore infinitely many solution exists.

68. Given $u(x) = F(x) + \int_{\log^z}^{x} u^{t-x} u(t)dt$ ...(1)

By comparing equation (1) with

$$u(x) = F(x) + \lambda \int_{\log z}^{x} k(x,t)u(t)\, dt$$

$$\lambda = 1 \quad ...(2)$$

$$k(x, t) = e^{t-x} \quad ...(3)$$

Let $k_m(x, t)$ be the mth integrated kernel, then

$$k_1(x, t) = k(x, t) \quad ...(4)$$

and $$k_m(x, t) = \int_t^x k(x,z)k_{m-1}(z,t)dz$$

$$m = 2, 3, \quad ...(5)$$

From equation. (2) and (3), we get

$$k_1(x, t) = k(x, t) = e^{t-x} \quad ...(6)$$

Putting $m = 2$ in equation (4) and using equation (6)

$$k_2(x, t) = \int_t^x k(x,z)k_1(z,t)dz$$

$$= \int_t^x e^{z-x}.e^{t-z}dz$$

$$= e^{t-x}\int_t^x dz$$

$$= (x - t)\, e^{t-x} \quad ...(7)$$

Next putting $m = 3$ in equation (5)

$$k_3(x, t) = \int_t^x k(x,z)k_2(z,t)dz$$

$$= \int_t^x e^{z-x}(z-t)e^{t-z}dz$$

$$= e^{t-x}\int_t^x (z-t)dz$$

$$= e^{t-x}\left[\frac{(z-t)^2}{2}\right]_t^x$$

$$= e^{t-x} : \frac{(x-t)^2}{2!} \quad ...(8)$$

Observing equation (6), (7) and (8) by mathematical induction

$$k_m(x, t) = e^{t-x} - \frac{(x-t)^{m-1}}{(m-1)!}$$

$$m = 1, 2, 3,... \quad ...(9)$$

By definition of Resolvent kernel,

$$R(x, t : \lambda) = \sum_{m=1}^{\infty} \lambda^{m-1}.k_m(x,t)$$

$$= \sum_{m=1}^{\infty} k_m(x,t) \text{ (using equation 2)}$$

$$\sum_{m=1}^{\infty} e^{t-x}\frac{(x-t)^{m-1}}{(m-1)!} \text{ (using equation 9)}$$

$$= e^{t-x}\sum_{m=1}^{\infty}\frac{(x-t)^{m-1}}{(m-1)!}$$

$$= e^{t-x}.\, e^{x-t} = e^{t-x+x-t} = e^0 = 1$$

71. Let $I = \iint_E ye^{-(x+y)}dxdy$

where $E = \{(x, y) \in \mathbb{R}^2 : 0 < x < y\}$

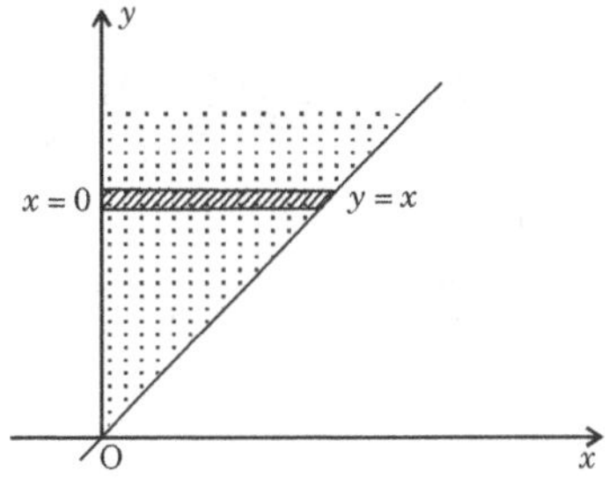

Fig.

$$I = \int_{y=0}^{\infty}\int_{x=0}^{y} ye^{-(x+y)}dxdy = \int_{y=0}^{\infty} y\left[\frac{e^{-x}}{-1}\right]_0^y e^{-y}dy$$

$$I = \int_{y=0}^{\infty} ye^{-y}e^{-x}\int_y^0 dy = \int_{y=0}^{\infty} ye^{-y}(1-e^{-y})dy$$

$$= \int_{y=0}^{\infty} (ye^{-y} - ye^{-2y})dy$$

$$= \int_{y=0}^{\infty} e^{-y}y^{2-1}dy - \int_0^{\infty} e^{-2y}y^{2-1}dy$$

$$= \frac{\overline{|2}}{1^2} - \frac{\overline{|2}}{2^2} \qquad \left[\because \int_0^{\infty} e^{-ax}x^{n-1}dx = \frac{\overline{|n}}{a^n}\right]$$

$$= 1 - \frac{1}{4} \qquad [\because \overline{|n+1} = n!\,\forall n \in I^+]$$

$$= \frac{3}{4}$$

75. Given that

$E = \{(x, y) \in R^2 : 0 \leq x \leq 1, 0 \leq y \leq x\}$

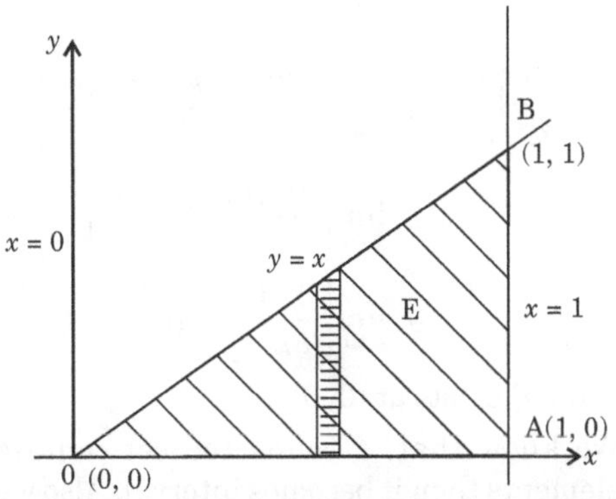

Fig.

Let $I = \iint_E (x+y)\,dxdy$

$$= \int_{x=0}^{1}\int_{y=0}^{x}(x+y)\,dxdy$$

$$= \int_{x=0}^{1}\left[xy+\frac{y^2}{2}\right]_0^x dx$$

$$= \int_{x=0}^{1}\left[x^2+\frac{x^2}{2}\right]dx$$

$$I = \int_{x=0}^{1}\frac{3x^2}{2}dx = \frac{3}{2}\left(\frac{x^3}{3}\right)_0^1 = \frac{1}{2}$$

76. Given that

$$f(x,y) = \begin{cases} \dfrac{2xy}{x^2+y^2} & (x,y)\neq(0,0) \\ 0 & (x,y)=(0,0) \end{cases}$$

$$\lim_{(x,y)\to(0,0)} f(x,y) = \lim_{(x,y)\to(0,0)}\left[\frac{2xy}{x^2+y^2}\right]$$

first we approach (0, 0) along y = mx then

$$\lim_{(x,y)\to(0,0)} f(x,y) = \lim_{(x,y)\to(0,0)}\left[\frac{2x.mx}{x^2+m^2x^2}\right]$$

$$= \lim_{x\to0}\left[\frac{2mx^2}{x^2+m^2x^2}\right]$$

$$= \lim_{x\to0}\left[\frac{2m}{1+m^2}\right] = \frac{2m}{1+m^2}$$

which is depends upon m.

$\therefore \lim_{(x,y)\to(0,0)} f(x,y)$ does not exist.

Hence $f(x, y)$ is not continous at $(x, y) = (0, 0)$ i.e. dis continous at (0, 0)

Now $\left(\frac{\partial f}{\partial x}\right)_{(0,0)} = \lim_{h\to0}\left[\frac{f(0+h,0)-f(0,0)}{h}\right]$

$$= \lim_{h\to0}\left[\frac{f(h,0)-f(0,0)}{h}\right]$$

$$= \lim_{h\to0}\left[\frac{(0-0)}{h}\right] = 0$$

$$\left(\frac{\partial f}{\partial y}\right)_{(0,0)} = \lim_{k\to0}\left[\frac{f(0,0+k)-f(0,0)}{k}\right]$$

$$= \lim_{k\to0}\left[\frac{f(0,k)-f(0,0)}{k}\right]$$

$$= \lim_{k\to0}\left[\frac{0-0}{k}\right] = 0$$

f_x and f_y exists at (0, 0)

77. We know that, a connected set contains two elements then it becomes interval. Also we know that every interval is uncountable.

80. The series $\sum_{n=1}^{\infty}\frac{x^n}{n}$ converges, each $x \in [-1, 1]$

82. Given that

$$F(x,y,z) = \frac{(x,y,z)}{(x^2+y^2+z^2)^{\frac{3}{2}}},\ (x,y,z)\in W \quad \text{... (1)}$$

and $w = \{(x,y,z)\in \mathbb{R}^3 : 1 \le x^2+y^2+z^2 \le 4\}$ ... (2)

The Gauss divergence theorem

$$\iint_S F.\hat{n}dS = \iiint_v \text{div}F dS \quad \text{... (3)}$$

$$\text{div } F = div\left[\frac{(x,y,z)}{(x^2+y^2+z^2)^{\frac{3}{2}}}\right]$$

$$= div\left(\frac{\bar{r}}{r^3}\right) \quad \left[\because \begin{array}{l} \bar{r} = (x,y,z) and \\ r^2 = x^2+y^2+z^2 \end{array}\right]$$

$$= div\left(\frac{x}{r^3}i+\frac{y}{r^3}j+\frac{z}{r^3}k\right)$$

$$= \nabla.\left(\frac{x}{r^3}i+\frac{y}{r^3}j+\frac{z}{r^3}k\right)$$

$$= \left(\frac{\partial}{\partial x}i+\frac{\partial}{\partial y}j+\frac{\partial}{\partial z}k\right).\left(\frac{x}{r^3}i+\frac{y}{r^3}j+\frac{z}{r^3}k\right)$$

$$= \frac{\partial}{\partial x}\left(\frac{x}{r^3}\right)+\frac{\partial}{\partial y}\left(\frac{y}{r^3}\right)+\frac{\partial}{\partial z}\left(\frac{z}{r^3}\right)$$

$$= \left[\frac{r^3.1-x.3r^2.\frac{\partial r}{\partial x}}{r^6}\right]+\left[\frac{r^3.1-y.3r^2.\frac{\partial r}{\partial y}}{r^6}\right]+\left[\frac{r^3.1-z.3r^2.\frac{\partial r}{\partial z}}{r^6}\right]$$

$$= \frac{3r^3-3r^2\left(x.\frac{x}{r}+y.\frac{y}{r}+z.\frac{z}{r}\right)}{r^6}$$

$$\left[\because \frac{\partial r}{\partial x}=\frac{x}{r}, \frac{\partial r}{\partial y}=\frac{y}{r}, \frac{\partial r}{rz}=\frac{z}{r}\right]$$

$$= \frac{3r^3-3r^3}{r^6} = 0$$

$\therefore$ div F = 0

using equation 4 in equation (3) we get

$$\iint_S F.\hat{n}ds = 0$$

85. On comparing the given functional with

$$\int_0^1 F(x, y, y^1)dx$$

$$F(x, y, y') = 3y^2 + 2x^3y \quad \text{... (1)}$$

The Eular's equation is

$$\frac{\partial F}{\partial y} - \frac{d}{dx}\left(\frac{\partial F}{\partial y}\right) = 0 \quad \text{... (2)}$$

from equation (1) $\frac{\partial F}{\partial y} = 6y,\ \frac{\partial F}{\partial y'} = 2x^3$

and $\frac{d}{dx}\left(\frac{\partial F}{\partial y'}\right) = 6x^2$

with these values equation (2) gives

$$6y - 6x^2 = 0 \Rightarrow y = x^2 \quad \text{... (3)}$$

Given $y(\alpha) = 1$

from equation (3) $1 = \alpha^2$

$$\alpha = \pm 1$$

86. Given that,

$s = \{(x, y) : f \text{ is continuous at the point } (x, y)\}$

then $s = \{(x, y), x \neq 0, y \neq 0\}$

$\therefore$ s is open

88. On comparing the given functional with

$\int_0^{\frac{\pi}{8}} F(x, y, y')dx$, we get

$$F(x, y, y') = (y')^2 + 2yy' - 16y^2 \quad \text{...(i)}$$

Euler's equation is

$$\frac{\delta F}{\delta y} - \frac{d}{dy}\cdot\left(\frac{\delta F}{\delta y'}\right) = 0 \quad \text{...(ii)}$$

From equation (*i*)

$$\frac{\delta F}{\delta y} = 2y' - 32y,$$

$$\frac{\delta F}{\delta y'} = 2y' + 2y$$

and $\frac{d}{dx}\left(\frac{\partial F}{\partial y'}\right) = 2y'' + 2y'$

With these values equation (*ii*) gives

$$2y' - 32y - 2y'' - 2y' = 0$$

$$y'' + 16y = 0$$

$$(D^2 + 16)y = 0 \quad \text{...(iii)}$$

The Auxiliary equation of equation (*iii*) is

$$m^2 + 16 = 0 \Rightarrow m = \pm 4i$$

$$CF = c_1 \cos 4x + c_2 \sin 4x$$

where c_1 and c_2 being arbitary constants and

$$P_1 = 0$$

$\therefore$ $y = cF + PI$

$$y = c_1 \cos 4x + c_2 \sin 4x \quad \text{...(iv)}$$

Putting $x = 0$ and $y = 0$ in equation (*iv*), we get

$$0 = c_1 1 + 0 \Rightarrow c_1 = 0 \quad \text{...(v)}$$

Putting $x = \frac{\pi}{8}$ and $y = 1$ in equation (*iv*), we get

$$1 = c_1 \cos \pi/2 + c_2 \sin \pi/2$$

$$\Rightarrow \quad 1 = c_2 \quad \text{...(vi)}$$

Using equations (*v*) and (*vi*) in equation (*iv*), we get

$$y = \sin 4x$$

90. $\oint_C -2ydx + (3x - 4y^2)dy + (z^2 + 3y)dz = 0$

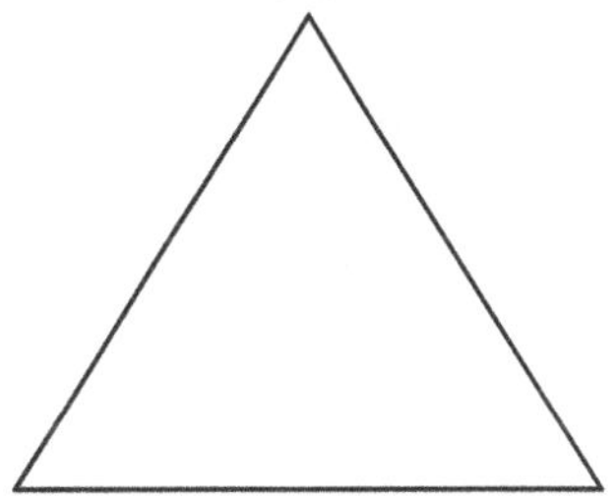

Fig.

98. Given $u(x) = \alpha\int_0^1 e^{x-t}u(t)dt$

$$\Rightarrow \quad u(x) = \alpha e^x \int_0^1 e^{-t}u(t)dt \quad \text{...(i)}$$

$$u_x = (\alpha e^x, c) \quad \text{...(ii)}$$

where $c = \int_0^1 e^{-t}u(t)dt$ ...(*iii*)

From equation (*ii*), $u(t) = \alpha e^t.\ c$ ...(*iv*)

Using equations (*iv*) and (*iii*) becomes

$$c = \int_0^1 e^{-t}\alpha e^t c dt$$

$$\Rightarrow \quad c = \alpha c\int_0^1 dt$$

$$\Rightarrow \quad c = \alpha c \Rightarrow (\alpha - 1)\, e = 0$$

For non-trival solution $c \neq 0$ therefore

$$\alpha - 1 = 0 \Rightarrow \alpha = 1$$

110. Here $c = (0, 0)$

$$u = (a_1, a_2) = \left(\frac{1}{\sqrt{2}}, \frac{1}{\sqrt{2}}\right)$$

$$\therefore \quad f'(c, u) = \lim_{h\to 0} f\frac{(c + hu) - f(c)}{h}$$

$$= \lim_{h\to 0} f\frac{[(0,0) + h(a_1, a_2) - f(0,0)]}{h}$$

$$= \lim_{h\to 0} f\frac{(ha_1, ha_2) - f(0,0)}{h}$$

$$= \lim_{h\to 0} \frac{\dfrac{h^2 a_1^2\ ha_2}{h^4 a_1^4 + h^2 a_2^2}}{h}$$

$$\Rightarrow \lim_{h\to 0} \frac{a_1^2 a_2}{h^2 a_1^4 + a_2^2}$$

$$\Rightarrow \frac{a_1^2 a_2}{a_2^2} = \frac{a_1^2}{a_2}$$

$$\Rightarrow \frac{\left(\frac{1}{\sqrt{2}}\right)^2}{\left(\frac{1}{\sqrt{2}}\right)} = \frac{1}{\sqrt{2}}$$

111. The Gauss Divergence Theorem

$$\iint_S F.\hat{n}\, ds = \iiint_V div\ F\, dv$$

given that

$$F(x, y, z) = xi + yj + (z - 2)k$$

$$\therefore \quad div\ F = \bar{\nabla}.F$$

$$= \left(\frac{\partial}{\partial x}i + \frac{\partial}{\partial y}j + \frac{\partial}{\partial z}k\right)(xi + yj + (z-2)k)$$

$$= \frac{\partial x}{\partial x} + \frac{\partial y}{\partial y} + \frac{\partial(z-2)}{\partial z}$$

$$= 1 + 1 + 1 = 3$$

∴ From Eqn. (i) we get

$$\iint F.n\, ds = \iiint_V 3dv = 3\iiint_V dv$$

$$= 3\left(\frac{2}{3}\pi.33\right)$$

[$\iiint_v dv$ = volume of the hemisphere of radius 3]

$$= 2\pi \times 27 = 54\pi$$

112. E is a non-measurable subset of [0, 1]

Let $P = E^\circ \cup \left\{\frac{1}{n} : n \in N\right\}$

and $Q = \bar{E} \cup \left\{\frac{1}{n} : n \in N\right\}$

Here E° is the interior of E, *i.e.* $E^\circ < E$ and $\bar{E}$ is the closure of E, *i.e.* $\bar{E} \approx E$

Hence, P is measurable but not Q.

113. $\displaystyle\int_0^\pi \int_x^\pi \int_0^2 \frac{\sin y}{y} dz\, dy\, dx$

$$= \int_{y=0}^{\pi} \int_{z=x}^{\pi} \int_{x=0}^{2} \frac{\sin y}{y} dz\, dy\, dx$$

= –4 (on integration)

114. $S = \left\{\frac{1}{n} : n \in N\right\} \cup \{0\} = 0, 1, \frac{1}{2}, \frac{1}{3}, ...$

$$T = \left\{n + \frac{1}{n} : n \in N\right\} = 2, \frac{5}{2}, \frac{10}{3}, ...$$

Hence by definition of complete, T and S both are complete.

116. Gauss divergence theorem

$$\iint_s F.\overset{a}{n}\, ds = \iiint_v F\, dv \qquad ...(i)$$

Here, $\bar{F} = \sin^2 xi + 2yj - z(1 + \sin 2x)\, k$

we have

$$div\ \bar{F} = \bar{\nabla} \times F$$

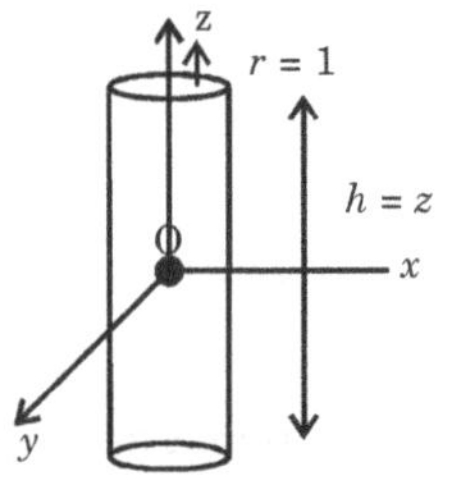

Fig

$$= \left(\frac{\partial}{\partial x}i + \frac{\partial}{\partial y}j + \frac{\partial}{\partial z}k\right)$$

$$\times [(\sin^2 xi + 2yj - z\,(1 + \sin 2x)k)]$$

$$= \frac{\partial}{\partial y}(\sin 2x) + \frac{\partial}{\partial y}(2y) + \frac{\partial}{\partial z}[-z(1+\sin 2x)]$$

$$= 2\sin x \cos x + 2 - (1 + \sin 2x)$$

$$= \sin 2x + 2 - 1 - \sin 2x = 1$$

From equation (*i*) we get

$$\iint_S [\sin^2 xi + 2yj - z(1+\sin 2x)k]\hat{n}\, dS$$

$$= \iiint_v 1.dv = \iiint_v dv$$

$$= \pi.1^2.2 = 2\pi$$

($\because$ volume of cylinder = $\pi r^2 h$)

117. We have

$$l_1 = \int_0^1 f(x)\, dx = \int_0^1 \frac{1}{\sqrt{x}} dx$$

$$= \lim_{\varepsilon\to 0} \int_{0+\varepsilon}^1 dx/\sqrt{x} = \lim_{\varepsilon\to 0} \left[2\sqrt{x}\right]_6^1$$

$$= 2\lim_{\varepsilon\to 0}\left[1\sqrt{\varepsilon}\right] = 2$$

Therefore, the given integral is convergent i.e., l, exists.

Now we have

$$l_2 = \int_1^\infty f(x) dx = \lim_{x\to\infty} \int_1^x \frac{dx}{\sqrt{x}}$$

$$= \lim_{x\to\infty}\left[\left(2\sqrt{x}\right)_1^x\right] = \lim_{x\to\infty}\left[2\left(\sqrt{x}-1\right)\right]$$

$$= \infty$$

Thus the limit does not exists finitely and therefore the given integral is divergent i.e the integral does not exists.

119. Given that

$$f(x, y) = \begin{cases} \dfrac{x^3}{x^2+y^2} & (x,y)\neq(0,0) \\ 0 & x,y=(0,0) \end{cases}$$

Clearly the directional derivation exists along any straight line

123. Given that $f(x) \begin{cases} \dfrac{1}{n} & if\ x = \dfrac{1}{n}\ n \in \text{N} \\ 0 & \text{otherwise} \end{cases}$

and $g(x) = \begin{cases} n & if\ n = \dfrac{1}{n}\ n \in \text{N} \\ 0 & \text{otherwise} \end{cases}$

we have

$$f(x) \begin{cases} 1 & , x=1 \\ 0 & , 1>x>1/2 \\ 1/2 & , x=1/2 \\ 0 & , 1/2>x>1/3 \\ 1/3 & , x=1/3 \\ \vdots & \vdots \\ 0 & , \dfrac{1}{n-1}>n>\dfrac{1}{n} \\ \dfrac{1}{n} & , n=\dfrac{1}{n} \\ \vdots & \vdots \end{cases}$$

124. Clearly $f(x)$ is discontinuous at $x = 1,\ 1, \frac{1}{2}, \frac{1}{3}, \frac{1}{4}\ldots$ i.e function have countable points of discontinue by. Thus $f(x)$ is Riemann – integrable

Now we have

$$g(x) \begin{cases} 1 & , x=1 \\ 0 & , 1>x>1/2 \\ 2 & , x=1/2 \\ 0 & , 1/2>x>1/3 \\ 3 & , x=1/3 \\ \vdots & \vdots \\ 0 & , \dfrac{1}{n-1}>n>\dfrac{1}{n} \\ n & , x=\dfrac{1}{n} \\ \vdots & \vdots \end{cases}$$

Clearly $f(x)$ is discontinuous at $x = 1, 1/2, 1/3, 1/4\ldots$ i.e., $f(x)$ have countable points of discontinuity by $f(x)$ is Riemann –integrable.

125. Let $f : \text{R}^3 \to \text{R}^3$ be defined by

$$f(x_1, x_2, x_3) = (x_2 + x_3, x_3 + x_1, x_1 + x_2)$$

$$\therefore \quad f_1(x_1, x_2, x_3) = x_2 + x_3$$

$$f_2(x_1, x_2, x_3) = x_3 + x_1$$

$$f_3(x_1, x_2, x_3) = x_1 + x_2$$

$$\therefore \quad \text{If} = \begin{vmatrix} \partial_1 f_1 & \partial_2 f_1 & \partial_3 f_1 \\ \partial_1 f_2 & \partial_2 f_2 & \partial_3 f_2 \\ \partial_1 f_3 & \partial_2 f_3 & \partial_3 f_3 \end{vmatrix}$$

$$= \begin{vmatrix} 0 & 1 & 1 \\ 1 & 0 & 1 \\ 1 & 1 & 0 \end{vmatrix}$$

$\therefore$ Thus first derivative of f is invertible every where.

133. $f = x^2 + xy + yz - 9 = 0$

grad $f = 2xi + (yi + xj) + (zj + yk)$

$= i(2x + y) + j\,(x + z) + yk$

grad f at point (1, 2, 3) is $4i + 4j + 2k$

The directional derivative of f is maximum in the direction of grad f

$= 4i + 4j + 2k$

$= 2i + 2j + k.$

134. $\text{I} = \int \nabla.(r^2 r)d\text{V} \qquad (\because \text{V} = r)$

$$= \int 5r^2 d\text{V}$$

$$= \int_0^{\pi}\int_0^{2\pi}\int_{\phi=0}^{2\pi} 5r^2.r^2 \sin\theta\, d\theta\, d\phi\, dr$$

$$= 128\pi$$

135. $$\text{I} = \int_{\Gamma} \frac{\cos z}{z^2} dz$$

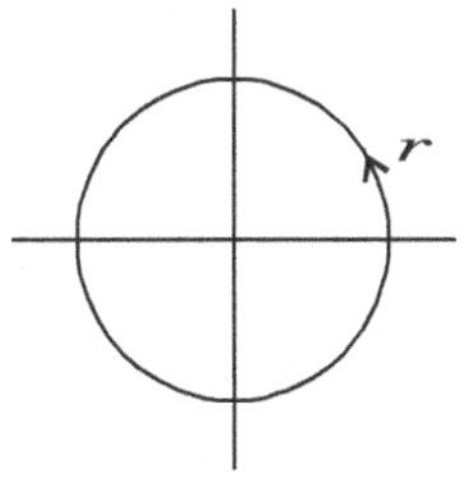

Residue at origin,

$$\text{R} = \underset{z\to 0}{\text{Lt}} \frac{d'}{dz'}(\cos z)$$

$$= \underset{z\to 0}{\text{Lt}} (-\sin z)$$

$$\therefore \quad \text{I} = 2\pi i,\ \text{R} = 0$$

137. By divergence theorem, we get

$$\iint_s \vec{r}.\hat{n} = \iiint_v \Delta.\vec{r}\, dv$$

$$= \iiint_v 3\, dv \qquad (\because \Delta.\vec{r} = 3)$$

= 3V, where V is the volume enclosed by s.

141. u is hazonomic on $\{(x, y) \mid x^2 + y^2 \le 1\}$

We know that

$$\iint_s \frac{\partial \vec{u}}{\partial n} d\vec{s} = \iint_s \left(\frac{\partial u}{\partial n}\hat{n}\right)\cdot \hat{n}\, ds$$

$$= \iint_s (\Delta u)\cdot \hat{n}\, ds$$

$$= \iiint_v \nabla.(\nabla u)\, dv,$$

by divergence theorem.

$$= \iiint_v \nabla^2 u\, dv$$

$= 0$ Since $\nabla^2 u = 0$ in v, u is harmonic inv.

153. By stoke's theorem, we have

$$\int_c v.dr = \iint_c (\text{curl}\, v).nds$$

So, $\quad I = \int_c v.dr$

where e is the boundary are $x^2 + y^2 = 9$.

$$I = \int_c (2yi + 3xj - z^2k)\,(idx + jdy)$$

$$= \int_c 2y\,dx + 3x\,dy \qquad [\text{on } x^2 + y^2 = 9, z = (0)$$

$$= 2\int_0^{2\pi} 3^2 \sin\theta.(-\sin\theta)\,d\theta + 3\int_0^{2\pi} 3^2 \cos\theta.\cos\theta\, d\theta$$

$$= -9\int_0^{2\pi} (1 - \cos 2\theta)\,d\theta + \frac{27}{2}\int_0^{2\pi} (1 - \cos 2\theta)\,d\theta$$

$$= -9[\theta]_0^{2\pi} + \frac{9}{2}[\sin 2\theta]_0^{2\pi} + \frac{27}{2}[\theta]_0^{2\pi} + \frac{27}{4}[\sin 2\theta]_0^{2\pi}$$

$$= \left[\frac{27}{2} - 9\right] 2\pi$$

$$= \mathbf{9\pi}$$

154. Here $\quad f_n(x) = \dfrac{nx}{n + x}$

Then $\quad f(x) = \underset{n\to\infty}{\text{Lt}} \dfrac{nx}{n + x}$

$$= \underset{n\to\infty}{\text{Lt}} \frac{nx}{n\left(1 + \frac{x}{n}\right)}$$

Let $\in > 0$ be given.

Then $|f_n(x) - f(x)] < \in$

$$\Rightarrow \left|\frac{nx}{n + x} - x\right| < \in$$

$$\Rightarrow \left|\frac{nx - nx - x^2}{n + x}\right| < \in$$

$$\Rightarrow \frac{x^2}{n + x} < \in$$

$$\Rightarrow (n + x) > \frac{x^2}{\in}$$

$$\Rightarrow n > \frac{x^2}{\in} - x \qquad ...(1)$$

The inequality (1) holds $\forall\ n \ge m$ where m is a positive integer just greater than $\dfrac{1}{\in}$.

In particular for $x = 0$, $m = 1$.

Hence the series converges uniformly on [0, 1].

■■

4

CHAPTER

Ordinary Differential Equations

2016

1. Let V be the set of all solutions of the equation $y'' + a y' + by = 0$ satisfying $y(0) = y(1)$, where a, b are positive real numbers. Then, dimension (V) is equal to ______.

2. Let $y'' + p(x) y' + q(x)y = 0$, $x \in (-\infty, \infty)$, where p(x) and q(x) are continuous functions. If $y_1(x) = \sin(x) - 2\cos(x)$ and $y_2(x) = 2\sin(x) + \cos(x)$ are two linearly independent solutions of the above equation, then $|4p(0) + 2q(1)|$ is equal to _____.

3. Consider the following statements P and Q:

(P) : $x^2y'' + xy' + \left(x^2 - \frac{1}{4}\right)y = 0$ has two linearly independent Frobenius series solutions near $x = 0$.

(Q) : $x^2 y' + 3\sin(x)\, y' + y = 0$ has two linearly independent Frobenius series solutions near $x = 0$.

Which of the above statements hold TRUE?

(*a*) both P and Q (*b*) only P

(*c*) only Q (*d*) Neither P nor Q

4. Let y be the solution of

$$y' + y = |x|, x \in \mathbb{R}$$
$$y(-1) = 0$$

Then y(1) is equal to

(*a*) $\frac{2}{e} - \frac{2}{e^2}$ (*b*) $\frac{2}{e} - 2e^2$

(*c*) $2 - \frac{2}{e}$ (*d*) $2 - 2e$

5. The difference between the least two eigenvalues of the boundary value problem

$y'' + \lambda y = 0, 0 < x < \pi$

$y(0) = 0, y'(\pi) = 0,$

is equal to ______________.

2015

6. The minimum possible order of a homogeneous linear ordinary differential equation with real constant coefficients having $x^2 \sin(x)$ as a solution is equal to ____

7. If $y(x)$ satisfies the initial value problem

$$(x^2 + y)dx = x\, dy,\ y(1) = 2,$$

then $y(2)$ is equal to _____

8. It is known that Bessel functions $J_n(x)$, for $n \geq 0$, satisfy the identity

$$e^{\frac{x}{2}\left(t-\frac{1}{t}\right)} = J_0(x) + \sum_{n=1}^{\infty} J_n(x)\left(t^n + \frac{(-1)^n}{t^n}\right)$$

for all $t > 0$ and $x \in \mathbb{R}$. The value of $J_0\left(\frac{\pi}{3}\right) + 2\sum_{n=1}^{\infty} J_{2n}\left(\frac{\pi}{3}\right)$ is equal to ______

2014

9. Let $y(x)$ be the solution to the initial value problem $\frac{dy}{dx} = \sqrt{y + 2x}$ subject to $y(1.2) = 2$. Using the Euler method with the step size $h = 0.05$, the approximate value of $y(1.3)$, correct to two decimal places, is__________.

10. The general solution to the ordinary differential equation

$$x^2\frac{d^2y}{dx^2} + x\frac{dy}{dx} + \left(4x^2 - \frac{9}{25}\right)y = 0$$ in terms of Bessel's functions, $J_\upsilon(x)$, is

(*a*) $y(x) = c_1J_{3/5}(2x) + c_2J_{-3/5}(2x)$

(*b*) $y(x) = c_1J_{3/10}(x) + c_2J_{-3/10}(x)$

(*c*) $y(x) = c_1J_{3/5}(x) + c_2J_{-3/5}(x)$

(*d*) $y(x) = c_1J_{3/10}(2x) + c_2J_{-3/10}(2x)$

11. If $y_1(x) = x$ is a solution to the differential equation $(1 - x^2)\frac{d^2y}{dx^2} - 2x\frac{dy}{dx} + 2y = 0$, then its general solution is

(*a*) $y(x) = c_1x + c_2\left(x\ln|1 + x^2| - 1\right)$

(*b*) $y(x) = c_1x + c_2\left(\ln\left|\frac{1-x}{1+x}\right| + 1\right)$

(*c*) $y(x) = c_1x + c_2\left(\frac{x}{2}\ln|1 - x^2| + 1\right)$

(*d*) $y(x) = c_1x + c_2\left(\frac{x}{2}\ln\left|\frac{1+x}{1-x}\right| - 1\right)$

12. The solution to the initial value problem $\frac{d^2y}{dt^2} + 2\frac{dy}{dt} + 5y = 3e^{-t}\sin t$, $y(0) = 0$ and $\frac{dy}{dt}(0) = 3$, is

(a) $y(t) = e^t(\sin t + \sin 2t)$

(b) $y(t) = e^{-t}(\sin t + \sin 2t)$

(c) $y(t) = 3e^t \sin t$

(d) $y(t) = 3e^{-t} \sin t$

2013

13. Assume that all the zeros of the polynomial $a_n x^n + a_{n-1}x^{n-1} + \ldots + a_1 x + a_0$ have negative real parts. If $u(t)$ is any solution to the ordinary differential equation

$$a_n \frac{d^n u}{dt^n} + a_{n-1}\frac{d^{n-1}u}{dt^{n-1}} + \ldots + a_1 \frac{du}{dt} + a_0 u = 0,$$

then $\lim_{t\to\infty} u(t)$ is equal to

(a) 0 (b) 1

(c) $n - 1$ (d) ∞

Statement for Linked Answer Questions 14 and 15:

Let $W(y_1, y_2)$ be the Wrönskian of two linearly independent solutions y_1 and y_2 of the equation $y'' + P(x)y' + Q(x)y = 0$.

14. The product $W(y_1, y_2)P(x)$ equals

(a) $y_2 y_1'' - y_1 y_2''$ (b) $y_1 y_2' - y_2 y_1'$

(c) $y_1' y_2'' - y_2' y_1''$ (d) $y_2' y_1' - y_1'' y_2''$

15. If $y_1 = e^{2x}$ and $y_2 = xe^{2x}$, then the value of $P(0)$ is

(a) 4 (b) –4

(c) 2 (d) –2

2012

16. If a transformation $y = uv$ transforms the given differential equation

$f(x)y'' - 4f'(x)y' + g(x)y = 0$ into the equation of the form $v'' + h(x)v = 0$, then u must be

(a) $\frac{1}{f^2}$ (b) xf

(c) $\frac{1}{2f}$ (d) f^2

17. The expression $\frac{1}{D_x^2 - D_y^2}\sin(x - y)$ is equal to

(a) $-\frac{x}{2}\cos(x - y)$

(b) $-\frac{x}{2}\sin(x - y) + \cos(x - y)$

(c) $-\frac{x}{2}\cos(x - y) + \sin(x - y)$

(d) $\frac{3x}{2}\sin(x - y)$

18. If $y = \sum_{m=0}^{\infty} c_m x^{r+m}$ is assumed to be a solution of the differential equation $x^2y'' - xy' - 3(1 + x^2)y = 0$, then the values of r are

(a) 1 and 3 (b) –1 and 3

(c) 1 and – 3 (d) –1 and – 3

19. The solution of the initial value problem $y'' + 2y' + 10y = 6\,\delta(t)$, $y(0) = 0$, $y'(0) = 0$, where $\delta(t)$ denotes the Dirac-delta function, is

(a) $2e^t \sin 3t$ (b) $6\,e^t \sin 3t$

(c) $2e^{-1} \sin 3t$ (d) $6e^{-t} \sin 3t$

20. Let $f(x)$ and $xf(x)$ be the particular solutions of a differential equation

$$y'' + R(x)y' + S(x)y = 0$$

Then the solution of the differential equation $y'' + R(x)y' + S(x)y = f(x)$ is

(a) $y = \left(-\frac{x^2}{2} + \alpha x + \beta\right) f(x)$

(b) $y = \left(\frac{x^2}{2} + \alpha x + \beta\right) f(x)$

(c) $y = (-x^2 + \alpha x + \beta)\, f(x)$

(d) $y = (x^3 + \alpha x + \beta)\, f(x)$

21. Let the Legendre equation $(1 - x^2)y'' - 2xy' + n(n + 1)y = 0$ have n^{th} degree polynomial solution $y_n(x)$ such that $y_n(1) = 3$. If $\int_{-1}^{1}\left(y_n^2(x) + y_{n-1}^2(x)\right)dx = \frac{144}{15}$, then n is

(a) 1 (b) 2

(c) 3 (d) 4

22. A particle of mass m is constrained to move on a circle with radius a which itself is roatating about its vertical diameter with a constant angular velocity ω. Assume that the initial angular velocity is zero and g is the acceleration due to gravity. If θ be the inclination of the radius vector of the particle with the axis of rotation and θ denotes the derivative of θ with respect to t, then the Lagrangian of this system is

(a) $\frac{1}{2}ma^2(\theta^2 + \omega^2\sin^2\theta) + mga\cos\theta$

(b) $\frac{1}{2}ma^2(\theta^2 + 2\omega\sin\theta) - mga\sin\theta$

(c) $\frac{1}{2}ma^2(\theta^2 + 2\omega^2\sin\theta) - mga\sin\theta$

(d) $\frac{1}{2}ma^2(\theta^2 + \omega\sin 2\theta) + mga\sin\theta$

2011

23. The initial value problem

$$x\frac{dy}{dx} = y + x^2, x > 0; y(0) = 0$$

has

(*a*) infinitely many solutions

(*b*) exactly two solutions

(*c*) a unique solution

(*d*) no solution

24. Let y be the solution of the initial value problem

$$\frac{d^2y}{dx^2} + y = 6\cos 2x, y(0) = 3, y'(0) = 1$$

Let the Laplace transform of y be F(s). Then, the value of F(1) is

(*a*) $\frac{17}{5}$ (*b*) $\frac{13}{5}$

(*c*) $\frac{11}{5}$ (*d*) $\frac{9}{5}$

25. Let y be a polynomial solution of the differential equation

$$(1 - x^2) y'' - 2xy' + 6y = 0$$

If $y(1) = 2$, then the value of the integral $\int_{-1}^{1} y^2 dx$ is

(*a*) $\frac{1}{5}$ (*b*) $\frac{2}{5}$

(*c*) $\frac{4}{5}$ (*d*) $\frac{8}{5}$

2010

26. The maximum number of linearly independent solutions of the differential equation $\frac{d^4y}{dx^4} = 0$, with the condition $y(0) = 1$, is

(*a*) 4 (*b*) 3

(*c*) 2 (*d*) 1

27. Let $y(x)$ be the solution of the initial value problem $y''' - y'' + 4y' - 4y = 0, y(0) = y'(0) = 2, y''(0) = 0$.

Then the value of $y\left(\frac{\pi}{2}\right)$ is

(*a*) $\frac{1}{5}\left(4e^{\frac{\pi}{2}} - 6\right)$ (*b*) $\frac{1}{5}\left(6e^{\frac{\pi}{2}} - 4\right)$

(*c*) $\frac{1}{5}\left(8e^{\frac{\pi}{2}} - 2\right)$ (*d*) $\frac{1}{5}\left(8e^{\frac{\pi}{2}} + 2\right)$

28. Let $y(x)$ be the solution of the initial value problem $x^2y'' + xy' + y = x, \quad y(1) = y'(1) = 1$.

Then the value of $y(e^{\frac{\pi}{2}})$ is

(*a*) $\frac{1}{2}\left(1 - e^{\frac{\pi}{2}}\right)$ (*b*) $\frac{1}{2}\left(1 + e^{\frac{\pi}{2}}\right)$

(*c*) $\frac{1}{2} + \frac{\pi}{4}$ (*d*) $\frac{1}{2} - \frac{\pi}{4}$

2009

29. If $D \equiv \frac{d}{dx}$ then the value of $\frac{1}{(xD+1)}(x^{-1})$ is

(*a*) $\log x$ (*b*) $\frac{\log x}{x}$

(*c*) $\frac{\log x}{x^2}$ (*d*) $\frac{\log x}{x^3}$

30. The equation $(\alpha xy^3 + y\cos x)\,dx + (x^2y^2 + \beta \sin x)\,dy = 0$ is exact for

(*a*) $\alpha = \frac{3}{2}, \beta = 1$ (*b*) $\alpha = 1, \beta = \frac{3}{2}$

(*c*) $\alpha = \frac{2}{3}, \beta = 1$ (*d*) $\alpha = 1, \beta = \frac{2}{3}$

31. If $y(x) = x$ is a solution of the differential equation $y'' - \left(\frac{2}{x^2} + \frac{1}{x}\right)(xy' - y) = 0, 0 < x < \infty$, then its general solution is

(*a*) $(\alpha + \beta e^{-2x})x$ (*b*) $(\alpha + \beta e^{2x})x$

(*c*) $\alpha x + \beta e^x$ (*d*) $(\alpha e^x + \beta)x$

32. Let $P_n(x)$ be the Legendre polynomial of degree n such that $P_n(1) = 1, n = 1, 2, \ldots\ldots$ If

$$\int_{-1}^{1}\left(\sum_{j=1}^{n}\sqrt{j(2j+1)}\,P_j(x)\right)^2 dx = 20,$$

then n =

(*a*) 2 (*b*) 3

(*c*) 4 (*d*) 5

Common Data for Questions 33–34

Let $y_1(x) = 1 + x$ and $y_2(x) = e^x$ be two solutions of $y''(x) + P(x)\,y'(x) + Q(x)\,y(x) = 0$.

33. P(x) =

(*a*) $1 + x$ (*b*) $-1 - x$

(*c*) $\frac{1+x}{x}$ (*d*) $\frac{-1-x}{x}$

34. The set of initial conditions for which the above differential equation has NO solution is

(*a*) $y(0) = 2, y'(0) = 1$

(*b*) $y(1) = 0, y'(1) = 1$

(*c*) $y(1) = 1, y'(1) = 0$

(*d*) $y(2) = 1, y'(2) = 2$

2008

35. Let y be a solution $y' = e^{-y^2} - 1$ on [0,1] which satisfies $y(0) = 0$. Then

(a) $y(x) > 0$ for $x > 0$

(b) $y(x) < 0$ for $x > 0$

(c) y changes sign in [0,1]

(d) $y \equiv 0$ for $x > 0$

36. For the equation $x(x-1)y'' + \sin(x)y' + 2x(x-1)y = 0$, consider the following statements

P : $x = 0$ is a regular singular point.

Q : $x = 1$ is a regular singular point.

Then

(a) both P and Q are true

(b) P is false but Q is true

(c) P is true but Q is false

(d) both P and Q are false

37. Let y_1 and y_2 be two linearly independent solutions of $y'' + (\sin x)y$, $0 \le x \le 1$.

Let $g(x) = W(y_1, y_2)(x)$ be the Wronskian of y_1 and y_2. Then

(a) $g' > 0$ on[0,1]

(b) $g' < 0$ on [0, 1]

(c) g' vanishes at only one point of [0, 1]

(d) g' vanishes at all points of [0, 1]

38. One particular solution of $y''' - y'' - y' + y = -e^x$ is a constant multiple of

(a) xe^{-x} (b) xe^{x}

(c) x^2e^{-x} (d) x^2e^{x}

39. Let $a, b \in \mathbb{R}$. Let $y = (y_1, y_2)^t$ be a solution of the system of equation $y_1' = y_2, y_2' = ay_1 + by_2$. Every solution $y(x) \to 0$ as $x \to \infty$ if

(a) $a < 0, b < 0$ (b) $a < 0, b > 0$

(c) $a > 0, b > 0$ (d) $a > 0, b < 0$

Statement for Linked Answer Questions 40 and 41:

Let $n \ge 3$ be an integer. Let y be the polynomial solution of $(1 - x^2)y'' - 2xy' + n(n-1)y = 0$ satisfying $y(1) = 1$.

40. Then the degree of y is

(a) n (b) $n - 1$

(c) less than $n - 1$ (d) greater than $n + 1$

41. If $I = \int_{-1}^{1} y(x)x^{n-3}dx$ and $J = \int_{-1}^{1} y(x)x^n dx$, then

(a) $I \neq 0, J \neq 0$ (b) $I \neq 0, J = 0$

(c) $I = 0, J \neq 0$ (d) $I = 0, J = 0$

2007

42. Suppose $y_p(x) = x\cos(2x)$ is a particular solution of $y'' + \alpha y = -4\sin(2x)$. Then the constant α equals

(a) -4 (b) -2

(c) 2 (d) 4

43. If $F(s) = \tan^{-1}(s) + k$ is the Laplace transform of some function $f(t)$, $t \ge 0$, then $k =$

(a) $-\pi$ (b) $-\frac{\pi}{2}$

(c) 0 (d) $\frac{\pi}{2}$

44. Let $Y(x) = (y_1(x), y_2(x)')$ and let $A = \begin{bmatrix} -3 & 1 \\ k & -1 \end{bmatrix}$

Further, let S be the set of values of k for which all the solutions of the system of equations $Y'(x) = AY(x)$ tend to zero as $x \to \infty$. Then S is given by

(a) $\{k : k \le -1\}$ (b) $\{k : k \le 3\}$

(c) $\{k : k < -1\}$ (d) $\{k : k < 3\}$

45. Let $P_n(x)$ be the Legendre polynomial of degree n and let

$$P_{m+1}(0) = -\frac{m}{m+1}P_{m+1}(0),\ m = 1, 2, .,.$$

If $P_n(0) = -\frac{5}{16}$, then $\int_{-1}^{1} P_n^2(x)dx =$

(a) $\frac{2}{13}$ (b) $\frac{2}{9}$

(c) $\frac{5}{16}$ (d) $\frac{2}{5}$

46. For which of the following pair of functions $y_1(x)$ and $y_2(x)$, continuous functions $p(x)$ and $q(x)$ can be determined on [–1, 1] such that $y_1(x)$ and $y_2(x)$ give two linearly independent solutions of

$y'' + p(x)y' + q(x)y = 0$, $x \in [-1, 1]$

(a) $y_1(x) = x\sin(x)$, $y_2(x) = \cos(x)$

(b) $y_1(x) = xe^x$, $y_2(x) = \sin(x)$

(c) $y_1(x) = e^{x-1}$, $y_2(x) = e^{x-1}$

(d) $y_1(x) = x^2$, $y_2(x) = \cos(x)$

47. Let $J_0(.)$ and $J_1(.)$ be the Bessel functions of the first kind of orders zero and one, respectively. If $\mathcal{L}(J_0(t)) = \frac{1}{\sqrt{s^2+1}}$, then $\mathcal{L}(J_1(t)) =$

(a) $\frac{s}{\sqrt{s^2+1}}$ (b) $\frac{1}{\sqrt{s^2+1}} - 1$

(c) $1 - \frac{1}{\sqrt{s^2+1}}$ (d) $\frac{s}{\sqrt{s^2+1}} - 1$

Statement for Linked Answer Questions 48 and 49:

Suppose the equation $x^2y'' - xy' + (1 + x^2)y = 0$ has a solution of the form $y = x^r \sum_{n=0}^{\infty} c_n x^n,\ c_0 \neq 0$.

48. The indicial equation for r is

(a) $r^2 - 1 = 0$ (b) $(r-1)^2 = 0$

(c) $(r+1)^2 = 0$ (d) $r^2 + 1 = 0$

49. For $n \geq 2$, the coefficients c_n will satisfy the relation

(a) $n^2c_n - c_{n-2} = 0$ (b) $n^2c_n + c_{n-2} = 0$

(c) $c_n - n^2 c_{n-2} = 0$ (d) $c_n + n^2 c_{n-2} = 0$

2006

50. For the ordinary differential equation

$$(x-1)\frac{d^2y}{dx^2} + (\cot \pi x)\frac{dy}{dx} + (\text{cosec}^2 \pi x)y = 0$$

Which of the following statements is true ?

(a) 0 is regular and 1 is irregular

(b) 0 is irregular and 1 is regular

(c) Both 0 and 1 are regular

(d) Both 0 and 1 are irregular

51. For the n-th Legendre polynomial $c_n \frac{d^n y}{dx^n}(x^2-1)^n$, the value of c_n is

(a) $\frac{1}{(n!2^n)}$ (b) $\frac{n!}{(2^n)}$

(c) $(n!)2^n$ (d) $\frac{2^n}{(n!)}$

52. Let $y_1(x)$ and $y_2(x)$ be two solutions of

$$(1-x^2)\frac{d^2y}{dx^2} - 2x\frac{dy}{dx} + (\sec x)y = 0$$

with Wronskian W(x). If $y_1(0) = 1$ $\left(\frac{dy_1}{dx}\right)_{x=0} = 0$ and $W\left(\frac{1}{2}\right) = \frac{1}{3}$, then $\left(\frac{dy_2}{dx}\right)_{x=0}$ equals

(a) $\frac{1}{4}$ (b) 1

(c) $\frac{3}{4}$ (d) $\frac{4}{3}$

53. If $y(x)$ is the solution of the differential equation $\frac{dy}{dx} = 2(1+y)\sqrt{y}$ satisfying $y(0) = 0;\ y\left(\frac{\pi}{2}\right) = 1$, then the largest interval (to the right of origin) on which the solution exists is

(a) $[0, 3\pi/4)$ (b) $[0, \pi)$

(c) $[0, 2\pi)$ (d) $[0, 2\pi/3)$

54. A particular solution of

$$x^2\frac{d^2y}{dx^2} + 2x\frac{dy}{dx} + \frac{y}{4} = \frac{1}{\sqrt{x}} \text{ is}$$

(a) $\frac{1}{2\sqrt{x}}$ (b) $\frac{\log x}{2\sqrt{x}}$

(c) $\frac{(\log x)^2}{2\sqrt{x}}$ (d) $\frac{(\log x)\sqrt{x}}{2}$

55. The initial value problem

$$x\frac{d^2y}{dx^2} + \frac{dy}{dx} + xy = 0;\ y(0) = 1,\ \left(\frac{dy}{dx}\right)_{x=0} = 0 \text{ has}$$

(a) a unique solution

(b) no solution

(c) infinitely many solutions

(d) two linearly independent solutions

56. An integrating factor for $(\cos y \sin 2x)dx + (\cos^2 y - \cos^2 x)dy = 0$ is

(a) $\sec^2 y + \sec y \tan y$

(b) $\tan^2 y + \sec y \tan y$

(c) $1/(\sec^2 y + \sec y \tan y)$

(d) $1/(\tan^2 y + \sec y \tan y)$

2005

57. In a sufficiently small neighbourhood around x = 2, the differential equation $\frac{dy}{dx} = \frac{y}{\sqrt{x}},\ y(2) = 4$ has

(a) no solution

(b) a unique solution

(c) exactly two solutions

(d) infinitely many solutions

58. The set of linearly independent solutions of the differential equation

$$\frac{d^4y}{dx^4} - \frac{d^2y}{dx^2} = 0 \text{ is}$$

(a) $\{1, x, e^x, e^{-x}\}$ (b) $\{1, x, e^{-x}, xe^{-x}\}$

(c) $\{1, x, e^x, xe^x$ (d) $\{1, x, e^x, xe^{-x}\}$

59. For the differential equation

$$x^2(1-x)\frac{d^2y}{dx^2} + x\frac{dy}{dx} + y = 0$$

(a) $x = 1$ is an ordinary point

(b) $x = 1$ is a regular singular point

(c) $x = 0$ is an irregular singular point

(d) $x = 0$ is an ordinary point

60. A curve γ in the xy-plane is such that the line joining the origin to any point P(x, y) on the curve and the line parallel to the y - axis through P are equally inclined to the tangent to the curve at P. Then , the differential equation of the curve γ is

(a) $x\left(\frac{dy}{dx}\right)^2 + 2y\left(\frac{dy}{dx}\right) = x$

(b) $x\left(\frac{dy}{dx}\right)^2 + 2y\left(\frac{dy}{dx}\right) = 0$

(c) $x\left(\frac{dx}{dy}\right)^2 + 2y\left(\frac{dx}{dy}\right) = 0$

(d) $x\left(\frac{dx}{dy}\right)^2 + 2y\left(\frac{dx}{dy}\right) = x$

61. Let $P_n(x)$ denote the Legendre polynomial of degree n. If

$$f(x) = \begin{cases} x, & -1 \le x \le 0 \\ 0, & 0 \le x \le 1 \end{cases}$$

and $f(x) = a_0 P_0(x) + a_1 P_1(x) + a_2 P_2(x) + \ldots$, then

(a) $a_0 = -\frac{1}{4}, a_1 = -\frac{1}{2}$

(b) $a_0 = -\frac{1}{4}, a_1 = \frac{1}{2}$

(c) $a_0 = \frac{1}{2}, a_1 = -\frac{1}{4}$

(d) $a_0 = -\frac{1}{2}, a_1 = -\frac{1}{4}$

62. If $J_n(x)$ and $Y_n(x)$ denote Bessel functions of order n of the first and the second kind, then the general solution of the differential equation $x\frac{d^2y}{dx^2} - \frac{dy}{dx} + xy = 0$ is given by

(a) $y(x) = \alpha x J_1(x) + \beta x Y_1(x)$

(b) $y(x) = \alpha J_1(x) + \beta Y_1(x)$

(c) $y(x) = \alpha J_0(x) + \beta Y_0(x)$

(d) $y(x) = \alpha x J_0(x) + \beta x Y_0(x)$

63. The general solution of the system of differential equations

$$y + \frac{dz}{dx} = 0$$

$$\frac{dy}{dx} - z = 0$$

is given by

(a) $y = \alpha e^x + \beta e^{-x}$, $z = \alpha e^x - \beta e^{-x}$

(b) $y = \alpha \cos x + \beta \sin x$, $z = \alpha \sin x - \beta \cos x$

(c) $y = \alpha \sin x - \beta \cos x$, $z = \alpha \cos x + \beta \sin x$

(d) $y = \alpha e^x - \beta e^{-x}$, $z = \alpha e^x + \beta e^{-x}$

64. It is required to find the solution of the differential equation

$$2x(2+x)\frac{d^2y}{dx^2} + 2(3+x)\frac{dy}{dx} - xy = 0$$

around the point x = 0. The roots of the indicial equation are

(a) $0, \frac{1}{2}$ (b) 0, 2

(c) $\frac{1}{2}, \frac{1}{2}$ (d) $0, -\frac{1}{2}$

2004

65. The orthogonal trajectories to the family of straight lines $y = k(x-1)$, $k \in R$, are given by

(a) $(x-1)^2 + (y-1)^2 = c^2$

(b) $x^2 + y^2 = c^2$

(c) $x^2 + (y-1)^2 = c^2$

(d) $(x-1)^2 + y^2 = c^2$

66. If $y = \varphi(x)$ is a particular solution of $y'' + (\sin x)y' + 2y = e^x$ and $y = \psi(x)$ is a particular solution of $y'' + (\sin x)y' + 2y = \cos 2x$, then a particular solution of $y'' + (\sin x)y' + 2y = e^x + 2\sin^2 x$, is given by

(a) $\varphi(x) - \psi(x) + \frac{1}{2}$ (b) $\psi(x) - \varphi(x) + \frac{1}{2}$

(c) $\varphi(x) - \psi(x) + 1$ (d) $\psi(x) - \varphi(x) + 1$

67. Let $y = \varphi(x)$ and $y = \psi(x)$ be solutions of $y'' - 2xy' + (\sin x^2)y = 0$

such that $\varphi(0) = 1$, $\varphi'(0) = 1$ and $\psi(0) = 1$, $\psi'(0) = 2$. Then the value of the Wronskian $W(\varphi, \psi)$ at $x = 1$ is

(a) 0 (b) 1

(c) e (d) e^2

68. The set of all eigenvalues of the Sturm-Liouville problem

$y'' + \lambda y = 0$, $y'(0) = 0$, $y'(\frac{\pi}{2}) = 0$, is given by

(a) $\lambda = 2n$, $n = 1,2,3, \ldots$

(b) $\lambda = 2n$, $n = 0,1,2,3, \ldots$

(c) $\lambda = 4n^2$, $n = 1,2,3, \ldots$

(d) $\lambda = 4n^2$, $n = 0,1,2,3, \ldots$

69. If $Y(p)$ is the Laplace transform of $y(t)$, which is the solution of the initial value problem $\frac{d^2y}{dt^2} + y(t) = \begin{cases} 0, & 0 < t < 2\pi \\ \sin t, & t > 2\pi \end{cases}$, with $y(0) = 1$ and $y'(0) = 0$, then $Y(p)$ equals

(a) $\frac{p}{1+p^2} + \frac{e^{-2\pi p}}{(1+p^2)^2}$ (b) $\frac{p+1}{1+p^2}$

(c) $\frac{p}{1+p^2} + \frac{e^{-2\pi p}}{(1+p^2)}$ (d) $\frac{p(1+p^2)+1}{(1+p^2)^2}$

70. If $y = \sum_{m=0}^{\infty} a_m x^m$ is a solution of $y'' + xy' + 3y = 0$, then $\frac{a_m}{a_{m+2}}$ equals

(a) $\frac{(m+1)(m+2)}{m+3}$ (b) $-\frac{(m+1)(m+2)}{m+3}$

(C) $-\frac{m(m+1)}{m+3}$ (d) $\frac{m(m-1)}{m+3}$

71. The indicial equation for: $x(1+x^2)y'' + (\cos x)y' + (1-3x+x^2)y = 0$, is

(a) $r^2 - r = 0$ (b) $r^2 + r = 0$

(c) $r^2 = 0$ (d) $r^2 - 1 = 0$

72. The general solution $\begin{pmatrix} x(t) \\ y(t) \end{pmatrix}$ of the system

$x = -x + 2y$

$y = 4x + y$

is given by

(a) $\begin{pmatrix} c_1e^{3t} - c_2e^{-3t} \\ 2c_1e^{3t} + c_2e^{-3t} \end{pmatrix}$ (b) $\begin{pmatrix} c_1e^{3t} \\ c_2e^{-3t} \end{pmatrix}$

(c) $\begin{pmatrix} c_1e^{3t} + c_2e^{-3t} \\ 2c_1e^{3t} + c_2e^{-3t} \end{pmatrix}$ (d) $\begin{pmatrix} c_1e^{3t} - c_2e^{-3t} \\ -2c_1e^{3t} + c_2e^{-3t} \end{pmatrix}$

2003

73. The orthogonal trajectory to the family of circles $x^2 + y^2 = 2\,cx$ (c arbitrary) is described by the differential equation.

(a) $(x^2 + y^2)\,y' = 2xy$ (b) $(x^2 - y^2)\,y' = 2xy$

(c) $(y^2 - x^2)\,y' = xy$ (d) $(y^2 - x^2)\,y' = 2xy$

74. Let $y_1(x)$ and $y_2(x)$ be solutions of $y''x^2 + y' + (\sin x)y = 0$, which satisfy the boundary conditions $y_1(0) = 0$, $y_1'(1) = 1$ and $y_2(0) = 1$, $y_2'(1) = 0$ respectively. Then

(a) y_1 and y_2 do not have common zeroes

(b) y_1 and y_2 have common zeroes

(c) either y_1 or y_2 has a zero of order 2

(d) both y_1 and y_2 have zeroes of order 2

75. For the Sturm Liouville problems : $(1+x^2)\,y'' + 2xy' + \lambda\, x^2y = 0$ with $y'(1) = 0$ and $y'(10) = 0$ the eigen-values, λ, satisfy

(a) $\lambda \geq 0$ (b) $\lambda < 0$

(c) $\lambda \neq 0$ (d) $\lambda \leq 0$

76. For the Initial Value Problem (I.V.P.) : $y' = f(x, y)$ with $y(0) = 0$, which of the following statements is true

(a) $f(x, y) = \sqrt{xy}$ satisfies Lipschitz's condition and so I.V.P. has unique solution

(b) $f(x, y) = \sqrt{xy}$ does not satisfy Lipschitz's condition and so I.V. P. has no solution

(c) $f(x, y) = |y|$ satisfies Lipschitz's condition and so I.V.P. has unique solution

(d) $f(x, y) = |y|$ does not satisfy Lipschitz's condition still I.V.P. has unique solution

77. All real solutions of the differential equation $y'' + 2ay' + by = \cos x$ (where a and b are real constants) are periodic if

(a) $a = 1$ and $b = 0$ (b) $a = 0$ and $b = 1$

(c) $a = 1$ and $b \neq 0$ (d) $a = 0$ and $b \neq 1$

78. Let $y = \Psi(x)$ be a bounded solution of the equation: $(1-x^2)\,y'' - 2xy' + 30y = 0$. Then

(a) $\int_{-1}^{1} x^3\psi(x)dx \neq 0$

(b) $\int_{-1}^{1} (1+x^3+x^4)\psi(x)dx \neq 0$

(c) $\int_{-1}^{1} x^5\psi(x)dx = 0$

(d) $\int_{-1}^{1} x^{2m}\psi(x)dx = 0$ for all $n \in \mathrm{N}$

79. $\int x^3 J_0(x)dx$ is equal to (upto a constant)

(a) $x\,J_0(x) - x^3\,J_1(x)$ (b) $x^2\,J_0(x) + J_1(x)$

(c) $x^3\,J_1(x) - 2x^2\,J_2(x)$ (d) $2x^2\,J_1(x) + x\,J_2(x)$

80. Let $y_1(x)$ and $y_2(x)$ be two linearly independent solutions of $xy'' + y' + x^2y = 0$, in the neighbourhood of $x = 0$. If $y_1(x)$ is a power series around $x = 0$, then

(a) $y_2(x..)$ is bounded around $x = 0$

(b) $y_2(x)$ is unbounded around $x = 0$

(c) $y_2(x)$ has power series solution

(d) $y_2(x)$ has solution of the form $\sum_{n=1}^{\infty} b_n x^{n+r}$, where $r \neq 0$, and $b_0 \neq 0$

81. Consider the following system of differential equations in $x(t)$, $y(t)$ and $z(t)$

$$\begin{bmatrix} x' \\ y' \\ z' \end{bmatrix} = \begin{bmatrix} 0 & 1 & 0 \\ 1 & 0 & 0 \\ 1 & 1 & 1 \end{bmatrix} \begin{bmatrix} x \\ y \\ z \end{bmatrix}$$

Then there exists a choice of 3 linearly independent vectors u, v, w in R^3 such that vectors, forming a fundamental set of solutions of the above system, are given by

(a) $e^{-t}\,u$, $e^t\,v$, $te^t\,w$ (b) $e^t\,u$, $te^t\,v$, $t^2e^t\,w$

(c) $e^{-t}\,u$, $te^{-t}v$, $e^t\,w$ (d) u, tv, $e^t\,w$

2002

82. Let n be a non-negative integer. The eigenvalues of the Sturm-Liouville problem?

$$\frac{d^2y}{dx^2} + \lambda y = 0,$$

with boundary conditions

$$y(0) = y(2\pi),\ \frac{dy}{dx}(0) = \frac{dy}{dx}(2\pi) \text{ are}$$

(a) n (b) $n^2\pi^2$

(c) $n\pi$ (d) n^2

83. The Bessel's function $\{J_0(\alpha_k x)\}_{k=1}^{\infty}$ with α_k denoting the *k-th* zero of $J_0(x)$ form an orthogonal system on [0, 1] with respect to weight function

(a) 1 (b) x^2

(c) x (d) $\sqrt{x}$

84. Linear combinations of solutions of an ordinary differential equation are also solutions if the differential equation is:

(a) Linear nonhomogeneous

(b) Linear homogeneous

(c) Nonlinear homogeneous

(d) Nonlinear nonhomogeneous

85. If the integrating factor of

$$(x^7y^2 + 3y)\,dx + (3x^8 y - x)\,dy = 0$$

is $x^m y^n$, then

(a) $m = -7, n = 1$ (b) $m = 1, n = -7$

(c) $m = n = 0$ (d) $m = n = 1$

86. The initial value problem

$$(x^2 - x)\frac{dy}{dx} = (2x - 1)y,\ y(x_0) = y_0$$

has a unique solution if (x_0, y_0) equals

(a) (2, 1)

(b) (1, 1)

(c) (0, 0)

(d) (0, 1)

87. Find the general solution of the differential equation

$$\frac{d^4y}{dx^4} - y = x \sin x.$$

88. Find the general solution of the differential equation

$$(x-1)^2\frac{d^2y}{dx^2} + (x-1)\frac{dy}{dx} - 4y = 0$$

in powers of $(x - 1)$ using the Frobenius method.

2001

89. Which of the following pair of functions is not a linearly independent pair of solutions of $y'' + 9y = 0$?

(a) $\sin 3x$, $\sin 3x - \cos 3x$

(b) $\sin 3x + \cos 3x$, $3 \sin x - 4 \sin^3 x$

(c) $\sin 3x$, $\sin 3x \cos 3x$

(d) $\sin 3x + \cos 3x$, $4 \cos^3 x - 3 \cos x$

90. Determine the type of the following differential equation

$$\frac{d^2y}{dx^2} + \sin(x + y) = \sin x$$

(a) Linear, homogeneous

(b) Non-linear, homogeneous

(c) Linear, non-homogeneous

(d) Non-linear, non-homogeneous

91. Which of the following is not an integrating factor of $xdy - ydx = 0$?

(a) $\frac{1}{x^2}$ (b) $\frac{1}{x^2 + y^2}$

(c) $\frac{1}{xy}$ (d) $\frac{x}{y}$

92. The general solution of the differential equation

$$\frac{dy}{dx} + \tan y \tan x = \cos x \sec y \text{ is}$$

(a) $2 \sin y = (x + c - \sin x \cos x) \sec x$

(b) $\sin y = (x + c) \cos x$

(c) $\cos y = (x + c) \sin x$

(d) $\sec y = (x + c) \cos x$

93. The eigenvalues of the Sturm Liouville system

$y'' + \lambda y = 0,\ 0 \le x \le \pi$

$y(0) = 0,\ y'(\pi) = 0$ are

(a) $\frac{n^2}{4}$ (b) $\frac{(2n-1)^2\pi^2}{4}$

(c) $\frac{(2n-1)^2}{4}$ (d) $\frac{n^2\pi^2}{4}$

94. The differential equation whose linearly independent solutions are $\cos 2x$, $\sin 2x$ and e^{-x} is

(a) $(D^3 + D^2 + 4D + 4)\,y = 0$

(b) $(D^3 - D^2 + 4D - 4)\,y = 0$

(c) $(D^3 + D^2 - 4D - 4)y = 0$

(d) $(D^3 - D^2 - 4D + 4)\,y = 0$

where $D = \frac{d}{x}$.

95. (*a*) Find the general solution of the differential equation

$$\frac{d^2y}{dx^2} + 4y = \sec^2 2x$$

using the method of variation of parameters.

(*b*) Construct Green's function for the boundary value problem,

$$y'' + y = -x, y(0) = y(\pi) = 0$$

if it exists.

2000

96. The particular solution of the equation $y' \sin x = y \ln y$ satisfying the initial condition $y\left(\frac{\pi}{2}\right) = e$, is

(*a*) $e^{\tan(x/2)}$ (*b*) $e^{\cot(x/2)}$

(*c*) $\ln \tan\left(\frac{x}{2}\right)$ (*d*) $\ln \cot\left(\frac{x}{2}\right)$

97. The differential equation $\frac{dy}{dx} = k(a - y)(b - y)$, when solved with the condition $y(0) = 0$, yields the result

(*a*) $\frac{b(a-y)}{a(b-y)} = e^{(a-b)kx}$ (*b*) $\frac{b(a-x)}{a(b-x)} = e^{(b-a)ky}$

(*c*) $\frac{a(b-y)}{b(a-y)} = e^{(b-a)kx}$ (*d*) $xy = ke$

98. The Sturm-Liouville problem : $y'' + \lambda^2 y = 0, y'(0) = 0, y(\pi) = 0$ has its eigenvectors given by $y =$

(*a*) $\sin\left(n + \frac{1}{2}\right)x$

(*b*) $\sin nx$

(*c*) $\cos\left(n + \frac{1}{2}\right)x$

(*d*) $\cos nx$; where $n = 0, 1, 2, \ldots$

99. Use the Laplace transform procedure to solve the initial value problem:

$ty''(t) + y'(t) + ty(t) = 0; y(0) = 1, y'(0) = k.$, ($k$ is a constant) [5]

100. Construct the Green's function for the boundary value problem:

$y''(x) + y(x) = -1; y(0) = 0, y\left(\frac{\pi}{2}\right) = 0$ and hence solve the equation.

ANSWERS

1. (1)	**2.** (2)	**3.** (*b*)	**4.** (*a*)	**5.** (2)	**6.** (6)	**7.** (6)	**8.** (1)	**9.** (2.2 to 2.22)	
10. (*a*)	**11.** (*d*)	**12.** (*b*)	**13.** (*a*)	**14.** (*a*)	**15.** (*b*)	**16.** (*d*)	**17.** (*a*)	**18.** (*b*)	**19.** (*)
20. (*b*)	**21.** (*b*)	**22.** (*a*)	**23.** (*a*)	**24.** (*b*)	**25.** (*d*)	**26.** (*a*)	**27.** (*c*)	**28.** (*b*)	**29.** (*b*)
30. (*c*)	**31.** (*b*)	**32.** (*d*)	**33.** (*d*)	**34.** (*a*)	**35.** (*d*)	**36.** (*a*)	**37.** (*c*)	**38.** (*d*)	**39.** (*a*)
40. (*a*)	**41.** (*b*)	**42.** (*d*)	**43.** (*b*)	**44.** (*b*)	**45.** (*a*)	**46.** (*c*)	**47.** (*c*)	**48.** (*b*)	**49.** (*b*)
50. (*d*)	**51.** (*a*)	**52.** (*a*)	**53.** (*c*)	**54.** (*c*)	**55.** (*b*)	**56.** (*a*)	**57.** (*b*)	**58.** (*a*)	**59.** (*b*)
60. (*b*)	**61.** (*b*)	**62.** (*a*)	**63.** (*c*)	**64.** (*b*)	**65.** (*d*)	**66.** (*c*)	**67.** (*c*)	**68.** (*c*)	**69.** (*a*)
70. (*b*)	**71.** (*c*)	**72.** (*a*)	**73.** (*b*)	**74.** (*b*)	**75.** (*a*)	**76.** (*c*)	**77.** (*b*)	**78.** (*d*)	**79.** (*c*)
80. (*c*)	**81.** (*a*)	**82.** (*d*)	**83.** (*c*)	**84.** (*b*)	**85.** (*a*)	**86.** (*b*)	**87.** (*)	**88.** (*)	**89.** (*c*)
90. (*b*)	**91.** (*d*)	**92.** (*b*)	**93.** (*c*)	**94.** (*a*)	**95.** (*a*) (*)	**95.** (*b*) (*)	**96.** (*a*)	**97.** (*a*)	**98.** (*b*)
99. (*b*)	**100.** (*b*)								

EXPLANATIONS

1. The auxiliary equation is

$m^2 + am + b = 0$, where a and b both are +ve real number.

Then roots of equation are complex numbers.

i.e. $m_1 = \alpha + i\beta$, $m = \alpha - i\beta$, where α and β in terms of a and b

$$y(x) = e^{\alpha x}(C_1 \cos \beta x + C_2 \sin \beta x)$$

$$y(0) = y(1)$$

$\Rightarrow$ This is only one independent solution

The dim (V) = 1

2. Let $y'' + p(x)\, y' + \Sigma(x)y = 0$, $x t (-\infty, \infty)$ where p(x) & q(x) are continuous functions. If $y_1(x) = \sin x - 2\cos x$ and $y_2(x) = 2\sin x + \cos x$ are two linearly independent solutions of the above equation, Then Coefficient of $y'' + p(x)\, y' + q(x)y = 0$, & $y'' + y = 0$ are equal, Then $p(x) = 0$ and $q(x) = 1$

Then $|4p(0) + 2q(1)| = 2$

3. For the statement P : equation

$$x^2y'' + xy' + \left(x^2 - \frac{1}{4}\right)y = 0$$

x = 0 is an regular singular point and using Frobenius series solution, we have indicial equation of the differential equation as

$$r^2 - \frac{1}{4} = 0 \quad \Rightarrow \quad r = \pm\frac{1}{2}$$

roots are distinct and not differ by an integer, then we have two independent solutions.

For the solution $x^2y'' + 3\sin(x)\, y' + y = 0$, x = 0 is an Irregulary singular point.

4.
$$\text{If} = e^{\int dx} = e^x$$

The solution is

$$ye^x = \int e^x |x| + c$$

Here we take $I = [-1, 1] \in \mathbb{R}$ then

$$ye^x = -\int_{-1}^{0} e^{-x}x dx + \int_0^1 e^x x\, dx$$

$$ye^x = e^{-1}(-2) + 1 + 1$$

$$= -2e^{-1} + 2$$

$$y(x) = \left(-\frac{2}{e} + 2\right)e^{-x}$$

$x \in [-1, 1]$

Then value $y(1) = \left(-\frac{2}{e} + 2\right)e^{-1}$

$$= -\frac{2}{e^2} + \frac{2}{e}$$

5. Here $y'' + \lambda y = 0$

We can neglect cases when. $\lambda < 0$, $\lambda = 0$, Now For $\lambda > 0$,

$$y = A\sin\sqrt{\lambda}x + B\cos\sqrt{\lambda}x$$

$$y(0) = \beta = 0$$

$$y'(x) = A\sqrt{\lambda}\cos\sqrt{\lambda}x$$

$$y'(\pi) = A\sqrt{\lambda}\cos\sqrt{\lambda}\pi = 0$$

$A \neq O$ (should not zero)

$$\cos\sqrt{\lambda}\pi = 0$$

$$\Rightarrow \quad \sqrt{\lambda}\pi = \left(n + \frac{1}{2}\right)\pi$$

$$\lambda_n = \left(n + \frac{1}{2}\right)^2$$

n = 0, 1, 2, ...

For n = 0, $\lambda_0 = \frac{1}{4}$

$$\lambda_1 = \frac{9}{4}$$

$$\Rightarrow \quad \lambda_1 - \lambda_0 = \frac{9}{4} - \frac{1}{4}$$

$$= \frac{8}{4} = 2$$

9. Given initial value problem is

$$\frac{dy}{dx} = \sqrt{y + 2x}$$

subject to $y(1.2) = 2$ and $h = 0.05$

Hence, $f(x, y) = \sqrt{y + 2x}$,

$$x_0 = 1.2,$$

$$y_0 = 2$$

and $h = 0.05$

By Euler method,

$$y_{n+1} = y_n + hf(x_n, y_n)$$

$$\therefore \quad y_1 = y_0 + hf(x_0, y_0)$$

$$= 2 + 0.05\sqrt{2 + 2(1.2)}$$

$= 2+0.05\sqrt{2+2.4}$

$= 2+0.05\sqrt{4.4}$

$= 2 + 0.05 \times 2.098$

$= 2.104$

$y_2 = y_1 + hf(x_1, y_1)$

$= 2.104+0.05\times\sqrt{2.104+2.50}$

$[x_1 = x_0 + h = 1.2 + 0.05 = 1.25]$

$= 2.104+0.05\sqrt{4.604}$

$= 2.104 + 0.05 \times 2.146$

$= 2.104 + 0.1073$

$y_2 = 2.21$

Hence approximate value $y(1.3)$ is 2.21.

10. Given ordinary differential equation is

$$x^2\frac{d^2y}{dx^2}+x\frac{dy}{dx}+\left(4x^2-\frac{9}{25}\right)y=0$$

It can be rewritten as

$$x^2\frac{d^2y}{dx^2}+x\frac{dy}{dx}+\left\{(2x)^2-\left(\frac{3}{5}\right)^2\right\}y=0$$

Which is a Bessel equation of order $\frac{3}{5}$.

$\therefore$ Its general solution is

$$y = c_1J_n(x)+c_2J_{-n}(x)$$

on putting $n = 3/5$ we get

$$y = C_1\, J_{3/5}(2x)+c_2\,J_{-3/5}(2x)$$

11. Given differential equation is

$$(1-x^2)\frac{d^2y}{dx^2}-2x\frac{dy}{dx}+2y = 0 \qquad ...(i)$$

and $y_1(x) = x$ is solution of (i)

Let $y = vy$, be the general solution of (i)

$$\text{Now, } v''+v'\left[\frac{2z'}{z}+p\right] = \frac{R}{z} \qquad ...(ii)$$

Differential equation (i) can be written as

$$\frac{d^2y}{dx^2}-\frac{2x}{1-x^2}\frac{dy}{dx}+\frac{2}{1-x^2}y = 0$$

Comparing this differential equation with

$$\frac{d^2y}{dx^2}+p(x)\frac{dy}{dx}+q(x)y=R$$

$$p = \frac{-2x}{1-x^2},$$

$$q = \frac{2}{1-x^2},\ R=0$$

put these values in (ii)

$$v''+v'\left[\frac{2}{x}-\frac{2x}{1-x^2}\right] = 0$$

$$\Rightarrow\ v''+v'\left[\frac{2-4x^2}{x(1-x^2)}\right] = 0$$

$$\Rightarrow\ \frac{v''}{v'} = -\left[\frac{2-4x^2}{x(1-x^2)}\right]$$

$$\Rightarrow\ \frac{v''}{v'} = -\frac{2}{x}+\frac{2x}{1-x^2}$$

On integrating, we get

$$\int\frac{v''}{v'}dv = -2\int\frac{1}{x}dx+\int\frac{2x}{1-x^2}dx$$

$$\Rightarrow\ \log v' = -2\log x-\log(1-x^2)+\log c_2$$

$$v' = \frac{c_2}{x^2(1-x^2)}$$

Again integrating we get

$$\int v_1'\,dv = \int c_2\left[\frac{1}{x^2}+\frac{1}{2(1-x)}+\frac{1}{2(1+x)}\right]$$

$$\Rightarrow\ v = c_2\left[-\frac{1}{x}-\frac{1}{2}\log x+\frac{1}{2}\log x\right]+c_1$$

$$\Rightarrow\ v = c_1+c_2\left[-\frac{1}{x}+\frac{1}{2}\log\left|\frac{1-x}{1+x}\right|\right]$$

Now, put v in

$$y = vy_1 = vx$$

$$\text{we get}\quad y(x) = c_1x+c_2\left[\frac{x}{2}\log\left|\frac{1-x}{1+x}\right|-1\right]$$

12. Given initial value problem is

$$\frac{d^2y}{dt^2}+2\frac{dy}{dt}+5y = 3e^{-t}\sin t,\ y(0)=0$$

$$\text{and}\quad \frac{dy(0)}{dt}=3$$

Auxiliary equation is

$$m^2 + 2m + 5 = 0$$

$$\Rightarrow\quad m = -1 \pm 2i$$

$$\text{C.F} = e^{-t}[c_1\cos 2t+c_2\sin 2t]$$

$$\text{Now,}\quad \text{PI} = \frac{1}{D^2+2D+5}\,3e^{-t}\sin t$$

$$= 3e^{-t}\frac{1}{(D-1)^2+2(D-1)+5}\sin t$$

$$= 3e^{-t}\frac{1}{D^2+4}\sin t$$

$$= 3e^{-t}\frac{\sin t}{-1^2+4} = e^{-t}\sin t$$

Hence, solution is

$$y(t) = e^{-t}[c_1 \cos 2t + c_2 \sin 2t + \sin t]$$

when $t = 0$, then $y(t) = 0$

$\therefore \quad 0 = e^{-0}[c_1 \cos 0 + c_2 \sin 0 + \sin 0]$

$\Rightarrow \quad c_1 = 0$

$$y'(t) = e^{-t}[-2c_1 \sin 2t + 2c_2 \cos 2t + \cos t] - e^{-t}[c_1 \cos 2t + c_2 \sin 2t + \sin t]$$

when $t = 0$, $y'(t) = 3$

$$\therefore \quad 3 = e^{-0}[-2c_1 \sin 0 + 2c_2 \cos 0 + \cos 0] - e^{-0}[c_1 \cos 0 + c_2 \sin 0 + \sin 0]$$

$\Rightarrow \quad 3 = 2c_2 + 1 \Rightarrow c_2 = 1$

Hence required solution is

$$y(t) = e^{-t}(\sin t + \sin 2t)$$

13. $a_n \dfrac{d^n u}{dt^n} + a_{n-1} \dfrac{d^{n-1}u}{dt^{n-1}} + \ldots\ldots + a_1 \dfrac{du}{dt} + a_0 u = 0$

$$a_n D^n + a_{n-1} D^{n-1} + \ldots\ldots + a_1 D + a_0 = 0$$

Given $a_n x^n + a_{n-1} x^{n-1} + \ldots\ldots + a_1 x + a_0$ have negative real part.

$$\lim_{t \to \infty} u(t) = 0$$

16. Given differential Equation

$$f(x)y'' - uf'(x)y' + g(x)y = 0 \quad \ldots (1)$$

put $y = uv$

$$f(x)[uv'' + 2u'v' + u''v] - uf'(x)[uv' + u'v] + g(x)\,4v = 0$$

$$f(x)\,uv'' + [2f(x)u' - uf'(x)u]\,v' + [f(x)u'' - uf'(x)\,u' + g(x)u]v = 0$$

$$v'' + \left[\frac{2f(x)u' - uf'(x)u}{f(x)u}\right]v' + \left[\frac{f(x)u'' - uf'(x)u' + q(x)u}{f(x)u}\right]v = 0 \quad \ldots (2)$$

by comparing it with

$$v'' + h(x)\,v = 0$$

we get

$$2f(x)\,u' - uf'(x)u = 0$$

$$\frac{u'}{u} = \frac{2f'(x)}{f(x)}$$

Integrate it

$$\ln u = 2 \ln f(x)$$

$$\ln u = \ln(f(x))^2$$

$$u = f^2$$

23. $\dfrac{xdy}{dx} = y = x^2,\ x > 0,$

$$y(0) = 0$$

$$(xD - 1)\,y = x^2$$

Let $x = e^z$ and $D^1 = xD$

then $(D^1 - 1)y = e^{2z}$

$$y.e^{-z} = \int e^{-z} \cdot e^{2z} dz + c_1$$

$$y = e^{2z} + c_1 e^z$$

$$y = x^2 + c_1 x$$

$$y(0) = 0$$

$$0 = 0.c_1$$

Hence c_1 can take any arbitary value.

Hence $y = x^2 + c_1 x$

$$c_1 \in R$$

i.e. infinitely many solution.

24. $y'' + y = 6 \cos 2x$

$$y(0) = 3,\ y'(0) = 1$$

$$S^2L\{y\} - Sy(0) - y'(0) + L\{y\} = 6L\{\cos 2x\}$$

$$S^2L\{y\} - 3S - 1 + L\{y\} = \frac{6.S}{S^2 + z^2}$$

$$L\{y\}(1 + S^2) = \frac{6S}{S^2 + 4} + 3S + 1$$

$$= \frac{6S + 3S^3 + 12.5 + S^2 + 4}{S^2 + 4}$$

$$L\{y\}(1 + S^2) = \frac{3S^3 + S^2 + 18S + 4}{S^2 + 4}$$

$$F(s) = L\{y\}$$

$$= \frac{3S^3 + S^2 + 185 + 4}{(S^2 + 4)(1 + S^2)}$$

$$F(1) = \frac{3 + 1 + 18 + 4}{(1 + 4)(1 + 1)}$$

$$= \frac{26}{10} = \frac{13}{5}$$

25. $(1 - x^2)y^{11} - 2xy^1 + 6y = 0$

$$y(1) = 2$$

then $\displaystyle\int_{-1}^{1} y^2 dx = 8/5$ (By integrating the differential equation)

26. $\dfrac{d^4 y}{dx^4} = 0$

$$D^4 y = 0$$

$$y = c_1 + c_2 x + c_3 x^2 + c_4 x^3$$

$$y(0) = 1$$

$\Rightarrow \quad c_1 = 1$

So $y = 1 + c_2x + c_3x^2 + c_4x^3$

$c_i \in R$

So maximum number of linearly independent solutions is 4.

27. $y''' - y'' 4y' - 4y = 0$

$y(0) = y'(0) = 2, y''(0) = 0$

$(D^3 - D^2 + 4D - 4)\, y = 0$

Auxillary equation $M^3 - M^2 + 4m - 4 = 0$

$M^2(m - 1) + 4(m - 1) = 0$

$M = 1, M = \pm 2i$

Solution $y = c_1e^x + c_2 \cos zx + c_3 \sin zx$

$y(\pi/2) = c_1e^{\pi/2} - c_2 + 0$

$= c_1e^{\pi/2} - c_2$

Now $y(0) = 2 = c_1 + c_2$

$y'(0) = 2 = c_1 + 2c_3$

$y''(0) = 0 = c_1 - 4c_2$

$\Rightarrow$ $5c_2 = 2 \Rightarrow c_2 = 2/5$

$c_1 = 2 - 2/5 = 8/5$

$c_3 = (2 - 2/5)/2 = 4/5$

so $y(\pi/2) = \dfrac{8e^{\pi/2}}{5} - 2/5 = \dfrac{1}{5}\left[8e^{\pi/2} - 2\right]$

28. $x^2y'' + xy' + y = x$

$y(1) = y'(1) = 1$

Let $x = e^z \Rightarrow xD = \theta;\ \theta = \dfrac{d}{dz}$

$[\theta(\theta - 1) + \theta + 1]\, y = e^z$

$(\theta^2 + 1)\, y = e^z$

$y = c_1 \cos z + c_2 \sin z + \dfrac{e^z}{2}$

$y = c_1 \cos(\ln x) + c_2 \sin(\ln x) + \dfrac{x}{2}$

$y(1) = c_1 \cos(0) + c_2 \sin(0) + 1/2$

$1 = c_1 + 1/2 \Rightarrow c_1 = 1/2$

$y'(x) = -c_1\dfrac{\sin(\ln x)}{x} + c_2\dfrac{\cos(\ln x)}{x} + \tfrac{1}{2}$

$y'(1) = 1 = c_2 + 1/2 \Rightarrow c_2 = 1/2$

so $y(e^{\pi/2}) = c_1 \cos\left(\ln e^{\pi/2}\right) + c_2 \sin\left(\ln e^{\pi/2}\right) + \dfrac{e^{\pi/2}}{2}$

$y(e^{\pi/2}) = \dfrac{1}{2} + \dfrac{e^{\pi/2}}{4} = \dfrac{1}{2}\left(e^{\pi/2} + 1\right)$

29. $\dfrac{1}{(xD+1)}x^{-1} = \dfrac{1}{D'+1}e^{-z}$

Let $x = e^z$ then $xD = D^1$

$= \dfrac{ze^{-z}}{1} = \log x.\dfrac{1}{x} = \dfrac{\log x}{x}$

30. $(\alpha, xy^3 + y \cos x)dx + (x^2y^2 + \beta \sin x)dy = 0$

is exact if $\dfrac{\partial M}{\partial y} = \dfrac{\partial N}{\partial x}$

where $M = \alpha\, xy^3 + y \cos x$

$N = x^2y^2 + \beta \sin x$

$3\alpha xy^2 + \cos x = 2xy^2 + \beta \cos x$

$\Rightarrow$ $\alpha = \dfrac{2}{3}$ and $\beta = 1$

31. If $y(x) = x$ is a solution of the differential equation

$y'' - \left(\dfrac{2}{x^2} + \dfrac{1}{x}\right)(xy' - y) = 0 \quad 0 < x < \infty$

then its general solution is $(\alpha + \beta e^{2x})x$

32. $P_n(x)$ be the legendre polynomial of degree n such that $P_n(1) = 1, n = 1, 2...$

if $\displaystyle\int_{-1}^{1}\left(\sum_{j=1}^{n}\sqrt{j(2j+1)}Pj(x)\right)^2 dx = 20;$

then $n = 5$

33. Let $y_1(x) = 1 + x$ and $y_2(x) = e^x$ be two solution of

$y'' + P(x)y' + Q(x)\, y = 0$

$y_1'' + P(x)\, y_1' + Q(x)y_1 = 0$

$y_2'' + P(x)y_2' + Q(x)y_2 = 0$

$0 + P(x) + Q(x)(1+ x) = 0$

$e^x[1+P(x)+Q(x)] = 0$

$P(x) + Q(x) = -x\, Q(x)$

$P(x) + Q(x) = -1$ as $e^x \neq 0$

$Q(x) = \dfrac{1}{x}$

$P(x) = -1 - \dfrac{1}{x} = \dfrac{-x-1}{x}$

34. Solution of differential equation is

$y = c_1(1 + x) + c_2e^x$

$y' = c_1 + c_2e^x$

for option (*a*) $y(0) = 2 \Rightarrow c_1 + c_2 = 2$

$y'(0) = 1 \Rightarrow c_1 + c_2 = 1$

which is not possible, so no solution.

35. Given that $y' = e^{-y^2} - 1$ on $[0, 1]$

with $y(0) = 0$

By Picard iterative method

$y_1 = y_0 + \displaystyle\int_0^x f(t_0, y_0)dt$

$= y_0 + \displaystyle\int_0^x (e^0 - 1)dt = 0 + 0 = 0$

$$y^2 = y_0 + \int_0^x f(t_0, y_1)dt$$

$$= 0 + \int_0^x (e^0 - 1)dt = 0 + 0 = 0$$

$y_3 = 0, y_4 = 0, \ldots\ldots$

So $\quad y \equiv 0, \forall\ x > 0$

36. Given that

$x(x-1)y'' + \sin x . y' + 2x(x-1)y = 0 \quad \ldots (1)$

$$y'' + \frac{\sin x}{x(x-1)} y' + 2y = 0$$

where $b_1(x) = \dfrac{\sin x}{x(x-1)}$, $b_2(x) = 2$

since $b_1(x)$ is not analytic at $x = 0$

and $\quad x = 1$

Hence $\quad x = 0$

and $\quad x = 1$ are singular point.

Now $\quad xb_1(x) = \dfrac{\sin x}{x(x-1)}$

which analytic at $x = 0$.

Hence $x = 0$ is a regular singular point.

Next $(x-1)b_1(x) = \dfrac{\sin x}{x}$

which is analytic at $x = 1$ Hence $x = 1$ is regular singular point. Thus $x = 0$ and $x = 1$ both are regular singular point of equation (1).

37. $\quad y'' + (\sin x)y = 0 \le x \le 1$

$$w(y_1, y_2) = ce^{-\int \sin x\, dx}$$

$$g = ce^{\cos}\ x$$

$$g' = -ce^{\cos x} \sin x$$

g' is zero at $x = 0$

38. $y''' - y'' - y' + y = -e^x$

$(D^3 - D^2 - D + 1)y = -e^x$

Particular Integral (PI)

$$= -\frac{1}{(D^3 - D^2 - D + 1)} e^x$$

$$= -x\frac{1}{3D^2 - 2D - 1} e^x$$

$$= \frac{-x^2e^x}{6D - 2} = 0 = \frac{-x^2e^x}{4}$$

So constant multiple of x^2e^x.

39. Let $a, b \in$ R. Let $y = \begin{bmatrix} y_1 \\ y_2 \end{bmatrix}$ be a solution of the system

$$y_1^1 = y_2$$

$$y_2^1 = ay_1 + by_2$$

and every solution $y(x) \to 0$ as $x \to \infty$

If $Dy_1 = y_2 \Rightarrow Dy_1 - y_2 = 0 \quad \ldots (1)$

$Dy_2 = ay_1 + by_2 - ay_1 + (D - b)y_2 = 0 \ldots (2)$

Now in equation (1) multiple by $(-a)$ and in equation (2) multiply by D, then subtracting them.

$$ay_2 - D(D - b)y_2 = 0$$

$$D^2y_2 - bDy_2 - ay_2 = 0$$

$$(D^2 - bD - a)y_2 = 0$$

$$y_2 = c_1e^{\lambda_1 x} + c_2e^{\lambda_2 x}$$

where λ_1 and λ_2 are roots of auxiliary equation.

$$m^2 - bm - a = 0$$

Now $\quad y_2 \to 0$ as $x \to \infty$

If $\quad \lambda_1 < 0$ and $\lambda_2 < 0$

i.e., $\quad \lambda_1 = \dfrac{b + \sqrt{b^2 + ua}}{2}$

$\lambda_2 = \dfrac{b - \sqrt{b^2 + ua}}{2}$

$b < 0$ and $b < -\sqrt{b^2 + 4a}$

and $\quad b^2 + 4a > 0$

$b^2 > -4a$

$\Rightarrow \quad a < 0$

$$c, \lambda, e^{\lambda_1 x} + c_2\lambda_2e^{\lambda_2 x} = ay_1 + b(c_1e^{\lambda_1 x} + c_2e^{\lambda_2 x})$$

$$y_1 = \frac{c_1(\lambda_1 - 1)e^{\lambda_1 x} + c_z(\lambda_2 - 1)e^{\lambda_2 x}}{a}$$

$y_1 \to 0$ as $x \to \infty$ if $\lambda_1 < 0, \lambda_2 < 0$

so $\quad a < 0$

and $\quad b < 0$

40. Let $n \ge 3$ be an integer. Let y be the polynomial solution of

$$(1 - x^2)y'' - 2xy' + n(n-1)y = 0$$

$y(1) = 1$ then the degree of y is n.

41. $I = \int_{-1}^{1} y(x).x^{n-3}dx \neq 0$

$J = \int_{-1}^{1} y(x).x^n dx = 0$

42. We have, $y_p(x) = -4\dfrac{1}{(D^2 + \alpha)}\sin 2x$

$$= -4 \times \frac{1}{2D}\sin 2x$$

$[\because (-2)^2 + \alpha = 0 \Rightarrow \alpha = 4]$

$= x \cos 2\lambda$

43. $L^{-1}\{\tan^{-1} s + k\}$

$$= -\frac{1}{t}L^{-1}\left[\frac{d}{ds}(\tan^{-1} s + k)\right]$$

$$= -\frac{1}{t}L^{-1}\left[\frac{1}{s^2+1}\right]$$

$$= -\frac{1}{t}[\sin t]$$

$$\Rightarrow \quad L\left[\frac{-\sin t}{t}\right] = -\int_{\infty}^{\infty}\frac{1}{s^2+1}ds$$

$$= -\tan^{-1} s\Big|_s^{\infty}$$

$$= \tan^{-1} 5\frac{\pi}{2}$$

$$= k = -\frac{\pi}{2}$$

44. We have, S = {K : K ⊆ 3}

∀ K ≤ 3 |A| > 0 and solution of $y'(x) = A_y(x)$

tend to zero as $x \to \infty$

45. $P_{m+1}(0) = \frac{-m}{m+1}P_{m-1}(0)$

let $m = 5$

$$\Rightarrow \quad P_6(0) = \frac{-5}{6}P_4(0)$$

$$= -\frac{5}{6} \times -\frac{3}{4} \times P_2(0)$$

$$= \frac{-5}{6} \times -\frac{3}{4} \times -\frac{1}{2}$$

$$= \frac{-5}{16}$$

$$\Rightarrow \quad n = 6$$

Now $\int_{-1}^{1} P^2{}_n(x)dx = \frac{2}{2n+1}$

$$\Rightarrow \quad \int_{-1}^{1} P_6^2(x)dx = \frac{2}{2.6+1}$$

$$= \frac{2}{13}$$

46. As p and q are continuous on [–1, 1]

⇒ linearly independent solution of

$y'' + p(x)y' + q(x)y = 0; x \in [-1, 1]$

Then $y_1 = e^{x-1}$

$y_2 = e^{x-1}$

One two linearly independent solutions, since

$w(y_1 . y_2) \neq 0, \forall [-1, 1]$

47. $L[j_0(t)] = \frac{1}{\sqrt{S^2+1}}$

and $J_0'(t) = -J_1(t)$

Now $L[J_0'(t)] = sL[J_0(t) - J_0(0)]$

$$\Rightarrow s\left(\frac{s}{\sqrt{s^2+1}}\right) - 1 = \frac{s}{\sqrt{s^2+1}} - 1$$

$$\Rightarrow L[-J_0'(t)] = \frac{-s}{\sqrt{s^2+1}} + 1$$

$$\Rightarrow L[J_1(t)] = 1 - \frac{s}{\sqrt{s^2+1}}$$

48. $x^2y'' - xy' + (1 + x^2)y = 0$ ...(*i*)

$$\Rightarrow y'' - \frac{1}{x}y' + \left(\frac{1+x^2}{x^2}\right)y = 0$$

$P(x) = -\frac{1}{x} \to -\infty$ as $x = 0$

$\phi(x) = \left(\frac{1}{x^2} + 1\right) \to \infty$ as $x = 0$

⇒ $x = 0$ is a singular point of the differential equation.

$xP(x) = -1$ at $x = 0$

$x^2\phi(x) = -1 + x^2 = 1$ at $x = 0$

⇒ $x = 0$ is a singular point of the given differential equation

Now let

$$y = \sum_{n=0}^{\infty} c_n y^{n+r}\ ;\ c_0 \neq 0$$

$$\frac{dy}{dx} = \sum_{n=0}^{\infty}(n+r)c_n x^{n+r-1}$$

$$\frac{d^2y}{dx^2} = \sum_{n=0}^{\infty}(n+r)(n+r-1)c_n x^{(n+r-2)}$$

From equation (*i*)

$$\sum(n+r-1)^2 c_n x^{n-r} + \sum c_n x^{n+r+2} = 0$$

Now equating the coefficient of lowest degree term both side by putting $n = 0$ in first summation,

we get $(r-1)^2 c_0 = 0$ but $c_0 \neq 0$

⇒ $(r-1)^2 = 0$ ...(*ii*)

which is the indicial equation.

49. Now, from equation (*ii*), we get

$r = 1, 1$

Now, comparing the coefficient of x^{n+r} both sides, we get $(n + r - 1)^2 c_n + c_n - 2 = 0$

let $r = 1$

$\Rightarrow \quad n^2 c_n + c_n - 2 = 0$

50. $\lim_{x\to 0} \frac{\cot AX}{X-1}$ i.e. limit does not exists so $x = 0$ is not a regular singular point.

$\lim_{x\to 1} \frac{\cot AX}{X}$ i.e, limit does not exists so $x = 1$ is also not a regular singular point.

51. n^{th} legendre's polynomial is

$$C_n \frac{d^n y}{dx^n}\left(x^2 - 1\right)^n$$

Then $\quad C_n = \frac{1}{n!\cdot 2^n}$

This is Rodrigues formulae.

52. $$w(y_1, y_2) = \begin{vmatrix} y_1 & y_2 \\ y_1' & y_2' \end{vmatrix}$$

and $$w = ce^{-\int P dx} = ce^{+\int \frac{2x}{1-x^2}dx}$$

$$= ce^{\ln\left(1-x^2\right)-1}$$

$$w = \frac{C}{\left(1-x^2\right)}, w\left(\tfrac{1}{2}\right)$$

$$= 1/3 = \frac{C}{1-\frac{1}{4}} = \frac{4C}{3}$$

$\Rightarrow \quad C = 1/4$

$$w = \frac{1}{4\left(1-x^2\right)},\ w\,(0, 0) = 1/4$$

$$1/4 = \begin{vmatrix} 1 & y_2 & (0) \\ 0 & y_2' & (0) \end{vmatrix}$$

$\Rightarrow \quad y_2'(0) = 1/4$

53. $$dy/dx = 2(1+y)\sqrt{y}$$

$$\frac{dy}{2(1+y)\sqrt{y}} = dx$$

let $\quad \sqrt{y} = t$

$$\Rightarrow \quad \frac{1}{2\sqrt{y}}dy = dt$$

$$\Rightarrow \quad \frac{dt}{1+t^2} = dx$$

$\Rightarrow \quad \tan^{-1} t = x + c$

$\Rightarrow \quad \tan^{-1}\sqrt{y} = x + c$

at $\quad x = \pi/2$ and $y = 1$;

$\tan^{-1}(1) = \pi/2 + c$

$\Rightarrow \quad n\pi + \pi/4 = \pi/2 + c$

$\Rightarrow \quad c = n\pi - \pi/4$

$x = 0, y = 0$

$\tan^{-1}(0) = 0 + c$

$c = n\pi$

i.e the solution exists for $(0, 2\pi)$

54. $(x^2 D^2 + 2xD + 1/4)y = \frac{1}{\sqrt{x}}$

let $\quad x = e^z, xD = \theta; \theta = d/dz$

$(4(D\,(D - 1)) + 8D + 1)y = 4e^{-z/2}$

$\Rightarrow (4D^2 - 4D + 8D + 1)y = 4e^{-z/2}$

Auxiliary equation is

$4m^2 + 4m + 1 = 0$

$(2m + 1)^2 = 0$

$m = -1/2, -1/2$

$CF = (C_1 + C_2 z)e^{-z/2}$

$$= 4\left(\frac{1}{(2D+1)^2}e^{-z/2}\right)$$

$$= 4z^2\frac{1}{2.2.2}e^{-z/2}$$

$$= \frac{4z^2}{8e^{z/2}} = \frac{4(\log x)^2}{8\sqrt{x}}$$

$$= \frac{(\log x)^2}{2\sqrt{x}}$$

55. $$y'' + \frac{1}{x}y' + y = 0$$

$P(x) = 1/x$

$$w(y_1, y_2) = ce^{-\int P dx} = C/x$$

which has no solution

56. $(\cos y \sin 2x)dx + (\cos^2 y - \cos^2 x)\, dy = 0$

$$\frac{\partial m}{\partial y} = -\sin y \sin 2x$$

$$\frac{\partial n}{\partial x} = \sin 2x$$

$$\frac{\frac{\partial m}{\partial y} - \frac{\partial n}{\partial x}}{m} = \frac{\sin 2x(1+\sin y)}{\cos y \sin 2x}$$

$$= \sec y + \tan y = f(y)$$

so $\sec^2 y + \sec y \tan y$ is integrating factor.

57. $$\frac{dy}{dx} = \frac{y}{\sqrt{x}}$$

$$\Rightarrow \quad \frac{1}{y} dy = x^{-1/2}\, dx$$

$$\Rightarrow \quad y = e^{2\sqrt{x}}.e^c$$

At $x = 2,\ y = 4$

$$\therefore \quad e^c = 4e^{-2\sqrt{2}}$$

$$\therefore \quad y = e^{2\sqrt{x}}.4e^{-2\sqrt{2}}$$

Hence, differential equation has a unique solution

58. Given : $D^4 - D^2 = 0$

$$\Rightarrow \quad D^2(D-1)(D+1) = 0$$

$$\Rightarrow \quad D = 0, 0, 1, -1$$

$$\therefore \quad y = 1 + C_1 x + C_2 e^x + C_3 e^{-x}$$

Hence, the set of linearly independent solutions is $\{1, x, e^{-x}, e^x\}$

59. Given : $x^2(1-x)\frac{d^2y}{dx^2} + x\frac{dy}{dx} + y = 0$

$$\Rightarrow \quad \frac{d^2y}{dx^2} + \frac{1}{x(1-x)}\frac{dy}{dx} + \frac{1}{x^2(1-x)}y = 0$$

$$\therefore \quad P = \frac{1}{x(1-x)}, \quad Q = \frac{1}{x^2(1-x)}$$

$$\Rightarrow \quad P - xQ = 0$$

Hence, solution of C.F. is $u = -x$

So, the $x = 1$ is a regular singular point.

60. Let equation of curve is $\gamma = f(X)$

Line joining origin to any point $P(x, y)$ on the curve.

Then equation of line is,

$$\gamma - y = \frac{y-0}{x-0}(X - x)$$

$$\Rightarrow \quad \gamma - y = \frac{y}{x}(X - x) \qquad ...(i)$$

Equation of line parallel to the y-axis is $X = 0$ ...(ii)

Gradient of this line is $m_2 = \infty$

$$\Rightarrow \quad \theta_2 = \frac{\pi}{2}$$

Tangent to the curve at $P(x, y)$ is

$$\gamma - y = f'(x)(X - x) \qquad ...(iii)$$

$$m_3 = f'(x)$$

$$\theta_3 = \tan^{-1} f'(x)$$

$$m_1 = \frac{y}{x}$$

$$\Rightarrow \quad \theta_1 = \tan^{-1}(y/x)$$

Now $\theta_1 - \theta_3 = \theta_3 - \theta_2$ (given)

$$\tan^{-1}\left(\frac{y}{x}\right) - \tan^{-1} f'(x) = \tan^{-1} f'(x) - \frac{\pi}{2}$$

or $$\tan^{-1} f'(x) - \tan^{-1}\left(\frac{y}{x}\right) = \frac{\pi}{2} - \tan^{-1} f'(x)$$

On solving, we get

$$x[f'(x)]^2 + 2y[f'(x)] = 0$$

i.e., $$x\left(\frac{dy}{dx}\right)^2 + 2y\left(\frac{dy}{dx}\right) = 0$$

61. $$f(x) = \begin{cases} x, & -1 \le x \le 0 \\ 0, & 0 \le x \le 1 \end{cases}$$

and $$f(x) = a_0 P_0(x) + a_1 P_1(x) + a_2 P_2(x) + ...$$

Now $$f(x) = \sum_{r=0}^{\infty} a_r P_r(x)$$

where, $$a_r = \left(r + \frac{1}{2}\right)\int_{-1}^{1} f(x)\, P_r(x)\, dx$$

$$= \frac{2r+1}{2}\left[\int_{-1}^{0} f(x)\, P_r(x)\, dx + \int_{0}^{1} f(x)\, P_r(x)\, dx\right]$$

$$= \frac{2r+1}{2}\left[\int_{-1}^{0} x\, P_r(x)\, dx + 0\right]$$

$$a_r = \frac{2r+1}{2}\int_{-1}^{0} x P_r(x)\, dx$$

$$a_0 = \frac{1}{2}\int_{-1}^{0} x(1)\, dx$$

$$= \frac{1}{2}\left[\frac{x^2}{2}\right]_{-1}^{0}$$

$$= -\frac{1}{4}$$

$$a_1 = \frac{3}{2}\int_{-1}^{0} x(x)\, dx$$

$$= \frac{3}{2}\cdot\frac{1}{3}\left[x^3\right]_{-1}^{0} = \frac{1}{2}$$

Hence, $a_0 = -\frac{1}{4}, a_1 = \frac{1}{2}$

63. $y = \alpha \sin x - \beta \cos x$ ...(i)

$z = \alpha \cos x + \beta \sin x$ ...(ii)

Differentiate equation (i) with respect to x, we get

$$\frac{dy}{dx} = \alpha \cos x + \beta \sin x = z$$

$$\frac{dy}{dx} - z = 0 \quad ...(iii)$$

Differentiate equation (ii) with respect to x, we get

$$\frac{dy}{dx} = -\alpha \sin x + \beta \cos x = -y$$

$$\Rightarrow \quad y + \frac{dy}{dx} = 0 \quad ...(iv)$$

Hence, equations (i) and (ii) are general solution of differential equations (iii) and (iv).

64. $$2x(2+x)\frac{d^2y}{dx^2} + 2(3+x)\frac{dy}{dx} - xy = 0$$

Let $2x(2+x) = v^2$

$\Rightarrow$ $2x^2 + 4x - v^2 = 0$

$$\Rightarrow \quad x = \frac{-4 \pm \sqrt{16+8v^2}}{4}$$

$$x = \frac{-2 \pm \sqrt{4+2v^2}}{2}$$

65. We have $y = k(x-1)\ k \in R$ ...(i)

$\Rightarrow$ $dy/dx = k$

$$\Rightarrow \quad dy/dx = \frac{y}{x-1} \quad ..(ii)$$

From Equation (i)

its orthogonal family is

$$-dx/dy = \frac{y}{(x-1)}$$

on integrating we have

$$\Rightarrow -\int (x-1)dx = \int y\,dy + c_1$$

$\Rightarrow$ $(x-1)^2 + y^2 = c_1 = c^2$.

66. If $y = \phi(x)$ is a particular solution of

$y'' + (\sin x)y' + 2y = e^x$

and $y = \psi(x)$

is a particular solution of

$y'' + (\sin x)\,y' + xy = \cos 2x$

Then, the particular solution of is

$\phi(x) - \psi(x) + 1$

as $y'' + (\sin x)y' + 2y = e^x + 2\sin^2 x$

$\Rightarrow y'' + (\sin x)\,y' + 2y = e^x - \cos 2x + 1$

$\Rightarrow \phi \cos - \psi(x) + 1 = y$

67. $w(x) = ce - \int p(x)\,dx$

$$\Rightarrow w(x) = ce^{x^2}$$

$$\Rightarrow \begin{vmatrix} \phi(x) & \psi(x) \\ \phi'(x) & \psi(x) \end{vmatrix} = ce^{x^2}$$

$$\text{at } x = 0, \begin{vmatrix} 1 & 1 \\ 1 & 2 \end{vmatrix} = ce^0 \Rightarrow c = 1$$

$$w(1) = 1.e^{1^2} = e$$

68. $y'' + \lambda y = 0$

$y'(0) = 0\ y'(\pi/2) = 0$

let $\lambda = \mu^2 > 0$

$\Rightarrow (D^2 + \mu^2)\,y = 0$

$\Rightarrow$ $y = c_1 \cos \mu x + c_2 \sin \mu x$

$\Rightarrow$ $y' = -c_1\mu \sin \mu x + c_2\,\mu \cos \mu x$

Now $y'(0) = 0 = c_2\mu$

$\Rightarrow$ $c_2 = 0$

$y'(\pi/2) = 0 = -c_1\mu \sin \mu\pi/2$

$\Rightarrow$ $c_1 \neq 0$ if sin

$\mu\pi/2 = 0 = \sin n\pi$

$\Rightarrow$ $\mu_1 = 2x$

so $\lambda = (2n)^2 = 4x^2,\ n \in N$

69. $$\frac{d^2y}{dt^2} + y(t) = \begin{bmatrix} 0 & 0 \le + \le 2\pi \\ \sin t & t > 2\pi \end{bmatrix}$$

taking Laplace in both sides

$$p^2y(p) - py(0) - y'(0) + y(p)$$

$$= \int_{2\pi}^{on} e^{-pt} \sin t dt \ p^2y(p) - y(1) + y(p)$$

$$= \left[\frac{e^{-pt}}{\sqrt{1+p^2}}(-p\sin t - \cos t)\right]_{2\pi}^{\infty}$$

$$\Rightarrow (p^2+1)\,y(p) - p = 0 \frac{-e^{-2\pi p}}{\sqrt{1+p^2}}(0-1)$$

$$y(p) = \frac{p}{1+p^2} + \frac{e^{-2\pi p}}{(1+p^2)^{3/2}}$$

70. $y'' + xy' + 3y = 0$ ...(i)

Here $$y = \sum_{m=0}^{\infty} a_m x^m$$

$$y' = \sum_{m=1}^{\infty} m a_m x^{m-1}$$

$$y'' = \sum m(m-1)a_m x^{m-2}$$

so equation (i) we get

$$\sum m(m-1)a_m x^{m-2} + \sum m a_m x^m + 3\sum a_m x^m = 0$$

$$\sum m(m-1)a_m x^{m-2} + \sum (m+3)a_m x^m = 0$$

$\Rightarrow (m+2)(m+1)\, a_m + 2 + cm + 3)a_m = 0$

$$\Rightarrow \quad \frac{a_m}{a_m+2} = \frac{-(m+2)(m+1)}{(m+3)}$$

71. $x(1+x^2)y'' + \cos(x)y' + (1-3x+x^2)y = 0$ ...(*i*)

$$y = \sum_{r=0}^{\infty} a_m x^{m+r}$$

$$y' = \sum_{r=0}^{\infty} (m+r)a_m x^{m+r-1}$$

$$y'' = \sum (m+r)(m+r-1)a_m x^{m+r-2}$$

Putting values of y, y', y''.

On equation (*ii*), we get

$$\sum (m+r)(m+r-1)a_m x^{m+r-1} \sum (m+r)$$

$$(m+r-1)a_m x^{m+r+2} + \sum (m+r)a_m$$

$$(\cos x)x^{m+r-1} + \sum a_m x^{m+r}$$

$$-3\sum a_m x^{m+r+1} + \sum a_m x^{m+r+2} = 0$$

Now equating coefficients of x^{r-1} to zero we get

$r(r-1)\, a_0 + ra_0 = 0$

$\Rightarrow (r^2 - r + r)\, a_0 = 0$

$r^2 a_0 = 0$

$r^2 = 0$ (indicial equation)

72. $\dfrac{dx}{dt} = -x + 2y$

$$\frac{dy}{dt} = 4x + y$$

$(D+1)x = 2y$ ...(*i*)

$(D-1)y = 4x$ ...(*ii*)

operating equation (*i*) by $(D-1)$

$(D^2-1)\, x = 2(D-1)y$

$= 2(4x)$

$\Rightarrow (D^2-1)\, x - 8x = 0$

$\Rightarrow \quad (D^2-9)n = 0$

$x = c_1 e^{3t} + + c_2 e^{-3t}$

$$\Rightarrow \quad \frac{dv}{dt} = 3c_1 e^{3t} - 3c_2 e^{-3t}$$

$$\Rightarrow \quad y = \frac{1}{2}\left(x + \frac{dx}{dt}\right) = 2c_1 e^{3t} - c_2 e^{-3t}$$

Replacing c_2 by $-c_2$ we have

$$\begin{pmatrix} x(t) \\ y(t) \end{pmatrix} = \begin{pmatrix} c_1 & e^{3t} & -c_2 e^{-3t} \\ 2c_1 & e^{3t} & +c_2 e^{-3t} \end{pmatrix}$$

73. Given, $x^2 + y^2 = 2cx$

$$\Rightarrow \quad c = \frac{x^2+y^2}{2x}$$

Differentiating with respect to x, we get

$$2x + 2y\frac{dy}{dx} = 2c$$

$$\Rightarrow \quad x + y\frac{dy}{dx} = c = \frac{x^2+y^2}{2x}$$

$$\Rightarrow \quad \frac{dy}{dx} = \frac{\frac{x^2+y^2}{2x}}{y} = \frac{y^2-x^2}{2xy}$$

Its orthogonal trajectory is given by $-\dfrac{dx}{dy}$

$$\therefore \quad -\frac{dx}{dy} = \frac{y^2-x^2}{2xy}$$

$$\Rightarrow \quad \frac{dy}{dx}(y^2-x^2) = -2xy$$

$\Rightarrow \quad y'(x^2-y^2) = 2xy$

76. By applying Lipsdiz condition

$$|f(x,y_1) - f(x,y_2)| = |x|\left|y_1^2 - y_2^2\right|$$

79. Sinced $\dfrac{d}{dx}\{x^n J_n(x)\} = x^n J_{n-1}(x)$

So $\int x^n J_{n-1}(x)dx = x^n J_n(x)$ ...(i)

$$\therefore \quad \int_0^x x^3 J_0(x)dx = \int_0^x x^2[xJ_0(x)]dx$$

$$= \left[x^2\{xJ_1(x)\}\right]_0^x - \int_0^x 2x\{xJ_1(x)\}dx$$

(Integrating by parts and using (*i*) for $n=1$)

$$= x^3 J_1(x) - 2\int_0^x x^2 J_1(x)dx$$

$$= x^3 J_1(x) - 2\,[x^2 J_2(x)]$$

80. $y = au + bx$

$$u = 1 - \frac{x^3}{3^2} + \frac{x^6}{3^4(\lfloor 2)^2} - \frac{9}{3^6(\lfloor 3)^2} + \ldots$$

and

$$v = u\log x + 2\left[\frac{x^3}{3^3} - \frac{1}{3^5(\lfloor 2)^2}\left(1+\frac{1}{2}\right)x^6 + \ldots\right]2$$

82. $y^{(2)} + \lambda y = 0$

where λ is a parameter.

The general solution is

$$y = C_1 \sin\sqrt{\lambda}x + C_2 \cos\sqrt{\lambda}x$$

Putting boundary conditions

$$y(0) = y(2\pi)$$

and $y'(0) = y'(2\pi)$

where $y^{(1)} = C_1\sqrt{\lambda}\cos\sqrt{\lambda}\,x - C_2\sqrt{\lambda}\sin\sqrt{\lambda}\,x$

we have $\lambda = n^2$

83. Because if λ_i and are λ_j are roots of equation. $J_n(\lambda a) = 0$, then

$$\int_0^a x J_n(\lambda_i x) J_n(\lambda_j x)\,dx$$

$$= \begin{cases} 0, & \text{if } i \neq j \text{(diff.roots)} \\ \frac{a^2}{2} J_{n+1}^2(\lambda_i a), & \text{if } i = j \text{(equal roots)} \end{cases}$$

For orthogonality of system on [0, 1], the weight function is x.

84. A linear homogenous equation can always be reduced to a linear differentiation equation with constant coefficients of the form (by substitution)

$$\frac{d^n y}{dx^n} + a_1\frac{d^{n-1}y}{dx^{n-1}} + a_2\frac{d^{n-2}y}{dx^{n-2}} + \ldots + a_1 y = x \quad \ldots(i)$$

$$f(D) = x$$

We will now show that if $y_1, y_2, \ldots, y_n$ are n linearly independent solutions of equation (i) then $c_1y_1 + c_2y_2 + \ldots + c_ny_n$ is also a solution of equation (i),

where $c_1, c_2, \ldots, c_n$ being arbitrary constants.

Since $y_1, y_2, \ldots, y_n$ are solution of (i),

we get

$$f(D)y_1 = 0,$$

$$f(D)y_2 = 0, \ldots, f(D)\,y_n = 0 \quad \ldots(ii)$$

$f(D)\,\{c_1y_1 + c_2y_2 + \ldots + c_ny_n\}$

$= f(D)\,(c_1y_1) + f(D)\,(c_2y_2) + \ldots + f(D)\,(c_ny_n)$

$= c_1f(D)y_1 + c_2f(D)\,y_2 + \ldots + c_n\,f(D)\,y_n$

$= c_1.0 + c_2.0 + \ldots + c_n.0$

$= 0$ (using(ii))

This proves that statement.

85. $(x^7y^2 + 3y)\,dx + (3x^8y - x)\,dy = 0 \quad \ldots(i)$

$\approx x^{\alpha}y^{\beta}\,(mydx + nxdy) + x^{\alpha'}x^{\beta'}\,(m'\,ydx + n'\,xdy) = 0 \ldots(ii)$

$x^7y\,(ydx + 3xdy) + (3ydx - xdy) = 0 \ldots(iii)$

Comparing equations (ii) and (iii);

we get

$$\alpha = 7 \quad \alpha' = 0$$

$$\beta = 1 \quad \beta' = 0$$

$$m = 1 \quad m' = 3$$

$$n = 3 \quad n' = -1$$

$\therefore$ I.F. of first term of (iii) is

$$x^{km-1-\alpha}\,y^{km-1-\beta} = x^{k-8}\,y^{3k-2}$$

I.F. of second term of (iii) is

$$x^{k'n'-1-\alpha'}y^{k'n'-1-\beta'} = x^{3k'-1}y^{-k'-1}$$

$\therefore$ $k - 8 = 3k' - 1$

and $3k - 2 = -k' - 1$

$$k = 3k' + 7$$

$$k = \frac{-k^1 + 1}{3}$$

$$3k' + 7 = \frac{-k' + 1}{3}$$

$$9k' + 21 = -k' + 1$$

$$10k' = -20$$

$$k' = -2$$

$$k = 1$$

$\therefore$ I. F $= x^{-7}y = x^m y^n$

$\Rightarrow$ $m = -7, n = 1$

86. $(x^2 - x)\dfrac{dy}{dx} = (2 - x^1)y$

Put $x^2 - x = t,\ 2x - 1 = \dfrac{dt}{dx}$

$\therefore$ $t\dfrac{dy}{dx} = y\dfrac{dt}{dx}$

$\Rightarrow$ $ydt = tdy$

$\Rightarrow$ $\dfrac{dt}{t} = \dfrac{dy}{y}$

Integrating,

$$\log\frac{y}{t} = \log c$$

$\Rightarrow$ $y = ct = c\,(x^2 - x)$

$$y(x_0) = c(x_0^2 - x_0) = y_0$$

$\Rightarrow$ $c = \dfrac{y_0}{x_0^2 - x_0}$

$$y = \frac{y_0}{x_0^2 - x_0}(x^2 - x)$$

It has unique solution if x_0, y_0 equals (1, 1)

95. (*a*) Given equation is

$$\frac{d^2y}{dx^2}+4y = \sec^2 2x$$

Here $m^2 + 4 = 0$

or $m = \pm 2i$

$\therefore$ $y = C_1 \cos 2x + C_2 \sin 2x$

Therefore Wronskian, $W = \begin{vmatrix} y_1 & y_2 \\ y_1' & y_2' \end{vmatrix}$

$$= \begin{vmatrix} \cos 2x & \sin 2x \\ -2\sin 2x & 2\cos 2x \end{vmatrix}$$

$= 2$

When P.I. $= -\cos 2x \int \frac{\sin 2x.\sec^2 2x}{2}dx$

$$+ \sin 2x \int \frac{\cos 2x.\sec^2 2x}{2}dx$$

$$= -\frac{\cos 2x}{2}.\frac{\sec 2x}{2}+\frac{\sin 2x}{2}.\frac{1}{2}\ln(\sec 2x+\tan 2x)$$

$$= -\frac{1}{4}+\frac{1}{4}\sin 2x \ln(\sec 2x+\tan 2x)$$

Hence complete solution is

$y = C_1 \cos 2x + C_2 \sin 2x + \frac{1}{4} \sin 2x \ln (\sec 2x + \tan 2x) - \frac{1}{4}$.

95. (*b*) Given equation is $y + y'' = -x$.

Using variation of parameters.

$\therefore$ $y = u_1 \cos x + u_2 \sin x$.

$$u_1' = -\frac{\sin x}{\cos x.\cos x-(-\sin x)\sin x}(-x)$$

$= x \sin x$

$$u_2' = -\frac{\cos x}{\cos x.\cos x-(-\sin x)\sin x}(-x)$$

$= x \cos x$.

Let us now solve for u_1 and u_2 by integrating their derivatives between 0 and x and between x and π respectively. Then $\cos^2 x + \sin^2 x$ is the Wronskian of the two solutions y_1 and y_2. We have using s as a dummy variable of integration.

$$u_1 = -\int_0^x \frac{\sin s.(-s)}{1}ds$$

$$= \int_0^x s\sin s\, ds.$$

$$= [\sin s - s\cos s]_0^x$$

$= \sin x - x \cos x$

and $$u_2 = -\int_x^\pi \frac{\cos(s)(-s)}{1}ds$$

$$= \int_x^\pi s\cos s\, ds$$

$$= [\cos s + s\sin s]_x^\pi$$

$= -1 - \cos x - x \sin x$

Hence, $y = u_1 \cos x + u_2 \sin x$

$= \sin x \cos x - x \cos^2 x - \sin x - \sin x \cos x - x \sin^2 x$

$= -x [\cos^2 x + \sin^2 x] - \sin x$

$= -(x + \sin x)$.

So, green function $g(x, s)$

$$= \begin{cases} -\sin s\cos x, & 0 \le x \le s \\ -\cos s \sin x, & s \le x \le \pi \end{cases}$$

This will possible if

$\underset{x\to s^+}{Lt}\, g_x(x,s) - \underset{x\to s^-}{Lt}\, g_x(x,s) = -1$ at $x = s$.

$\therefore$ $\underset{x\to s^+}{Lt} - \cos s\cos x - \underset{x\to s^-}{Lt} - \sin s(-\sin x)$

$= -\cos^2 s - \sin^2 s = -1$.

Thus continuity is satisfied.

Hence required green function is

$$g(x, s) = \begin{cases} -\sin s\cos x, & 0 \le x \le s \\ -\cos s \sin x, & s \le x \le \pi. \end{cases}$$

99. Given

$ty''(t) + y'(t) + ty(t) = 0; y(0) = 1, y'(0) = k$

Taking Laplace transform of both sides, we have

$L\{t\, y''(t)\} + L\{y'(t)\} + L\{t\, y(t)\} = 0$

$$\Rightarrow -\frac{d}{ds}\left[s^2\bar{y}-sy(0)-y'(0)\right]+\left[s\bar{y}-y(0)\right]-\frac{d\bar{y}}{ds}=0$$

Using given values

$$-\frac{d}{ds}\left[s^2\bar{y}-s-k\right]+\left[s\bar{y}-1\right]-\frac{d\bar{y}}{ds}=0$$

$$\Rightarrow -2s.\bar{y}-s^2\frac{d\bar{y}}{ds}+1+s\bar{y}-1-\frac{d\bar{y}}{ds}=0$$

$$\Rightarrow (s^2+1)\frac{d\bar{y}}{ds}+s\bar{y}=0$$

Separating the variables

$$\int\frac{d\bar{y}}{y}+\int\frac{s ds}{s^2+1}=0$$

Integrating, we get

$$\log \bar{y} + \frac{1}{2} \log (s^2 + 1) = \log c$$

$$\Rightarrow \qquad \bar{y} = \frac{c}{\sqrt{s^2+1}}$$

Taking Laplace inverse

$$y = C\, J_0(x)$$

But $y(0) = C\, J_0(0)$,

i.e., $C = 1$

$\therefore \quad y = J_0(x)$

100. Given equation is

$$y''(x) + y(x) = -1$$

Using variation of parameters

Here

$$y = u_1 \cos x + u_2 \sin x.$$

$$\therefore \quad u_1' = \frac{\sin x}{\cos x \cos x - (-\sin x)\sin x}(-1)$$

$$= \sin x$$

and

$$u_2' = \frac{\cos x}{\cos x \cos x - (-\sin x)\sin x}(-1)$$

$$= \cos x$$

Using s as a dummy variable

$$g(x, s) = \begin{cases} -\sin s \cos x, & 0 \le x \le s \\ -\cos s \sin x, & s \le x \le \pi/2 \end{cases}$$

For continuity

$$\underset{x \to s^+}{\text{Lt}}\, g_x(x,s) - \underset{x \to \bar{s}}{\text{Lt}}\, g_x(x,s)$$

$$= \underset{x \to s^+}{\text{Lt}} -\cos^2 s - \underset{x \to \bar{s}}{\text{Lt}} \sin^2 s$$

$$= -1$$

Hence $g(x, s)$ holds all the properties of green function

Hence

$$g(x, s) = \begin{cases} -\sin s \cos x, & 0 \le x \le s \\ -\cos s \sin x, & s \le x \le \pi/2 \end{cases}$$

■■

5 CHAPTER Algebra

2016

1. Let F be a field of order 32. Then the number of non-zero solutions $(a, b) \in F$ F of the equation $x^2 + x y + y^2 = 0$ is equal to ________.
2. Let $u(x, y) = x^3 + a x^2 y + b x y^2 + 2 y^3$ be a harmonic function and $v(x, y)$ its harmonic conjugate. If $v(0, 0) = 1$, then $| a + b + v(1, 1)|$ is equal to _______.

2015

3. Let $c \in \mathbb{Z}_3$ be such that $\dfrac{Z_3[X]}{(X^3 + c X + 1)}$ is a field. Then c is equal to ________
4. The number of ring homomorphisms from $\mathbb{Z}_2 \times \mathbb{Z}_2$ to $\mathbb{Z}_4$ is equal to _______
5. Let $G = \{e, x, x^2, x^3, y, xy, x^2y, x^3y\}$ with $o(x) = 4$, $o(y) = 2$ and $xy = yx^3$. Then the number of elements in the center of the group G is equal to
   (a) 1 (b) 2
   (c) 4 (d) 8
6. Let $p(x) = 9x^5 + 10x^3 + 5x + 15$ and $q(x) = x^3 - x^2 - x - 2$ be two polynomials in $\mathbb{Q}[x]$. Then, over $\mathbb{Q}$,
   (a) $p(x)$ and $q(x)$ are both irreducible
   (b) $p(x)$ is reducible but $q(x)$ is irreducible
   (c) $p(x)$ is irreducible but $q(x)$ is reducible
   (d) $p(x)$ and $q(x)$ are both reducible

2014

7. The number of non-isomorphic groups of order 10 is _______
8. Let a,b,c,d be real numbers with $a < c < d < b$. Consider the ring $C[a, b]$ with pointwise addition and multiplication.
   If $S = \{f \in C[a, b] : f(x) = 0 \text{ for all } x \in [c, d]\}$, then
   (a) S is NOT an ideal of $C[a, b]$
   (b) S is an ideal of $C[a, b]$ but NOT a prime ideal of $C[a, b]$
   (c) S is prime ideal of $C[a, b]$ but NOT a maximal ideal of $C[a, b]$
   (d) S is a maximal ideal of $C[a, b]$
9. Let R be a ring. If $R[x]$ is a principal ideal domain, then R is necessarily a
   (a) Unique Factorization Domain
   (b) Principal Ideal Domain
   (c) Euclidean Domain
   (d) Field
10. Let $\mathbb{F}_{125}$ be the field of 125 elements. The number of non-zero elements $\alpha \in \mathbb{F}_{125}$ such that $\alpha^5 = \alpha$ is _______

2013

11. Suppose that R is a unique factorization domain and that $a, b \in R$ are distinct irreducible elements. Which of the following statements is **TRUE**?
    (a) The ideal $\langle 1 + a \rangle$ is a prime ideal
    (b) The ideal $\langle a + b \rangle$ is a prime ideal
    (c) The ideal $\langle 1 + ab \rangle$ is a prime ideal
    (d) The ideal $\langle a \rangle$ is not necessarily a maximal ideal
12. Which of the following groups has a proper subgroup that is **NOT** cyclic?
    (a) $\mathbb{Z}_{15} \times \mathbb{Z}_{77}$ (b) S_3
    (c) $(\mathbb{Z},+)$ (d) $(\mathbb{Q},+)$
13. The number of group homomorphisms from $\mathbb{Z}_3$ to $\mathbb{Z}_9$ is ________
14. Let G be a group of order 231. The number of elements of order 11 in G is ______
15. Which of the following is a field?
    (a) $\mathbb{C}[x]/\langle x^2 + 2 \rangle$ (b) $\mathbb{Z}[x]/\langle x^2 + 2 \rangle$
    (c) $\mathbb{Q}[x]/\langle x^2 - 2 \rangle$ (d) $\mathbb{R}[x]/\langle x^2 - 2 \rangle$
16. Let $x_0 = 0$. Define $x_{n+1} = \cos x_n$ for every $n \geq 0$. Then
    (a) $\{x_n\}$ is increasing and convergent
    (b) $\{x_n\}$ is decreasing and convergent
    (c) $\{x_n\}$ is convergent and $x_{2n} < \lim_{m\to\infty} x_m < x_{2n+1}$ for every $n \in \mathbb{N}$
    (d) $\{x_n\}$ is not convergent
17. The number of non-isomorphic abelian groups of order 24 is ______
18. Which of the following groups contains a unique normal subgroup of order four?
    (a) $\mathbb{Z}_2 \oplus \mathbb{Z}_4$
    (b) The dihedral group, D_4, of order eight
    (c) The quaternion group, Q_8
    (d) $\mathbb{Z}_2 \oplus \mathbb{Z}_2 \oplus \mathbb{Z}_2$

2012

19. Let $R = \mathbb{Z} \times \mathbb{Z} \times \mathbb{Z}$ and $I = \mathbb{Z} \times \mathbb{Z} \times \{0\}$. Then which of the following statement is correct?

(*a*) I is a maximal ideal but not a prime ideal of R.

(*b*) I is a prime ideal but not a maximal ideal of R.

(*c*) I is both maximal ideal as well as a prime ideal of R.

(*d*) I is neither a maximal ideal nor a prime ideal of R.

20. The order of the smallest possible non trivial group containing elements x and y such that $x^7 = y^2 = e$ and $yx = x^4y$ is

(*a*) 1 (*b*) 2
(*c*) 7 (*d*) 14

21. The number of 5-Sylow subgroup (*s*) in a group of order 45 is

(*a*) 1 (*b*) 2
(*c*) 3 (*d*) 4

22. Let $\omega = \cos\frac{2\pi}{3} + i\sin\frac{2\pi}{3}$, $M = \begin{pmatrix} 0 & i \\ i & 0 \end{pmatrix}$,

$N = \begin{pmatrix} \omega & 0 \\ 0 & \omega^2 \end{pmatrix}$ and $G = \langle M, N \rangle$ be the group generated by the matrices M and N under matrix multiplication. Then

(*a*) $G/Z(G) \cong C_6$ (*b*) $G/Z(G) \cong S_3$
(*c*) $G/Z(G) \cong C_2$ (*d*) $G/Z(G) \cong C_4$

23. The flux of the vector field $\vec{u} = x\hat{i} + y\hat{j} + z\hat{k}$ flowing out through the surface of the ellipsoid $\frac{x^2}{a^2} + \frac{y^2}{b^2} + \frac{z^2}{c^2} = 1, a > b > c > 0$, is

(*a*) πabc (*b*) $2\pi abc$
(*c*) $3\pi abc$ (*d*) $4\pi abc$

2011

24. The number of irreducible quadratic polynomials over the field of two elements F_2 is

(*a*) 0 (*b*) 1
(*c*) 2 (*d*) 3

25. The number of elements in the conjugacy class of the 3-cycle (2 3 4) in the symmetric group S_6 is

(*a*) 20 (*b*) 40
(*c*) 120 (*d*) 216

26. Let P = (0, 1) Q = [0, 1]; U = (0, 1); S = [0, 1], T = R and A = {P, Q, U, S, T}. The equivalence relation 'homeomorphism' induces which one of the following as the partition of A?

(*a*) {P, Q, U, S}, {T} (*b*) {P, T}, {Q}, {U}, {S}
(*c*) {P, T}, {Q, U, S} (*d*) {P, T}, {Q, U}, {S}

27. If Z [*i*] is the ring of Gaussian integers, the quotient Z [*i*]/(3 – *i*) is isomorphic to

(*a*) Z (*b*) Z/3Z
(*c*) Z/4Z (*d*) Z/10Z

28. For the rings $L = \frac{R[x]}{\langle x^2 - x + 1 \rangle}$;

$M = \frac{R[x]}{\langle x^2 + x + 1 \rangle}$; $N = \frac{R[x]}{\langle x^2 + 2x + 1 \rangle}$

which one of the following is **TRUE?**

(*a*) L is isomorphic to M; L is not isomorphic to N; M is not isomorphic to N

(*b*) M is isomorphic to N; M is not isomorphic to L; N is not isomorphic to L

(*c*) L is isomorphic to M; M is isomorphic to N

(*d*) L is not isomorphic to M; L is not is isomorphic to N; M is not isomorphic to N

2010

29. Which one of the following groups is simple?

(*a*) S_3 (*b*) $GL(2, \mathbb{R})$
(*c*) $\mathbb{Z}_2 \times \mathbb{Z}_2$ (*d*) A_5

30. Consider the algebraic extension $E = \mathbb{Q}(\sqrt{2}, \sqrt{3}, \sqrt{5})$ of the field $\mathbb{Q}$ of rational numbers. Then $[E : \mathbb{Q}]$, then degree of E over $\mathbb{Q}$, is

(*a*) 3 (*b*) 4
(*c*) 7 (*d*) 8

31. Let G_1 be an abelian group of order 6 and $G_2 = S_3$. For $j = 1, 2$, let P_j be the statement:
"G_j has a unique subgroup of order 2". Then

(*a*) both P_1 and P_2 hold

(*b*) neither P_1 nor P_2 holds

(*c*) P_1 holds but not P_2

(*d*) P_2 holds but not P_1

32. Let G be the group of all symmetries of the square. Then the number of conjugate classes in G is

(*a*) 4

(*b*) 5

(*c*) 6

(*d*) 7

33. Consider the polynomial ring $\mathbb{Q}[x]$. The ideal of $\mathbb{Q}[x]$ generated by $x^2 - 3$ is

(*a*) maximal but not prime

(*b*) prime but not maximal

(*c*) both maximal and prime

(*d*) neither maximal nor prime

2009

34. $\dfrac{\mathbb{Z}_2[x]}{\langle x^3+x^2+1\rangle}$ is

(a) a field having 8 elements

(b) a field having 9 elements

(c) an infinite field

(d) NOT a field

35. The number of elements of a principal ideal domain can be

(a) 15 (b) 25

(c) 35 (d) 36

36. Which one of the following ideals of the ring $\mathbb{Z}[i]$ of Gaussian integers is NOT maximal ?

(a) $\langle 1+i\rangle$ (b) $\langle 1-i\rangle$

(c) $\langle 2+i\rangle$ (d) $\langle 3+i\rangle$

37. If Z(G) denotes the centre of a group G, then the order of the quotient group $\dfrac{G}{Z(G)}$ cannot be

(a) 4 (b) 6

(c) 15 (d) 25

38. Let $Aut(G)$ denote the group of automorphisms of a group G. Which one of the following is NOT a cyclic group ?

(a) $Aut(\mathbb{Z}_4)$ (b) $Aut(\mathbb{Z}_6)$

(c) $Aut(\mathbb{Z}_8)$ (d) $Aut(\mathbb{Z}_{10})$

2008

39. Let G = R\ {0} and H = {–1, 1} be groups under multipilication. Then the map φ G → H defined by $\varphi(x) = \dfrac{x}{|x|}$ is

(a) not a homomorphism

(b) a one - one homomorphism, which is not onto

(c) an onto homomorphism, which is not one-one

(d) an isomorphism

40. The number of maximal ideals in Z_{27} is

(a) 0 (b) 1

(c) 2 (d) 3

41. Let G be a group of order 45. Let H be a 3-Sylow subgroup of G and K be a 5-Sylow subgroup of G. Then

(a) both H and K are normal in G

(b) H is normal in G but K is not normal in G

(c) H is not normal in G but K is normal in G

(d) both H and K are not normal in G

42. The ring $Z\left[\sqrt{-11}\right]$ is

(a) a Euclidean Domain

(b) a Principal Ideal Domain, but not a Euclidean Domain

(c) a Unique Factorization Domain, but not a Principal Ideal Domain

(d) not a Unique Factorization Domain

43. Let R be a Principal Ideal Domain and a, b any two non-unit elements of R. Then the ideal generated by a and b is also generated by

(a) $a + b$ (b) ab

(c) gcd(a, b) (d) lcm(a, b)

44. Consider the action of S_4, the symmetric group of order 4, on $Z[x_1, x_2, x_3, x_4]$ given by $\sigma.\ p(x_1, x_2, x_3, x_4) = p(x_{\sigma(1)}, x_{\sigma(2)}, x_{\sigma(3)}, x_{\sigma(4)})$ for $\sigma \in S_4$.
Let $H \subseteq S_4$ denote the cyclic subgroup generated by (1423). Then the cardinality of the orbit $O_H(x_1x_3 + x_2x_4)$ of H on the polynomial $x_1x_3 + x_2x_4$ is

(a) 1 (b) 2

(c) 3 (d) 4

2007

45. The value of α for which G = {α, 1, 3, 9, 19, 27} is a cyclic group under multiplication modulo 56 is

(a) 5 (b) 15

(c) 25 (d) 35

46. Consider Z_{24} as the additive group modulo 24. Then the number of elements of order 8 in the group Z_{24} is

(a) 1 (b) 2

(c) 3 (d) 4

47. Let U(n) be the set of all positive integers less than n and relatively prime to n. Then U(n) is a group under multiplication modulo n. For n = 248, the number of elements in U(n) is

(a) 60 (b) 120

(c) 180 (d) 240

48. Let R [x] be the polynomial ring in x with real coefficients and let I = $\langle x^2 + 1\rangle$ be the ideal generated by the polynomial $x^2 + 1$ in R [x]. Then

(a) I is a maximal ideal

(b) I is a prime ideal but NOT a maximal ideal

(c) I is NOT a prime ideal

(d) R [x] / I has zero divisors

49. Consider Z_5 and Z_{20} as rings modulo 5 and 20, respectively. Then the number of homomorphisms $\varphi : Z_5 \to Z_{20}$ is

(a) 1 (b) 2

(c) 4 (d) 5

50. Let Q be the field of rational numbers and consider Z_2 as a field modulo 2. Let $f(x) = x^3 - 9x^2 + 9x + 3$. Then $f(x)$ is

(*a*) irreducible over Q but reducible over Z_2

(*b*) irreducible over both Q and Z_2

(*c*) reducible over Q but irreducible over Z_2

(*d*) reducible over both Q and Z_2

51. Consider Z_5 as a field modulo 5 and let

$f(x) = x^5 + 4x^4 + 4x^3 + 4x^2 + x + 1$.

Then the zero of $f(x)$ over Z_5 are 1 and 3 with respective multiplicity

(*a*) 1 and 4 (*b*) 2 and 3

(*c*) 2 and 2 (*d*) 1 and 2

2006

52. Let G be a cyclic group of order 8, then its group of automorphisms has order

(*a*) 2 (*b*) 4

(*c*) 6 (*d*) 8

53. Let M_3 (R) be the ring of all 3 × 3 real matrices. If I, J $\subseteq M_3$ (R) are defined as

$$I = \left\{ \begin{pmatrix} a & b & c \\ 0 & 0 & 0 \\ 0 & 0 & 0 \end{pmatrix} \mid a,b,c \in R \right\},$$

$$J = \left\{ \begin{pmatrix} a & 0 & 0 \\ b & 0 & 0 \\ c & 0 & 0 \end{pmatrix} \mid a,b,c \in R \right\},$$

then,

(*a*) I is a right ideal and J a left ideal

(*b*) I and J are both left ideals

(*c*) I and J are both right ideals

(*d*) I is a left ideal and J a right ideal

54. Let F_4, F_8 and F_{16} be finite fields of 4, 8 and 16 elements respectively. Then,

(*a*) F_4 is isomorphic to a subfield of F_8

(*b*) F_8 is isomorphic to a subfield of F_{16}

(*c*) F_4 is isomorphic to a subfield of F_{16}

(*d*) none of the above

55. Let G be the group with the generators *a* and *b* given by

$$G = \langle a,b : a^4 = b^2 = 1,\ ba = a^{-1}b \rangle.$$

If Z(G) denotes the centre of G, then G/Z(G) is isomorphic to

(*a*) the trivial group

(*b*) C_2, the cyclic group of order 2

(*c*) $C_2 \times C_2$

(*d*) C_4

56. Let I denote the ideal generated by $x^4 + x^3 + x^2 + x + 1$ in $Z_2[x]$ and F $Z_2[x]$ /I. Then,

(*a*) F is an infinite field

(*b*) F is a finite field of 4 elements

(*c*) F is a finite field of 8 elements

(*d*) F is a finite field of 16 elements

57. Let bijections *f* and *g* : R/ {0, 1} → R/{0,1} be defined by $f(x) = 1/(1-x)$ and $g(x) = x/(x-1)$, and let G be the group generated by *f* and *g* under composition of mappings. It is given that G has order 6. Then,

(*a*) G and its automorphism group are both Abelian

(*b*) G and its automorphism group are both non-Abelian

(*c*) G is Abelian but its automorphism group is non-Abelian

(*d*) G is non-Abelian but its auto-morphism group is Abelian

58. Let R = $\{\alpha_0 + \alpha_1 i + \alpha_2 j + \alpha_3 k : \alpha_0, \alpha_1, \alpha_2, \alpha_3 \in Z_3\}$ be the ring of quaternions over Z_3, where $i^2 = j^2 = k^2 = ijk = -1$; $ij = -ji = k$; $jk = -kj = i$; $ki = -ik = j$. Then,

(*a*) R is a field

(*b*) R is a division ring

(*c*) R has zero divisors

(*d*) none of the above

2005

59. Let D_8 denote the group of symmetries of square (dihedral group). The minimal number of generators for D_8 is

(*a*) 1 (*b*) 2

(*c*) 4 (*d*) 8

60. Let the set $\frac{Z}{nZ}$ denote the ring of integers modulo n under addition and multiplication modulo n. Then $\frac{Z}{9Z}$ is not a subring of $\frac{Z}{12Z}$ because

(*a*) $\frac{Z}{9Z}$ is not a subset of $\frac{Z}{12Z}$

(*b*) G.C.D. (9,12) = 3 ≠ 1

(*c*) 12 is not a power of 3

(*d*) 9 does not divide 12

61. Consider the following statements.

S : Every nonabelian group has a nontrivial abelian subgroup T : Every nontrivial abelian group has a cyclic subgroup. Then

(*a*) both S and T are false

(*b*) S is true and T is false

(*c*) T is true and S is false

(*d*) both S and T are true

62. Let S_{10} denote the group of permutations on ten symbols {1,2, ..., 10}. The number of elements of S_{10} commuting with the element σ = (1 3 5 7 9)is

(*a*) 5 ! (*b*) 5.5 !

(*c*) 5 ! 5 ! (*d*) $\frac{10!}{5!}$

63. Match the following in an integral domain.

U. The only nilpotent element(s) a. 0

V. The only idempotent element (s) b. 1

W. The only unit and idempotent element (s) c. 0,1

(*a*) U –*a*; V –*b*; W –*c*

(*b*) U –*b*; V –*c*; W –*a*

(*c*) U –*c*; V –*a*; W –*b*

(*d*) U –*a*; V –*c*; W –*b*

64. Let Z be the ring of integers under the usual addition and multiplication. Then every nontrivial ring homomorphism $f : Z \to Z$ is

(*a*) both injective and surjective

(*b*) injective but not surjective

(*c*) surjective but not injective

(*d*) neither injective nor surjective

2004

65. Let I be the set of irrational real numbers and let $G = I \cup (0)$. Then, under the usual addition of real numbers, G is

(*a*) a group, since **R** and **Q** are groups under addition

(*b*) a group, since the additive identity is in G

(*c*) not a group, since addition on G is not a binary operation

(*d*) not a group, since not all elements in G have an inverse

66. In the group (Z, +), the subgroup generated by 2 and 7 is

(*a*) Z (*b*) 5Z

(*c*) 9Z (*d*) 14Z

67. Let G and H be two groups. The groups $G \times H$ and $H \times G$ are isomorphic

(*a*) for any G and any H

(*b*) only if one of them is cyclic

(*c*) only if one of them is abelian

(*d*) only if G and H are isomorphic

68. Let $H = Z_2 \times Z_6$ and $K = Z_2 \times Z_4$. Then

(*a*) H is isomorphic to K since both are cyclic

(*b*) H is isomorphic to K since 2 divides 6 and g.c.d. (3, 4) = 1

(*c*) H is not isomorphic to K since K is cyclic whereas H is no

(*d*) H is not isomorphic to K since there is no homomorphism from H to K

69. Suppose G denotes the multiplicative group (–1, 1) and $S = (z \in C : |z| = 1)$. Let G act on S by complex multiplication. Then the cardinality of the orbit of *i* is

(*a*) 1 (*b*) 2

(*c*) 5 (*d*) infinite

70. The number of 5-Sylow subgroups of Z_{20} is

(*a*) 1

(*b*) 4

(*c*) 5

(*d*) 6

71. Let $S = \left\{\begin{pmatrix} a & b \\ 0 & c \end{pmatrix} : a, b, c \in R\right\}$ be the ring under matrix addition and multiplication.

Then the subset $\left\{\begin{pmatrix} 0 & P \\ 0 & 0 \end{pmatrix} : P \in R\right\}$ is

(*a*) not an ideal of S

(*b*) an ideal but not a prime ideal of S

(*c*) is a prime ideal but not a maximal ideal of S

(*d*) is a maximal ideal of S

72. Consider $S = C[x^{-5}]$, complex polynomials is x^5, as a subset of $T = C[x]$, the ring of all complex polynomials. Then

(*a*) S is neither an ideal nor a subring of T

(*b*) S is an ideal, but not a subring of T

(*c*) S is a subring but not an ideal of T

(*d*) S is both a subring and an ideal of T

73. Which of the following statements is true about $S = Z[x]$?

(*a*) S is an Euclidean domain since all its ideals are principal

(*b*) S is an Euclidean domain since Z is an Euclidean domain

(*c*) S is not an Euclidean domain since S is not even an integral domain

(*d*) S is not an Euclidean domain since it has non-principal ideals

2003

74. The number of groups of order n (upto isomorphism) is

(*a*) finite for all values of n

(*b*) finite only for finitely many values of n

(*c*) finite for infinitely many values of n

(*d*) infinite for some values of n

75. The set of all real 2×2 invertible matrices acs on R^2 by matrix multiplication. The number of orbits for this action is

(*a*) 1 (*b*) 2

(*c*) 4 (*d*) infinite

76. Any subgroup of Q (the group of rational numbers under addition) is

(*a*) cyclic and finitely generated but not abelian and normal

(*b*) cyclic and abelian but not finitely generated and normal

(c) abelian and normal but not cyclic and finitely generated

(*d*) finitely generated and normal but not cyclic and abelian

77. Let σ and τ be the permutations defined by

$$\sigma = \begin{pmatrix} 1 & 2 & 3 & 4 & 5 & 6 & 7 & 8 & 9 \\ 1 & 3 & 5 & 7 & 9 & 6 & 4 & 8 & 2 \end{pmatrix}$$

$$\text{and } \tau = \begin{pmatrix} 1 & 2 & 3 & 4 & 5 & 6 & 7 & 8 & 9 \\ 7 & 8 & 3 & 4 & 9 & 6 & 5 & 2 & 1 \end{pmatrix}$$

Then

(*a*) σ and τ generate the group of permutations on {1, 2, 3, 4, 5, 6, 7, 8, 9}

(*b*) σ is contained in the group generated by τ

(*c*) τ is contained in the group generated by σ

(*d*) σ and τ are in the same conjugacy class

78. Upto isomorphism, the number of abelian groups of order 10^5 is

(*a*) 2

(*b*) 5

(*c*) 7

(*d*) 49

79. Set of multiples of 4 forms an ideal in Z, the ring of integers under usual addition and multiplication. This ideal is

(*a*) a prime ideal but not a maximal ideal

(*b*) a maximal ideal but not a prime ideal

(*c*) both a prime ideal and a maximal ideal

(*d*) neither a prime ideal nor a maximal ideal

80. Let C [0, 1] be the set of all continuous functions defined on the interval [0, 1]. On this set, define addition and multiplication pointwise. Then C [0, 1] is

(*a*) a group but not a ring

(*b*) a ring but not an integral domain

(*c*) a field

(*d*) an integral domain but not a field

2002

81. Let G be a cyclic group of order 6. Then the number of elements $g \in G$ such that $G = \langle g \rangle$ is

(*a*) 5 (*b*) 3

(*c*) 4 (*d*) 2

82. The number of elements of order 5 in the symmetric group S_5 is

(*a*) 5 (*b*) 20

(*b*) 24 (*c*) 12

83. The order of the element $(\overline{2}, \overline{2})$ in $Z_4 \times Z_6$ is

(*a*) 2 (*b*) 6

(*c*) 4 (*d*) 12

84. Which of the following Banach spaces is not separable?

(*a*) $L^1[0, 1]$ (*b*) $L^\infty[0, 1]$

(*c*) $L^2[0, 1]$ (*d*) $C[0, 1]$

85. Let G be a group of order 30. Let A and B be normal subgroups of orders 2 and 5 respectively. Then the order of the group G/AB is

(*a*) 10 (*b*) 3

(*c*) 2 (*d*) 5

86. Let m and n be coprime natural numbers. Then the kernel of the ring homomorphism $\phi : Z \to Z_m \times Z_n$, defined by $\phi(x) = (\overline{x}, \overline{x})$, is

(*a*) mZ (*b*) mnZ

(*c*) nZ (*d*) Z

87. Let p be a prime and q be a prime divisor of $2^p - 1$. Find the order of $\overline{2}$ (the residue class of 2) in the multiplicative group G of non zero residue classes of integers modulo q. Conclude that $q > p$.

2001

88. Let G be a group of order 49. Then

(*a*) G is abelian

(*b*) G is cyclic

(*c*) G is non-abelian

(*d*) centre of G has order 7

89. The polynomial $f(x) = x^5 + 5$ is

(*a*) irreducible over C

(*b*) irreducible over R

(*c*) irreducible over Q

(*d*) not irreducible over Q

where Q denotes the field of rational number.

90. Let (Z, +) denote the group of all integers under addition. Then the number of all automorphisms of (Z, +) is

(*a*) 1 (*b*) 2

(*c*) 3 (*d*) 4

91. Let G be a finite group of order 200. Then the number of subgroups of G of order 25 is

(*a*) 1 (*b*) 4

(*c*) 5 (*d*) 10

92. If p is prime, and Z_{p^4} denote the ring of integers modulo p^4, then the number of maximal ideals in Z_{p^4} is

(*a*) 4 (*b*) 2

(*c*) 3 (*d*) 1

93. Show that the alternating group An, $n \geq 3$ is generated by all cycles of length 3.

94. Let R be a commutative principal ideal domain with identity $1 \neq 0$ and let P be a non-zero prime ideal fo R. Show that P is a maximal ideal of R.

2000

95. Let G be the additive group of integers I and G′ be the multiplicative group of the fourth roots of unity. Let $f: G \rightarrow G'$ be a homomorphism mapping given by $f(n) = i^n$; where $i = \sqrt{-1}$. Then the Kernel of f is

(*a*) empty set

(*b*) $\{4m \,;\, m \in I\}$

(*c*) $\{(2m)^2 + 1 : m, \in I\}$

(*d*) $\{2m + 1 : m \in I\}$

96. Prove that the set A of all 2 × 2 matrices of the form $\begin{bmatrix} a & 0 \\ b & 0 \end{bmatrix}$ where $a, b \in I$, the set of integers, is a left ideal but not a right ideal in the ring R of all 2 × 2 matrices over I.

97. Show that if p is a prime number, then any group G of order $2p$ has a normal subgroup of order p.

ANSWERS

1. (0) **2.** (10) **3.** (2) **4.** (1) **5.** (*b*) **6.** (*c*) **7.** (1.99 to 2.01) **8.** (*b*) **9.** (*d*)

10. (3.99 to 4.01) **11.** (*d*) **12.** (*d*) **13.** (3) **14.** (10) **15.** (*c*) **16.** (*c*) **17.** (3)

18. (Marks to all) **19.** (*b*) **20.** (*b*) **21.** (*a*) **22.** (*b*) **23.** (*d*) **24.** (*c*) **25.** (*b*) **26.** (*d*)

27. (*d*) **28.** (*a*) **29.** (*d*) **30.** (*d*) **31.** (*c*) **32.** (*c*) **33.** (*c*) **34.** (*a*) **35.** (*b*) **36.** (*d*)

37. (*c*) **38.** (*c*) **39.** (*c*) **40.** (*b*) **41.** (*a*) **42.** (*b*) **43.** (*c*) **44.** (*b*) **45.** (*c*) **46.** (*d*)

47. (*c*) **48.** (*a*) **49.** (*d*) **50.** (*a*) **51.** (*) **52.** (*b*) **53.** (*a*) **54.** (*c*) **55.** (*c*) **56.** (*d*)

57. (*b*) **58.** (*b*) **59.** (*b*) **60.** (*b*) **61.** (*d*) **62.** (*c*) **63.** (*a*) **64.** (*c*) **65.** (*c*) **66.** (*d*)

67. (*d*) **68.** (*d*) **69.** (*b*) **70.** (*a*) **71.** (*b*) **72.** (*a*) **73.** (*d*) **74.** (*a*) **75.** (*b*) **76.** (*c*)

77. (*d*) **78.** (*b*) **79.** (*d*) **80.** (*d*) **81.** (*d*) **82.** (*b*) **83.** (*b*) **84.** (*c*) **85.** (*b*) **86.** (*b*)

87. (*) **88.** (*a*) **89.** (*a*) **90.** (*b*) **91.** (*a*) **92.** (*b*) **93.** (*) **94.** (*) **95.** (*b*) **96.** (*)

97. (*)

EXPLANATIONS

1. Order of field f = 32 i.e 0(f) = 32

O(F|{0}) = 31 which is prime

Let $x \neq 0, y \neq 0$

$$x^2 + xy + y^2 = 0$$

$$= \frac{(x^3 - y^3)}{x - y} = 0$$

$\Rightarrow$ $x^3 = y^3$

$\Rightarrow$ $x = y$

(as $x \to x^3$ is injective mapping)

$\Rightarrow$ $x^2 + xy + y^2 = 0$

$\Rightarrow$ $3x^2 = 0$

$\Rightarrow$ x = 0 which is contradition.

$\Rightarrow$ There exists no non-zero solution.

2. $u_x = 3x^2 + 2axy + by^2$

$u_y = ax^2 + 2bxy + 6y^2$

$u_y = -v_x$

$\Rightarrow$ $u_x = v_x = -ax^2 - 2bxy - 6y^2$

integrating

$$v(x, y) = -\frac{a}{3}x^3 - bx^2y - 6xy^2 + f(y)$$

$$v(1, 1) = -\frac{a}{3} - b - 6 + f(1)$$

$$a + b + v(1,1) = a + b - \frac{a}{3} - b - 6 + f(1)$$

$$a + b + v(1, 1) = \frac{2}{3}a - 6 + f(1)$$

Here $v_y = -bx^2 - 12xy + f'(y)$

$\Rightarrow$ $3x^2 + 2axy + by^2 = -bx^2 - 12xy + f'(y)$

$f'(y) = (3 + b)x^2 + (12 + 2a)xy + by^2$

should be function of y only

$3 + b = 0$ & $12 + 2a = 0$

$\Rightarrow$ $b = -3, a = -6$

$\Rightarrow$ $f'(y) = -6y^2$

$v(x, y) = x^3 + 6x^2y - 6xy^2 - 3y + c$

$\Rightarrow$ $v(0, 0) = C$

$\Rightarrow$ $v(1, 1) = 1 + 6 - 6 - 3 = -1$

$|a + b + v(1, 1)| = |-6 -3 -1| = 10$

7. Number of non-isomorphic group of order 10 is 2. Which are z_5 z_5 and z_{10}.

8. We have, $a < c < d < b$. Ring $c[a, b]$ with pointwise addition and multiplication.

If $S = \{f \in C[a, b] : f(x) = 0$ for all $x \in [c, d]\}$, then S is an ideal of $C[a, b]$ but not a prime ideal of $C[a, b]$.

9. If $R[x]$ is principal ideal domain, then R is necessarily a field.

10. Given, F_{125} be the field of 125 elements.

$\alpha \in F_{125}$ such that $\alpha^5 = \alpha$ then number of non-zero elements α is 4.

11. For unique factorization domain and distinct irreducible elements the idea $\langle a \rangle$ is not necessarily a maximal ideal.

12. $\mathbb{Z}_{15} \times \mathbb{Z}_{77}$, S_3, $(\mathbb{Z}_0 t)$ are cyclic

13. The number of group homomorphism from $\mathbb{Z}_3$ to $\mathbb{Z}_9$ is 3.

14. Group of order = 231

Number of elements = $231 - (11)^2 = 10$

15. $\mathbb{Q}[x]/\langle x^2 - 2 \rangle$ is a field.

16. $x_0 = 0$

$x_{n+1} = \cos x_n$

$x_n = \cos x_{n-1}$

$\{x_n\}$ convergent.

$$x_{2n} < \lim_{m \to \infty} x_m < x_{2n+1} \quad \text{for } n \in \mathbb{N}$$

17. The number of non-isomorphic abelian groups of order 24 is 3.

18. Question is incomplete.

19. We have

$$R = Z \times Z \times Z$$

and $I = Z \times Z \times \{0\}$

we know that, {0} is prime ideal of Z.

Hence I is prime ideal of R.

Now $J = Z \times Z \times 2Z$

is also be an ideal of R

and $I \subseteq J$

Hence I is not maximal ideal of R.

20. The order of smallest possible non-trival group containing elements x and y such that $x^7 = y^2 = e$ and $yx = x^4y$ is 2

21. Here $1 + \frac{5k}{9} = 0$

where $k = 0, 1, 2...$

$\therefore$ Number of 5 – sylow subgroup in a group of order 45 is one.

22. Given, $W = \cos\frac{2\pi}{3} + i\sin\frac{2\pi}{3}$

$$M = \begin{bmatrix} 0 & i \\ i & 0 \end{bmatrix}; N = \begin{bmatrix} w & 0 \\ 0 & w^2 \end{bmatrix}$$

and G = <M, N> be the group generated by M and N under Matrix multiplication

Now M, N $\in$ G

$$MN = \begin{bmatrix} 0 & i \\ i & 0 \end{bmatrix}\begin{bmatrix} w & 0 \\ 0 & w^2 \end{bmatrix} = \begin{bmatrix} 0 & iw^2 \\ iw & 0 \end{bmatrix}$$

and $$NM = \begin{bmatrix} w & 0 \\ 0 & w^2 \end{bmatrix}\begin{bmatrix} 0 & i \\ i & 0 \end{bmatrix} = \begin{bmatrix} 0 & iw \\ iw^2 & 0 \end{bmatrix}$$

$\therefore$ MN $\neq$ NM, Hence G is non-abelian group.

Therefore $\frac{G}{Z(G)}$ is non cyclic group.

Hence $\frac{G}{Z(G)} = S_3$.

24. Since $x^2 + 1$ and $x^2 + x + 1$ are only irreducible quadratic polynomial over z_2. Therefore number of irreducible quadratic polynomial over F_2 are 2.

25. Given (2, 3, 4) = (1)(2, 3, 4)(5).(6)

The number of elements in the conjugacy class of 3 cycle (2, 3, 4) in the symmetric group S_6 is

$$\frac{6!}{3!\,|\,3!\,|\,3!} = \frac{6!}{3 \cdot 3!} = \frac{6 \cdot 5 \cdot 4}{3} = 40$$

27. Quotient ring $\frac{Z[i]}{\langle 3-i \rangle}$

Now $3 - i + \lt 3 - i \gt = 0 + \lt 3 - i \gt$ as

$\lt 3 - i\gt$ is and ideal generated by $3 - i$

Hence $3 - i = 0$

$3 = i$

$9 = -1$

$10 = 0$

Hence number of element in $\frac{\mathbb{Z}[i]}{\langle 3-i \rangle}$ is 10

But $\mathbb{Z}$ has infinitely many elements

$\frac{\mathbb{Z}}{3\mathbb{Z}} \cong \mathbb{Z}_3$ has only three elements

$\frac{\mathbb{Z}}{4\mathbb{Z}} \cong \mathbb{Z}_4$ has only four elements

$\frac{\mathbb{Z}}{10\mathbb{Z}} \cong \mathbb{Z}_{10}$ has 10 element

So $\frac{Z[i]}{\langle 3-i \rangle} \cong \frac{Z}{10z}$

28. Given Rings are

$$L = \frac{R[x]}{\langle x^2 - x + 1 \rangle}$$

$$M = \frac{R[x]}{\langle x^2 + x + 1 \rangle}$$

$$N = \frac{R[x]}{\langle x^2 + 2x + 1 \rangle}$$

Here $x^2 - x + 1$; $x^2 + x + 1$ are irreducible order R

Hence L is isomorphic to M.

Now $x^2 + 2x + 1 = (x + 1)^2$ which is reducible over $\mathbb{R}$. Hence L is not isomorphic to N and M is not isomorphic to N.

29. A group is simple if its only normal subgroups are the identity subgroup and the group itself

Here A_5 has no proper normal subgroups. Therefore A_5 is a Simple group.

30. The degree of extension (E) over Q

$$= \left[Q\left(\sqrt{2}, \sqrt{3}, \sqrt{5}\right), Q\right] = 2 \times 2 \times 2 = 8$$

31. Let G_1 be an abelian group of order 6 and

$G_2 = S_3$ for $j = 1, 2\ldots$

P_j be the statement

G_j has unique subgroup of order 2

Now since G_1 is an abelian group of order 6. Hence G_1 is cyclic because $O(G_1) = 6 = 2.3$ and $2/3 - 1$. Therefore G_1 has a unique subgroup of order z because corresponding to every diviser of the order of a cyclic group. There must exists a unique subgroup Hence statement P_1 hold.

Now $G_2 = S_3 = \{I, (12), (13), (123), (132)\}$

$H_1 = \{I, (12)\}$

$H_2 = \{I, (13)\}$

$H_3 = \{I, (23)\}$

are subgroup of s_3 of order 2. Therefore G_2 has 3 subgroups of order 2. Hence statement P_2 does not hold.

32. Number of conjugacy classes in G is 6.

33. Given polynomial ring is $Q(x)$. Let I be the ideal generated by $x^2 - 3$

i.e. $I = \lt x^2 - 3\gt$

Now $x^2 - 3 = 0$

$x^2 = 3$

$x = \pm\sqrt{3} \notin Q$

Hence $x^2 - 3$ is irreducible over Q.

Therefore $I = \lt x^2 - 3\gt$ is prime ideal and also it is maximal ideal.

34. $$\frac{z_2(x)}{\langle x^3 + x^2 + 1 \rangle} = \{(ax^2 + bx + c) + \langle x^3 + x^2 + 1 \rangle : a, b, c \in z_2\}$$

The number of choice for a, b, c are 2, 2, 2 respectively

Then the cardinality of $\frac{z_2}{\langle x^3 + x^2 + 1 \rangle}$ is given by $2.\,2.\,2 = 2^3 = 8$

35. The number of elements of a principal ideal domain must be of the form P^n.

Therefore the number of elements of a principal ideal domain can be 25.

[$\because$ $25 = 5^2$, 5 is prime]

36. Given ring is $\mathbb{Z}[i]$

Consider $I = \langle 3+i \rangle$

Here $3+i = (2-i)(1+i)$

$(2-i)(1+i) \in I$

but $2-i \notin I$ also $1+i \notin I$

Hence $I = \langle 3+i \rangle$ is not prime ideal and hence I is not maximal ideal.

37. Since 0(15) group is cyclic

$\Rightarrow \frac{G}{Z(G)}$ is cyclic

$\Rightarrow$ G is abelian

If G is abelian

$\frac{G}{Z(G)} = 1$

$\Rightarrow$ G is non-abelian.

38. Let Aut(G) denote the group of automorphism of a group

then $\text{Aut}(\mathbb{Z}\,n) \cong U(n)$

$\text{Aut}(\mathbb{Z}\,u) \cong U(u) = \{1, 3\}$

which is a cyclic group.

Next $\text{Aut}(\mathbb{Z}_6) \cong U(6) = \{1, 5\}$

which is a cyclic group.

Next. $\text{Aut}(\mathbb{Z}_8) \cong U(8) = \{1, 3, 5, 7\}$

$<1> = \{1\}$

$<3> = \{3, 1\}$

$<5> = \{5, 1\}$

$<7> = \{7, 1\}$

so that $U(8) \neq <a>$ for any a in U(8)

$\text{Aut}(\mathbb{Z}_8) \cong U(8)$ is not cyclic group.

Next $\text{Aut}(\mathbb{Z}_{10}) \cong U(10) = \{1, 3, 7, 9\}$

Here $<3> = \{3^1, 3^2, 3^3, 3^4\}$

$= \{3, 9, 7, 1\}$

$U(10) = <3>$

$\text{Aut}(\mathbb{Z}_{10}) \cong U(10)$ is cyclic group.

39. Since $\phi(x) = \frac{x}{|x|} = \begin{cases} 1 & x > 0 \\ -1 & x < 0 \end{cases}$

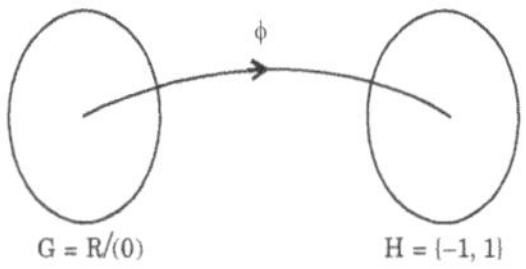

Fig.

clearly $\phi : G \to H$ is an onto homomorphism which is not one-one

40. Let $x < 27$ be a prime numner then

$<x>$ is maximal iff gcd $(x, 27) \neq 1$

Therefore the prime numbers less than 27 are 2, 3, 5, 7, 11, 13, 17, 19, 27 out of these prime numbers 3 in such that

$<3, 27> = 3 \neq 1$

Hence the number of maximal ideals is 1.

41. Given that

$O(G) = 45 = 3^2 \times 5$

$\therefore$ Number of 3. sylow subgroup.

$= 1 + 3k/5, k = 0, 1, 2\ldots$

$= 1$(unique)

$\therefore$ 3-sylow subgroup H and G is normal in G.

Next, Number of 5-sylow subgroup.

$= 1 + 5k/g, k = 0, 1, 2\ldots$

$= 1$(unique)

$\therefore$ 5-sylow subgroup k of G is normal in G.

42. The ring $Z\left[\sqrt{-11}\right]$ is a principal ideal domain but not a euclidean domain.

43. Let R be a principal ideal domain and a_1 b any two non-unit elemets of R. Then, the ideal generated by a is $<a>$ and the ideal generated by b is $<b>$. Now the ideal generated by a and b is $<a> \cap <b> = <g\,cd\,(a, b)>$ = ideal generated by gcd (a, b).

44. Given, the action of s_4, the symmetric group of order u on $z[x_1, x_2, x_3, x_4]$ given by.

$\sigma.P\,(x_1, x_2, x_3, x_4) = P\{x_{\sigma(1)}, x_{\sigma(2)}, x_{\sigma(3)}, x_{\sigma(4)}\} \;\forall\, \sigma \in s_4$

Let $H \subseteq S_4$ denote the cyclic subgroup generated by (1423) i.e.

$H = \{(1423), (1423)^2 = e\}$

$\therefore OH(x_1x_3 + x_2x_4)$

$= \{(1423)(x_1x_3 + x_2x_4), e(x_1x_3 + x_2x_4)\}$

$= \{x_4x_1 + x_3x_2, x_1x_3 + x_2x_4\}$

$\therefore$ Cardinality of OH $(x_1x_3 + x_2x_4) = 2$

45. Since, G is group under x_{56}, therefore G is closed under x_{56}.

we have $3x_{56}27 = 81 \pmod{56}$

$= 25 \in G$

$\therefore \alpha = 25$

46. The number of elements of order 8 in the group z_{24} under addition modulo 24.

$= \phi(8) \Rightarrow 4$

47. The order of $U(n) = \phi(n)$

$= \phi(248) = \phi(2^3 \times 31)$

$= \phi(2)^3\,\phi(31)$

$= 6 \times 30 = 180$

48. Let A is an ideal of R[x] that properly contains $\langle x^2+1\rangle$ we will prove that A = R[x] by showing that A contains some non-zero real number c_1 which is a constant polynomial $ln\ (x) = c$, for all x, then $1 = \left(\frac{1}{c}\right) c \in$ A and therefore A = R[x]. To this end, let $f(x) \in$ A but $f(x) \not\subset \langle x^2 + 1\rangle$ then

$f(x) = q(x)(x^2 + 1) + r(x)$

where $r(x) \neq 0$ and degree $r(x) < 2$ it follows that

$$r(x) = ax + b$$

where a and b are not both 0 and

$ax + b = r(x) = f(x) - q(x)\ (x^2 + 1) \in$ A

Hence, $a^2x^2 - b^2 = (ax + b)(ax - b) \in$ A

and $a^2\ (x^2 + 1) \in$ A

$0 \in a^2 + b^2 = (a^2x^2 + a^2) - (a^2x^2 - b^2) \in$ A

49. First we determine all group homomorphism from z_5 to z_{20} such homomorphism is completly specified by the image of 1, that is if 1 maps to a, then x maps to x_a then $|a|$ divide both 5 and 20. So $|a| = 1, 5$

Thus a = 0, 4, 8, 12 or 16

This gives us a list of candidates for the group homomorphism that each of these five possibilities yields an operation-preserving well defined function can now be verified by direct calculation {i.e., gcd (5, 20) = 5}

Now we determine all ring homomor-phism form z_5 to z_{10} from above the only group homomorphism from z_5 to z_{20} are $x \to ax$, where a = 0, 4, 8, 12 or 16 but since 1.1 = 1 in z_5 : we must have $a.a = a$ in z_{20}. This requirement rules and 4, 8, 12 as possibilities for a. Finally simple calculation shows that each of the remaining two choices does yields a ring homomorphism.

50. Let Q be the field of relational number and z be the field modulo 2.

Let $f(x) = x^3 - 9x^2 + 9x + 3$

Here, $\frac{3}{3}, \frac{3}{-9}$ but $\frac{3}{1}$ and $\frac{9}{3}$

Hence by Einstein's criterion $f(x)$ is irreducible over Q.

Next $z_2 = \{0, 1\}$

$\therefore\quad f(0) = 0^3 - 9 \times 0^2 + 9 \times 0 + 3$

$= 3 \neq 0$

$\therefore$ 0 is not root of $f(x)$

$f(1) = 1^3 - 9 \times 1^2 + 9 \times 1 + 3$

$= 4 \neq 0$

$\therefore$ 1 is also not be a root of $f(x)$. Hence $f(x)$ is irreducible over z_2.

51. Let z_5 be a field modulo 5 and

$f(x) = x^5 + 4x^4 + 4x^3 + 4x^2 + x + 1$

Since 1 is root of $f(x)$

$\therefore\quad f(1) = 0$

Now

$f'(x) = 5x^4 + 16x^3 + 12x^2 + 8x + 1$

$= x^3 + 2x^2 + 3x + 1$

$\therefore\quad f'(1) = 1^3 + 2 \times 1^2 + 3 \times 1 + 1$

$= 7 = 2 \pmod 2$

$f'(x) = 3x^2 + 4x + 3$

$\therefore\quad f'(1) = 3 \times 1^2 + 4 \times 1 + 3$

$= 10 \equiv 0 \pmod 5$

$\therefore$ multiplicity of 1 is 2

Next, since 3 is root by $f(x)$

$\therefore\quad f(3) = 0$

Now

$f'(x) = 5x^4 + 16x^3 + 12x^2 + 8x + 1$

$= x^3 + 2x^2 + 3x + 1$

$\therefore\quad f'(x) = 3^3 + 2 \times 3^2 + 3 \times 3 + 1$

$= 55 \cong 0 \pmod 5$

$\therefore$ multiplicity of 3 is 1.

No option match.

52. The number of isomorphism (automor-phism) from G $\to$ G (where G is a cycle group of order n) $= \phi(n)$

Therefore the number of automorphism on a cyclic group of order $8 = \phi(8) = 4$

Hence, the group of automorphism has order = 4

53. We have

$$\begin{bmatrix} x & y & z \\ u & v & w \\ r & s & t \end{bmatrix}\begin{bmatrix} a & b & c \\ 0 & 0 & 0 \\ 0 & 0 & 0 \end{bmatrix} = \begin{bmatrix} ax & bx & cx \\ au & bu & cu \\ ar & br & cr \end{bmatrix} \notin \ell$$

and $$\begin{bmatrix} a & b & c \\ 0 & 0 & 0 \\ 0 & 0 & 0 \end{bmatrix}\begin{bmatrix} x & y & z \\ u & v & w \\ r & s & t \end{bmatrix} = \begin{bmatrix} ax & ay & az \\ 0 & 0 & 0 \\ 0 & 0 & 0 \end{bmatrix} \in \ell$$

$\therefore$ l is right ideal

Again $$\begin{bmatrix} a & 0 & 0 \\ b & 0 & 0 \\ c & 0 & 0 \end{bmatrix}\begin{bmatrix} x & y & z \\ u & v & w \\ r & s & t \end{bmatrix} = \begin{bmatrix} ax & ay & az \\ bx & by & bz \\ cx & cy & cz \end{bmatrix} \notin \ell$$

and $$\begin{bmatrix} x & y & z \\ u & v & w \\ r & s & t \end{bmatrix}\begin{bmatrix} a & 0 & 0 \\ b & 0 & 0 \\ c & 0 & 0 \end{bmatrix} = \begin{bmatrix} ax+by+cz & 0 & 0 \\ au+bv+cw & 0 & 0 \\ ar+bs+ct & 0 & 0 \end{bmatrix} \in \ell$$

$\therefore$ T is left ideal

54. given that$0(F_4) = 2^2$

$$0(F_8) = 2^3$$

$$0(F_{16}) = 2^4$$

The power divisors = order of subfield

Divisor of 4 = 2, 1

Thus, $0(2^2)$ and $0(2^1)$ are subfields.

55. Let G be the group with generators a and b given by

$$G < a.\ b: a^4 = b^2 = 1, ba = a^{-1} b>$$

if $z(G)$ denotes the centre of a,

then $G/z(G)$ is isomorphic to $C_2 \times C_2$

56. Let z denote the ideal generated by

$x^4 + x^3 + x^2 + x + 1$ in $z_2[x]$

i.e., $l = <x^4 + x^3 + x^2 + x + 1>$

$$f(x) = x^4 + x^3 + x^2 + x + 1$$

$$\therefore \quad f(0) = 0^4 + 0^3 + 0^2 + 0 + 1$$

$$= 1 \neq 0$$

$$f(1) = 1^4 + 1^3 + 1^2 + 1 + 1$$

$$= 5 \equiv 1 \pmod 2$$

$$\therefore \quad f(x) = x^4 + x^3 + x^2 + x + 1$$

is irreducible over $Z_2[x]$

$$l = <x^4 + x^3 + x^2 + x + 1>$$

is prime ideal in $z_2[x]$

$$\therefore \quad F = \frac{z_2[x]}{z} = \frac{z_2[x]}{\langle x^4 + x^3 + x^2 + x + 1 \rangle}$$

is field with $2^4 = 16$ elements

57. Let bijections f and g: R|{0, 1} → R|{0, 1} be defined by

$$f(x) = \frac{1}{1-x}$$

$$g(x) = \frac{x}{(x-1)}$$

$$\therefore \quad (fog)(x) = f(g(x)) = \frac{f(x}{x-1)}$$

$$= \frac{1}{1-\frac{x}{x-1}} = \frac{x-1}{-1} = 1 - x$$

and $(gof)(x) = g(f(x))$

$$= g\left(\frac{1}{1-x}\right) = \frac{\frac{1}{1-x}}{\frac{1}{1-x}-1} = \frac{\frac{1}{1-x}}{\frac{1-1+x}{1-x}}$$

$$= \frac{1}{x}$$

$$\therefore \quad (gof) \neq (fog)$$

∴ G is non-abelian

also its automorphism group is non-abelian therefore, G and its automorphism group are both non-abelian.

58. Let $R = \{\alpha_0 + \alpha_1 j + \alpha_2 j + \alpha_3 k : \alpha_0, \alpha_1, \alpha_2, \alpha_3 \in z_3\}$ be the rign of quaternions over z_3, where

$$i^2 = j^2 = k^2 = ijk = -1$$

$$ij = -ji = k; jk = -kj = i;$$

$$ki = -ik = j$$

Then, r is division ring

59. D_8 is the group of symmetries of a square (dihedral group)

So, the minimal number of generators for D_8 is 2.

60. Multiplication identity = 1

But G.C.D of 9 and 12 = 3 ≠ 1

So $\frac{Z}{9Z}$ is not a subring of $\frac{Z}{12Z}$

61. Every non-abelian group has nontrivial abelian subgroup and every nontrivial abelian group has a cyclic subgroup. Both statements are true.

62. S_{10} is the group of permutations on ten symbols {1, 2, ...10}. Then, the number of elements of S_{10} commuting with the element $\sigma = (1, 3, 5, 7, 9)$ = 5! 5!

63. The only nilpotent element → 0

The only idempotent element → 1

The only unit and idempotent element → 0, 1

64. Z is the ring of integers under the usual addition and multiplication. Then every nontrivial ring homomorphism $f : Z \to Z$ must be onto but not one-one, i.e., must be surjective but not injective.

65. Given that, $G = I \cup \{0\}$

where, I is an irrational number.

Then, $2+\sqrt{3}$, $2-\sqrt{3} \in G$, as $2+\sqrt{3}$ and $2-\sqrt{3}$ are irrational number now.

$2+\sqrt{3}+2-\sqrt{3} = 4 \notin G$, as 4 is not an irrational number. Hence, G is not group since, addition on G is not a binary operation

66. Since, LCM(2, 7) = 14 therefore, the subgroup of z generated by 2 and 7 is 14 Z.

67. We know that

$$G_1 \times H_1 \cong G_2 \times H_2$$

$$\text{iff } G_1 \cong G_2 \text{ and } H_1 \cong H_2$$

$$\Rightarrow \quad G \times H \cong H \times G \text{ iff } G \cong H$$

68. $H = Z_2 \times Z_6$ and $K = Z_2 \times Z_4$ are not isomorphic since there is no homo morphism from H to K.

69. Suppose G denotes the multiplicative group [–1, 1] and $S = [z \in \mathbb{C} : |z| = 1]$ let G acts on S by complex multiplication, then

or bit $(i) = [-1.i, 1.i] = [-1, i]$

∴ Cardinality of orbit of $i = 2$

70. The number of 5 – 9y low subgroup of Z_{20}

$$= 1 + 5\,k/4$$

$$K = 0, 1, 2... = 1$$

71. Let $S = \left\{\begin{bmatrix} a & b \\ 0 & c \end{bmatrix} : a, b, c \in R\right\}$ be the ring under matrix addition and multiplication let.

$$A = \left\{\begin{bmatrix} 0 & p \\ 0 & 0 \end{bmatrix} : p \in R\right\}$$

Then $\begin{bmatrix} 0 & p \\ 0 & 0 \end{bmatrix}\begin{bmatrix} a & b \\ 0 & c \end{bmatrix} = \begin{bmatrix} 0 & pc \\ 0 & 0 \end{bmatrix} \in A$

and $\begin{bmatrix} a & b \\ 0 & c \end{bmatrix}\begin{bmatrix} 0 & p \\ 0 & 0 \end{bmatrix} = \begin{bmatrix} 0 & ap \\ 0 & 0 \end{bmatrix} \in A$

$\therefore$ A is an ideal of S

Now $\begin{bmatrix} 0 & a \\ 0 & 0 \end{bmatrix}\begin{bmatrix} 0 & 0 \\ 0 & c \end{bmatrix} = \begin{bmatrix} 0 & ac \\ 0 & o \end{bmatrix} \in A$

but $\begin{bmatrix} 0 & 0 \\ 0 & c \end{bmatrix} \notin A$

Hence A is not prime ideal.

Thus. $A = \left\{\begin{pmatrix} 0 & p \\ 0 & 0 \end{pmatrix} : p \in R\right\}$

is an ideal of S but not prime ideal of S.

72. Consider $S = C[x^5]$

= complex poly-nomial in x^5 as a subset of T = C[x], the ring of all complex polynomials.

Let $x^5 \in C(x^5)$

but $x^5.x^5 = x^{10} \in C(x^5)$

$\therefore$ $C[x^5]$ is not subring of $T = C[x^5]$

let $x^5 \in C[x^5]$ and $1 + x \in T = C[x]$

but $x^5\,(1+x)\,x^5 = x^5 + x^6 \notin C[x^5]$

and $(1 + x)\,x^5 = x^5 + x^6 \notin C[x^5]$

Hence $S = C[x^5]$ if s not an ideal of $T = C[x]$

73. We know that F(x) is principal ideal domain iff F is field.

$\therefore$ Z[x] is not principal ideal domain because Z is not field now, we know that every Euclidean domain is principal ideal domain.

$\therefore$ Not principal ideal domain

$\Rightarrow$ Not Euclidean domain.

$\therefore$ Z(x) is not Euclidean domain since it has non principal ideal.

76. Q is abelian infinits group

So all subgroups of Q are abeliana and normal not finitely generated.

79. Since 4 is not prime

So 4z is not maximum ideal

Also take $a = z, b = z \Rightarrow ab = 4$

Now $a, b \in z$

and $ab \in 4z$

But neither a nor b belong to 4z.

So, 4z is neither prime nor maximal ideal.

80. + is defined

and $f.g. = 0$

$\Rightarrow$ either $f = 0$ or $g = 0$

$\Rightarrow$ it is an integral domain but not field

81. Coprime of 6 are 1 & 5 only

So 2 elements.

82. $$(S_5) = \underline{|5} = 120$$

$\therefore$ Number of elements of order, 5

$$= \frac{120}{5} = 24$$

85. A and B are normal subgroups of G.

and $O(A) = 2$

$O(B) = 5$

Since 2 & 5 are relatively prime so

$O(A \cap B) = 1$

and $O(AB) = \dfrac{O(A).O(B)}{O(A \cap B)} = 10$

Now, A and B are normal subgroups

So, AB is normal subgroup in G.

So, $O\left(\dfrac{G}{AB}\right) = O\left(\dfrac{G}{AB}\right)$

$$= \frac{30}{10} = 3$$

94. Here it is sufficient to show that the maximal ideal P of commutative ring R is prime. For this suppose $ab \in P$ yet $a \notin P$.

Consider the set M+ (a) which consists of all sum $x + ra$ of an element $x \in P$ and a multiple $ra(r \in R)$ of a. This is an ideal, because for any $x, x' \in P$ and $r, r' \in R$,

we have

$(x + ra) + (x' + r'a) = (x + x') + (r + r')\,a$ where $(x + x') \in P$ and $(r + r') \in R$, and for any $v \in R$.

$v(x + ra) = vx + (vr)\,a$

where $(vx) \in P$ and $vr \in R$. This ideal P + (a) properly contains $a \notin P$. Since P is a maximal ideal. That gives us

$$P + (a) = R$$

and so $1 = x + ra$ for some $x \in r$, e $\in$ R

Finally, since $ab \in P$ by hypothesis.

This implies

$$b = 1b = (x + ra)b$$
$$= xb + rab \in P + P = P$$ This shows that ideal P is prime.

96. Let R be the ring of all 2 × 2 matrices with element as integers for addition and multiplication of matrices as the two ring operations. Let M be the subset of R consisting of matrices of the form $\begin{bmatrix} a & 0 \\ b & 0 \end{bmatrix}$ where $a, b \in I$

We have to show M is a half ideal of ring R.

Let $$A = \begin{bmatrix} a_1 & 0 \\ b_1 & 0 \end{bmatrix}$$

and $$B = \begin{bmatrix} a_2 & 0 \\ b_2 & 0 \end{bmatrix}$$ be any two elements of M.

Then $$A - B = \begin{bmatrix} a_1 - a_2 & 0 \\ b_1 - a_2 & 0 \end{bmatrix} \in M$$

Since $a_1 - a_2 \in I$, $b_1 - b_2 \in I$

So M is a subgroup of the additive group of the ring R.

Now Let $P = \begin{bmatrix} w & x \\ y & z \end{bmatrix}$ be any element of R

and $A = \begin{bmatrix} a & 0 \\ b & 0 \end{bmatrix}$ be any element of M.

Then $$PA = \begin{bmatrix} w & x \\ y & z \end{bmatrix}\begin{bmatrix} a & 0 \\ b & 0 \end{bmatrix}$$

$$= \begin{bmatrix} wa + xb & 0 \\ ya + zb & 0 \end{bmatrix} \in M$$

Therefore M is a left ideal of R.

Now we have to show M is not right ideal of R.

Since $\begin{bmatrix} 1 & 0 \\ 1 & 0 \end{bmatrix} \in R$ and $\begin{bmatrix} 2 & 4 \\ 3 & 5 \end{bmatrix} \in R$

Its product $\begin{bmatrix} 1 & 0 \\ 1 & 0 \end{bmatrix}\begin{bmatrix} 2 & 4 \\ 3 & 5 \end{bmatrix} = \begin{bmatrix} 2 & 4 \\ 3 & 5 \end{bmatrix} \notin M$

Hence M is not right ideal of R.

97. Here p is a prime number and G is a group of order $2p$.

Since G is a finite group of order $2p$. Then by the definition of subgroup order of subgroup be divisor of order of G.

Hence G has a subgroup of order 2 or p.

If H_1 and H_2 are subgroup, then $0(H_1) = 2$, $0(H_2) = p$ obviously.

But $$0\left(\frac{G}{H}\right) = \frac{0(G)}{0(H)}$$

$$= \frac{2p}{p} = 2 \text{ i.e., } 0(H_1)$$

Hence by definition of normal subgroup G has a normal subgroup of order p.

■■

6 CHAPTER Functional Analysis

2016

1. $f : [0, 1] \to [0, 1]$ is called a shrinking map if $|f(x) - f(y)| < |x - y|$ for all $x, y \in [0, 1]$ and a contraction if there exists an $\alpha < 1$ such that $|f(x) - f(y)| \le \alpha |x - y|$ for all $x, y \in [0, 1]$
   Which of the following statements is TRUE for the function $f(x) = x - \dfrac{x^2}{2}$?
   (a) f is both a shrinking map and a contraction
   (b) f is a shrinking map but NOT a contraction
   (c) f is NOT a shrinking map but a contraction
   (d) f is Neither a shrinking map nor a contraction
2. The remainder when 98! is divided by 101 is equal to ____________.
3. Let G be a group whose presentation is
   $G = \{x, y \mid x^5 = y^2 = e, \quad x^2y = yx\}$.
   Then G is isomorphic to
   (a) $\mathbb{Z}_5$
   (b) $\mathbb{Z}_{10}$
   (c) $\mathbb{Z}_2$
   (d) $\mathbb{Z}_{30}$

2015

4. Let $V = C^1[0, 1]$, $X = \left(C[0,1], \|\ \|_\infty\right)$ and $Y = \left(C[0,1], \|\ \|_2\right)$. Then V is
   (a) dense in X but NOT in Y
   (b) dense in Y but NOT in X
   (c) dense in both X and Y
   (d) neither dense in X nor dense in Y
5. Let $T = \left(C[0,1], \|\ \|_\infty\right) \to \mathbb{R}$ be defined by $T(f) = \int_0^1 2xf(x)dx$ for all $f \in C[0, 1]$. Then $\|T\|$ is equal to ________
6. Let $H = \left\{(x_n) \in l_2 : \sum_{n=1}^{\infty} \dfrac{x_n}{n} = 1\right\}$. Then H
   (a) is bounded
   (b) is closed
   (c) is a subspace
   (d) has an interior point

2014

7. Which of the following statements about the spaces ℓ^p and $L^p[0, 1]$ is **TRUE**?
   (a) $\ell^3 \subset \ell^7$ and $L^6[0, 1] \subset L^9[0, 1]$
   (b) $\ell^3 \subset \ell^7$ and $L^9[0, 1] \subset L^6[0, 1]$
   (c) $\ell^7 \subset \ell^3$ and $L^6[0, 1] \subset L^9[0, 1]$
   (d) $\ell^7 \subset \ell^3$ and $L^9[0, 1] \subset L^6[0, 1]$
8. Consider $C[-1, 1]$ equipped with the supremum norm given by $\|f\|_\infty = \sup\{|f(t)| : t \in [-1, 1]\}$ for $f \in C[-1, 1]$. Define a linear functional T on $C[-1, 1]$ by
   $$T(f) = \int_{-1}^{0} f(t)dt - \int_{0}^{1} f(t)dt \text{ for all } f \in C[-1, 1].$$
   Then the value of $\|T\|$ is _____
9. Let $X = C^1[0, 1]$. For each $f \in X$, define
   $p_1(f) := \sup\{|f(t)| : t \in [0, 1]\}$
   $p_2(f) := \sup\{|f'(t)| : t \in [0, 1]\}$
   $p_3(f) := p_1(f) + p_2(f)$
   Which of the following statements is **TRUE**?
   (a) (X, p_1) is a Banach space
   (b) (X, p_2) is a Banach space
   (c) (X, p_3) is NOT a Banach space
   (d) (X, p_3) does NOT have denumerable basis

2013

10. Let X be a compact Hausdorff topological space and let Y be a topological space. Let $f : X \to Y$ be a bijective continuous mapping. Which of the following is **TRUE**?
    (a) f is a closed map but not necessarily an open map
    (b) f is an open map but not necessarily a closed map
    (c) f is both an open map and a closed map
    (d) f need not be an open map or a closed map
11. Let $\mathcal{H}$ be a Hilbert space and let $\{e_n : n \ge 1\}$ be an orthonormal basis of $\mathcal{H}$. Suppose $T : \mathcal{H} \to \mathcal{H}$ is a bounded linear operator. Which of the following **CANNOT** be true?
    (a) $T(e_n) = e_1$ for all $n \ge 1$
    (b) $T(e_n) = e_{n+1}$ for all $n \ge 1$
    (c) $T(e_n) = \sqrt{\dfrac{n+1}{n}}\, e_n$ for all $n \ge 1$
    (d) $T(e_n) = e_{n-1}$ for all $n \ge 2$ and $T(e_1) = 0$

2012

12. Let H be a Hilbert space and $S^{\perp}$ denote the orthogonal complement of a set $S \subseteq H$. Which of the following is **INCORRECT**?

(a) For $S_1, S_2 \subseteq H$; $S_1 \subseteq S_2 \Rightarrow S_1^{\perp} \subseteq S_2^{\perp}$

(b) $S \subseteq (S^{\perp})^{\perp}$

(c) $\{0\}^{\perp} = H$

(d) $S^{\perp}$ is always closed

13. Let H be a complex Hilbert space, $T: H \to H$ be a bounded linear operator and let T^* denote the adjoint of T. Which of the following statements are always **TRUE**?

$P: \forall x, y \in H, \langle Tx, y\rangle = \langle x, T^* y\rangle$

$Q: \forall x, y \in H, \langle x, Ty\rangle = \langle T^* x, y\rangle$

$R: \forall x, y \in H, \langle x, Ty\rangle = \langle x, T^* y\rangle$

$S: \forall x, y \in H, \langle Tx, Ty\rangle = \langle T^* x, T^* y\rangle$

(a) P and Q (b) P and R

(c) Q and S (d) P and S

2011

14. Let $x = (x_1, x_2, ...) \in l^4$, $x \neq 0$. For which one of the following values of p, the series $\sum_{i=1}^{\infty} x_i y_i$ converges for every

$y = (y_1, y_2, ...) \in l^p$?

(a) 1 (b) 2

(c) 3 (d) 4

15. Let H be a complex Hilbert space and H^* be its dual. The mapping $\phi: H \to H^*$ defined by $\phi(y) = f_y$ where $f_y(x) = \langle x, y\rangle$ is

(a) not linear but onto

(b) both linear and onto

(c) linear but not onto

(d) neither linear nor onto

16. A horizontal lever is in static equilibrium under the application of vertical forces F_1 at a distance l_1 from the fulcrum and F_2 at a distance l_2 from the fulcrum. The equilibrium for the above quantities can be obtained if

(a) $F_1 l_1 = 2F_2 l_2$ (b) $2F_1 l_1 = F_2 l_2$

(c) $F_1 l_1 = F_2 l_2$ (d) $F_1 l_1 < F_2 l_2$

17. Assume F to be a twice continuously differentiable function. Let J(y) be a functional of the form

$$\int_0^1 F(x, y')\, dx, \quad 0 \le x \le 1$$

defined on the set of all continuously differentiable functions y on [0 1] satisfying $y(0) = a$, $y(1) = b$. For some arbitrary constant c, a necessary condition for y to be an extremum of J is

(a) $\frac{\partial F}{\partial x} = c$ (b) $\frac{\partial F}{\partial y'} = c$

(c) $\frac{\partial F}{\partial y} = c$ (d) $\frac{\partial F}{\partial x} = 0$

18. Let $e_i = (0, ... 0, 1, 0, ...)$ (i.e., e_i is the vector with 1 at the ith place and 0 elsewhere) for $i = 1, 2, ...$

Consider the statements:

P: $\{f(e_i)\}$ converges for every continuous linear functional on l^2.

Q: $\{e_i\}$ converges in l^2.

Then, which of the following holds?

(a) Both P and Q are TRUE

(b) P is TRUE but Q is not TRUE

(c) P is not TRUE but Q is TRUE

(d) Neither P nor Q is TRUE

2010

19. Which one of the following sets of functions is NOT orthogonal (with respect to the L^2-inner product) over the given interval?

(a) $\{\sin nx : n \in \mathbb{N}\}, -\pi < x < \pi$

(b) $\{\cos nx : n \in \mathbb{N}\}, -\pi < x < \pi$

(c) $\{x^{2n+\frac{1}{2}} : n \in \mathbb{N}\}, -1 < x < 1$

(d) $\{x^{2n+1} : n \in \mathbb{N}\}, -1 < x < 1$

20. Let X and Y be normed linear spaces and $\{T_n\}$ be a sequence of bounded linear operators from X to Y. Consider the statements:

$P: \{\|T_n x\| : n \in \mathbb{N}\}$ is bounded for each $x \in X$

$Q: \{\|T_n\| : n \in \mathbb{N}\}$ is bounded

Which one of the following is correct?

(a) If P implies Q, then both X and Y are Banach spaces

(b) If P implies Q, then only one of X and Y is a Banach space

(c) If X is a Banach space, then P implies Q

(d) If Y is a Banach space, then P implies Q

21. Let $X = C[0, 1]$ with the norm $\|x\|_1 = \int_0^1 |x(t)|\, dt$, $x \in C[0, 1]$ and $\Omega = \{f \in X' \; \|f\| = 1\}$, where X' denotes the dual space of X. Let $C(\Omega)$ be the linear space of continuous functions on Ω with the norm $\|u\| = \sup_{s \in \Omega} |u(s)|$, $u \in C(\Omega)$. Then (*a*) X is linearly isometric with $C(\Omega)$

(*b*) X is linearly isometric with a proper subspace of $C(\Omega)$

(*c*) there does not exist a linear isometry from X into $C(\Omega)$

(*d*) every linear isometry from X to $C(\Omega)$ is onto

22. Let $X = \mathbb{R}$ equipped with the topology generated by open intervals of the form (a, b) and sets of the form $(a, b) \cap \mathbb{Q}$. Then which one of the following statements is correct?

(*a*) X is regular (*b*) X is normal

(*c*) $X \setminus \mathbb{Q}$ is dense in X (*d*) $\mathbb{Q}$ is dense in X

23. Let $X = \mathbb{N}$ be equipped with the topology generated by the basis consisting of sets $A_n = \{n, n+1, n+2, ...\}, n \in \mathbb{N}$. Then X is

(*a*) Compact and connected

(*b*) Hausdorff and connected

(*c*) Hausdorff and compact

(*d*) Neither compact nor connected

2009

24. Consider the metrics

$$d_2(f, g) = \left(\int_a^b |f(t) - g(t)|^2 \, dt \right)^{1/2}$$

and $d_\infty(f, g) = \sup_{t \in [a,b]} |f(t) - g(t)|$ on the space $X = C[a, b]$ of all real valued continuous functions on $[a, b]$. Then which of the following is TRUE?

(*a*) Both (X, d_2) and (X, d_∞) are complete.

(*b*) (X, d_2) is complete but (X, d_∞) is NOT complete.

(*c*) (X, d_∞) is complete but (X, d_2) is NOT complete.

(*d*) Both (X, d_2) and (X, d_∞) are NOT complete.

25. Let $\{e_n\}_{n=1}^{\infty}$ be an orthonormal sequence in a Hilbert space H and let $x (\neq 0) \in H$. Then

(*a*) $\lim_{n \to \infty} \langle x, e_n \rangle$ does not exist

(*b*) $\lim_{n \to \infty} \langle x, e_n \rangle = \|x\|$

(*c*) $\lim_{n \to \infty} \langle x, e_n \rangle = 1$

(*d*) $\lim_{n \to \infty} \langle x, e_n \rangle = 0$

26. Let $f : (c_{00}, \|\cdot\|_1) \to \mathbb{C}$ be a non-zero continuous linear functional. The number of Hahn-Banach extensions of f to $(\ell^1, \|\cdot\|_1)$ is

(*a*) one (*b*) two

(*c*) three (*d*) infinite

27. If $I : (\ell^1, \|\cdot\|_2) \to (\ell^1, \|\cdot\|_1)$ is the identity map, then

(*a*) both I and I^{-1} are continuous

(*b*) I is continuous but I^{-1} is NOT continuous

(*c*) I^{-1} is continuous but I is NOT continuous

(*d*) neither I nor I^{-1} is continuous

28. Let X and Y be Banach spaces and let $T : X \to Y$ be a linear map. Consider the statements :

P : If $x_n \to x$ in X then $Tx_n \to T_x$ in Y.

Q : If $x_n \to x$ in X and $Tx_n \to y$ in Y then $Tx = y$.

Then

(*a*) P implies Q and Q implies P

(*b*) P implies Q but Q does not imply P

(*c*) Q implies P but P does not imply Q

(*d*) neither P implies Q nor Q implies P

29. The extremal of the functional

$$\int_0^1 \left(y + x^2 + \frac{y'^2}{4} \right) dx, \; y(0) = 0, y(1) = 0 \text{ is}$$

(*a*) $4(x^2 - x)$ (*b*) $3(x^2 - x)$

(*c*) $2(x^2 - x)$ (*d*) $x^2 - x$

2008

30. For $1 \le p \le \infty$ $\| \ \|_p$ denote the p - norm on R^2. If $\| \ \|_p$ satisfies the parallelogram law, the p is equal to

(*a*) 1 (*b*) 2

(*c*) 3 (*d*) ∞

31. Let $f : l^2 \to R$ be defined by $f(x_1, x_2, ...) = \sum_{n=1}^{\infty} \frac{x_n}{2^{n/2}}$ for $(x_1, x_2, ...) \in l^2$. Then $\|f\|$ is equal to

(*a*) $\frac{1}{2}$ (*b*) 1

(*c*) 2 (*d*) $\frac{1}{\sqrt{2} - 1}$

32. Consider R^3 with norm $\| \ \|_1$, and the linear transformation $T : R^3 \to R^3$ defined by the 3×3 matrix $\begin{pmatrix} 1 & 1 & 3 \\ 2 & 2 & 2 \\ 1 & 3 & -3 \end{pmatrix}$. Then the operator norm of $\|T\|$ of T is equal to

(*a*) 6

(*b*) 7

(*c*) 8

(*d*) $\sqrt{42}$

33. Consider R^2 with norm $\| \|_\infty$, and let $Y = \{(y_1, y_2) \in R^2 : y_1 + y_2 = 0\}$. If $g : Y \to R$ is defined by $g(y_1, y_2) = y_2$ for $(y_1\, y_2) \in y$, then

(*a*) g has no Hahn-Banach extension to R^2

(*b*) g has a unique Hahn-Banach extension to R^2

(*c*) every linear functional $f : R^2 \to R$ satisfying $f(-1, 1) = 1$ is a Hahn-Banach extension of g to R^2

(*d*) the functionals $f_1, f_2 : R^2 \to R$ given by $f_1(x_1, x_2) = x_2$ and $f_2(x_1, x_2) = -x_1$ are both Hahn-Banach extensions of g to R^2

34. Let X be a Banach space and Y be a normed linear space. Consider a sequence (F_n) of bounded linear maps from X to Y such that for each fixed $x \in X$, the sequence $(F_n(x))$ is bounded in Y. Then

(*a*) for each fixed $x \in X$, the sequence $(F_n(x))$ is convergent in Y

(*b*) for each fixed $n \in N$, the set $\{F_n(x) : x \in X)$ is bounded in Y

(*c*) the sequence $(\|F_n\|)$ is bounded in R

(*d*) the sequence (F_n) is uniformly bounded on X

35. Let $H = L^2([0, \pi])$ with the usual inner product. For $n \in N$, let

$$u_n(t) = \frac{\sqrt{2}}{\sqrt{\pi}} \sin nt, t \in [0, \pi],$$

and $$E = \{u_n : n \in N\}.$$

Then

(*a*) E is not a linearly independent subset of H.

(*b*) E is a linearly independent subset of H, but is not an orthonormal subset of H.

(*c*) E is an orthonormal subset of H, but is not an orthonormal basis for H.

(*d*) E is an orthonormal basis for H.

36. The functional $\int_0^1 (y'^2 + x^3)dx$, given $y(1) = 1$, achieves its

(*a*) weak maximum on all its extremals

(*b*) weak minimum on all its extremals

(*c*) weak maximum on some, but not on all of its extremals

(*d*) weak minimum on some, but not on all of its extremals

Common Data for Questions 37, 38 :

Let $X = C^1([0, 1])$ and $Y = C([0, 1])$, both with the sup norm. Define $F : X \to Y$ by $F(x) = x + x'$ and $f(x) = x(1) + x'(1)$ for $x \in X$.

37. Then

(*a*) F and f are continuous

(*b*) F is continuous and f is discontinuous

(*c*) F is discontinuous and f is continuous

(*d*) F and f are discontinuous

38. Then

(*a*) F and f are closed maps

(*b*) F is a closed map and f is not a closed map

(*c*) F is not a closed map and f is a closed map

(*d*) neither F nor f is a closed map

2007

39. For a positive integer n, let $f_n : R \to R$ be defined by

$$f_n(x) = \begin{cases} \frac{1}{4n+5}, & \text{if } 0 \le x \le n, \\ 0, & \text{otherwise,} \end{cases}$$

Then $\{f_n(x)\}$ converges to zero

(*a*) uniformly but NOT in L^1 norm

(*b*) uniformly and also in L^1 norm

(*c*) pointwise but NOT uniformly

(*d*) in L^1 norm but NOT pointwise

40. Let P_1 and P_2 be two projection operators on a vector space. Then

(*a*) $P_1 + P_2$ is a projection if $P_1 P_2 = P_2 P_1 = 0$

(*b*) $P_1 - P_2$ is a projection if $P_1 P_2 = P_2 P_1 = 0$

(*c*) $P_1 + P_2$ is a projection

(*d*) $P_1 - P_2$ is a projection

41. Consider the Hilbert space

$$l^2 = \left\{X = \{x_n\} : x_n \in R, \sum_{n=1}^{\infty} x_n^2 < \infty\right\}$$

Let $E = \left\{\{x_n\} : |x_n| \le \frac{1}{n}, \text{for all } n\right\}$ be a subset of l^2.

Then

(*a*) $E^\circ = \left\{X : |x_n| < \frac{1}{n}, \text{for all } n\right\}$

(*b*) $E^\circ = E$

(*c*) $E^\circ = \{X : |x_n| < \frac{1}{n}$ for all but finitely many $n\}$

(*d*) $E^\circ = \phi$

42. Let X and Y be normed linear spaces and let $T : X \to Y$ be a linear map. Then T is continuous if

(*a*) Y is finite dimensional

(*b*) X is finite dimensional

(*c*) T is one to one

(*d*) T is onto

43. Let X be a normed linear space and let $E_1, E_2 \subseteq X$. Define
$E_1 + E_2 = \{x + y : x \in E_1, y \in E_2\}$.
Then $E_1 + E_2$ is
(a) open if E_1 or E_2 is open
(b) NOT open unless both E_1 and E_2 are open
(c) closed if E_1 or E_2 is closed
(d) closed if both E_1 and E_2 are closed

44. The functional $\int_0^1 (1+x)(y')^2\,dx,\ y(0) = 0, y(1) = 1,$ possesses
(a) strong maxima
(b) strong minima
(c) weak maxima but NOT a strong maxima
(d) weak minima but NOT a strong minima

Common Data Questions

Common Data for Questions 45, 46, 47 :

Let P[0, 1] = $\{p : p$ is a polynomial function on $[0, 1]\}$. For $p \in P[0, 1]$, define
$||P|| = \sup\{|p(x)| : 0 \le x \le 1\}$.
Consider the map $T : P[0, 1] \to P[0, 1]$ defined by

$$(Tp)(x) = \frac{d}{dx}(p(x)).$$

Then P[0,1] is a normed linear space and T is a linear map. The map T is said to be closed if the set $G = \{(p, Tp) : p \in P[0,1]\}$ is closed subset of $P[0, 1] \times P[0, 1]$.

45. The linear map T is
(a) one to one and onto
(b) one to one but NOT onto
(c) onto but NOT one to one
(d) neither one to one nor onto

46. The normed linear space P[0, 1] is
(a) a finite dimensional normed linear space which is NOT a Banach space
(b) a finite dimensional Banach space
(c) an infinite dimensional normed linear space which is NOT a Banach space
(d) an infinite dimensional Banach space

47. The map T is
(a) closed and continuous
(b) neither continuous nor closed
(c) continuous but NOT closed
(d) closed but NOT continuous

2006

48. Consider the Hilbert space

$$l^2 = \left\{(x_1, x_2 \ldots) | x_i \in R, i = 1, 2, \ldots \text{ and} \sum_{i=1}^{\infty} x_i^2, < \infty\right\}$$

under the inner product

$$\langle (x_1, x_2, \ldots), (y_1, y_2 \ldots)\rangle = \sum_{i=1}^{\infty} x_i y_i .$$

Let S $\{(x_1, x_2, \ldots) \in l^2 \mid \sum_{n=1}^{\infty} \frac{x_n}{n} = 0\}$. Then the number of interior points of S is
(a) 0
(b) non zero but finite
(c) countably infinite
(d) uncountably infinite

49. Let C([0, 1]) be the space of all real valued continuous functions on [0,1] with the norm $\|f\|_\infty = \{|f(x)| : x \in [0,1]\}$. sup Consider the subspace $P_n([0,1])$ of all polynomials of degree less than or equal to n and the subspace P([0,1]) of all polynomials on [0,1]. Then,
(a) P_n ([0,1]) is closed in C([0,1]) but not P ([0,1])
(b) P([0,1]) is closed in C ([0,1]) but not P_n([0,1])
(c) both P([0,1]) and P_n([0,1]) are closed in C([0,1])
(d) neither P([0,1]) nor P_n([0,1]) is closed in C([0,1])

50. Consider the inner product space P([0,1]) of all real polynomials on [0,1] with the inner product

$$\langle f, g\rangle = \int_0^1 f(x)g(x)dx \text{ and } V = \text{span } \{t^2\} .$$

Let $h(t) \in V$ be such that
$\|(2t-1) - h(t)\| \le \|(2t-1) - x(t)\|$ for $x(t) \in V$.
Then, $h(t)$ is
(a) $\frac{5}{6}t^2$
(b) $\frac{5}{3}t^2$
(c) $\frac{5}{12}t^2$
(d) $\frac{5}{24}t^2$

51. Consider the sequence of continuous linear operators $T_n : l^2 \to l^2$ defined by
$T_n(x) = (0, 0, ., .0; x_{n+1}, x_{n+2}, x_{n+3}, .)$.
for every $x = (x_1, x_2, .) \in l^2$ and $n \in N$. Then, for every $x \neq 0$ in l^2
(a) both $\|T_n\|$ and $\|T_n(x)\|$ converge to 0
(b) neither $\|T_n\|$ nor $\|T_n(x)\|$ converges to 0
(c) $\|T_n\|$ converges to 0 but not $\|T_n(x)\|$
(d) $\|T_n(x)\|$ converges to 0 but not $\|T_n\|$

52. Let the continuous linear operator $T : l^2 \to l^2$ be defined by

$T(x_1, x_2, .) = (0, x_1, 0, x_3, 0, x_5, 0)$.

Then,

(*a*) T is compact but not T^2

(*b*) T^2 is compact but not T

(*c*) both T and T^2 are compact

(*d*) neither T nor T^2 is compact

Statement for Linked Answer Questions 53 & 54 :

Let H be an infinite dimensional Hilbert space and f be a continuous linear functional on H such that $\|f\| = 1$. Define $W = \{x \in H : f(x) = 1\}$. The interior and the boundary of the closed unit ball U of H are denoted by U° and ∂U respectively.

53. Which of the following is correct ?

(*a*) $U^\circ \cap W = \phi$ and $W \cap \partial U = \phi$

(*b*) $U^\circ \cap W \neq \phi$ and $W \cap \partial U \neq \phi$

(*c*) $U^\circ \cap W = \phi$ and $W \cap \partial U \neq \phi$

(*d*) $U^\circ \cap W \neq \phi$ and $W \cap \partial U \neq \phi$

54. The number of points in $W \cap U$ is

(*a*) 0

(*b*) 1

(*c*) not one but countable

(*d*) uncountable

Statement for Linked Answer Questions 55 & 56 :

Let $p(x) = c_0 + c_1 x$ minimize $\langle f(x) - p(x), \ f(x) - p(x) \rangle$ $= \int_{-1}^{1} (f(x) - p(x))^2 dx$ overall polynomials of degree less than or equal to 1.

55. The best choice of coefficients c_0, c_1 is

(*a*) $\langle f,1 \rangle, \langle f,x \rangle$ (*b*) $\langle f,1 \rangle, \frac{2}{3}\langle f,x \rangle$

(*c*) $\frac{1}{2}\langle f,1 \rangle, \frac{3}{2}\langle f,x \rangle$ (*d*) $\frac{2}{3}\langle f,1 \rangle, \frac{2}{3}\langle f,x \rangle$

56. If $f(x) = x^2 + x$, then $p(x)$ is given by

(*a*) $\left(1 + \frac{x}{3}\right)$

(*b*) $\frac{1}{3}(1 + 3x)$

(*c*) $\frac{1}{3}(1 + x)$

(*d*) $\frac{2}{3}(1 + x)$

2005

57. Let C[0, 1], be the space of all continuous real valued functions on [0,1]. The identity map I : $(C[0,1], \|\cdot\|_\infty) \to (C[0,1], \|\cdot\|_1)$ is

(*a*) continuous but not open

(*b*) open but not continuous

(*c*) both continuous and open

(*d*) neither continuous nor open

58. Consider the Hilbert space

$l^2 = \{(x_1, x_2 ....), x_i \in C$ for all i and $\sum_{i=1}^{\infty} |x_i|^2 < \infty\}$

with the inner product $\langle (x_1, x_2 ....)(y_1, y_2 ....) \rangle = \sum_{i=1}^{\infty} x_i \bar{y}_i$. Define $T : l^2 \to l^2$ by

$T((x_1, x_2, ...)) = (x_1, \frac{x_2}{2}, \frac{x_3}{3}, ...)$. Then T is

(*a*) neither self-adjoint nor unitary

(*b*) both self-adjoint and unitary

(*c*) unitary but not-adjoint

(*d*) self-adjoint but unitary

59. Let X = C[0, 1] be the space of all real valued continuous functions on [0, 1] Let $T : X \to R$ be a linear functional defined by T (f) = f(1).Let $X_1 = (X, \|\cdot\|_1)$ and $X_2 = (X, \|\cdot\|_\infty)$. Then T iscontinuous

(*a*) on X_1 but not on X_2

(*b*) on X_2 but not on X_1

(*c*) on both X_1 and X_2

(*d*) neither on X_1 nor on X_2

60. Let $X = (C[0,1], \|\cdot\|_p)$, $1 \leq p \leq \infty$ and

$f_n(t) \begin{cases} n(1 - nt) & \text{if } 0 \leq t \leq 1/n \\ 0 & \text{if } 1/n < t \leq 1 \end{cases}$ if

$S = \{f_n \in X : n > 1\}$, then S is

(*a*) bounded if $p = 1$

(*b*) bounded if $p = 2$

(*c*) bounded if $p = \infty$

(*d*) unbounded for all p

Statement for Linked Answer Questions 61a and 61b :

Let H be a real Hilbert space, $p \in H$, $p \neq 0$ and $G = \{x \in H : \langle x, p \rangle = 0\}$ and $q \in H/G$.

61a. The orthogonal projection of q onto G is

(*a*) $q - \frac{\langle q, p \rangle p}{\|p\|^2}$ (*b*) $q - \frac{\langle q, p \rangle p}{\|p\|}$

(*c*) $q - \langle q, p \rangle p$ (*d*) $q - \langle q, p \rangle \|p\| p$

61b. In particular, if H = $L_2[0, 1]$, G = $\{f\in L_2[0,1] : \int_0^1 x\, f(x)dx=0\}$ and $q = x^2$, then the orthogonal of q onto G is

(a) $x^2 - \frac{3}{4}x$ (b) x^2-3x

(c) $x^2-\frac{3}{5}x$ (d) $x^2-\frac{3}{2}x$

2004

62. Consider R^2 with $\|\cdot\|_1$ norm and M = $\{(x, 0)\} : x \in R\}$. Define $g : M \to R$ by $g(x, y) = x$. Then a Hahn-Banach extension f of g is given by

(a) $f(x, y) = 2x$

(b) $f(x, y) = x + y$

(c) $f(x, y) = x - 2y$

(d) $f(x, y) = x + 2y$

63. Let X be an inner product space and $S \subset X$. Then it follows that

(a) $S\perp$ has nonempty interior

(b) $S\perp = \{0\}$

(c) $S\perp$ is a closed subspace

(d) $(S\perp)\perp = S$

64. Let X be the space of bounded real sequences with sup norm. Define a linear operator $T : X \to X$ by

$T(x) = \left(\frac{x_1}{1}, \frac{x_2}{2}, \ldots\right)$ for $x = (x_1, x_2, \ldots) \in X$. Then

(a) T is bounded but not one to one

(b) T is one to one but not bounded

(c) T is bounded and its inverse (from range of T) exists but is not bounded

(d) T is bounded and its inverse (from range of T) exists and is bounded

65. Let X be the space of real sequences having finitely many non-zero terms with $\|\cdot\|_p$, $1 \le p < \infty$. Then

(a) f is continuous only for $p = 1$

(b) f is continuous only for $p = 2$

(c) f is continuous only for $p = \infty$

(d) f is not continuous for any p, $1 \le p \le \infty$

66. Let X = C^1 [0, 1] with the norm $\|x\| = \|x\|_\infty + \|x'\|_\infty$ (where x' is the derivative of x) and Y = $C^1[0, 1]$ with sup norm. If T is the identity operator from X into Y, then

(a) T and T^{-1} are continuous

(b) T is continuous but T^{-1} is not

(c) T^{-1} is continuous but T is not

(d) neither T nor T^{-1} is continuous

67. Let X = C[–1, 1] with the inner product defined by

$$\langle x,y\rangle = \int_{-1}^{1} x(t)y(t)\, dt.$$

Let Y be the set of all odd functions in X. Then

(a) $Y\perp$ is the set of all even functions in X

(b) $Y\perp$ is the set of odd functions in X

(c) $Y\perp = \{0\}$

(d) $Y\perp$ is the set of all constant functions in X

68. Let X = l^2, the space of all square-summable sequences with

$$\|x\| = \sqrt{\sum_{i=1}^{\infty} |x_i|^2}, \text{ for } x = (x_i) \in X.$$

Define a sequence (T_n) of linear operators on X by $T_n(x) = (x_1, x_2, \ldots, x_n, 0, 0, \ldots)$. Then

(a) T_n is an unbounded operator for sufficiently large n

(b) T_n is bounded but not compact for all n

(c) T_n is compact for all n but $\lim_{n\to\infty} T_n$ is not compact

(d) T_n is compact for all n and so is $\lim_{n\to\infty} T_n$

2003

69. Let l_2 be the set of real sequenc $\{x_n\}$ such that $\sum_{n=1}^{\infty} |x_n|^2 < \infty$. For x in l_2 define $\|x\|^2 = \sum_{n=1}^{\infty} |x_n|^2$. Consider the set S = $\{x \in l_2$ such that $|x| < 1\}$. Then

(a) interior of S is compact

(b) S is compact

(c) closure of S is compact

(d) closure of S is not compact

70. On X = C [0, 1] define $T : X \to X$ by $T(f)(x) = \int_0^x f(t)dt$, for all f in X. Then

(a) T is one-one and onto

(b) T is one-one but not onto

(c) T is not one-one but onto

(d) T is neither one-one nor onto

71. Let X = C^1 [0,1] and Y = C [0, 1] both having the norm $|f| = \sup\{|f(x)|, 0 \le x \le 1\}$.

Define $T : X \to Y$ by $T(f) = f'$, where f' denotes the derivative of f. Then T is

(a) linear and continuous

(b) not linear but continuous

(c) is linear and not continuous

(d) is not linear and not continuous

72. Let B *a* Banach space (not finite dimensional) and $T : B \to B$ be a continuous operator such that the range of T is B and $T(x) = 0 \Rightarrow x = 0$. Then

(*a*) T maps bounded sets to compact sets

(*b*) T^{-1} maps bounded sets to compact sets

(*c*) T^{-1} maps bounded sets to bounded sets

(*d*) T maps compact sets to opoen sets

73. Let the sequence $\{e_n\}$ be a complete orthonormal set in a Hilbert space H. Then

(*a*) for all bounded linear operators T on H, the sequence $\{Te_n\}$ is convergent in H

(*b*) for the identity operator I on H the sequence $\{Ie_n\}$ is convergent in H

(*c*) for all bounded linear functionals *f* on H the sequence $\{fe_n\}$ is convergent in R

(*d*) none of the above

74. Let $A : H \to H$ by any bounded linear operator on a complex Hilbert space H such that $|Ax\| = \|A * x|$ for all *x* in H, where A* is the adjoint of A. If there is a non zero *x* in H such that $A^*(x) = (2 + 3i)x$, then A is

(*a*) an unitary operator on H

(*b*) a self-adjoint operator on H but not unitary

(*c*) a self-adjoint operator on H but not normal

(*d*) a normal operator

2002

75. Consider the Banach space C[0, π] with the supremum norm. The norm of the linear functional l : C[0, *n*] → R, given by $l(f) = \int_0^{\pi} f(x)\sin^2 x\,dx$, is

(*a*) 1 (*b*) $\frac{\pi}{2}$

(*c*) π (*d*) 2π

76. Let X be an infinite dimensional Banach space. Prove that X can not have countable dimension as a vector space.

2001

77. Given a nontrivial normed linear space, the nontriviality of its dual space is assured by

(*a*) the Hahn-Banach Theorem

(*b*) the Principle of Uniform Bo-undedness

(*c*) the Open Mapping Theorem

(*d*) the Closed Graph Theorem

78. All norms on a normed vector space X are equivalent provided

(*a*) X is reflexive

(*b*) X is complete

(*c*) X is finite dimensional

(*d*) X is an inner product space

79. The space l_p is a Hilbert space if and only if

(*a*) $p > 1$

(*b*) p = even

(*c*) $P = \infty$

(*d*) $p = 2$

80. In an inner product space X, fix $b \in X$ and define $f(x) = \langle x, b \rangle$ where $\langle x, b \rangle$ is the innerproduct of *x* with *b*. Show that *f* is a continuous linear functional and $\|f\| = \|b\|$.

2000

81. The norm of the linear functional *f* defined on C [-1, 1] by

$$f(x) = \int_{-1}^{0} x(t)\,dt - \int_{0}^{1} x(t)\,dt \text{ is}$$

(*a*) zero (*b*) one

(*c*) two (*d*) three

Where C [–1, 1] denotes a Banach space of all real valued functions *x*(*t*) on [–1, 1] with norm given by $\|x\| = \max_{t \in [-1,1]} |x(t)|$

82. Show that in an inner product space, $x \perp y$ (*x* is orthogonal to *y*) if and only if we have $\|x + \alpha y\| = \|x - \alpha y\|$ for all scalars α.

83. If (x_n) in a Banach space (*x*, | | . | |) is such that $(f(x_n))$ is bounded for all $f \in X'$, the dual of X, then using uniform boundedness theorem, show that $(\| x_n \|)$ is bounded. [5]

84. Let X be the normed space whose points are sequences of complex numbers $x = (\xi_j)$ with only finitely many non-zero terms and norm defined by $\| x \| = j \sup |\xi_j|$ Let $T : X \to X$ is defined by

$$y = Tx = \left(\xi_1, \frac{1}{2}\xi_2, \frac{1}{3}\xi_3, \ldots\right),$$

show that T is linear and bounded but T^{-1} is unbounded. Does this contradict the open mapping theorem ? [5]

ANSWERS

1. (*b;d*)	**2.** (50)	**3.** (*c*)	**4.** (*c*)	**5.** (1)	**6.** (*b*)	**7.** (*b*)	**8.** (1.99 to 2.01)		**9.** (*d*)
10. (*d*)	**11.** (*a*)	**12.** (*a*)	**13.** (*a*)	**14.** (*a*)	**15.** (*b*)	**16.** (*c*)	**17.** (*b*)	**18.** (*b*)	**19.** (*c*)
20. (*c*)	**21.** (*c*)	**22.** (*d*)	**23.** (*b*)	**24.** (*a*)	**25.** (*c*)	**26.** (*b*)	**27.** (*a*)	**28.** (*?*)	**29.** (*d*)
30. (*b*)	**31.** (*b*)	**32.** (*c*)	**33.** (*d*)	**34.** (*b*)	**35.** (*a*)	**36.** (*b*)	**37.** (*b*)	**38.** (*b*)	**39.** (*b*)
40. (*b*)	**41.** (*a*)	**42.** (*c*)	**43.** (*b*)	**44.** (*b*)	**45.** (*c*)	**46.** (*a*)	**47.** (*a*)	**48.** (*d*)	**49.** (*c*)
50. (*b*)	**51.** (*b*)	**52.** (*a*)	**53.** (*d*)	**54.** (*b*)	**55.** (*b*)	**56.** (*c*)	**57.** (*a*)	**58.** (*d*)	**59.** (*d*)
60. (*b*)	**61a.** (*b*)	**61b.** (*c*)	**62.** (*d*)	**63.** (*a*)	**64.** (*d*)	**65.** (*b*)	**66.** (*a*)	**67.** (*a*)	**68.** (*c*)
69. (*c*)	**70.** (*a*)	**71.** (*b*)	**72.** (*d*)	**73.** (*a*)	**74.** (*c*)	**75.** (*a*)	**76.** (*)	**77.** (*a*)	**78.** (*d*)
79. (*d*)	**80.** (*)	**81.** (*d*)	**82.** (*)	**83.** (*)	**84.** (*)				

EXPLANATIONS

1.
$$|f(x) - f(y)| = \left|(x-y) - \left(\frac{x^2}{2} - \frac{y^2}{2}\right)\right|$$
$$\leq |x-y| + \left|\left(\frac{x^2}{2} - \frac{y^2}{2}\right)\right|$$
$$\leq |x-y|\left|\left(1 + \frac{1}{2}|x+y|\right)\right|$$

Since $\alpha = 1 + \frac{1}{2}|x+y| \geq 1 \;\forall\; x, y \in [0, 1]$

$\therefore$ f is shrinking map but not a contraction if $\alpha = 1$ or f is neither shrinking map nor a contraction if $\alpha > 1$

2. Since $(p-1)! = (p-1) \bmod p$

$\Rightarrow$ $(p-2)! = 1 \bmod p$

taking $p = 101 \Rightarrow 99! = 1 \bmod 101$

$\Rightarrow$ $98! \times 99 = 1 \bmod 101$

We know that, $99 \times 50 = 1 \bmod 101$

$\Rightarrow$ $98! = 50 \bmod 101$

So the remainder is 50.

3. Here $G = \{x, y \mid x^5 = y^2 = e, x^2y = yx\}$ is dihedral group of order 2.

So G is isomorphic to Z_2.

7. The true statement about the space l^P and $L^P[0, 1]$ is $l^3 \subset l^7$ and $L^9[0, 1] \subset L^6[0, 1]$

8. Given, suprememum norm

$$\|f\|_\infty = \sup\{|f(t)| : t \in [-1,1]\} \text{ for } f \in C[-1,1]$$

T is a linear functional on $C[-1, 1]$ such that

$$T(f) = \int_\pi^0 f(t)\,dt - \int_0^1 f(t)\,dt$$

for all $f \in C[-1, 1]$

$\therefore$ The value of $\|T\|$ is 2.

9. Given, $X = c'[0, 1]$

for each $f \in X$, $P_1(f) = \sup\{|f(t)| : t \in [0, 1]\}$

$P_2(f) = \sup\{|f'(t)| : t \in [0, 1]\}$

$P_3(f) = p_1(f) + p_2(f)$

Then, (X, P_3) does not have denumerable basis.

10. $f : X \to Y$ be bijective continous mapping where X = compact Hausdorff topological space

Y = topological space.

So, f need not be an open map or a closed map.

11. H be a Hilbent space.

let $\{e_n : n \geq 1\}$ be an orthonormal basis of H.

$T : H \to H \to$ bounded linear operator

So $T(e_n) = e_{n+1}$ for all $n \geq 1$

$T(e_n) = e_1\ n \geq 1$ is not true.

12. Given that, H be a Hilbert space and $S \subseteq H$ such that

$$S^{\perp} = \{V \in H : \langle V, W \rangle = 0\ \forall\ W \in S\}$$

Let $S_1, S_2 \subseteq H$

such that $S_1 \subseteq S_2$

Let $V \in S_2^{\perp}$

$\Rightarrow$ $V \perp W, \forall\ W \in S_2$

$\Rightarrow$ $V \perp W, \forall\ W \in S_1$ ($\because S_1 \subseteq S_2$)

$\Rightarrow$ $V \in S_1^{\perp}$

$\Rightarrow$ $S_2^{\perp} \subseteq S_1^{\perp}$

15. Let x, y $\in$ H

Then $\phi(x+y) = f_{(x+y)}$ ...(*i*)

Now $f_{(x+y)}(t) = \langle t, x+y \rangle,\ \forall t \in H$

$= \langle t, x \rangle + \langle t, y \rangle,\ \forall t \in H$

$= f_x(t) + f_y(t)$

$f_{x+y} = f_x + f_y$

$= \phi_x + \phi_y$ ...(*ii*)

from equation (*i*) & (*ii*), we get

$$\phi(x+y) = \phi(x) + \phi(y).\ \forall x, y \in H$$

Hence ϕ is linear map.

Let f be an arbitrary functional in H. Then by Riesz representation theorem. There exists a unique vector such that $f(x) = \langle x. y \rangle$, $\forall \in$ H.

By definition of $f(y)$, we have $f = f_y$ and $\phi(y) = f_y = f$ thus ϕ is onto.

16. The equilibrium can be obtained if

$$F_1 l_1 = F_2 l_2$$

17. Sin 0, F is independent of y, therefore

$$\frac{\partial F}{\partial y} = 0 \quad ...(1)$$

The Euler's equation is

$$\frac{\partial F}{\partial y} - \frac{d}{dx}\left(\frac{\partial F}{\partial y'}\right) = 0 \quad ...(2)$$

using equation (1) & (2)

$$0 - \frac{d}{dx}\left(\frac{\partial F}{\partial y'}\right) = 0$$

by integrating both sides wrt. x, we get

$$\frac{\partial F}{\partial y'} = C$$

29. On comparing the given functional with $\int_0^1 f(x, y, y')\theta\, dx$

$$f(x, y, y') = y + x^2 + \frac{y'^2}{4} \quad ...(1)$$

The Eular's Equation is

$$\frac{\partial F}{\partial y} - \frac{d}{dx}\left(\frac{\partial F}{\partial y}\right) = 0 \quad ...(2)$$

From equation (2)

$$\frac{\partial F}{\partial y} = 1, \quad \frac{\partial F}{\partial y'} = \frac{y'}{2}$$

and $$\frac{d}{dx}\left(\frac{\partial F}{\partial y}\right) = \frac{y''}{2}$$

with these values equation (2) gives

$$1 - \frac{y''}{2} = 0$$

$\Rightarrow$ $y'' - 2 = 0$

$y'' = 2$

By integrating, $y' = 2x + A$

again integrating on both sides,

$$y = \frac{2x^2}{2} + Ax + B$$

$$y = x^2 + Ax + B \quad ...(3)$$

Put $x = 0$ in equation (3)

$y(0) = B = 0$

Put $x = 1$ in equation (3)

$y(1) = 1 + A = 0$

$A = -1$

Put the value of A and B in equation (3)

$$y = x^2 - x$$

36. Given function is

$$I(y) = \int_0^1 (y'^2 + x^3)dx \quad ...(1)$$

with $y(1) = 1$

Here $F(x, y, y') = y'^2 + x^3$

$$\frac{\partial F}{\partial y} = 0$$

$$\frac{\partial F}{\partial y'} = 2y^1$$

Eualr's equation is

$$\frac{\partial F}{\partial y} - \frac{d}{dx}\left(\frac{\partial F}{\partial y'}\right) = 0$$

$$2y^1 = c$$

$$y^1 = \frac{c}{2}$$

$$y = c_1 x + c_2 \quad \text{... (2)}$$

Now $y(1) = 1$ implies

$$1 = c_1 + c_2 \quad \text{... (3)}$$

from equation (2), we have

$$P = c_1 \quad \text{... (4)}$$

Therefore weiertrass function is

$$F(x, y, p, y') = F(x, y, y^1) - F(x, y, p) - (y^1 - p)\, Fp(x, y, p)$$

$$= y^{12} + x^3 - p^2 - x^3 - (y' - p)\, 2p$$

$$= y'^2 - p^2 - 2y'p + 2p^2$$

$$= (y' - p)^2$$

$$= (y' - c_1)^2 \ \forall\ y' \qquad (\because p = c_1)$$

$$\geq 0 \ \forall y'$$

Therefore given functional (i) has strong minima on all its externals.

41. Consider the Hilbert space

$$l^2 = \left\{x, (x_n) : x_n \in R, \sum_{n=1}^{\infty} x_n^2 < 8\right\}$$

and let

$$E = \{\{x_n\} : | x_n | < 1 | n, \forall n\}$$

be a subset of l^2. Then,

$$E^0 = \{x_n : | x_n | < 1 | n, \forall n\}$$

44. Given functional is

$$l(y) = \int_0^1 (1 + x)(y')^2 dx \quad ...(i)$$

with $y(0) = 0$,

$y(1) = 1$

Here $F(x, y, y') = (1' \, tx)\, y'^2$

which is independent of y

Hence, $\dfrac{\partial F}{\partial y'} = c(\text{constant})$

$$\Rightarrow \quad 2y'(1 + x) = c$$

$$y' = \frac{c}{2(1+x)}$$

$$= \frac{c_1}{(1+x)}$$

On integrating we get

$$y = c_1\, l_n\,(1 + x) \quad ...(ii)$$

Now, $y(0) = 0$

$$0 = c_1\, l_n(1 + x)$$

$$y(1) = 1$$

$$1 = c_1\, l_n(1 + x)$$

$$p = \frac{c_1}{(1+x)}$$

Therefore, Weierstrass function is

$$F(x, y, p, y') = F(x, y, y') - F(x, y, p) - (y' - p)\, Fp\,(x, y, p)$$

$$= \frac{\sin x + \cos x}{\left[\int_0^{2\pi} (\sin x + \cos x)^2 dx\right]^{\frac{1}{2}}}$$

$$= \frac{\sin x + \cos x}{\left[\int_0^{2\pi} (1 + \sin 2x) dx\right]^{\frac{1}{2}}}$$

$$= \frac{\sin x + \cos x}{\left[\left(x - \frac{\cos 2x}{2}\right)_0^{2\pi}\right]^{\frac{1}{2}}}$$

$$= \frac{\sin x + \cos x}{\sqrt{2x}}$$

Again, the normalized eigen function corresponding to eigen function $y_2(x)$ is

$$\phi_2(x) = \frac{y_2(x)}{\left\{\int_0^{2\pi} [y_2(x)]^2 dx\right\}^{\frac{1}{2}}}$$

$$= \frac{\sin x - \cos x}{\left[\int_0^{2\pi} (\sin x - \cos x)^2 dx\right]^{\frac{1}{2}}}$$

$$= \frac{\sin x - \cos x}{\left[\int_0^{2\pi}(1-\sin 2x)dx\right]^{\frac{1}{2}}}$$

$$\Rightarrow \quad = \frac{\sin x - \cos x}{\left[\left(x+\frac{\cos 2x}{2}\right)_0^{2\pi}\right]^{\frac{1}{2}}}$$

$$= \frac{\sin x - \cos x}{\sqrt{2\pi}}$$

Also $\quad f_1 = \int_0^{2\pi} f(x)\,\phi_1(x)dx$

$= \int_0^{2\pi} \frac{(\sin x + \cos x)}{\sqrt{2\pi}} dx$ [let $f(x) = 1$]

$= 0$

$= (1 + x)y'^2 - (1 + x)\, p^2 - (y' - p)\, 2p\, (1 + x)$

$= (1 + x)(y'^2 - p^2 - 2py' + 2p^2)$

$= (1 + x)(y'^2 - 2py' + p^2)$

$= (y' - p)^2(1 + x)$

$= \left[y' - \frac{c_1}{1+x}\right]^2 (1+x) \geq 0, \forall y'$

Hence given functional has strong minima.

45. We have

$$\int_{-1}^{1} f(x)dx = \frac{3}{2}f\left(-\frac{1}{3}\right) + kf\left(\frac{1}{3}\right) + \frac{1}{2}f(1)$$

We obtain

for $f(x) = 1$, $2 = \frac{3}{2}\times 1 + k \times 1 + \frac{1}{2}\times 1$

$\Rightarrow 2 = \frac{3}{2} + k + \frac{1}{2} \Rightarrow k = 0$

46. We have, $\begin{bmatrix} 1 & 4 & 3 \\ 2 & 7 & 9 \\ 5 & 8 & a \end{bmatrix}$

$$= \begin{bmatrix} l_{11} & 0 & 0 \\ l_{21} & l_{22} & 0 \\ l_{31} & l_{32} & -5^3 \end{bmatrix}\begin{bmatrix} 1 & u_{12} & u_{13} \\ 0 & 1 & u_{23} \\ 0 & 0 & 1 \end{bmatrix}$$

$$\Rightarrow \begin{bmatrix} l_{11} & l_{11}u_{12} & l_{11}u_{13} \\ l_{21} & l_{21}u_{12}+l_{22} & l_{21}u_{13}+l_{22}u_{23} \\ l_{31} & l_{31}u_{12}+l_{32} & l_{31}u_{13}+l_{32}u_{23}-53 \end{bmatrix}$$

$\Rightarrow \quad l_{11} = 1, l_{21} = 2, l_{31} = 5$

$l_{11}u_{12} = 4 \Rightarrow u_{12} = \frac{4}{1} = 4$

$l_{11}u_{13} = 3 \Rightarrow u_{13} = \frac{3}{1} = 3$

$l_{21}u_{12} + l_{22} = 7 \Rightarrow l_{22} = 7 - 8 = -1$

$l_{21}u_{13} + l_{22}u_{23} = 9 \Rightarrow u_{23} = \frac{9-6}{-1} = -3$

$l_{31}u_{12} + l_{32} = 9 \Rightarrow u_{23} = \frac{9-6}{-1} = -3$

$l_{31}u_{12} + l_{32} = 8 \Rightarrow l_{32} = 8 - 20 = -12$

$l_{31}u_{13} + l_{32}u_{23} - 53 = a$

$\Rightarrow 5 \times 3 + (-12) \times (-3) - 53 = a$

$a = -2$

50. P(0, 1) be the inner product space of all real polynomials on (0, 1) with

$$\langle f. g\rangle = \int_0^1 f(x).g(x)$$

and $\quad V = \text{spam}(t^2)$

Let $h(t) \in V$ be such that

$$||(2t-1) - h(t)|| = ||(2t-1) - x(t)||$$

for $x(t) \in V$

Then, $\quad h(t) = 5/3\, t^2$

51. Consider the sequence of continuous linear opeartors.

$Tn : l^2 \to l^2$ difined by

$Tn(x) = (0, 0, \ldots 0, x_{u+n}, x_n + 2, x_{n+3}, .)$.

for every $x = (x_1, x_2 .) \in l^2$ and $n \in N$

Then for every $x \neq 0$ in l^2 neither

$||Tn||$ nor $|T_n(x)|$ converges to 0.

52. We have continuous linear operator

$T : l^2 \to l^2$ difined by

$$T(x_1\, x_2 \ldots) = (0, x_1, 0, x_3, 0, x_5, 0\ldots)$$

Then, t is compact but not T^2.

57. C[0, 1] is the space of all continuous real valued functions on [0, 1].

Then identify map $I : (C[0, 1], \|\cdot\|_\infty) \to (C[0, 1], \|\cdot\|_1)$ is continuous but not open.

64. Let x be the space of bounded real sequences with sub-norm. Define a linear operator

$$T : X \to X \text{ by}$$

$$T(X) = \left(\frac{x_1}{1}\frac{x_2}{2}, \ldots\right)$$

for $\quad x = (x_1, x_2, x_3.) \in X$

Then, T is bounded and its inverse (from range of T) exists is bounded.

65. Let X be the space of real sequences having finitely many non-zero terms with $\| \|_p$, $1 \le p \le \infty$.

Then, f is continuous iff $p = 2$

66. We have X = C[0, 1] with the norms

$$\|x\| = \|x\|_\infty + \|x'\|_\infty$$

where x' is the derivative of x

and Y = c'[0, 1] with sub norm.

if $T : X \Rightarrow Y$ is an identity operator then T and T^{-1} both are continuous.

67. We have X = C[–1, 1]

with the inner product defined by

$$<x, y> = \int_{-1}^{1} x(t)y(t)dt$$

and y be the set of all odd functions in x

we know that,

$$\int_{-1}^{+1} x(t)y(t)dt = 0$$

if $x(t)$ is an even function as $y(t)$ is an odd function.

Hence, $(x, y) = 0$

if $x(t)$ is an even function and $x(t) \in Y^\perp$

$\therefore$ $Y^\perp$ is set of all even function in X.

68. We have $X = l^2$

The space of all square summable sequence with

$$\|x\| = \sqrt{\sum_{i=1}^{\infty} |x_i|^2} \qquad \text{for } x = (x_i) \in X$$

Define a sequance $[T_n]$ of linear operater on X by $T_n(x) = (x_1, x_2, x_3 . x_n, 0, 0.)$.

Then, T_n is compact but $\lim_{n\to\infty} T_n$ is not compact $n > \infty$.

80. We have $f(x) = \langle x, b\rangle \; \forall \in X$. To show that f is a continuous linear functional on inner product space X.

Let $x_1, x_2 \in X$ and α, β be two scalars.

$f(\alpha x_1 + \beta x_2) = \langle \alpha x_1 + \beta x_2, b\rangle$

$= \alpha\,(x_1, b) + \beta\,(x_2, b)$[By linear property of product space]

$= \alpha f(x_1) + \beta f(x_2)$

Hence f is linear.

Now we have to show f is continuous.

For every $x \in X$, we have $f(x) = \langle x, b\rangle$

$\Rightarrow \quad |f(x)| = |\langle x, b\rangle|$

$\le \|x\| \, \|b\|$ [By Schwarz inequality]

Let $\|b\| = K$. then $K \ge 0$.

$$|f(x)| \le K\,\|x\| \;\forall\, x \in X$$

Therefore the function f is bounded and every bounded function is continuous. Hence f is continuous. Therefore f is continuous linear functional on inner product space X. Now we shall prove

$$\|f\| = \|b\|$$

Since $|f(x)| \le \|x\| \, \|b\|$

[By Schwarz inequality] ... (1)

By definition, $\|x\| = \text{Sup}\{|f(x)| : \|x\| \le 1\}$

If $\|x\| \le 1$, then

$$\|x\| \, \|b\| \le \|b\|$$

$\therefore \quad |f(x)| \le \|b\| \;\forall\, x$ such that $\|x\| \le 1$

$\Rightarrow \text{Sup}\,\{|f(x)| : \|x\| \le 1\} \le \|b\|$

$\Rightarrow \quad \|f\| \le \|b\|$ ...(2)

Now we shall show that the relation (2) takes the form on an equality. If $b = 0$ then

$$\|b\| = 0.$$

Also if $b = 0$ then

$$f(x) = \langle x, b\rangle = \langle x, 0\rangle = 0$$

$$\forall\, x \in X.$$

Therefore f is zero function and $\|f\| = 0$

i.e. if $b = 0$

then $\|b\| = \|f\| = 0$

Let us now take $b \ne 0$. Then X is not a zero space.

$\therefore \quad \|f\| = \sup\,\{|f(x)| : \|x\| = 1)$ ... (3)

Since $b \ne 0$, therefore $\dfrac{b}{\|b\|}$ is a unit vector.

$$\therefore \quad \|f\| \ge \left| f\left(\frac{b}{\|b\|}\right) \right|$$

$$= \left\langle \frac{b}{\|b\|}, b \right\rangle$$

$$= \frac{1}{\|b\|}(b, b)$$

$$= \frac{1}{\|b\|}\|b\|^2$$

$$= \|b\|$$

Thus $\|f\| \geq \|b\|$ ... (4)

From equation (2) and (4) we conclude that

$$\|f\| = \|b\|.$$

82. If $\|x+\alpha y\| = \|x-\alpha y\| \ \forall$ scalars α.

i.e. $\|x+\alpha y\|^2 = \|x-\alpha y\|^2$

$\Rightarrow \|x\|^2 + 2\alpha x.y + \alpha^2\|y\|^2$

$= \|x\|^2 - 2\alpha.x.y + \alpha^2\|y\|$

$\Rightarrow 2\alpha\, x\,.\,y = 0$

$\Rightarrow x\,.\,y = 0$

i.e. x and y are perpendicular Conversely if x and y are perpendicular

i.e., $x\,.\,y = 0$

Then, $\|x\|^2 + \alpha^2\|y\|^2 + 2\alpha\, x.y$

$= \|x\|^2 + \alpha^2\|y\|^2 - 2\alpha\, x.y$

$\Rightarrow \|x+\alpha y\|^2 = \|x-\alpha y\|^2$

$\Rightarrow \|x+\alpha y\| = \|x-\alpha y\|$

83. We have $(f(x_n))$ is bounded for all $f \in X'$, the dual of X

i.e. $f(x_n)$ is bounded for all $f \in X$.

Then we have to show that $(\|x_n\|)$ is bounded. For this we use natural imbedding

$$x \to F_{x_n}$$

By uniform bounded theorem, F is defined by

$$F_{x_n}(f) = f(x_n)$$

Hence $f(x_n) = \{f(x_n)\}$ is bounded for each f is equivalent to the assumption that $\{F_{x_n}(f)\}$ is bounded set for each $f \in X$. Since $(X, \|.\|)$ is a banach space, then from uniform bounded theorem $\{F_{x_n}\}$ is bounded set in X.

i.e., $\{\|F_{x_n}\|\}$ is a bounded set. Since the natural imbedding preserves norms.

$\therefore \|F_{x_n}\| = \|x_n\|$ for each $x_n \in X$

Hence $(\|x_n\|)$ is bounded. **Proved.**

■■

7

CHAPTER

Numerical Analysis

2016

1. Let {X,Y,Z} be a basis of $\mathbb{R}^3$. Consider the following statements P and Q:

(P) : {X + Y, Y + Z, X – Z] is a basis of $\mathbb{R}^3$.

(Q) : {X + Y + Z, X + 2Y – Z, X – 3Z] is a basis of $\mathbb{R}^3$.

Which of the above statements hold TRUE?

(*a*) both P and Q (*b*) only P

(*c*) only Q (*d*) Neither P nor Q

2. Let the polynomial x^4 be approximated by a polynomial of degree ≤ 2, which interpolates x^4 at x = – 1,0 and 1. Then, the maximum absolute interpolation over the interval [–1,1] is equal to ________________.

3. Let y(t) be a continuous function on [0, ∞]. If

$$y(t) = t(1 - 4\int_0^t y(x)dx) + 4\int_0^t x\,y(x)dx,$$

then $\int_0^{\pi/2} y(t)dt$ is equal to ________.

4. Let the integral

$$I = \int_0^4 f(x)dx, \text{ where } f(x) = \begin{cases} x & 0 \le x \le 2 \\ 4 - x & 2 \le x \le 4 \end{cases}$$

Consider the following statements P and Q:

(P) : If I_2 is the value of the integral obtained by the composite trapezoidal rule with two equal sub-intervals, then I_2 is exact.

(Q) : If I_3 is the value of the integral obtained by the composite trapezoidal rule with three equal sub-intervals, then I_3 is exact.

Which of the above statements hold TRUE?

(*a*) both P and Q (*b*) only P

(*c*) only Q (*d*) Neither P nor Q

5. For the fixed point iteration $x_{k+1} = g(x_k)$, k = 0, 1, 2,...., consider the following statements P and Q:

(P) : If $g(x) = 1 + \frac{2}{x}$ then the fixed point iteration converges to 2 for all $x_0 \in [1, 100]$.

(Q) : If $g(x) = \sqrt{2 + x}$ then the fixed point iteration converges to 2 for all $x_0 \in [0, 100]$.

Which of the above statements hold TRUE?

(*a*) both P and Q (*b*) only P

(*c*) only Q (*d*) Neither P nor Q

2015

6. Suppose that the Newton-Raphson method is applied to the equation $2x^2 + 1 - e^{x^2} = 0$ with an initial approximation x_0 sufficiently close to zero. Then, for the root $x = 0$, the order of convergence of the method is equal to ___

7. If the trapezoidal rule with single interval [0, 1] is exact for approximating the integral $\int_0^1 (x^3 - cx^2)dx$, then the value of c is equal to ________

8. If, for some α, β ∈ $\mathbb{R}$, the integration formula

$$\int_0^2 p(x)dx = p(\alpha) + p(\beta)$$

holds for all polynomials $p(x)$ of degree at most 3, then the value of $3(\alpha - \beta)^2$ is equal to ____________

9. Let $p(x)$ be the polynomial of degree at most 3 that passes through the points(–2, 12), (–1, 1), (0, 2) and (2, – 8). Then the coefficient of x^3 in $p(x)$ is equal to _____.

2014

10. Let $\alpha \in \mathbb{R}$. If αx is the polynomial which interpolates the function $f(x) = \sin \pi x$ on [–1, 1] at all the zeroes of the polynomial $4x^3 - 3x$, then α is _______

11. Using the Newton-Raphson method with the initial guess $x^{(0)} = 6$, the approximate value of the real root of $x \log_{10} x = 4.77$, after the second iteration, is _________

12. Let the following discrete data be obtained from a curve $y = y(x)$:

x :	0	0.25	0.5	0.75	1.0
y :	1	0.9896	0.9589	0.9089	0.8415

Let S be the solid of revolution obtained by rotating the above curve about the x-axis between $x = 0$ and $x = 1$ and let V denote its volume. the approximate value of V, obtained using Simpson's $\frac{1}{3}$ rule, is _________

13. Using the Gauss-Seidel iteration method with the initial guess $\{x_1^{(0)} = 3.5, x_2^{(0)} = 2.25, x_3^{(0)} = 1.625\}$, the second approximation $\{x_1^{(2)}, x_2^{(2)}, x_3^{(2)}\}$ for the solution to the system of equations

$$2x_1 - x_2 = 7$$
$$-x_1 + 2x_2 - x_3 = 1$$
$$-x_2 + 2x_3 = 1,$$

is

(a) $x_1^{(2)} = 5.3125, x_2^{(2)} = 4.4491, x_3^{(2)} = 2.1563$

(b) $x_1^{(2)} = 5.3125, x_2^{(2)} = 4.3125, x_3^{(2)} = 2.6563$

(c) $x_1^{(2)} = 5.3125, x_2^{(2)} = 4.4491, x_3^{(2)} = 2.6563$

(d) $x_1^{(2)} = 5.4991, x_2^{(2)} = 4.4491, x_3^{(2)} = 2.1563$

14. The fourth order Runge-Kutta method given by

$$u_{j+1} = u_j + \frac{h}{6}[K_1 + 2K_2 + 2K_3 + K_4]$$

$j = 0, 1, 2, ...,$

is used to solve the initial value problem $\frac{du}{dt} = u, u(0) = \alpha.$

If $u(1)= 1$ is obtained by taking the step size $h = 1$, then the valued of K_4 is_____

15. A particle P of mass m moves along the cycloid $x = (\theta - \sin\theta)$ and $y = (1 + \cos\theta)$, $0 \le \theta \le 2\pi$. Let g denote the acceleration due to gravity. Neglecting the frictional force, the Lagranian associated with the motion of the particle P is:

(a) $m(1 - \cos\theta)\,\dot{\theta}^2 - mg\,(1 + \cos\theta)$

(b) $m(1 + \cos\theta)\,\dot{\theta}^2 + mg\,(1 + \cos\theta)$

(c) $m(1 + \cos\theta)\,\dot{\theta}^2 + mg\,(1 - \cos\theta)$

(d) $m(\theta + \sin\theta)\,\dot{\theta}^2 - mg\,(1 + \cos\theta)$

2012

16. Given the data:

x	1	2	3	4	5
y	–1	2	–3	4	–5

If the derivative of $y(x)$ is approximated as:

$$y'(x_k) \approx \frac{1}{h}\left(\Delta y_k + \frac{1}{2}\Delta^2 y_k - \frac{1}{4}\Delta^3 y_k\right),$$

then the value of $y'(2)$ is

(a) 4 (b) 8

(c) 12 (d) 16

17. The root of the equation $xe^x = 1$ between 0 and 1, obtained by using two iterations of bisection method, is

(a) 0.25 (b) 0.50

(c) 0.75 (d) 0.65

18. Using Euler's method taking step size = 0.1, the approximate value of y obtained corresponding to $x = 0.2$ for the initial value problem $\frac{dy}{dx} = x^2 + y^2$ and $y(0) = 1$, is

(a) 1.322 (b) 1.122

(c) 1.222 (d) 1.110

19. Consider the system of equations

$$\begin{bmatrix} 5 & -1 & 1 \\ 2 & 4 & 0 \\ 1 & 1 & 5 \end{bmatrix}\begin{bmatrix} x \\ y \\ z \end{bmatrix} = \begin{bmatrix} 10 \\ 12 \\ -1 \end{bmatrix}$$

Using Jacobi's method with the initial guess $\left[x^{(0)}\ y^{(0)}\ z^{(0)}\right]^T = [2.0\ 3.0\ 0.0]^T$, the approximate solution $[x^{(2)}\ y^{(2)}\ z^{(2)}]^T$ after two iterations, is

(a) $[2.64\ \ -1.70\ \ -1.12]^T$

(b) $[2.64\ -1.70\ \ 1.12]^T$

(c) $[2.64\ \ 1.70\ \ -1.12]^T$

(d) $[2.64\ \ 1.70\ \ 1.12]^T$

2011

20. While solving the equation $x^2 - 3x + 1 = 0$ using the Newton-Raphson method with the initial guess of a root as 1, the value of the root one iteration is

(a) 1.5 (b) 1

(c) 0.5 (d) 0

21. Consider the system of equations

$$\begin{bmatrix} 5 & 2 & 1 \\ -2 & 5 & 2 \\ -1 & 2 & 8 \end{bmatrix}\begin{bmatrix} x_1 \\ x_2 \\ x_3 \end{bmatrix} = \begin{bmatrix} 13 \\ -22 \\ 14 \end{bmatrix}$$

With the initial guess of the solution $\left[x_1^{(0)}, x_2^{(0)}, x_3^{(0)}\right]^T = [1, 1, 1]^T$, the approximate value of the solution $\left[x_1^{(1)}, x_2^{(1)}, x_3^{(1)}\right]^{1T}$ after one iteration by the Gauss-Seidel method is

(a) $[2, -4.4, 1.625]^T$

(b) $[2, -4, -3]^T$

(c) $[2, 4.4, 1.625]^T$

(d) $[2, -4, 3]^T$

22. Let y be the solution of the initial value problem

$$\frac{dy}{dx} = (y^2 + x)\ ;\ y(0) = 1$$

Using Taylor series method of order 2 with the step size $h = 0.1$, the approximate value of $y(0.1)$ is

(a) 1.315 (b) 1.415

(c) 1.115 (d) 1.215

23. The value of the integral

$$I = \int_{-1}^{1} \exp\left(x^2\right) dx$$

using a rectangular rule is approximated as 2. Then, the approximation error $|I - 2|$ lies in the interval

(a) (2e, 3e) (b) (2/3, 2e)

(c) (e/8, 2/3) (d) (0, e/8)

2010

24. The numerical value obtained by applying the two-point trapezoidal rule to the integral $\int_0^1 \frac{\ln(1+x)}{x} dx$ is

(a) $\frac{1}{2}(\ln 2 + 1)$ (b) $\frac{1}{2}$

(c) $\frac{1}{2}(\ln 2 - 1)$ (d) $\frac{1}{2}\ln 2$

25. Let $l_k(x)$, $k = 0, 1..., n$ denote the Lagrange's fundamental polynomials of degree n for the nodes $x_0, x_1,..., x_n$. Then the value of $\sum_{k=0}^{n} l_k(x)$ is

(a) 0 (b) 1

(c) $x^n + 1$ (d) $x^n - 1$

Statement for Linked Answer Q. (26 – 27)

For a differentiable function $f(x)$, the integral $\int_0^h f(x)\,dx$ is approximated by the formula $h[a_0 f(0) + a_1 f(h)] + h^2[b_0 f'(0) + b_1 f'(h)]$, which is exact for all polynomials of degree at most 3.

26. The values of a_1 and b_1 respectively are

(a) $\frac{1}{2}$ and $-\frac{1}{12}$ (b) $-\frac{1}{12}$ and $\frac{1}{2}$

(c) $\frac{1}{2}$ and $\frac{1}{12}$ (d) $\frac{1}{12}$ and $\frac{1}{2}$

27. The values of a_0 and b_0 respectively are

(a) $\frac{1}{2}$ and $\frac{1}{2}$ (b) $\frac{1}{12}$ and $-\frac{1}{12}$

(c) $\frac{1}{2}$ and $\frac{1}{12}$ (d) $\frac{1}{2}$ and $-\frac{1}{12}$

28. Four weightless rods form a rhombus PQRS with smooth hinges at the joints. Another weightless rod joins the midpoints E and F of PQ and PS respectively. The system is suspended from P and a weight 2W is attached to R. If the angle between the rods PQ and PS is 2θ, then the thrust in the rod EF is

(a) W tan θ (b) 2W tan θ

(c) 2W cot θ (d) 4W tan θ

2009

29. For what values of α and β, the quadrature formula $\int_{-1}^{1} f(x)dx \approx \alpha f(-1) + f(\beta)$ is exact for all polynomials of degree ≤ 1 ?

(a) α = 1, β = 1

(b) α = –1, β = 1

(c) α = 1, β = –1

(d) α = –1, β = –1

30. Let $f : [0, 4] \to \mathbb{R}$ be a three times continuously differentiable function. Then the value of $f[1, 2, 3, 4]$ is

(a) $\frac{f''(\xi)}{3}$ for some $\xi \in (0, 4)$

(b) $\frac{f''(\xi)}{6}$ for some $\xi \in (0, 4)$

(c) $\frac{f'''(\xi)}{3}$ for some $\xi \in (0, 4)$

(d) $\frac{f'''(\xi)}{6}$ for some $\xi \in (0, 4)$

31. Let $\phi : [0, 1] \to \mathbb{R}$ be three times continuously differentiable. Suppose that the iterates defined by $x_{n+1} = \phi(x_n)$, $n \geq 0$ converge to the fixed point ξ of φ. If the order of convergence is three then

(a) $\phi'(\xi) = 0, \phi''(\xi) = 0$

(b) $\phi'(\xi) \neq 0, \phi''(\xi) = 0$

(c) $\phi'(\xi) = 0, \phi''(\xi) \neq 0$

(d) $\phi'(\xi) \neq 0, \phi''(\xi) \neq 0$

32. Let $f : [0, 2] \to \mathbb{R}$ be a twice continuously differentiable function.

If $\int_0^2 f(x)dx \approx 2f(1)$, then the error in the approximation is

(a) $\frac{f'(\xi)}{12}$ for some $\xi \in (0, 2)$

(b) $\frac{f'(\xi)}{2}$ for some $\xi \in (0, 2)$

(c) $\frac{f''(\xi)}{3}$ for some $\xi \in (0, 2)$

(d) $\frac{f''(\xi)}{6}$ for some $\xi \in (0, 2)$

33. A simple pendulum, consisting of a bob of mass m connected with a string of length a, is oscillating in a vertical plane. If the string is making an angle θ with the vertical, then the expression for the Lagrangian is given as

(a) $ma^2\left(\dot{\theta}^2 - \frac{2g}{a}\sin^2\left(\frac{\theta}{2}\right)\right)$

(b) $2mga\sin^2\left(\frac{\theta}{2}\right)$

(c) $ma^2\left(\frac{\dot{\theta}^2}{2} - \frac{2g}{a}\sin^2\left(\frac{\theta}{2}\right)\right)$

(d) $\frac{ma}{2}\left(\dot{\theta}^2 - \frac{2g}{a}\cos\theta\right)$

2008

34. Consider the initial value problem $\frac{dy}{dx} = f(x,y)$, $y(x_0) = y_0$. The aim is to compute the value of $y_1 = y(x_1)$, where $x_1 = x_0 + h$ $(h > 0)$. At $x = x_1$, if the value of y_1 is equated to the corresponding value of the straight line passing through (x_0, y_0) and having the slope equal to the slope of the curve $y(x)$ at $x = x_0$, then the method is called

(a) Euler's method

(b) Improved Euler's method

(c) Backward Euler's method

(d) Taylor series method of order 2

35. The possible values of α for which the variational problem $J[y(x)] = \int_0^1 (3y^2 + 2x^3y')dx, y(\alpha) = 1$ has extremals are

(a) –1, 0 (b) 0, 1

(c) –1,1 (d) –1, 0, 1

36. The integral equation

$x(t) = \sin t + \lambda \int_0^1 (s^2t^3 + e^{s^2+t^3})x(s)ds,\ 0 \le t \le 1, \lambda \in$ R, $\lambda \ne 0$ has a solution for

(a) all non-zero values of λ

(b) no value of λ

(c) only countably many positive values of λ

(d) only countably many negative values of λ

37. The integral equation

$x(t) - \int_0^1 [\cos t \sec s\, x(s)]ds = \sin h\, t, 0 \le t \le 1$, has

(a) no solution

(b) a unique solution

(c) more than one but finitely many solution

(d) infinitely many solutions

38. If $y_{i+1} = y_i + h\,\varphi(f, x_i, y_i, h)$, $i = 1, 2, \ldots$, where $\varphi(f, x, y, h) = af(x, y) + bf(x + h, y + hf(x, y))$, is a second order accurate scheme to solve the initial value problem $\frac{dy}{dx} = f(x, y)$, $y(x_0) = y_0$, then a and b, respectively, are

(a) $\frac{h}{2}, \frac{h}{2}$ (b) 1, –1

(c) $\frac{1}{2}, \frac{1}{2}$ (d) $h, -h$

39. If a quadrature formula $\frac{3}{2}f\left(-\frac{1}{3}\right) + Kf\left(\frac{1}{3}\right) + \frac{1}{2}f(1)$ that approximates $\int_{-1}^{1} f(x)dx$, is found to be exact for quadratic polynomials, then the value of K is

(a) 2 (b) 1

(c) 0 (d) –2

40. If $\begin{pmatrix} 1 & 4 & 3 \\ 2 & 7 & 9 \\ 5 & 8 & a \end{pmatrix} = \begin{pmatrix} 1_{11} & 0 & 0 \\ 1_{21} & 1_{22} & 0 \\ 1_{31} & 1_{32} & -53 \end{pmatrix} \begin{pmatrix} 1 & u_{12} & u_{13} \\ 0 & 1 & u_{23} \\ 0 & 0 & 1 \end{pmatrix}$ then the value of a is

(a) –2 (b) –1

(c) 1 (d) 2

41. Using the least squares method, if a curve $y = ax^2 + bx + c$ is fitted to the collinear data points (–1, –3), (1, 1), (3, 5) and (7, 13), then the triplet (a, b, c) is equal to

(a) (–1, 2, 0) (b) (0, 2, –1)

(c) (2, –1, 0) (d) (0, –1, 2)

42. A quadratic polynomial $p(x)$ is constructed by interpolating the data points (0, 1), (1, e) and (2, e^2). If $\sqrt{e}$ is approximated by using $p(x)$, then its approximate value is

(a) $\frac{1}{8}(3 + 6e - e^2)$ (b) $\frac{1}{8}(3 - 6e - 2e^2)$

(c) $\frac{1}{8}(3 - 6e - e^2)$ (d) $\frac{1}{8}(3 + 6e - 2e^2)$

2007

43. Let $f(x) = x^{10} + x - 1, x \in$ R and let $x_k = k, k = 0, 1, 2, \ldots, 10$. Then the value of the divided difference $f[x_0, x_1, x_2, x_3, x_4, x_5, x_6, x_7, x_8, x_9, x_{10}]$ is

(a) – 1 (b) 0

(c) 1 (d) 10

44. The smallest degree of the polynomial that interpolates the data

x	–2	–1	0	1	2	3
$f(x)$	– 58	–21	–12	–13	– 6	27

is

(a) 3 (b) 4

(c) 5 (d) 6

45. Suppose that x_0 is sufficiently close to 3. Which of the following iterations $x_{n+1} = g(x_n)$ will converge to the fixed point $x = 3$?

(a) $x_{n+1} = -16 + 6x_n + \frac{3}{x_n}$

(b) $x_{n+1} = \sqrt{3 + 2x_n}$

(c) $x_{n+1} = \frac{3}{x_n - 2}$

(d) $x_{n+1} = \frac{x_n^2 - 2}{2}$

46. Consider the quadrature formula, $\int_{-1}^{1} |x| f(x)\,dx \approx \frac{1}{2}[f(x_0) + f(x_1)]$

where x_0 and x_1 are quadrature points. Then the highest degree of the polynomial, for which the above formula is exact, equals

(a) 1 (b) 2

(c) 3 (d) 4

Statement for Linked Answer Questions 47 and 48:

A particle of mass m slides down without friction along a curve $z = 1 + \frac{x^2}{2}$ in the xz-plane under the action of constant gravity. Suppose the z-axis points vertically upwards. Let $\dot{x}$ and $\ddot{x}$ denote $\frac{dx}{dt}$ and $\frac{d^2x}{dt^2}$, respectively.

47. The Lagrangian of the motion is

(a) $\frac{1}{2}m\dot{x}^2(1+x^2) - mg\left(1+\frac{x^2}{2}\right)$

(b) $\frac{1}{2}m\dot{x}^2(1+x^2) + mg\left(1+\frac{x^2}{2}\right)$

(c) $\frac{1}{2}m\dot{x}^2x^2 - mg\left(1+\frac{x^2}{2}\right)$

(d) $\frac{1}{2}m\dot{x}^2(1-x^2) - mg\left(1+\frac{x^2}{2}\right)$

48. The Lagrangian equation of motion is

(a) $\ddot{x}(1 + x^2) = -x(g + \dot{x}^2)$

(b) $\ddot{x}(1 + x^2) = x(g + \dot{x}^2)$

(c) $\ddot{x} = -gx$

(d) $\ddot{x}(1 - x^2) = -x(g + \dot{x}^2)$

2006

49. Let $f(x)$ be a differentiable function such that $\frac{d^3f}{dx^3} = 1$ for all $x \in [0, 3]$. If $p(x)$ is the quadratic polynomial which interpolates $f(x)$ at $x = 0, x = 2$ and $x = 3$, then $f(1) - p(1)$ equals

(a) 0

(b) 1/3

(c) 1/6

(d) 2/3

50. Let $h(x)$ be a twice continuously differentiable function on [1, 2] with fixed point α. Then, the sequence of iterates $x_{n+1} = h(x_n)$ converges to α quadratically, provided

(a) $\frac{dh}{dx}(\alpha) \neq 0$

(b) $\frac{dh}{dx}(\alpha) \neq \frac{d^2h}{dx^2}(\alpha) = 0$

(c) $\frac{dh}{dx}(\alpha) \neq 0, \frac{d^2h}{dx^2}(\alpha) \neq 0$

(d) $\frac{dh}{dx}(\alpha) = 0, \frac{d^2h}{dx^2}(\alpha) \neq 0$

51. Consider the initial value problem (IVP):

$$\frac{dy}{dx} = f(x, y(x)),\ y(x_0) = y_0.$$

Let $y_1 = y_0 + w_1k_1 + 3k_2$ approximate the solution of the above IVP at $x_1 = x_0 + h$ with $k_1 = hf(x_0, y_0)$, $k_2 = hf(x_0 + (h/6),\ y_0 + (k_1/6))$ and h being the step-size. If the formula for y_1 yields a second order method, then the value of w_1 is

(a) –1 (b) –2

(c) 3 (d) $\frac{1}{6}$

2005

52. An iterative method to find the nth root $(n \in N)$ of a postive number a is given by $x_{k+1} = \frac{1}{2}\left[x_k + \frac{a}{x_k^{n-1}}\right]$. A value of n for which this iterative method fails to converge is

(a) 1 (b) 2

(c) 3 (d) 8

53. Suppose the function u (x) interpolates f (x) at $x_0, x_1, x_2, \ldots, x_{n-1}$ and the function v(x)interpolates f (x) at $x_1, x_2, \ldots x_{n-1}, x_n$. Then, a function F (x) which interpolatcs f(x) at all the points $x_0, x_1, x_2, \ldots x_{n-1}, x_n$ is given by

(a) $E(x) = \dfrac{(x_n - x)u(x) - (x - x_0)v(x)}{(x_n - x_0)}$

(b) $F(x) = \dfrac{(x_n - x)u(x) + (x - x_0)v(x)}{(x_n - x_0)}$

(c) $F(x) = \dfrac{(x_n - x)v(x) + (x - x_0)u(x)}{(x_n - x_0)}$

(d) $F(x) = \dfrac{(x_n - x)v(x) - (x - x_0)u(x)}{(x_n - x_0)}$

54. Suppose the iterates x_n generated by $x_{n+1} = x_n - \dfrac{2f(x_n)}{f'(x_n)}$ where f' denotes the derivative of f, converges to a double zero x = a of f(x). Then the convergence has order

(a) 1 (b) 2

(c) 3 (d) 1.6

55. Suppose the matrix $M = \begin{pmatrix} 2 & \alpha & -1 \\ \alpha & 2 & 1 \\ -1 & 1 & 4 \end{pmatrix}$ has a unique Cholesky decomposition of the form $M = LL^T$, where L is a lower triangular matrix. The range of values of α is

(a) $-2 < \alpha < 2$

(b) $\alpha > 2$

(c) $-2 < \alpha < 3/2$

(d) $3/2 < \alpha < 2$

56. The Runge-Kutta method of order four is used to solve the differential equation

$$\frac{dy}{dx} = f(x), \quad y(0) = 0$$

with step size h. The solution at x = h is given by

(a) $y(h) = \dfrac{h}{6}\left[f(0) + 4f(\tfrac{h}{2}) + f(h)\right]$

(b) $y(h) = \dfrac{h}{6}\left[f(0) + 2f(\tfrac{h}{2}) + f(h)\right]$

(c) $y(h) = \dfrac{h}{6}\left[f(0) + f(h)\right]$

(d) $y(h) = \dfrac{h}{6}\left[2f(0) + f(\tfrac{h}{2}) + 2f(h)\right]$

57. The values of the constants α, β, x_1 for which the quadrature formula

$$\int_0^1 f(x)dx = \alpha f(0) + \beta f(x_1)$$

is exact for polynomials of degree as high as possible , are

(a) $\alpha = \frac{2}{3}, \beta = \frac{1}{4}, x_1 = \frac{3}{4}$

(b) $\alpha = \frac{3}{4}, \beta = \frac{1}{4}, x_1 = \frac{2}{3}$

(c) $\alpha = \frac{1}{4}, \beta = \frac{3}{4}, x_1 = \frac{2}{3}$

(d) $\alpha = \frac{2}{3}, \beta = \frac{3}{4}, x_1 = \frac{1}{4}$

Statement for Linked Answer Questions 58a and 58b :

It is required to solve the system SX = T, where

$S = \begin{pmatrix} 2 & -1 & 1 \\ 2 & 2 & 2 \\ -1 & -1 & 2 \end{pmatrix}$, $T = \begin{pmatrix} -1 \\ 4 \\ -5 \end{pmatrix}$ by the Gauss- Seidel iteration onethod.

58a. Suppose S is written in the form $S = M - L - U$, where, M is a diagonal matrix, L is a strictly lower triangular matrix and U is a strictly upper triangular matrix. If the iteration process is expressed as $X_{n+1} = QX_n + F$, then Q is given by

(a) $Q = (M + L)^{-1}U$

(b) $Q = M^{-1}(L + U)$

(c) $Q = (M - L)^{-1}U$

(d) $Q = M^{-1}(L - U)$

58b. The matrix Q is given by

(a) $Q = \begin{pmatrix} 0 & \frac{1}{2} & -\frac{1}{2} \\ 0 & -\frac{1}{2} & -\frac{1}{2} \\ 0 & 0 & -\frac{1}{2} \end{pmatrix}$

(b) $Q = \begin{pmatrix} 0 & 0 & 0 \\ \frac{1}{2} & -\frac{1}{2} & 0 \\ -\frac{1}{2} & -\frac{1}{2} & -\frac{1}{2} \end{pmatrix}$

(c) $Q = \begin{pmatrix} 0 & -\frac{1}{2} & \frac{1}{2} \\ 0 & \frac{1}{2} & \frac{1}{2} \\ 0 & 0 & \frac{1}{2} \end{pmatrix}$

(d) $Q = \begin{pmatrix} 0 & 0 & 0 \\ -\frac{1}{2} & \frac{1}{2} & 0 \\ \frac{1}{2} & \frac{1}{2} & \frac{1}{2} \end{pmatrix}$

2004

59. An iterative scheme is given by $x_{n+1} = \frac{1}{5}\left(16 - \frac{12}{x_n}\right)$, $n \in N \cup (0)$. Such a scheme, with n suitable x_0, will

(*a*) not converge (*b*) converge to 1.6

(*c*) converge to 1.8 (*d*) converge to 2

60. To find the positive square root of $a > 0$ by solving $x^2 - a = 0$ by the Newton-Raphson method, if x_n denotes the nth iterate with $x_0 > 0, x_0 \neq \sqrt{a}$, then the sequence $(x_n, n \geq 1)$ is

(*a*) strictly decreasing

(*b*) strictly increasing

(*c*) constant

(*d*) not convergent

61. In solving the ordinary differential equation $y' = 2x, y(0) = 0$ using Euler's method, the iterates y_n, $n \in N$ satisfy

(*a*) $y_n = x_n^2$ (*b*) $y_n = 2x_n$

(*c*) $y_n = x_n x_{n-1}$ (*d*) $y_n = x_{n-1} + x_n$

2003

62. Let M be the length of the initial interval $[a_0, b_0]$ containing a solution of $f(x) = 0$. Let $[x_0, x_1, x_2,..\}$. represent the successive points generated by the bisection method. Then the minimum number of iterations required to guarantee an approximation to the solution with an accuracy of ε is given by

(*a*) $-2 - \frac{\log\left(\frac{\varepsilon}{M}\right)}{\log 2}$ (*b*) $-2 + \frac{\log\left(\frac{\varepsilon}{M}\right)}{\log 2}$

(*c*) $-2 + \frac{\log(M\varepsilon)}{\log 2}$ (*d*) $-2 - \frac{\log\left(\frac{\varepsilon}{M}\right)}{(\log 2)^2}$

63. On evaluating $\int_1^2\int_1^2 \frac{1}{(x+y)}dxdy$ numerically by Trapezoidal rule one would get the value

(*a*) $\frac{17}{48}$ (*b*) $\frac{11}{48}$

(*c*) $\frac{21}{48}$ (*d*) $\frac{17}{52}$

64. If the scheme corresponding to the Newton-Raphson method for solving the system of nonlinear equation : $x^2 + y^2 - 10 = 0, x^2 y - 3 = 0$ is

$x^{k+1} = x^k + \{f(x,y)\}_{(x^k, y^k)}$ and y^{k+1}

$= y^k + \{g(x,y)\}_{(x^k, y^k)}$

then $f(x, y)$ and $g(x, y)$ are respectively given by

(*a*) $-\frac{(x^2+y^2-10)}{2x}$ and $-\frac{x^2y-3}{x^2}$

(*b*) $\frac{x^2(y^2-x^2+10)-6y}{2x(x^2-y^2)}$ and $\frac{y^3-10y+3}{x^2-y^2}$

(*c*) $\frac{x^2(3y^2-x^2-10p+6y)}{2x(x^2-y^2)}$ and $\frac{y^3-10y+3}{x^2-y^2}$

(*d*) $-(x^2 + y^2 - 10)$ and $-(x^2y - 3)$

65. A lower bound on the polynomial interpo-lation error $e_2(\bar{x})$ for $f(x) = ln(x)$, with $x_0 = 2, x_1 = 2, x_2 = 4$ and $\bar{x} = \frac{5}{4}$ is given by

(*a*) $\frac{1}{256}$ (*b*) $\frac{1}{64}$

(*c*) $\frac{1}{512}$ (*d*) 0

66. Consider the Quadrature formula

$$\int_0^h f(x)dx = \left\{\alpha f(0) + \beta f\left(\frac{3h}{4}\right) + \gamma f(h)\right\}h$$

The values of α, β, γ for which this is exact for polynomials of as high degree as possible, are

(*a*) $\alpha = \frac{5}{18}, \beta = \frac{8}{9}, \gamma = -\frac{1}{6}$

(*b*) $\alpha = \frac{1}{2}, \beta = -\frac{1}{4}, \gamma = \frac{3}{4}$

(*c*) $\alpha = 0, \beta = 1, \gamma = -\frac{1}{4}$

(*d*) $\alpha = 1, \beta = 2, \gamma = 3$

67. Consider the (Cholesky's) algorithm given below for LL^T decomposition of a Symmetric Positive Definite matrix A:

Compute $L_{11} = A_{11}^{1/2}$

For $i = 2$ to N
Computer $L_{i,1} = A_{i,1}/L_{i,1}$

For $i = 2$ to N

Computer $L_{j,j} = \left(A_{j,j} - \sum_{m=1}^{j-1} L_{j,m}^2\right)^{1/2}$

Right alternative for filling the shaded box to complete the above algorithm is

(a) For $i = j + 1$ to N
Compute $L_{j,j} = \frac{1}{L_{j,j}}\left(A_{i,j} - \sum_{m=1}^{j-1} L_{i,m}L_{j,m}\right)$

(b) For $i = j$ to N
Compute $L_{i,j} = \frac{1}{L_{j,j}}\left(A_{i,j} - \sum_{m=1}^{j-1} L_{i,m}L_{j,m}\right)$

(c) For $i = j$ to N
Compute $L_{i,j} = \frac{1}{L_{j,j}}\left(A_{i,j} - \sum_{m=1}^{j-1} L_{i,m}L_{j,m}\right)$

(d) For $i = j + 1$to N
Compute $L_{i,j} = \frac{1}{L_{j,j}}\left(A_{i,j} - \sum_{m=1}^{j-1} L_{i,m}^2\right)$

2002

68. If $f(x)$ has an isolated zero of multiplicity 3 at $x = \xi$, and the iteration

$$x_{n+1} = x_n - \frac{3f(x_n)}{f^1(x_n)}, n = 0, 1, 2, \ldots$$

converges to ξ, then the rate of convergence is

(a) linear

(b) faster than linear but slower than quadratic

(c) quadratic

(d) cubic

69. The best possible error estimate in the Gauss-Hermite formula with 3 points, for calculating the integral $\int_{-\infty}^{\infty} x^4 e^{-x^2} dx$ is

(a) 0 (b) 0.30

(c) 0.65 (d) 1.20

70. The fourth divided difference of the polynomial $3x^3 + 11x^2 + 5x + 11$ over the points $x = 0, 1, 4, 6,$ and 7 is

(a) 18 (b) 11

(c) 3 (d) 0

71. The polynomial of least degree inter-polating the data (0, 4), (1, 5), (2, 8), (3, 13) is

(a) 4 (b) 3

(c) 2 (d) 1

72. For the matrix

$$\begin{bmatrix} 0 & 1 & -1 & 1 \\ 1 & 0 & 0 & 2 \\ -1 & 0 & 0 & 0 \\ 1 & 2 & 0 & 0 \end{bmatrix}$$

the bound for the eigenvalues predicted by Gershgorin's theorem is

(a) 3 (b) 1

(c) 2 (d) 4

73. Determine the LU decomposition of the matrix

$$A = \begin{bmatrix} 5 & -2 & -3 \\ 20 & -5 & -13 \\ 35 & -5 & -17 \end{bmatrix}$$

with L having all its diagonal entries1; and hence solve the system $AX = [0\ 2\ 13]^t$.

74. Using the Runge-Kutta method of order 4 and taking the step size $h = 0.1$, determine $y(0.1)$, where $y(x)$ is the solution of

$$\frac{dy}{dx} + 2xy^2 = 0, \; y(0) = 1.$$

2001

75. If Δ and ∇ are the forward and the backward difference operators respec-tively, then $\Delta - \nabla$ is equal to

(a) $-\Delta\,\nabla$ (b) $\Delta\,\nabla$

(c) $\Delta + \nabla$ (d) $\frac{\Delta}{\nabla}$

76. One root of the equation $e^x - 3x^2 = 0$ lies in the interval (3, 4). The least number of iterations of the bisection method so that $|\text{error}| \leq 10^{-3}$ are

(a) 10 (b) 8

(c) 6 (d) 4

77. The least squares approximation of first degree to the function $f(x) = \sin x$ over the interval $\left[-\frac{\pi}{2}, \frac{\pi}{2}\right]$ is

(a) $\frac{24x}{\pi^3}$ (b) $\frac{24x}{\pi^2}$

(c) $\frac{24x}{\pi}$ (d) $24x$

78. The order of the numerical diffrentiation formula

$$f'(x_0) = \frac{1}{12h^2}[-\{f(x_0-2h) + f(x_0+2h)\} + 16\{f(x_0-h) + f(x_0+h)\} - 30f(x_0)]$$ is

(a) 2 (b) 3

(c) 4 (d) 1

79. The method

$$y_n + 1 = y_n + \frac{1}{4}(k_1 + 3k_2), \; n = 0, 1, \ldots$$

$$k_1 = hf(x_n, y_n)$$

$$k_2 = hf\left(x_n + \frac{2h}{3}, y_n + \frac{2}{3}k_1\right)$$

is used to solve the initial value problem

$y' = f(x, y) = -10y, \; y(0) = 1$

The method will produce stable results if the step size h satisfies

(a) $0.2 < h < 0.5$ (b) $0 < h < 0.5$

(c) $0 < h < 1$ (d) $0 < h < 0.2$

80. Find the value of p such that the integration method

$$\int_{x_0}^{x_1} f(x)dx = \frac{h}{2}[f(x_0)+f(x_1)]+ph^3[f''(x_0)+f''(x_1)]$$

where $x_1 = x_0 + h$, provides exact result for highest degree polynomial. Find also the order of the method and the error term.

81. Set up the Gauss-Siedel iteration scheme in matrix form to solve the system of equations

$$\begin{pmatrix} 4 & 1 & 2 \\ 1 & 5 & 1 \\ 2 & 1 & 4 \end{pmatrix} x = \begin{pmatrix} -1 \\ 5 \\ 3 \end{pmatrix}$$

Is this method convergent ? If yes, find its rate of convergence.

2000

82. The smallest value of $x(|x| < 1)$ correct to two decimal places satisfying the equation

$$x - \frac{x^3}{3} + \frac{x^5}{10} - \frac{x^7}{42} + \frac{x^9}{216} - \frac{x^{11}}{1320} + \ldots = 0.4431135 \text{ is}$$

(*a*) 0.58 (*b*) 0.47

(*c*) 0.44 (*d*) 0.88

83. The Jacobi's iteration method for the set of equations

$x_1 + ax_2 = 2,\ 2ax_1 + x_2 = 7,\ \left(a \neq \frac{1}{\sqrt{2}}\right)$ converges for

(*a*) all values of a (*b*) $a = 1$

(*c*) $|a| < \frac{1}{\sqrt{2}}$ (*d*) $\frac{1}{\sqrt{2}} < a < \sqrt{\frac{3}{2}}$

84. The interpolating polynomial of highest degree which corresponds the functional values $f(-1) = 9, f(0) = 5, f(2) = 3, f(5) = 15$, is

(*a*) $x^3 + x^2 + 2x + 5$

(*b*) $x^2 - 3x + 5$

(*c*) $x^4 + 4x^3 + 5x^2 + 5$

(*d*) $x + 5$

85. Evaluate $\int_0^{\frac{\pi}{2}} \sqrt{1-0.162\sin^2\phi}\, d\phi$ by Simpson's one-third rule by taking the step sizes as $\frac{\pi}{12}$.

86. Determine the step-size that can be used to evaluate the integration $\int_1^2 \frac{dx}{x}$ by using Simpson's one-third rule so that the truncation error is less than 5×10^{-4} and hence evaluate the integral.[5]

87. Solve

$$\frac{d^2y}{dx^2} = x\frac{dy}{dx} - y;$$

$y(0) = 3,\ y'(0) = 0,$

to approximate $y(0.1)$ by using fourth order Range-Kutta method. [5]

ANSWERS

1. (*c*)	**2.** (0.25)	**3.** (0.50)	**4.** (*b*)	**5.** (*a*)	**6.** (1)
7. (1.5)	**8.** (4)	**9.** (–2)	**10.** (0.46 to 0.48)	**11.** (6.07 to 6.09)	**12.** (2.81 to 2.83)
13. (*b*)	**14.** (1.01 to 1.03)				

15. (*a*)	**16.** (*b*)	**17.** (*c*)	**18.** (*c*)	**19.** (*c*)	**20.** (*d*)	**21.** (*a*)	**22.** (*c*)	**23.** (*b*)	**24.** (*d*)
25. (*b*)	**26.** (*a*)	**27.** (*c*)	**28.** (*c*)	**29.** (*a*)	**30.** (*d*)	**31.** (*a*)	**32.** (*d*)	**33.** (*c*)	**34.** (*b*)
35. (*c*)	**36.** (*a*)	**37.** (*d*)	**38.** (*a*)	**39.** (*c*)	**40.** (*a*)	**41.** (*a*)	**42.** (*b*)	**43.** (*b*)	**44.** (*a*)
45. (*b*)	**46.** (*a*)	**47.** (*a*)	**48.** (*a*)	**49.** (*d*)	**50.** (*c*)	**51.** (*d*)	**52.** (*a*)	**53.** (*d*)	**54.** (*d*)
55. (*c*)	**56.** (*a*)	**57.** (*b*)	**58.** (*b*)	**58b.** (*c*)	**59.** (*b*)	**60.** (*b*)	**61.** (*c*)	**62.** (*a*)	**63.** (*a*)
64. (*b*)	**65.** (*c*)	**66.** (*b*)	**67.** (*d*)	**68.** (*a*)	**69.** (*c*)	**70.** (*d*)	**71.** (*b*)	**72.** (*c*)	**73.** (*)
74. (*)	**75.** (*b*)	**76.** (*d*)	**77.** (*)	**78.** (*a*)	**79.** (*d*)	**80.** (*)	**81.** (*)	**82.**	(*b*)
83. (*c*)	**84.** (*b*)	**85.** (*)	**86.** (*)	**87.** (*)					

EXPLANATIONS

1. Here {X + Y, Y + Z, X – Z] are not independent because

$\alpha(X + Y) + \beta(Y + Z) + \gamma(X - Z) = 0$

$\Rightarrow \alpha = \beta = \gamma \neq 0$

But {X + Y + Z, X + 2Y – Z, X – 3Z} are independent and span $\mathbb{R}^3$, then {X + Y + Z, X + 2Y – Z, X – 3Z} is a basis of $\mathbb{R}^3$.

2. Error = $|f(x) - p(x)| \leq \frac{1}{8}(x_1 - x_0)^2 M_2$

Where $|f''(x)| \leq M_2 \;\forall\; x[x_0, x_1]$

$\Rightarrow M_2 = 1$

$\therefore$ Error $\leq \frac{1}{8}(1+1).1 = \frac{2}{8} = \frac{1}{4} = 0.25$

Thus, the maximum interpolation error over the interval [-1, 1] is equal to 0.25.

3. $y(t) = t + \int_0^t 4(x-t)y(x)dx$ is a volterra integral equation

Here $f(t) = t, \lambda = 1$

$k(t, x) = 4(x - t)$

and Resolvent kernel R(t, x : 1) is given by

$R(t, x : 1) = 2 \sin 2(x - t)$

Then solution is

$$y(t) = t + \int_0^t 2\sin 2(x-t)x\, dx$$

$$= t - t + \frac{1}{2}\sin 2t$$

$$= \frac{1}{2}\sin 2t$$

$$\int_0^{\pi/2} y(t)dt = \frac{1}{2}\int_0^{\pi/2} \sin 2t\, dt = \frac{1}{2} = 0.5$$

4. $I = \int_0^4 f(x)dx = \int_0^2 xdx + \int_2^4 (4-x)dx = 4$

$$I_2 = \frac{h}{2}[(y_0 + y_2) + 2y_1] = 4$$

$$I_3 = \frac{h}{2}[(y_0 + y_3) + 2(y_1 + y_2)] = 8$$

So, I_2 is exact.

Therefore only (P) is true.

5. Using theorem

Let g be a continuous function on the closed interval [a, b] with g : [a, b] → [a, b] and suppose that g′ is continuous on the open interval (a, b) with $|g'(x)| \leq k < 1$ for all $x \in (a, b)$.

If $g'(p) \neq 0$. Then for any $p_0 \in [a, b]$, the sequence $p_n = p_{n-1}$ converges only linearly to the fixed point P using above statement, Both P and Q are true.

10. The value of α lies between 0.46 to 0.48.

11. Given, $x_0 = 6$

$f(x) = x\log_{10} x - 4.77$

$$f'(x) = x \cdot \frac{1}{x} + \log x = 1 + \log x$$

By Newton Raphson method,

$$x_{n+1} = x_n - \frac{f(x_n)}{f'(x_n)}$$

Now, $$x_1 = 6 - \frac{6\log 6 - 4.77}{1 + \log 6}$$

$$= 6 - \frac{6 \times 0.778 - 4.77}{1 + 0.778}$$

$$= 6 - \frac{4.67 - 4.77}{1.78}$$

$$= 6 + \frac{0.1}{1.78} = 6.056$$

$$x_2 = x_1 - \frac{f(x_1)}{f'(x_1)}$$

$$= 6.056 - \frac{4.74 - 4.77}{1 + 0.782}$$

$$= 6.057 + \frac{0.03}{1.78}$$

$= 6.056 + 0.016$

$= 6.07$

12. Here, $h = 0.25, y_0 = 1,$

$y_1 = 0.9896, y_2 = 0.9589$

$y_3 = 0.9089, y_4 = 0.8415$

Then the required volume of solid generated

$$= \int_0^1 \pi y^2 dx$$

$$= \pi\frac{h}{3}\left[\left(y_0^2 + y_4^2\right) + 4\left(y_1^2 + y_3^2\right) + 2y_2^2\right]$$

$$= \frac{0.25\pi}{3}\left[\left\{1 + (0.8415)^2\right\} + 4\left\{(0.9896)^2 + (0.9089)^2\right\} + 2(0.9589)^2\right]$$

$$= \frac{0.25\pi}{3}(10.77)$$

$= 0.2618 \times 10.77$

$= 2.82$

13. Given, $\{x_1^{(0)} = 3.5, x_2^{(0)} = 2.25, x_3^{(0)} = 1.625\}$

and equations are

$$2x_1 - x_2 = 7$$
$$-x_1 + 2x_2 - x_3 = 1$$
$$-x_2 + 2x_3 = 1$$

We can write these equation as

$$x_1 = \frac{7+x_2}{2}$$

$$x_2 = \frac{1+x_1+x_3}{2}$$

$$x_3 = \frac{1+x_2}{2}$$

Now, $x_1^{(1)} = \frac{7+x_2^{(0)}}{2} = \frac{7+2.25}{2}$

$$= \frac{9.25}{2} = 4.625$$

$$x_2^{(1)} = \frac{1+x_1^{(1)}+x_3}{2}$$

$$= \frac{1+4.625+1.625}{2}$$

$$= \frac{7.25}{2} = 3.625$$

$$x_3^{(1)} = \frac{1+x_2^{(1)}}{2}$$

$$= \frac{1+3.625}{2} = \frac{4.625}{2} = 2.3125$$

Now, $x_1^{(2)} = \frac{7+x_2^{(1)}}{2}$

$$= \frac{7+3.625}{2} = \frac{10.625}{2} = 5.3125$$

$$x_2^{(2)} = \frac{1+x_1^{(2)}+x_3^{(1)}}{2}$$

$$= \frac{1+5.3125+2.3125}{2}$$

$$= \frac{8.625}{2} = 4.3125$$

$$x_3^{(2)} = \frac{1+x_2^{(2)}}{2}$$

$$= \frac{1+4.3125}{2} = 2.6563$$

Hence, $x_1^{(2)} = 5.315, x_2^{(2)}$

$= 4.3125, x_3^{(2)} = 2.6563$

14. Given initial value problem is

$$\frac{du}{dt} = v\,,\ u(0) = \alpha \text{ and } h = 1$$

i.e., $f(t, u) = u$ and $t_0 = 0, \mu_0 = \alpha$

$$k_1 = hf(t_0 u_0) = 1f(n) = 1.\alpha = \alpha$$

$$k_2 = hf\left(t_0 + \frac{1}{2}, u_0 + \frac{1}{2}k_1\right)$$

$$= 1.f\left[\frac{1}{2}, \alpha + \frac{1}{2}\alpha\right] = f\left[\frac{1}{2}, \frac{3}{2}\alpha\right]$$

$\Rightarrow$ $k_2 = \frac{3}{2}\alpha$

$$k_3 = hf\left[t_0 + \frac{1}{2}, \mu_0 + \frac{1}{2}k_2\right]$$

$$= 1f\left[\frac{1}{2}, \alpha + \frac{1}{2}\frac{3}{2}\alpha\right] = f\left[\frac{1}{2}, \frac{7}{2}\alpha\right]$$

$$\Rightarrow k_3 = \frac{7}{2}\alpha$$

Now, $k_4 = f[t_0 + h, u_0 + k_3]$

$$= f\left[1, \alpha + \frac{7}{4}\alpha\right] = f\left[1, \frac{11}{4}\alpha\right]$$

$$\Rightarrow k_4 = \frac{11}{4}\alpha$$

$\therefore$ $u_1 = u_0 + \frac{1}{6}[k_1 + 2k_2 + 2k_3 + k_4]$

$$= \alpha + \frac{1}{6}\left[\alpha + 3\alpha + 7\alpha + \frac{11}{4}\alpha\right]$$

$\Rightarrow$ $u_1 = \alpha + \frac{41}{24}\alpha = \frac{65}{24}\alpha$

By given condition,

$$u_1 = 1$$

$$1 = \frac{65}{24}\alpha$$

$\Rightarrow$ $\alpha = \frac{24}{65} = 0.37$

$\therefore$ $k_4 = \frac{11}{4} \times 0.37 = 1.02$

16. We have

x	y	Δy	$\Delta^2 y$	$\Delta^3 y$	$\Delta^4 y$
1	–1				
		3			
2	2		–8		
		–5		20	
3	–3		12		–48
		7		–28	
4	4		–16		
		–9			
5	–5				

Hence $\Delta y_1 = -5$

$\Delta^2 y_1 = 12$

$\Delta^3 y_1 = -28$

Now $x_0 = 1$ and $h = 1$

$x_1 = x_0 + h = 1 + 1 = 2$

$$y'(x_1) = \frac{1}{h}\left[\Delta y_1 + \frac{1}{2}\Delta^2 y_1 - \frac{1}{4}\Delta^3 y_1\right]$$

$$y'(2) = \frac{1}{1}\left[-5 + \frac{1}{2}\times 12 - \frac{1}{4}(-28)\right]$$

$= -5 + 6 + 7$

$= 8$

17. Let $f(x) = xe^x - 1$

$f(0) = -1 < 0$

and $f(1) = 0$

Hence $x_1 = \dfrac{0+1}{2} = 0.5$

$f(x_1) = 0.5e^{0.5} - 1$

$= -0.175 < 0$

$x_2 = \dfrac{0.5+1}{2}$

$= 0.75$

18. $\dfrac{dy}{dx} = x^2 + y^2$

$x_0 = 0, y_0 = 1, h = 0.1$

$f(x, y) = x^2 + y^2$

$y_1 = y(x_1) = y_0 + hf(x_0, y_0)$

$= 1 + 0.1\,(0^2 + 1^2)$

$= 1 + 0.1 = 1.1$

$y_2 = y(x_2) = y(0.2)$

$= y_1 + hf(x_1, y_1)$

$= 1.1 + 0.1\,[(0.1)^2 + (1.1)^2]$

$= 1.1 + 0.1\,[0.01 + 1.21]$

$= 1.222.$

19. Given system of equation is

$$\begin{bmatrix} 5 & -1 & 1 \\ 2 & 4 & 0 \\ 1 & 1 & 5 \end{bmatrix}\begin{bmatrix} x \\ y \\ z \end{bmatrix} = \begin{bmatrix} 10 \\ 12 \\ -1 \end{bmatrix}$$

$5x - y + z = 10$

$2x + 4y = 12$

$x + y + 5z = -1$

$$x = 2 + \frac{1}{5}y - \frac{1}{5}z$$

$$y = 3 - \frac{1}{2}x$$

$$z = -\frac{1}{5} - \frac{1}{5}x - \frac{1}{5}y$$

Now the initial Guess is

$[x^{(0)}, y^{(0)}\, z^{(0)}]^T = [2.0, 3.0, 0.0]^T$

$$x^{(1)} = 2 + \frac{3}{5} - 0 = 2 + 0.6 = 2.6$$

$$y^{(1)} = 3 - \frac{2}{2} = 3 - 1 = 2.0$$

$$z^{(1)} = -\frac{1}{5} - \frac{2}{5} - \frac{3}{5} = -1.2$$

Now $x^{(2)} = 2 + \dfrac{2}{5} + \dfrac{1.2}{5}$

$= 2.64$

$$y^{(2)} = 3 - \frac{1}{2}\times 2.6$$

$= 1.70$

$$z^{(2)} = -\frac{1}{5} - \frac{1}{5}x - \frac{1}{5}y$$

$$= -\frac{1}{5} - \frac{1}{5}\times 2.6 - \frac{1}{5}\times 2$$

$= -1.12$

$[x^{(2)}\, y^{(2)}\, z^{(2)}]^T = [2.64\ 1.70 - 1.12]^T$

20. Given $x_0 = 1$

and $f(x) = x^2 - 3x + 1 \quad \therefore f(1) = -1$

$f^1(x) = 2x - 3 \quad \therefore f^1(1) = -1$

$$x_1 = x_0 - \frac{f(x_0)}{f^1(x_0)}$$

$$= 1 - \frac{(-1)}{(-1)} = 0$$

21. Given system of equations

$$\begin{bmatrix} 5 & 2 & 1 \\ -2 & 5 & 2 \\ -1 & 2 & 8 \end{bmatrix}\begin{bmatrix} x_1 \\ x_2 \\ x_3 \end{bmatrix} = \begin{bmatrix} 13 \\ -22 \\ 14 \end{bmatrix}$$

$5x_1 + 2x_2 + x_3 = 13$

$-2x_1 + 5x_2 + 2x_3 = -22$

$-x_1 + 2x_2 + 8x_3 = 14$

$$x_1 = \frac{13}{5} - \frac{2}{5}x_2 - \frac{1}{5}x_3$$

$$x_2 = \frac{-22}{5} + \frac{2}{5}x_1 - \frac{2}{5}x_3$$

$$x_3 = \frac{14}{8} + \frac{1}{8}x_1 - \frac{2}{8}x_2$$

Now initial Guess is

$$[x^{(0)}\ y^{(0)}\ z^{(0)}] = [1\ 1\ 1]^T$$

$$x_1^{(1)} = \frac{13}{5} - \frac{2}{5}\times 1 - \frac{1}{5}\times 1$$

$$= 2.0$$

$$x_2^{(1)} = \frac{-22}{5} + \frac{2}{5}\times 1 - \frac{2}{5}\times 1$$

$$= -4.4$$

$$x_3^{(1)} = \frac{14}{8} + \frac{1}{8}\times 1 - \frac{2}{8}\times 1$$

$$= 1.625$$

$$[x_1^{(1)}\ x_2^{(1)}\ x_3^{(1)}]^T = [2, -4.4\ \ 1.625]^T$$

22. Given $\frac{dy}{dx} = (y^2 + x)$

$$x_0 = 0, y_0 = 1 \text{ and } h = 0.1$$

$$\frac{d^2y}{dx^2} = 2y\frac{dy}{dx} + 1$$

$$= 2y(y^2 + x) + 1$$

$$= 2y^3 + 2xy + 1$$

$\therefore$ $y_1 = y(x) = y(0.1)$

$$= y_0 + (0.1 - 0)\left(\frac{dy}{dx}\right)_{y_0, x_0} + \frac{(0.1-0)^2}{2^1}\left(\frac{d^2y}{dx^2}\right)_{x_0, y_0}$$

$$= 1 + (0.1) \times (1^2 + 0) + \frac{(0.1)^2}{2}\left[(2.1)^3 + 2.0 + 1\right]$$

$$= 1 + 0.1 + 0.01 \times \frac{3}{2}$$

$$= 1.115$$

25. If $l_R(x)$, $k = 0, 1, 2, ..n$ denote the lagrange's fundamental polynomial of degree n for the model $x_0, x_1 \dots x_n$ then

$$\sum_{k=0}^{n} l_k(x) = 1$$

and $$l_i(x_i) = \begin{cases} 0 & i \neq \\ 1 & i = j \end{cases}$$

26. $$\int_0^h f(x)dx = h[a_0 f(0) + a_1 f(h)] + h^2 [b_0 f^1(0) + b_1 f^1(h)] \quad \dots (1)$$

for $f(x) = 1$,

$$h = h[a_0 + a_1]$$

$$\Rightarrow \quad a_0 + a_1 = 1 \quad \dots (2)$$

for $f(x) = x$

$$\frac{h^2}{2} = h[a, h] + h^2[b_0 + b_1]$$

$$2a_1 + 2b_0 + 2b_1 = 1 \quad \dots (3)$$

for $f(x) = x^2$,

$$\frac{h^3}{3} = h(a_1 h^2) + h^2(2b_1 h)$$

$$3a_1 + 6b_1 = 1 \quad \dots (4)$$

for $f(x) = x^3$,

$$\frac{h^4}{4} = h[a, h^3] + h^2[3b_1, h]$$

$$4a_1 t\ 12b_1 = 1 \quad \dots (5)$$

by solving (2), (3), (4) & (5) we get

$$a_0 = 1/2, b_0 = 1/12$$

$$a_1 = \frac{1}{2}, b_1 = -1/12$$

27. From above statement

$$a_0 = 1/2$$

$$b_0 = \frac{1}{2}$$

29. We have $\int_{-1}^{1} f(x)dx = \alpha f(-1) + f(\beta)$

for $f(x) = 1, 2 = \alpha + 1 \Rightarrow \alpha = 1$

for $f(x) = x, 0 = \alpha(-1) + \beta$

$\Rightarrow$ $\beta = \alpha = 1$

Hence $\alpha = \beta = 1$

30. Let $f: [0, 4] \to \mathbb{R}$ be a three times continuously differentiable function. Then the value of (1, 2, 3, 4) is $\frac{f''(\xi_1)}{6}$ for some $\xi_1 \in (0, 4)$.

32. If $f: [0, 2] \to \mathbb{R}$ be a twice continuously differentiable function

If $\int_0^2 f(x)dx = 2f(1)$

$$x_0 = 0, x_1 = z,$$

$$h = 2 - 0 = 2$$

$\therefore$ Error constant

$$C = \int_{x_0}^{x_1} x^2 dx - \frac{h}{2}[x_0^2 + x_1^2]$$

$$= \frac{1}{3}[x_1^3 - x_0^3] - \frac{h}{2}[x_0^2 + x_1^2]$$

$$= \frac{1}{3}[2^3 - 0] - \frac{2}{2}[0 + 2^2]$$

$$= \frac{8}{3} - 4 = -\frac{4}{3}$$

Trancation error becomes

$$R_1 = \frac{c}{2} f''(\xi_1)$$

for some $\xi_1 \in (0, 2) = -\frac{4}{6} f''(\xi_1)$

for some $\xi_1 \in (0, 2) \cong \frac{f''(\xi)}{6}$

for some $\xi_1 \in (0, 2)$

33. The displacement OA = s is given by

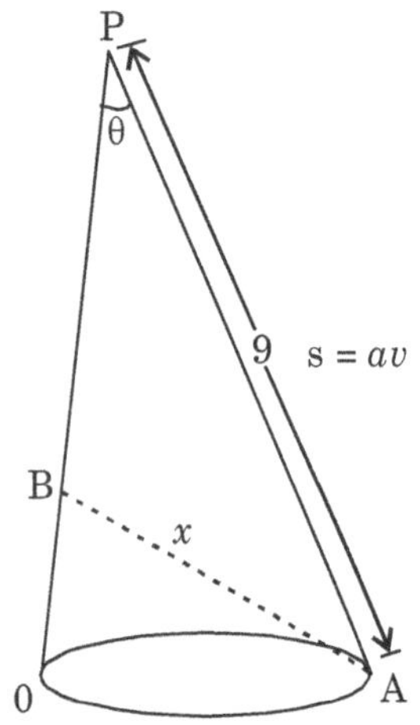

Fig.

Hence $V = \frac{ds}{dt} = \frac{d(av)}{dt} = a\frac{d\theta}{dT}$

$= a\dot{\theta}$

The kinetic energy of the motion is

$$T = \frac{1}{2}MV^2 = \frac{1}{2}m(a\dot{\theta})^2 = \frac{1}{2}ma^2\dot{\theta}^2$$

If the potential energy of the system, when bob is at O is zero, then the potential energy when the bob is at A, is given by

$$V = mg(OB) = mg(OP - OB)$$
$$= mg(a - a\cos\theta)$$
$$= mg\,a(1 - \cos\theta)$$

Hence the lagrangian of the motion is

$$L = T - V$$

$$= \frac{1}{2}ma^2\dot{\theta}^2 - mga(1 - \cos\theta)$$

$$= ma^2\left[\frac{\dot{\theta}^2}{2} - \frac{g}{a}\left(2\sin^2\frac{\theta}{2}\right)\right]$$

$$= ma^2\left[\frac{\dot{\theta}^2}{2} - \frac{2g}{a}\sin^2\frac{\theta}{2}\right]$$

34. Given that $\frac{dy}{dx} = f(x, y), y(x_0) = y_0$ be an initial value problem.

The aim is to compute the value of $y_1 = y(x_1)$ where $x_1 = x_0 + h (h > 0)$. $Ax = x_1$.

If the value of y_1 is equated to the corresponding value of the straight line passing through (x_0, y_0) and having the slope equal to the slope of the curve $y(x)$ at $x = x_0$ then method is called improved Eular's Method.

35. On comparing the given functional with

$$\int_0^1 F(x, y, y^1)dx$$

$$F(x, y, y') = 3y^2 + 2x^3y \qquad \text{... (1)}$$

The Eular's equation is

$$\frac{\partial F}{\partial y} - \frac{d}{dx}\left(\frac{\partial F}{\partial y}\right) = 0 \qquad \text{... (2)}$$

from equation (1) $\frac{\partial F}{\partial y} = 6y, \frac{\partial F}{\partial y'} = 2x^3$

and $\frac{d}{dx}\left(\frac{\partial F}{\partial y'}\right) = 6x^2$

with these values equation (2) gives

$$6y - 6x^2 = 0 \Rightarrow y = x^2 \qquad \text{... (3)}$$

Given $y(\alpha) = 1$

from equation (3) $1 = \alpha^2$

$\alpha = \pm 1$

36. Given

$$x(t) = \sin t + \lambda\int_0^1 [s^2t^3 + e^{s^2} + t^3]x(s)ds$$

$$x(t) = \sin t + \lambda\left[t^3\int_0^1 s^2 \times (s)ds + e^{t^3}\int_0^1 e^{s^2} x(s)ds\right] \qquad \text{... (1)}$$

$$x(t) = \sin t\ \lambda\ (t^3c, + e^{t^3}\ c_2) \qquad \text{... (2)}$$

where $c_1 = \int_0^1 s^2 x(s)ds \qquad \text{... (3)}$

$c_2 = \int_0^1 e^{s^2} x(s)ds \qquad \text{... (4)}$

form equation (2) we have

$$x(s) = \sin s + \lambda\left(s^3c_1 + e^{s^3}c_2\right) \qquad \text{... (5)}$$

using equation (5) and (3) reduces to

$$c_1 = \int_0^1 s^2\left[\sin s + \lambda\left(s^3c_1 + e^{s^3}(2)\right)\right]ds$$

$$c_1 = \int_0^1 s^2 \sin s ds + \lambda c_1 \int_0^1 s^5 ds + \lambda c_z \int_0^1 s^2 e^{s^3} ds$$

$$c_1 = \left[-s^2 \cos s + 2s \sin s - 2\cos s\right]_0^1$$

$$+\lambda c_1 \left[\frac{s^6}{6}\right]_0^1 + \frac{\lambda c_2}{3}\left[e^{s^3}\right]_0^1$$

$$c_1 = [-\cos 1 + 2\sin 1 - 2\cos 1] + \frac{\lambda}{6}c_1 + \frac{\lambda(e-1)}{3}c_2$$

$$\left(1 - \frac{\lambda}{6}\right)c_1 + \frac{(1-e)\lambda}{3}c_2 = 2\sin 1 - 3\cos 1$$

using equation (5) and (4) reduces to

$$c_2 = \int_0^1 e^{s^2}\left[\sin s + \lambda(s^3 c_1 + e^{s^3} c_2)\right]ds$$

$$= \int_0^1 e^{s^2} \sin ds + \lambda c_1 \int_0^1 e^{s^2} s^3 ds + \lambda c_2 \int e^{s^3 + s^2} ds$$

39. Given

$$\int_{-1}^{1} f(x)dx = -\frac{3}{2}f\left(-\frac{1}{3}\right) + kf\left(\frac{1}{3}\right) + \frac{1}{2}f(1)$$

we obtain

$$\text{for } f(x) = 1,\ 2 = \frac{3}{2} \times 1 + k \times 1 + \frac{1}{2} \times 1$$

$$g = \frac{3}{2} + k + \frac{1}{2}$$

$$k = 0$$

40. Given that $\begin{bmatrix} 1 & 4 & 3 \\ 2 & 7 & 9 \\ 5 & 8 & 9 \end{bmatrix}$

$$= \begin{bmatrix} l_{11} & 0 & 0 \\ l_{21} & l_{22} & 0 \\ l_{31} & l_{32} & -53 \end{bmatrix}\begin{bmatrix} 1 & \mu_{12} & \mu_{13} \\ 0 & 1 & \mu_{23} \\ 0 & 0 & 1 \end{bmatrix}$$

$$= \begin{bmatrix} l_{11} & l_{11}\mu_{12} & l_{11}\mu_{13} \\ l_{21} & l_{21}\mu_{12} + l_{22} & l_{21}\mu_{13} + l_{22}\mu_{23} \\ l_{31} & l_{31}\mu_{12} + \mu_{32} & l_{31}\mu_{13} + l_{32}\mu_{23} - 53 \end{bmatrix}$$

$l_{11} = 1,\ l_{21} = 2,\ l_{31} = 5$

$$l_{11}\mu_{12} = 4 \Rightarrow \mu_{12} = \frac{4}{1} = 4$$

$$l_{11}\mu_{13} = 3 \Rightarrow \mu_{13} = \frac{3}{1} = 3$$

$$l_2 u_{12} + l_{22} = 7 \Rightarrow l_{22} = 7 - 8 = -1$$

$$l_{21}\mu_{13} + l_{22} = \mu_{23} = 9 \Rightarrow \mu_{23} = \frac{9-6}{-1} = -3$$

$$l_{31}\mu_{12} + l_{32} = 8 \Rightarrow l_{32} = 8 - 20 = -12$$

$$l_{31}\mu_{13} + l_{32}\mu_{23} - 53 = a$$

$$5 \times 3 + (-12) \times (-3) - 53 = 9$$

$$a = -2$$

44. We have

x	$f(x)$	D $f(x)$	D² $f(x)$	D³ $f(x)$
– 2	– 58			
– 1	– 21	37	28	18
– 1	– 21	9		
0	– 12	– 1	– 10	18
1	– 13	7	8	18
2	– 6	33	26	
3	27			

since $D^3 f(x)$ is constant. Hence, polynomial must be of degree 3.

45. Let x_n converges to x, then

$$x_n + 1 = \sqrt{3 + 2x_n}$$

$$\Rightarrow \quad x = \sqrt{3 + 2x}$$

$$\Rightarrow \quad x^2 - 2x - 3 = 0$$

$$x = 3, -2$$

Hence x_n converges to $x_0 = 3$.

Alternative method

we have $\quad x_n + 1 = \sqrt{3 + 2x_n}$

then $\quad \phi(x) = \sqrt{3 + 2x_n}$

$$\Rightarrow \quad \phi'(x) = \frac{1}{\sqrt{3 + 2x_n}}$$

$$|\phi'(x)| = \left|\frac{1}{\sqrt{3 + 2x_n}}\right| < 1$$

let $x_0 = 2.9$

$$x_1 = \sqrt{3 + 2x_0} = 2.9664$$

$$x_2 = \sqrt{3 + 2x_1} = 2.9888$$

$$x_3 = \sqrt{3 + 2x_2} = 2.9962$$

$$x_4 = \sqrt{3 + 2x_3} = 2.9988$$

$$x_5 = \sqrt{3 + 2x_4} = 2.9996$$

$$x_6 = \sqrt{3 + 2x_5} = 2.9999$$

Therefore, $x = 3$

46. Given quadrature formula is

$$\int_{-1}^{+1} |x| f(x)dx \cong \frac{1}{2}[f(x_0) + f(x_1)]$$

$$\Rightarrow \quad \int_{-1}^{0} xf(x)dx + \int_{0}^{1} xf(x)dx$$

$$\cong \frac{1}{2}[f(x_0) + f(x_1)]$$

Taking $f(x) = 1$

$$\frac{1}{2}+\frac{1}{2} \cong \frac{1}{2}[1+1] \Rightarrow 1 \cong 1$$

Taking $f(x) = x$

$$-\frac{1}{3}+\frac{1}{3} \cong \frac{1}{2}[x_0 + x_1]$$

$$\therefore \quad = \frac{1}{2}[-1+1]$$

$$\Rightarrow \quad 0 \cong 0$$

Taking $f(x) = x^2$

$$\frac{1}{4}+\frac{1}{4} \cong \frac{1}{2}\left[x_0^2 + x_1^2\right]$$

$$= \frac{1}{2}[1+1] = 1$$

$\Rightarrow \frac{1}{2} \cong 1$ which is contradiction

$\therefore$ Highest degree is 1.

47. Given that the particle of mass m slides down without friction along a curve

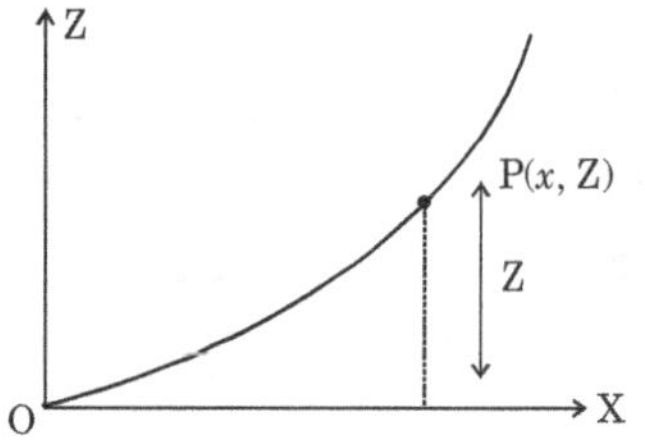

Fig.

$$z = 1+\frac{x^2}{2}$$

Let $p(x, y)$ be the position of the particle at any instant, then, kinetic energy of the particle is

$$T = \frac{1}{2}m(\dot{x}^2 + \dot{z}^2)$$

$$= \frac{1}{2}m(\dot{x}^2 + x^2\dot{x}_2) \qquad (\because \dot{z} = x\dot{x})$$

$$= \frac{1}{2}m\dot{x}^2(1+x^2)$$

and the potential energy of the particle is

$$v = mgz = mg\left(1+\frac{x^2}{2}\right)$$

Hence the Lagrangian of the motion is

$$L = T - V$$

$$= \frac{1}{2}m\dot{x}^2(1+x^2) - mg\left(1+\frac{x^2}{2}\right)$$

48. The Lagranges equation of motion is

$$\frac{d}{dt}\left(\frac{\partial L}{\partial \dot{x}}\right) - \frac{\partial L}{\partial x} = 0$$

$$\Rightarrow \frac{d}{dt}[m\dot{x}(1+x^2)] - m\dot{x}^2 x - mgx = 0$$

$$\Rightarrow \ddot{x}(1+x^2) + 2\dot{x}^2 x - \dot{x}^2 - x - gx = 0$$

$$\Rightarrow \ddot{x}(1+x^2) = -x[\dot{x}^2 + g]$$

51. Given initial value problem is

$$dy/dx = f[x, y(x)],\ y(x_0) = y_0$$

Then $\quad y_1 = y_0 + \frac{1}{2}(k_1 + k_2),$

where $\quad k_1 = hf(x_0, y_0)$

$\quad k_2 = hf(x_0 + h, y_0 + k_1)$

Hence by comparison

$$w = 1//6$$

52.

$$x_{k+1} = \frac{1}{2}\left[x_k + \frac{a}{x_k^{n-1}}\right]$$

$$x_{1+1} = \frac{1}{2}\left[x_1 + \frac{a}{x_1^{n-1}}\right]$$

$$x_{2+1} = \frac{1}{2}\left[x_2 + \frac{a}{x_2^{n-1}}\right]$$

$$x_{3+1} = \frac{1}{2}\left[x_3 + \frac{a}{x_3^{n-1}}\right]$$

But for $\quad n = 1, x_{k+1} = \frac{1}{2}[x_k + a]$

Hence $n = 1$, this fails to converge.

55.

$$M = \begin{bmatrix} 2 & \alpha & -1 \\ \alpha & 2 & 1 \\ -1 & 1 & 4 \end{bmatrix}$$

L is a lower triangular matrix

Then $\quad L = \begin{bmatrix} 2 & 0 & 0 \\ \alpha & 2 & 0 \\ -1 & 1 & 4 \end{bmatrix},$

and $\quad L^T = \begin{bmatrix} 2 & \alpha & -1 \\ 0 & 2 & 1 \\ 0 & 0 & 4 \end{bmatrix}$

$$\Rightarrow \quad LL^T = \begin{bmatrix} 2 & 0 & 0 \\ \alpha & 2 & 0 \\ -1 & 1 & 4 \end{bmatrix} \begin{bmatrix} 2 & \alpha & -1 \\ 0 & 2 & 1 \\ 0 & 0 & 4 \end{bmatrix}$$

$$= \begin{bmatrix} 4 & 2\alpha & -2 \\ 2\alpha & \alpha^2+4 & -\alpha+2 \\ -2 & -\alpha+2 & 18 \end{bmatrix}$$

But, by a unique cholesky decomposition of the form

$M = LL^T$

Then by this relation, the range of values of α is $-2 < \alpha < 3/2$.

56. $$\frac{dy}{dx} = f(x)$$

step size $= h$, $y(0) = 0$, $x_0 = 0$

By Rungee-Kutta of the fourth order

$$K_1 = h\, f(x_0, h_0) = h\, [f(x_0)] = h\, f(0)$$

$$K_2 = hf\left(x_0 + \frac{1}{2}h, y_0 + \frac{1}{2}K_1\right)$$

$$= h\, f\left(x_0 + \frac{1}{2}h\right)$$

$$= h\, f\left(\frac{h}{2}\right)$$

$$K_3 = hf\left(x_0 + \frac{1}{2}h, y_0 + \frac{1}{2}K_2\right)$$

$$= h\, f\left(\frac{h}{2}\right)$$

$$K_4 = hf\,(x_0 + h, y_0 + K_3) = hf(h)$$

Hence by the fourth order Runge-Kutta formulae

The solution at $x = h$

$$y_1 = y_0 + \frac{1}{6}(K_1 + 2K_2 + 2K_3 + K_4)$$

$$\Rightarrow \quad y(h) = 0 + \frac{1}{6}\left(hf(0) + 2hf\left(\frac{h}{2}\right) + 2hf\left(\frac{h}{2}\right) + hf(h)\right)$$

$$\Rightarrow \quad y(h)\, \frac{h}{6} = [f(0) + 4f\left(\frac{h}{2}\right) + f(h)]$$

57. Given, Quadrature formula

$$\int_0^1 f(x)\, dx = \alpha\, f(0) + \beta\, f(x_1)$$

This is exact for polynomials of degree as high as possible, only for

$$\alpha = \frac{3}{4}, \beta = \frac{1}{4}, x_1 = \frac{2}{3}$$

60. we have $f(x) = x^2 - a$

Now by Newton-Raphson Method

$$x_n = x_{n-1} - \frac{f(x)}{f'(x)}$$

$$x_{n-1} = \frac{x^2_{n-1} - a}{2x_{n-a}} \quad \Rightarrow \quad \frac{x^2_{n-1} + a}{2x_{n-1}}$$

$$\Rightarrow \quad x_n = \frac{x^2_{n-1} + a}{2x_{n-1}}$$

$$\Rightarrow \quad x_1 = \frac{x_0^2 + a}{2x_0}$$

$$x_2 = \frac{x_1^2 + a}{2x_1}$$

$$x_3 = \frac{x_2^2 + a}{2x_2}$$

$$x_4 = \frac{x_3^2 + a}{2x_3} \quad +$$

$\vdots \quad \vdots \qquad \vdots$

from above it is clear that

$x_0 < x_1 < x_2 < x_3 < x_4 < \ldots$

Hence the sequence x_n, $n \geq 1$ is an increasing sequence.

61. Given that

$$dy \,|\, dx = 2x, \text{ with } y(0) = 0$$

$$\Rightarrow \quad f(x, y) = 2x, x_0 = 0\; y_0 = 0$$

Now taking $h = 1$

$\therefore \quad y(1) = y_1 = y_0 + h\, f(x_0, y_0)$

$= 0 + 1 \times 2 \times 2 = 0 = 0.1$

$y(2) = y_2 = y_1 + h\, f(x_1, y_1)$

$= 0 + 1 \times 2 \times 1 = 2 = 1.2$

$y(3) = y_3 = y_2 + h\, f(x_2, y_2)$

$= 2 + 1 \times 2 \times 2 = 6 = 2.3$

$\therefore \quad y(4) = y_4 = y_3 + h\, f(x_3, y_3)$

$= 6 + 1 \times 2 \times 3 = 12 = 3.4$

$\therefore \quad y(5) = y_5 = y_4 + h\, f(x_4, y_4)$

$= 12 + 1 \times 2 \times 4 = 20 = 4.5$

$\vdots \quad \vdots \quad \vdots \quad \vdots \quad \vdots$

Hence, from above it is clear that

$$y_{(n)} = y_n = x_{n-1}\, x_n$$

62. Required : $x_n - x_{n-1} \leq \in$

$$x_n = \frac{x_{n-1} + x_{n-2}}{2}$$

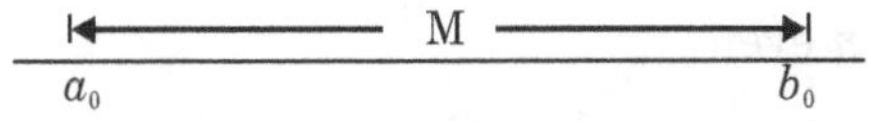

$$x_0 = \frac{a_0 + b_0}{2}$$

or $\dfrac{x_{n-1} + x_{n-2}}{2} - x_{n-1} \leq \in$

or $\dfrac{x_{n-2} + x_{n-1}}{2} \leq \in$

or $-\left(\dfrac{x_{n-1} - x_{n-2}}{2}\right) \leq \in$

or $\dfrac{x_{n-2} - \left(\dfrac{x_{n-2} + x_{n-3}}{2}\right)}{2} \leq \in$

or $\dfrac{x_{n-2} - x_{n-3}}{2^2} \leq \in$

$\vdots \qquad \vdots$

or $(-1)^{n-1}\left(\dfrac{x_{n-(n-1)} - x_{n-n}}{2^{n-1}}\right) \leq \in$

or $(-1)^{n-1}\dfrac{(x_1 - x_0)}{2^{n-1}} \leq \in$

Now $x_1 = \dfrac{x_0 + a_0}{2}$

$$x_1 - x_0 = \frac{x_0 + a_0}{2} - x_0$$

$$= \frac{a_0 - x_0}{2}$$

$$= \frac{a_0 - \left(\dfrac{a_0 + b_0}{2}\right)}{2}$$

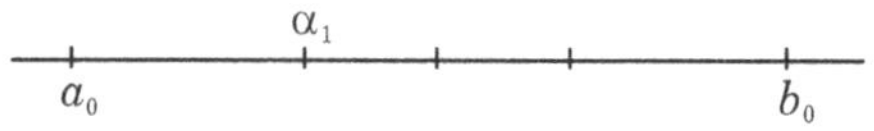

$$= \frac{a_0 - b_0}{2^2}$$

$$= \frac{-M}{2^2}$$

or $(-1)^{n-1}\left(-\dfrac{M}{2^2}\right) \leq \in$

or $\dfrac{(-1)^n M}{2^{n+1}} \leq \in$

$\dfrac{(-1)^n}{2^n} \cdot \dfrac{M}{2} \leq \in$

or $\left(\dfrac{-1}{2}\right)^n \leq \dfrac{2 \in}{M}$

For n even

or $\dfrac{1}{2^n} \leq \dfrac{2 \in}{M}$

or $2^n \geq \dfrac{M}{2 \in}$

or $n \ln^2 \geq \ln\left(\dfrac{M}{2 \in}\right)$

or $n \ln^2 \geq -\ln\left(\dfrac{2 \in}{M}\right)$

or $n \geq \dfrac{-\ln^2 - \ln\left(\dfrac{\in}{M}\right)}{\ln_2}$

or $\dfrac{x_0 + b_0}{2}$

$$x_1 - x_0 = \frac{x_0 + b_0}{2} - x_0$$

$$= \frac{b_0 - x_0}{2}$$

$$= \frac{b_0 - \left(\dfrac{a_0 + b_0}{2}\right)}{2}$$

$$= \frac{b_0 - a_0}{2^2}$$

$$= \frac{M}{2^2}$$

or $\dfrac{(-1)^{n-1}}{2^{n-1}} \dfrac{M}{2^2} \leq \in$

or $(-1)^{n-1}\dfrac{M}{2^{n+1}} \leq \in$

or $\dfrac{(-1)^{n-1}}{2^{n-1}} \dfrac{M}{2^2} \leq \in$

or $\dfrac{(-1)^{n-1}}{2^{n-1}} \leq \dfrac{2^2 \in}{M}$

For odd n

$$\frac{1}{2^{n-1}} \leq \frac{2^2 \in}{M}$$

or $2^{n+1} \geq \dfrac{M}{\in}$

or $(n + 1) \geq \dfrac{-\ln\left(\dfrac{\in}{M}\right)}{\ln 2}$

or $n \geq -1 - \dfrac{\ln \in / M}{\ln 2}$

63. Let $z = \frac{1}{x+y}$; take $h = k = 0.2$

$x \backslash y$	$y_0 = 1$	$y_1 = 1.2$	$y_2 = 1.4$	$y_3 = 1.6$	$y_4 = 1.8$	$y_5 = 2.0$	A_x
1	$\frac{1}{2}$	$\frac{1}{2.2}$	$\frac{1}{2.4}$	$\frac{1}{2.6}$	$\frac{1}{2.8}$	$\frac{1}{3}$	0.4059
1.2	$\frac{1}{2.2}$	$\frac{1}{2.4}$	$\frac{1}{2.6}$	$\frac{1}{2.8}$	$\frac{1}{3}$	$\frac{1}{3.2}$	0.3751
1.4	$\frac{1}{2.4}$	$\frac{1}{2.6}$	$\frac{1}{2.8}$	$\frac{1}{3}$	$\frac{1}{3.2}$	$\frac{1}{3.4}$	0.3486
1.6	$\frac{1}{2.6}$	$\frac{1}{2.8}$	$\frac{1}{3}$	$\frac{1}{3.2}$	$\frac{1}{3.4}$	$\frac{1}{3.6}$	0.3257
1.8	$\frac{1}{2.8}$	$\frac{1}{3}$	$\frac{1}{3.2}$	$\frac{1}{3.4}$	$\frac{1}{3.6}$	$\frac{1}{3.8}$	03056
2.0	$\frac{1}{3}$	$\frac{1}{3.2}$	$\frac{1}{3.4}$	$\frac{1}{3.6}$	$\frac{1}{3.8}$	$\frac{1}{4}$	0.2878

Applying trapezoidal rule to each row for $h = 0.2$ we find $A_1, A_{1.2}, A_{1.4}, A_{1.6}, A_{1.8}$ and A_2 as given in the above table.

Then, again by Trapezoidal rule, we get

$$\int_1^2\int_1^2 \frac{dxdy}{x+y} = 0.2\ [\frac{1}{2}\ (0.4059 + .2878) + (0.3751 + 0.3486 + 0.3257 + 0.3056)]$$

$$= 0.3404 \approx \frac{17}{18}$$

66. $\int_0^h f(x)dx = \left\{\alpha f(0) + \beta + \left(\frac{3h}{4}\right) + \gamma f(h)\right\}h$

Choosing $f(x) = 1, x, x^2$, etc. we get

When $f(x) = 1$

$$h = h[\alpha + \beta + \gamma]$$

$\therefore \quad \alpha + \beta + \gamma = 1$

When $f(x) = x$

$$\frac{h^2}{2} = h\left[0 + \beta\frac{3h}{4} + \gamma h\right]$$

When $f(x) = x^2$

$$\frac{h^2}{3} = h\left[0 + \beta\frac{9h^2}{16} + \gamma h^2\right]$$

Solving, we get

$$\alpha = \frac{1}{2},$$

$$\beta = -\frac{1}{4},$$

and $\gamma = \frac{3}{4}$

68. Rate of convergence of Newton's formula when there exists multiple roots :

we have $x_{n+1} = x_n - \frac{f(x_n)}{f'(x_n)}$

i.e., $a + \epsilon_{n+1} = a + \epsilon_n - \frac{f(a+\epsilon_n)}{f'(a+\epsilon_n)}$

$$= \epsilon_n \frac{f(a) + \epsilon_n f'(a) + \frac{1}{2}\epsilon_n^2 f''(a) + \ldots}{f'(a) + \epsilon_n f''(a) + \frac{1}{2}\epsilon_n^2 f''(a) + \ldots}$$

$$= \epsilon_n - \frac{\frac{1}{2}\epsilon_n^2 f''(a) + \ldots}{\epsilon_n . f''(a) + \ldots}$$

$[\because f(a) = 0, f'(a) = 0]$

$$= \epsilon_n - \epsilon_n \frac{\frac{1}{2} f''(a) + \ldots}{f''(a) + \ldots}$$

$$= \frac{1}{2}\epsilon_n$$

If $x = a$ is the root of multiplicity $m > 1$, then the speed of convergence is given by

$$\epsilon_{n+1} \approx \frac{m-1}{m}\epsilon_n$$

Here $m = 3$

$\therefore \quad \epsilon_{n+1} \approx \frac{2}{3}\epsilon_n$, which is also linear.

70. (None of these)

$$f(x) = 3x^3 + 11x^2 + 5x + 11$$

Newton's Divided difference table of fourth order : -

x	$f(x)$	$\Delta f(x)$	$\Delta^2 f(x)$	$\Delta^3 f(x)$	$\Delta^4 f(x)$
0	11	$\frac{30-11}{1-0} = 9$	$\frac{123-9}{4-0} = 28.5$		
1	30	$\frac{399-30}{4-1} = 123$	$\frac{343-123}{6-1} = 44$	$\frac{44-28.5}{6-0} = 2.583$	$\frac{3-2.583}{7} = 0.059$
4	399	$\frac{1085-399}{6-4} = 343$	$\frac{529-343}{7-4} = 62$	$\frac{62-44}{7-1} = 3$	
6	1085	$\frac{1614-1885}{7-6} = 529$			
7	1614				

Fourth divided difference = **0.059**

80. We have

$$\int_{x_0}^{x_1} f(x)dx = \int_{x_0}^{x_0+h} f(x)dx$$

$$= \frac{h}{2}[f(x_0) + f(x_1)] + ph^3 [f''(x_0) + f''(x_1)]$$

$$= \frac{h}{2}[f(x_0) + f(x_1)] + ph^3 f''(x_0) + ph^3 f''(x_1)$$

$$= \frac{h}{2}[f(x_0) + f(x_0 + h)] + ph^3 f''(x_0) + ph^3 f''(x_0 + h)$$

$$= \frac{h}{2}[f(x_0) + f(x_0) + \Delta f(x_0)] + ph\, \Delta^2 f(x_0)$$

$$+ ph\left[\Delta^2 f(x_0) - \frac{2}{24}\Delta^4 f(x_0) + \ldots\right]$$

$$= \frac{h}{2}[f(x_0) + \Delta f(x_0) + 2\,ph\, \Delta^2 f(x_0) - \frac{ph}{12}\Delta^4 f(x_0) + \quad \ldots(i)$$

But we know that by Newton's interpolation formula

$$\int_{x_0}^{x_0+h} f(x)dx$$

$$= h\left[f(x_0) + \frac{1}{2}\Delta f(x_0) - \frac{1}{12}\Delta^2 f(x_0) + \ldots\right] \ldots(ii)$$

Since integration method provides exact result for highest degree polynomial. So equating equations (*i*) and (*ii*), we get

$$2P = -\frac{1}{12}$$

or $$P = -\frac{1}{24}$$

81. The given system of equations are

$$4x + y + 2z = -1$$
$$x + 5y + z = 5$$
$$2x + y + 4z = 3$$

i.e. $$x = \frac{1}{4}[-1 - y - 2z]$$

$$y = \frac{1}{5}[5 - z - x]$$

$$z = \frac{1}{4}[3 - 2x - y]$$

We start the iteration by putting $y = 0$, $z = 0$.

First approximation of x

$$= x^{(1)} = -\frac{1}{4} = -0.25$$

Substitute $x = -0.25$ and $z = 0$ in second equation, we get First approximation of y

$$= y^{(1)} = \frac{1}{5}[5 - 0 + 0.25]$$

$$= \frac{1}{5} \times 5.25$$

$$= 1.05$$

Substituting $x = 0.25$

and $y = 1.05$in third equation.

First approximation of z

$$= z^{(1)} = \frac{1}{4}[3 + 0.5 - 1.05]$$

$$= \frac{1}{4}[3.50 - 1.05]$$

$$= \frac{2.45}{4}$$

$$= 0.6125.$$

Second approximation of x

$$x^{(2)} = \frac{1}{4}[-1 - 1.05 - 2 \times 0.6125]$$

$$= -\frac{3.275}{4} = -0.81875$$

Second approximation of y

$$y^{(2)} = \frac{1}{5}[5 - 0.6125 + 0.81875]$$

$$= 1.04125$$

Second approximation of z

$$z^{(2)} = \frac{1}{4}[3 + 2 \times 0.81875 - 1.04125]$$

$$= 0.8990625$$

Here – 0.81875, 1.04125, 0.8990625 are sufficiently close to taken as a solution of given system.

85. Here, $\quad I = \int_0^{\pi/2} \sqrt{1 - 0.162\sin^2\phi}\, d\phi$

$$= \int_0^{\pi/2} \sqrt{1 - 0.081(1 - \cos 2\phi)}d\phi$$

$$= \int_0^{\pi/2} \sqrt{1 - 0.081 + 0.081\cos 2\phi}d\phi$$

$$= \int_0^{\pi/2} \sqrt{0.919 + 0.081\cos 2\phi}d\phi$$

$$= \frac{h}{3}[(y_0 + y_6) + 4(y_1 + y_3 + y_5) + 2(y_2 + y_4)]$$

where $\quad h = \frac{\pi}{12}$

and $\quad y_0 = 1$

$$y_1 = \sqrt{0.919 + 0.081\cos 30°} = 0.9945$$

$$y_2 = \sqrt{0.919 + 0.081\cos 60°} = 0.9795$$

$$y_3 = \sqrt{0.919 + 0.081\cos 90°} = 0.9586$$

$$y_4 = \sqrt{0.919 + 0.081\cos 120°} = 0.9372$$

$$y_5 = \sqrt{0.919 + 0.081\cos 150°} = 0.9213$$

$$y_6 = \sqrt{0.919 + 0.081\cos 180°} = 0.9154$$

$\therefore$

$$I = \frac{\pi}{36}[17.2464]$$

$$= \mathbf{1.5056}$$

86. By simpson's $\frac{1}{3}$ rule.

$$\int_{x_0}^{x_0+nh} f(x)dx = \frac{h}{3}[f(x_0) + f(x_0 + nh) + 4\{f(x_0 + h) + f(x_0 + 3h) + ...\} + 2\{f(x_0 + 2h) + f(x_0 + 4h) + ...\} + ...]$$

Putting $\quad x_0 = 1, n = 2n, 1 + 2nh = 2$

So, $\quad h = \frac{2-1}{2n} = \frac{1}{2n}$

Putting $n = 1$, i.e., we divide whole range into two equal parts by three points x_0, x_1, x_2.

Thus $\quad \int_1^2 \frac{dx}{x} = \int_{x_0}^{x_2} f(x)dx$ where

$$f(x) = \frac{1}{x},$$

$$x_0 = 1, x_2 = 2.$$

$$= \frac{b-a}{2n}[f(x_0) + 4f(x_1) + f(x_2)]$$

$$= \frac{2-1}{6}\left[\frac{1}{1} + 4.\frac{1}{3/2} + \frac{1}{2}\right]$$

$$= 0.69444$$

Actual value of

$$\int_1^2 \frac{dx}{x} = [\log_e x]_1^2$$

$$= \log_e 2$$

$$= 0.69315$$

$\therefore \quad$ error $= 0.69315 - 0.69444$

$$= 0.000129$$

$$= 1.29 \times 10^{-4} < 5 \times 10^{-4}.$$

Hence the step size is

$$h = \frac{2-1}{2} = \frac{1}{2}$$

87. Substituting $\frac{dy}{dx} = z = f(x, y, z)$, then equation becomes

$$\frac{d^2y}{dx^2} = xz - y$$

$$= g(x, y, z)$$

The initial conditions are

$$x = 0, y = 3, z = 0$$

also $h = 0.1$

So, $k_1 = hf(x, y, z)$

$= hz = 0.1 \times 0 = 0$

$$k_2 = hf\left(x+\frac{h}{2}, y+\frac{k_1}{2}, z+\frac{m_1}{2}\right)$$

$$= h\left(z+\frac{m_1}{2}\right)$$

$= 0.1(0 - 0.15)$

$= - 0.015$

$$k_3 = hf\left(x+\frac{h}{2}, y+\frac{k_2}{2}, z+\frac{m_2}{2}\right)$$

$$= h\left(z+\frac{m_2}{2}\right)$$

$$= 0.1\left(-\frac{0.30075}{2}\right)$$

$= - 0.0150375$

$k_4 = hf(x + h, y + k_3, z + m_3)$

$= h(z + m_3)$

$= 0.1 (- 0.298498125)$

$= - 0.0298498125$

$m_1 = hg(x, y, z)$

$= h(xz - y)$

$= 0.1(0 - 3)$

$= - 0.3$

$$m_2 = hg\left(x+\frac{h}{2}, y+\frac{k_1}{2}, z+\frac{m_1}{2}\right)$$

$$= h\left[\left(x+\frac{h}{2}\right)\left(z+\frac{m_1}{2}\right)-\left(y+\frac{k_1}{2}\right)\right]$$

$= 0.1 [(0.05) (- 0.15) - 3]$

$= - 0.30075$

$$m_3 = hg\left(x+\frac{h}{2}, y+\frac{k_2}{2}, z+\frac{m_2}{2}\right)$$

$$= h\left[\left(x+\frac{h}{2}\right)\left(z+\frac{m_2}{2}\right)-\left(y+\frac{k_2}{2}\right)\right]$$

$$= (0.1)\left[\left(\frac{0.1}{2}\right)\left(\frac{-0.30075}{2}\right)-(2.9925)\right]$$

$= - 0.298498125$

$m_4 = hg(x + h, y + k_3, z + m_3)$

$= h[(x + h) (z + m_3) - (y + k_3)]$

$= 0.1[(0.1) (- 0.298498125) - (2.9849625)]$

$= - 0.3014812312.$

This gives at $x = 0.1$

$$y(0.1) = y(0) + \frac{1}{6}[k_1 + 2k_2 + 2k_3 + k]$$

$$= 3 + \frac{1}{6}[0 + 2 \times (- 0.015)$$

$$+ 2 \times (- 0.0150375) + (- 0.0298498125)]$$

$$= 3 + \frac{1}{6}[- 0.0075 - 0.030075$$

$$- 0.029849812]$$

$= 3 + (- 0.011237468)$

$= 2.988762532.$

$$z(0.1) = z(0) + \frac{1}{6}[m_1 + 2m_2 + 2m_3 + m_4]$$

$$= 0 + \frac{1}{6}[- 0.3 + 2 \times (- 0.30075) +$$

$$2(- 0.298498125) - 0.3014812312]$$

$$= \frac{1}{6}[- 0.3 - 0.6015 - 0.59699625$$

$$- 0.3014812312]$$

$= - 0.300162913.$

8

CHAPTER

Partial Differential Equations

2016

1. Let γ be the curve which passes through (0,1) and intersects each curve of the family $y = c\,x^2$ orthogonally. Then γ also passes through the point

(a) $(\sqrt{2}, 0)$ (b) $(0, \sqrt{2})$

(c) (1, 1) (d) (–1, 1)

2. Let

$$S(x) = a_0 + \sum_{n=1}^{\infty}(a_n \cos(nx) + b_n \sin(nx))$$

be the Fourier series of the 2π periodic function defined by $f(x) = x^2 + 4\sin(x)\cos(x), -\pi \le x \le \pi$. Then

$$\left|\sum_{n=0}^{\infty} a_n - \sum_{n=1}^{\infty} b_n\right|$$

is equal to __________.

3. The number of roots of the equation $x^2 - \cos(x) = 0$ in the interval $\left[-\frac{\pi}{2}, \frac{\pi}{2}\right]$ is equal to ___.

2015

4. Let $\Omega = \{(x, y) \in \mathbb{R}^2 \mid x^2 + y^2 < 1\}$ be the open unit disc in R^2 with boundary $\partial\Omega$. If $u(x, y)$ is the solution of the Dirichlet problem

$$u_{xx} + u_{yy} = 0 \quad \text{in } \Omega$$
$$u(x, y) = 1 - 2y^2 \quad \text{on } \partial\Omega,$$

then $u\left(\frac{1}{2}, 0\right)$ is equal to

(a) – 1 (b) $\frac{-1}{4}$

(c) $\frac{1}{4}$ (d) 1

5. Let $u(x, t), x \in \mathbb{R}, t \ge 0$, be the solution of the initial value problem

$$u_{\tau\tau} = u_{xx}$$
$$u(x, 0) = x$$
$$u_{\tau}(x, 0) = 1$$

Then $u(2, 2)$ is equal to __________.

6. Let $u(x, y) = 2f(y)\cos(x - 2y), (x, y) \in \mathbb{R}^2$, be a solution of the initial value problem

$$2u_x + u_y = u$$
$$u(x, 0) = \cos(x).$$

Then $f(1)$ is equal to

(a) $\frac{1}{2}$ (b) $\frac{e}{2}$

(c) e (d) $\frac{3e}{2}$

2014

7. If $u(x, t)$ is the D' Alembert's solution to the wave equation $\frac{\partial^2 u}{\partial t^2} = \frac{\partial^2 u}{\partial x^2}$, $x \in \mathbb{R}, t > 0$, with the condition $u(x, 0) = 0$ and $\frac{\partial u}{\partial t}(x, 0) = \cos x$, then $u\left(0, \frac{\pi}{4}\right)$ is _____

8. The solution to the integral equation $\varphi(x) = x + \int_0^x \sin(x - \xi)\varphi(\xi)\,d\xi$ is

(a) $x^2 + \frac{x^3}{3}$ (b) $x - \frac{x^3}{3!}$

(c) $x + \frac{x^3}{3!}$ (d) $x^2 - \frac{x^3}{3!}$

9. The inverse Laplace transform of $\frac{2s^2 - 4}{(s-3)(s^2 - s - 2)}$ is

(a) $(1+t)e^{-t} + \frac{7}{2}e^{-3t}$ (b) $\frac{e^t}{3} + te^{-1} + 2t$

(c) $\frac{7}{2}e^{3t} - \frac{e^{-1}}{6} - \frac{4}{3}e^{2t}$ (d) $\frac{7}{2}e^{-3t} - \frac{e^t}{6} - \frac{4}{3}e^{-2t}$

10. The integral surface of the first order partial differential equation

$$2y(z-3)\frac{\partial z}{\partial x} + (2x - z)\frac{\partial z}{\partial y} = y(2x - 3)$$

passing through the curve $x^2 + y^2 = 2x$, $z = 0$ is

(a) $x^2 + y^2 - z^2 - 2x + 4z = 0$

(b) $x^2 + y^2 - z^2 - 2x + 8z = 0$

(c) $x^2 + y^2 + z^2 - 2x + 16z = 0$

(d) $x^2 + y^2 + z^2 - 2x + 8z = 0$

11. The boundary value problem, $\frac{d^2\varphi}{dx^2} + \lambda\varphi = x$; $\varphi(0) = 0$ and $\frac{d\varphi}{dx}(1) = 0$, is converted into the integral equation $\varphi(x) = g(x) + \lambda\int_0^1 k(x,\xi)\varphi(\xi)d\xi$,

where the kernel $k(x, \xi) = \begin{cases} \xi, 0 < \xi < x \\ x, x < \xi < 1 \end{cases}$

Then $g\left(\frac{2}{3}\right)$ is ________

12. Consider the heat equation

$$\frac{\partial u}{\partial t} = \frac{\partial^2 u}{\partial x^2},\quad 0 < x < \pi,\ t > 0.$$

with the boundary conditions $u(0, t) = 0$, $u(\pi, t) = 0$ for $t > 0$ and the initial condition $u(x, 0) = \sin x$.

Then $u\left(\frac{\pi}{2}, 1\right)$ is _____

2013

13. Let $u(x, t)$ be the solution to the wave equation

$$\frac{\partial^2 u}{\partial x^2}(x, t) = \frac{\partial^2 u}{\partial t^2}(x, t),$$

$u(x, 0) = \cos(5\pi x)$, $\frac{\partial u}{\partial t}(x, 0) = 0$

Then, the value of $u(1,1)$ is ________

2012

14. The function $u(r, \theta)$ satisfying the Laplace equation

$$\frac{\partial^2 u}{\partial r^2} + \frac{1}{r}\frac{\partial u}{\partial r} + \frac{1}{r^2}\frac{\partial^2 u}{\partial \theta^2} = 0, e < r < e^2$$

subject to the conditions $u(e, \theta) = 1$, $u(e^2, \theta) = 0$ is

(a) $\text{In}(e/r)$ (b) $\text{In}(e/r^2)$

(c) $\text{In}(e^2/r)$ (d) $\sum_{n=1}^{\infty}\left(\frac{r-e^2}{e-e^2}\right)\sin n\theta$

15. The functional

$$\int_0^1 \left(y'^2 + (y + 2y')y'' + kxyy' + y^2\right)dx,$$

$y(0) = 0, y(1) = 1, y'(0) = 2, y'(1) = 3$

is path independent if k equals

(a) 1 (b) 2

(c) 3 (d) 4

16. The integral surface satisfying the partial differential equation $\frac{\partial z}{\partial x} + z^2\frac{\partial z}{\partial y} = 0$ and passing through the straight line $x = 1, y = z$ is

(a) $(x - 1)z + z^2 = y^2$ (b) $x^2 + y^2 - z^2 = 1$

(c) $(y - z)x + x^2 = 1$ (d) $(x - 1)z^2 + z = y$

17. The diffusion equation

$$\frac{\partial^2 u}{\partial x^2} = \frac{\partial u}{\partial t}, u = u(x, t), u(0, t) = 0 = u(\pi, t),$$

$u(x, 0) = \cos x \sin 5x$

(a) $\frac{e^{-36t}}{2}[\sin 6x + e^{20t}\sin 4x]$

(b) $\frac{e^{-36t}}{2}[\sin 4x + e^{20t}\sin 6x]$

(c) $\frac{e^{-20t}}{2}[\sin 3x + e^{15t}\sin 5x]$

(d) $\frac{e^{-36t}}{2}[\sin 5x + e^{20t}\sin x]$

2011

18. The partial differential equation

$$x^2\frac{\partial^2 z}{\partial x^2} - (y^2 - 1)x\frac{\partial^2 z}{\partial x\partial y} + y(y-1)^2\frac{\partial^2 z}{\partial y^2} + x\frac{\partial z}{\partial x} + y\frac{\partial z}{\partial y} = 0$$

is hyperbolic in a region in the XY - plane if

(a) $x \neq 0$ and $y = 1$ (b) $x = 0$ and $y \neq 1$

(c) $x \neq 0$ and $y \neq 1$ (d) $x = 0$ and $y = 1$

19. The integral surface for the Cauchy problem

$$\frac{\partial z}{\partial x} + \frac{\partial z}{\partial y} = 1$$

which passes through the circle $z = 0$, $x^2 + y^2 = 1$ is

(a) $x^2 + y^2 + 2z^2 + 2zx - 2yz - 1 = 0$

(b) $x^2 + y^2 + 2z^2 + 2zx + 2yz - 1 = 0$

(c) $x^2 + y^2 + 2z^2 - 2zx - 2yz - 1 = 0$

(d) $x^2 + y^2 + 2z^2 + 2zx + 2yz + 1 = 0$

20. The vertical displacement $u(x, t)$ of an infinitely long elastic string is governed by the initial value problem

$$\frac{\partial^2 u}{\partial t^2} = 4\frac{\partial^2 u}{\partial x^2}, -\infty < x < \infty, t > 0,$$

$$u(x, 0) = -x \text{ and } \frac{\partial u}{\partial t}(x, 0) = 0$$

The value of $u(x, t)$ at $x = 2$ and $t = 2$ is equal to

(a) 2 (b) 4

(c) -2 (d) -4

21. A massless wire is bent in the form of a parabola $z = r^2$ and a bead slides on it smoothly. The wire is rotated about z-axis with a constant angular acceleration α. Assume that m is the mass of the bead, ω is the initial angular velocity and g is the acceleration due to gravity. Then, the Lagrangian at any time t is

(a) $\frac{m}{2}\left[\left(\frac{dr}{dt}\right)^2(1+4r^2)+r^2(\omega+\alpha t)^2+2gr^2\right]$

(b) $\frac{m}{2}\left[\left(\frac{dr}{dt}\right)^2(1+4r^2)-r^2(\omega+\alpha t)^2+2gr^2\right]$

(c) $\frac{m}{2}\left[\left(\frac{dr}{dt}\right)^2(1+4r^2)-r^2(\omega+\alpha t)^2-2gr^2\right]$

(d) $\frac{m}{2}\left[\left(\frac{dr}{dt}\right)^2(1+4r^2)+r^2(\omega+\alpha t)^2-2gr^2\right]$

22. On the interval [0, 1], let y be a twice continuously differentiable function which is an extremal of the functional

$$J(y) = \int_0^1 \frac{\sqrt{1+2y'^2}}{x}\,dx$$

with $y(0) = 1$, $y(1) = 2$. Then, for some arbitrary constant c, y satisfies

(a) $y'^2(2-c^2x^2) = c^2x^2$ (b) $y'^2(2+c^2x^2) = c^2x^2$

(c) $y'^2(1-c^2x^2) = c^2x^2$ (d) $y'^2(1+c^2x^2) = c^2x^2$

2010

23. The general solution of the partial differential equation $\frac{\partial^2 z}{\partial x \partial y} = x + y$ is of the form

(a) $\frac{1}{2}xy(x+y) + F(x) + G(y)$

(b) $\frac{1}{2}xy(x-y) + F(x) + G(y)$

(c) $\frac{1}{2}xy(x-y) + F(x)\,G(y)$

(d) $\frac{1}{2}xy(x+y) + F(x)G(y)$

24. Let H, T and V denote the Hamiltonian, the kinetic energy and the potential energy respectively of a mechanical system at time t. If H contains t explicitly, then $\frac{\partial H}{\partial t}$ is equal to

(a) $\frac{\partial T}{\partial t}+\frac{\partial V}{\partial t}$ (b) $\frac{\partial T}{\partial t}-\frac{\partial V}{\partial t}$

(c) $\frac{\partial V}{\partial t}-\frac{\partial T}{\partial t}$ (d) $-\frac{\partial V}{\partial t}-\frac{\partial T}{\partial t}$

25. The Euler's equation for the variational problem:

Minimize $I[y(x)] = \int_0^1 (2x - xy - y')\,y'dx$, is

(a) $2y'' - y = 2$ (b) $2y'' + y = 2$

(c) $y'' + 2y = 0$ (d) $2y'' - y = 0$

26. Consider the wave equation $\frac{\partial^2 u}{\partial t^2} = 4\frac{\partial^2 u}{\partial x^2}$, $0 < x < \pi$, $t > 0$, with $u(0, t) = u(\pi, t) = 0$, $u(x, 0) = \sin x$ and $\frac{\partial u}{\partial t} = 0$ at $t = 0$. Then $u\left(\frac{\pi}{2}, \frac{\pi}{2}\right)$ is

(a) 2 (b) 1

(c) 0 (d) –1

2009

27. The integral surface satisfying the equation $y\frac{\partial z}{\partial x} + x\frac{\partial z}{\partial y} = x^2 + y^2$ and passing through the curve $x = 1 - t$, $y = 1 + t$, $z = 1 + t^2$ is

(a) $z = xy + \frac{1}{2}(x^2 - y^2)^2$

(b) $z = xy + \frac{1}{4}(x^2 - y^2)^2$

(c) $z = xy + \frac{1}{8}(x^2 - y^2)^2$

(d) $z = xy + \frac{1}{16}(x^2 - y^2)^2$

28. For the diffusion problem $u_{xx} = u_t$ ($0 < x < \pi$, $t > 0$), $u(0, t) = 0$, $u(\pi, t) = 0$ and $u(x, 0) = 3\sin 2x$, the solution is given by

(a) $3e^{-t}\sin 2x$ (b) $3e^{-4t}\sin 2x$

(c) $3e^{-9t}\sin 2x$ (d) $3e^{-2t}\sin 2x$

2008

29. The solution of $xu_x + yu_y = 0$ is of the form

(a) $f(y/x)$ (b) $f(x+y)$

(c) $f(x-y)$ (d) $f(xy)$

30. If the partial differential equation $(x-1)^2u_{xx} - (y-2)^2u_{yy} + 2xu_x + 2yu_y + 2xyu = 0$ is parabolic in $S \subseteq R^2$ but not in $R^2 \setminus S$, then S is

(a) $\{(x,y) \in R^2 : x = 1 \text{ or } y = 2\}$

(b) $\{(x,y) \in R^2 : x = 1 \text{ and } y = 2\}$

(c) $\{(x,y) \in R^2 : x = 1\}$

(d) $\{(x,y) \in R^2 : y = 2\}$

31. The characteristic curve of $2yu_x + (2x + y^2)u_y = 0$ passing through (0, 0) is

(a) $y^2 = 2(e^x + x - 1)$ (b) $y^2 = 2(e^x - x + 1)$

(c) $y^2 = 2(e^x - x - 1)$ (d) $y^2 = 2(e^x + x + 1)$

32. The initial value problem $u_x + u_y = 1$, $u(s, s) = \sin s$, $0 \le s \le 1$, has

(a) two solutions

(b) a unique solution

(c) no solution

(d) infinitely many solutions

33. Let $u(x, t)$ be the solution of $u_{tt} - u_{xx} = 1, x \in R, t > 0$, with $u(x, 0) = 0, u_t(x, 0) = 0, x \in R$. Then $u\left(\frac{1}{2}, \frac{1}{2}\right)$ is equal to

(*a*) $\frac{1}{8}$ (*b*) $-\frac{1}{8}$

(*c*) $\frac{1}{4}$ (*d*) $-\frac{1}{4}$

Statement for Linked Answer Questions 34 and 35:

Consider the boundary value problem

$u_{xx} + u_{yy} = 0, x \in (0, \pi), y \in (0, \pi),$

$u(x, 0) = u(x, \pi) = u(0, y) = 0.$

34. Any solution of this boundary value problem is of the form

(*a*) $\sum_{n=1}^{\infty} a_n \sinh nx \sin ny$

(*b*) $\sum_{n=1}^{\infty} a_n \cosh nx \sin ny$

(*c*) $\sum_{n=1}^{\infty} a_n \sinh nx \cos ny$

(*d*) $\sum_{n=1}^{\infty} a_n \cosh nx \cos ny$

35. If an additional boundary condition $u_x(\pi, y) = \sin y$ is satisfied, then $u\left(x, \frac{\pi}{2}\right)$ is equal to

(*a*) $\frac{\pi}{2}(e^{\pi} - e^{-\pi})(e^{\pi} - e^{-\pi})$

(*b*) $\frac{\pi(e^{x} + e^{-x})}{(e^{\pi} - e^{-\pi})}$

(*c*) $\frac{\pi(e^{x} - e^{-x})}{(e^{\pi} + e^{-\pi})}$

(*d*) $\frac{\pi}{2}(e^{\pi} + e^{-\pi})(e^{x} + e^{-x})$

2007

36. Let $u(x, y) = f(xe^y) + g(y^2 \cos(y))$, where f and g are infinitely differentiable functions. Then the partical differential equation of minimum order satisfied by u is

(*a*) $u_{xy} + xu_{xx} = u_x$

(*b*) $u_{xy} + xu_{xx} = xu_x$

(*c*) $u_{xy} - xu_{xx} = u_x$

(*d*) $u_{xy} - xu_{xx} = xu_x$

37. Let $u(x, y)$ be the solution to the Cauchy problem $xu_x + u_y = 1, u(x, 0) = 2 \ln(x), x > 1$.

Then $u(e, 1) =$

(*a*) -1 (*b*) 0

(c) 1 (d) e

38. Consider the Neumann problem

$u_{xx} + u_{yy} = 0, 0 < x < \pi, -1 < y < 1,$

$u_x, (0, y) = u_x = (\pi, y) = 0,$

$u_y(x, -1) = 0, u_y(x, 1) = \alpha + \beta \sin(x).$

The problem admits solution for

(*a*) $\alpha = 0, \beta = 1$ (*b*) $\alpha = -1, \beta = \frac{\pi}{2}$

(c) $\alpha = 1, \beta = \frac{\pi}{2}$ (*d*) $\alpha = 1, \beta = -\pi$

Statement for Linked Answer Questions 39 and 40:

Let $u(x, t)$ be the solution of the one dimensional wave equation

$u_{tt} - 4u_{xx} = 0, -\infty < x < \infty, t > 0,$

$$u(x, 0) = \begin{cases} 16 - x^2, & |x| \le 4, \\ 0, & \text{otherwise,} \end{cases}$$

and $u_t(x, 0) = \begin{cases} 1, & |x| \le 2 \\ 0, & \text{otherwise,} \end{cases}$

39. For $1 < t < 3$, $u(2, t) =$

(*a*) $\frac{1}{2}\left[16 - (2 - 2t)^2\right] + \frac{1}{2}[1 - \min\{1, t - 1\}]$

(*b*) $\frac{1}{2}\left[32 - (2 - 2t)^2 - (2 + 2t)^2\right] + t$

(c) $\frac{1}{2}\left[32 - (2 - 2t)^2 - (2 + 2t)^2\right] + 1$

(*d*) $\frac{1}{2}\left[16 - (2 - 2t)^2\right] + \frac{1}{2}[1 - \max\{1 - t, -1\}]$

40. The value of $u_t(2, 2)$

(*a*) equals – 15

(*b*) equals – 16

(c) equals 0

(*d*) does NOT exist

2006

41. In the region $x > 0, y > 0$, the partial differential equation

$$(x^2 - y^2)\frac{\partial^2 u}{\partial x^2} + 2(x^2 + y^2)\frac{\partial^2 u}{\partial x \partial y} + (x^2 - y^2)\frac{\partial^2 u}{\partial y^2} = 0$$

(*a*) changes type

(*b*) is elliptic

(*c*) is parabolic

(*d*) is hyperbolic

42. Consider the partial differential equation $\frac{\partial u}{\partial t}+u\frac{\partial u}{\partial x}=0$ satisfying the initial condition $u(x, 0) = \alpha + \beta x$. If $u(x, t) = 1$ along the characteristic $x = t + 1$, then

(*a*) $\alpha = 1, \beta = 1$ (*b*) $\alpha = 2, \beta = 0$

(*c*) $\alpha = 0, \beta = 0$ (*d*) $\alpha = 0, \beta = 1$

43. Let $u(x, t)$ be the solution of the initial value problem

$$\frac{\partial^2 u}{\partial t^2}-\frac{\partial^2 u}{\partial x^2}=0;\ u(x,0)=\sin x;\ \frac{\partial u}{\partial t}(x,0)=1$$

Then, $u\left(\pi,\frac{\pi}{2}\right)$ equals

(*a*) $\frac{\pi}{2}$ (*b*) $1-\left(\frac{\pi}{2}\right)$

(*c*) 1 (*d*) $1+\pi$

44. Let $u(x, t)$ be the bounded solution of $\frac{\partial u}{\partial t}-\frac{\partial^2 u}{\partial x^2}=0$ with $u(x, 0) = \frac{e^{2x}-1}{e^{2x}+1}$. Then, $\lim_{t\to+\infty} u(1, t)$ equals

(*a*) $-\frac{1}{2}$ (*b*) $\frac{1}{2}$

(*c*) -1 (*d*) 1

45. Let $u(x, y)$ be a solution of Laplace's equation on $x^2 + y^2 \le 1$. If

$$u(\cos\theta, \sin\theta)=\begin{cases}\sin\theta & \text{for } 0\le\theta\le\pi\\ 0 & \text{for } \pi\le\theta\le 2\pi,\end{cases}$$

then $u(0, 0)$ equals

(*a*) $\frac{1}{\pi}$ (*b*) $\frac{2}{\pi}$

(*c*) $\frac{1}{(2\pi)}$ (*d*) $\frac{\pi}{2}$

46. Let PQRS be a rectangle in the first quadrant whose adjacent sides PQ and QR have slopes 1 and –1 respectively. If $u(x, t)$ is a solution of $\frac{\partial^2 u}{\partial t^2}-\frac{\partial^2 u}{\partial x^2}=0$ and $u(P) = 1$, $u(Q) = -\frac{1}{2}$, $u(R) = \frac{1}{2}$, then $u(S)$ equals

(*a*) 2 (*b*) 1

(*c*) $\frac{1}{2}$ (*d*) $-\frac{1}{2}$

Statement for Linked Answer Questions 47 and 48:

Consider the partial differential equation

$$x\frac{\partial u}{\partial y}-y\frac{\partial u}{\partial x}=u$$

47. The characteristic curves for the above equation in the (x, y) plane are

(*a*) straight lines with slopes 1

(*b*) straight lines with slopes –1

(*c*) circles with center at the origin

(*d*) circles touching y-axis and centered on x-axis

48. If $u(x, y)$ is a solution to the above equation with $u(x, 0)=\sin\left(\frac{\pi}{4}x\right)$, then $u\left(\frac{1}{\sqrt{2}},\frac{1}{\sqrt{2}}\right)$ equals

(*a*) $\frac{1}{\sqrt{2}}e^{\frac{\pi}{4}}$ (*b*) $\frac{\pi}{4}e^{\frac{\pi}{\sqrt{2}}}$

(*c*) $\frac{1}{\sqrt{2}}e^{\frac{1}{\sqrt{2}}}$ (*d*) $\frac{\pi}{4}e^{\frac{\pi}{4}}$

2005

49. The integral surface of the partial differential equation $x\frac{\partial u}{\partial x}+y\frac{\partial u}{\partial y}=0$ satisfying the condition $u(1, y) = y$ is given by

(*a*) $u(x, y)=\frac{y}{x}$

(*b*) $u(x, y)=\frac{2y}{x+1}$

(*c*) $u(x, y)=\frac{y}{2-x}$

(*d*) $u(x, y) = y + x - 1$

50. If f(x) and g(y) are arbitrary functions, then the general solution of the partial differential equation $u\frac{\partial^2 u}{\partial x\partial y}-\frac{\partial u}{\partial x}\frac{\partial u}{\partial y}=0$ is given by

(*a*) $u(x, y) = f(x) + g(y)$

(*b*) $u(x, y) = f(x + y) + g(x - y)$

(*c*) $u(x, y) = f(x)\,g(y)$

(*d*) $u(x, y) = xg(y) + y f(x)$

51. The partial differential equation

$$x\frac{\partial^2 u}{\partial x^2}+2xy\frac{\partial^2 u}{\partial x\partial y}+y\frac{\partial^2 u}{\partial y^2}+x\frac{\partial u}{\partial y}+y\frac{\partial u}{\partial x}=0$$

is

(*a*) elliptic in the region $x < 0$, $y < 0$, $xy > 1$

(*b*) elliptic in the region $x > 0$, $y > 0$, $xy > 1$

(*c*) parabolic in the region $x < 0$, $y < 0$, $xy > 1$

(*d*) hyperbolic in the region $x<0$, $y < 0$, $xy > 1$

52. A function u (x,t)satisfies the wave equation

$$\frac{\partial^2 u}{\partial t^2} = \frac{\partial^2 u}{\partial x^2},\ 0 < x < 1,\ t > 0.$$

If $u\left(\frac{1}{2},0\right) = \frac{1}{4}, u\left(1,\frac{1}{2}\right) = 1$ and $u\left(0,\frac{1}{2}\right) = \frac{1}{2}$,

then $u\left(\frac{1}{2},1\right)$ is

(a) $\frac{7}{4}$ (b) $\frac{5}{4}$

(c) $\frac{4}{5}$ (d) $\frac{4}{7}$

53. The Fourier transform F (ω) of f(x). $-\infty < x < \infty$ is defined by

$$F(\omega) = \frac{1}{2\pi}\int_{-\infty}^{\infty} f(x)e^{-i\omega x}dx$$

The Fourier transform with respect to x of the solution u(x, y)of the boundary value problem

$$\frac{\partial^2 u}{\partial x^2} + \frac{\partial^2 u}{\partial y^2} = 0, -\infty < x < \infty,\ y > 0$$

$$u(x,0) = f(x), -\infty < x < \infty$$

which remains bounded for large y is given by

$$U(\omega, y) = F(\omega)e^{-|\omega| y}.$$

Then, the solution u (x, y)is given by

(a) $u(x,y) = \frac{1}{\pi}\int_{-\infty}^{\infty} \frac{f(x-z)}{y^2+z^2}dz$

(b) $u(x,y) = \frac{1}{\pi}\int_{-\infty}^{\infty} \frac{f(x+z)}{y^2+z^2}dz$

(c) $u(x,y) = \frac{y}{\pi}\int_{-\infty}^{\infty} \frac{f(x-z)}{y^2+z^2}dz$

(d) $u(x,y) = \frac{y}{\pi}\int_{-\infty}^{\infty} \frac{f(x+z)}{y^2+z^2}dz$

54. It is required to solve the Laplace equation

$$\frac{\partial^2 u}{\partial x^2} + \frac{\partial^2 u}{\partial y^2} = 0,\quad 0 < x < a, 0 < y < b,$$

satisfying the boundary conditions

u(x, 0) = 0, u(x, b) = 0, u(0, y) = 0 and u(a, y) = f(y).

If c_n's are constants, then the equation and the homogeneous boundary conditions determine the fundamental set of solutions of the form

(a) $u(x,y) = \sum_{n=1}^{\infty} c_n \sinh\frac{n\pi x}{b}\sin\frac{n\pi y}{b}$

(b) $u(x,y) = \sum_{n=1}^{\infty} c_n \sin\frac{n\pi x}{b}\sin\frac{n\pi y}{b}$

(c) $u(x,y) = \sum_{n=1}^{\infty} c_n \sin\frac{n\pi x}{b}\sinh\frac{n\pi y}{b}$

(d) $u(x,y) = \sum_{n=1}^{\infty} c_n \sinh\frac{n\pi x}{b}\sinh\frac{n\pi y}{b}$

Statement for Linked Answer Questions 55a and 55b :

Consider the one dimensional heat equation $\frac{\partial u}{\partial t} = \frac{\partial^2 u}{\partial x^2}$, $0 < x < 1, t > 0$ with the initial condition $u(x, 0) = 2\cos^2 \pi x$ and the boundary conditions $\frac{\partial u}{\partial t}(0,t) = 0 = \frac{\partial u}{\partial x}(1, t)$.

55a. The temperature u (x,t) is given by

(a) $u(x, t) = 1 - e^{-4\pi^2 t}\cos 2\pi x$

(b) $u(x, t) = 1 + e^{-4\pi^2 t}\cos 2\pi x$

(c) $u(x, t) = 1 - e^{-4\pi^2 t}\sin 2\pi x$

(d) $u(x, 1) = 1 + e^{-4\pi^2 t}\sin 2\pi x$

55b. The heat flux F at $(\frac{1}{4}, t)$ is given by

(a) $F = 2\pi\, e^{-4\pi^2 t}$ (b) $F = -2\pi\, e^{-4\pi^2 t}$

(c) $F = 4\pi\, e^{-2\pi^2 t}$ (d) $F = -4\pi\, e^{-2\pi^2 t}$

2004

56. In the (x, t) plane, the characteristics of the initial value problem $u_t + uu_x = 0$, with $u(x, 0) = x, 0 \le x \le 1$, are

(a) parallel straight lines

(b) straight lines which intersect at (0, – 1)

(c) non-intersecting parabolas

(d) concentric circles with centre at the origin

57. Suppose $u(x, y)$ satisfies Laplace's equation : $\nabla^2 u = 0$ in R^2 and $u = x$ on the unit circle. Then, at the origin

(a) u tends to infinity

(b) u attains a finite minimum

(c) u attains a finite maximum

(d) u is equal to 0

58. The characteristic curves of the partial differential equation

$(2x + u)\, u_x + (2y + u)\, u_y = u,$

passing through (1, 1) for any arbitrary initial values prescribed on a non-characteristic curve are given by

(*a*) $x = y$ (*b*) $x^2 + y^2 = 2$

(*c*) $x + y = 2$ (*d*) $x^2 - xy + y^2 = 1$

59. The solution of Laplace's equation

$$\frac{\partial^2 u}{\partial r^2} + \frac{1}{r}\frac{\partial u}{\partial r} + \frac{1}{r^2}\frac{\partial^2 u}{\partial \theta^2} = 0$$

in the unit disk with boundary conditions $u(1, \theta) = 2\cos^2\theta$ is given by

(*a*) $1 + r^2 \cos 2\theta$ (*b*) $1 + \ln r + r\cos 2\theta$

(*c*) $2r^3 \cos^2\theta$ (*d*) $1 - r^2 + 2r^2\cos^2\theta$

60. For the heat equation $\dfrac{\partial u}{\partial t} = \dfrac{\partial^2 u}{\partial x^2}$ on $R \times [0, T]$, with $u(x, 0) = u_0(x)$, $u_0 \in L^2(R)$,

(*a*) the solution is reversible in time

(*b*) if $u_0(x)$ has compact support, so does $u(x, t)$ for any given t

(*c*) if $u_0(x)$ is discontinuous at a point, so is $u(x, t)$ for any given t

(*d*) if $u_0(x) \geq 0$ for all x, then $u(x, t) \geq 0$ for all x and $t > 0$

61. If $u(x, t)$ satisfies the wave equation

$\dfrac{\partial^2 u}{\partial t^2} = c^2 \dfrac{\partial^2 u}{\partial x^2}$, $x \in R, t > 0$, with initial conditions

$$u(x, 0) = \begin{cases} \sin\dfrac{\pi x}{c}, & 0 \leq x \leq c \\ 0 & elsewhere \end{cases},$$

and $u_t(x, 0) = 0$ for all x, then for a given $t > 0$,

(*a*) there are values of x at which $u(x, t)$ is discontinuous

(*b*) $u(x, t)$ is continuous, but $u_x(x, t)$ is not continuous

(*c*) $u(x, t)$, $u_x(x, t)$ are continuous, but $u_{xx}(x, t)$ is not continuous

(*d*) $u(x, t)$ is smooth for all x

2003

62. Complete integral for the partial differential equation $z = px + qy - \sin(pq)$ is

(*a*) $z = ax + by + \sin(ab)$

(*b*) $z = ax + by - \sin(ab)$

(*c*) $z = ax + y + \sin(b)$

(*d*) $z = x + by - \sin(a)$

63. Pick the region in which the following differential equation is hyperbolic

$$yu_{xx} + 2\,xy\, u_{xy} + x\, u_{yy} = u_x + u_y$$

(*a*) $xy \neq 1$ (*b*) $xy \neq 0$

(*c*) $xy > 1$ (*d*) $xy > 0$

64. Let $u = \psi(x, t)$ be the solution to the initial value problem

$u_{tt} = u_{xx}$ for $-\infty < x < \infty, t > 0$

with $u(x, 0) = \sin(x)$, $u_1(x, 0) = \cos(x)$ then the value of $\psi(\pi/2, \psi/6)$ is

(*a*) $\dfrac{\sqrt{3}}{2}$ (*b*) $\dfrac{1}{2}$

(*c*) $\dfrac{1}{\sqrt{2}}$ (*d*) 1

65. Consider the boundary value problem

$u_{xx} + u_{yy} = 0$ in $\Omega = \{(x, y); x^2 + y^2 < 1\}$ with $\dfrac{\partial u}{\partial n} = x^2 + y^2$ on the boundary of Ω

$\left(\dfrac{\partial u}{\partial n}\text{ denotes the normal derivative of } u\right)$.

Then its solution $u(x, y)$

(*a*) is unique and is identically zero

(*b*) is unique upto a constant

(*c*) does not exist

(*d*) is unique and non-zero

66. The Cauchy problem $u_x - u_y = 2$ with the Cauchy data on $T : (s, -s, 2s)$ has

(*a*) one solution

(*b*) two solutions

(*c*) no solution

(*d*) infinite solutions

67. Let $u(r, \theta, z, t)$ be the solution to the heat conduction problem

$u_t = u_{xx}$ in $\Omega \times [0, T]$, where $\Omega = \{(r, \theta, z) \mid 0 < r_1 \leq r \leq r_2, 0 \leq \theta \leq 2\pi, 0 \leq z \leq L\}$ with compatible initial and boundary conditions :

$u(r, \theta, z, 0) = \begin{cases} 0 & \text{in the interior of } \Omega \\ g(\theta) & \text{on } \partial\Omega \end{cases}$ and $u(r, \theta, z, t) = f(\theta)$ on $\partial\Omega$ for $t > 0$

Further, if $M = \max\{u, (r, \theta, z, T) \mid (r, \theta, z) \in \Omega\}$,

$M_1 = \max\{u(r, \theta, z, T) \mid r = r_1, 0 \leq \theta \leq 2\pi, 0 < z < L\}$

$M_2 = \max\{u(r, \theta, z, T) \mid r = r_2, 0 \leq \theta \leq 2\pi, 0 < z < L\}$

then

(*a*) $M_1 \leq M \leq M_2$

(*b*) $M_2 \leq M \leq M_1$

(*c*) $M \leq \max(M_1, M_2)$

(*d*) $M \geq \max(M_1, M_2)$

2002

68. Which of the following, concerning the solution of the Neumann problem for Laplace's equation, on a smooth bounded domain, is true ?

(*a*) Solution is unique

(*b*) Solution is unique upto an additive constant

(*c*) Solution is unique upto a multipli-cative constant

(*d*) No conclusion can be drawn about uniqueness

69. Which of the following satisfies the heat equation (without source terms and with diffusion constant 1) in one space dimension?

(*a*) $\sin\left(\frac{x^2}{4t}\right)$ (*b*) $e^t \sin x$

(*c*) $x^2 - t$ (*d*) $\frac{e^{-x^2/4t}}{\sqrt{t}}$

70. Which of the following is elliptic ?

(*a*) Laplace equation (*b*) Wave equation

(*c*) Heat equation (*d*) $u_{xx} + 2u_{xy} - 4u_{yy} = 0$

71. Solve the initial value problem

$$\frac{\partial^2 u}{\partial t^2} - \frac{\partial^2 u}{\partial x^2} = 0,$$

$$t > 0,\ x \in (-\infty, \infty)$$

$$u(x, 0) = x, \frac{\partial u}{\partial t}(x,0) = \frac{x}{1+x^2}$$

72. Consider the initial value problem

$$\frac{\partial u}{\partial y} + u\frac{\partial u}{\partial x} = 0,$$

$$y > 0,\ x \in \mathrm{R},$$

$$u(x, 0) = f(x).$$

Show that the solution is constant along the characteristics. Hence deduce that if f is decreasing monotonically, the solution cannot exist as a single valued function for all $y > 0$.

2001

73. The solution of the initial value problem $u_{tt} = 4u_{xx},\ t > 0, -\infty < x < \infty$ satisfying the conditions

$u(x, 0) = x,\ u_t(x, 0) = 0$ is

(*a*) x (*b*) $\frac{x^2}{2}$

(*c*) $2x$ (*d*) $2t$

74. The general integral of the partial differential equation

$(y + zx)z_x - (x + yz)z_y = x^2 - y^2$ is

(*a*) $F(x^2 + y^2 + z^2, xy + z) = 0$

(*b*) $F(x^2 + y^2 - z^2, xy + z) = 0$

(*c*) $F(x^2 - y^2 - z^2, xy + z) = 0$

(*d*) $F(x^2 + y^2 + z^2, xy - z) = 0$

where F is an arbitrary function.

75. Find the region in which the partial differential equation

$$u_{xx} - yu_{xy} + xu_x + yu_y + u = 0$$

is hyperbolic and reduce it to a canonical form.

2000

76. The equation $x^2(y - 1)Z_{xx} - x(y^2 - 1)Z_{xy} + y(y^2 - 1)Z_{yy} + Z_x = 0$ is hyperbolic in the entire xy plane except along

(*a*) x-axis

(*b*) y-axis

(*c*) a line parallel to y-axis

(*d*) a line parallel to x-axis

77. The solution of the Cauchy problem $u_{yy}(x, y) - u_{xx}(x, y) = 0$; $u(x, 0) = 0$, $u_y(x, 0) = x$ is $u(x, y) =$

(*a*) $\frac{x}{y}$ (*b*) xy

(*c*) $xy + \frac{x}{y}$ (*d*) 0

78. The characteristics curves of the equation $x^2u_{xx} - y^2u_{yy} = x^2y^2 + x$; $x > 0$, $u = (x, y)$ are

(*a*) rectangular hyperbola

(*b*) parabola

(*c*) circle

(*d*) straight line

79. Use Lagrange's method to solve the equation.

$$\begin{vmatrix} x & y & z \\ \alpha & \beta & \gamma \\ \frac{\partial z}{\partial x} & \frac{\partial z}{\partial y} & -1 \end{vmatrix} = 0;\ \text{where } z = z(x, y)$$ [5]

80. (*a*) Reduce the equation

$u_{xx}(x, y) - u_{yy}(x, y) - \frac{2}{x}u_x = 0$ to a possible canonical form. [3]

(*b*) Reduce the following heat conduction problem with non-homogeneous boundary conditions:

$u_t(x, t) - u_{xx}(x, t) = 0;\ 0 < x < \pi,\ t > 0,$

$u(0, t) = 0,\ u(\pi, t) = 10,$

$u(x, 0) = f(x)$

to a problem with homogeneous boundary conditions. [2]

ANSWERS

1. (*a*)	**2.** (2)	**3.** (2)	**4.** (*c*)	**5.** (4)	**6.** (*b*)	**7.** (0.69 to 0.72)		**8.** (*c*)	**9.** (*d*)
10. (*a*)	**11.** (–0.29 to –0.27)		**12.** (0.36 to 0.38)		**13.** (1)	**14.** (*c*)		**15.** (*b*)	**16.** (*d*)
17. (*a*)	**18.** (*c*)	**19.** (*c*)	**20.** (*b*)	**21.** (*d*)	**22.** (*)	**23.** (*a*)	**24.** (*a*)	**25.** (*b*)	**26.** (*d*)
27. (*d*)	**28.** (*b*)	**29.** (*a*)	**30.** (*b*)	**31.** (*a*)	**32.** (*d*)	**33.** (*a*)	**34.** (*a*)	**35.** (*c*)	**36.** (*c*)
37. (*a*)	**38.** (*b*)	**39.** (*b*)	**40.** (*a*)	**41.** (*d*)	**42.** (*d*)	**43.** (*a*)	**44.** (*a*)	**45.** (*b*)	**46.** (*a*)
47. (*c*)	**48.** (*a*)	**49.** (*a*)	**50.** (*c*)	**51.** (*d*)	**52.** (*c*)	**53.** (*b*)	**54.** (*c*)	**55a.** (*b*)	**55b.** (*b*)
56. (*d*)	**57.** (*d*)	**58.** (*a*)	**59.** (*a*)	**60.** (*c*)	**61.** (*d*)	**62.** (*b*)	**63.** (*c*)	**64.** (*a*)	**65.** (*b*)
66. (*b*)	**67.** (*a*)	**68.** (*b*)	**69.** (*d*)	**70.** (*a*)	**71.** (*)	**72.** (*)	**73.** (*a*)	**74.** (*b*)	**75.** (*)
76. (*b*)	**77.** (*b*)	**78.** (*a*)	**79.** (*)	**80.** (*)					

''– Marks to all*

EXPLANATIONS

1. Given curve

$$y = cx^2$$

$$\Rightarrow \quad \frac{y}{x^2} = c$$

$$\Rightarrow \quad y' = \frac{2y}{x}$$

is differential equation for known curve.

For orthogonal curve, the differential equation is

$$y' = -\frac{1}{f(x,y)}$$

$$\Rightarrow \quad y' = -\frac{x}{2y}$$

$$\Rightarrow \quad y^2 = -\frac{x^2}{2} + c_1 \qquad ...(1)$$

Since it passes through (0, 1) $\Rightarrow c_1 = 1$

$\therefore$ The equation of curve is

$$y^2 = -\frac{x^2}{2} + 1$$

which also satisfies $(\sqrt{2}, 0)$.

$\therefore$ It also passes through $(\sqrt{2}, 0)$

2. $a_0 = \frac{1}{2n}\int_{-n}^{n} f(x)dx$

$$= \frac{1}{2n}\int_{-n}^{n} (x^2 + 2\sin 2x)dx = \frac{n^2}{3}$$

$$a_n = \frac{1}{n}\int_{-n}^{n} f(x)\cos nx\, dx = \frac{(-1)^n 4}{n^2} \quad n = 1, 2, ...$$

$$b_n = b_2 = 2, b_n = 0 \text{ if } n \neq 2 \qquad n = 1, 2, ...$$

$$\text{Then} \sum_{n=0}^{\infty} a_n - \sum_{n=0}^{\infty} b_n = a_0 + \sum_{n=0}^{\infty} a_n - \sum_{n=0}^{b_n} b_n$$

$$\left|\sum_{n=0}^{\infty} a_n - \sum_{n=0}^{b_n} b_n\right| = \left|\frac{n^2}{3} - \frac{n^2}{3} - 2\right| = |-2| = 2$$

3. Let $f(x) = x^2 - \cos x$

$f(0) = -1$

$$f\left(\frac{\pi}{2}\right) = \frac{\pi}{4}$$

$$= +\text{ve}, f\left(\frac{\pi}{4}\right) = \frac{\pi}{16} - \frac{1}{\sqrt{2}} < 0$$

So only one root of f(x) lies in $\left[0, \frac{\pi}{2}\right]$.

Similarly only one root of f(x) lies in $\left[-\frac{\pi}{2}, 0\right]$.

Hence two roots of f(x) lies in $\left[-\frac{\pi}{2}, \frac{\pi}{2}\right]$

7. Standard wave equation is

$$\frac{\partial^2 u}{\partial t^2} = c^2 \frac{\partial^2 u}{\partial x^2} \qquad ...(i)$$

Given, wave equation is

$$\frac{\partial^2 u}{\partial t^2} = \frac{\partial^2 u}{\partial x^2} \qquad ...(ii)$$

On comparing equation (*i*) and (*ii*), we get

$$c^2 = 1$$

$$\Rightarrow \quad c = 1$$

Also, given, $u(x, 0) = 0 = f(x)$

and $\frac{\partial u}{\partial t}(x,0) = \cos x = g(x)$

So, its solution is

$$u\left(0,\frac{\pi}{4}\right) = \frac{1}{2}(0+0)+\frac{1}{2}\int_{-\pi/4}^{\pi/4} g(\xi)d\xi$$

$$= \left[\because u(x,t)=\frac{1}{2}[f(x+ct)+f(x-ct)] + \frac{1}{2c}\int_{x-ct}^{x+ct} g(\xi)d(\xi)\right]$$

$$= \frac{1}{2}\int_{-\pi/4}^{\pi/4} \cos\xi\, d\xi$$

$$= \frac{1}{2}\times 2\int_{0}^{\pi/4} \cos\xi\, d\xi$$

$$= [\sin\xi]_0^{\pi/4}$$

$$= \sin\frac{\pi}{4}-\sin 0$$

$$= \frac{1}{\sqrt{2}}-0$$

$$= \frac{1}{1.414} = 0.7072 \text{ or } 0.71$$

9. We have,

$$\frac{2s^2-4}{(s-3)(s^2-s-2)} = \frac{2s^2-4}{(s-3)(s-2)(s+1)}$$

By partial fractions,

$$\frac{2s^2-4}{(s-3)(s-2)(s+1)} = \frac{A}{s-3}+\frac{B}{s-2}+\frac{C}{s+1}$$

$$\Rightarrow 2s^2-4 = A(s-2)(s+1) + B(s-3)(s+1) + C(s-3)(s-2)$$

On putting $s = 2$, we get, $B = -\frac{4}{3}$

On putting $s = 3$, we get, $A = \frac{7}{2}$

On putting $s = -1$, we get, $C = -\frac{1}{6}$

$$\therefore \frac{2s^2-4}{(s-3)(s-2)(s+1)} = \frac{7}{2(s-3)}-\frac{4}{3(s-2)}-\frac{1}{6(s+1)}$$

Now, $\mathcal{L}^{-1}\left\{\frac{2s^2-4}{(s-3)(s-2)(s+1)}\right\}$

$$= \frac{7}{2}\mathcal{L}^{-1}\left\{\frac{1}{s-3}\right\}-\frac{4}{3}\mathcal{L}^{-1}\left\{\frac{1}{s-2}\right\}-\frac{1}{6}\mathcal{L}^{-1}\left\{\frac{1}{s+1}\right\}$$

$$= \frac{7}{2}e^{3t}-\frac{4}{3}e^{2t}-\frac{1}{6}e^{-t}$$

12. Given heat equation is

$$\frac{\partial u}{\partial t} = \frac{\partial^2 u}{\partial x^2},\ 0 < x < \pi,\ t > 0 \quad ...(i)$$

Let us assume that

$u(x, t) = X(x)T(t)$ is the solution of equation (*i*)

$$\frac{\partial u}{\partial t} = X\frac{dT}{dt},$$

$$\frac{\partial u}{\partial x} = T\frac{dX}{dx},\ \frac{\partial^2 u}{\partial x^2} = T\frac{d^2X}{dx^2}$$

Then equation (*i*) reduces to

$$X\frac{dT}{dt} = T\frac{d^2X}{dx^2}$$

i.e. $$\frac{1}{X}\frac{d^2X}{dx^2} = \frac{1}{T}\frac{dT}{dt} = \lambda \text{ (constant)}$$

By boundary condition,

$$u(0, t) = 0,\ u(\pi, t) = 0$$

$$u(0, t) = 0 = X(0)T(t)$$

$$\Rightarrow \quad X(0) = 0 \text{ since } T(t) \neq 0$$

$$u(\pi, t) = 0 = X(\pi)\, T(t)$$

$$\Rightarrow \quad X(\pi) = 0 \text{ since } T(t) \neq 0$$

Hence, $\frac{d^2X}{dx^2} - \lambda X(x) = 0$

and $X(0) = 0,\ X(\pi) = 0$

This is sturm-liouville problem

for $\lambda < 0$ is $\lambda = -\mu^2$

we get $\frac{d^2X}{dx^2} + \mu^2 X(x) = 0$

Solution is $X(x) = c_1 \cos\mu x + c_2 \sin\mu x$

using $X(0) = 0$, $\boxed{0 = c_1}$

and $X(\pi) = 0$

$$\Rightarrow \quad 0 = c_2 \sin\mu\pi$$

$$\Rightarrow \quad \sin\mu\pi = 0 \qquad [\because c_2 \neq 0]$$

$$\Rightarrow \quad \mu\pi = n\pi$$

$$\Rightarrow \quad \mu = n,\ \lambda = -n^2$$

Hence $X(x) = c_2 \sin nx \quad ...(i)$

Again, $\frac{1}{T}\frac{dT}{dt} - \lambda = 0$

$\Rightarrow \quad \frac{dT}{dt} + n^2\, T(t) = 0$

$\Rightarrow \quad T(t) = c_3\, e^{-n^2 t}$

$\therefore \quad u(x, t) = X(x)\, T(t)$

$= c_2 \sin nx \cdot c_3 e^{-n^2 t}$

[using equation (*i*)]

$u(x, t) = c\sin nx\, e^{-n^2 t} \quad ...(ii)$

$[\because c_2\, c_3 = c \text{ (constant)}]$

using $u(x, 0) = \sin x$, we get $\sin x = c \sin nx$

on comparing we get $c = 1, n = 1$

Then, $u\left(\frac{\pi}{2}, 1\right) = 1.\sin\frac{\pi}{2} e^{-1} = e^{-1}$

[using equation (*ii*)]

$= \frac{1}{e} = 0.36$

16. Given partial differential equation.

$$\frac{\partial z}{\partial x} + z^2 \frac{\partial z}{\partial y} = 0$$

$$P + z^2 q = 0 \quad ...(1)$$

Auxiliary Equation of equation (1) is

$$\frac{dx}{1} = \frac{dy}{z^2} = \frac{dz}{0} \quad ...(2)$$

$\Rightarrow \quad dz = 0$

By integrating,

$$z = c_1 \quad ...(3)$$

Now taking ; $\frac{dx}{1} = \frac{dy}{z^2}$

$$dx = \frac{dy}{c_1^2}$$

$$c_1^2 dx = dy$$

By integrating

$$c_1^2 x = y + c_2$$

$$z^2 x - y = c_2 \quad ...(4)$$

now Applying $x = 1, y = z$

$$z^2 - z = c_2 \quad ...(5)$$

from equation (4) and (5), we get

$$z^2 x - y = z^2 - z$$

$$(x - 1)z^2 + z = y$$

17. Given diffusion equation is

$$\frac{\partial^2 u}{\partial x^2} = \frac{\partial u}{\partial t} \quad ...(1)$$

with $u = u(x, t)$, $\alpha = 1$, $I = \pi$

$u(0, t) = 0 = u(\pi, t)$

$u(x, 0) = \cos x \sin 5x$

The general solution of Equation (1) is

$$u(x, t) = \sum_{n=0}^{\infty} D_n \sin\left(\frac{n\pi x}{\pi}\right) e^{\frac{-n^2 \pi^2}{\pi^2} t}$$

$$= \sum_{n=0}^{\infty} D_n \sin(nx) e^{-n^2 t}$$

Now $\quad u(x, 0) = \cos x \sin 5x$

$$\cos x \sin 5x = \sum_{n=0}^{\infty} D_n \sin(nx)$$

$$D_n = \frac{2}{\pi}\int_0^{\pi} \cos x \sin 5x \sin nx\, dx$$

$$= \frac{2}{\pi}\int_0^{\pi} \frac{1}{2}[\sin 6x + \sin ux] \sin nx\, dx$$

$$= \frac{1}{\pi}\left[\int_0^{\pi} \sin 6x \sin nx\, dx + \int_0^{\pi} \sin ux \sin nx\, dx\right]$$

$\therefore D_0 = 0,\ D_1 = 0,\ D_2 = 0,\ D_3 = 0,\ D_4 = 1,$
$D_5 = 0, D_6 = 1, D_7 = D_8 = ... = 0$

Solution of equation (i) is

$$u(x, t) = e^{-16t} \sin 4x + e^{-36t} \sin 6x$$

$$= e^{-36t} [\sin 6x + e^{20t} \sin 4x].$$

18. Given partial differential equation

$$\frac{x^2 d^2 z}{\partial x^2} - \left(y^2 - 1\right) x \frac{\partial^2 z}{\partial x \partial y} + y\left(y - 1\right)^2 \frac{\partial^2 z}{\partial y^2}$$

$$+ x\frac{\partial z}{\partial x} + y\frac{\partial z}{\partial y} = 0$$

is hyperbolic in a region in the *xy*-plane if.

$$S^2 - 4RT > 0$$

where $\quad R = x^2$

$S = -(y^2 - 1)x$

$T = y(y - 1)^2$

$(y^2 - 1)^2 x^2 - 4x^2 y (y - 1)^2 > 0$

$(y - 1)^2 x^2 [y^2 + 2y + 1 - 4y] > 0$

$x^2 (y - 1)^2 (y - 2)^2 > 0$

$x \neq 0, y \neq 1, 2$

19. $\quad P + q = 1$

By Eular's equation

$$\frac{dx}{1} = \frac{dy}{1} = \frac{dz}{1}$$

$x - y = c_1$ and $z - y = c_2$

$z - y = \phi(x - y)$

$z = y + \phi(x - y)$

is the general integral

Now the curve is $z = 0$

$$x^2 + y^2 = 1$$

$$z = 0, x = \cos t, y = \sin t$$

$$z = y + \phi(x - y) \quad \text{(given)}$$

$$0 = \sin t + \phi(\cos t - \sin t)$$

$$\phi(\cos t - \sin t) = -\sin t$$

$$\phi(\sin t) = -\cos t + \sin t$$

$$\phi(s) = -\sqrt{1 - S^2} + S$$

{Let $\sin t = s$}

so general integral

$$z = y + \phi(x - y)$$

$$z = y - \sqrt{1 - (x - y)^2} + (x - y)$$

$$(z - x)^2 = 1 - (x - y)^2$$

$$z^2 + x^2 - 2zx = 1 - x^2 - y^2 + 2xy$$

$$2x^2 + y^2 + z^2 - 2xy - 2zx - 1 = 0$$

$$x^2 + y^2 + 2z^2 - 2xy - 2zx - 1 = 0$$

20. $u_{tt} = 4u_{xx'} - \infty < x < \infty, t > 0$

$$u(x, 0) = -x, u_t(x, 0) = 0$$

$u(x, t)$ at $x = 2$ and $t = 2$

$$u(x, t) = \begin{cases} \frac{1}{2}\{f(x + ct) + f(x - ct)\}, x \ge ct \\ \frac{1}{2}\{f(x + ct) - f(x - ct)\}, x \le ct \end{cases}$$

$$= \begin{cases} \frac{1}{2}(-x - ct - x + ct) x \ge ct \\ \frac{1}{2}(-x + ct + ct - x) x \le ct \end{cases}$$

$$= \begin{cases} -x & x \ge ct \\ ct & x \le ct \end{cases}$$

$4(2, 2) = 4$

22. On comparing the given functional with

$$\int_0^1 F(x_1 y_1 y^1) dx$$

$$F(x, y, y^1) = \frac{\sqrt{1 + y^{12}}}{x} \quad \dots (1)$$

The Eular's equation

$$\frac{\partial F}{\partial y} - \frac{d}{dx}\left(\frac{\partial F}{\partial y'}\right) = 0 \quad \dots (2)$$

From equation (1)

$$\frac{\partial F}{\partial y} = 0, \frac{\partial F}{\partial y^1}$$

$$= \frac{1}{2}\frac{(1 + y^{12})^{-1/2}}{x}, 2y^1$$

$$= \frac{y^1}{x(1 + y^{12})^{1/2}}$$

Since $\frac{\partial F}{\partial y} = 0$ therefore equation (2) gives

$$0 - \frac{d}{dx}\left(\frac{\partial F}{\partial y^1}\right) = 0$$

By Integrating

$$\frac{\partial F}{\partial y^1} = C$$

$$\frac{y^1}{x(1 + y^{12})^{1/2}} = C$$

$$y^1 = cx(1 + y^{12})^{1/2}$$

$$y^{12} = c^2x^2(1 + y^{12})$$

$$y^{12}(1 - c^2x^2) = c^2x^2$$

23. $z_{xy} = x + y$

$$z_y = \frac{x^2}{2} + xy + \phi_1(y)$$

$$z = \frac{x^2 y}{2} + \frac{xy^2}{2} + \int \phi_1(y) dy + \phi_2(x)$$

$$z = \frac{1}{2}xy[x + y] + F(x) + G(y)$$

24. We know that

$$H = T + V$$

where T is kinetic energy and V is potential energy Differentiate with respect to time.

$$\frac{\partial H}{\partial t} = \frac{\partial T}{\partial t} + \frac{\partial V}{\partial t}$$

25. On comparing the given variational problem with

$$\int_0^1 (2x - xy - y')y' dx$$

$$F(x, y, y') = (2x - xy - y')y' \quad \dots (1)$$

Eular's equation is

$$\frac{\partial F}{\partial y} - \frac{d}{dx}\left(\frac{\partial F}{\partial y'}\right) = 0 \quad \dots (2)$$

From equation (1) $\frac{\partial F}{\partial y} = -xy^1$, $\frac{\partial F}{\partial y}$

$$= 2x - xy - 2y'$$

and $\frac{d}{dx}\left(\frac{\partial F}{\partial y'}\right) = 2 - xy' - y - 2y''$

From equation (2)

$$-xy' - (2 - xy' - y - 2y'') = 0$$

$$xy' + 2 - xy' - y - 2y'' = 0$$

$$2y'' + y = 2$$

26.
$$4_{tt} = 4xx^1 \qquad 0 < x < \pi, t > 0$$
$$4(0, t) = u(\pi, t) = 0$$
$$4(u, 0) = \sin x$$
$$u_t(x_1, 0) = 0, \text{ then } u(\pi/2, \pi/2)$$
$$u(x, t) = \begin{cases} \frac{1}{2}\left[4(x-ct)+u(x+ct)\right], x \ge ct \\ \frac{1}{2}\left[4(x+ct)-u(ct-x)\right], x \le ct \end{cases}$$
$$= \begin{cases} \frac{1}{2}\left[\sin(x-2t)+\sin(x+2t)\right] x \ge 2t \\ \frac{1}{2}\left[\sin(x+2t)-\sin(2t-x)\right], x \le 2t \end{cases}$$
$$= \begin{cases} \frac{1}{2}\left[2\sin x\cos 2t\right] x \ge ct \\ \frac{1}{2}\left[2\sin x\cos 2t\right] x \le 2t \end{cases}$$
$$= \sin x \cos 2t$$
$$4(\pi/2, \pi/2) = 1.(-1) = -1$$

27. $yp + xq = x^2 + y^2$
$$\frac{dx}{y} = \frac{dy}{x} = \frac{dz}{x^2+y^2}$$
$$xdx - ydy = 0$$
$$\Rightarrow \quad x^2 - y^2 = c_1$$
$$\frac{ydx + xdy - dz}{x^2+y^2-(x^2+y^2)} = \frac{dx}{y}$$
$$ydx + xdy - dz = 0$$
$$dz = d(xy)$$
$$z = xy + c_z$$
$$z - xy = \phi(x^2 - y^2)$$
be general integral
$$x = 1 - t$$
$$y = 1 + t$$
$$z = 1 + t^2$$
Now the general integral given,
$$z = xy + \phi(x^2 - y^2)$$
$$1 + t^2 = 1 - t^2 + \phi(-4t)$$
$$\phi(-4t) = t^2$$
$$\phi(c) = \frac{c^2}{16}$$
so
$$z = xy + \frac{(x^2-y^2)^2}{16}$$
be the integral surface.

28.
$$U_{xx} = U_{t'} \ (0 < x < \pi, t > 0)$$
$$U(0, t) = 0, U(\pi, t) = 0$$
$$U(x, 0) = 3 \sin 2x = f(x)$$
$$U(x, t) = \sum_{n=1}^{\infty} a_n \exp\left(\frac{-n^2\pi^2 t}{\pi^2}\right)\sin\left(\frac{n\pi x}{\pi}\right)$$
$$f(x) = \sum_{n=1}^{\infty} a_n \sin\left(\frac{n\pi x}{\pi}\right)$$
$$3 \sin 2x = \sum_{n=1}^{\infty} a_n \sin nx$$
$$a_z = 3$$
and $\quad a_n = 0 \ \forall n \in N \ \{z\}$

and $a_n = \frac{2}{\pi}\int_0^{\pi} 3\sin 2x.\sin\left(\frac{n\pi x}{\pi}\right)dx$
$$= \frac{2}{\pi}\int_0^{\pi} 3\sin 2x.\sin nx dx$$
$$= \frac{3}{\pi}\int_0^{\pi} [\cos(n-2)x - \cos(n+2)x]dx$$
$$= \frac{3}{\pi}\left[\frac{\sin(n-2)\pi}{(n-2)} - \frac{\sin(n+2)\pi}{(n+2)}\right]$$
$$a_z = 3 \text{ and}$$
$$a_n = 0 \ \forall \ n \in N - \{2\}$$

so, $u(x, t) = a_z e^{-z^2} t \sin 2x = 3e^{-ut} \sin 2x$.

29. Given that $x4_x + y4_y = 0$

the Lagranges auxiliary equation is
$$\frac{dx}{dx} = \frac{dy}{y} = \frac{dy}{0}$$
$$\frac{y}{x} = c_1 \text{ and } u = c_2$$
$$u = f\left(\frac{y}{x}\right)$$

30. The partial differential equation $(x-1)^2 4_{xx} - (y-2)^2 4_{yy} + 2x4_x + 2y4_y + 2xy4 = 0$ is parabolic in $S \le R^2$ but not in $\frac{R^2}{S}$ then S can be obtained by the equation.
$$S^2 - 4RT = 0$$
where
$$R = (x-1)^2$$
$$T = -(y-2)^2$$
$$S = 0$$
$$\Rightarrow 0 - 4(x-1)^2 (y-2)^2 = 0$$
$$x = 1, y = 2$$
$$S = \{(x, y) : x = 1 \text{ and } y = 2\}$$

31. As only (*a*) satisfying as a solution to given partial differential equation

32. $4x + 4y = 1$, $\mu(s, s) = \sin s$

$$\frac{dx}{1} = \frac{dy}{1} = \frac{dy}{1}$$

$$(x - y) = c_1 \; 4 - y = c_2$$

$$c_2 = \phi(c_1)$$

$$\mu - y = \phi(x - y)$$

$$\mu = y + \phi(x - y)$$

Now $\mu(s, s) = \sin s$

$$\sin s = s + \phi(0)$$

$$\phi(0) = \sin s - s$$

so infinitely many solutions.

33. $\mu_{tt} - \mu_{xx} = 1, x \in R, t > 0$

with $\mu(x, 0) = 0 = f(x)$

$\mu_t(x_t, 0) = 0 = g(x)$

$$\mu(x, t) = \frac{1}{2}[f(x+ct)+f(x-ct)] + \frac{1}{2c}\int_{x-ct}^{x+ct} g(s)ds + \frac{1}{2c}\int_{x-c(t-\tau)}^{x+c(t-\tau)} f(s,\tau)dsd\tau$$

$$= \frac{1}{2}[0+0] + \frac{1}{2.1}\int_{x-t}^{x+t} ods + \frac{1}{2}\int_{x-(t-\tau)}^{x+(t-\tau)} 1dsd\, J\int_0^t$$

$$= \frac{1}{2}\int_0^t 2(t-\tau)d\tau$$

$$= \frac{1}{2} \times 2\left[t^2 - \frac{t^2}{2}\right]$$

$$= \frac{t^2}{2} \quad 4\left(\frac{1}{2}, \frac{1}{2}\right) = \frac{1}{8}$$

34. $u_{xx} + u_{yy} = 0 \quad x \in (0, \pi), y \in (0, \pi)$

$u(x, 0) = u(x, \pi) = u(0, y) = 0$

so solution is

$$u(x, y) = \sum_{n=1}^{\infty} a_n \sin\left(\frac{n\pi y}{b}\right)\sinh\left(\frac{n\pi(x-a)}{b}\right)$$

Here $b = \pi$ and $a = 0$

$$\text{so } u(x, y) = \sum_{n=1}^{\infty} a_n \sin ny.\sinh nx$$

$$= \sum_{n=1}^{\infty} a_n \sin ny.\sinh nx$$

35. $u_x(x, y) = \sum_{n=1}^{\infty} na_n \sin ny.\cosh nx$

$$a_n = \frac{-2}{\pi}\int_0^{\pi} \sin y \sin\left(\frac{n\pi y}{\pi}\right)dy$$

$$= \begin{cases} \pi & \text{for } n = 1 \\ 0 & \text{for } n \neq 0 \end{cases}$$

so $u(x, y) = a_1 \text{siny}. \sin hx$

now $u_x(x, y) = \sin y .\cos h\, x$

$$= a, \sin y. \cos hx$$

$$a_1 = \frac{1}{\cosh x}$$

so $u(x, y) = \pi \sin y.\dfrac{\sinh x}{\cosh x}$

$$= \pi \sin y. \tan hx$$

$$= \pi \sin y\left(\frac{e^x - e^{-x}}{e^{\pi} + e^{-\pi}}\right)$$

$$u\left(x, \frac{\pi}{2}\right) = \pi\left(\frac{e^x - e^{-x}}{e^{\pi} + e^{-\pi}}\right)$$

36. $U(x, y) = f(x e^y) + g(y^2 \cos y)$

$$u_{xy} = e^y f'(xe^y) + xe^{2y} f'(xe^x) \quad \ldots(i)$$

$$u_{xy} = e^2 y f'(xe^y)$$

$$u_x = e^y f'(xe^y)$$

$$\Rightarrow u_{xy} - xu_{xx} = 4x$$

39. $u_{tt} - 4u_{xx} = 0 - \infty < x < \infty, t > 0$

$$u(x, 0) = \begin{bmatrix} 16 - x^2, & |x| \leq 4 \\ 0 & \text{otherwise} \end{bmatrix}$$

$$= f(x)$$

$$ut(x, 0) = \begin{bmatrix} 1, & |x| \leq 2 \\ 0, & \text{otherwise} \end{bmatrix}$$

$$= g(x)$$

$$u(x, t) = \frac{1}{2}[f(x-2t) + f(x+2t)] + \frac{1}{4}\int_{x-2t}^{x+2t} g(s)ds$$

$$u(2, t) = \frac{1}{2}[f(2-2t) + f(2+2t)] + \frac{1}{4}\int_{2-2t}^{2+2t} g(s)ds$$

$$= \frac{1}{2}[16-(2-2t)^2 + 16-(2+2t)^2] + \frac{1}{4}\int_{2-2t}^{2+2t} 1ds$$

$$= \frac{1}{2}[32-(2-2t)^2-(2+2t)^2] + \frac{1}{4}[2+2t-2+2t]$$

$$= \frac{1}{2}[32-(2-2t)^2-(2+2t)^2] + t$$

40. $u_t(2, t) = \dfrac{1}{2}[+4(2-2t) - 4(2+2t)] + 1$

$$u_t(2, 2) = \frac{1}{2}[4(2-4) - 4(2+4)] + 1$$

$$= \frac{1}{2}[-8-24] + 1 = -15 \Rightarrow -15$$

41. We have

$(x^2 - y^2)\ 4xx + 2(x^2 + y^2)\ 4xy + (x^2 - y^2)\ 4xy = 0$

$4(x^2 + y^2)^2 - 4(x^2 - y^2)^2$

Here, $R = (x^2 - y^2)$

$S = 2(x^2 + y^2)$

and $T = (x^2 - y^2)$

$\therefore \quad S^2 - 4RT = 4(x^4 + y^4 + 2x^2y^2) - 4(x^4 + y^4 - 2x^2y^2)$

$= x^2y^2 > 0$ as $x > 0, y > 0$

Hence the given partial differential equation is hyperbolic.

42. We have

$ut + uun = 0$

Lagranges auxiliary equation is

$$\frac{dt}{1} = \frac{du}{0} = \frac{dx}{u}$$

Now $du = 0 \Rightarrow u = C_1$

and $$\frac{dt}{1} = \frac{dx}{u}$$

$$\Rightarrow \int dt = \int \frac{1}{C_1}\,dx$$

$\Rightarrow \quad x - C_1 t = C_2$

$\Rightarrow \quad u = \phi(x - ut)$

But $u(x, 0) = \alpha + \beta x = \phi(x) \quad ...(i)$

along $x = t + 1$

$u(x, t) = \phi(t + 1 - t) = 1$

$\Rightarrow \quad \phi(1) = 1$

$\Rightarrow \quad \phi(x) = x = \beta x + \alpha$

$\Rightarrow \quad \alpha = 0, \beta = 1$

43. $u_{tt} = u_{xx}$, $u(x, 0) = \sin x$

$u_t(x, 0) = 1$

$$u(x, t) = \frac{1}{2}[f(x-t) + f(x+t) + \frac{1}{2}\int_{x-t}^{x+t} 1ds$$

$$= \frac{1}{2}[\sin(x - t) + \sin(x + t)] + \frac{1}{2} \times 2t$$

$$= \frac{1}{2}[2 \sin x \cos t] + t$$

$= \sin x \cos t + t$

$u(\pi, \pi/2) = \pi/2$

44. $u_t = u_{xx}'$

$$\Rightarrow \quad u(x, 0) = \frac{e^{2x} - 1}{e^{2x} + 1}, \text{ then}$$

$$\lim_{t\to\infty} u(1,t) = -1/2$$

as $$u(x, t) = \sum_{n=1}^{\infty} a_n \exp\left(\frac{-n^2\pi^2 t}{\pi^2}\right) \sin\left(\frac{n\pi x}{\pi}\right)$$

$$= \sum_{n=1}^{\infty} a_n \exp\left(-n^2 t\right) \sin(nx)$$

45. $$u(\cos\theta, \sin\theta) = \begin{cases} \sin\theta & 0 \le \theta \le \pi \\ 0 & \pi \le \theta \le 2\pi \end{cases}$$

circle in $x^2 + y^2 \le 1$

$$u(1, \theta) = \begin{cases} \sin\theta, & 0 \le \theta \le \pi \\ 0 & \pi \le \theta \le 2\pi \end{cases}$$

$a_0 = 1/\pi,\ a_n = 0$

$b_n = 0,\ \forall n \in N$

so $u(0, 0) = 2/\pi$

46. $u(P) + u(R) = u(Q) + u(S)$

$\Rightarrow \quad 1 + 1/2 = -1/2 + u(S)$

$\Rightarrow \quad u(S) = 2$

47. $xuy - yux = u$

$-yp + xq = u$

$$\frac{dx}{-y} = dy/x = du/u$$

$xdx + ydy = 0$

$x^2 + y^2 = c_1$

48. $$u(x, 0) = \sin\frac{\pi}{4}x$$

Then, $$u\left(\frac{1}{\sqrt{2}}, \frac{1}{\sqrt{2}}\right) = \frac{1}{\sqrt{2}}e^{\pi/4}$$

49. Let $$u(x, y) = \frac{y}{x}$$

$$\frac{\partial u}{\partial x} = -\frac{y}{x^2}, \text{ and } \frac{\partial u}{\partial y} = \frac{1}{x}$$

$$\Rightarrow \quad x.\frac{\partial u}{\partial x} + y.\frac{\partial u}{\partial y} = 0$$

Also, $u(1, y) = \frac{y}{1} = y$

50. Let $u = f(x)\,g(y)$

$$\therefore \quad \frac{\partial u}{\partial x} = f'(x)g(y), \text{ and } \frac{\partial u}{\partial y} = f(x)g'(y)$$

and $$\frac{\partial^2 u}{\partial x\,\partial y} = f'(x)\,g'(y)$$

$$\Rightarrow u\frac{\partial^2 u}{\partial x\,\partial y} - \frac{\partial u}{\partial x}\frac{\partial u}{\partial y} = f(x)\,g(y).f'(x)\,g'(y) - f(x)\,g(y).f'(x)\,g'(y) = 0$$

51. $x\frac{\partial^2 u}{\partial x^2} + 2xy\frac{\partial^2 u}{\partial x\partial y} + y\frac{\partial^2 u}{\partial y^2} + x\frac{\partial u}{\partial y} + y\frac{\partial u}{\partial x} = 0$

If $r = \frac{\partial^2 u}{\partial x^2}, s = \frac{\partial^2 u}{\partial x\partial y}, t = \frac{\partial^2 u}{\partial y^2}$

$p = \frac{\partial u}{\partial x}, \quad q = \frac{\partial u}{\partial y}$

i.e. $\quad xr + 2xys + yt + xq + yp = 0$

compare with

$$Rr + Ss + Tt + f(x, y, z, p, q) = 0$$

$$R = x, \quad S = 2xy, \quad T = y$$

Now λ the quadratic

$$R\lambda^2 + S\lambda + T = 0$$

$$x\lambda^2 + 2xy\lambda + y = 0$$

$$\Rightarrow \quad \lambda = \frac{-2xy \pm \sqrt{4x^2y^2 - 4xy}}{2x}$$

$$\lambda = \frac{-xy \pm \sqrt{x^2y^2 - xy}}{x}$$

But $\quad x^2y^2 - xy > 0$

$\Rightarrow \quad xy\,(xy - 1) > 0$

because $\sqrt{x^2y^2 - xy}$ is always positive

Hence, function is hyperbolic in the region $x < 0$, $y < 0$, $xy > 1$.

55a. $u(x, t) = 1 + e^{-4\pi^2 t}\cos 2\pi x \quad ...(i)$

$$\frac{\partial u}{\partial x} = -e^{-4\pi^2 t}\,.\,2\pi\sin 2\pi x \quad ...(ii)$$

Initial condition

$u(x, 0) = 2\cos^2 \pi x$ satisfies

boundary conditions,

$$\frac{\partial u}{\partial x}(0, t) = 0 = \frac{\partial u}{\partial x}(1, t)$$

are also satisfies by equation (*ii*).

55b. Heat flux $= \left(\frac{\partial u}{\partial x}\right)_{\left(\frac{1}{4}, t\right)}$

$= -2\pi\, e^{-4\pi^2 t}\sin 2\pi\,.\,\frac{1}{4}$ (By equation (*ii*))

$= -\,2\pi\, e^{-4\pi^2 t}$

56. $4_t + 4ux = 0$ with $u(x, 0) = x$

$$\frac{dt}{1} = \frac{dx}{4} = \frac{du}{0}$$

$\Rightarrow x - 4t = c_1$ and $u = c_2$

$\Rightarrow u = \phi(x - ut)$

Now $u(x, 0) = x \Rightarrow x = \phi(x)$

$u = x - ut$ be the solution and

$x - ut = c_1$

and $\quad u = c_2$ intersect at $(0, -1)$

57. Suppose, $u(x, y)$ satisfies Laplace's equation i.e., $\nabla^2 u = 0$

In R^2 and $u = 0$ on the unit circle. There at the origin u is equal to 0.

58. $(2x+u)u_x + (2y + u)u_y = u$

$$\frac{dx}{2x + u} = \frac{dy}{2y + u} = \frac{du}{u}$$

$$\Rightarrow \quad \frac{dx - dy}{2(x - y)} = \frac{du}{u}$$

$$\Rightarrow \quad u = c_1(x - y)^{1/2}$$

so, if $(1, 1)$, $u(1, 1) = 0$

$\Rightarrow \quad x = y$

59. $\frac{\partial^2 u}{\partial r^2} + \frac{1}{r}\frac{\partial u}{\partial r} + \frac{1}{r^2}\frac{\partial^2 u}{\partial \theta^2} = 0$

$u(1, \theta) = 2\cos^2\theta$

so $\quad u(r, \theta) = 1 + r^2\cos^2\theta$

as $u(r, \theta) = \frac{a_0}{2} + \sum_{n=1}^{\infty}\left(\frac{r}{a}\right)^n (a_n\cos n\theta + b_n\sin n\theta)$

where $a_n = \frac{1}{\pi}\int_0^{2\pi} f(\theta)\cos n\theta\, d\theta$

$n = 0, 1, 2, ...$

$b_n = \frac{1}{\pi}\int_0^{2\pi} f(\theta)\sin n\theta\, d\theta$

$n = 1, 2, ...$

60. If $u_0(x)$ is discontinuous at a point, so it is for any given t.

61. $\frac{\partial^2 u}{\partial t^2} = c^2\frac{\partial^2 u}{\partial \times 2}, x \in R, t > 0$

with initial condition

$$u(x, 0) = \begin{cases} \sin\frac{\pi x}{c}, & 0, \le x \le c \\ 0, & \text{otherwise} \end{cases} \quad \textit{and}$$

$ut\,(x, 0) = 0, \forall - x.$

then for a given $t > 0$ $u(x, t)$

$$= \frac{1}{2}\left[\sin\left(\frac{\pi(x - ct)}{c}\right) + \sin\left(\frac{\pi(x + ct)}{c}\right)\right]$$

$\Rightarrow u(x, t)$ is smooth for all x.

62. $z = px + qy - \sin pq$...(*i*) Equation (*i*) is of the clairaut's is form.

So its complete equation is obtained by merely replacing p and q by a and b respectively.

∴ Complete integeral is

$$z = ax + by - \sin(ab).$$

69. Heat equation is given by

$$\frac{\partial U}{\partial t} = c^2 \frac{\partial^2 U}{\partial x^2};\ c^2 = 1$$

Let $$U = \frac{e^{-x^2}}{\sqrt{t}}$$

$$\frac{\partial U}{\partial t} = \frac{\sqrt{t}.e^{-x^2/4t}\left(\frac{x^2}{4t^2}\right) - e^{-\frac{x^2}{4t}\frac{1}{2\sqrt{t}}}}{t}$$

$$= \frac{e^{-x^2/4t}}{\sqrt{t}}\left[\frac{x^2}{4t^2} - \frac{1}{2t}\right]$$

$$= u\left[\frac{x^2}{4t^2} - \frac{1}{2t}\right]$$

$$\frac{\partial U}{\partial x} = \frac{1}{\sqrt{t}} \cdot e^{-\frac{x^2}{4t}}\left(\frac{2x}{4t}\right)$$

$$= U\left(-\frac{x}{2t}\right)$$

$$\frac{\partial^2 U}{\partial x^2} = \frac{\partial U}{\partial x}\left(-\frac{x}{2t}\right) - U\left(\frac{1}{2t}\right)$$

$$= U\left\{\frac{x^2}{4t^2} - \frac{1}{2t}\right\}$$

$$\therefore \quad \frac{\partial U}{\partial t} = \frac{\partial^2 U}{\partial x^2}$$

70. Laplace equation $\Delta^2 \psi = 0$ is the elliptic equation occuring most frequently in physical problems.

75. The general linear partial differential equation

$A u_{xx} + B u_{xy} + C u_{yy} + F(x, y, u, u_x, u_y) = 0$

represents hyperbolic if

$$B^2 - 4AC > 0$$

i.e. $y^2 - 4 . 1 . 0 > 0$

$\Rightarrow \quad y^2 > 0.$

i.e. given partial differential equation is hyperbolic in above x-axis region.

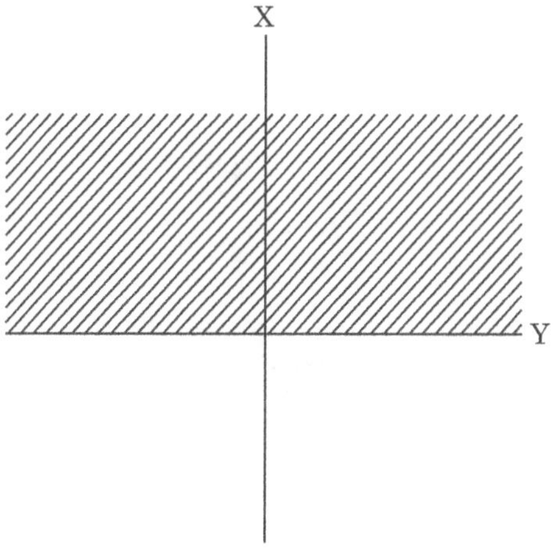

Fig.

79. Given equation is

$$\begin{bmatrix} x & y & z \\ \alpha & \beta & \gamma \\ \frac{\partial z}{\partial x} & \frac{\partial z}{\partial y} & -1 \end{bmatrix} = 0$$

$$\Rightarrow x\left[-\beta - \gamma\frac{\partial z}{\partial y}\right] - y\left[-\alpha - \gamma\frac{\partial z}{\partial x}\right] + z\left[\alpha\frac{\partial z}{\partial y} - \beta\frac{\partial z}{\partial x}\right] = 0$$

$$\Rightarrow -\beta x - x\gamma\frac{\partial z}{\partial y} + \alpha y + y\gamma\frac{\partial z}{\partial x} + \alpha z\frac{\partial z}{\partial y} - \beta z\frac{\partial z}{\partial x} = 0$$

$$\Rightarrow (y\gamma - \beta z)\frac{\partial z}{\partial x} + (\alpha z - x\gamma)\frac{\partial z}{\partial y} = \beta x - \alpha y$$

Here subsidiary equations are

$$\frac{dx}{(y\gamma - \beta z)} = \frac{dy}{(\alpha z - x\gamma)} = \frac{dz}{(\beta x - \alpha y)}$$

Using multipliers x, y and z, we get

$$\text{each fraction} = \frac{xdx + ydy + zdz}{0}$$

$\Rightarrow xdx + ydy + zdz = 0$

On integration, we get

$$x^2 + y^2 + z^2 = c. \quad \text{... (1)}$$

Again using multipliers, α, β and γ, we get

$$\text{each fraction} = \frac{\alpha dx + \beta dy + \gamma dz}{0}$$

$\Rightarrow \alpha dx + \beta dy + \gamma dz = 0$

On integration, we get

$$\alpha x + \beta y + \gamma z = b \quad \text{... (2)}$$

From equations (1) and (2), the required solution is

$$x^2 + y^2 + z^2 = f(\alpha x + \beta y + \gamma z).$$

80(*a*). We choose two new variables

$$p = p(x, y)$$

and $$q = q(x, y)$$

Then $$\frac{\partial u}{\partial x} = \frac{\partial u}{\partial p}\cdot\frac{\partial p}{\partial x} + \frac{\partial u}{\partial q}\cdot\frac{\partial q}{\partial x}$$

$$= U_p \cdot p_x + U_q q_x \quad \text{...(1)}$$

$$\frac{\partial^2 u}{\partial x^2} = U_{pp}p_y^2 + 2U_{Pq}p_x q_x$$

$$+ U_{qq}q_x^2 + U_P p_{xx} + U_q q_{xx} \quad \text{...(2)}$$

Similarly $$\frac{\partial^2 u}{\partial y^2} = U_{pp}p_y^2 + 2U_{Pq}p_y q_y$$

$$+ U_{qq}q_y^2 + U_P p_{yy} + U_q q_{yy} \quad \text{...(3)}$$

Using equations (1), (2) and (3) in given equation

$$U_{PP}p_x^2 + 2U_{Pq}p_x q_x + U_{qq}q_x^2 + U_P p_{xx}$$

$$+ U_q q_{xx} - U_{PP}p_y^2 - 2U_{Pq}p_y q_y - U_{qq}q_y^2$$

$$- U_P p_{yy} - U_q q_{yy} - \frac{2}{x}U_P p_x$$

$$- \frac{2}{x}U_q q_x = 0.$$

$$\Rightarrow (U_{PP}p_x^2 - U_{PP}p_y^2 + U_p p_{xx} - U_P p_{yy} - \frac{2}{x}U_P P_x)$$

$$+ (U_{qq}q_x^2 + U_q q_{xx} - U_{qq}q_y^2 - U_q q_{yy} - \frac{2}{x}U_q q_x)$$

$$+ (2U_{pq}P_x q_x - 2U_{pq}P_y q_y) = 0$$

$$\Rightarrow (p_x^2 - p_y^2)U_{PP} + 2(p_x q_x - p_y q_y)U_{pq}$$

$$+ (q_x^2 - q_y^2)U_{qq} + (P_{xx} - P_{yy} - \frac{2}{x}P_x)U_P$$

$$+ (q_{xx} - q_{yy} - \frac{2}{x}\cdot q_x)U_q = 0$$

This is required canonical form.

9 CHAPTER Topology

2016

1. Let (z_n) be a sequence of distinct points in $D(0, 1) = \{z \in \mathbb{C} \mid |z| < 1\}$ with $\lim_{n\to\infty} z_n = 0$. Consider the following statements P and Q:

(P) : There exists a unique analytic function f on D(0, 1) such that $f(z_n) = \sin(z_n)$ for all n.

(Q) : There exists an analytic function f on D (0, 1) such that $f(z_n) = 0$ if n is even and $f(z_n) = 1$ if n is odd.

Which of the above statements hold TRUE?

(*a*) both P and Q (*b*) only P

(*c*) only Q (*d*) Neither P nor Q

2. Let $(\mathbb{R}, \tau)$ be a topological space with the cofinite topology. Every infinite subset of $\mathbb{R}$ is

(*a*) Compact but NOT connected

(*b*) Both compact and connected

(*c*) NOT compact but connected

(*d*) Neither compact nor connected

3. Let M be the set of all n × n real matrices with the usual norm topology. Consider the following statements P and Q:

(P) : The set of all symmetric positive definite matrices in M is connected

(Q) : The set of all invertible matrices in M is compact.

Which of the above statements hold TRUE?

(*a*) both P and Q

(*b*) only P

(*c*) only Q

(*d*) Neither P nor Q

4. Consider the following statements P and Q:

(P) : If H is a normal subgroup of order 4 of the symmetric group S_4, then $S_4/_H$ is abelian.

(Q) : If Q = {±1, ±i, ±j, ±k} is the quaternion group, then $Q/\{-1, 1\}$ is abelian.

Which of the above statements hold TRUE?.

(*a*) both P and Q

(*b*) only P

(*c*) only Y

(*d*) Neither P nor Q

2015

5. Let X be a connected topological space such that there exists a non-constant continuous function $f : X \to \mathbb{R}$, where $\mathbb{R}$ is equipped with the usual topology. Let $f(X) = \{f(x) : x \in X\}$. Then

(*a*) X is countable but $f(X)$ is uncountable

(*b*) $f(X)$ is countable but X is uncountable

(*c*) both $f(X)$ and X are countable

(*d*) both $f(X)$ and X are uncountable

6. Let τ_1 be the usual topology on $\mathbb{R}$. Let τ_2 be the topology on $\mathbb{R}$ generated by

$B = \{[a, b) \subset \mathbb{R} : -\infty < a < b < \infty\}$. Then the set

$\{x \in \mathbb{R} : 4\sin^2 x \le 1\} \cup \left\{\frac{\pi}{2}\right\}$ is

(*a*) closed in $(\mathbb{R}, \tau_1)$ but NOT in $(\mathbb{R}, \tau_2)$

(*b*) closed in $(\mathbb{R}, \tau_2)$ but NOT in $(\mathbb{R}, \tau_1)$

(*c*) closed in both $(\mathbb{R}, \tau_1)$ and $(\mathbb{R}, \tau_2)$

(*d*) neither closed in $(\mathbb{R}, \tau_1)$ nor closed in $(\mathbb{R}, \tau_2)$

2014

7. Let X be a set with at least two elements. Let τ and τ' be two topologies on X such that $\tau' \ne \{\phi, X\}$. Which of the following conditions is necessary for the identity function $id : (X, \tau) \to (X, \tau')$ to be continuous?

(*a*) $\tau \subseteq \tau'$

(*b*) $\tau' \subseteq \tau$

(*c*) no conditions on τ and τ'

(*d*) $\tau \cap \tau' = \{\phi, X\}$

2013

8. Consider $\mathbb{R}^2$ with the usual topology. Which of the following statements are **TRUE** for all A, B $\subseteq \mathbb{R}^2$?

$P : \overline{A \cup B} = \overline{A} \cup \overline{B}$.

$Q : \overline{A \cap B} = \overline{A} \cap \overline{B}$.

$R : (A \cup B)^\circ = A^\circ \cup B^\circ$.

$S : (A \cap B)^\circ = A^\circ \cap B^\circ$.

(*a*) P and R only (*b*) P and S only

(*c*) Q and R only (*d*) Q and S only

2012

9. In a topological space, which of the following statements is NOT always true :

(*a*) Union of any finite family of compact sets is compact.

(*b*) Union of any family of closed sets is closed.

(*c*) Union of any family of connected sets having a non empty intersection is connected.

(*d*) Union of any family of dense subsets is dense.

10. Consider the following statements :

P : The family of subsets $\left\{A_n = \left(-\frac{1}{n}, \frac{1}{n}\right), n = 1, 2, \ldots\right\}$ satisfies the finite intersection property.

Q : On an infinite set X, a metric $d : X \times X \to R$ is defined as $d(x, y) = \begin{cases} 0, & x = y \\ 1, & x \neq y \end{cases}$.

The metric space (X, d) is compact.

R : In a Frechet (T_1) topological space, every finite set is closed.

S : If $f : R \to X$ is continuous, where R is given the usual topology and (X, τ) is a Hausdorff (T_2) space, then f is a one-one function.

Which of the above statements are correct?

(*a*) P and R (*b*) P and S

(*c*) R and S (*d*) Q and S

11. Let X = {*a*, *b*, *c*} and let $\Im$ = {ϕ, {*a*}, {*b*}, {*a*, *b*}, X} be a topology defined on X. Then which of the following statements are **TRUE**?

P : (X, $\Im$) is a Hausdorff space.

Q : (X, $\Im$) is a regular space.

R : (X, $\Im$) is a normal space.

S : (X, $\Im$) is a connected space.

(*a*) P and Q (*b*) Q and R

(*c*) R and S (*d*) P and S

12. Consider the statements

P : If X is a normed linear space and $M \subseteq X$ is a subspace, then the closure $\overline{M}$ is also a subspace of X.

Q : If X is a Banach space and $\sum x_n$ is an absolutely convergent series in X, then $\sum x_n$ is convergent.

R : Let M_1 and M_2 be subspaces of an inner product space such that $M_1 \cap M_2 = \{0\}$. Then $\forall\, m_1 \in M_1, m_2 \in M_2$; $\|m_1 + m_2\|^2 = \|m_1\|^2 + \|m_2\|^2$.

S : Let $f : X \to Y$ be a linear transformation from the Banach Space X into the Banach space Y. If f is continuous, then the graph of f is always compact.

The correct statements amongst the above are :

(*a*) P and R only (*b*) Q and R only

(*c*) P and Q only (*d*) R and S only

2011

13. For which subspace $X \subseteq R$ with the usual topology and with $\{0, 1\} \subseteq X$, will a continuous function $f : X \to \{0, 1\}$ satisfying $f(0) = 0$ and $f(1) = 1$ exist?

(*a*) X = [0, 1] (*b*) X = [–1, 1]

(*c*) X = R (*d*) $[0, 1] \not\subset X$

14. Suppose X is a finite set with more than five elements. Which of the following is **TRUE**?

(*a*) There is a topology on X which is T_3

(*b*) There is a topology on X which is T_2 but not T_3

(*c*) There is a topology on X which is T_1 but not T_2

(*d*) There is no topology on X which is T_1

2010

Common Data for Q. (15 - 16)

Let $X = \mathbb{N} \times \mathbb{Q}$ with subspace topology of the usual topology on $\mathbb{R}^2$ and $P = \left\{\left(n, \frac{1}{n}\right) : n \in \mathbb{N}\right\}$.

15. In the space X ,

(*a*) P is closed but not open

(*b*) P is open but not closed

(*c*) P is both open and closed

(*d*) P is neither open nor closed

16. The boundary of P in X is

(*a*) an empty set (*b*) a singleton set

(*c*) P (*d*) X

2009

17. The subspace $\mathbb{Q} \times [0, 1]$ of $\mathbb{R}^2$ (with the usual topology) is

(*a*) dense in $\mathbb{R}^2$ (*b*) connected

(*c*) separable (*d*) compact

18. Consider the topology $\tau = \{G \subseteq \mathbb{R} : \mathbb{R} \setminus G \text{ is compact in } (\mathbb{R}, \tau_u)\} \cup \{\phi, \mathbb{R}\}$ on $\mathbb{R}$, where τ_u is the usual topology on $\mathbb{R}$ and ϕ is the empty set. Then $(\mathbb{R}, \tau)$ is

(*a*) a connected Hausdorff space

(*b*) connected but NOT Hausdorff

(*c*) Hausdorff but NOT connected

(*d*) neither connected nor Hausdorff

19. Let

$\tau_1 = \{G \subseteq \mathbb{R} : G \text{ is finite or } \mathbb{R}\backslash G \text{ is finite}\}$

and

$\tau_2 = \{G \subseteq \mathbb{R} : G \text{ is countable or } \mathbb{R}\backslash G \text{ is countable}\}$.

Then

(*a*) neither τ_1 nor τ_2 is a topology on $\mathbb{R}$

(*b*) τ_1 is a topology on $\mathbb{R}$ but τ_2 is NOT a topology on $\mathbb{R}$

(*c*) τ_2 is a topology on $\mathbb{R}$ but τ_1 is NOT a topology on $\mathbb{R}$

(*d*) both τ_1 and τ_2 are topologies on $\mathbb{R}$

2008

20. Let X be a non-empty set. Let $\Im_1$ and $\Im_2$ be two topologies on X such that $\Im_1$ is strictly contained in $\Im_2$. If $I : (x, \Im_1) \to (x, \Im_2)$ is the identity map, then

(*a*) both I and I^{-1} are continuous

(*b*) both I and I^{-1} are not continuous

(*c*) I is continuous but I^{-1} is not continuous

(*d*) I is not continuous but I^{-1} is continuous

21. Let X = R and let $\Im = \{U \subseteq X : X - U \text{ is finite}\} \cup \{\phi, X\}$.

The sequence $1, \frac{1}{2}, \frac{1}{3}, \ldots, \frac{1}{n}, \ldots$ in $(X, \Im)$

(*a*) converges to 0 and not to any other point of X

(*b*) does not converge to 0

(*c*) converges to each point to X

(*d*) is not convergent in X

22. Let $E = \{(x, y) \in R^2 : |x| \le 1, |y| \le 1\}$. Define f : $E \to R$ by $f(x, y) = \frac{x + y}{1 + x^2 + y^2}$. Then the range of f is a

(*a*) connected open set

(*b*) connected closed set

(*c*) bounded open set

(*d*) closed and unbounded set

23. Let X = {1, 2, 3} and $\Im = \{\phi, \{1\}, \{2\}, \{1, 2\}, \{2, 3\}, \{1, 2, 3\}\}$. The topological space $(X, \Im)$ is said to have the property P if for any two proper disjoint closed subsets Y and Z of X, there exist disjoint open sets U, V such that $Y \subseteq U$ and $Z \subseteq V$. Then the topological space $(X, \Im)$

(*a*) is T_1 and satisfies P

(*b*) is T_1 and does not satisfy P

(*c*) is not T_1 and satisfies P

(*d*) is not T_1 and does not satisfy P

Common Data for Questions 24, 25, 26:

Let X = C([0, 1]) with sup norm $\| \; \|_\infty$.

24. Let $S = \{x \in X : \|x\|_\infty \le 1\}$. Then

(*a*) S is convex and compact

(*b*) S is not convex but compact

(*c*) S is convex but not compact

(*d*) S is neither convex nor compact

25. Which one of the following is true?

(*a*) $C^\infty([0, 1])$ is dense in X

(*b*) X is dense in $L^\infty([0, 1])$

(*c*) X has a countable basis

(*d*) There is a sequence in X which is uniformly Cauchy on [0,1] but does not converge uniformly on [0, 1]

26. Let $I = \{x \in X : x(0) = 0\}$. Then

(*a*) I is not an ideal of X

(*b*) I is an ideal, but not a prime ideal of X

(*c*) I is a prime ideal, but not a maximal ideal of X

(*d*) I is a maximal ideal of X

2007

27. Consider R^2 with the usual topology. Let $S = \{(x, y) \in R^2 : x \text{ is an integer}\}$. Then S is

(*a*) open but NOT closed

(*b*) both open and closed

(*c*) neither open nor closed

(*d*) closed but NOT open

28. Suppose $X = \{\alpha, \beta, \delta\}$. Let

$\Im_1 = \{\phi, X, \{\alpha\}, (\alpha, \beta)\}$ and $\Im_2 = \{\phi, X, \{\alpha\}, \{\beta, \delta\}\}$.

Then

(*a*) both $\Im_1 \cap \Im_2$ and $\Im_1 \cup \Im_2$ are topologies

(*b*) neither $\Im_1 \cap \Im_2$ nor $\Im_1 \cup \Im_2$ is a topology

(*c*) $\Im_1 \cup \Im_2$ is a topology but $\Im_1 \cap \Im_2$ is NOT a topology

(*d*) $\Im_1 \cap \Im_2$ is a topology but $\Im_1 \cup \Im_2$ is NOT a topology

29. Let $S = \{0, 1, 1), (1, 0, 1), (-1, 2, 1)\} \subseteq R^3$. Suppose R^3 is endowed with the standard inner product $\langle , \rangle$. Define $M = \{x \in R^3 : \langle x, y \rangle = 0 \text{ for all } y \in S\}$. Then the dimension of M equals

(*a*) 0 (*b*) 1

(*c*) 2 (*d*) 3

30. Let X be an uncountable set and let $\mathfrak{I} = \{U \subseteq X : U = \phi \text{ or } U^c \text{ is finite}\}$. Then the topological space $(X, \mathfrak{I})$

(*a*) is separable

(*b*) is Hausdorff

(*c*) has a countable basis

(*d*) has a countable basis at each point

31. Suppose $(X, \mathfrak{I})$ is a topological space. Let $\{S_n\}_{n\geq 1}$ be a sequence of subsets of X.

Then

(*a*) $(S_1 \cup S_2)^\circ = S_1^\circ \cup S_2^\circ$

(*b*) $\left(\bigcup_n S_n\right)^\circ = \bigcup_n S_n^\circ$

(*c*) $\overline{\bigcup_n S_n} = \bigcup_n \overline{S_n}$

(*d*) $\overline{S_1 \cup S_2} = \overline{S_1} \cup \overline{S_2}$

2006

32. Let τ_1 be the usual topology on R. Define another topology τ_2 on R by

$\tau_2 = \{U \subseteq R \mid U^c$ is either finite or empty or whole of R$\}$,

where U^c denotes the complement of U in R. If I : $(R, \tau_1) \to (R, \tau_2)$ is the identity map, then

(*a*) I is continuous but not I^{-1}

(*b*) I^{-1} is continuous but not I

(*c*) both I and I^{-1} are continuous

(*d*) neither I nor I^{-1} is continuous

33. Let τ_1 be the usual topology on R. Define another topology τ_2 on R by

$\tau_2 = \{U \subseteq R \mid U^c$ is either countable or empty or whole of R$\}$

Then, Z is

(*a*) closed in (R, τ_1) but not in (R, τ_2)

(*b*) closed in (R, τ_2) but not in (R, τ_1)

(*c*) closed in both (R, τ_1) and (R, τ_2)

(*d*) closed neither in (R, τ_1) nor in (R, τ_2)

34. Consider R^2 with the usual topology. The complement of N × N is

(*a*) open but not connected

(*b*) connected but not open

(*c*) both open and connected

(*d*) neither open nor connected

2005

35. Under the usual topology in R^3, if $O = \{(x, y, z) \in R^3 : x^2 + y^2 < 1\}$ and $F = \{(x, y, z) \in R^3 : z = 0\}$, then $O \cap F$ is

(*a*) both open and closed

(*b*) neither open nor closed

(*c*) open but not closed

(*d*) closed but not open

36. Consider R and S^1 with the usual topology where S^1 is the unit circie in R^2. Then

(*a*) there is no continuous map from S^1 to R

(*b*) any continuous map from $S^1$to R is the zero map

(*c*) any continuous map from $S^1$to R is a constant map

(*d*) there are nonconstant continuous map from S^1 to R

37. Consider R with the usual topology and R^ω ,the countable product of R with product topology. If $D_n = [-n,n] \subseteq R$ and $f : R^\omega \to R$ is a continuous map, then

$f\left(\prod_{n\in N} D_n\right)$ is of the form

(*a*) $[a, b]$ for some $a \leq b$

(*b*) (a, b) for some $a < b$

(*c*) Z

(*d*) R

38. Let R^2 denote the plane with the usual topology and $U = \{(x,y) \in R^2 : xy < 0\}$. Denote the number of connected components of U and $\overline{U}$ (the closure of U) by α and β respectively. Then

(*a*) $\alpha = \beta = 1$ (*b*) $\alpha = 1, \beta = 2$

(*c*) $\alpha = 2, \beta = 1$ (*d*) $\alpha = \beta = 2$

39. Under the usual topology on R^3, the map $f : R^3 \to R^3$ defined by $f(x, y, z) = (x + 1, y - 1, z)$ is

(*a*) neither open nor closed

(*b*) open but not closed

(*c*) both open and closed

(*d*) closed but not open

2004

40. In R^2 with usual topology, the set $U = \{(x, -y) \in R^2 : x = 0, 1, -1 \text{ and } y \in N\}$ is

(*a*) neither closed nor bounded

(*b*) closed but not bounded

(*c*) bounded but not closed

(*d*) closed and bounded

41. In R^3 with usual topology, let $V = \{(x, y, z) \in R^3 : x^2 + y^2 + z^2 = 1, y \neq 0)$ and $W = \{(x,y,z) \in R^3 : y = 0\}$. Then $V \cup W$ is

(a) connected and compact

(b) connected but not compact

(c) compact but not connected

(d) neither connected nor compact

42. In R with the usual topology, the set $U = \{x \in R : -1 \leq x \leq 1, x \neq 0)$ is

(a) neither Hausdorff nor first countable

(b) Hausdorff but not first countable

(c) first countable but not Hausdorff

(d) both Hausdorff and first countable

43. Suppose $U = \{x \in Q : 0 \leq x \leq 1\}$ and $V = \{x \in Q : 0 < x < 2\}$. Let n and m be the number of connected components of U and V respectively. Then

(a) $m = n = 1$ (b) $m = n \neq 1$

(c) $m = 2n$, m, n finite (d) $m > 2n$

44. Let $f : [0, 1] \to R$ be the continuous function defined by

$$f(x) = \frac{(x-1)(x-2)}{(x-3)(x-4)}.$$

Then the maximal subset of R on which f has a continuous extension is

(a) $(-\infty, 3)$ (b) $(-\infty, 3) \cup (4, \infty)$

(c) $\frac{R}{\{3,4\}}$ (d) R

45. Suppose $U = \left(0, \frac{1}{2}\right) \times \left(0, \frac{1}{2}\right)$,

$V = \left(-\frac{1}{2}, 0\right) \times \left(-\frac{1}{2}, 0\right)$ and D be the open unit disk with centre at origin of R^2. Let f be a real valued continuous function on D such that $f(U) = 0$. Then it follows that

(a) $f(v) = 0$ for every v in V

(b) $f(v) \neq 0$ for every v in V

(c) $f(v) = 0$ for some v in V

(d) f can assume any real value on V

2003

46. Let $Q = \{(x, y)$ in $R^2 \mid x \geq 0, y \geq 0\}$ be the first quadrant in R^2 with usual topology. Then Q is closed because

(a) it is compact

(b) it does not contain all its limit points

(c) its complement is open

(d) it is connected

47. Let $X = [0, 1] \times [0, 2] \times \ldots \times [0, 10]$ and $f : X \to R$ be a continuous function. Then $f(X)$ is

(a) $[r_1, r_2] \cup [r_3, r_4]$ for some r_1, r_2, r_3, r_4 in R such that $r_1 < r_2 < r_3 \leq r_4$

(b) $(-\infty, r]$ for some r in R

(c) $[r_1, r_2]$ for some r_1, r_2 in R such that $r_1 \leq r_2$

(d) $(-\infty, r_1] \cup [r_2, \infty)$ for some r_1, r_2 in R such that $r_1 \leq r_2$

48. Consider the following statements concerning topological spaces

(P) Continuous image of a non-compact space is non-compact

(Q) Every metrizable space is normal Then

(a) both P and Q are true

(b) P is true and Q is false

(c) P is false and Q is true

(d) both P and Q are false.

49. In R^3, with the usual topology, let B be the unit closed ball with center at the origin, and T be the closure of an inscribed tetrahedron. Let $f : T \to R$ be any continuous function. Then

(a) f has an extension to $B \Rightarrow f$ is a constant function

(b) not every f has an extension to B

(c) f always has an extension to B

(d) if f has an extension to B then $f(T) \subseteq [0, 1]$

50. Let PQR be a triangle in R^2 with the usual topology. Define

X = *Int* (PQR) ∪ (P, Q, R).

Then the number of connected components of X is

(a) 1 (b) 2

(c) 3 (d) 4

51. In R^2 with the usual topology, let $X = \{(x, |x|)$ such that $-1 \leq x \leq 1\}$. Let $p : X \to [-1, 1]$ be the map defined by $p(x, y) = x$ for all (x, y) in X. Then p is

(a) a homoomorphism as p is one-one, onto and continuous

(b) a homoomorphism as both p and p^{-1} are one-one, onto and continuous

(c) not a homoomorphism as p is not continous

(d) not a homoomorphism as p^{-1} is not continuous

2002

52. The topology on the real line R generated by left-open right-closed intervals (a, b) is

(a) strictly coarser than the usual topology

(b) strictly finer than the usual topology

(c) not comparable with the usual topology

(d) same as the usual topology

9.6 Topology

53. Let X, Y be topological spaces and $f : X \to Y$ be a continuous and bijective map. Then f is a homeomorphism, if

(*a*) X and Y are compact

(*b*) X is Hausdorff and Y is compact

(*c*) X is compact and Y is Hausdorff

(*d*) X and Y are Hausdorff

54. Show that X is Hausdorff topological space if and only if the diagonal A defined by

$$\Delta = \{(x, y) \in X \times X \mid x = y\}$$

is a closed subset of $X \times X$ (with product topology).

2001

55. Let $T : C^n \to C^n$ be a linear operator having n distinct eigenvalues. Then

(*a*) T is invertible

(*b*) T is invertible as well as diagona-lizable

(*c*) T is not diagonalizable

(*d*) T is diagonalizable

56. A metric space is always

(*a*) first countable (*b*) second countable

(*c*) Lindelof (*d*) separable

57. Let X be the indiscrete space and Y a T_0 space. If $f : X \to Y$ is continuous, then

(*a*) X must be a one-point space

(*b*) Y must be discrete

(*c*) f must be a constant

(*d*) Y must be a one-point space

58. Let X be a group with identity e and let $p : X \to R$ be a function satisfying

(*i*) $p(x) \geq 0$ forall $x \in X$, $p(x) = 0$ if $x = e$

(*ii*) $p(xy) \leq p(x) + p(y)$ for all $x, y \in X$

(*iii*) $p(x^{-1}) = p(x)$, for all $x \in X$.

Define $d(x, y) = p(x^{-1} y)$. Show that d is a metric on X.

2000

59. The topology τ on the real line R generated by the class $\Im$ of all closed intervals $[d, d + l]$ with length l is

(*a*) indiscrete

(*b*) discrete

(*c*) standard topology

(*d*) neither discrete nor Housdorff

60. Let norms $\|x\|_1 = \sum_{i=1}^{n} |\xi i|$ and $\|x\|_2 = \left(\sum_{i=1}^{n} |\xi i|^2\right)^{\frac{1}{2}}$ induce topologies τ_1 and τ_2 on R^n, the n-dimensional Euclidean space, then

(*a*) τ_1 is weaker than τ_2

(*b*) τ_1 is stronger than τ_2

(*c*) τ_1 is equivalent to τ_2

(*d*) τ_1 and τ_2 are incomparable

61. Let A be a subset of a topological space (X, τ) and τ_A be the relative topology on A. Then A is τ - connected if and only if A is τ_A - connected. Prove this. [5]

ANSWERS

1. (*b*)	**2.** (*b*)	**3.** (*b*)	**4.** (*c*)	**5.** (*d*)	**6.** (*c*)	**7.** (*b*)	**8.** (*b*)	**9.** (*d*)	**10.** (*a*)
11. (*c*)	**12.** (*c*)	**13.** (*d*)	**14.** (*a*)	**15.** (*c*)	**16.** (*b*)	**17.** (*a*)	**18.** (*a*)	**19.** (*d*)	**20.** (*d*)
21. (*a*)	**22.** (*c*)	**23.** (*c*)	**24.** (*c*)	**25.** (*d*)	**26.** (*c*)	**27.** (*b*)	**28.** (*a*)	**29.** (*c*)	**30.** (*c*)
31. (*d*)	**32.** (*d*)	**33.** (*b*)	**34.** (*b*)	**35.** (*b*)	**36.** (*a*)	**37.** (*a*)	**38.** (*b*)	**39.** (*b*)	**40.** (*b*)
41. (*c*)	**42.** (*d*)	**43.** (*a*)	**44.** (*b*)	**45.** (*b*)	**46.** (*a*)	**47.** (*d*)	**48.** (*d*)	**49.** (*d*)	**50.** (*c*)
51. (*c*)	**52.** (*d*)	**53.** (*c*)	**54.** (*)	**55.** (*b*)	**56.** (*a*)	**57.** (*c*)	**58.** (*)	**59.** (*b*)	**60.** (*c*)
61. (*)									

EXPLANATIONS

2. Let A be any non-empty infinite subset of $\mathbb{R}$ and U be an open cover of A. Let V be any open set in U, Then $\frac{A}{V}$ is finite. So we can finite some finitely many open set from U to cover $\frac{A}{V}$.

Therefore every open cover has a finite sub cover. So A is compact, but A is arbitrary, so every subset of $\mathbb{R}$ is compact.

Next Let U and V are disjoint non-empty set in X s.t U & V

$U \cup V = X$

$U = X - F_U$ and $V - X - F_V$ for some finite subset F_U and F_V since U & V are disjoints so $V < F_U$ & $V < F_V$

But $X = U \cup V \leq F_V \cup F_U$ which is finite we get a contradiction

$\therefore$ X is connected.

Hence every infinite subset of $\mathbb{R}$ with cofinite topology is compact and connected.

3. The set of all symmetric positive definite matrices is a convex set. Thus there should be a path connecting any two matrices is that set i.e it is connected. But the set of all invertible matrices in M is unbounded, so it is not compact

Hence only P is true.

4. $O(S_4) = 4! = 24$ and $O(H) = 4$

But the H does not contain every element of S_4 of the form $xyx^{-1}y^{-1}$, where $x, y \in S_4$

So $S^4/_H$ is non-abelian group.

Order of quaternion group is 8 and $O\left(\frac{Q}{\{-1,1\}}\right) = 4$

So $O\left(\frac{Q}{\{-1,1\}}\right)$ is an abelian group.

Hence only Q is true.

7. τ and τ' be two topologies on X. i.e., (X, τ) and (X, τ') are topological space.

The identity function $I : (XI(\tau), \tau) \to (X, \tau')$

By definition of continuity in topological space, the mapping $f : x \to y$ is continuous iff the inverse image under f of any open set in y is open in x.

Now, I is continuous iff $H \in I' \Rightarrow I[H] \in \tau$.

But $I^{-1}(H) = H$ since I is identify map

Hence, I is continuous iff $H \in \tau' \Rightarrow H \in \tau$ i.e. iff $\tau' \subseteq \tau$.

8.
$$\overline{A \cup B} = \bar{A} \cup \bar{B}$$
$$(A \cap B)^\circ = A^\circ \cap B^\circ$$

So P and S are true.

9. Let $\{A_\alpha : \alpha \in \wedge$ where $\wedge$ is index set$\}$ be any family of dense subset of a topological space $(x, \exists)$

Then $\bar{A}_\alpha = x, \forall \alpha \in \wedge$

Now
$$\overline{\bigcup_{\alpha \in \wedge} A_\alpha} = \bigcup_{\alpha \in \wedge} \bar{A}_\alpha = X$$

Therefore, union of any family of dense subsets is dense.

11. Let $x = \{a, b, c\}$

$$y = \{\phi, \{a\}, \{b\}, \{a, b\}, x\}$$

Then there exists open set $\{a\}$ containing a but there does not exists open set containing. Such that there intersection is empty. Hence, (x, y) is not a Hansdorff space.

Let $a \in x$ and $\{b, c\}$ be a closed set of x such that $a \notin \{b, c\}$, then there exists an open set $\{a\}$, containing a but there does not exists any open set containing closed set $\{b, c\}$ such that there intersection is empty.

Hence (x, y) is not a regular space there fore (x, y) is a normal space as well as connected space.

20. Let x be a non-empty set Let Y_1 and Y_2 be two topologies on X such that Y_1 is strictly contained in Y_2. If $I : (X, Y_1) \to (X, Y_2)$ is the identity map then I is not continuous but I^{-1} is continuous.

22. Given that

$$f(x, y) = \frac{x + y}{1 + x^2 + y^2}$$
$$|f(x, y)| = \frac{|x + y|}{|1 + x^2 + y^2|}$$

$< 1 [\because |x + 1| < |1 + x^2 + y^2|]$

$\therefore \quad |f(x, y)| < 1 \forall (x, y) \in R^2$

$f(x, y)$ is bounded.

27. We know that all the subsets of a topological space are either open or closed.

Now $S = \{(x, y)\} \in R^2 : x$ is an integer $\}$ is open as well as closed. As, $R^2 - s$ is closed as well as open.

28. Given that $X = \{\alpha, \beta, \delta\}$

Also $J_1 = \{\phi, x, \{\alpha\}, \{\alpha, \beta\}\}$

$J_2 = \{\phi, x, \{\alpha\}, \{\beta, \delta\}\}$

Then $J_1 \cup J_2 = \{\phi, x, \{\alpha\}, \{\alpha, \beta\}, \{\beta, \delta\}\}$

is a topology on x.

Also $J_1 \cap J_2 = \{\phi, x, \{\alpha\}\}$ is a topology on x.

Hence $J_1 \cup J_2$ and $J_1 \cap J_2$ both are topologies on x.

29. We have

$s = \{(0, 1, 1),(1, 0, 1),(-1, 2, 1)\} \subseteq R^3$

and $M = \{x \in R^3 : < x, y > = 0, \forall y \in s$

$$i.e., M = \left\{ \begin{pmatrix} x_1 \\ x_2 \\ x_3 \end{pmatrix} : x_2 + x_3 \right.$$

$$\left. = \phi, x_1 + x_3 = 0, -x_1 + 2x_2 + x_3 = 0 \right\}$$

$$\text{i.e.,} \begin{bmatrix} 0 & 1 & 1 \\ 1 & 0 & 1 \\ -1 & 2 & 1 \end{bmatrix} \begin{bmatrix} x_1 \\ x_2 \\ x_3 \end{bmatrix} = \begin{bmatrix} 0 \\ 0 \\ 0 \end{bmatrix}$$

$$= \begin{bmatrix} 0 & 1 & 1 \\ 1 & 0 & 1 \\ 0 & 2 & 2 \end{bmatrix} \begin{bmatrix} x_1 \\ x_2 \\ x_3 \end{bmatrix}$$

$$= \begin{bmatrix} 0 \\ 0 \\ 0 \end{bmatrix}$$

$$\Rightarrow \begin{bmatrix} 0 & 1 & 1 \\ 1 & 0 & 1 \\ 0 & 0 & 0 \end{bmatrix} \begin{bmatrix} x_1 \\ x_2 \\ x_3 \end{bmatrix} = \begin{bmatrix} 0 \\ 0 \\ 0 \end{bmatrix}$$

$$\Rightarrow \left. \begin{matrix} x_2 + x_3 = 0 \\ x_1 + x_3 = 0 \end{matrix} \right]$$

$\Rightarrow x_1 = x_2 = c_1$

and $x_3 = c$

Hence $M = \{(c_1, c_1, c): c \in R ; c_1 \in R\}$

so $\dim (m) = 2$

30. Since x is an uncountable set and

$J = \{u \subseteq x ; u = \phi$ or $\cup^c$ is finite$\}$

Hence, topological space (X, T) has a countable basis.

31. Since $S_1 \subset \bar{S}_1$ and $\bar{S}_1 \subset \bar{S}_2$,

we have $S_1 \cup S_2 \subset \bar{S}_1 \cup \bar{S}_2$ Being a union of two closed sets $\bar{S}_1 \cup \bar{S}_2$ is a closed set.

Hence $\overline{S_1 \cup S_2} \subset \overline{S_1 \cup S_2}$

Next $S_1 \subset S_1 \cup S_2$, $S_2 \subset S_1 \cup S_2$ imply that $\bar{S}_1 \subset \overline{S_1 \cup S_2}$, $\bar{S}_2 \subset \overline{S_1 \cup S_2}$ and $\bar{S}_1 \cup \bar{S} = \overline{S_1 \cup S_2}$

Therefore, $\overline{S_1 \cup S_2} = \bar{S}_1 \cup \bar{S}_2$

32. We have topology J_2 on R by

$J_2 = \{ V \subseteq R\}$ V^C is either finite or empty or whole of R$\}$

Where V^C denotes the complement of V in R and J_1 is a usual topology on R if

$l : (R_1 J_1) \rightarrow (R_1 J_2)$

is the identity map, then neither l nor l^{-1} is continuous.

33. Given that J is usual topology on R and $J_2 = \{V \subseteq R\}$ V^C is either contable or empty set or whole R$\}$

is a topology on R.

Then, z is closed in $(R_1 J_2)$ but not in $(R_1 J_1)$

34. Concider R^2 with usual topology, then complement of $N \times N$ is connected but not open.

35. $O = \{(x, y, z) \in R^3 : x^2 + y^2 < 1\}$

i.e., it is a sphere of radius less than 1.

$F = \{(x, y, z) \in R^3 : z = 0\}$

*i.e.,*it is a plane of equation $z = 0$

Hence, $O \cap F$ is neither open nor closed.

36. R and S′ are usual topology.

Then there is no continuous map from S^1 to R because S^1 is the unit circle which lies in R^2.

37. R is the usual topology and R^ω is the countable product of R with product topology. If $D_n = [-n, n] \subseteq R$ and $f : R^\omega \rightarrow R$ is a continuous map, then $f(\prod_{n \in N} D_n)$ must be in the form of $[a, b]$ for some $a \leq b$.

38. Let R^2 denote the usual topology

and $U = \{(x, y) \in R^2 : xy < 0\}$

then $\bar{U} = \{(y, x) \in R^2 : xy < 0\}$

Now the number of connected components of U and $\bar{U}$

i.e. $\alpha = 1, \beta = 2$.

39. $f : R^3 \rightarrow R^3$

$f(x, y, z) = (x + 1, y - 1, z)$

$\Rightarrow a_1(x + 1) + a_2(y - 1) + a_3 z = 0$

$\Rightarrow a_1 = 0, a_2 = 0, a_3 = 0$

40. Consider R^2 with usual topology the set

$U = \{(x, -y) \in R^2 : x = 0, 1, -1,$ and $y \in N\}$

is closed but not bounded

41. Consider R^3 with usual topology, let

$V = \{(x, y, z) \in R^3 : x^2 + y^2 + z^2 = 1, y \neq 0\}$

and $W = \{(x, y, z) \in R^3 : y = 0\}$

Then $V \cup W$ is compact but not connected.

42. Consider R with usual topology and

$U = \{x \in R : -1 \le x \le 1, x \ne 0\}$

Here $-\frac{1}{z} \ne -\frac{1}{z}$

but $\frac{1}{z}, -\frac{1}{z} \in U$

and $-\frac{1}{z} \in [-1, 0]$

and $\frac{1}{z} \in (0, 1)$

Now, (–1, 0) and (0, 1) are disjoint set.

Hence U is Hausdorff and first countable

43. We have $U = \{x \in Q : 0 \le x \le 1\}$

and $V = \{x \in Q : 0 < x < 2\}$

if n and m are connected components of and V_1 then

$$n = m = 1$$

61. Since two non empty subsets of A is said to be τ-separated if and only if they are τ_A-separated. If A is τ-connected i.e. A cannot be the union of two τ-separated sets. So it cannot be the union of two τ_A-separated sets.

Hence A is τ_A-connected space. Con-versely, if τ_A is connected then there is no union of two τ_A-separated sets, as above there is no union of two τ-separated sets. Hence A is τ-connected.

10 CHAPTER

Probability and Statistics

2016

1. Let the probability density function of a random variable X be

$$f(x) = \begin{cases} x & 0 \le x < \frac{1}{2} \\ c(2x-1)^2 & \frac{1}{2} < x \le 1 \\ 0 & \text{otherwise} \end{cases}$$

Then, the value of c is equal to ________.

2. Let $X_1, X_2, X_3, \ldots X_n$ be a random sample from the following probability density function for $0 < \mu < \infty$, $0 < \alpha < 1$.

$$f(x;\mu,\alpha) = \begin{cases} \frac{1}{\Gamma(\alpha)}(x-\mu)^{\alpha-1}e^{-(x-\mu)}; & x > \mu \\ 0 & \text{otherwise} \end{cases}$$

Here α and μ are unknown parameters. Which of the following statements is TRUE?

(*a*) Maximum likelihood estimator of only μ exists

(*b*) Maximum likelihood estimator of only α exists

(*c*) Maximum likelihood estimators of both μ and α exist

(*d*) Maximum likelihood estimator of Neither μ nor α exists

3. Suppose X and Y are two random variables such that aX + bY is a normal variable for all $a, b \in \mathbb{R}$. Consider the following statements P, Q, R and S:

(P) : X is a standard normal random variable.

(Q) : The conditional distribution of X given Y is normal.

(R) : The conditional distribution of X given X + Y is normal.

(S) : X – Y has mean 0.

Which of the above statements ALWAYS hold TRUE?

(*a*) both P and Q

(*b*) both Q and R

(*c*) both Q and S

(*d*) both P and S

4. Let X be a random variable with the following cumulative distribution function:

$$F(x) = \begin{cases} 0 & x < 0 \\ x^2 & 0 \le x < \frac{1}{2} \\ \frac{3}{4} & \frac{1}{2} \le x < 1 \\ 1 & x \ge 1 \end{cases}$$

Then $P\left(\frac{1}{4} < X < 1\right)$ is equal to ______.

2015

5. Let X be a random variable having the distribution function

$$F(x) = \begin{cases} 0 & \text{if } x < 0 \\ \frac{1}{4} & \text{if } 0 \le x < 1 \\ \frac{1}{3} & \text{if } 1 \le x < 2 \\ \frac{1}{2} & \text{if } 2 \le x < \frac{11}{3} \\ 1 & \text{if } x \ge \frac{11}{3} \end{cases}$$

Then E(X) is equal to _____

6. Let $x_1 = 2.2$, $x_2 = 4.3$, $x_3 = 3.1$, $x_4 = 4.5$, $x_5 = 1.1$ and $x_6 = 5.7$ be the observed values of a random sample of size 6 from a $U(\theta - 1, \theta + 4)$ distribution, where $\theta \in (0, \infty)$ is unknown. Then a maximum likelihood estimate of θ is equal to

(*a*) 1.8 (*b*) 2.3

(*c*) 3.1 (*d*) 3.6

7. In an experiment, a fair die is rolled until two sixes are obtained in succession. The probability that the experiment will end in the fifth trial is equal to

(*a*) $\frac{125}{6^5}$ (*b*) $\frac{150}{6^5}$

(*c*) $\frac{175}{6^5}$ (*d*) $\frac{200}{6^5}$

8. Let $X \sim B\left(5, \frac{1}{2}\right)$ and $Y \sim U(0,1)$. Then $\frac{P(X+Y \le 2)}{P(X+Y \ge 5)}$ is equal to ________

9. Let the random variable X have the distribution function

$$F(x) = \begin{cases} 0 & \text{if } x < 0 \\ \frac{x}{2} & \text{if } 0 \le x < 1 \\ \frac{3}{5} & \text{if } 1 \le x < 2 \\ \frac{1}{2} + \frac{x}{8} & \text{if } 2 \le x < 3 \\ 1 & \text{if } x \ge 3 \end{cases}$$

Then $P(2 \le X < 4)$ is equal to ________

10. Let $X \sim$ Poisson (λ), where $\lambda > 0$ is unknown. If $\delta(X)$ is the unbiased estimator of $g(\lambda) = e^{-\lambda}(3\lambda^2 + 2\lambda + 1)$, then $\sum_{k=0}^{\infty} \delta(k)$ is equal to ________

11. Let X and Y be independently distributed central chi-squared random variables with degrees of freedom m (≥ 3) and n (≥ 3), respectively. If $E\left(\frac{X}{Y}\right) = 3$ and $m + n = 14$, then $E\left(\frac{Y}{X}\right)$ is equal to

(a) $\frac{2}{7}$ (b) $\frac{3}{7}$

(c) $\frac{4}{7}$ (d) $\frac{5}{7}$

12. Let $\Omega = (0, 1]$ be the sample space and let P(.) be a probability function defined by

$$P((0, x]) = \begin{cases} \frac{x}{2} & \text{if } 0 \le x < \frac{1}{2} \\ x & \text{if } \frac{1}{2} \le x \le 1 \end{cases}$$

Then $P\left(\left\{\frac{1}{2}\right\}\right)$ is equal to ________

13. Let $X_1 \ldots X_n$ be a random sample from $N(\mu, 1)$ distribution, where $\mu \in \left\{0, \frac{1}{2}\right\}$.

For testing the null hypothesis $H_0 : \mu = 0$ against the alternative hypothesis $H_1 : \mu = \frac{1}{2}$, consider the critical region

$$R = \left\{(x_1, x_2, \ldots, x_n) : \sum_{i=1}^{n} x_i > c\right\},$$

where c is some real constant. If the critical region R has size 0.025 and power 0.7054, then the value of the sample size n is equal to ____________

14. Let X and Y be two random variables having the joint probability density function

$$f(x, y) = \begin{cases} 2 & \text{if } 0 < x < y < 1 \\ 0 & \text{otherwise.} \end{cases}$$

Then the conditional probability $P\left(X \le \frac{2}{3} \mid Y = \frac{3}{4}\right)$ is equal to

(a) $\frac{5}{9}$ (b) $\frac{2}{3}$

(c) $\frac{7}{9}$ (d) $\frac{8}{9}$

15. Let $X_1, X_2, \ldots$ be a sequence of independent and identically distributed random variables with $P(X_1 = 1) = \frac{1}{4}$ and $P(X_1 = 2) = \frac{3}{4}$. If $\bar{X}_n = \frac{1}{n}\sum_{i=1}^{n} X_i$, for $n = 1, 2, \ldots$, then $\lim_{n\to\infty} P(\bar{X}_n \le 1.8)$ is equal to________.

16. Let X_1, X_2 and X_3 be independent and identically distributed random variables with $E(X_1) = 0$ and $E(X_1^2) = \frac{15}{4}$.

If $\psi : (0, \infty) \to (0, \infty)$ is defined through the conditional expectation

$$\psi(t) = E(X_1^2 \mid X_1^2 + X_2^2 + X_3^2 = t), t > 0,$$

then $E(\psi((X_1 + X_2)^2))$ is equal to ________.

2014

17. The time to failure, in months, of light bulbs manufactured at two plants A and B obey the exponential distribution with means 6 and 2 months respectively. Plant B produces four times as many bulbs as plant A does. Bulbs from these plants are indistinguishable. They are mixed and sold together. Given that a bulb purchased at random is working after 12 months, the probability that it was manufactured at plant A is ____

18. Let X, Y be continuous random variables with joint density function

$$f_{xy}(x, y) = \begin{cases} e^{-y}(1 - e^{-x}) \text{ if } 0 < x < y < \infty \\ e^{-x}(1 - e^{-y}) \text{ if } 0 < y \le x < \infty \end{cases}$$

The value of $E[X + Y]$ is ________

19. Suppose that X is a population random variable with probability density function

$$f(x; \theta) = \begin{cases} \theta x^{\theta - 1} & \text{if } 0 < x < 1 \\ 0 & \text{otherwise,} \end{cases}$$

where θ is a parameter. In order to test the null hypothesis $H_0 : \theta = 2$, against the alternative hypothesis $H_1 : \theta = 3$, the following test is used:

Reject the null hypothesis if $X_1 \geq \frac{1}{2}$ and accept otherwise, where X_1 is a random sample of size 1 drawn from the above population. Then the power of the test is ________

20. Suppose that $X_1, X_2, ..., X_n$ is a random sample of size n drawn from a population with probability density function

$$f(x;\theta) = \begin{cases} \frac{x}{\theta^2} e^{-\frac{x}{\theta}} & \text{if } x > 0 \\ 0 & \text{otherwise,} \end{cases}$$

where θ is a parameter such that $\theta > 0$. The maximum likelihood estimator of θ is

(*a*) $\frac{\sum_{i=1}^{n} X_i}{n}$ (*b*) $\frac{\sum_{i=1}^{n} X_i}{n-1}$

(*c*) $\frac{\sum_{i=1}^{n} X_i}{2n}$ (*d*) $\frac{2\sum_{i=1}^{n} X_i}{n}$

2013

21. Suppose the random variable U has uniform distribution on [0,1] and X = –2 log U. The density of X is

(*a*) $f(x) = \begin{cases} e^{-x} \text{ if } x > 0 \\ 0 \quad \text{otherwise} \end{cases}$

(*b*) $f(x) = \begin{cases} 2e^{-x} \text{ if } x > 0 \\ 0 \quad \text{otherwise} \end{cases}$

(*c*) $f(x) = \begin{cases} \frac{1}{2} e^{\frac{-2x}{2}} \text{ if } x > 0 \\ 0 \quad \text{otherwise} \end{cases}$

(*d*) $f(x) = \begin{cases} 1/2 & \text{if } x \in [0,2] \\ 0 & \text{otherwise} \end{cases}$

22. Suppose X is a random variable with $P(X = k) = (1-p)^k p$ for $k \in \{0,1,2, ...\}$ and some $p \in (0,1)$. For the hypothesis testing problem

$$H_0: p = \frac{1}{2} H_1 : p \neq \frac{1}{2}$$

consider the test "Reject H_0 if $X \leq A$ or if $X \geq B$",. where A < B are given positive integers. The type-I error of this test is

(*a*) $1 + 2^{-B} - 2^{-A}$ (*b*) $1 - 2^{-B} + 2^{-A}$

(*c*) $1 + 2^{-B} - 2^{-A-1}$ (*d*) $1 - 2^{-B} + 2^{-A-1}$

23. For each $\lambda > 0$, let X_λ be a random variable with exponential density $\lambda e^{-\lambda x}$ on$(0, \infty)$. Then, Var(log X_λ)

(*a*) is strictly increasing in λ

(*b*) is strictly decreasing in λ

(*c*) does not depend on λ

(*d*) first increases and then decreases in λ

24. Let X be an arbitrary random variable that takes values in{0,1, ...,10}. The minimum and maximum possible values of the variance of X are

(*a*) 0 and 30

(*b*) 1 and 30

(*c*) 0 and 25

(*d*) 1 and 25

Common Data for Questions 25 and 26:

Let $X_1, X_2, ..., X_n$ be an i.i.d. random sample from exponential distribution with mean . In other words, they have density

$$f(x) = \begin{cases} \frac{1}{\mu} e^{-x/\mu} \text{ if } x > 0 \\ 0 \quad \text{otherwise} \end{cases}$$

25. Which of the following is **NOT** an unbiased estimate of μ?

(*a*) X_1

(*b*) $\frac{1}{n-1}(X_2 + X_3 + ... + X_n)$

(*c*) $n.(\min\{X_1, X_2, ..., X_n\})$

(*d*) $\frac{1}{n}\max\{X_1, X_2, ..., X_n\}$

26. Consider the problem of estimating μ. The m.s.e (mean square error) of the estimate

$T(X) = \frac{X_1 + X_2 + ... + X_n}{n+1}$ is

(*a*) μ^2 (*b*) $\frac{1}{n+1}\mu^2$

(*c*) $\frac{1}{(n+1)^2}\mu^2$ (*d*) $\frac{n^2}{(n+1)^2}\mu^2$

2012

27. A continuous random variable X has the probability density function

$$f(x) = \begin{cases} \frac{3}{5} e^{\frac{3}{5}x}, & x > 0 \\ 0, & x \leq 0. \end{cases}$$

The probability density function of $Y = 3X + 2$ is

(*a*) $f(y) = \begin{cases} \frac{1}{5} e^{-\frac{1}{5}(y-2)}, & y > 2 \\ 0, & y \leq 2 \end{cases}$

(*b*) $f(y) = \begin{cases} \frac{2}{5} e^{-\frac{2}{5}(y-2)}, & y > 2 \\ 0, & y \leq 2 \end{cases}$

(c) $f(y) = \begin{cases} \frac{3}{5}e^{-\frac{3}{5}(y-2)}, & y > 2 \\ 0, & y \le 2 \end{cases}$

(d) $f(y) = \begin{cases} \frac{4}{5}e^{-\frac{4}{5}(y-2)}, & y > 2 \\ 0, & y \le 2 \end{cases}$

28. A simple random sample of size 10 from $N(\mu, \sigma^2)$ gives 98% confidence interval (20.49, 23.51).

Then the null hypothesis $H_0 : \mu = 20.5$ against $H_A : \mu \neq 20.5$

(a) can be rejected at 2% level of significance

(b) cannot be rejected at 5% level of significance

(c) can be rejected at 10% level of significance

(d) cannot be rejected at any level of significance

29. If a random variable X assumes only positive integral values, with the probability

$$P(X = x) = \frac{2}{3}\left(\frac{1}{3}\right)^{x-1}, x = 1, 2, 3, ...$$

then E(X) is

(a) $\frac{2}{9}$ (b) $\frac{2}{3}$

(c) 1 (d) $\frac{3}{2}$

30. The probability density function of the random variable X is

$$f(x) = \begin{cases} \frac{1}{\lambda}e^{-x/\lambda}, & x > 0 \\ 0, & x \le 0, \end{cases}$$

where $\lambda > 0$. For testing the hypothesis $H_0 : \lambda = 3$ against $H_A : \lambda = 5$, a test is given as "Reject H_0 if $X \ge 4.5$". The probability of type I error and power of this test are, respectively,

(a) 0.1353 and 0.4966

(b) 0.1827 and 0.379

(c) 0.2021 and 0.4493

(d) 0.2231 and 0.4066

Statement for Linked Answer Questions 31 and 32 :

The joint probability density function of two random variables X and Y is given as

$$f(x, y) = \begin{cases} \frac{6}{5}\left(x + y^2\right), & 0 \le x \le 1, 0 \le y \le 1 \\ 0, & \textit{elsewhere} \end{cases}$$

31. E(X) and E(Y) are, respectively,

(a) $\frac{2}{5}$ and $\frac{3}{5}$ (b) $\frac{3}{5}$ and $\frac{3}{5}$

(c) $\frac{3}{5}$ and $\frac{6}{5}$ (d) $\frac{4}{5}$ and $\frac{6}{5}$

32. Cov (X, Y) is

(a) – 0.01 (b) 0

(c) 0.01 (d) 0.02

2011

33. Which of the following functions is a probability density function of a random variable X?

(a) $f(x) = \begin{cases} x(2-x), & 0 < x < 2 \\ 0, & \textit{elsewhere} \end{cases}$

(b) $f(x) = \begin{cases} x(1-x) & 0 < x < 1 \\ 0, & \textit{elsewhere} \end{cases}$

(c) $f(x) = \begin{cases} 2xe^{-x^2}, & -1 < x < 1 \\ 0 & \text{elsewhere} \end{cases}$

(d) $f(x) = \begin{cases} 2xe^{-x^2}, & x > 0 \\ 0 & \text{elsewhere} \end{cases}$

34. Let X_1, X_2, X_3 and X_4 be independent standard normal random variables. The distribution of

$$W = \frac{1}{2}\{(X_1 - X_2)^2 + (X_3 - X_4)^2\}$$

is

(a) N (0, 1) (b) N (0, 2)

(c) χ_2^2 (d) χ_4^2

35. For $n \ge 1$, let $\{X_n\}$ be a sequence of independent random variables with

$$P(X_n = n) = P(X_n = -n) = \frac{1}{2n^2}$$

$$P(X_n = 0) = 1 - \frac{1}{n^2}$$

Then, which of the following statements is **TRUE** for the sequence $\{X_n\}$?

(a) Weak Law of Large Numbers holds but Strong Law of Large Number does not hold

(b) Weak Law of Large Number does not hold but Strong Law of Large Number holds

(c) Both Weak Law of Large Number and Strong Law of Large Number hold

(d) Both Weak Law of Large Number and Strong Law of Large Numbers do not hold

36. The time to failure (in hours) of a component is a continuous random variable T with the probability density function

$$f(t) = \begin{cases} \frac{1}{10} e^{-\frac{t}{10}}, & t > 0 \\ 0, & t \le 0. \end{cases}$$

Ten of these components are installed in a system and they work independently. Then, the probability that **NONE** of these fail before ten hours, is

(*a*) e^{-10} (*b*) $1 - e^{-10}$
(*c*) $10\,e^{-10}$ (*d*) $1 - 10e^{-10}$

37. Let X be the real normed linear space of all real sequences with finitely many non-zero terms, with supremum norm and $T : X \to X$ be a one to one and onto linear operator defined by

$$T(x_1, x_2, x_3 \ldots) = \left(x_1, \frac{x_2}{2^2}, \frac{x_3}{3^2}\right)$$

Then, which of the following is **TRUE**?

(*a*) T is bounded but T^{-1} is not bounded
(*b*) T is not bounded but T^{-1} is bounded
(*c*) Both T and T^{-1} are bounded
(*d*) Neither T nor T^{-1} is bounded

Common Data for Questions 38 and 39:

Let X and Y be two continuous random variables with the joint probability density function

$$f(x, y) = \begin{cases} 2, & 0 < x + y < 1, \quad x > 0, y > 0, \\ 0, & \text{elsewhere} \end{cases}$$

38. $P\left(X + Y < \frac{1}{2}\right)$ is

(*a*) $\frac{1}{4}$ (*b*) $\frac{1}{2}$
(*c*) $\frac{3}{4}$ (*d*) 1

39. $E\left(X \mid Y = \frac{1}{2}\right)$ is

(*a*) $\frac{1}{4}$ (*b*) $\frac{1}{2}$
(*c*) 1 (*d*) 2

2010

40. Let E and F be any two events with $P(E \cup F) = 0.8$, $P(E) = 0.4$ and $P(E|F) = 0.3$. Then P(F) is

(*a*) $\frac{3}{7}$ (*b*) $\frac{4}{7}$
(*c*) $\frac{3}{5}$ (*d*) $\frac{2}{5}$

41. Let X have a binomial distribution with parameters n and p, where n is an integer greater than 1 and $0 < p < 1$. If $P(X = 0) = P(X = 1)$, then the value of p is

(*a*) $\frac{1}{n-1}$ (*b*) $\frac{n}{n+1}$
(*c*) $\frac{1}{n+1}$ (*d*) $\frac{1}{1+n^{\frac{1}{n-1}}}$

42. Let X have a binomial distribution with parameters n and p, $n = 3$. For testing the hypothesis $H_0 : p = \frac{2}{3}$ against $H_1 : p = \frac{1}{3}$, let a test be : "Reject H_0 if $X \ge 2$ and accept H_0 if $X \le 1$". Then the probabilities of Type I and Type II errors respectively are

(*a*) $\frac{20}{27}$ and $\frac{20}{27}$ (*b*) $\frac{7}{27}$ and $\frac{20}{27}$
(*c*) $\frac{20}{27}$ and $\frac{7}{27}$ (*d*) $\frac{7}{27}$ and $\frac{7}{27}$

Common Data for Q. (43 - 44)

Let X and Y be continuous random variables with the joint probability density function

$$f(x, y) = \begin{cases} ae^{-2y}, & 0 < x < y < \infty \\ 0, & \text{otherwise.} \end{cases}$$

43. The value of a is

(*a*) 4 (*b*) 2
(*c*) 1 (*d*) 0.5

44. The value of $E(X \mid Y = 2)$ is

(*a*) 4 (*b*) 3
(*c*) 2 (*d*) 1

2009

45. Let F, G and H be pairwise independent events such that $P(F) = P(G) = P(H) = \frac{1}{3}$ and $(F \cap G \cap H) = \frac{1}{4}$. Then the probability that at least one event among F, G and H occurs is

(*a*) $\frac{11}{12}$ (*b*) $\frac{7}{12}$
(*c*) $\frac{5}{12}$ (*d*) $\frac{3}{4}$

46. Let X be a random variable such that $E(X^2) = E(X) = 1$. Then $E(X^{100}) =$

(*a*) 0
(*b*) 1
(*c*) 2^{100}
(*d*) $2^{100} + 1$

47. For which of the following distributions, the weak law of large numbers does NOT hold ?

(*a*) Normal

(*b*) Gamma

(*c*) Beta

(*d*) Cauchy

48. Let X be a non-negative integer valued random variable with $E(X^2) = 3$ and $E(X) = 1$. Then

$$\sum_{i=1}^{\infty} i\, P(X \geq i) =$$

(*a*) 1 (*b*) 2

(*c*) 2 (*d*) 4

49. Let X be a random variable with probability density function $f \in \{f_0, f_1\}$, where

$$f_0(x) = \begin{cases} 2x, & \text{if } 0 < x < 1 \\ 0, & \text{otherwise} \end{cases}$$

and

$$f_1(x) = \begin{cases} 3x^2, & \text{if } 0 < x < 1 \\ 0_{xn} & \text{otherwise} \end{cases}$$

For testing the null hypothesis $H_0 : f \equiv f_0$ against the alternative hypothesis $H_1 : f \equiv f_1$ at level of significance $\alpha = 0.19$, the power of the most powerful test is

(*a*) 0.729 (*b*) 0.271

(*c*) 0.615 (*d*) 0.385

50. Let X and Y be independent and identically distributed U(0, 1) random variables. Then

$$P\left(Y < \left(X - \frac{1}{2}\right)^2\right) =$$

(*a*) $\frac{1}{12}$ (*b*) $\frac{1}{4}$

(*c*) $\frac{1}{3}$ (*d*) $\frac{2}{3}$

Common Data for Questions 51–52

Let X and Y be random variables having the joint probability density function

$$f(x,y) = \begin{cases} \dfrac{1}{\sqrt{2\pi y}} e^{\frac{-1}{2y}(x-y)^2}, & \text{if } -\infty < x < \infty, 0 < y < 1 \\ 0, & \end{cases}$$

51. The variance of the random variable X is

(*a*) $\frac{1}{12}$ (*b*) $\frac{1}{4}$

(*c*) $\frac{7}{12}$ (*d*) $\frac{5}{12}$

52. The covariance between the random variables X and Y is

(*a*) $\frac{1}{3}$ (*b*) $\frac{1}{4}$

(*c*) $\frac{1}{6}$ (*d*) $\frac{1}{12}$

2008

53. Let $X_1, X_2, \ldots, X_{10}$ be a random sample from $N(80, 3^2)$ distribution. Define

$$S = \sum_{i=1}^{10} U_i \text{ and } T = \sum_{i=1}^{10}\left(U_i - \frac{S}{10}\right)^2$$

where $U_i = \frac{X_i - 80}{3}$, $i = 1, 2, \ldots, 10$.

Then the value of E(ST) is equal to

(*a*) 0 (*b*) 1

(*c*) 10 (*d*) $\frac{80}{3}$

54. Two (distinguishable) fair coins are tossed simultaneously. Given that ONE of them lands up head, the probability of the OTHER to land up tail is equal to

(*a*) $\frac{1}{3}$ (*b*) $\frac{1}{2}$

(*c*) $\frac{2}{3}$ (*d*) $\frac{3}{4}$

55. Consider the function

$$f(x) = \begin{cases} k(x - [x]), & 0 \leq x < 2 \\ 0, & \text{otherwise,} \end{cases}$$

where $[x]$ is the integral part of x. The value of k for which the above function is a probability density function of some random variable is

(*a*) $\frac{1}{4}$ (*b*) $\frac{1}{2}$

(*c*) 1 (*d*) 2

56. For two random variables X and Y, the regression lines are given by $Y = 5X - 15$ and $Y = 10X - 35$. Then the regression coefficient of X on Y is

(*a*) 0.1 (*b*) 0.2

(*c*) 5 (*d*) 10

57. In an examination there are 80 questions each having four choices. Exactly one of these four choices is correct and the other three are wrong. A student is awarded 1 mark for each correct answer, and – 0.25 for each wrong answer. If a student ticks the answer of each question randomly, then the expected value of his/her total marks in the examination is

(*a*) –15 (*b*) 0

(*c*) 5 (*d*) 20

58. Let $X_1, X_2, \ldots, X_n$ be a random sample from uniform distribution on $[0, \theta]$. Then the maximum likelihood estimator (MLE) of θ based on the above random sample is

(a) $\frac{2}{n}\sum_{i=1}^{n} X_i$

(b) $\frac{1}{n}\sum_{i=1}^{n} X_i$

(c) Min $\{X_1, X_2, \ldots, X_n\}$

(d) Max $\{X_1, X_2, \ldots, X_n\}$

Statement for Linked Answer Questions 59 and 60:

Let a random variable X follow the exponential distribution with mean 2. Define $Y = [X - 2 \mid X > 2]$.

59. The value of $P(Y \geq t)$ is

(a) $e^{-\frac{t}{2}}$ (b) e^{-2t}

(c) $\frac{1}{2}e^{-\frac{t}{2}}$ (d) $\frac{1}{2}e^{-t}$

60. The value of E(Y) is equal to

(a) $\frac{1}{4}$ (b) $\frac{1}{2}$

(c) 1 (d) 2

2007

61. Let X and Y be jointly distributed random variables having the joint probability density function

$$f(x, y) = \begin{cases} \frac{1}{\pi}, & \text{if } x^2 + y^2 \leq 1, \\ 0, & \text{otherwise} \end{cases}$$

Then $P(Y > \max(X, -X)) =$

(a) $\frac{1}{2}$ (b) $\frac{1}{3}$

(c) $\frac{1}{4}$ (d) $\frac{1}{6}$

62. Let $X_1, X_2, \ldots$ be a sequence of independent and identically distributed chi-square random variables, each having 4 degrees of freedom.

Define $S_n = \sum_{i=1}^{n} X_1^2$, $n = 1, 2\ldots$

If $\frac{S_n}{n} \xrightarrow{p} \mu$, as $n \to \infty$, then =

(a) 8 (b) 16

(c) 24 (d) 32

63. Let A B and C be three events such that

$P(A) = 0.4$, $P(B) = 0.5$, $P(A \cup B) = 0.6$, $P(C) = 0.6$ and $P(A \cap B \cap C^c) = 0.1$.

Then $P(A \cap B \mid C) =$

(a) $\frac{1}{2}$ (b) $\frac{1}{3}$

(c) $\frac{1}{4}$ (d) $\frac{1}{5}$

64. Consider two identical boxes B_1 and B_2, where the box B_i ($i = 1, 2$) contains $i + 1$ red and $5 - i - 1$ white balls. A fair die is cast. Let the number of dots shown on the top face of the die be N. If N is even or 5, then two balls are drawn with replacement from the box B_1, otherwise, two balls are drawn with replacement from the box B_2. The probability that the two drawn balls are of different colours is

(a) $\frac{7}{25}$ (b) $\frac{9}{25}$

(c) $\frac{12}{25}$ (d) $\frac{16}{25}$

65. Let $X_1, X_2, \ldots$ be a sequence of independent and identically distributed random variables with

$P(X_1 = -1) = P(X_1 = 1) = \frac{1}{2}$.

Suppose for the standard normal random variable Z, $P(-0.1 < Z \leq 0.1) = 0.08$.

If $S_n = \sum_{i=1}^{n^2} X_i$, then $\lim_{n\to} P\left(S_n > \frac{n}{10}\right) =$

(a) 0.42 (b) 0.46

(c) 0.50 (d) 0.54

66. Let $X_1, X_2, \ldots, X_5$ be a random sample of size 5 from a population having standard normal distribution. Let

$\overline{X} = \frac{1}{5}\sum_{i=1}^{5} X_i$ and $T = \sum_{i=1}^{5}\left(X_i - \overline{X}\right)^2$

Then $E(T^2 \overline{X}^2) =$

(a) 3 (b) 3.6

(c) 4.8 (d) 5.2

67. Let $x_1 = 3.5$, $x_2 = 7.5$ and $x_3 = 5.2$ be observed values of a random sample of size three from a population having uniform distribution over the interval $(\theta, \theta + 5)$, where $\theta \in (0, \infty)$ is unknown and is to be estimated. Then which of the following is NOT a maximum likelihood estimate of θ ?

(a) 2.4 (b) 2.7

(c) 3.0 (d) 3.3

Common Data for Questions 68 and 69:

Let X and Y be jointly distributed random variables such that the conditional distribution of Y, given X = x, is uniform on the interval $(x-1, x+1)$. Suppose E (X) = 1 and Var (X) = $\frac{5}{3}$.

68. The mean of the random variable Y is

(a) $\frac{1}{2}$ (b) 1

(c) $\frac{2}{3}$ (d) 2

69. The variance of the random variable Y is

(a) $\frac{1}{2}$ (b) $\frac{2}{3}$

(c) 1 (d) 2

2006

70. Let X, Y and Z be events which are mutually independent, with probabilities a, b, c respectively. Let the random variable N denote the number of X, Y or Z which occur. Then, the probability that N = 2 is

(a) $ab + bc + ca - abc$ (b) $ab + bc + ca - 3abc$

(c) $2(a + b + c) - abc$ (d) $ab + bc + ca$

71. Assume that 45 percent of the population favours a certain candidate in an election. If a random sample of size 200 is chosen, then the standard deviation of the number of members of the sample that favours the candidate is

(a) 6.12 (b) 5.26

(c) 8.18 (d) 7.04

72. Let X and Y be independent Poisson random variables with parameters 1 and 2 respectively.

Then, P is $\left(X = 1 \mid \frac{X+Y}{2} = 2\right)$

(a) 0.426 (b) 0.293

(c) 0.395 (d) 0.512

73. Let T denote the number of times we have to roll a fair dice before each face has appeared at least once and let N denote the number of different faces appearing in the first six rolls. Then E (T | N = 3) is

(a) 9 (b) 15

(c) 16 (d) 17

74. Let there be three types of light bulbs with lifetimes X, Y and Z having exponential distributions with mean θ, 2θ and 3θ respectively. Then, the maximum likelihood estimator of θ based on the observation X, Y and Z is

(a) $\frac{(X + 2Y + 3Z)}{3}$ (b) $3(X + 2Y + 3Z)$

(c) $\frac{1}{3}\left(X + \frac{Y}{2} + \frac{Z}{3}\right)$ (d) $\frac{1}{6}\left(X + \frac{Y}{2} + \frac{Z}{3}\right)$

75. Let Z be the vertical coordinate, between −1 and 1, of a point chosen uniformly at random on the surface of a unit sphere in R^3.

Then, $P\left(-\frac{1}{2} \le Z \le \frac{1}{2}\right)$ is

(a) $\frac{5}{6}$ (b) $\left(\frac{\sqrt{3}}{2}\right)$

(c) $\frac{3}{4}$ (d) $\frac{1}{2}$

76. Let the marks obtained in the half-yearly and final examinations in a large class have an approximately bivariate normal distribution with the following parameters

	Mean	Deviation
Marks (half yearly)	60	18
Marks (final exam)	55	20
Correlation :	0.75.	

Then, estimate of the average final examination score of students who were above average on the half-yearly examination is

(a) 60 (b) 67

(c) 70 (d) 72

77. Let V_1, V_2, V_5 be 5 independent uniform (0, 1) variables and let $V_{(1)} < V_{(2)} < .... < V_{(5)}$ be their order statistics. Then, for $0 < x < y < 1$, the joint density $f(x, y)$ of $(V_{(2)}, V_{(4)})$ is given by

(a) $(5!)xy(1-x)(1-y)$

(b) $\frac{x(y-x)(1-y)}{(5!)}$

(c) $(5!)x(y-x)(1-y)$

(d) $\frac{xy(1-x)(1-y)}{(5!)}$

2005

78. Let $A_1, A_2, ... A_n$ be n independent events which the probability of occurence of the event A_i given by $P(A_i) = 1 - \frac{1}{\alpha^i}$, $\alpha > l$, $i = 1, 2, ...n$. Then the probability that at least one of the events occurs is

(a) $1 - \frac{1}{\alpha^{\frac{n(n+1)}{2}}}$ (b) $\frac{1}{\alpha^{\frac{n(n+1)}{2}}}$

(c) $\frac{1}{\alpha^n}$ (d) $1 - \frac{1}{\alpha^n}$

79. The life time of two brands of bulbs X and Y are exponentially distributed with a mean life time of 100 hours. Bulb X is switched on 15 hours after bulb Y has been switched on. The probability that the bulb X fails before Y is

(a $\frac{15}{100}$ (b) $\frac{1}{2}$

(c) $\frac{85}{100}$ (d) 0

80. A random sample of size n is chosen from a population with probability density

function $f(x,\theta)=\begin{cases}\frac{1}{2}e^{-(x-\theta)}, & x\geq\theta\\ \frac{1}{2}e^{(x-\theta)}, & x<\theta\end{cases}$ Then,

the maximum likelihood estimator of θ is the

(a) mean of the sample

(b) standard deviation of the sample

(c) median of the sample

(d) maximum of the sample

81. Let X_1, X_2, X_3 be a random sample of size 3 chosen from a population with probability distribution $P(X = 1) = P$ and $P(X = 0) = 1 - p = q$, $0 < p < 1$. The sampling distribution f(.)of the statistic Y = Max $\{X_1, X_1, X_3\}$ is

(a) $f(0) = p^3$; $f(1) = 1 - p^3$

(b) $f(0) = q$; $f(1) = p$

(c) $f(0) = q^3$; $f(1) = 1 - q^3$

(d) $f(0) = p^3 + q^3$; $f(1) = 1 - p^3 - q^3$

82. Let $\{X_n\}$ be a sequence of independent random variables with

$$p(X_n=n^\alpha)= p(X_n=-n^\alpha)= \frac{1}{2}.$$

The sequence $\{X_n\}$obeys the weak law of large numbers if

(a) $\alpha<\frac{1}{2}$ (b) $\alpha=\frac{1}{2}$

(c) $\frac{1}{2}<\alpha\leq 1$ (d) $\alpha>1$

83. Let X be a random variable with $P(X = 1) = P$ and $p(X = 0) = 1 - p = q$, $0 < p < 1$. If μ_n denotes the nth moment about the mean, then $\mu_{2n+1}= 0$ if and only if

(a) $p=\frac{1}{4}$ (b) $p=\frac{1}{3}$

(c) $p=\frac{2}{3}$ (d) $p=\frac{1}{2}$

Statement for Linked Answer Questions 84a and 84b :

Let the random variables X and Y be independent Poisson variates with parameters $\lambda_1$and λ_2 respectively.

84a. The conditional distribution of X given X+ Y is

(a) Poisson (b) hypergeometric

(c) Geometric (d) binomial

84b. The regression equation of X on X + Y is given by

(a) $E(X|X+Y) = XY\frac{\lambda_1}{\lambda_1+\lambda_2}$

(b) $E(X|X+Y) = (X+Y)\frac{\lambda_2}{\lambda_1+\lambda_2}$

(c) $E(X|X+Y) = (X+Y)\frac{\lambda_1}{\lambda_1+\lambda_2}$

(d) $E(X|X+Y) = XY\frac{\lambda_2}{\lambda_1+\lambda_2}$

2004

85. Suppose X is a random variable, c is a constant and $a_n = E(X - c)^n$ is finite for all $n \geq 1$. Then $P(X = c) =1$ if and only if $a_n = 0$ for

(a) at least one $n \geq 1$

(b) at least one odd n

(c) at least one even n

(d) at least two values of n

86. If the random vector $(X_1, X_2)^T$ has a bivariate normal distribution with mean vector (, $)^T$ and the matrix $((E(X_iX_j))_{1\leq i,j\leq 2}$ equals $\begin{pmatrix}\alpha_1 & \mu^2\\ \mu^2 & \alpha_2\end{pmatrix}$, where $\in$ R and $\alpha_1, \alpha_2, > \mu^2$ then X_1 and X_2 are

(a) independent for all α_1 and α_2

(b) independent if and only if $\alpha_1 = \alpha_2$

(c) uncorrelated, but not independent for all α_1, α_2

(d) uncorrelated if and only if $\alpha_1= \alpha_2$ and in this case they are not independent

87. If the cost matrix for an assignment problem is given by

$$\begin{pmatrix}a & b & c & d\\ b & c & d & a\\ c & d & a & b\\ d & a & b & c\end{pmatrix}$$

where a, b, c, d > 0, then the value of the assignment problem is

(a) a + b + c + d (b) min {a, b, c, d}

(c) max {a, b, c, d} (d) 4 min (a, b, c, d)

88. Suppose X is a random variable and f, $g : \mathbb{R} \to \mathbb{R}$ are measurable functions such that $f(X)$ and $g(X)$ are independent, then

(*a*) X is degenerate

(*b*) both $f(X)$ and $g(X)$ is degenerate

(*c*) either $f(X)$ or $g(X)$ is degenerate

(*d*) X, $f(X)$ and $g(X)$ could all be non-degenerate

89. Suppose $X_1, X_2, \ldots X_n$ is a random sample from a $N(\mu, \sigma^2)$ distribution, where is known, but σ^2 is not. If $\bar{X} = \frac{1}{n}\sum_{i=0}^{n} X_i$ and $S = \sqrt{\frac{1}{n}\sum_{i=0}^{n}(X_i - \mu)^2}$, then the pair $(\bar{X}, S)$ is

(*a*) complete and sufficient

(*b*) complete but not sufficient

(*c*) sufficient but not complete

(*d*) neither sufficient nor complete

90. If X and Y are random variables with $0 < \text{Var}(X), \text{Var}(Y) < \infty$, consider the statements : (I) Var (E(Y/X)) = Var(Y) and (II) the correlation co-efficient between X and Y is ± 1. Then

(*a*) (I) implies (II) and (II) implies (I)

(*b*) (I) implies (II) but (II) does not imply (I)

(*c*) (II) implies (I) but (I) does not imply (II)

(*d*) neither does (I) imply (II) nor does (II) imply (I)

91. If the random variable X has a Poisson distribution with parameter λ and the parametric space has three elements 3, 4 and k, then to test the null hypothesis $H_0 : \lambda = 3$ *vs.* the alternative hypothesis $H_1 : \lambda \neq 3$, a uniformly most powerful test at any level $\alpha \in (0.1)$ exists for any sample size

(*a*) for all $k \neq 3, 4$

(*b*) if and only if $k > 4$

(*c*) if and only if $k < 3$

(*d*) if and only if $k > 3$

92. Suppose the random variable X has a uniform distribution P_θ in the interval $[\theta - 1, \theta + 1]$, where $\theta \in Z$. If a random sample of size n is drawn from this distribution, then P_θ almost surely for all $\theta \in Z$, a Maximum likelihood estimator (MLE) for θ

(*a*) exists and is unique

(*b*) exists but may or may not be unique

(*c*) exists but cannot be unique

(*d*) does not exist

93. A χ^2(chi-squared) test for independence between two attributes X and Y is carried out at 2.5% level of significance on the following 2 × 2 contingency table showing frequencies

X/Y	X_1	X_2
Y_1	1	0
Y_2	1	d

If the upper 2.5% point of the χ_1^2 distribution is given as 5.0, then the hypothesis of independence is to be rejected if and only if

(*a*) $d > 1$ (*b*) $d > 3$

(*c*) $d > 5$ (*d*) $d > 9$

2003

94. Let X_1 and X_2 be independent binomial random variables with $E(X_i) = n_i p$ and $var(X_i) = n_i p(1 - p)$ $0 < p < 1$, $i = 1, 2$. Then the distribution of the random variable $Z = n_1 + n_2 - X_1 - X_2$ is

(*a*) binomial with mean $(n_1 + n_2)p$

(*b*) binomial with mean $(n_1 + n_2)(1 - p)$

(*c*) Poisson with mean $(n_1 + n_2)p$

(*d*) Poisson with mean $(n_1 + n_2)(1 - p)$

95. Let –2, 5, –6, 9, –5, –9 be the observed values of a radnom sample of size 6 from a distribution having probability density function, $f_\theta(x) = \begin{cases} e^{-(x-\theta)} & \text{if } x > \theta \\ 0 & \text{otherwise} \end{cases}$

Then the maximum likelihood estimate of θ is

(*a*) 9 (*b*) – 9

(*c*) $-\frac{4}{3}$ (*d*) $\frac{4}{3}$

96. E_1, E_2 are independent events such that

$P(E_1) = \frac{1}{4}, P(E_2 / E_1) = \frac{1}{2}$ and $P(E_1 / E_2) = \frac{1}{4}$.

Define random variables X and Y by

$$X = \begin{cases} 1 \text{ if } E_1 \text{ occurs} \\ 0 \text{ if } E_1 \text{ does not occur}' \end{cases}$$

$$Y = \begin{cases} 1 \text{ if } E_2 \text{ occurs} \\ 0 \text{ if } E_2 \text{ does not occur} \end{cases}$$

Consider the following statements

α : X is uniformly distributed on the set (0, 1)

β : X and Y are identically distributed

γ : $P(X^2 + Y^2 = 1) = 1/2$

δ : $P(XY = X^2Y^2) = 1$

Choose the correct combination

(*a*) (α, β) (*b*) (α, γ)

(*c*) (β, γ) (*d*) (γ, δ)

97. Let X and Y be the time (in hours) taken. by Saurabh and Sachin to solve a problem. Suppose that each of X and Y are uniformly distributed over the interval [0, 1]. Assume that Saurabh and Sachin start to solve the problem independently. Then, the probability that the problem will be solved in less than 20 minutes is

(*a*) $\frac{1}{3}$ (*b*) $\frac{5}{9}$

(*c*) $\frac{8}{9}$ (*d*) $\frac{4}{9}$

98. The value of the limit

$$\lim_{n\to\infty}\sum_{j=n}^{4n}\binom{4n}{j}\left(\frac{1}{4}\right)^{j}\left(\frac{3}{4}\right)^{4n-j} \text{ equals}$$

(*a*) 0 (*b*) $\frac{1}{4}$

(*c*) $\frac{1}{2}$ (*d*) $\frac{3}{4}$

99. Let $f(x)$ and $g(x)$ be two probability mass functions (*p.m.f*) defined by

$$f(x) = \frac{1}{6}, x = 1,2,3,4,5,6 \text{ and}$$

$$g(x) = \begin{cases} 1/12, \text{ if } x = 1, 2 \\ 1/2 \quad \text{if } x = 3 \\ 1/9, \text{ if } x = 4, 5, 6 \end{cases}$$

Let X be a random sample of size one from a distribution having *p.m.f.* $h(x) \in \{f(x), g(x)\}$. To test the hypothesis $H_0 : h = f$ *vs* $H_1 : h = g$, a most powerful test of size $\alpha = 1/6$ rejects H_0 *iff*

(*a*) $x = 1$ (*b*) $x = 2$

(*c*) $x = 3$ (*d*) $x \in \{4, 5, 6\}$

2002

100. Let $P(X = n) = \frac{\lambda}{n^2(n+1)}$, where λ is an appropriate constant. Then E(X) is

(*a*) $2\lambda + 1$ (*β*) λ

(*c*) ∞ (*d*) 2λ.

101. Let *x* be a non-optimal feasible solution of a linear programming maximization problem and y a dual feasible solution. Then

(*a*) The primal objective value at *x* is greater than the dual objective value at *y*

(*b*) The primal objective value at *x* could equal the dual objective value at *y*

(*c*) The primal objective value at *x* is less than the dual objective value at *y*

(*d*) The dual could be unbounded

102. A lot of 1000 screws contains 1% with major defects and 5 % with minor defects. If 50 screws are picked at random and inspected, then the ordered pair (expected number of major defectives, expected number of minor defectives) is

(*a*) (1, 5) (*b*) (2.5, 0.5)

(*c*) (0.5, 2.5) (*d*) (5, 1)

103. The sample correlation of the trans-formed random variables $aX + b$ and $cY + d$ is same as that of X and Y provided

(*a*) $ac < 0; b, d \in (0, \infty)$

(*b*) $ac < 0; b, d \in (-\infty, 0)$

(*c*) $ac > 0; b, d \in R$

(*d*) $ac < 0; b, d \in R$

104. There are two identical locks, with two identical keys, and the keys are among the six different ones which a person carries in his pocket. In a hurry he drops one key somewhere. Then the probability that the locks can still be opened by drawing one key at random is equal to

(*a*) $\frac{1}{3}$ (*b*) $\frac{5}{6}$

(*c*) $\frac{1}{30}$ (*d*) $\frac{1}{12}$

105. Let $X_1, X_2, .., X_{100}$ be independent and identical Poisson random variables with parameter λ = 0.03. Let $S = \sum_{i=1}^{100} X_i$. Use the Central Limit Theorem to evaluate $P(\{S \geq 3\})$ and compare the result with the exact probability of the event $\{S \geq 3\}$.

106. Let $X_1, X_2, ..X_n$ be a random sample from exponential density $f_\theta(x) = \theta e^{-\theta x}$, $x \geq 0$, $\theta > 0$. Find the maximum likelihood estimate (MLE) of θ. Also, find the MLE of $P_\theta(X_1 \geq 1)$. Further show that both the estimators are consistent.

107. (*a*) Let $X \sim B(n_1, p_1)$ and $Y \sim B(n_2, p_2)$, where p_1 and p_2 are unknowns. Further, let X and Y be statistically independent. Construct an approximate 100 $(1 - \alpha)$% confidence interval for $(p_1 - p_9)$.

(*b*) An antibiotic for pneumonia was injected into 100 patients with kidney malfunctions (uremic patients) and into 100 patients with no kidney malfunctions (normal patients). Some allergic reaction developed in 38 of the uremic patients and in 21 of the normal patients. Use the result in part (a) to construct a 95% confidence interval for the difference between the two population proportions (Use the appropriate table value $Z_{0.025} = 1.960$, $Z_{0.05} = 1.645$).

2001

108. The random variable X has a t-dis-tribution with v degrees of freedom. Then the probability distribution of X^2 is

(*a*) chi-square distribution with 1 degree of freedom

(*b*) chi-square distribution with v degrees of freedom

(*c*) F-distribution with $(1, v)$ degrees of freedom

(*d*) F-distribution with $(v, 1)$ degrees of freedom

109. Let (X, Y) be the co-ordinates of a point chosen at random inside the disc $x^2 + y^2 \le r^2$ where $r > 0$. The probability that $Y > mX$ is

(*a*) $\frac{1}{2^r}$ (*b*) $\frac{1}{2}$

(*c*) $\frac{1}{2^m}$ (*d*) $\frac{1}{2^{m+r}}$

110. Let (X, Y) be a two-dimensional random variable such that

$E(X) = E(Y) = 3$, $Var(X) = Var(Y) = 1$ and $Cov(X, Y) = \frac{1}{2}$.

Then $P(|X - Y| > 6)$ is

(*a*) less than $\frac{1}{6}$ (*b*) equal to $\frac{1}{2}$

(*c*) equal to $\frac{1}{3}$ (*d*) greater than $\frac{1}{2}$

111. The number N of the persons getting injured in a bomb blast at a busy market place is a random variable having a Poisson distribution with parameter λ (≥ 1). A person injured in the explosion may either suffer a minor injury requiring first aid or suffer a major injury requiring hospitalisation. Let the number of persons with minor injury be N_1 and the conditional distribution of N_1 given N be

$$P\left(N_1 = \frac{i}{N}\right) = \frac{1}{N}, t = 1, 2, ..., N$$

Find the expected number of persons requiring hospitalisation in a bomb blast.

112. Let $X_1, X_2, ..., X_{200}$ be identically and independently distributed random variables each with mean 0 and variance 1. Show that

$$\sqrt{\frac{\pi}{2}}\, P(|X_1 X_2 + X_3 X_4 + ..+ X_{199} X_{200}| < 10)$$

is approximately equal to $\int_0^1 e^{\frac{-x^2}{2}} dx$.

113. The following table gives the scores on some scale of four ability groups taught by three different teaching methods

	Teaching method		
Ability group	A	B	C
1	5	9	4
2	8	7	2
3	12	15	7
4	7	11	9

Test whether or not the teaching methods are equally effective. You may use appropriate values from the following upper percentile values of F-distribution for your test

$F_{2,6,.01} = 10.92$, $F_{3,6,.01} = 9.78$, $F_{2,6,.05} = 5.14$ $F_{3,6,.05} = 4.76$.

2000

114. The probability that exactly one of the events E or F occurs is equal to

(*a*) P(E) + P(F) – P(EF)

(*b*) P(E) + P(F) – 2 P(EF)

(*c*) $P(EF^C) + P(E^CF)$

(*d*) P(E) + P(F)

115. If $\{A_n, n \ge 1\}$ is a sequence of events, then

$\lim_{x\to\infty} P(A_n) = P\left(\lim_{x\to\infty} A_n\right)$ if

(*a*) $\{A_n\}$ is an increasing sequence of events

(*b*) $\{A_n\}$ is a decreasing sequence of events

(*c*) $\{A_n\}$ is neither increasing nor decreasing sequence of events

(*d*) none of these

116. Suppose that the five random variables $X_1, .., X_5$ are independent and each has standard normal distribution. A constant C such that the random variable $\frac{C(X_1 + X_2)}{\left(X_3^2 + X_4^2 + X_5^2\right)^{\frac{1}{2}}}$ will have a *t*-distribution, has the value

(*a*) $\frac{\sqrt{3}}{2}$ (*b*) $\sqrt{\frac{3}{2}}$

(*c*) $\frac{3}{2}$ (*d*) $\sqrt{\frac{2}{3}}$

117. Suppose that $X_1, .., X_n$ are random variables such that the variance of each variable is 1 and the correlation between each pair of different variables is $\frac{1}{4}$. Then Var $(X_1 + X_2 + .. + X_n)$ is

(*a*) $\frac{n(n+1)}{2}$ (*b*) $\frac{n(n+2)}{4}$

(*c*) $\frac{n(n+3)}{4}$ (*a*) $\frac{n(n+3)}{2}$

118. Let X and Y have joint probability density function $f_{X,Y}(x, y) = 2e^{-(x+y)}, 0 < x < y, 0 < y$.
Find P(Y < 3X).

119. Let $X_1, X_2 ., X_n$ be a random sample from a poisson distribution with parameter $\theta > 0$. Find the uniformly minimum variance unbiased estimator (UMVUE) of $P(X \le 1) = (1 + \theta)e^{-\theta}$.

120. Let $X_1, X_2, .X_n$ be a random sample from a distribution that is normally distributed with mean θ_1 and variance θ_2. Find a best test of the simple hypothesis $H_0: \theta_1 = 0, \theta_2 = 1$ against the alternative simple hypothesis $H_1: \theta_1 = 1, \theta_2 = 4$.

ANSWERS

1. (5.25)	**2.** (*d*)	**3.** (*b*)	**4.** (0.68)	**5.** (2.25)	**6.** (*a*)	**7.** (*c*)	**8.** (6)	**9.** (0.4)	**10.** (9)
11. (*d*)	**12.** (0.25)	**13.** (25)	**14.** (*d*)	**15.** (1)	**16.** (2.5)	**17.** (0.92 to 0.94)		**18.** (3.99 to 4.01)	
19. (0.86 to 0.88)		**20.** (*c*)	**21.** (*c*)	**22.** (*c*)	**23.** (*c*)	**24.** (*c*)	**25.** (*d*)	**26.** (*b*)	**27.** (*a*)
28. (*b*)	**29.** (*d*)	**30.** (*d*)	**31.** (*b*)	**32.** (*a*)	**33.** (*d*)	**34.** (*c*)	**35.** (*a*)	**36.** (*a*)	**37.** (*c*)
38. (*b*)	**39.** (*a*)	**40.** (*b*)	**41.** (*c*)	**42.** (*c*)	**43.** (*a*)	**44.** (*d*)	**45.** (*a*)	**46.** (*b*)	**47.** (*d*)
48. (*c*)	**49.** (*b*)	**50.** (*a*)	**51.** (*d*)	**52.** (*b*)	**53.** (*a*)	**54.** (*b*)	**55.** (*c*)	**56.** (*a*)	**57.** (*c*)
58. (*d*)	**59.** (*a*)	**60.** (*d*)	**61.** (*c*)	**62.** (*b*)	**63.** (*b*)	**64.** (*d*)	**65.** (*b*)	**66.** (*a*)	**67.** (*c*)
68. (*b*)	**69.** (*a*)	**70.** (*b*)	**71.** (*d*)	**72.** (*d*)	**73.** (*a*)	**74.** (*b*)	**75.** (*c*)	**76.** (*b*)	**77.** (*c*)
78. (*a*)	**79.** (*c*)	**80.** (*b*)	**81.** (*d*)	**82.** (*c*)	**83.** (*a*)	**84a.** (*d*)	**84b.** (*b*)	**85.** (*a*)	**86.** (*c*)
87. (*d*)	**88.** (*b*)	**89.** (*a*)	**90.** (*d*)	**91.** (*d*)	**92.** (*c*)	**93.** (*a*)	**94.** (*b*)	**95.** (*c*)	**96.** (*a*)
97. (*b*)	**98.** (*b*)	**99.** (*c*)	**100.** (*b*)	**101.** (*c*)	**102.** (*b*)	**103.** (*b*)	**104.** (*a*)	**105.** (*)	**106.** (*)
107a. (*)	**107b.** (*)	**108.** (*b*)	**109.** (*c*)	**110.** (*)	**111.** (*)	**112.** (*)	**113.** (*)	**114.** (*c*)	**115.** (*d*)
116. (*a*)	**117.** (*d*)	**118.** (*)	**119.** (*)	**120.** (*)					

EXPLANATIONS

1. $\int_{-\infty}^{\infty} f(x)dx = 1$

$\Rightarrow \int_0^{\frac{1}{2}} x dx + \int_{\frac{1}{2}}^{1} c(2x-1)^2 dx = 1$

$\Rightarrow c = 5.25$

2. After the simplification, we make conclusion MLE does not exists for both μ & α.

3. We can see that sum as well as the difference of two independent normal variates is also normal variate.

X - Y is not necessary has mean O (in general) S is not true similarly P is also not true.

4. $P\left(\frac{1}{4} < X < 1\right) = F\left(\frac{1}{2}\right) - F\left(\frac{1}{4}\right)$

$= \frac{3}{4} - \frac{1}{16} = \frac{11}{16} \approx 0.68$

21. For uniform distribution

$f(x) = \frac{1}{b-a} \quad a < x < b$

$0 \quad x < a, \quad \text{or } x > 6$

here $f(x) = 1 \quad 0 < x < 1$

$0 \quad x < 0 ; x > 1$

$X = -2\log U$

$u = e^{-x/2}$

Density of X is $\left|\frac{du}{dx}\right|$

$$= \frac{1}{2}e^{-x/2} \quad \text{for } x > 0$$

$$0 \qquad \text{otherwise}$$

23. X_λ random variable with $\lambda e^{-\lambda x}(0, \infty)$

Var (log X_λ) = E($\log^2 X_\lambda$) – [E(log X_λ)]^2

after solving it

Var (log X_λ) does not depend on λ.

24. Random variable {0, 1, ... 10}

Variance of X = E(X^2) –E^2(X)

Minimum var (X) = 0

Maximum var(X) = 25

27. The result found by substituting

$$x = \frac{(y-2)}{3}$$

and transforming the domain for y.

28. μ lies in 98% confidence interval, so the H_0 cannot be rejected at 2% level of significance and therefore it cannot be rejected at 5% level of significance also.

30. Given that

$$f(x) = \frac{1}{\lambda}e^{\frac{-x}{\lambda}} \quad x > 0$$

$$\text{Therefore type 1 error} = P\left[reject\frac{H_0}{H_0}\right]$$

$$= P\left[x > \frac{4.5}{\lambda} = 3\right]$$

$$= \int_{4.5}^{\infty} \frac{1}{3}e^{\frac{-x}{3}}\,dx = 0.2231$$

$$\text{Similarly, Power} = P\left[accept\frac{H_1}{H_1}\right]$$

$$= P\left[x > \frac{4.5}{\lambda} = 5\right]$$

$$= \int_{4.5}^{\infty} \frac{1}{5}e^{-\frac{x}{5}}dx$$

$$= 0.4066.$$

31. The marginal distribution of x.

$$f(x) = \int_0^1 \frac{6}{5}(x+y^2)dy$$

$$= \frac{6}{5}\left[x+\frac{1}{3}\right] \quad 0 < x < 1$$

$$\text{Therefore } E(x) = \int_0^1 x\frac{6}{5}\left[x+\frac{1}{3}\right]dx = \frac{3}{5}$$

Similarly we can calculate E(y) by making marginal distribution of y.

$$E(y) = \frac{3}{5}$$

32. $$E(xy) = \int_0^1\int_0^1 xy\frac{6}{5}(x+y^2)dxdy$$

$$= \int_0^1 x\frac{6}{5}\left[\frac{xy^2}{2}+\frac{y^4}{4}\right]_0^1 dx$$

$$= \frac{7}{20}$$

$$\text{cov}(x, y) = E[xy] - E(x)\,E(y)$$

$$= \frac{7}{20} - \frac{3}{5}\times\frac{3}{5}$$

$$= -\frac{1}{100}$$

$$= -0.01$$

33. The two properties of pdf $f(x)$ of an random variable are

(i) $f(x) > 0$ (ii) $\int f(x)dx = 1$ in the given domain of random variable. Function given in (d) satisfy these two properties.

34. Result follows from properties of chi-square distribution.

35. For this sequence weak law of large number holds but strong law of large numbers does not hold.

36. P(one component does not fail before 10h)

$$= P(t > 10) = e^{-1}$$

⇒ P(none of the components does not fail before 10h) = e^{-1}

38. $$P(x + y < 1/2) = P\left[x+y<\frac{1}{2}/x<y\right] + P\left[x+y<\frac{1}{2}/x>y\right]$$

$$= 2\int_0^{1/2}\int_0^{1/2-x} 2dy = 1/2$$

39. The conditional distribution of x given y is

$$f\left(\frac{x}{y}\right) = \frac{f(x,y)}{f(y)}$$

where $f(y) = \int_0^{1-y} 2dx = 2(1-y) \quad 0 < y < 1$

so $f\left(\frac{x}{y}\right) = \frac{1}{1-y} \qquad 0 < x < 1-y$

Therefore $E\left[\frac{x}{y} = \frac{1}{2}\right] = \int_0^{1/2} 2x dx = 1/4$

40. $P(F) = \frac{P(EUF) - P(E)}{1 - P(E/F)}$

so $P(F) = \frac{0.8 - 0.4}{1 - 0.3} = \frac{4}{7}$

41. Let $q = 1 - P$

then from $P(X = 0) = P(X = 1)$

we get $q^n = nPq^{n-1}$

i.e $P = \frac{1}{n+1}$

42. Type I error= $P\left[\text{reject}\frac{H_0}{H_1}\right]$

$= P\left[\frac{x \geq 2}{P} = \frac{2}{3}\right]$

$= \binom{3}{2}\left(\frac{2}{3}\right)^2 + \binom{3}{3}\left(\frac{2}{3}\right)^3$

$= \frac{20}{27}$

Type II error = $P\left[\text{reject}\frac{H_1}{H_1}\right]$

$= P\left[\frac{x > 1}{P} = \frac{1}{3}\right]$

$= 1 - \binom{3}{0}\left(\frac{1}{3}\right)^0\left(\frac{2}{3}\right)^3 + \binom{3}{1}\left(\frac{1}{3}\right)\left(\frac{2}{3}\right)^2$

$= \frac{7}{27}$

43. according to property of joint pdf

$\iint_{xy} f(x,y)\,dxdy = 1$

so in this case $\int_0^{\infty}\int_x^{\infty} ae^{-2y} dxdy = 1$

or $\frac{a}{4} = 1 \Rightarrow a = 4$

44. The conditional distribution of x given y is

$$f\left(\frac{x}{y}\right) = \frac{f(x,y)}{f(y)}$$

where $f(y) = \int_0^4 4e^{-2y} dx, \; 0 < y < \infty$

$f(y) = 4ye^{-2y}, 0 < y < \infty$

so $f\left(\frac{x}{y}\right) = \frac{1}{y}, 0 < x < y$

therefore

$$E\left[\frac{x}{y} = 2\right] = \int_0^2 x.\frac{1}{2}dx = 1$$

48. Given $\sum_{i=1}^{x} iP(x \geq i)$

$= 1[P(1)+P(2)+ \dots] + 2[P(2) + P(3) + \dots]$
$+ 3\,[P(3) + P(4) + \dots]$

$= 1[P(1)]+(1 + 2).\,P(2) + (1 + 2 + 3).\,P(3) \dots]$

$= \sum_{x=1}^{\infty} \frac{1}{2}x(x+1)P(x) = \frac{1}{2}[E(x^2) + E(x)]$

$= 2.$

49. According to Neyman Pearson's lemma most powerful critical region for testing the said hypothesis is

$\frac{f_0}{f_1} < c \Rightarrow \frac{2x}{3x^2} < c \Rightarrow x > k$

where k is given by

$P\left(\text{reject}\frac{H_0}{H_0}\right) = 0.19$

i.e., $\int_k^1 2x dx = 0.19 \Rightarrow k = 0.9$

therefore power $P\left(\text{reject}\frac{H_0}{H_1}\right)$

i.e., $\int_{0.9}^1 3x^2 dx = 0.271$

50. The distribution of x and y are define as

$$f(x) = \begin{cases} 1 & 0 < x < 1 \\ 0 & \text{otherwise} \end{cases}$$

$$f(y) = \begin{cases} 1 & 0 < y < 1 \\ 0 & \text{otherwise} \end{cases}$$

Therefore $P\left(y < \left(x - \frac{1}{2}\right)^2\right)$

$$= \int_0^1 \int_0^{\left(x-\frac{1}{2}\right)^2} 1.dydx$$

$$= \int_0^1 \left(x - \frac{1}{2}\right)^2 dx$$

$$= \frac{1}{12}$$

53. S = 10, sample mean, while T = 10 sample variance and E(S) = 0 therefore cov(S, T) = 0 implies E(ST) = 0

54. The two coins are independent therefore event of one coins does not depend on other.

56. Regression line x on y is either may be first or second.

But if we take the first line as x on y. Then the product of coefficients comes out to be more than 1, which is not possible. It mean the second line is the regression line x and y and from this line regression coefficient x on y = 0.1

57. The expected total marks

= 80 × expected marks in one question

$$= 80 \times \left[1.\frac{1}{4} + (-0.25).\frac{3}{4}\right] = 5$$

58. The uniform distribution has pdf.

$$f\left(\frac{x}{\theta}\right) = \begin{cases} \frac{1}{\theta} & 0 \le x \le \theta \\ 0 & otherwise \end{cases}$$

the likelihood function

$$\psi(\theta) = \prod_{i=1}^{n} f\left(\frac{xi}{\theta}\right)$$

$$= \frac{1}{\theta^n} I(X_1 \ldots X_n \in [0, \theta])$$

$$= \frac{1}{\theta^n} I[\max(X_1 \ldots X_n) \le \theta]$$

Here the indicator function I(A) equals to life event A happens and O otherwise.

What the indicator above means is that the likelihood will be equal to 0 if at least one of the factors is 0 and this will happen if atleast one observation Xi will fall outside of the allowed interval [0, θ] Another way to say it is that the mximum among observations will exceed θ.

i.e., $\psi(\theta) = 0$, if $\theta < \max(x_1 . x_n)$ and

$$\psi(\theta) = \frac{1}{\theta^n} \text{ if } \theta \ge \max(x_1 . x_n)$$

Therefore, $\theta = \max(x_1 . x_n)$ is MLE of θ.

59. The distribution of y is same as x.

(The memory lessness property of exponential distribution)

i.e., pdf of y is given by.

$$f(y) = \frac{1}{2} e^{\frac{-y}{2}}, y > 0$$

so $$p(y \ge t) = \int_t^\infty \frac{1}{2} e^{-\frac{y}{2}} dy = e^{\frac{-t}{z}}$$

60. With the same conclusion

$$E(y) = E(x) = 2.$$

70. Here N = 2 means that two event occur and one does not occur, if x and y occurs and z does not occur then,

$$\text{Probability} = ab(1 - c)$$
$$= ab - abc$$

if y and z occurs and x does not occur

Then, $$\text{Probability} = bc(1 - a)$$
$$= bc - abc$$

if x and z occurs and y does not occur

Then $$\text{Probability} = ca(1 - b)$$
$$= ca - abc$$

Therefore, required probability that (N = 2)

$$= ab - abc + bc - abc + ca - abc$$
$$= ab + bc + ca - 3abc$$

71. Given that n = 200,

P = 45%

= 45/100 = 0.45

and q = 1 – P = 1 – 0.45

= 0.55

Therefore mean = nP

= 200 × 0.45 = 90

and variance = nPq

= 200 × 0.55 × 0.45

= 49.5

Therefore standard deviation

$$= \sqrt{\text{variance}} = \sqrt{npq}$$

$$= \sqrt{49.5} \equiv 7.04$$

72. We have, $\frac{x+y}{2} = 2 \Rightarrow x + y = 4$

When $x = 1$, we get

$1 + y = 4 \Rightarrow y = 3$

given that for x, $\lambda = 1$ and for y, $\lambda = 2$

Therefore, by using Poisson's distribution

$$P(x) = \frac{e^{-\lambda}\lambda^x}{x!}$$

we get $P\left(x=1\left|\frac{x+y}{2}=2\right.\right)$

$$= \frac{e^{-1}(1)^1}{1!} + \frac{e^{-2}(2)^3}{3!}$$

$$\cong 0.5$$

78. Probability that at least one of the events occurs

$$= 1 - \frac{1}{\alpha^{\frac{n(n+1)}{2}}}$$

because $\left[\frac{1}{\alpha_1}(1+2+\ldots\ldots n+1)\right] = \frac{1}{\alpha^{n+1}}$

79. Probability that the bulb X fails before Y

$$= \frac{100-15}{100} = \frac{85}{100}$$

80. The maximum likelihood estimator of θ is the standard deviation of the sample.

81. Let X_1, X_2, X_3 be a random sampling of size 3 chosen from a population with probability distribution

$P(X = 1) = p$ and $P(X = 0) = 1 - p = q, 0 < p < 1$

Then the sampling distribution $f(\cdot)$ of the statistic

$Y = \text{Max}\{X_1, X_2, X_3\}$ is

$f(0) = p^3 + q^3$

and $f(1) = 1 - p^3 - q^3$

85. Suppose X is a random variable, C is a constant and $a_n = E(x - c)^n$ is finite for all $n \geq 1$. Then, $P(x = c) = 1$

if and only if $a_n = 0$ for atleast $n \geq 1$.

87. Given cost matrix of assignment problem

is $\begin{bmatrix} a & b & c & d \\ b & c & d & a \\ c & d & a & b \\ d & a & b & c \end{bmatrix}$ let min

$(a, b, c, d) = a$ then, optimal table is

$$\begin{bmatrix} 0 & b-a & c-a & d-a \\ b-a & c-a & d-a & 0 \\ c-a & d-a & 0 & b-a \\ d-a & 0 & b-a & c-a \end{bmatrix}$$

Hence by Hungarian method cost

$= a + a + a + a = 4a$

$= 4\min(a, b, c, d)$

88. Given that x is random variable and $f.g.$ R → R are measurable functions such that $f(X)$ and $g(X)$ are independent, then both $f(X)$ and $g(X)$ are degenerate.

101. Weak duality theorem : Let x_0 be a feasible solution of the primal problems.

$f(x) = cx$

Subject to $AX \leq b; X \geq 0$.

where x^T and $c \in R^n$, $b^T \in R^m$ and A is are $m \times n$ real matrix. If w_0 be a feasible solution of the dual of the primal namely.

Mini. $g(w) = b^T w$ subject to $A^T w \geq c^T$,

$w \geq 0$

where $w^T \in R^m$

then $cX_0 \leq b^T w_0$.

Proof: Since X_0 and w_0 are the feasible solution to the primal and its dual respectively, we must have

$$AX_0 \leq b, X_0 \geq 0$$

and

$$A^T w_0 \geq C^T, w_0 \geq 0$$

Thus $c \leq w_0{}^T A$

or $c \times 0 \leq w_0{}^T AX_0 \leq w_0{}^T b$

or $c \times 0 \leq b^T w_0$

Equality sign holds only if both one optimal solutions. Hence if x be a non-optimal feasible solution of a L.P. maximum Problem and y a dual feasible solution, then $cX_0 < b^T w_0$

i.e. the Primal objective value at x is less than the dual objective value at y.

104. Required Probability

$$= \frac{2}{5}\cdot\frac{1}{5} + \frac{4}{6}\cdot\frac{2}{5}$$

$$= \frac{1}{15} + \frac{4}{15}$$

$$= \frac{5}{15} = \frac{1}{3}$$

111. Given the parameter of poisson distribution is λ and probability of minor injury.

$$P(N_1) = \frac{1}{N} \text{ and } n = N.$$

$$\therefore \quad \lambda = nP = N \cdot \frac{1}{N} = 1$$

Now, $$P(r) = \frac{\lambda^r e^{-\lambda}}{r!} = \frac{(1)^r e^{-1}}{r!} = \frac{e^{-1}}{r!}$$

So, probability of major accidents (which requires hospitalisation)

$$= 1 - P \text{ (minor accidents)}$$

$$= 1 - \frac{e^{-1}}{r!}$$

For $r = 1, 2, ...N.$

$$P(1) = 1 - \frac{e^{-1}}{1!} = 1 - \frac{1}{2.71} = 0.9963$$

$$P(2) = 1 - \frac{e^{-1}}{2!} = 1 - \frac{1}{2 \times 2.71} = 0.8154.$$

....

....

and so on.

112. We have given the random variables $X_1, X_2, ...$ X_{200} each with mean 0.

$$\therefore \quad f(x) = \frac{1}{\sigma\sqrt{2\pi}} e^{-x^2/2\sigma^2}$$

Since $\sigma^2 = 1$(given)

$$\therefore \quad f(x) = \frac{1}{\sqrt{2\pi}} e^{-x^2/2}$$

So, the probability $P(|X_1X_2 + X_3X_4 + ... + X_{199}X_{200}|$ $< 10)$

$$= \int_{-1}^{1} \frac{1}{\sqrt{2\pi}} e^{-x^2/2} dx$$

$$= \frac{2}{\sqrt{2\pi}} \int_0^1 e^{-x^2/2} dx$$

$$\Rightarrow \sqrt{\frac{\pi}{2}} P(|X_1X_2 + X_3X_4 + ... + X_{199}X_{200}| < 10)$$

$$= \int_0^1 e^{-x^2/2} dx. \textbf{ Ans.}$$

11

CHAPTER

Linear Programming

2016

1. Let $T : l_2 \to l_2$ be defined by

$T((x_1, x_2,\ldots,x_n,..)) = (x_2 - x_1, x_3 - x_2,\ldots, x_{n+1} - x_n,\ldots).$

Then

(*a*) $\|T\| = 1$

(*b*) $\|T\| > 2$ but bounded

(*c*) $1 < \|T\| \le 2$

(*d*) $\|T\|$ is unbounded

2. Let $X_1, X_2, X_3,\ldots$ be a sequence of i.i.d. random variables with mean 1. If N is a geometric random variable with the probability mass function $P(N = k) = \frac{1}{2^k}$; k = 1, 2, 3... and it is independent of the X'_is, then $E(X_1 + X_2 + \ldots + X_N)$ is equal to ________.

3. Let X_1 be an exponential random variable with mean 1 and X_2 a gamma random variable with mean 2 and variance 2. If X_1 and X_2 are independently distributed, then $P(X_1 < X_2)$ is equal to ____________.

4. Let $X_1, X_2, X_3,\ldots$ be a sequence of i.i.d. uniform (0, 1) random variables. Then, the value of

$$\lim_{n\to\infty} P(-\ln(1-X_1) - \ldots - \ln(1-X_n) \ge n)$$

is equal to ________.

5. Lex X be a standard normal random variable. Then, $P(X < 0 \| [x] | = 1)$ is equal to

(*a*) $\dfrac{\Phi(1) - \frac{1}{2}}{\Phi(2) - \frac{1}{2}}$

(*b*) $\dfrac{\Phi(1) + \frac{1}{2}}{\Phi(2) + \frac{1}{2}}$

(*c*) $\dfrac{\Phi(1) - \frac{1}{2}}{\Phi(2) + \frac{1}{2}}$

(*d*) $\dfrac{\Phi(1) + 1}{\Phi(2) + 1}$

6. Let $X_1, X_2, X_3, \ldots\ldots X_N$ be a random sample from the probability density function

$$f(x) = \begin{cases} \alpha\, a e^{-\alpha x} + (1-\theta)2\alpha e^{-2\alpha x}; & x \ge 0 \\ 0 & \text{otherwise} \end{cases}$$

where $\alpha > 0$, $0 \le \theta \le 1$ are parameters. Consider the following testing problem:

$H_0: \theta = 1, \alpha = 1$ versus $H_1 : \theta = 0, \alpha = 2$.

Which of the following statements is TRUE?

(*a*) Uniformly Most Powerful test does NOT exist

(*b*) Uniformly Most Powerful test is of the form $\sum_{i=1}^{n} X_i > c$, for some $0 < c < \infty$

(*c*) Uniformly Most Powerful test is of the form $\sum_{i=1}^{n} X_i < c$, for some $0 < c < \infty$

(*d*) Uniformly Most Powerful test is of the form $c_1 < \sum_{i=1}^{n} X_i < c_2$, for some $0 < c_1 < c_2 < \infty$

7. Let $X_1, X_2, X_3,\ldots$ be a sequence of i.i.d. $N(\mu, 1)$ random variables. Then,

$$\lim_{n\to\infty} \frac{\sqrt{\pi}}{2n} \sum_{i=1}^{n} E(|X_i - \mu|)$$

is equal to __________.

8. Let $X_1, X_2, X_3, \ldots X_n$ be a random sample from uniform $[1, \theta]$, for some $\theta > 1$. If $X_{(n)}$ = Maximum $(X_1, X_2, X_3, \ldots, X_n)$, then the UMVUE of θ is

(*a*) $\dfrac{n+1}{n} X_{(n)} + \dfrac{1}{n}$

(*b*) $\dfrac{n+1}{n} X_{(n)} - \dfrac{1}{n}$

(*c*) $\dfrac{n}{n+1} X_{(n)} + \dfrac{1}{n}$

(*d*) $\dfrac{n}{n+1} X_{(n)} + \dfrac{n+1}{n}$

9. Let $x_1 = x_2 = x_3 = 1$, $x_4 = x_5 = x_6 = 2$ be a random sample from a Poisson random variable with mean θ, where $\theta \in \{1, 2\}$. Then, the maximum likelihood estimator of θ is equal to _____.

2015

10. The Lagrangian of a system in terms of polar coordinates (r, θ) is given by

$$L = \frac{1}{2}m\dot{r}^2 + \frac{1}{2}m\left(\dot{r}^2 + r^2\dot{\theta}^2\right) - mgr\left(1-\cos(\theta)\right),$$

where m is the mass, g is the acceleration due to gravity and $\dot{s}$ denotes the derivative of s with respect to time. Then the equations of motion are

(a) $2\ddot{r} = r\dot{\theta}^2 - g\left(1-\cos(\theta)\right)$,

$\frac{d}{dt}\left(r^2\dot{\theta}\right) = -g\, r\sin(\theta)$

(b) $2\ddot{r} = r\dot{\theta}^2 + g\left(1-\cos(\theta)\right)$,

$\frac{d}{dt}\left(r^2\dot{\theta}\right) = -g\, r\sin(\theta)$

(c) $2\ddot{r} = r\dot{\theta}^2 - g\left(1-\cos(\theta)\right)$,

$\frac{d}{dt}\left(r^2\dot{\theta}\right) = g\, r\sin(\theta)$

(d) $2\ddot{r} = r\dot{\theta}^2 + g\left(1-\cos(\theta)\right)$,

$\frac{d}{dt}\left(r^2\dot{\theta}\right) = g\, r\sin(\theta)$

11. Consider the linear programming problem

Maximize $3x + 9y$,

subject to $2y - x \le 2$

$3y - x \ge 0$

$2x + 3y \le 10$

$x, y \ge 0.$

Then the maximum value of the objective function is equal to _____

2014

12. Let E_1 and E_2 be two non empty subsets of a normed linear space X and let $E_1 + E_2 := \{x + y \in X : x \in E_1 \text{ and } y \in E_2\}$.

Then which of the following statements is **FALSE**

(a) If E_1 and E_2 are convex, then $E_1 + E_2$ is convex

(b) If E_1 or E_2 is open, then $E_1 + E_2$ is open

(c) $E_1 + E_2$ must be closed if E_1 and E_2 are closed

(d) If E_1 is closed and E_2 is compact, then $E_1 + E_2$ is closed

13. If X_1, X_2 is a random sample of size 2 from an $N(0, 1)$ population, then $\frac{(X_1 + X_2)^2}{(X_1 - X_2)^2}$ follows

(a) $\chi^2_{(2)}$ (b) $F_{2,2}$

(c) $F_{2,1}$ (d) $F_{1,1}$

14. Let $Z \sim N(0, 1)$ be a random variable. Then the value of $E\,[\max\{Z, 0\}]$ is

(a) $\frac{1}{\sqrt{\pi}}$ (b) $\sqrt{\frac{2}{\pi}}$

(c) $\frac{1}{\sqrt{2\pi}}$ (d) $\frac{1}{\pi}$

15. Consider the following linear programming problem:

Minimize $x_1 + x_2$

Subject to:

$2x_1 + x_2 \ge 8$

$2x_1 + 5x_2 \ge 10$

$x_1, x_2 \ge 0$

The optimal value to this problem is ___

16. Consider the following linear programming problem:

Minimize: $x_1 + x_2 + 2x_3$

Subject to $x_1 + 2x_2 \ge 4$

$x_2 + 7x_3 \le 5$

$x_1 - 3x_2 + 5x_3 = 6$

$x_1, x_2 \ge 0$, x_3 is unrestricted

The dual to this problem is:

Maximize : $4y_1 + 5y_2 + 6y_3$

Subject to $y_1 + y_3 \le 1$

$2y_1 + y_2 - 3y_3 \le 1$

$7y_2 + 5y_3 = 2$

and further subject to:

(a) $y_1 \ge 0, y_2 \le 0$ and y_3 is unrestricted

(b) $y_1 \ge 0, y_2 \ge 0$ and y_3 is unrestricted

(c) $y_1 \ge 0, y_3 \le 0$ and y_2 is unrestricted

(d) $y_3 \ge 0, y_2 \le 0$ and y_1 is unrestricted

2013

17. Consider the linear programming problem:

Maximize $x + \frac{3}{2}y$

subject to $2x + 3y \le 16$,

$x + 4y \le 18$,

$x \ge 0, y \ge 0.$

If S denotes the set of all solutions of the above problem, then

(a) S is empty

(b) S is a singleton

(c) S is a line segment

(d) S has positive area

18. Consider the following linear programming problem:

Maximize $x + 3y + 6z - W$

subject to $5x + y + 6z + 7W \le 20$,

$6x + 2y + 2z + 9W \le 40$,

$x \ge 0, y \ge 0, z \ge 0, W \ge 0$.

Then the optimal value is ______

2012

19. For the linear programming problem

Maximize $z = x_1 + 2x_2 + 3x_3 - 4x_4$

Subject to $2x_1 + 3x_2 - x_3 - x_4 = 15$

$6x_1 + x_2 + x_3 - 3x_4 = 21$

$8x_1 + 2x_2 + 3x_3 - 4x_4 = 30$

$x_1, x_2, x_3, x_4 \ge 0$,

$x_1 = 4, x_2 = 3, x_3 = 0, x_4 = 2$ is

(*a*) an optimal solution

(*b*) a degenerate basic feasible solution

(*c*) a non-degenerate basic feasible solution

(*d*) a non-basic feasible solution

20. Which one of the following statement is **TRUE**?

(*a*) A convex set cannot have infinite many extreme points.

(*b*) A linear programming problem can have infinite many extreme points.

(*c*) A linear programming problem can have exactly two different optimal solutions.

(*d*) A linear programming problem can have a non-basic optimal solution.

21. The following table gives the unit transportation costs, the supply at each origin and the demand of each destination for a transportation problem.

		Destination				
		D_1	D_2	D_3	D_4	Supply
	O_1	3	4	8	7	60
Origin	O_2	7	3	7	6	80
	O_3	3	9	3	4	100
Demand		40	70	50	80	

Let x_{ij} denote the number of units to be transported from origin i to destination j. If the u-v method is applied to improve the basic feasible solution given by $x_{12} = 60$, $x_{22} = 10$, $x_{23} = 50$, $x_{24} = 20$, $x_{31} = 40$ and $x_{34} = 60$, then the variable entering and leaving the basis, respectively, are

(*a*) x_{11} and x_{24}

(*b*) x_{13} and x_{23}

(*c*) x_{14} and x_{24}

(*d*) x_{33} and x_{24}

2011

22. The Linear Programming Problem:

Maximize $z = x_1 + x_2$

subject to $x_1 + 2x_2 \le 20$

$x_1 + x_2 \le 15$

$x_2 \le 6$

$x_1, x_2 \ge 0$

(*a*) has exactly one optimum solution

(*b*) has more than one optimum solutions

(*c*) has unbounded solution

(*d*) has no solution

23. Consider the Primal Linear Programming Problem:

$$P: \begin{cases} \text{Maximize } z = c_1x_1 + c_2x_2 + \ldots + c_nx_n \\ \text{subject to} \\ a_{11}x_1 + a_{12}x_2 + \ldots + a_{1n}x_n \le b_1 \\ a_{21}x_1 + a_{22}x_2 + \ldots + a_{2n}x_n \le b_2 \\ \vdots \qquad \vdots \qquad \vdots \\ a_{m1}x_1 + a_{m2}x_2 + \ldots + a_{mn}x_n \le b_m \\ x_j \ge 0, j = 1, \ldots, n. \end{cases}$$

The Dual of P is

$$D: \begin{cases} \text{Minimize } z' = b_1w_1 + b_2w_2 + \ldots + b_mw_m \\ \text{subject to} \\ a_{11}w_1 + a_{21}w_2 + \ldots + a_{m1}w_m \ge c_1 \\ a_{12}w_1 + a_{22}w_2 + \ldots + a_{m2}w_m \ge c_2 \\ \vdots \qquad \vdots \qquad \vdots \\ a_{1n}w_1 + a_{2n}w_2 + \ldots + a_{mn}w_m \le c_n \\ w_i \ge 0, i = 1, \ldots, m. \end{cases}$$

Which of the following statements is **FALSE?**

(*a*) If P has an optimal solution, then D also has an optimal solution

(*b*) The dual of the dual problem is a primal problem

(*c*) If P has an unbounded solution, then D has no feasible solution

(*d*) If P has no feasible solution, then D has a feasible solution

24. We have to assign four jobs I, II, III, IV to four workers A, B C and D. The time taken by different workers (in hours) in completing different jobs is given below :

		I	II	III	IV
	A	5	3	2	8
Workers	B	7	9	2	6
	C	6	4	5	7
	D	5	7	7	8

The optimal assignment is as follows:

Job III to worker A; Job IV to worker B; Job II to worker C and Job I to worker D and hence the time taken by different workers in completin different jobs is now changed as:

		I	II	III	IV
	A	5	3	2	5
Workers	B	7	9	2	3
	C	4	2	3	2
	D	5	7	7	5

Then the minimum time (in hours) taken by the workers to complete all the jobs is

(*a*) 10 (*b*) 12

(*c*) 15 (*d*) 17

25. The following table shows the information on the availability of supply to each warehouse, the requirement of each market and unit transportation cost (in rupees) from each warehouse to each market.

	Market				
	M_1	M_2	M_3	M_4	Supply
Warehouse W_1	6	3	5	4	22
Warehouse W_2	5	9	2	7	15
Warehouse W_3	5	7	8	6	8
Requirement	7	12	17	9	

The present transportation schedule is as follows: W_1 to M_2: 12 units; W_1 to M_3: 1 unit; W_1 to M_4: 9 units; W_2 to M_3: 15 units; W_3 to M_1:7 units and W_3 to M_3 : 1 unit. Then the minimum total transportation cost (in rupees) is

(*a*) 150 (*b*) 149

(*c*) 148 (*d*) 147

2010

26. For the linear programming problem

Minimize $z = x - y$, subject to $2x + 3y \leq 6$, $0 \leq x \leq 3$, $0 \leq y \leq 3$,

the number of extreme points of its feasible region and the number of basic feasible solutions respectively, are

(*a*) 3 and 3 (*b*) 4 and 4

(*c*) 3 and 5 (*d*) 4 and 5

27. Which one of following statements is correct?

(*a*) If a Linear Programming Problem (LPP) is infeasible, then its dual is also infeasible

(*b*) If an LPP is infeasible, then its dual always has unbounded solution

(*c*) If an LPP has unbounded solution, then its dual also has unbounded solution

(*d*) If an LPP has unboundd solution, then its dual is infeasible

28. The following table gives the cost matrix of a transportation problem

4	5	6
3	2	2
1	1	2

The basic feasible solution given by $x_{11} = 3, x_{13} = 1, x_{23} = 6, x_{31} = 2, x_{32} = 5$ is

(*a*) degenerate and optimal

(*b*) optimal but not degenerate

(*c*) degenerate but not optimal

(*d*) neither degenerate nor optimal

29. If z^* is the optimal value of the linear programming problem

Maximize $z = 5x_1 + 9x_2 + 4x_3$

subject to $x_1 + x_2 + x_3 = 5$

$4x_1 + 3x_2 + 2x_3 = 12$

$x_1, x_2, x_3 \geq 0,$

then

(*a*) $0 \leq z^* < 10$ (*b*) $10 \leq z^* < 20$

(*c*) $20 \leq z^* < 30$ (*d*) $30 \leq z^* < 40$

2009

30. Which one of the following is TRUE ?

(*a*) Every linear programming problem has a feasible solution.

(*b*) If a linear programming problem has an optimal solution then it is unique.

(*c*) The union of two convex sets is necessarily convex.

(*d*) Extreme points of the disk $x^2 + y^2 \leq 1$ are the points on the circle $x^2 + y^2 = 1$.

31. The dual of the linear programming problem :

Minimize $\mathbf{c}^T \mathbf{x}$ subject to $A\mathbf{x} \geq \mathbf{b}$ and $x \geq 0$ is

(*a*) Maximize $\mathbf{b}^T \mathbf{w}$ subject to $A^T w \geq c$ and $\mathbf{w} \geq \mathbf{0}$

(*b*) Maximize $\mathbf{b}^T \mathbf{w}$ subject to $A^T w \leq c$ and $\mathbf{w} \geq \mathbf{0}$

(*c*) Maximize $\mathbf{b}^T \mathbf{w}$ subject to $A^T w \leq c$ and $\mathbf{w}$ is unrestricted

(*d*) Maximize $\mathbf{b}^T \mathbf{w}$ subject to $A^T w \geq c$ and $\mathbf{w}$ is unrestricted

32. For a fixed $t \in \mathbb{R}$, consider the linear programming problem :

$$\begin{aligned} \text{Maximize} \quad & z = 3x + 4y \\ \text{subject to} \quad & x + y \le 100 \\ & x + 3y \le t \\ \text{and} \quad & x \ge 0, y \ge 0 \end{aligned}$$

The maximum value of z is 400 for t =

(*a*) 50 (*b*) 100

(*c*) 200 (*d*) 300

33. The minimum value of

$z = 2x_1 - x_2 + x_3 - 5x_4 + 22x_5$

subject to $x_1 - 2x_4 + x_5 = 6$

$x_2 + x_4 - 4x_5 = 3$

$x_3 + 3x_4 + 2x_5 = 10$

$x_j \ge 0, j = 1, 2 ...., 5$

is

(*a*) 28 (*b*) 19

(*c*) 10 (*d*) 9

34. Using the Hungarian method, the optimal value of the assignment problem whose cost matrix is given by

5	23	14	8
10	25	1	23
35	16	15	12
16	23	11	7

is

(*a*) 29 (*b*) 52

(*c*) 26 (*d*) 44

2008

35. Let $c_{ij} \ge 2$ be the cost of the $(i, j)^{th}$ cell of an assignment problem. If a new cost matrix is generated by the elements $c_{ij}^* = \frac{1}{2}c_{ij} + 1$, then

(*a*) optimal assignment plan remains unchanged and cost of assignment decreases

(*b*) optimal assignment plan changes and cost of assignment decreases

(*c*) optimal assignment plan remains unchanged and cost of assignment increases

(*d*) optimal assignment plan changes and cost of assignment increases

36. Let a primal linear programming problem admit an optimal solution. Then the corresponding dual problem

(*a*) does not have a feasible solution

(*b*) has a feasible solution but does not have any optimal solution

(*c*) does not have a convex feasible region

(*d*) has an optimal solution

37. The cost matrix of a transportation problem is given by

1	2	3	4
4	3	2	1
0	2	2	1

The following are the values of variables in a feasible solution.

$x_{12} = 6, x_{23} = 2, x_{24} = 6, x_{31} = 4, x_{33} = 6$

Then which of the following is correct?

(*a*) The solution is degenerate and basic

(*b*) The solution is non-degenerate and basic

(*c*) The solution is degenerate and non-basic

(*d*) The solution is non-degenerate and non-basic

38. The maximum value of $z = 3x_1 - x_2$ subject to $2x_1 - x_2 \le 1$, $x_1 \le 3$ and $x_1, x_2 \ge 0$ is

(*a*) 0 (*b*) 4

(*c*) 6 (*d*) 9

39. Consider the problem of maximizing $z = 2x_1 + 3x_2 - 4x_3 + x_4$ subject to

$$\begin{aligned} x_1 + x_2 + x_3 &= 2, \\ x_1 - x_2 + x_3 &= 2, \\ 2x_1 + 3x_2 + 2x_3 - x_4 &= 0, \\ x_1, x_2, x_3, x_4 &\ge 0, \end{aligned}$$

Then

(*a*) (1, 0, 1, 4) is a basic feasible solution but (2, 0, 0, 4) is not

(*b*) (1, 0, 1, 4) is not a basic feasible solution but (2, 0, 0, 4) is

(*c*) neither (1, 0, 1, 4) nor (2, 0, 0, 4) is a basic feasible solution

(*d*) both of (1, 0, 1, 4) and (2, 0, 0, 4) are basic feasible solutions

2007

40. Consider the linear programming problem,

Max. $z = c_1x_1 + c_2x_2, c_1, c_2 > 0,$

subject to $x_1 + x_2 \le 3$

$2x_1 + 3x_2 \le 4$

$x_1, x_2 \ge 0.$

Then,

(*a*) the primal has an optimal solution but the dual does NOT have an optimal solution

(*b*) both the primal and the dual have optimal solutions

(*c*) the dual has an optimal solution but the primal does NOT have an optimal solution

(*d*) neither the primal nor the dual have optimal solutions

41. For each $a \in R$, consider the linear programming problem

Max. $z = x_1 + 2x_2 + 3x_3 + 4x_4$

subject to $ax_1 + 2x_3 \le 1$

$x_1 + ax_2 + 3x_4 \le 2$

$x_1, x_2, x_3, x_4 \ge 0.$

Let $S = \{a \in R :$ the given LP problem has a basic feasible solution$\}$. Then

(*a*) $S = \phi$ (*b*) $S = R$

(*c*) $S = (0, \infty)$ (*d*) $S = (-\infty, 0)$

42. Consider the linear programming problem

Max. $z = x_1 + 5x_2 + 3x_3$

subject to $2x_1 - 3x_2 + 5x_1 \le 3$

$3x_1 + 2x_3 \le 5$

$x_1, x_2, x_3, \ge 0.$

Then the dual of this LP problem

(*a*) has a feasible solution but does NOT have a basic feasible solution

(*b*) has a basic feasible solution

(*c*) has infinite number of feasiblel solutions

(*d*) has no feasible solution

43. Consider a transportation problem with two warehouses and two markets. The warehouse capacities are $a_1 = 2$ and $a_2 = 4$ and the market demands are $b_1 = 3$ and $b_2 = 3$. Let x_{ij} be the quantity shipped from warehouse i to market j and c_{ij} be the corresponding unit cost. Suppose that $c_{11} = 1$, $c_{21} = 1$ and $c_{22} = 2$. Then $(x_{11}, x_{12}, x_{21}, x_{22}) = (2, 0, 1, 3)$ is optimal for every

(*a*) $c_{12} \in [1, 2]$ (*b*) $c_{12} \in [0, 3]$

(*c*) $c_{12} \in [1, 3]$ (*d*) $c_{12} \in [2, 4]$

2006

44. For a linear programming primal maximization problem P with dual Q, which of the following statements is correct?

(*a*) The optimal values of P and Q exist and are the same

(*b*) Both optimal values exist and the optimal value of P is less than the optimal value of Q

(*c*) P will have an optimal solution, if and only if Q also has an optimal solution

(*d*) Both P and Q cannot be infeasible

45. Let a convex set in 9-dimensional space be given by the solution set of the following system of linear inequalities

$$\sum_{j=1}^{3} x_{ij} = 1, i = 1, 2, 3$$

$$\sum_{j=1}^{3} x_{ij} = 1, j = 1, 2, 3$$

$$x_{ij} \ge 0, i, j = 1, 2, 3$$

Then, the number of extreme points of this set is

(*a*) 3 (*b*) 4

(*c*) 9 (*d*) 6

46. Consider the linear programming problem

Max $c_1x_1 + c_2x_2 + c_3x_3$

s.t $x_1 + x_2 + x_3 \le 4$

$x_1 \le 2$

$x_3 \le 3$

$3x_1 + x_3 \le 7$

$x_1, x_2, x_3 \ge 0.$

If (1, 0, 3) is an optimal solution, then

(*a*) $c_1 \le c_2 \le c_3$

(*b*) $c_3 \le c_1 \le c_2$

(*c*) $c_2 \le c_3 \le c_1$

(*d*) $c_2 \le c_1 \le c_3$

47. Let the convex set S be given by the solution set of the following system of linear inequalities in the sixteen variables $\{x_{ij} : i, j = 1,.,4\}$

$$\sum_{j=1}^{4} x_{ij} = 3, i = 1, .., 4$$

$$\sum_{j=1}^{4} x_{ij} = 3, j = 1, .., 4$$

$$x_{ij} \ge 0, i, j = 1, .., 4.$$

Then, the dimension of S is equal to

(*a*) 4 (*b*) 9

(*c*) 8 (*d*) 12

Statement for Linked Answer Q. 48 & 49 :

Consider the Linear Programming Problem P:

Max $c_1x_1 + c_2x_2 + ... + c_nx_n$

s.t. $\sum_{j=1}^{n} a_{ij}x_j \le b_i, i = 1,..., m,$

$x_j \ge 0, j = 1, ., n,$

with m constraints in n non-negative variables.

48. Let $x^* = (x_1^*, x_2^*, \ldots, x_n^*)$ be an optimal extreme point solution to P with $x_1^*, x_2^*, x_3^*, \ldots, x_n^* > 0$. Then, out of the m constraints $\sum_{i=1}^{n} a_{ij}x_i \le b_i \; i = 1, \ldots, m$, the number of constraints not satisfied with equality at x^* is

(*a*) at most $m - 4$ (*b*) at most $n - 4$

(*c*) equal to $m - 3$ (*d*) equal to $m - 2$

49. Treat c_i's, a_{ij} 's as fixed and consider the problem P for different values of b_i's. Let P be unbounded for some set of parameters $b_1, b_2, \ldots, b_m$. 'Then

(*a*) $n > m$

(*b*) P is either unbounded or infeasible for every choice of b_i's

(*c*) $m > n$

(*d*) P has an optimal solution for some choice of b_i's

2005

50. Consider the following Linear Programming Problem (LPP) :

Minimize $z = 2x_1 + 3x_2 + x_3$

subject to $x_1 + 2x_2 + 2x_3 - x_4 + x_5 = 3$

$2x_1 + 3x_2 + 4x_3 + x_6 = 6$

$x_i \ge 0, i = 1, 2, \ldots 6.$

A nondegenerate basic feasible solution $(x_1, x_2, x_3, x_4, x_5, x_6)$ is

(*a*) (1, 0, 1, 0, 0, 0)

(*b*) (1, 0, 0, 0, 0, 7)

(*c*) (0, 0, 0, 0, 3, 6)

(*d*) (3, 0, 0, 0, 0, 0)

51. The unit cost c_{ij} of producing product i at plant j is given by the matrix :

$$\begin{pmatrix} 14 & 12 & 16 \\ 21 & 9 & 17 \\ 9 & 7 & 5 \end{pmatrix}$$

The total cost of optimal assignment is

(*a*) 20 (*b*) 22

(*c*) 25 (*d*) 28

52. Consider the following primal Linear Programming Problem (LPP).

Maximize $z = 3x_1 + 2x_2$

subject to $x_1 - x_2 \le 1$

$x_1 + x_2 \ge 3$

$x_1, x_2 \ge 0$

The dual of this problem has

(*a*) infeasible optimal solution

(*b*) unbounded optimal objective value

(*c*) a unique optimal solution

(*d*) infinitely many optimal solutions

53. The cost matrix of a Transportation Problem is given by

6	4	1	5
8	9	2	7
4	3	6	2

The following values of the basic variables were obtained at the first iteration :

$x_{11} = 6, x_{12} = 8, x_{22} = 2, x_{23} = 14, x_{33} = 1, x_{34} = 4.$

Then

(*a*) the current solution is optimal

(*b*) the current solution is nonoptimal and the entering and leaving variables are x_{31} and x_{33} respectively

(*c*) the current solution is nonoptimal and the entering and leaving variables are x_{21} and x_{12} respectively

(*d*) the current solution is nonoptimal and the entering and leaving variables are x_{14} and x_{12} respectively

54. In a balanced transportation problem, if all the unit transportation costs c_{ij} are decreased by a nonzero constant α, then in the optimal solution of the revised problem

(*a*) the values of the decision variables and the objective value remain unchanged

(*b*) the values of the decision variables change but the objective value remains unchanged

(*c*) the values of the decision variables remain unchanged but the objective value changes

(*d*) the values of the decision variables and the objective value change

55. Consider the following Linear Programming Problem (LPP).

Maximize $z = 3x_1 + x_2$

subject to $x_1 + 2x_2 \le 5$

$x_1 + x_2 - x_3 \le 2$

$7x_1 + 3x_2 - 5x_3 \le 20$

$x_1, x_2, x_3 \ge 0.$

The nature of the optimal solution to the problem is

(*a*) nondegenerate alternative optima

(*b*) degenerate alternative optima

(*c*) degenerate unique optimal

(*d*) nondegenerate unique optimal

2004

56. Consider the Linear Programming Problem (LPP)

Maximize x_1,

subject to : $3x_1 + 4x_2 \leq 10$, $5x_1 - x_2 \leq 9$, $3x_1 - 2x_2 \geq -2$, $x_1 - 3x_2 \leq 3$, $x_1, x_2 \geq 0$.

The value of the LPP is

(*a*) $\frac{9}{5}$ (*b*) 2

(*c*) 3 (*d*) $\frac{10}{3}$

2003

57. Suppose that the linear programming problem P : Min $z = c^1 x$ s.t. $Ax \geq b$, $x \geq 0$, where A is an $m \times n$ matrix, c an $n \times 1$ vector and b an $m \times 1$ vector, is being solved by the Dual Simplex Algorithm. Then

(*a*) the value of the primal objective function increases at every iteration

(*b*) the algorithm will always terminate with an optimal solution for the dual

(*c*) the algorithm will always terminate with an optimal solution to the primal

(*d*) it is not always possible to obtain a starting basis for this Algorithm

58. Consider the transportation problem given below. The bracketed elements in the table indicate a feasible solution and the elements on the left hand corner are the costs c_{ij}

			a_i
2	5	1	1
(1)			2
1	3	4	
	(1)	(1)	3
b_j 1	1	1	

(*a*) this solution is a basic feasible solution

(*b*) this solution can be made basic feasible

(*c*) this is an optimal solution

(*d*) the problem does not have an optimal solution

59. Consider the linear programming problem P_I : Min $z = c' x$ s.t. $Ax = b$, $x \geq 0$, where A is an $m \times n$ matrix, $m \leq n$, c and x are $n \times 1$ vectors and b an $m \times 1$ vector. Let K denote the set of feasible solutions for P_1. Then,

(*a*) the number of positive x_j's in any feasible solution of P_I can never exceed m, and if it is less than m, the feasible solution is a degenerate basic feasible solution

(*b*) every feasible solution of P1 in which m variables are positive is a basic feasible solution and ${}^nC_m$ is the total number of basic feasible solutions

(*c*) in solving P_1 by the simplex algorithm a new basis and a new extreme point of the constraint set are generated after every pivot step

(*d*) K is a convex set and if the value of the objective function at an extreme point x^* of K is better than its values at all the neighbouring extreme points, then x^* is an optimal solution of P1

60. Consider the linear programming formulation (P2) of optimally assigning n men to n jobs with respect to some costs $\{c_{ij}\}_{i,j} = {}^n_1$. Let A denote the coefficient matrix of the constraint set. Then,

(*a*) rank of A is $2n–1$ and every basic feasible solution of P2 is integer valued

(*b*) rank of A is $2n–1$ and every basic feasible solution of P2 is integer valued

(*c*) rank of A is $2n$ and every basic feasible solution of P2 is integer valued

(*d*) rank of A is $2n$ and every basic feasible solution of P2 is not integer valued

61. Simplex tableau for phase I of the simplex algorithm for a linear programming problem is given below (x_3, x_4, x_5 are artificial variables)

Basis	x_1	x_2	x_3	x_4	x_5	RHS
$Z_j - C_J$	0	0	–2	–2	0	0
x_1	1	0	3/5	1/5	0	2
x_2	0	1	–2/5	1/5	0	0
x_3	0	0	–1	–1	1	0

Choose the correct statement

(*a*) the tableau does not show the end of phase I, since the artificial variable x_5 is in the basis

(*b*) the tableau does show the end of phase I since the value of the phase I objective function is zero

(*c*) the constraints for the original linear programming problem are not redundant

(*d*) the original linear programming problem does not have a feasible solution

62. Given below is the final tableau of a linear programming problem (x_4 and x_5 are slack variables)

Basis	x_1	x_2	x_3	x_4	x_5	RHS
Z_j–C_J	0	0	3	5	1	8
x_1	1	0	1	4	–1	2
x_2	0	1	2	–1	1	3

If the right hand side vector $\begin{pmatrix}1\\3\end{pmatrix}$ of the problem gets changed to $\begin{pmatrix}1+\theta\\3\end{pmatrix}$, then the current basic feasible solution is optimal for

(*a*) all $\theta \le 2$

(*b*) all $\theta \ge -\dfrac{1}{4}$

(*c*) all $\theta \in \left[-\dfrac{1}{2}, 2\right]$

(*d*) no non-zero value of θ

2002

63. The system $Ax \le 0$, where A is an $n \times n$ matrix,

(*a*) may not have a nonzero solution

(*b*) always has a nonzero solution

(*c*) always has at least 2 linearly independent solutions

(*d*) always has at least n linearly independent solutions

64. Consider the following linear program

$$\text{P Max} : \sum_{j=1}^{n} c_j x_j \text{ subject to}$$

$$\sum_{j=1}^{n} a_{ij}x_j \le b_i, 1 \le i \le m \text{ and } x_j \ge 0,\ 1 \le j \le n.$$

Suppose that we are keeping the c_j's and a_{ij}'s fixed and varying the b_i's. Suppose that P is unbounded for some set of the parameter values b_i. Then, for every choice of b_i's,

(*a*) P is unbounded or infeasible

(*b*) P is unbounded

(*c*) The dual problem to P has a finite optimum

(*d*) The dual problem to P is unbounded

65. Consider the Linear Program

$$\text{Max} \sum_{i=1}^{4} c_i x_i$$

Subject to

$$\sum_{i=1}^{4} a_i x_i \le a_0,$$

$0 \le x_1, x_2, x_3, x_4 \le 1.$

where $a_i > 0$, $c_i > 0$ for $i = 1, 2, 3, 4$

and $a_0 > 0$

(*i*) Write the dual of this Linear Programming Problem.

(*ii*) Assuming

$$\frac{c_1}{a_1} \ge \frac{c_2}{a_2} \ge \frac{c_3}{a_3} \ge \frac{c_4}{a_4}$$

$a_1 + a_2 \le a_0$, and $a_1 + a_2 + a_3 > a_0$,

show that the feasible solution

$$x_1 = x_2 = 1,$$

$$x_3 = \frac{a_0 - a_1 - a_2}{a_3}, = 0,$$

is an optimal solution.

66. Consider the optimal assignment problem, in which n persons $P_1, P_2,.., P_n$ are to be assigned n jobs $J_1, J_2,.., J_n$ and where the effectiveness rating of the person P_i for the job J_j is $a_{ij} > 0$. The objective is to find an assignment of persons to jobs, that is, a permutation $\sigma : \{1, 2,..., n\} \to \{1, 2,... , n\}$ which assigns person P_i to job $J_{\sigma(i)}$, so as o maximize the total effectiveness $\sum_{i=1}^{n} \alpha_{i\alpha(i)}$. Show that in any optimal assignment, at least one person is assigned a job at which he is best.

2001

67. Let $S_1 = \{(x, y) \in R^2 : x^2 + y^2 \le 1\}$ and $S_2 = \{(x, y) \in R^2 : y \le x^2\}$. Then

(*a*) S_1 and S_2 both are convex sets

(*b*) S_1 is a convex set but S_2 is not a convex set

(*c*) S_2 is a convex set but S_1 is not a convex set

(*d*) neither S_1 nor S_2 is a convex set

68. Let T be the matrix (occuring in a typical transportation problem) given by

$$\begin{pmatrix} 1 & 1 & 0 & 0 \\ 0 & 0 & 1 & 1 \\ 1 & 0 & 1 & 0 \\ 0 & 1 & 0 & 1 \end{pmatrix}$$

Then

(*a*) Rank T = 4 and T is unimodular

(*b*) Rank T = 4 and T is not unimodular

(*c*) Rank T = 3 and T is unimodular

(*d*) Rank T = 3 and T is not unimodular

69. Consider the primal problem (LP)

max $4x_1 + 3x_2$

subject to

$x_1 + x_2 \leq 8$

$2x_1 + x_2 \leq 10$

$x_1 \geq 0, x_2 \geq 10$

together with its dual (LD). Then

(*a*) (LP) and (LD) both are infeasible

(*b*) (LP) and (LD) both are feasible

(*c*) (LP) is feasible but (LD) is infeasible

(*d*) (LP) is infeasible but (LD) is feasible

70. Let Z* denote the optimal value of LPP

max $Z = 4x_1 + 6x_2 + 2x_3$

such that

$3x_1 + 2x_2 + x_3 = 12$

$x_1 \geq 0, x_2 \geq 0, x_3 \geq 0.$

Then

(*a*) $10 \leq Z^* \leq 20$

(*b*) $20 < Z^* \leq 30$

(*c*) $30 < Z^* \leq 40$

(*d*) $Z^* > 40$

2000

71. Solve the following linear programming problem using the Simplex method.

Minimize $f = -40x_1 - 100x_2$

Subject to

$10x_1 + 5x_2 \leq 2500,$

$4x_1 + 10x_2 \leq 2000,$

$2x_1 + 3x_2 \leq 900,$

$x_1 \geq 0, x_2 \geq 0.$

ANSWERS

1. (c)	**2.** (2)	**3.** (0.5)	**4.** (0.5)	**5.** (*a*)	**6.** (*c*)	**7.** (0.70)	**8.** (*b*)	**9.** (2)	**10.** (*a*)
11. (24)	**12.** (*c*)	**13.** (*d*)	**14.** (*c*)	**15.** (4.24 to 4.26)		**16.** (*a*)	**17.** (*c*)	**18.** (60)	**19.** (*d*)
20. (*d*)	**21.** (*a*)	**22.** (*b*)	**23.** (*b*)	**24.** (*b*)	**25.** (*b*)	**26.** (*a*)	**27.** (*d*)	**28.** (*b*)	**29.** (*d*)
30. (*b*)	**31.** (*b*)	**32.** (*d*)	**33.** (*d*)	**34.** (*a*)	**35.** (*b*)	**36.** (*d*)	**37.** (*b*)	**38.** (*b*)	**39.** (*d*)
40. (*b*)	**41.** (*b*)	**42.** (*d*)	**43.** (*d*)	**44.** (*c*)	**45.** (*b*)	**46.** (*d*)	**47.** (*a*)	**48.** (*d*)	**49.** (*b*)
50. (*c*)	**51.** (*c*)	**52.** (*a*)	**53.** (*c*)	**54.** (*a*)	**55.** (*a*)	**56.** (*b*)	**57.** (*b*)	**58.** (*b*)	**59.** (*a*)
60. (*a*)	**61.** (*b*)	**62.** (*c*)	**63.** (*d*)	**64.** (*c*)	**65.** (*)	**66.** (*)	**67.** (*b*)	**68.** (*c*)	**69.** (*b*)
70. (*b*)	**71.** (*)								

EXPLANATIONS

1. $$||T(x)|| = \left(\sum_{n=1}^{\infty} |x_{n+1} - x_n|^2\right)^{\frac{1}{2}}$$

$$\leq \left(\sum_{n=1}^{\infty} |x_{n+1}|^2\right)^{\frac{1}{2}} + \left(\sum_{n=1}^{\infty} |x_n|^2\right)^{\frac{1}{2}}$$

$$\Rightarrow \quad ||x|| < ||Tx|| \leq 2\,||x|| \;\forall x$$

$$\Rightarrow \quad 1 < \frac{||Tx||}{||x||} \leq 2 \;\forall x$$

$$\Rightarrow \quad 1 < ||T|| \leq 2$$

2. $$P(N = k) = \frac{1}{2^k}$$

$$E(N) = \sum_{L=1}^{\infty} k.\frac{1}{2^k}$$

$$= \sum_{L=1}^{\infty} \frac{1}{2^{k-1}} = 2$$

Now $X_1, X_2, X_3, \ldots X_N$ are geometric random variable.

With $E(X_1') = 2,\ i = 1, 2, 3, \ldots..N$

by khinchin's theorem,

$$\frac{1}{n}\sum_{L=1}^{n} x_i \xrightarrow{P} E(Y_i) = 2$$

$$\Rightarrow E[X_1 + X_2 + \ldots + X_n] \to E(y_1) = 2$$

3. X_1 is an exponential random variable with mean 1 and X_2 a gamma variable with mean 2 and variance 2.

$$E(X_1) = \frac{1}{\lambda_1} = 1 \qquad \Rightarrow \lambda_1 = 1$$

$$E(X_2) = \frac{n}{\lambda_1} = 2 \qquad \Rightarrow \lambda_2 = 1$$

$$V(X_2) = \frac{n}{\lambda_2} = 2$$

If X_1 and X_2 are independently distributed, then,

$$P(X_1 < X_2) = \frac{\lambda_1}{\lambda_1 + \lambda_2}$$

$$= \frac{1}{1+1} = \frac{1}{2} = 0.5$$

4. X_1 is uniform (0, 1) random variables, then

$$Y_i = -\ln(1 - X_1)$$

Exponential random variable with mean 1 and variance 1

$$E(Y_i) = 1, \quad V(Y_i) = 1$$

$S_n = Y_1 + Y_2 + \ldots + Y_n$, by central limit theorem

$$\lim_{n\to\infty} P(S_n \leq n) \to \frac{1}{2}$$

$$\lim_{n\to\infty} P(S_n \geq n) \to \frac{1}{2}$$

6. Here $f(x) = \begin{cases} \theta\,\alpha\, e^{-\alpha x} + (1-\theta)2\alpha e^{-2\alpha x} & x \geq 0 \\ 0 & \text{otherwise} \end{cases}$

$H_0 : \theta = 1, \alpha = 1$

$H_1 : \theta = 0, \alpha = 2$

Under H_0, $f(x) = e^{-x}$

Under H_1, $f(x) = 4 . e^{-4x}$

Complete p.d.f.

$$f(x) = e^{-x} + 4e^{-4x}, \text{ then}$$

$$L = e^{-\Sigma x_i}$$

$$\ln L = -\Sigma x_i$$

$$P[\text{Rej } H_0 \,|\, H_0] = \alpha$$

$$P[-\Sigma x_i \,|\, H_0] = \alpha$$

After the simplification we have

$$-\Sigma x_i < c \Rightarrow \Sigma x_i < c$$

7. $X_1, X_2 - X_n$ be a sequence of i.i.d $N(\mu, 1)$ random variable

$$E[\,|X_i - \mu|\,] = \int_{-\infty}^{\infty} |x - \mu| f(x)dx$$

$$= \frac{1}{\sigma\sqrt{2n}} \int_{-\infty}^{\infty} |x - \mu| e^{-\frac{(x=\mu)^2}{2\sigma^2}} dx$$

$$= \frac{\sigma}{\sqrt{2n}} \int_{-\infty}^{\infty} |z| e^{-\frac{z^2}{2}} dz$$

$$= \frac{2\sigma}{\sqrt{2n}} \int_{-\infty}^{\infty} |z|\, e^{-\frac{z^2}{2}} dz$$

$$(\text{Here } \sigma = 1) = \sqrt{\frac{2}{n}}\sigma$$

$$= \sqrt{\frac{2}{n}}\, 0 < z < \infty \;|z| = 2.$$

$$\sum_{i=1}^{n} |x_i - \mu| = \sqrt{\frac{2}{n}}\eta$$

$$\lim_{n\to\infty} \frac{\sqrt{n}}{2n} \sum_{i=1}^{n} |x_i - \mu| = \lim_{n\to\infty} \frac{\sqrt{n}}{2n} \times \frac{\sqrt{2}}{\sqrt{n}} n$$

$$= \frac{1}{\sqrt{2}} \approx 0.70$$

8. Here, $X_1, X_2 \ldots X_n$ is a random sample from Uniform $[1, \theta]$, $\theta > 1$.

we define $f(x, \theta) = \begin{cases} \dfrac{1}{\theta - 1}, & 1 < x < \theta, \theta > 1 \\ 0 & \text{otherwise} \end{cases}$

We have seen that in sampling from $U[1, \theta]$ population, the statistic :

$X_{(n)} = \text{Max}\{X_i\}$ is sufficient and complete, for $\theta 1 \leq L \leq n$.

Also $\quad E[X_n] = \dfrac{n}{n+1}\theta + \dfrac{1}{n+1}$

$\Rightarrow \quad E\left\{\dfrac{n+1}{n}X_{(n)} - \dfrac{1}{n}\right\} = \theta$

$\Rightarrow \quad \dfrac{n+1}{n}X_{(n)} - \dfrac{1}{n}$ is an MVU estimator of θ.

9. $l'(\theta) = \dfrac{1}{\theta}\sum_{i=1}^{n} x_i - n = \dfrac{9}{\theta} - 6$

For maximum, $l'(\theta) = 0 \Rightarrow \theta = 1.5$

But $\theta \in (1, 2)$

Hence maximum likelihood estimator of θ is 2.

12. '$E_1 + E_2$ must be closed if E_1 and E_2 are closed'. This statement is false.

13. Given, X_1, X_2 is a random sample of size 2 from an $\mathcal{N}(0, 1)$

So, $\dfrac{(X_1 + X_2)^2}{(X_1 - X_2)^2}$ follows $F_{1,1}$.

14. Given, a random variable Z such that $Z \sim \mathcal{N}(0, 1)$

Then $E\,[\max\{Z, 0\}] = \dfrac{1}{\sqrt{2\pi}}$

15. Given linear programming problem is

$$z = \text{minimize } x_1 + x_2$$

subject to $\quad 2x_1 + x_2 \geq 8$

$2x_1 + 5x_2 \geq 10$

$x_1 x_2 \geq 0$

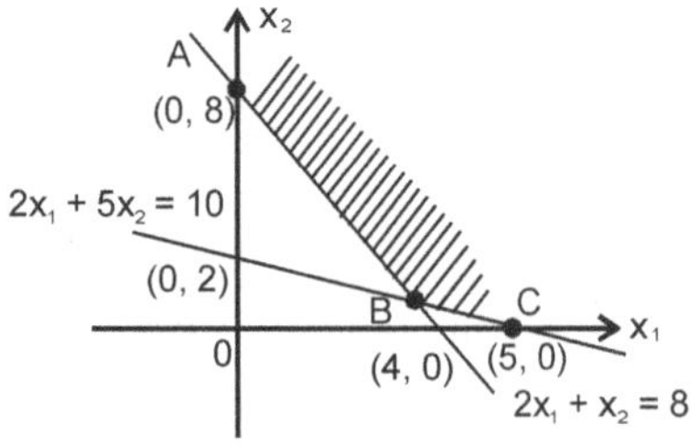

On plotting above inequalities we get the adjoining graph. The optimal region is ABC (shaded region) whose corner points are A (0, 8), B $\left(\dfrac{15}{4}, \dfrac{1}{2}\right)$ and C(5, 0)

Corner point	Optimal value
A (0, 8)	0 + 8 = 8
B $\left(\dfrac{15}{4}, \dfrac{1}{2}\right)$	$\dfrac{15}{4} + \dfrac{1}{2} = \dfrac{17}{4} = 4.25$ (minimum)
C (5, 0)	5 + 0 = 5

Hence, required optimal value is 4.25.

17. Maximize $x + \dfrac{3}{2}y$

Subject to $2x + 3y \leq 16$

$x + 4y \leq 18$

$x \geq 0,\ y \geq 0$

S denotes a line segment

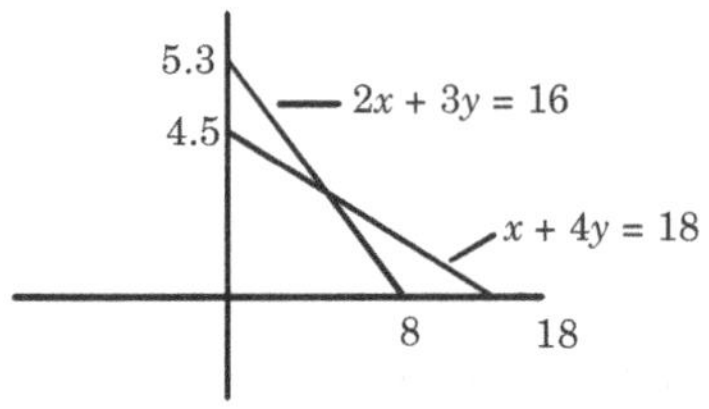

22. Given LPP is

$$\text{Max } z = x_1 + x_2$$

subject to $x_1 + 2x_2 \leq 20$

$x_1 + x_2 \leq 15$

$x_2 \leq 6$

$x_1, x_2 \geq 0$

The group is given by

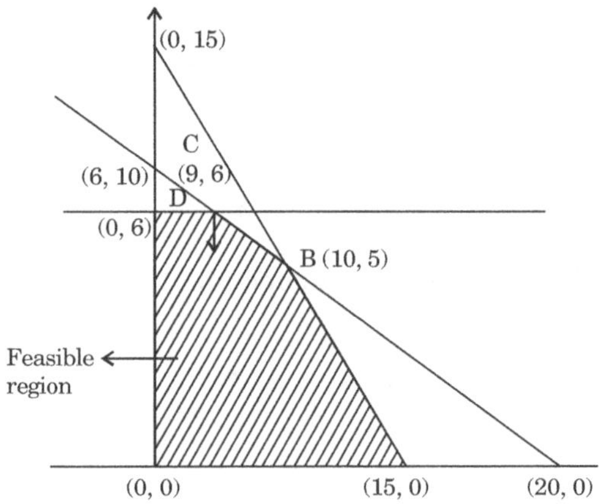

Now $\quad (z)_{(0,0)} = 0 + 0 = 0$

$(z)_{(15,0)} = 15 + 0 = 15$

$(z)_{(10,5)} = 10 + 5 = 15$

$(z)_{(9,6)} = 9 + 6 = 15$

$(z)_{(0,6)} = 0 + 6 = 6$

Therefore maximum value of z is obtained at every point lie on the line $x_1 + x_2 \leq 15$ between B and C.

Hence Given LPP has more than one optimum solution.

23. The dual of dual problem is a primal problem.

26. Given Linear programming problem is

minimize $z = x - y$

subject to $2x + 3y \leq 6$

$0 \leq x \leq 3$

$0 \leq y \leq 3$

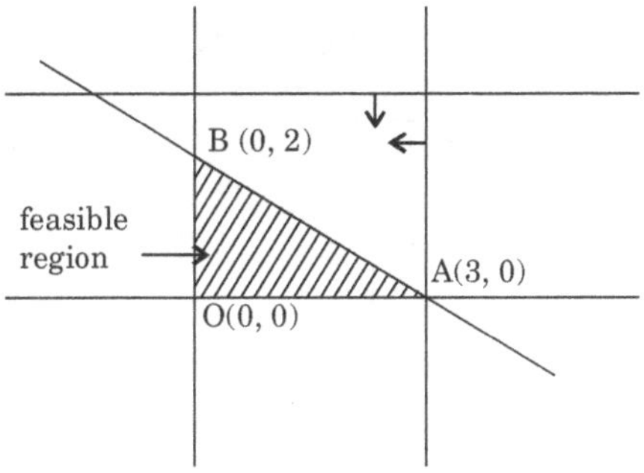

Fig.

Therefore, the number of extreme points on its feasible region is 3. Also the number of basic feasible solution is 3, which are

$x = y = 0, x = 3, y = 0, x = 0, y = 2$

27. If an LPP has unbounded solution then its dual is infeasible.

29. Given LPP is

$$\text{Max } z = 5x_1 + 9x_2 + 4x_3$$

Subject to

$$x_1 + x_2 + x_3 = 5$$

$$4x_1 + 3x_2 + 2x_3 = 12$$

$$x_1, x_2, x_3 \geq 0$$

	C_j		5	9	4	
B_V	C_B	X_B	x_1	x_2	x_3	Min Ratio
x_2	9	2	1	1	1	
x_3	4	3	4	3	2	
	$z_j -$	c_j	20	12	13	

since $z_j - c_j > 0$

Hence it is an optimal table

$$z^* \max z = 5 \times 0 + 9 \times 2 + 4 \times 3$$
$$= 18 + 12 = 30$$
$$30 \leq z^* \leq 40$$

31. The dual of LPP minimize $c^T x$ subject to $Ax \geq b$ and $x \geq 0$ is maximize $b^T w$ subject to $A^T w \leq c$ and $w \geq 0$.

32. Given LPP is

$$\text{Max } z = 3x + 4y$$

subject to $x + y \leq 100$

$x + 3y \leq t$

$x \geq 0, y \geq 0$

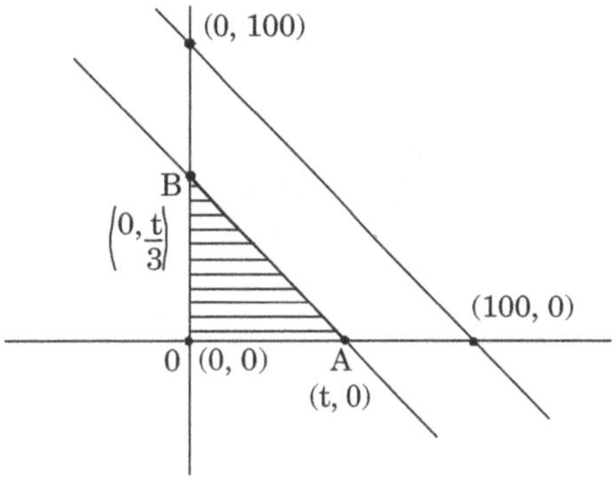

Fig.

$$(z)_{t,0} = 3t = 400$$

$$\Rightarrow \quad t = \frac{400}{3}$$

$$(z)_{0,\frac{t}{3}} = \frac{4t}{3} = 400$$

$$t = \frac{3 \times 400}{4} = 300$$

34. Given Cost Matrix

5	23	14	8
10	25	1	23
35	16	15	12
16	23	11	7

By Hungarian Method,

0	18	9	3
9	24	0	22
23	4	3	0
9	16	4	0

Since the number of dotted lines is not equal to the order of cost matrix. Hence solution is not optimal.

Now, the new optimal table is

0	12	9	3
9	20	0	22
23	0	3	0
9	16	4	0

Therefore, the solution is optimal. The optimal value is 5 + 1 + 16 + 7 = 29

38. Given LPP is

max $Z = 3x_1 - x_2$

subject to $2x_1 - x_2 \le 1$

$x_1 \le 3$

$x_1, x_2 \ge 0$

The graph is given below.

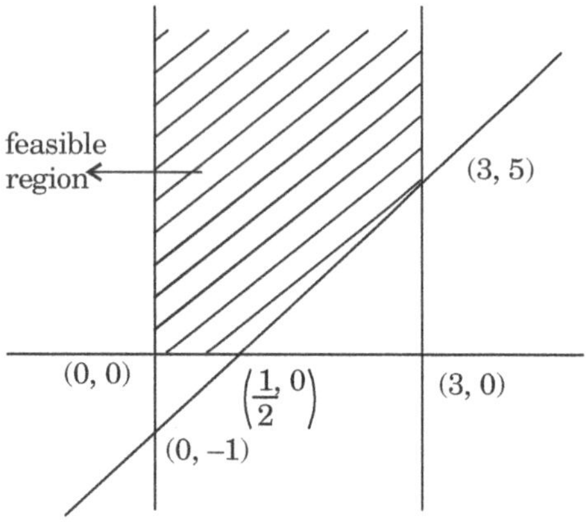

Fig.

$(Z)(0, 0) = 0$

$(Z)\left(\frac{1}{2}, 0\right) = 3 \times \frac{1}{2}$

$= \frac{3}{2}$

$(Z)_{(3, 5)} = 3 \times 3 - 5 = 4$

max $z = 4$

39. Given LPP is

max $Z = 2x_1 + 3x_2 - 4x_3 + x_4$

subject to $x_1 + x_2 + x_3 = 2$

$x_1 - x_2 + x_3 = 2$

$2x_1 + 3x_2 + 2x_3 - x_4 = 0$

$x_1, x_2, x_3, x_4 \ge 0$

Let $x_2 = 0$ then

$x_1 + x_3 = 2$

$2x_1 + 2x_3 - x_4 = 0$

which satisfied by (1, 0, 1, 4) and (2, 0, 0, 4)

Hence (1, 0, 1, 4) and (2, 0, 0, 4) are basic feasible solution.

40. Given LPP is

max $z = c_1x_1 + c_2x_2, c_1, c_2 > 0$

Subject to $x_1 + x_2 \le 3$

$2x_1 + 3x_2 \le 4$

$x_1 . x_2 \ge 0$

Then graph of LPP is

$\therefore \quad (z)(0, 0) = c_1 \times 0 + c_2 \times 0$

$= 0$

$(z)(2, 0) = 2c_1$

$(z)\left(0, \frac{4}{3}\right) = \frac{4}{3}c_2$

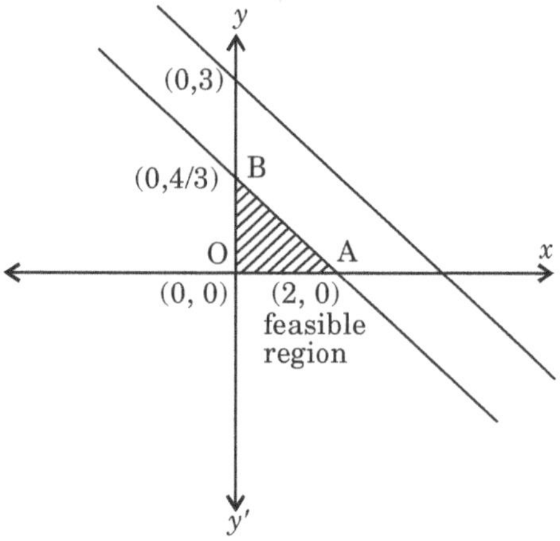

Fig.

Therefore, given LPP has an optimal solution depending on c_1 and c_2.

Now the dual LPP of the given primal LPP is

min $z_w = 3w_1 + 4w_2$

subject to $w_1 + 2w_2 \ge c_1$

$w_1 + 3w_2 \ge c_2$

$w_1, w_2 \ge 0$

Clearly the dual has also an optimal solution.

41. Given LPP is

max $z = x_1 + 2x_2 + 3x_3 + 4x_4$

subject to $ax_1 + 2x_3 \le 1$

$x_1 + ax_2 + 3x_4 \le 2$

$x_1, x_2, x_3, x_4 \ge 0$

where $a \in R$

Then subset form of LPP is

max $z = x_1 + 2x_2 + 3x_3 + 4x_4 + 0x_5 + 0x_6$

subject to

$ax_1 + 0x_2 + 2x_3 + 0x_4 + x_5 + 0x_6 = 1$

$x_1 + ax_2 + 0x_3 + 3x_4 + 0x_5 + x_6 = 2$

$x_1, x_2, x_3, x_4, x_5 x_6 \ge 0$

B_V	c_j		1	2	3	4	0	0	Mim Ratio
	c_B	x_B	x_1	x_2	x_3	x_4	x_5	x_6	
x_5	0	1	a	0	2	0	1	0	–
x_6	0	2	1	a	0	3	0	1	$\frac{2}{3}$–4
	z_j –	c_j	–1	–2	–3	–4	1	1	
x_5	0	1	a	0	2	0	1	0	$\frac{1}{2}$–
x_4	4	$\frac{2}{3}$	$\frac{1}{3}$	$\frac{a}{3}$	0	1	0	$\frac{1}{3}$	–
	z_j –	c_j	$\frac{1}{3}$	$\frac{4a}{2}-2$	–39	0	0	$\frac{4}{3}$	
x_3	3	$\frac{1}{2}$	$\frac{9}{2}$	0	1	0	$\frac{1}{2}$	0	
x_4	4	$\frac{2}{3}$	$\frac{1}{3}$	$\frac{a}{3}$	0	1	0	$\frac{4}{3}$	
	z_j –	c_j	$\left(\frac{9a+2}{6}\right)$	$\left(\frac{4a}{3}-2\right)$	(0)	(0)	$\left(\frac{3}{2}\right)$	$\left(\frac{4}{3}\right)$	

Therefore, the given LPP has an optional. solution for any $a \in$ R Hence, S = R.

42. Given LPP is

max $\quad z = x_1 + 5x_2 + 3x_3$

subject to $\quad 2x_1 - 3x_2 + 5x_3 \le 3$

$3x_1 + 2x_3 \le 5$

$x_1, x_2, x_3 \ge 0$

The dual of LPP is

min $\quad z_w = 3w_1 + 5w_2$

Subject to $\quad 2w_1 + 3w_2 \ge 1$

$-3w_1 \ge 5$

$5w_1 + 2w_2 \ge 3$

$w_1, w_2 \ge 0$

whose graph is given.

if is clear from the figure that the closet extreme point of feasible region is in fourth quadrant. Hence,

$$w_2 < 0$$

which contradict the fact that $w_2 \ge 0$

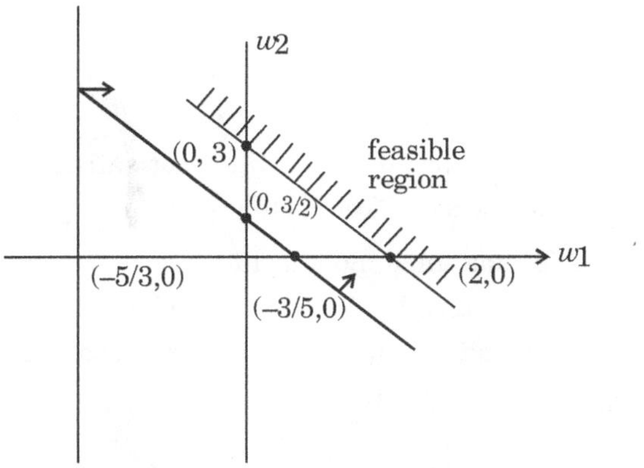

Fig.

Therefore, the dual of LPP has no feasible solution.

44. For a linear programming primal maximization problem P with dual Q.P will have an optimal solution if and only if Q also has an optimal solution.

45. The number of extreme point of the given set is 4.

46. Given LPP is

$$\max z = c_1x_1 + c_2x_2 + c_3x_3$$

Subject to

$$x_1 + x_2 + x_3 \le 4$$

$$x_1 \le 2, x_3 \le 3,$$

$$3x_1 + x_3 \le 7$$

$$x_1, x_2, x_3 \ge 0$$

For (1, 0, 3) is an optimal solution

we get $x_2 = 0$

$\therefore$ C_2 is arbitrary

Now, $x_3 > x_1$

we get $c_3 > c_1$

Hence, the required condition is

$$c_2 \le c_1 \le c_3$$

47. The dimension of S is 4.

48. $x^* = (x_1^*, x_2^*, ..x_n^*)$ is an optimal extreme point solution to P with $x_1^*, x_2^*, ..x_n^* > 0$

Then, out of the m constraints

$$\sum_{i=1}^{n} a_{ij}xj \le bj, \qquad i = 1, 2, ...m$$

The number of constraints not satisfied with equality at x^* is equal to m–2

49. If P has unbounded solution for some sets of parameters $b_1, b_2, b_3, ..bm$. Then P is either unbounded or infeasible for every choice of b_i's.

50.

$$x_1 + 2x_2 + 2x_3 - x_4 + x_5 = 3$$

$$2x_1 + 3x_2 + 4x_3 + x_6 = 6$$

Minimize $z = 2x_1 + 3x_2 + x_3$

Hence only feasible solution will be (0, 0, 0, 0, 3, 6) which satisfy the above equations

52.

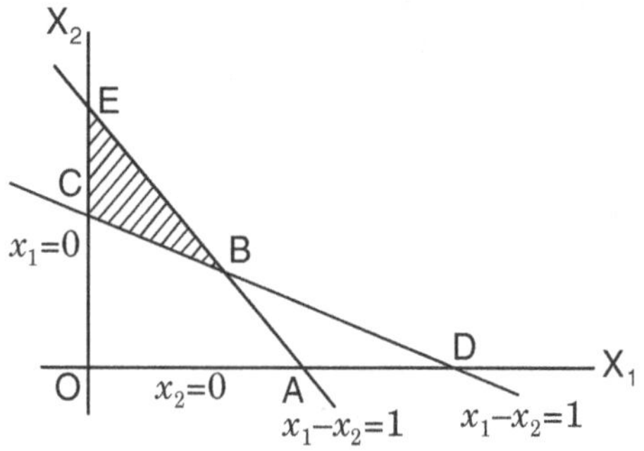

Maximize $z = 3x_1 + 2x_2$

subject to $x_1 - x_2 \le 1$

$x_1 + x_2 \ge 3$

$x_1, x_2 \ge 0$

Hence $x_1 - x_2 = 1$

$x_1 + x_2 = 3$

$x_1 = 0$

$x_2 = 0$

So by graph, this problem has infeasible optimal solution

53. By Vogel's Approximation method

Row Difference

6	4	1	5	3
8	9	2	7	5
4	3	6	2	1
2	1	1	3	

Column difference 2 1 1 3

Hence the current given solution is non-optimal and the entering and leaving variables are x_{21}, and x_{12} respectively.

54. In a balanced transportation problem, if all the unit transportation costs c_{ij} are decreased by a nonzero constant α, then, in the optimal solution of the revised problem, the values of the decision variables and the objective value remain unchanged.

56. Given LPP is

$$\max z = x_1$$

subject to $3x_1 + 4x_2 \le 10$, $5x_1 - x_2 \le 9$

$3x_1 - 2x_2 \le -2$ or $-3x_1 + 2x_2 \le 2$

$x_1 - 3x_2 \le 3$ $x_1, x_2 \ge 0$

whose graph is

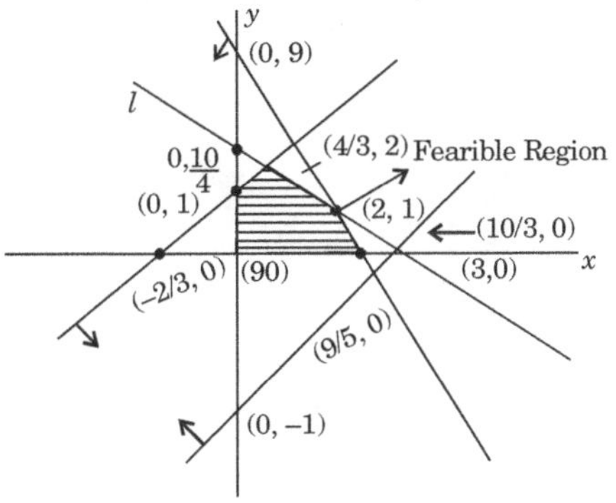

Fig

$\therefore$ $(z)(0, 0) = 0, (z)\left(\frac{9}{5^{10}}\right) = \left(\frac{9}{5}\right)$

$(z)(2, 1) = 2$

$(z)\left(\frac{4}{3}, 0\right) = \frac{4}{3}$, $(z)(0, 1) = 0$

$\therefore$ $\max z = 2$

SOLVED PAPER-2017

QUESTIONS

1. Consider the vector space $V = \{a_0 + a_1x + a_2x^2 : a_i \in \mathbb{R} \text{ for } i = 0, 1, 2\}$ of polynomials of degree at most 2. Let $f: V \to \mathbb{R}$ be a linear functional such that $f(1+x) = 0, f(1-x^2) = 0$ and $f(x^2 - x) = 2$. Then $f(1 + x + x^2)$ equals ______.

2. Let A be a 7×7 matrix such that $2A^2 - A^4 = I$, where I is the identity matrix. If A has two distinct eigen values and each eigenvalue has geometric multiplicity 3, then the total number of nonzero entries in the Jordan canonical form of A equals__________.

3. Let $f(z) = (x^2 + y^2) + i2xy$ and $g(z) = 2xy + i(y^2 - x^2)$ for $z = x + iy \in \mathbb{C}$. Then, in the complex plane $\mathbb{C}$,

(*a*) *f* is analytic and *g* is NOT analytic

(*b*) *f* is NOT analytic and *g* is analytic

(*c*) neither *f* nor *g* is analytic

(*d*) both *f* and *g* are analytic

4. If $\sum_{n=-\infty}^{\infty} a_n(z-2)^n$ is Laurent series of the function

$f(z) = \dfrac{z^4 + z^3 + z^2}{(z-2)^3}$ for $z \in \mathbb{C}/\{2\}$, then a_{-2} equal ___.

5. Let $f_n : [0, 1] \to \mathbb{R}$ be given by $f_n(x) = \dfrac{2x^2}{x^2 + (1-2nx)^2}$,

$n = 1, 2, \ldots$. Then the sequence (f_n)

(*a*) converges uniformly on [0, 1]

(*b*) does NOT converge uniformly on [0, 1] but has a subsequence that converges uniformly on [0, 1]

(*c*) does NOT converge pointwise on [0, 1]

(*d*) converges pointwise on [0, 1] but does NOT have a subsequence that converges uniformly on [0, 1]

6. Let $C : x^2 + y^2 = 9$ be the circle in $\mathbb{R}^2$ oriented positively.

The $\dfrac{1}{\pi}\oint_C (3y - e^{\cos x^2})dx + \left(7x + \sqrt{y^4 + 11}\right)dy$ equal __________.

7. Consider the following statements :

(P) There exists an unbounded subset of $\mathbb{R}$ whose Lebesgue measure is equal to 5.

(Q) If $f : \mathbb{R} \to \mathbb{R}$ is continuous and $g : \mathbb{R} \to \mathbb{R}$ is such that $f = g$ almost everywhere on $\mathbb{R}$, then g must be continuous almost everywhere on $\mathbb{R}$.

Which of the above statements hold TRUE?

(*a*) Both P and Q (*b*) Only P

(*c*) Only Q (*d*) Neither P nor Q

8. If $x^3 y^2$ is an integrating factor of

$(6y^2 + a\,xy)dx + (6xy + b\,x^2)dy = 0$,

where $a, b \in \mathbb{R}$, then

(*a*) $3a - 5b = 0$ (*b*) $2a - b = 0$

(*c*) $3a + 5b = 0$ (*d*) $2a + b = 0$

9. If $x(t)$ and $y(t)$ are the solutions of the system $\dfrac{dx}{dt} = y$ and $\dfrac{dy}{dt} = -x$ with the initial conditions $x(0) = 1$ and $y(0) = 1$, then $x\left(\dfrac{\pi}{2}\right) + y\left(\dfrac{\pi}{2}\right)$ equals________.

10. If $y = 3e^{2x} + e^{-2x} - \alpha x$ is the solution of the initial value problem

$$\frac{d^2y}{dx^2} + \beta y = 4\alpha x,\ y(0) = 4 \text{ and } \frac{dy}{dx}(0) = 1,$$

where $\alpha, \beta \in \mathbb{R}$, then

(*a*) $\alpha = 3$ and $\beta = 4$

(*b*) $\alpha = 1$ and $\beta = 2$

(*c*) $\alpha = 3$ and $\beta = -4$

(*d*) $\alpha = 1$ and $\beta = -2$

11. Let G be a non-abelian group of order 125. Then the total number of elements in $Z(G) = \{x \in G : gx = xg \text{ for all } g \in G\}$ equals ________.

12. Let F_1 and F_2 be subfields of a finite field F consisting of 2^9 and 2^6 elements, respectively. Then the total number of elements in $F_1 \cap F_2$ equals _______.

13. Consider the normed linear space $\mathbb{R}^2$ equipped with the norm given by $\|(x, y)\| = |x| + |y|$ and the subspace $X = \{(x, y) \in \mathbb{R}^2 : x = y\}$. Let f be the linear functional on X given by $f(x, y) = 3x$. If $g(x, y) = \alpha x + \beta y$, $\alpha, \beta \in \mathbb{R}$, is a Hahn-Banach extension of f no $\mathbb{R}^2$, then $\alpha - \beta$ equals ________.

14. For $n \in \mathbb{Z}$, define $c_n = \frac{1}{\sqrt{2\pi}} \int_{-\pi}^{\pi} e^{i(n-i)x} dx$, where $i^2 = -1$. The $\sum_{n \in \mathbb{Z}} |c_n|^2$ equals

(*a*) $\cosh(\pi)$ (*b*) $\sinh(\pi)$

(*c*) $\cosh(2\pi)$ (*d*) $\sinh(2\pi)$

15. If the fourth order divided difference of $f(x) = \alpha x^4 + 5x^3 + 3x + 2$, $\alpha \in \mathbb{R}$, at the points 0.1, 0.2, 0.3, 0.4, 0.5 is 5, then α equals ________.

16. If the quadrature rule $\int_0^2 f(x)dx \approx c_1 f(0) + 3f(c_2)$, where $c_1, c_2 \in \mathbb{R}$, is exact for all polynomials of degree ≤ 1, then $c_1 + 3c_2$ equals ______.

17. If $u(x, y) = 1 + x + y + f(xy)$, where $f: \mathbb{R}^2 \to \mathbb{R}$ is a differentiable function, then u satisfies

(*a*) $x\frac{\partial u}{\partial x} - y\frac{\partial u}{\partial y} = x^2 - y^2$

(*b*) $x\frac{\partial u}{\partial x} - y\frac{\partial u}{\partial y} = 0$

(*c*) $x\frac{\partial u}{\partial x} - y\frac{\partial u}{\partial y} = x - y$

(*d*) $y\frac{\partial u}{\partial x} - x\frac{\partial u}{\partial y} = x - y$

18. The partial differential equation

$$x\frac{\partial^2 u}{\partial x^2} + (x - y)\frac{\partial^2 u}{\partial x \partial y} - y\frac{\partial^2 u}{\partial y^2} + \frac{1}{4}\left(\frac{\partial u}{\partial y} - \frac{\partial u}{\partial x}\right) = 0 \text{ is}$$

(*a*) hyperbolic along the line $x + y = 0$

(*b*) elliptic along the line $x - y = 0$

(*c*) elliptic along the line $x + y = 0$

(*d*) parabolic along the line $x + y = 0$

19. Let X and Y be topological spaces and let $f: X \to Y$ be a continuous surjective function. Which one of the following statements is TRUE?

(*a*) If X is separable, then Y is separable

(*b*) If X is first countable, then Y is first countable

(*c*) If X is Hausdorff, then Y is Hausdorff

(*d*) If X is regular, then Y is regular

20. Consider the topology $T = \{U \subseteq \mathbb{Z} : \mathbb{Z} \setminus U \text{ is finite or } 0 \notin U\}$ on $\mathbb{Z}$. Then, the topological space $(\mathbb{Z}, T)$ is

(*a*) compact but NOT connected

(*b*) connected but NOT compact

(*c*) both compact and connected

(*d*) neither compact nor connected

21. F(x) be the distribution function of a random varibale X. Consider the functions :

$G_1(x) = (F(x))^3, x \in \mathbb{R}$,

$G_2(x) = 1 - (1 - F(x))^5, x \in \mathbb{R}$,

Which of the above functions are distribution functions?

(*a*) Neither G_1 nor G_2

(*b*) Only G_1

(*c*) Only G_2

(*d*) Both G_1 and G_2

22. Let $X_1, X_2, \ldots, X_n$ $(n \geq 2)$ be independent and identically distributed random variables with finite variance σ^2 and let $\bar{X} = \frac{1}{n}\sum_{i=1}^{n} X_i$. Then the covariance between $\bar{X}$ and $X_1 - \bar{X}$ is

(*a*) 0 (*b*) $-\sigma^2$

(*c*) $\frac{-\sigma^2}{n}$ (*d*) $\frac{\sigma^2}{n}$

23. Let $X_1, X_2, \ldots, X_n$ $(n \geq 2)$ be a random sample from a $N(\mu, \sigma^2)$ population, where $\sigma^2 = 144$. The smallest n such that the length of the shortest 95% confidence interval for μ will not exceed 10 is ________.

24. Consider the linear programming problem (LPP):

Maximize $4x_1 + 6x_2$

Subject to $x_1 + x_2 \leq 8$,

$2x_1 + 3x_2 \geq 18$,

$x_1 \geq 6$, x_2 is unrestricted in sign.

Then the LPP has

(*a*) no optimal solution

(*b*) only one basic feasible solution and that is optimal

(*c*) more than one basic feasible solution and a unique optimal solution

(*d*) infinitely many optimal solutions

25. For a linear programming problem (LPP) and its dual, which one of the following is NOT TRUE?

(*a*) The dual of the dual is primal

(*b*) If the primal LPP has an unbounded objective function, then the dual LPP is infeasible

(*c*) If the primal LPP is infeasible, then the dual LPP must have unbounded objective function

(*d*) If the primal LPP has a finite optimal solution, then the dual LPP also has a finite optimal solution

26. If U and V are the null spaces of $\begin{bmatrix} 1 & 1 & 0 & 0 \\ 0 & 0 & 1 & 1 \end{bmatrix}$ and $\begin{bmatrix} 1 & 2 & 3 & 2 \\ 0 & 1 & 2 & 1 \end{bmatrix}$, respectively, then the dimension of the subspace U + V equals _______.

27. Given two $n \times n$ matrices A and B with entries in $\mathbb{C}$, consider the following statements:

P : If A and B have the same minimal polynomial, then A is similar to B.

Q : If A and n distinct eigen values, then there exists $u \in \mathbb{C}^n$ such that $u, Au, \ldots, A^{n-1}u$ are linearly independent.

Which of the above statements hold TRUE?

(*a*) Both P and Q (*b*) Only P

(*c*) Only Q (*d*) Neither P nor Q

28. Let $A = (a_{ij})$ be a 10×10 matrix such that $a_{ij} = 1$ for $i \neq j$ and $a_{ii} = \alpha + 1$, where $\alpha > 0$. Let λ and μ be the largest and the smallest eigen values of A, respectively. If $\lambda + \mu = 24$, then α equals ______.

29. Let C be the simple, positively oriented circle of radius 2 centered at the origin in the complex plane. Then

$\frac{2}{\pi i}\int_C \left(ze^{(1/z)} + \tan\left(\frac{z}{2}\right) + \frac{1}{(z-1)(z-3)^2} \right) dz$ equals ___.

30. Let Re(z) and Im(z), respectively, denote the real part and the imaginary part of a complex number z. Let $T : \mathbb{C} \cup \{\infty\} \to \mathbb{C} \cup \{\infty\}$ be the bilinear transformation such that T(6) = 0, T(3 – 3i) = i and T(0) = ∞.

Then, the image of $D = \{z \in \mathbb{C} : |z - 3| < 3\}$ under the mapping w = T(z) is

(*a*) $\{w \in \mathbb{C} : \text{Im}(w) < 0\}$ (*b*) $\{w \in \mathbb{C} : \text{Re}(w) < 0\}$

(*c*) $\{w \in \mathbb{C} : \text{Im}(w) > 0\}$ (*d*) $\{w \in \mathbb{C} : \text{Re}(w) > 0\}$

31. Let (x_n) and (y_n) be the sequences in a complete metric space (X, d) such that $d(x_n, x_{n+1}) \leq \frac{1}{n^2}$ and $d(y_n, y_{n+1}) \leq \frac{1}{n}$ for all $n \in \mathbb{N}$. Then

(*a*) both (x_n) and (y_n) converge

(*b*) (x_n) converges but (y_n) need NOT converge

(*c*) (y_n) converges but (x_n) need NOT converge

(*d*) Neither (x_n) nor (y_n) converges

32. Let $f : [0,1] \to \mathbb{R}$ be given by $f(x) = 0$ if x is rational, and if x is irrational than $f(x) = 9^n$, where n is the number of zeroes immediately after the decimal point in the decimal representation of x. Then the Lebesgue integral $\int_0^1 f(x)dx$ equals ________.

33. Let $f : \mathbb{R}^2 \to \mathbb{R}$ be defined by

$$f(x, y) = \begin{cases} \sin\left(\frac{y^2}{x}\right)\sqrt{x^2 + y^2}, & x \neq 0, \\ 0, & x = 0. \end{cases}$$

Then, at (0, 0),

(*a*) f is continuous and the directional derivative of f does NOT exist in some direction

(*b*) f is NOT continuous and the directional derivatives of f exist in all directions

(*c*) f is NOT differentiable and the directional derivatives of f exist in all directions

(*d*) f is differentiable

34. Let D be the region in R^2 bounded by the parabola $y^2 = 2x$ and the line $y = x$. Then $\iint_D 3xy\, dx\, dy$ equals ________.

35. Let $y_1(x) = x^3$ and $y^2(x) = x^2|x|$ for $x \in \mathbb{R}$.

Consider the following statements :

P : $y_1(x)$ and $y_2(x)$ are linearly independent solution of $x^2\frac{d^2y}{dx^2} - 4x\frac{dy}{dx} + 6y = 0$ on $\mathbb{R}$.

Q : The Wronskian $y_1(x)\frac{dy_2}{dx}(x) - y_2(x)\frac{dy_1}{dx}(x) = 0$ for all $x \in \mathbb{R}$.

Which of the above statements hold TRUE?

(*a*) Both P and Q (*b*) Only P

(*c*) Only Q (*d*) Neither P nor Q

36. Let α and β with $\alpha > \beta$ be the roots of the indicial equation of

$$(x^2 - 1)^2\frac{d^2y}{dx^2} + (x+1)\frac{dy}{dx} - y = 0 \text{ at } x = -1.$$

The $\alpha - 4\beta$ equals ________.

37. Let S_9 be the group of all permutations of the set {1, 2, 3, 4, 5, 6, 7, 8, 9}. Then the total number of elements of S_9 that commute with $\tau = (1\,2\,3)(4\,5\,6\,7)$ in S_9 equals ________.

38. Let $\mathbb{Q}[x]$ be the ring of polynomials over $\mathbb{Q}$. Then the total number of maximal ideals in the quotient ring $\dfrac{\mathbb{Q}[x]}{(x^4-1)}$ equals ________/

39. Let $\{e_n : n \in \mathbb{N}\}$ be an orthonormal basis of a Hilbert space H. Let $T_n : H \to H$ be given by $T_x = \sum_{n=1}^{\infty} \frac{1}{n}\langle x, e_n\rangle e_n$. For each $n \in \mathbb{N}$, define

$T_n : H \to H$ by $T_n x = \sum_{j=1}^{n} \frac{1}{j}\langle x, e_j\rangle e_j$.

Then

(*a*) $\|T_n - T\| \to 0$ as $n \to \infty$

(*b*) $\|T_n - T\| \not\to 0$ as $n \to \infty$ but for each $x \in H$, $\|T_n x - T_x\| \to 0$ as $n \to \infty$

(*c*) for each $x \in H$, $\|T_n x - Tx\| \to 0$ as $n \to \infty$ but the sequence $(\|T_n\|)$ is unbounded

(*d*) there exist $x, y \in H$ such that $\langle T_n x, y\rangle \not\to \langle Tx, y\rangle$ as $n \to \infty$

40. Consider the subspace $V = \left\{(x_n) \in \ell^2 : \sum_{n=1}^{\infty}|x_n| < \infty\right\}$ of the Hilbert space ℓ^2 of all square summable real sequences. For $n \in \mathbb{N}$, define $T_n : V \to \mathbb{R}$ by $T_n((x_k)) = \sum_{i=1}^{n} x_i$.

Consider the following statements :

P : $\{T_n : n \in \mathbb{N}\}$ is pointwise bounded on V.

Q : $\{T_n : n \in \mathbb{N}\}$ is uniformly bounded on $\{x \in V : \|x\|_2 = 1\}$

Which of the above statements hold TRUE?

(*a*) Both P and Q

(*b*) Only P

(*c*) Only Q

(*d*) Neither P nor Q

41. Let $p(x)$ be the polynomial of degree at most 2 that interpolates and data (–1, 2), (0, 1) and (1, 2). If $q(x)$ is a polynomial of degree at most 3 such that $p(x) + q(x)$ interpolates and data (–1, 2), (0, 1), (1, 2) and (2, 11), then $q(3)$ equals ________.

42. Let J be the Jacobi iteration matrix of the linear system $\begin{bmatrix} 1 & 2 & 1 \\ 2 & 1 & 2 \\ -4 & 2 & 1 \end{bmatrix}\begin{bmatrix} x \\ y \\ z \end{bmatrix} = \begin{bmatrix} 1 \\ 2 \\ 3 \end{bmatrix}$.

Consider the following statements :

P : One of the eigenvalues of J lies in the interval [2, 3].

Q : The jacobi iteration converges for the above system.

Which of the above statements hold TRUE?

(*a*) Both P and Q (*b*) Only P

(*c*) Only Q (*d*) Neither P nor Q

43. Le $u(x, y)$ be the solution of $x\frac{\partial u}{\partial x} + y\frac{\partial u}{\partial y} = 4u$ satisfying the condition $u(x, y) = 1$ on the circle $x^2 + y^2 = 1$. Then $u(2, 2)$ equals ________.

44. Let $u(r, \theta)$ be the bounded solution of the following boundary value problem in polar coordinates :

$$r^2\frac{\partial^2 u}{\partial r^2} + r\frac{\partial u}{\partial r} + \frac{\partial^2 u}{\partial \theta^2} = 0,\ 0 < r < 2$$

and $0 \le \theta \le 2\pi$,

Then $u\left(1, \frac{\pi}{2}\right) + u\left(1, \frac{\pi}{4}\right)$ equals

(*a*) 1 (*b*) $\frac{9}{8}$

(*c*) $\frac{7}{8}$ (*d*) $\frac{3}{8}$

45. Let T_u and T_d denote the usual topology and the discrete topology on R, respectively, Consider the following three topologies :

T_1 = Usual topology on $\mathbb{R}^2 = \mathbb{R} \times \mathbb{R}$,

T_2 = Topology generated by the basis $\{U \times V : U \in T_d, V \in T_u\}$ on $\mathbb{R} \times \mathbb{R}$,

T_3 = Dictionary order topology on $\mathbb{R} \times \mathbb{R}$.

Then

(*a*) $T_3 \subsetneq T_1 \subseteq T_2$ (*b*) $T_1 \subsetneq T_2 \subsetneq T_3$

(*c*) $T_3 \subseteq T_2 \subsetneq T_1$ (*d*) $T_1 \subsetneq T_2 = T_3$

46. Let X be a random variable with probability mass function

$$p(n) = \left(\frac{3}{4}\right)^{n-1}\left(\frac{1}{4}\right) \text{ for } n = 1, 2, \ldots .$$

Then $E(X - 3 \mid X > 3)$ equals ________.

47. Let X and Y be independent and identically distributed random variables with probability mass function $p(n) = 2^{-n}$, $n = 1, 2, ...$,

Then $P(X \geq 2Y)$ equals (rounded to 2 decimal places)________.

48. Let X_1, X_2, ... be sequence of independent and identically distributed Poisson random variables with mean 4. Then

$$\lim_{n\to\infty} P\left(4 - \frac{2}{\sqrt{n}} < \frac{1}{n}\sum_{i=1}^{n} X_i < 4 + \frac{2}{\sqrt{n}}\right) \text{equals\_\_\_\_\_\_.}$$

49. Let X and Y be independent and identically distributed exponential random variables with probability density function

$$f(x) = \begin{cases} e^{-x}, & x > 0 \\ 0, & \text{otherwise.} \end{cases}$$

Then P (max(X, Y) < 2) equals (rounded to 2 decimal places) _________.

50. Let E and F be any two events with $P(E) = 0.4$, $P(F) = 0.3$ and $P(F|E) = 3\,P(F|E^c)$. The $P(E|F)$ equals (rounded to 2 decimal places) ________.

51. Let X_1, X_2, ... X_m $(m \geq 2)$ be a random sample from a binomial distribution with parameters $n = 1$ and p, $p \in (0, 1)$, and let $\bar{X} = \frac{1}{m}\sum_{i=1}^{m} X_i$. Then a uniformly minimum variance unbiased estimator for $p(1-p)$ is

(*a*) $\frac{m}{m-1}\bar{X}(1-\bar{X})$ (*b*) $\bar{X}(1-\bar{X})$

(*c*) $\frac{m-1}{m}\bar{X}(1-\bar{X})$ (*d*) $\frac{1}{m}\bar{X}(1-m\bar{X})$

52. Let X_1, X_2, ... X_9 be a random sample from a $N(0, \sigma^2)$ population. For testing $H_0 : \sigma^2 = 2$ against $H_1 : \sigma^2 = 1$, the most powerful test rejects H_0 if $\sum_{i=1}^{9} X_i^2 < c$, where c is to be chosen such that the level of significance is 0.1. Then the power of this test equals_________.

53. Let X_1, X_2, ..., X_n $(n \geq 2)$ be a random sample from a $N(\theta, \theta)$ population, where $\theta > 0$, and let $W = \frac{1}{n}\sum_{i=1}^{n} X_i^2$. Then the maximum likelihood estimator of θ is

(*a*) $\frac{1}{2}+\frac{1}{2}\sqrt{1-4W}$ (*b*) $\frac{1}{2}+\frac{1}{2}\sqrt{1+4W}$

(*c*) $\frac{-1}{2}+\frac{1}{2}\sqrt{1-4W}$ (*d*) $\frac{-1}{2}+\frac{1}{2}\sqrt{1+4W}$

54. Consider the following transportation problem. The entries inside the cells denote per unit cost of transportation from the destinations.

		Destination			
		1	2	3	Supply
	1	4	3	6	20
Origin	2	7	10	5	30
	3	8	9	7	50
	Demand	10	30	60	

The optimal cost of transportation equals ______.

55. Consider the linear programming problem (LPP):

Maximum $k\,x_1 + 5\,x_2$

Subject to $x_1 + x_2 \leq 1$,

$2\,x_1 + 3\,x_2 \leq 1$,

$x_1, x_2 \geq 0$.

If $x^* = (x_1^*, x_2^*)$ is an optimal solution of the above LPP with $k = 2$, then the largest value of k (rounded to 2 decimal places) for which x^* remains optimal equals ______.

56. The ninth and the tenth of this month are Monday an Tuesday _________.

(*a*) figuratively (*b*) retrospectively

(*c*) respectively (*d*) rightfully

57. It is _______ to read this year's textbook _______ the last year's.

(*a*) easier, than (*b*) most easy, than

(*c*) easier, from (*d*) easiest, from

58. A rule states that in order to drink beer, one must be over 18 years old. In a bar, there are 4 people. P is 16 years old, Q is 25 years old, R is drinking milkshake and S drinking a beer. What must be checked to ensure that the rule being followed ?

(*a*) Only P's drink

(*b*) Only P's drink and S's age

(*c*) Only S's age

(*d*) Only P's drink, Q's drink and S's age

59. Fatima starts from point P, goes North for 3 km, and then East for 4 km to reach point Q. She then turns to face point P and goes 15 km in that direction. She then goes North for 6 km. How far is she from point P, and in which direction should she go to reach point P?

(*a*) 8 km, East

(*b*) 12 km, North

(*c*) 6 km, East

(*d*) 10 km, North

60. 500 students are taking one or more courses out of Chemistry, Physics, and Mathematics. Registration records indicate course enrolment as follows : Chemistry (329), Physics (186), Mathematics (295), Chemistry and Physics (83), Chemistry and Mathematics (217), and Physics and Mathematics (63). How many students are taking all 3 subjects ?

(*a*) 37 (*b*) 43

(*c*) 47 (*d*) 53

61. "If you are looking for a history of India, or for an account of the rise and fall of the British Raj, or for the reason of the cleaving of the subcontinent into two mutually antagonistic parts and the effects this mutilation will have in the respective sections, and ultimately on Asia, you will not find it in these pages ; for thought I have spent a lifetime in the country, I lived too near the seat of events, and was too intimately associated with the actors, to get the perspective needed for the impartial recording of these matters."

Which of the following statements best reflects the author's opinion?

(*a*) An intimate association does not allow for the necessary perspective.

(*b*) Matters are recorded with an impartial perspective.

(*c*) An intimate association offers an impartial perspective.

(*d*) Actors are typically associated with the impartial recording of matters.

62. Each of P, Q, R, S, W, X, Y and Z has been married at most once. X and Y are married and have two children P and Q. Z is the grandfather of the daughter S of P. Further, Z and W are married and are parents of R. Which one of the following must necessarily be FALSE?

(*a*) X is the mother-in-law of R

(*b*) P and R are not married to each other

(*c*) P is a son of X and Y

(*d*) Q cannot be married to R

63. 1200 men and 500 women can build a bridge in 2 weeks. 900 men and 250 women will take 3 weeks to build the same bridge. How many men will be needed to build the bridge in one week?

(*a*) 3000 (*b*) 3300

(*c*) 3600 (*d*) 3900

64. The number of 3-digit number such that the digit 1 is never to the immediate right of 2 is

(*a*) 781 (*b*) 791

(*c*) 881 (*d*) 891

65. A contour line joins locations having the same height above the mean sea level. The following is a contour plot of a geographical region. Contour lines are shown at 25 m intervals in this plot.

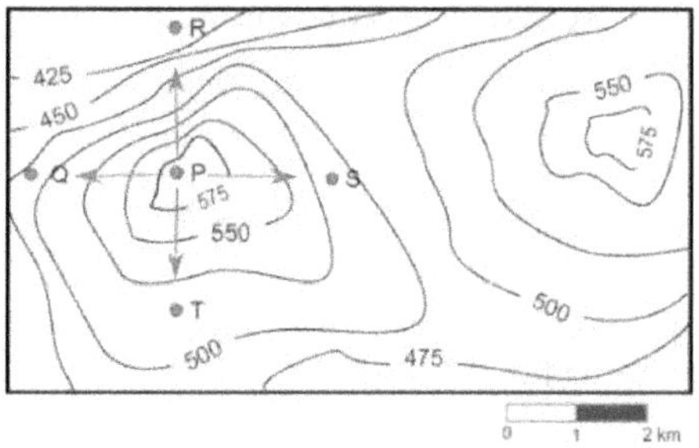

Which of the following is the steepest path leaving from P?

(*a*) P to Q (*b*) P to R

(*c*) P to S (*d*) P to T

ANSWERS

1. (1 to 1) **2.** (8 to 8) **3.** (*b*) **4.** (48 to 48) **5.** (*d*) **6.** (36 to 36) **7.** (*b*) **8.** (*a*)

9. (0 to 0) **10.** (*c*) **11.** (5 to 5) **12.** (8 to 8) **13.** (0 to 0) **14.** (*d*) **15.** (5 to 5) **16.** (1 to 1)

17. (*c*) **18.** (*d*) **19.** (*a*) **20.** (*a*) **21.** (*d*) **22.** (*a*) **23.** (23 to 23)

24. (*b*) **25.** (*c*) **26.** (3 to 3) **27.** (*c*) **28.** (7 to 7) **29.** (3 to 3) **30.** (*d*) **31.** (*b*)

32. (9 to 9) **33.** (*c*) **34.** (2 to 2) **35.** (*a*) **36.** (2 to 2) **37.** (24 to 24) **38.** (3 to 3)

39. (*a*) **40.** (*b*) **41.** (24 to 24) **42.** (*b*) **43.** (64 to 64) **44.** (*c*)

45. (*d*) **46.** (4 to 4) **47.** (0.27 to 0.30) **48.** (0.67 to 0.70) **49.** (0.73 to 0.77)

50. (0.65 to 0.68) **51.** (*a*) **52.** (0.49 to 0.51) **53.** (*d*) **54.** (590 to 590)

55. (3.32 to 3.34) **56.** (*c*) **57.** (*a*) **58.** (*b*) **59.** (*a*) **60.** (*d*) **61.** (*a*)

62. (*d*) **63.** (*c*) **64.** (*c*) **65.** (*b*)

EXPLANATIONS

1. $\alpha(1+x)+\beta(1-x^2)+\gamma(x^2-x)=0$

$\Rightarrow \alpha=\beta=\gamma=0$

$\Rightarrow \{1+x,\ 1-x^2,\ x^2-x\}$ is a basis of vector space V.

Here $1+x+x^2 \in V$

$\Rightarrow 1+x+x^2 = \frac{3}{2}(1+x)-\frac{1}{2}(1-x^2)+\frac{1}{2}(x^2-x)$

$= \frac{3}{2}\cdot 0 - \frac{1}{2}\cdot 0 + \frac{1}{2}\cdot 2 = 1$

2. If A has two distinct eigen values λ_1 and λ_2 (say) and each eigenvalues has geometric multiplicity. Then A has following Jordan cannonical form as

$$J = \begin{bmatrix} \lambda_1 &&&&&& \\ & \lambda_1 &&&&& \\ && \lambda_1 &&&& \\ &&& \lambda_2 &&& \\ &&&& \lambda_2 && \\ &&&&& \lambda_2 & 1 \\ &&&&&& \lambda_2 \end{bmatrix}_{7 \times 7}$$

so total number of non-zero entries is equal to B.

3. $f(z) = (x^2+y^2)+i2xy$

$u = x^2+y^2,\ v = 2xy$

$\Rightarrow u$ and v does not satisfy CR equations.

$(u_y \neq -v_x)$

$\Rightarrow f(z)$ is not analytic.

Next, for $g(z)$ we have

$u = 2xy,\ v = (y^2-x^2)$

Here $u_x,\ v_x,\ u_y,\ v_y$ exists and continuous on Ψ and satisfy CR equations

$\Rightarrow g(z)$ is analytic on Ψ.

4. We know that

$a_{-2} = \frac{1}{2\pi i}\int_C \frac{f(z)}{(Z-Z_0)^{-2H}}\,dZ$,

where C : $|Z| = 3$ in +ve.

$f(z) = \frac{z^4+z^3+z^2}{(z-2)^3}$

So, we have

$= \frac{1}{2\pi i}\int_C \frac{(z^4+z^3+z^2)}{(z-2)^2}\,dZ$

Using extension of CI.F., we obtain

$= \frac{1}{2\pi i}\times 2\pi i \times g'(2)$, where $g(z) = z^4+z^3+z^2$

$= 4\cdot 2^3 + 3\cdot 2^2 + 2\cdot 2$

$= 48$

5. $\lim_{n\to\infty} f_n(x) = \lim_{n\to\infty} \frac{2x^2}{x^2+(1-2nx)^2} = 0$

$\Rightarrow \langle f_n(x)\rangle$ converges point wise on [0, 1]

For uniform converges:

$$M'_n = \underset{x\in[0,1]}{Sup}\left|\frac{2x^2}{x^2+(1-2nx)^2}\right|$$

$\left[\frac{2x^2}{x^2+(1-2nx)^2}\right.$ attains the maximum value 2 at $\left. x=\frac{1}{2n}\right]$

$M_n = 2$

$\lim_{n\to\infty} M_n \not\to 0$ as $n \to 0$

Hence $\langle f_n\rangle$ is not uniformely convergent in any interval containing the origin.

6. By using green's theorem,

$$\frac{1}{n}\oint_C \left(3y - e^{\cos x^2}\right)dx + \left(7x+\sqrt{y^4+11}\right)dy$$

$$= \frac{4}{n}\iint_R dxdy \qquad R: x^2+9^2 = 9$$

$$= \frac{4}{\not\pi}\cdot\not\pi(3)^2 = 4\cdot 9 = 36$$

7. If g is continuous almost every where, then g is discontinuous on a set of measure zero.

8. If x^3y^2 is an I.F. of

$$\left(6y^2+axy\right)dx + \left(6xy+bx^2\right)dy = 0$$

$$\Rightarrow x^3y^2\left(6y^2+axy\right)dx + x^3y^2\left(6xy+bx^2\right)dy = 0$$

becomes exact

$$\Rightarrow \frac{\partial}{\partial y}\left(6x^3y^4+ax^4y^3\right) = \frac{\partial}{\partial x}\left(6x^4y^3+bx^5y^2\right)$$

$$\Rightarrow 24y^3x^3 + 3ax^4y^2 = 24y^3x^3 + 5bx^4y^2$$

$$\Rightarrow (3a-5b)x^4y^2 = 0$$

$$\Rightarrow 3a - 5b = 0$$

9. $\frac{d^2x}{dt^2} = \frac{dy}{dt} = -x \Rightarrow \frac{d^2x}{dt} + x = 0$

$$\Rightarrow x(t) = \left(C_1\cos t + C_2\sin t\right)$$

$$\Rightarrow x(0) = 1 = C_1$$

$$y = \frac{dx}{dt} = -C_1\sin t + C_2\cos t$$

$$y(0) = 1 = C_2$$

$$\Rightarrow x(t) = \cos t + \sin t$$

$$y(t) = -\sin t + \cos t$$

$$x\left(\frac{\pi}{2}\right) + y\left(\frac{\pi}{2}\right) = 2\cos\left(\frac{\pi}{2}\right) = 2\cdot 0 = 0$$

10. $y = 3e^{2x} + e^{-2x} - \alpha x$ is solution of IVP

$\frac{d^2y}{dx^2} + \beta y = 4\alpha x$, y(0)=4 &

$\frac{dy}{dx}(0) = 1$, $\alpha, \beta \leftarrow R$

$\frac{dy}{dx} = .6e^{2x} - 2e^{-2x} - \alpha$ ..(1)

$\frac{d^2y}{dx^2} = 12e^{2x} + 4e^{-2x}$ ..(2)

Using y, y', y'' in I.V.P., we have

$(12+3\beta)e^{2x} + (4+\beta)e^{-2x} - \alpha\beta x = 4\alpha x$ ..(3)

From (1)

$\frac{dy}{dx}(0) = 1 = 6 - 2 - \alpha \Rightarrow \alpha = 3$

Now, from (3), we have

$$(12+3\beta)e^{2x} + (4+\beta)e^{-2x} - 3\beta x = 12x$$

$$\Rightarrow \beta = -4.$$

11. Z(G) is a subgroup of G

O(2(G) divides order of G

$\Rightarrow$ O(Z(G)) = 5

$\Rightarrow$ there are five elements in Z(G).

12. Number of elements in $F_1 \cap F_2 = p^t$, where t = g.c.d (r, s) and number of elements in F_1 is p^r and in F_2 is p^s.

13. $f(x, y) = g(x, y)\ \forall\ (x, y) \in x$

and $\| f \| = \| g \|$

14. $\sum_{-\infty}^{\infty} |c_n|^2 = \frac{1}{2\pi}\int_{-\pi}^{\pi} |f(x)|^2\, dx,$

$$c_n = \frac{1}{2\pi}\int_{-\pi}^{\pi} f(x)e^{-inx}dx$$

15. Fourth order divided difference of f(x) is

$$f[x_0, x_1x_2...x_4] = \frac{1}{4!}f^{iv}(0.1) = 5$$

Here $f^{iv}(x) = 4!\,\alpha$

$$\Rightarrow f^{iv}(0.1) = 4!\,\alpha \Rightarrow \frac{1}{4!}.4!\alpha = 5 \Rightarrow \alpha = 5$$

16. Making the method exact for polynomials of degree ≤ 1. we obtain

for $f(x) = 1 : 2 = G + 3.1 \Rightarrow G = -1$

$$f(x) = x : 2 = (-1).0 + 3C_2 \Rightarrow C_2 = \frac{2}{3}$$

Then $C_1 + 3C_2 = (-1) + 3.\frac{2}{3} = 1$

17. $\frac{\partial u}{\partial x} = 1 + yf'$ ...(1)

$\frac{\partial u}{\partial y} = 1 + xf'$ ...(2)

Multiply x & y respectively to (1) & (2), and substracting, we have

$$x\frac{\partial u}{\partial x} + y\frac{\partial u}{\partial y} = x - y$$

18. Compare the given equation

$$x\frac{\partial^2 u}{\partial x^2} + (x-y)\frac{\partial^2 u}{\partial x \partial y} - y\frac{\partial^2 u}{\partial y^2} + \frac{1}{4}\left(\frac{\partial u}{\partial x} - \frac{\partial u}{\partial x}\right) = 0$$

with $A\frac{\partial^2 u}{\partial x^2} + 2B\frac{\partial^2 u}{\partial x \partial y} + C\frac{\partial^2 u}{\partial y^2}$

$$+F\left(x, y, a, \frac{\partial u}{\partial x}, \frac{\partial u}{\partial y}\right) = 0$$

we have $A = x, B = \frac{(x-y)}{2}, C = -y$

so $AC - B^2 = -xy - \frac{(x-y)^2}{4}$

$$= -\frac{1}{4}[xy + (x - y^2)]$$

$$= -\frac{1}{4}[(x + y^2)] \qquad \text{if } x + y = 0$$

$AC - B^2 = 0$

$\Rightarrow$ The given equation is prabolic along the line $x + y = 0$.

19. Continuous image of separable is separable.

$\therefore$ *f*(*x*) is separable and since *f* is onto

$\therefore$ *y* is separable

20. T is cofinite topology on Z, so it is compact but not connected.

21. Since X is random variable and F(*x*) is the distribution function of *x*. Then G_1 and G_2 are also distribution function, being a composition of distribution function.

22. $Cov(\bar{X}, X_1 - \bar{X})$

$$= E[\{\bar{X} - E(\bar{X})\}\ \{(X_1 - \bar{X}) - E(X_1 - \bar{X})\}]$$

23. By using *z*-test, $H_0 : \mu = 10$

$H_0 : \mu < 10$ (lest tailed)

24. Using graphical method,

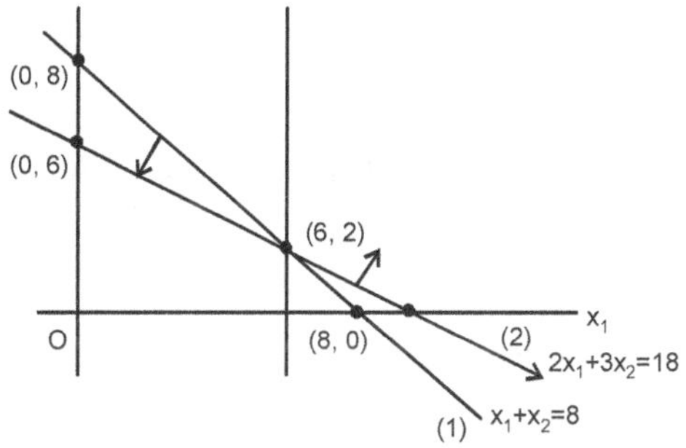

From the figure, use have seen that there is only one feasible solution is (6, 2) and that is optimal

25. Statement (A) is true by the theorem

The dual of dual is primal

Statement (B) is also that, because if the primal problem has an unbounded solution, than dual problem has no feasible solution.

Statement (C) if primal LPP has no feasible solution

Than dual has either no feasible solution or has unbounded solution.

so statement (C) is not true

Statement (D) also true.

26. dim U = 2

dim V = 2

Null space of $U \cap V$

$= \{(\alpha, \beta, \gamma, \delta) \mid \alpha\,(1,1,0,0) + \beta(0,0,1,)$

$+\gamma\,(12,3,2) + \delta\,(0,1,2,) = (0,0,0)\}$

$= \{(\alpha, \beta, \gamma, \delta) \mid \alpha + \gamma = 0, \alpha + 2\gamma + \delta = 0$

$\beta + 3\gamma + 2\delta = 0, \beta + 2\gamma + \delta = 0\}$

$= \{(\alpha, \beta, \gamma, \delta) \mid \alpha = -\gamma, \delta = -\gamma\ \beta = -\gamma\}$

$= \{(-\gamma, -\gamma, -\gamma, -\gamma,) \mid \gamma \in R\}$

$= \{\gamma\,(-1, -1, -1, -1,) \mid \gamma \in R\}$

$\dim (U \cap V) = 1$

$\dim (U + V) = \dim U + \dim V - \dim (U \cap V)$

$= 2 + 2 - 1 = 3.$

27. Statement (P) is not true because similar matrices have the same characteristic polynonial and hance the same eigenvalues.

Statement (Q) is true.

28. By Gershgorin's theorem, the eigen values of matrix A lies inside the circle

$$|\lambda i - (\alpha+1)| \le 9 \quad ...(i),$$

for all eigen values

and largest eigen values of A is

$$|\lambda| \le \sum_{L=1}^{10} |a_{ij}| \quad \forall\, j = 1 \text{ to } 10$$

so, $|\lambda| \le \alpha + 10 \quad ...(ii),$

and largest and smallest eigen values of A satisfy the

$$\lambda + \mu = 24 \quad ...(iii),$$

using (i), (ii) & (iii), we have

$$\alpha = 7$$

29. $\dfrac{2}{\pi i}\displaystyle\int_C \left(ze^{(1/z)} + \tan\left(\frac{z}{2}\right) + \frac{1}{(z-1)(z-3)^2} \right) dz = 3$

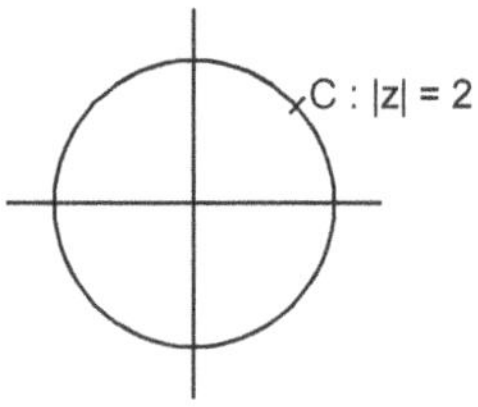

Let $f(z) = ze^{\frac{1}{z}}$, $g(z) = \tan\dfrac{z}{2}$,

and $h(z) = \dfrac{1}{(z-1)(z-3)^2}$

$$\int_C \big(f(z) + g(z) + h(z)\big)dz$$

$$= \int_C f(z)dz + \int_C g(z)\,dz + \int_C h(z)dz$$

For $\displaystyle\int_{C:|z|=2} Ze^{\frac{1}{z}}\,dz$

$$e^{\frac{1}{z}} = 1 + \frac{1}{z} + \frac{1}{2!}\frac{1}{z^2} + \frac{1}{3!}\frac{1}{z^3} + ...$$

$$ze^{\frac{1}{z}} = z + 1 + \frac{1}{2!}\frac{1}{z} + ...$$

$\operatorname*{Res}_{z=0} ze^{\frac{1}{z}} = \dfrac{1}{2!}$, So by Cauchy Residue's theorem

$$\int ze^{\frac{1}{z}} dz = 2\pi i . \frac{1}{2!} = \pi i$$

For $\displaystyle\int_{C:|z|=2} \tan\frac{z}{2} dz = 0$

(By Cauchy's theorem, $f(z) = \tan\dfrac{z}{2}$ is analytic on and inside C. All the singularity lies outside C)

For $\displaystyle\int \frac{1}{(z-1)(z-3)^2} dz = 2\pi i\left[\operatorname*{Res}_{Z=1} f(z)\right]$

$$= 2\pi i\left(\frac{1}{(1-3)^2}\right) = 2\pi i . \frac{1}{4} = \frac{\pi i}{2}$$

$$\int_C \left(ze^{\frac{1}{z}} + \tan\frac{z}{2} + \frac{1}{(z-1)(z-3)^2} \right) dz$$

$$= \pi i + 0 + \frac{\pi i}{2} = \frac{3\pi i}{2}$$

Hence

$$\frac{2}{\pi i}\int_C \left(ze^{\frac{1}{z}} + \tan\frac{z}{2} + \frac{1}{(z-1)(z-3)^2} \right) dz$$

$$= \frac{\cancel{2}}{\cancel{\pi i}}\left(\frac{3\cancel{\pi i}}{\cancel{2}}\right) = 3$$

30. Here we choose $z_1 = 6$, $z_2 = 3 - 3i$, $z_3 = 0$

$w_1 = 0$, $w_2 = i$, $w_3 = \infty$

Substituting these points in

$$\frac{(w - w_1)(w_2 - w_3)}{(w_1 - w_2)(w_3 - w)} = \frac{(z - z_1)(z_2 - z_3)}{(z_1 - z_2)(z_3 - z)} \quad ...(i)$$

Since, $w_3 = \infty$, we take the quotient involving w_3 in (1) as (–1).

Thus

$$\frac{(w-0)(-1)}{(0-i)} = \frac{(z-6)(3-3i-0)}{(6-3+3i)(0-z)}$$

$$\Rightarrow w = \frac{z-6}{-z} = -1+\frac{6}{z}$$

which is the required bilinear transformation that maps the D into $\{w \in C : \text{Re}(w) > 0\}$.

31. (x_n) is a Cauchy sequence in (x, d) but (y_n) need not be Cauchy in (x, d).

32. $\int_0^1 f(x)dx = \lim_{r\to\infty} \int_{\frac{1}{9^r}}^1 f\,dx$

33. $f_x(0,0) = \lim_{h\to 0} \frac{f(h,0)-f(0,0)}{h}$

$= \lim_{h\to 0} \frac{0-0}{h} = 0$

$f_y(0,0) = \lim_{k\to 0} \frac{f(0,k)-f(0,0)}{k} = \lim_{k\to 0} \frac{0-0}{k} = 0$

if the function f is differentiable at (0, 0), then by definition

$f(h, k) - f(0, 0) = 0.h + 0.k + h\phi + k\phi$.

$\Rightarrow f$ is not differential at origin but directional derivatives of f exists in all directions.

34.

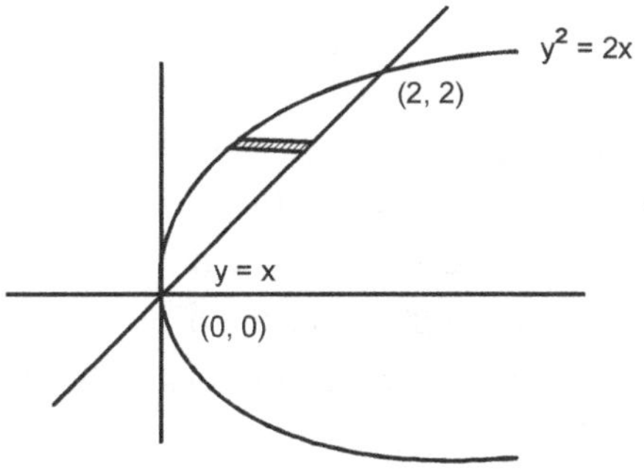

$\iint_D 3xy\,dxdy$

$= 3\int_{y=0}^{2} \int_{x=\frac{y^2}{2}}^{y} xy\,dxdy$

$= \frac{3}{2}\int_{y=0}^{2} y\left[x^2\right]_{\frac{y^2}{2}}^{y} dy$

$= \frac{3}{2}\int_{y=0}^{2} \left[y^3 - \frac{y^5}{4}\right] dy$

$= \frac{3}{2}\left[\frac{y^4}{4} - \frac{y^6}{24}\right]_0^2$

$= \frac{3}{2}\times\left(4-\frac{8}{3}\right)$

$= \frac{3}{2}\times\frac{4}{3} = 2$

35. Both the statements are true

$y_1 = x^3$, $\qquad y_2 = x^2\,|x|$

$y'_1 = 3x^3$, $\qquad y'_2 = 3x^2\,|x|$

Woronskian of y_1 & y_2 is

$$W(y_1, y_2) = \begin{vmatrix} y_1 & y_2 \\ \frac{dy_1}{dx} & \frac{dy_2}{dx} \end{vmatrix}$$

$= y_1(x)\frac{dy_2}{dx} - y_2(x)\frac{dy_1}{dx}$

$= x^3(3x\,|x|) - x^2\,|x|\,(3x^2)$

$= 0$

$\forall \in R$

But the function $y_1 = x_3$ & $y_2 = x_2|x|$ are not linearly dependent on any interval $a < x < b$ which includes $x = 0$.

36. Put $x + 1 = t$, then $x = (t-1)$, $dx = dt$

so $(x^2-1)^2 = t^2(t-2)^2$

Then given equation

$(x^2-1)^2\frac{d^2y}{dx^2} + (x+1)\frac{dy}{dx} - y = 0$ becomes

$t^2(t-2)^2\frac{d^2y}{dt^2} + t\frac{dy}{dx} - y = 0 \qquad ...(1)$

Let $y(t) = \sum_{n=0}^{\infty} c_n t^{n+r}$ be the series solution of (1).

Subsituting y, y', y'' in (1), we have

$t^2(t-2)^2\sum(n+r)(n+r-1)c_n t^{n+r-2}$

$+t\sum(n+r)c_n t^{n+r-1} - \sum c_n t^{n+r} = 0$

$\Rightarrow$ or

$\sum c_n(n+r)(n+2+1)t^{n+r+2}$

$-4\sum c_n(n+r)(n+r-1)t^{n+r+1}$

$+4\sum c_n(n+r)(n+r-1)t^{n+r}$

$+\sum(n+r)c_n t^{n+r} - \sum c_n t^{n+r} = 0$

indical equation is obtaing by equating to zero the coefficient of lowest power of t namely t^r (n = 0) i.e.

$$4r(r-1)+r-1=0$$

$$\Rightarrow r=1, r=-\frac{1}{4}$$

Here $\alpha = 1$, $\beta = -\frac{1}{4}$

so $\alpha - 4\beta = 1-4\left(-\frac{1}{4}\right) = 2.$

37. The set of elements of S_9 commuting with τ is centralizer.

Number of elements of S_9 commuting with τ =

order of centralizer of $S_9 = \frac{9!}{15120} = 24$

38. $\left(\frac{\mathbb{Q}[x]}{<x^4-1>}\right)/\left(I/<x^4-1>\right) \cong \frac{\mathbb{Q}[x]}{I}$, where I is an ideal of $\mathbb{Q}[x]$ and $<x^4-1> \subseteq I$

$\Rightarrow \frac{\mathbb{Q}[x]}{I}$ is field and $\mathbb{Q}[x]$ is P.I.D.

Let I = $<h(x)>$ where $h(x)$ is irreducible in $\mathbb{Q}[x]$.

i.e. $h(x)$ can be (x^2+1), $(x-1)$, $(x+1)$

39. $T_n(x) = \sum_{j=1}^{n} \frac{1}{j} <x, e_j> e_j$

$$\Rightarrow \lim_{n\to\infty} T_n(x) = \lim_{n\to\infty} \sum_{j=1}^{n} \frac{1}{j} <x, e_j> e_j$$

$$= \sum_{n=1}^{\infty} \frac{1}{n} <x, e_n> e_n$$

$$= T(x)$$

40. $\| T_n((x_k)) \| = \left|\sum_{i=1}^{n} x_i\right| \le \sum_{i=1}^{n} |x_i| < \infty.$

Let $x \in V$ such that $\|x\|_2 = 1$

$$\Rightarrow \|(x_n)\|_2 = 1$$

$$\Rightarrow (\Sigma |x_i|^2)^{1/2} = 1$$

$$\Rightarrow \Sigma |x_i|^2 = 1$$

$\therefore$ $\{T_n\}$ is not uniformly bounded in $\{x \in V : \|x\|_2 = 1\}$

But point-wise bounded on V.

41. $p(x) = \left(\frac{x^2-x}{2}\right)(2) + \left(\frac{x^2-1}{-1}\right)(1) + \frac{(x+1)x}{2\times 1}(2) =$

$x^2 + 1$

$p(x) + q(x)$

$$= \frac{x(x-1)(x-2)}{(-1)(-2)(-3)}(2)$$

$$+ \frac{(x+1)(x-1)(x-2)}{(1)(-1)(-2)}(1)$$

$$+ \frac{(x+1)x(x-2)}{(2)(1)(-1)}(2)$$

$$+ \frac{(x+1)(x-1)x}{(3)(2)(1)}(11)$$

$$= x^3 + x^2 - x + 1$$

$$\Rightarrow q(x) = x^3 - x$$

42. Interation matrix of given linear system

$$= J = -\begin{bmatrix} 1 & 0 & 0 \\ 0 & 1 & 0 \\ 0 & 0 & 1 \end{bmatrix} \begin{bmatrix} 0 & 2 & 1 \\ 2 & 0 & 2 \\ -4 & 2 & 0 \end{bmatrix}$$

$$= \begin{bmatrix} 0 & -2 & -1 \\ -2 & 0 & -2 \\ 4 & -2 & 0 \end{bmatrix}$$

For the eigenvalues of J :

$$|J - \lambda J| = 0 \Rightarrow \begin{vmatrix} -\lambda & -2 & -1 \\ -2 & -\lambda & -2 \\ 4 & -2 & 0-\lambda \end{vmatrix} = 0$$

$$\Rightarrow \lambda^3 \; 4\lambda - 12 = 0$$

We assume $(\lambda) = \lambda^3 - 4\lambda - 12$

$$f(2) = 8 - 12 - 12 < 0$$

$$f(3) = 27 - 24 = 3 > 0$$

$\Rightarrow$ one of the eigen values of J lies in the interval [2, 3].

so statement P is true.

Next, by the theorem, A neccessary and sufficient condition for convergence of an interation method is that the eigenvalues of iteration matrix satisfy

$$|\lambda_i(J)| < |$$

so statement Q is not true.

43. By lagrange equation

$$\underset{(i)}{\frac{dx}{x}} = \underset{(ii)}{\frac{dy}{y}} = \underset{(iii)}{\frac{du}{4u}}$$

Taking (ii) & (iii), we have

$$\frac{dx}{x} = \frac{dy}{y} \Rightarrow \frac{y}{x} = c_1 \qquad ...(i)$$

Similarly, Taking (i) & (ii), we have

$$\frac{u}{x^4} = c_2 \qquad ...(ii)$$

The general solution is

$\frac{u}{x^4} = \phi\left(\frac{y}{x}\right)$, where ϕ is an arbitary function,

$$u(x, y) = x^4\phi\left(\frac{y}{x}\right)$$

$$u(1, 1) = 1 = (1)^4\phi(1) \Rightarrow \phi(1) = 1$$

$$u(2, 2) = 2^4\phi\left(\frac{2}{2}\right) \Rightarrow 2^4\,\phi(1) = 2^4 \times 1 = 64$$

44. The value of $U\left(1, \frac{\pi}{2}\right) + 4\left(1, \frac{\pi}{4}\right) = \frac{7}{8}$

The given problem is Dirichlet problem of a circle as

$$\left.\begin{array}{l} u_{r_2} + \frac{1}{r}u_{r_1} + \frac{1}{r^2}\mu_{\theta\theta} = 0,\ 0 < r < a,\ 0 < \theta \le 2\pi \\ u(a, \theta) = f(\theta) \text{ for all } \theta \text{ is } (0, 2\pi) \end{array}\right\}$$

The general solution of θ is

$$u(r, \theta) = \frac{90}{2} +$$

$$\sum_{n=1}^{\infty}\left(\frac{r}{a}\right)^n (a_n \cos n\theta + b_n \sin n\theta)$$

using boundary conditions, we obtain

$$u\left(1, \frac{\pi}{2}\right) + u\left(1, \frac{\pi}{4}\right) = \frac{7}{8}$$

45. Usual topology on $\mathbb{R}^2$ is proper subset of topology generated by the basis $\{U \times V : U \in T_d, V \in T_u\}$ on $\mathbb{R} \times \mathbb{R}$ which is equal to dictionary order topology on $\mathbb{R} \times \mathbb{R}$.

46. Using expectations of conditional probability.

47. $P(X \ge 2Y) = \sum_{1}^{\infty}\sum_{2y}^{\infty} 2^{-x}$

48. $\lim_{x \to \infty} P\left[4 - \frac{2}{\sqrt{n}} < \frac{1}{n}\sum x_i < 4 + \frac{2}{\sqrt{n}}\right]$

$= 2\phi(1) = 0.68$

49. $P(\max(x, y) < 2)$

$= P(x < 2)\, P(y < 2)$

$= \left(\int_0^2 e^{-x}dx\right)^2$

$= 0.74$

50. $P(F/E) = 3P(F/E^C)$

$\Rightarrow P(E \cap F) = 2P(F \cap E^C)$

$\Rightarrow 3P(E \cap F) = 2P(F)$

$\Rightarrow P(E \cap F) = 0.2$

$\Rightarrow P(E/F) = \frac{0.2}{0.3} = 0.66$

54.

Origin \ Destination	1	2	3	Supply
1	4	3 [20]	6	~~20~~
2	7	10	5 [30]	~~30~~
3	8 [10]	9 [10]	7 [50]	~~50~~ ~~20~~ ~~10~~
Demand	~~10~~	~~30~~ ~~10~~	~~60~~ ~~30~~	

So, optimal cost of transportation equals to

$= 3 \times 20 + 5 \times 30 + 7 \times 30 + 8 \times 10 + 9 \times 10$

$= 60 + 150 + 210 + 80 + 90$

$= 590$

55.

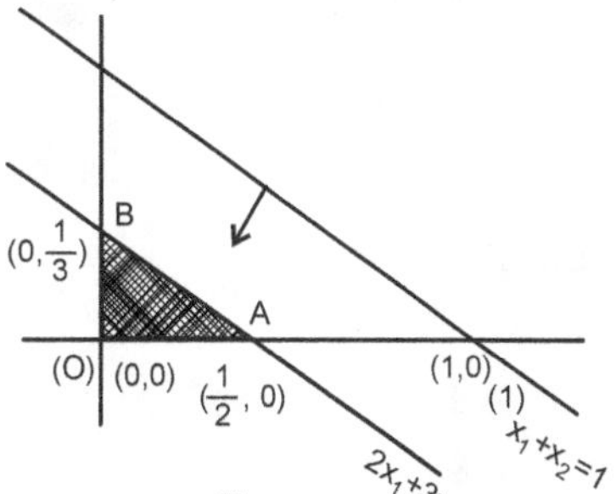

Fig.

SF denote the feasible region of given L.P.P. optimal value of L.P.P exists at corner points.

So,

O (0, 0) – K.0 + 5.0 = 0

$A\left(\frac{1}{2},0\right) - K.\frac{1}{2}+0 = \frac{K}{2}$

$B\left(0,\frac{1}{3}\right) - K.0 + 5.\frac{1}{3} = \frac{5}{3}$

If optimal solution of given L.P.P exists for K = 2,

So, $\frac{K}{2} > \frac{5}{3}$

$\Rightarrow K > \frac{5}{3}\times 2 = \frac{10}{3} = 3.32$

56. respectively

57. easier, than

58. P = 16 years

Q = 25 years

R = milkshake

S = Bear

With above known values, for the rule to be followed we have to check. P's drink and Sage because he is drinking beer.

59.

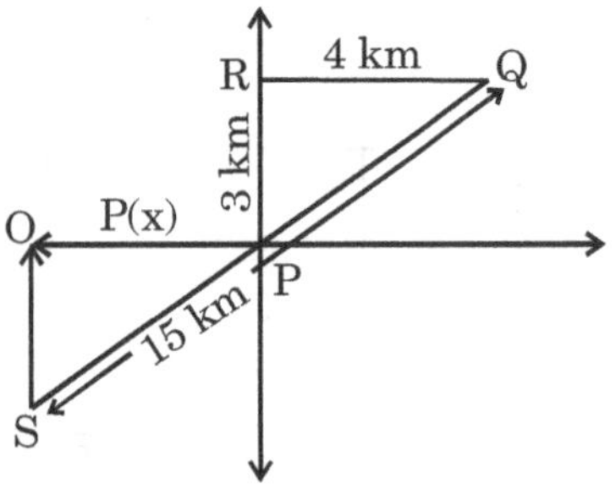

In ΔPQR

By pythagorus

$(4)^2 + (3)^2 = PQ^2$

PQ = 5 km

In Now PS = QS – PQ

= 15 – 5 = 10 km.

In ΔPOS

$x^2 = (10)^2 - (6)^2 = 64$

= 8 km. (East)

60. $P(A \cap B \cap C) = P((A) + P(B) + P(C)$

$-[P(A \cap B) + P(B \cap C) + P(A \cap C)]$

$-P(A \cap B \cap C)$

$500 = 329 + 186 + 295 - [83 + 217 + 63]$

$-P(A \cap B \cap C)$

$P(A \cap B \cap C) = 53.$

61. An intimate association does not allow for the necessary perspective.

62. With diagram:

X and Y are married and have 2 children P and Q

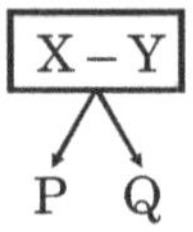

S is daughter of P and Z is S' grandfather

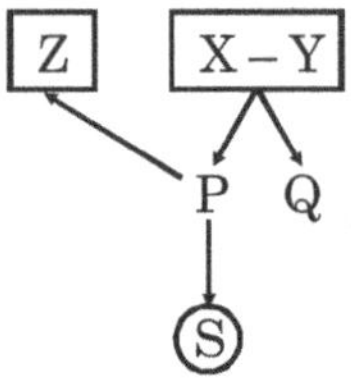

Z is married to W

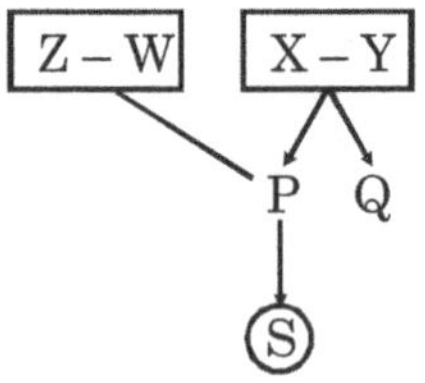

W and Z are parents of R

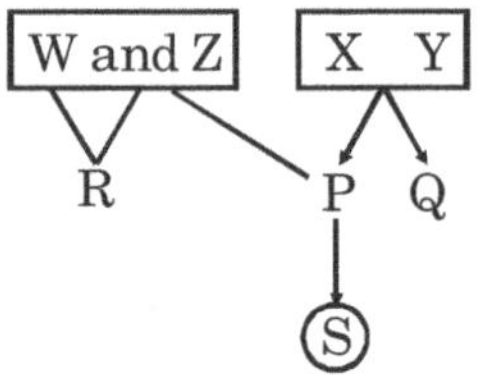

We can simply

Z and P are married and are parents of S. Hence above conditions prove d is the answer.

63. Turn week to reciprocals to make into 1

$1200\ M + 500\ W = \frac{1}{2}$

$900\ M + 250\ W = \frac{1}{3}$

Now 2(1200 M + 500 W) = 1

3(900 M + 250 W) = 1

Which becomes

$2400\ M + 1000\ W = 1$

$2700\ M + 750\ W = 1$

equating $2700\ M - 2400\ M$

$= 100\ W - 750\ W = 1000\ W - 750\ W$

$300\ M - 250\ W \Rightarrow W = \frac{300}{250} = \frac{6}{5}M.$

Put $W = \frac{6}{5}M$ in equation equal to 1 week

$2400M + 1000 \times \frac{6}{5}M = 1$

$M = 3600$

64. 3 digit number

can be filled from number 0 to 9 hence

| – | – | – | in 10 ways.

Hundredth place – can't have 0 and 1, hence can be filled in 8 ways.

Ten's place – can't have 1 or 2, hence can be filled in 8 ways.

One's place – It can only be filled in 1 way.

So, number becomes 881.

65. P to R is the steepest path because the path from P to R erasses the most number of contour lines which are 25 metres away.

SOLVED PAPER-2018

GENERAL APTITUDE SECTION

Q.1 – Q. 5 : carry one mark each

1. "The dress ________ her so well that they all immediately ________ her on her appearance."

The words that best fill the blanks in the above sentence are

(*a*) complemented, complemented

(*b*) complimented, complemented

(*c*) complimented, complimented

(*d*) complemented, complimented

2. "The judge's standing in the legal community, though shaken by false allegations of wrongdoing, remained ________."

The word that best fills the blank in the above sentence is

(*a*) undiminished (*b*) damaged

(*c*) illegal (*d*) uncertain

3. Find the missing group of letters in the following series :

BC, FGH, LMNO, _____

(*a*) UVWXY (*b*) TUVWX

(*c*) STUVW (*d*) RSTUV

4. The perimeters of a circle, a square and an equilateral triangle are equal. Which one of the following statements is true?

(*a*) The circle has the largest area.

(*b*) The square has the largest area.

(*c*) The equilateral triangle has the largest area.

(*d*) All the three shapes have the same area.

5. The value of the expression

$$\frac{1}{1+\log_u vw}+\frac{1}{1+\log_v wu}+\frac{1}{1+\log_w uv} \text{ is } \_\_\_\_\_\_.$$

(*a*) -1 (*b*) 0

(*c*) 1 (*d*) 3

Q. 6 – Q. 10 carry two marks each.

6. Forty students watched films A, B and C over a week. Each student watched either only one film or all three. Thirteen students watched film A, sixteen students watched film B and nineteen students watched film C. How many students watched all three films?

(*a*) 0 (*b*) 2

(*c*) 4 (*d*) 8

7. A wire would enclose an area of 1936 m^2, if it is bent into a square. The wire is cut into two pieces. The longer piece is thrice as long as the shorter piece. The long and the short pieces are bent into a square and a circle, respectively. Which of the following choices is closest to the sum of the areas enclosed by the two pieces in square meters?

(*a*) 1096 (*b*) 1111

(*c*) 1243 (*d*) 2486

8. A contract is to be completed in 52 days and 125 identical robots were employed, each operational for 7 hours a day. After 39 days, five-seventh of the work was completed. How many additional robots would be required to complete the work on time, if each robot is now operational for 8 hours a day?

(*a*) 50 (*b*) 89

(*c*) 146 (*d*) 175

9. A house has a number which needs to be identified. The following three statements are given that can help in identifying the house number.

i. If the house number is a multiple of 3, then it is a number from 50 to 59.

ii. If the house number is NOT a multiple of 4, then it is a number from 60 to 69.

iii. If the house number is NOT a multiple of 6, then it is a number from 70 to 79.

What is the house number?

(*a*) 54 (*b*) 65

(*c*) 66 (*d*) 76

10. An unbiased coin is tossed six times in a row and four different such trials are conducted.

One trial implies six tosses of the coin. If H stands for head and T stands for tail, the following are the observations from the four trials:

(1) HTHTHT (2) TTHHHT

(3) HTTHHT (4) HHHT__ __.

Which statement describing the last two coin tosses of the fourth trial has the highest probability of being correct?

(*a*) Two T will occur.

(*b*) One H and one T will occur.

(*c*) Two H will occur.

(*d*) One H will be followed by one T.

MATHEMATICS

Q.1 – Q.25 carry one mark each

1. The principal value of $(-1)^{(-2i/\pi)}$ is

(a) e^2 (b) e^{2i}

(c) e^{-2i} (d) e^{-2}

2. Let $f : \mathbb{C} \to \mathbb{C}$ be an entire function with $f(0) = 1$, $f(1) = 2$ and $f'(0) = 0$. If there exists $M > 0$ such that $|f''(z)| \le M$ for all $z \varepsilon \mathbb{C}$, then $f(2) =$

(a) 2 (b) 5

(c) $2 + 5i$ (d) $5 + 2i$

3. In the Laurent series expansion of $f(z) = \dfrac{1}{z(z-1)}$ valid for $|z-1| > 1$; the coefficient of $\dfrac{1}{z-1}$ is

(a) – 2 (b) – 1

(c) 0 (d) 1

4. Let X and Y be metric spaces, and let $f : X \to Y$ be a continuous map. For any subset S of X; which one of the following statements is true?

(a) If S is open, then f(S) is open

(b) If S is connected, then f(S) is connected

(c) If S is closed, then f(S) is closed

(d) If S is bounded, then f(S) is bounded

5. The general solution of the differential equation $xy' = y + \sqrt{x^2 + y^2}$ for $x > 0$ is given by (with an arbitrary positive constant k)

(a) $ky^2 = x + \sqrt{x^2 + y^2}$ (b) $kx^2 = x + \sqrt{x^2 + y^2}$

(c) $kx^2 = y + \sqrt{x^2 + y^2}$ (d) $ky^2 = y + \sqrt{x^2 + y^2}$

6. Let $p_n(x)$ be the polynomial solution of the differential equation $\dfrac{d}{dx}[(1-x^2)y'] + n(n+1)y = 0$ with $p_n(1) = 1$ for n = 1, 2, 3, ……, If $\dfrac{d}{dx}[p_{n+2}(x) - p_n(x)] = \alpha_n p_{n+1}(x)$ then α_n is

(a) 2n (b) 2n + 1

(c) 2n + 2 (d) 2n + 3

7. In the permutation group S_6, the number of elements of order 8 is

(a) 0

(b) 1

(c) 2

(d) 4

8. Let R be a commutative ring with 1 (unity) which is not a field. Let $I \subset R$ be a proper ideal such that every element of R not in I is invertible in R: Then the number of maximal ideals of R is

(a) 1 (b) 2

(c) 3 (d) infinite

9. Let $f : \mathbb{R} \to \mathbb{R}$ be a twice continuously differentiable function. The order of convergence of the secant method for finding root of the equation $f(x) = 0$ is

(a) $\dfrac{1+\sqrt{5}}{2}$ (b) $\dfrac{2}{1+\sqrt{5}}$

(c) $\dfrac{1+\sqrt{5}}{3}$ (d) $\dfrac{3}{1+\sqrt{5}}$

10. The Cauchy problem $uu_x + yu_y = x$ with $u(x, 1) = 2x$; when solved using its characteristic equations with an independent variable t, is found to admit of a solution in the form

$$x = \frac{3}{2}se^t - \frac{1}{2}se^{-t}, y = e^t, u = f(s,t)$$

Then $f(s, t) =$

(a) $\dfrac{3}{2}se^t + \dfrac{1}{2}se^{-t}$ (b) $\dfrac{1}{2}se^t + \dfrac{3}{2}se^{-t}$

(c) $\dfrac{1}{2}se^t - \dfrac{3}{2}se^{-t}$ (d) $\dfrac{3}{2}se^t - \dfrac{1}{2}se^{-t}$

11. An urn contains four balls, each ball having equal probability of being white or black. Three black balls are added to the urn. The probability that five balls in the urn are black is

(a) 2/7 (b) 3/8

(c) 1/2 (d) 5/7

12. For a linear programming problem, which one of the following statements is FALSE?

(a) If a constraint is an equality, then the corresponding dual variable is unrestricted in sign

(b) Both primal and its dual can be infeasible

(c) If primal is unbounded, then its dual is infeasible

(d) Even if both primal and dual are feasible, the optimal values of the primal and the dual can differ

13. Let $A = \begin{bmatrix} a & 2f & 0 \\ 2f & b & 3f \\ 0 & 3f & c \end{bmatrix}$, where a, b, c, f are real numbers and $f \neq 0$. The geometric multiplicity of the largest eigenvalue of A equals ________.

14. Consider the subspaces

$$W_1 = \{(x_1, x_2, x_3) \in \mathbb{R}^3 : x_1 = x_2 + 2x_3\}$$

$$W_2 = \{(x_1, x_2, x_3) \in \mathbb{R}^3 : x_1 = 3x_2 + 2x_3\}$$

of $\mathbb{R}^3$. Then the dimension of $W_1 + W_2$ equals____

15. Let V be the real vector space of all polynomials of degree less than or equal to 2 with real coefficients. Let $T : V \to V$ be the linear transformation given by $T(p) = 2p + p'$ for $p \in V$,

where p' is the derivative of p. Then the number of nonzero entries in the Jordan canonical form of a matrix of T equals.

16. Let $I = [2, 3)$, J be the set of all rational numbers in the interval $[4, 6]$, K be the Cantor (ternary) set, and let $L = \{7 + x : x \varepsilon K\}$. Then the Lebesgue measure of the set $I \cup J \cup L$ equals _______.

17. Let $u(x, y, z) = x^2 - 2y + 4z^2$ for $(x, y, z) \in \mathbb{R}^3$. Then the directional derivative of u in the direction $\frac{3}{5}\hat{i} - \frac{4}{5}\hat{k}$ at the point (5, 1, 0) is____.

18. If the Laplace transform of $y(t)$ is given by $Y(s) = L(y(t)) = \frac{5}{2(s-1)} - \frac{2}{s-2} + \frac{1}{2(s-3)}$, then

$y(0) + y'(0) =$ ____________.

19. The number of regular singular points of the differential equation

$$[(x-1)^2 \sin x]y'' + [\cos x \sin(x-1)]y' + (x-1)y = 0$$

in the interval $\left[0, \frac{\pi}{2}\right]$ is equal to ________.

20. Let F be a field with 7^6 elements and let K be a subfield of F with 49 elements. Then the dimension of F as a vector space over K is______.

21. Let $C([0, 1])$ be the real vector space of all continuous real valued functions on [0; 1]; and let T be the linear operator on $C([0, 1])$ given by

$$(Tf)(x) = \int_0^1 \sin(x+y) f(y)\,dy, \quad x \in [0,1].$$

Then the dimension of the range space of T equals

________________.

22. Let $a \in (-1, 1)$ be such that the quadrature rule

$\int_{-1}^{1} f(x)dx \simeq f(-a) + f(a)$ is exact for all polynomials of degree less than or equal to 3. Then $3a^2 =$ ____.

23. Let X and Y have joint probability density function given by

$$f_{X,Y}(x, y) = \begin{cases} 2, & 0 \le x \le 1 - y, 0 \le y \le 1 \\ 0, & \text{otherwise.} \end{cases}$$

If f_Y denotes the marginal probability density function of Y, then $f_Y(1/2) =$_______ .

24. Let the cumulative distribution function of the random variable X be given by

$$F_X(x) = \begin{cases} 0, & x < 0, \\ x, & 0 \le x < 1/2 \\ (1+x)/2, & 1/2 \le x < 1, \\ 1, & x \ge 1. \end{cases}$$

Then $\mathbb{P}(X = 1/2) =$ ______________.

25. Let $\{X_j\}$ be a sequence of independent Bernoulli random variables with $\mathbb{P}(X_j = 1) = 1/4$ and let $Y_n = \frac{1}{n}\sum_{j=1}^{n} X_j^2$. Then Y_n converges, in probability, to _____________.

Q. 26 – Q. 55 carry two marks each

26. Let Γ be the circle given by $z = 4e^{i\theta}$; where θ varies from 0 to 2π. Then $\oint_\Gamma \frac{e^z}{z^2 - 2z} dz =$

(a) $2\pi i(e^2 - 1)$ (b) $\pi i(1 - e^2)$

(c) $\pi i(e^2 - 1)$ (d) $2\pi i(1 - e^2)$

27. The image of the half plane Re(z) + Im(z) > 0 under the map $w = \frac{z-1}{z+i}$ is given by

(a) $\text{Re}(w) > 0$ (b) $\text{Im}(w) > 0$

(c) $|w| > 1$ (d) $|w| < 1$

28. Let $D \subset \mathbb{R}^2$ denote the closed disc with center at the origin and radius 2. Then $\iint_D e^{-(x^2+y^2)}\,dxdy =$

(a) $\pi(1 - e^{-4})$ (b) $\frac{\pi}{2}(1 - e^{-4})$

(c) $\pi(1 - e^{-2})$ (d) $\frac{\pi}{2}(1 - e^{-2})$

29. Consider the polynomial $p(X) = X^4 + 4$ in the ring $\mathbb{Q}[X]$ of polynomials in the variable X with coefficients in the field $\mathbb{Q}$ of rational numbers. Then

(a) the set of zeros of $p(X)$ in $\mathbb{C}$ forms a group under multiplication

(b) $p(X)$ is reducible in the ring $\mathbb{Q}[X]$

(c) the splitting field of $p(X)$ has degree 3 over $\mathbb{Q}$

(d) the splitting field of $p(X)$ has degree 4 over $\mathbb{Q}$

30. Which one of the following statements is true?

(a) Every group of order 12 has a non-trivial proper normal subgroup

(b) Some group of order 12 does not have a non-trivial proper normal subgroup

(c) Every group of order 12 has a subgroup of order 6

(d) Every group of order 12 has an element of order 12

31. For an odd prime p, consider the ring $\mathbb{Z}[\sqrt{-p}] = \{a + b\sqrt{-p} : a, b \in \mathbb{Z}\} \subseteq \mathbb{C}$. Then the element 2 in $\mathbb{Z}[\sqrt{-p}]$ is

(a) a unit (b) a square

(c) a prime (d) irreducible

32. Consider the following two statements:

P : The matrix $\begin{bmatrix} 0 & 5 \\ 0 & 7 \end{bmatrix}$ has infinitely many LU factorizations, where L is lower triangular with each diagonal entry 1 and U is upper triangular.

Q : The matrix $\begin{bmatrix} 0 & 0 \\ 2 & 5 \end{bmatrix}$ has no LU factorization, where L is lower triangular with each diagonal entry 1 and U is upper triangular.

Then which one of the following options is correct?

(a) P is TRUE and Q is FALSE

(b) Both P and Q are TRUE

(c) P is FALSE and Q is TRUE

(d) Both P and Q are FALSE

33. If the characteristic curves of the partial differential equation $xu_{xx} + 2x^2u_{xy} = u_x - 1$ are $\mu(x, y) = c_1$ and $v(x, y) = c_2$, where c_1 and c_2 are constants, then

(a) $\mu(x,y) = x^2 - y, v(x,y) = y$

(b) $\mu(x,y) = x^2 + y,\ v(x,y) = y$

(c) $\mu(x,y) = x^2 + y, v(x,y) = x^2$

(d) $\mu(x,y) = x^2 - y, v(x,y) = x^2$

34. Let $f : X \to Y$ be a continuous map from a Hausdorff topological space X to a metric space Y. Consider the following two statements:

P : f is a closed map and the inverse image $f^{-1}(y) = \{x \in X : f(x) = y\}$ is compact for each $y \in$ Y.

Q : For every compact subset $K \subset Y$, the inverse image $f^{-1}(K)$ is a compact subset of X:

Which one of the following is true?

(a) Q implies P but P does NOT imply Q

(b) P implies Q but Q does NOT imply P

(c) P and Q are equivalent

(d) neither P implies Q nor Q implies P

35. Let X denote $\mathbb{R}^2$ endowed with the usual topology. Let Y denote $\mathbb{R}$ endowed with the co-finite topology. If Z is the product topological space $Y \times Y$, then

(a) the topology of X is the same as the topology of Z

(b) the topology of X is strictly coarser (weaker) than that of Z

(c) the topology of Z is strictly coarser (weaker) than that of X

(d) the topology of X cannot be compared with that of Z

36. Consider $\mathbb{R}^n$ with the usual topology for n = 1, 2, 3. Each of the following options gives topological spaces X and Y with respective induced topologies. In which option is X homeomorphic to Y?

(a) $X = \{(x, y, z) \in \mathbb{R}^3 : x^2 + y^2 = 1\}$,

$Y = \{(x, y, z) \in \mathbb{R}^3 : z = 0, x^2 + y^2 \neq 0\}$

(b) $X = \{(x, y) \in \mathbb{R}^2 : y = \sin(1/x), 0 < x \le 1\}$

$\cup \{(x, y) \in \mathbb{R}^2 : x = 0, -1 \le y \le 1\}$,

$Y = [0,1] \subseteq \mathbb{R}$

(c) $X = \{(x, y) \in \mathbb{R}^2 : y = x\sin(1/x), 0 < x \le 1\}$,

$Y = [0,1] \subseteq \mathbb{R}$

(d) $X = \{(x, y, z) \in \mathbb{R}^3 : x^2 + y^2 = 1\}$,

$Y = \{(x, y, z) \in \mathbb{R}^3 : x^2 + y^2 = z^2 \neq 0\}$

37. Let $\{X_i\}$ be a sequence of independent Poisson (λ) variables and let $W_n = \frac{1}{n}\sum_{i=1}^{n} X_i$. Then the limiting distribution of $\sqrt{n}(W_n - \lambda)$ is the normal distribution with zero mean and variance given by

(a) 1 (b) $\sqrt{\lambda}$

(c) λ (d) θ^2

38. Let $X_1, X_2, \ldots\ldots, X_n$ be independent and identically distributed random variables with probability density function given by

$$f_X(x;\theta) = \begin{cases} \theta e^{-\theta(x-1)}, & x \ge 1, \\ 0 & \text{otherwise.} \end{cases}$$

Also, let $\overline{X} = \frac{1}{n} = \sum_{n=1}^{n} X_i$. Then the maximum likelihood estimator of θ is

(a) $1/\overline{X}$ (b) $(1/\overline{X}) - 1$

(c) $1/(\overline{X} - 1)$ (d) $\overline{X}$

39. Consider the Linear Programming Problem (LPP):

Maximize $\alpha x_1 + x_2$

Subject to $2x_1 + x_2 \le 6,$

$-x_1 + x_2 \le 1,$

$x_1 + x_2 \le 4$

$x_1 \ge 0,\ x_2 \ge 0$

where α is a constant. If $(3, 0)$ is the only optimal solution, then

(a) $\alpha < -2$ (b) $-2 < \alpha < 1$

(c) $1 < \alpha < 2$ (d) $a > 2$

40. Let $M_2(\mathbb{R})$ be the vector space of all 2×2 real matrices over the field $\mathbb{R}$. Define the linear transformation $S : M_2(\mathbb{R}) \to M_2(\mathbb{R})$ by $S(X) = 2X + X^T$, where X^T denotes the transpose of the matrix X: Then the trace of S equals _____.

41. Consider $\mathbb{R}^3$ with the usual inner product. If d is the distance from (1, 1, 1) to the subspace $\{(1,1,0),(0,1,1)\}$ of $\mathbb{R}^3$, then $3d^2 =$__________.

42. Consider the matrix $A = I_9 - 2u^T u$ with $u = \frac{1}{3}[1,1,1,1,1,1,1,1,1]$, where I_9 is the 9×9 identity matrix and u^T is the transpose of u. If λ and μ are two distinct eigenvalues of A, then $|\lambda - \mu| =$ ________.

43. Let $f(z) = z^3 e^{z^2}$ for $z \in \mathbb{C}$ and let Γ be the circle $z = e^{i\theta}$; where θ varies from 0 to 4π : Then

$$\frac{1}{2\pi i}\oint_{\Gamma} \frac{f'(z)}{f(z)} dz = \text{\_\_\_\_\_\_\_\_}.$$

44. Let S be the surface of the solid

$V = \{(x,y,z) : 0 \le x \le 1, 0 \le y \le 2, 0 \le z \le 3\}$.

Let $\hat{n}$ denote the unit outward normal to S and let

$$\hat{F}(x,y,z) = x\hat{i} + y\hat{j} + z\hat{k},\quad (x,y,z) \in V$$

Then the surface integral $\iint_S \vec{F} \cdot \hat{n}\, dS$ equals __________.

45. Let A be a 3×3 matrix with real entries. If three solutions of the linear system of differential equations $\dot{x}(t) = Ax(t)$ are given by

$$\begin{bmatrix} e^t - e^{2t} \\ -e^t + e^{2t} \\ e^t + e^{2t} \end{bmatrix} \begin{bmatrix} -e^{2t} - e^{-t} \\ e^{2t} - e^{-t} \\ e^{2t} + e^{-t} \end{bmatrix} \text{ and } \begin{bmatrix} e^{-t} + 2e^t \\ e^{-t} - 2e^t \\ -e^{-t} + 2e^t \end{bmatrix}$$

then the sum of the diagonal entries of A is equal to __________.

46. If $y_1(x) = e^{-x^2}$ is a solution of the differential equation $xy'' + \alpha y' + \beta x^3 y = 0$ for some real numbers α and β, then $\alpha\beta =$__________ .

47. Let $L^2([0, 1])$ be the Hilbert space of all real valued square integrable functions on [0, 1] with the usual inner product. Let ϕ be the linear functional on $L^2([0, 1])$ defined by $\phi(f) = \int_{1/4}^{3/4} 3\sqrt{2} f\, d\mu$, where μ denotes the Lebesgue measure on [0, 1]. Then $\|\phi\| =$________ .

48. Let U be an orthonormal set in a Hilbert space H and let $x \in H$ be such that $\|x\| = 2$.

Consider the set $E = \left\{u \in U : |\langle x,u\rangle| \ge \frac{1}{4}\right\}$.

Then the maximum possible number of elements in E is __________.

49. If $p(x) = 2 - (x+1) + x(x+1) - \beta x(x+1)(x-\alpha)$ interpolates the points (x, y) in the table

x	–1	0	1	2
y	2	1	2	–7

then $\alpha + \beta =$_________ .

50. If $\sin(\pi x) = a_0 + \sum_{n=1}^{\infty} a_n \cos(n\pi x)$, for $0 < x < 1$, then $(a_0 + a_1)\pi =$_______ .

51. For n = 1, 2, ..., let $f_n(x) = \dfrac{2nx^{n-1}}{1+x}, x \in [0,1]$. Then

$\lim_{x\to\infty} \int_0^1 f_n(x)dx =$ ________.

52. Let X_1, X_2, X_3, X_4 be independent exponential random variables with mean 1. 1/2, 1/3, 1/4, respectively. Then $Y = \min(X_1, X_2, X_3, X_4)$ has exponential distribution with mean equal to ______________.

53. Let X be the number of heads in 4 tosses of a fair coin by Person 1 and let Y be the number of heads in 4 tosses of a fair coin by Person 2. Assume that all the tosses are independent. Then the value of $\mathbb{P}(X = Y)$ correct up to three decimal places is ________.

54. Let X_1 and X_2 be independent geometric random variables with the same probability mass function given by $\mathbb{P}(X = k) = p(1-p)^{k-1}, k = 1, 2, \ldots$ Then the value of $\mathbb{P}(X_1 = 2 | X_1 + X_2 = 4)$ correct up to three decimal places is _________.

55. A certain commodity is produced by the manufacturing plants P_1 and P_2 whose capacities are 6 and 5 units, respectively. The commodity is shipped to markets M_1, M_2, M_3 and M_4 whose requirements are 1, 2, 3 and 5 units, respectively. The transportation cost per unit from plant P_i to market M_j is as follows:

	M_1	M_2	M_3	M_4	
P_1	1	3	5	8	6
P_2	2	5	6	7	5
	1	2	3	5	

Then the optimal cost of transportation is ____.

ANSWERS

General Aptitude (GA)

1. (*d*)	**2.** (*a*)	**3.** (*b*)	**4.** (*a*)	**5.** (*c*)	**6.** (*c*)	**7.** (*c*)	**8.** (*a*)	**9.** (*d*)	**10.** (*b*)

Technical Section

1. (*a*)	**2.** (*b*)	**3.** (*c*)	**4.** (*b*)	**5.** (*c*)
6. (*d*)	**7.** (*a*)	**8.** (*)	**9.** (*a*)	**10.** (*a*)
11. (*b*)	**12.** (*d*)	**13.** (1 to 1)	**14.** (3 to 3)	**15.** (5 to 5)
16. (1 to 1)	**17.** (6 to 6)	**18.** (1 to 1)	**19.** (2 to 2)	**20.** (3 to 3)
21. (2 to 2)	**22.** (1 to 1)	**23.** (1 to 1)	**24.** (0.25 to 0.25)	**25.** (0.25 to 0.25)
26. (*c*)	**27.** (*d*)	**28.** (*a*)	**29.** (*b*)	**30.** (*a*)
31. (*d*)	**32.** (*b*)	**33.** (*a*)	**34.** (*c*)	**35.** (*c*)
36. (*a*)	**37.** (*c*)	**38.** (*c*)	**39.** (*d*)	**40.** (10 to 10)
41. (1 to 1)	**42.** (2 to 2)	**43.** (6 to 6)	**44.** (18 to 18)	**45.** (2 to 2)
46. (4 to 4)	**47.** (3 to 3)	**48.** (64 to 64)	**49.** (3 to 3)	**50.** (2 to 2)
51. (1 to 1)	**52.** (0.1 to 0.1)	**53.** (0.272 to 0.274)	**54.** (0.332 to 0.334)	**55.** (57 to 57)

* *indicate none of the Answer is correct.*

EXPLANATIONS

GENERAL APTITUDE

3. The given series is

BC, FGH LMNO TUVWX

$\therefore$ Option (*b*) is correct.

4. Perimeter of circle, square and equilateral triangle are equal

$\therefore$ $P_C = P_S = P_t$

$2\pi r = 4S = 3a = K$ (Let) ...(i)

where '*r*' is radius of cirlce

'*s*' is side of square

and '*a*' is side of equilateral triangle

from (*i*) $r = \frac{k}{2\pi}$, $s = \frac{k}{4}$ and $a = \frac{k}{3}$

Now area of circle $= \pi r^2 = \frac{\pi k^2}{4\pi^2} = \frac{k^2}{4\pi}$

Area of square $= \frac{k}{4} \times \frac{k}{4} = \frac{k^2}{16}$

and area of equilateral triangle $= \frac{\sqrt{3}}{4}\left(\frac{k}{3}\right)^2 = \frac{\sqrt{3}\,k^2}{36}$

$\therefore$ $\frac{k^2}{4\pi} > \frac{k^2}{16} > \frac{\sqrt{3}k^2}{36}$

$\therefore$ Circle has largest area.

5. $\frac{1}{1+\log_u^{vw}} + \frac{1}{1+\log_v^{wu}} + \frac{1}{1+\log_w^{uv}}$

$= \frac{1}{\log_u^u + \log_u^{vw}} + \frac{1}{\log_v^v + \log_v^{wu}} + \frac{1}{\log_w^w + \log_w^{uv}}$

$$= \frac{1}{\log_u^{urw}} + \frac{1}{\log_v^{uvw}} + \frac{1}{\log_w^{uvw}}$$

$$= \log_{uvw}^{u} + \log_{uvw}^{v} + \log_{uvw}^{w}$$

$$= \log_{uvw}^{uvw} = 1$$

$\therefore$ Option (*c*) is correct.

6.

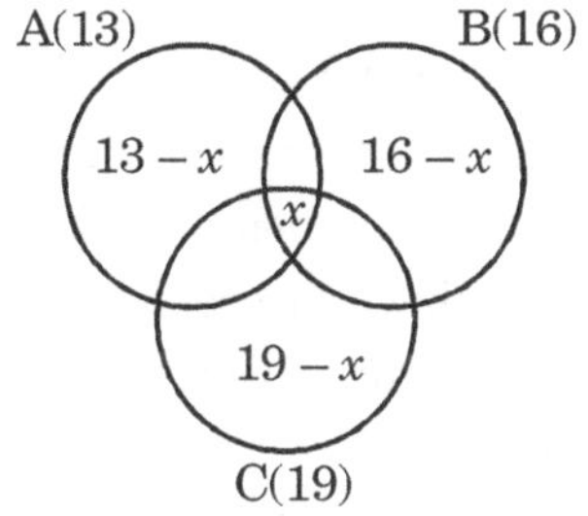

$\therefore \quad (13 - x) + x + (16 - x) + (19 - x) = 40$

$\therefore \quad 13 - x + x + 16 - x + 19 - x = 40$

$48 - 2x = 40$

$\therefore \quad 8 = 2x$

$\therefore \quad x = 4$

Hence '4' students watched all three films.

$\therefore$ Option (*c*) is correct.

7.

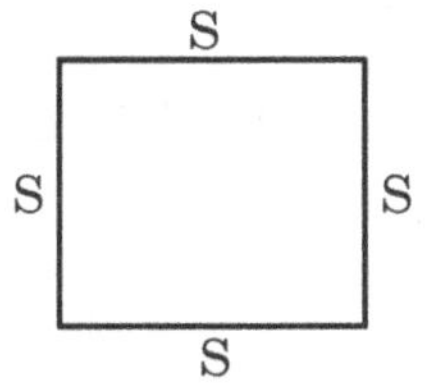

Area enclosed by wire = 1936

$\therefore \quad S^2 = 1936$

$\therefore \quad S = \sqrt{1936}$

$\therefore \quad \boxed{S = 44}$

Now perimeter (length of wire) = 4 × 44 = 176 m

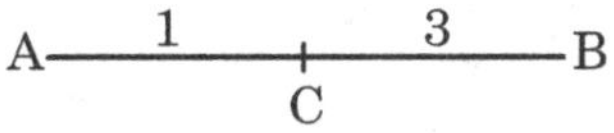

$\therefore \quad AC = \frac{1}{4} \times 176 = 44$

and $\quad BC = \frac{3}{4} \times 176 = 132$

Now BC is bent to form square.

$\therefore$ Area enclosed by square is = 33 × 33 = 1089 m^2

and AC is bent to form a circle

Now $\quad AC = 2\pi r$

$\therefore \quad 44 = 2 \times \frac{22}{7} \times r$

$\therefore \quad r = 7$

$\therefore$ Area enclosed by circle = πr^2

$$= \frac{22}{7} \times 7 \times 7 = 154 \text{ m}^2$$

$\therefore$ Sum of total area = 1089 + 154

= 1243 m^2

$\therefore$ Option (*c*) is correct.

8. According to Men-day-work concept

$$\frac{M_1 \times D_1 \times T_1}{W_1} = \frac{M_2 \times D_2 \times T_2}{W_2}$$

Now according to question,

$$\therefore \quad \frac{125 \times 39 \times 7}{5/7} = \frac{(125 + x) \times 13 \times 8}{(2/7)}$$

$$\therefore \quad \frac{125 \times 39 \times 7}{5} = \frac{(125 + x) \times 13 \times 8}{2}$$

$\therefore \quad 25 \times 39 \times 7 = 52(125 + x)$

$\therefore \quad x = 6.25 \approx 7$

9. From statement-1

Possible house number are 51, 54, 57

From statement-2

Possible house number are 61, 62, 63, 65, 66, 67, 69

From statement-3

Possible house number are 70, 71, 73, 74, 75, 76, 77, 79

From above statement, option (*d*) satisfies all the three statements.

$\therefore$ Option (*d*) is correct.

10. From the fourth trial outcomes are

H, H, H, T, ______, ______

Now possible outcomes of the last two coins tosses of the fourth trial are {HH, HT, TH, TT}

Out of 4 possibility cases, one 'H' and one 'T' of occurences will be highest.

$\therefore$ Option (*b*) is correct.

MATHEMATICS

1. We know that $Z^{\alpha} \equiv e^{\alpha \log z}$ .... (*i*)

where, Z and α are Complex number

Compairing $(-1)^{(-2i/\pi)}$ with Equation (*i*)

$\therefore z = -1, \quad \alpha = -2i/\pi$

We know that, $\log Z = ln|Z| + i(\text{Arg } Z + 2n\pi)$

For Principal value, n = 0

$\log Z = ln|Z| + i \text{ Arg }(Z) \qquad$ since $Z = -1 + o \cdot i$

$$\Rightarrow \log Z = ln|-1| + i\left(\pi + \tan^{-1}\frac{y}{x}\right)$$

$$\therefore \text{Arg}(z) = \pi + \tan^{-1}\frac{y}{x}$$

$\Rightarrow \log Z = 0 + i(\pi + 0)$

$\Rightarrow \log Z = i\pi$

Now from enquation (i), We get

$Z^{\alpha} = e^{-2i/\pi . i\pi} = e^2$

$\Rightarrow Z^{\alpha} = e^2$

Hence Principal Value of $(-1)^{(-2i/\pi)}$ is e^2

2. if $f : \mathbb{C} \to \mathbb{C}$ is an entire and bounded then f is Constant. therefore f'' is a Constant

Let $f''(Z) = a$, for some Constant a

$\Rightarrow f'(Z) = aZ + b$ .... (i)

$\Rightarrow f(Z) = a\frac{z^2}{2} + bZ + c$ .... (ii)

given that, f(0) = 1, f(1) = 2 and $f'(0) = 0$

$\Rightarrow C = 1$

$2 = \frac{a}{2} + b + 1$

$\Rightarrow a + 2b = 2$ .... (iii)

$f'(0) = 0 \Rightarrow b = 0$

therefore, a = 2

Now, $f(Z) = 2\frac{Z^2}{2} + 0 + 1$

$\Rightarrow f(Z) = Z^2 + 1$

$\Rightarrow f(2) = 4 + 1 = 5$

Hence, f(2) = 5

3. The Laurent Series expansion of

$f(z) = \frac{1}{Z(z-1)}$

Let $Z - 1 = u$

$f(u) = \frac{1}{u(u+1)}$

$f(u) = \frac{1}{u^2\left(1 + \frac{1}{u}\right)}$

$= \frac{1}{u^2}\sum_{n=0}^{\infty}(-1)^n\left(\frac{1}{u}\right)^n$

$= \sum_{n=0}^{\infty}(-1)^n \frac{1}{u^2 . u^n}$

$f(u) = \sum_{n=0}^{\infty}(-1)^n \frac{1}{u^{n+2}}$

$f(Z) = \sum_{n=0}^{\infty}(-1)^n \frac{1}{(Z-1)^{n+2}}$

Hence, the Coefficient of $\frac{1}{Z-1} = 0$

4. By theorem, Let X and Y be the metric Spaces. Let $f : X \to Y$ be a Continuous function, if Sc X is a Connected then f(s) a Connected in Y

So, by the above theorem

Hence, option (*b*) is Correct.

5. We have,

$xy' = y + \sqrt{x^2 + y^2}$ for $x > 0$

$\frac{dy}{dx} = \frac{y + \sqrt{x^2 + y^2}}{x}$ ...(i)

Let $y = ux$

$\frac{dy}{dx} = u + \frac{x\,du}{dx}$

now putting in eqn (*i*)

$u + x\frac{du}{dx} = \frac{ux + \sqrt{x^2 + u^2x^2}}{x}$

$x\frac{du}{dx} = \sqrt{1 + u^2}$

$\frac{du}{\sqrt{1+u^2}} = \frac{dx}{x}$

on taking integration both side

$\left(u + \sqrt{1+u^2}\right) = kx$

$\frac{y}{x} + \sqrt{1 + \frac{y^2}{x^2}} = kx$

$y + \sqrt{x^2 + y^2} = kx^2$

Hence $kx^2 = y + \sqrt{x^2 + y^2}$

6. Let $P_n(x)$ be the polynomial solution of the differential equation

$\frac{d}{dx}\left[(1 - x^2)y'\right] + n(n+1)y = 0$

with $P_n(1) = 1$ for $n = 1, 2, 3 ...$

Then $P_n(x) = \frac{1}{2^n n!}\frac{d^n}{dx^n}(x^n - 1)^n, n = 0,1,2...$

The reccurrance relation satisfies by $P_n(x)$ is

$P'_{n+1}(x) - P'_{n-1}(x) = (2n+1)P_n(x),\ n = 1,2\cdots$

take $n = n + 1$,

$P'_{n+2}(x) - P'_n(x) = (2(n+1)+1)P_{n+1}(x),\ n = 1, 2\cdots$

$\Rightarrow \frac{d}{dx}\left[P_{n+2}(x) - P_n(x)\right] = (2n+3)\ P_{n+1}(x),\ n = 1, 2\ldots$

$\therefore\ \alpha_n = 2n+3.$

Hence option (*d*) is correct.

7. Clearly the number of elements of under 8 in the Permutation group $S_6 = 0$

So, the option (*a*) is correct.

9. We know that

$$x_{n+1} = x_n - \frac{f(x_n)(x_n - x_{n-1})}{f(n_n) - f(n_{n-1})} \quad \ldots(1)$$

Let ξ be the root of $f(n) = 0$, then

$f(\xi) = 0$ and $e_n = \xi - x_n$.

$$\therefore\ \left.\begin{aligned} x_{n+1} &= e_{n+1} + \xi \\ x_n &= e_n + \xi \\ x_{n-1} &= e_{n-1} + \xi \end{aligned}\right\} \quad \ldots(2)$$

$$\therefore\ e_{n+1} = \frac{e_{n-1}f(x_n) - f(x_{n-1})e_n}{f(x_n) - f(x_{n-1})} \quad \ldots(3)$$

By mean value theorem, if a x_n in the interval of x_n and ξ such that

$$f'(x_n) = \frac{f(x_n) - f(\xi)}{x_n - \xi}$$

but since $f(\xi) = 0$, $x_n - \xi = e_n$

$$\therefore\ f'(x_n) = \frac{f(x_n)}{e_n}$$

$$\Rightarrow f(x_n) = e_n f'(x_n) \quad \ldots(4)$$

$$\Rightarrow f(x_{n-1}) = e_{n-1} f'(x_{n-1}) \quad \ldots(5)$$

Therefore from equation 3, we get

$$e_{n+1} = e_n \cdot e_{n-1} \frac{f'(x_n) - f'(x_{n-1})}{f(x_n) - f(x_{n-1})}$$

i.e. $e_{n+1} \propto e_n \cdot e_{n-1}$ ...(6)

By definition, the rate of convergence of secant method is of order *p* if

$$e_n \propto e_{n-1}^p$$

i.e. $e_{n+1} \propto e_n^p$ ...(7)

$$\Rightarrow e_n^p \propto e_{n-1} e_{n-1}$$

$$\Rightarrow e_n \propto e_{n-1}^{\left(\frac{p+1}{p}\right)} \quad \ldots(8)$$

therefore $p = \left(\frac{p+1}{p}\right)$

$\Rightarrow \quad p^2 - p - 1 = 0$

$$\Rightarrow \quad p = \frac{1 \pm \sqrt{5}}{2}$$

but $p > 0$. Hence

$$p = \frac{1+\sqrt{5}}{2}$$

Hence option (*a*) is Correct.

10. The Cauchy problem $uu_x + yu_y = x$ with $u(n, 1) = 2x$, when solved using its characteristic equation with an independent variable *t*, then

$$n = \frac{3}{2}se^t - \frac{1}{2}se^{-t} = \frac{1}{2}s\ \ (3e^t - e^{-t})$$

$$y = e^t$$

$$u = f(s,t) = \frac{3}{2}se^t + \frac{1}{2}se^{-t}$$

$$= \frac{1}{2}s(3e^t + e^{-t})$$

$\therefore$ Option (*a*) is correct.

11. The required Probability = 3/8

$\therefore$ Option (*b*) is Correct.

13. Let $A = \begin{pmatrix} a & 2f & 0 \\ 2f & b & 3f \\ 0 & 3f & c \end{pmatrix}$ where

$a, b, c, f \in \mathbb{R}$ and $f \neq 0$

Here, A is Symmetric matrix, i.e., $A = A^1$

So A is diagonalizable matrix.

We know that, A Square matrix is a diagonalizable $\Leftrightarrow$ Algebraic multiplicity of $\lambda i =$ geometric multiplicity of λi where i = 1, 2, 3,

Since A is diagonalizable matrix, so it has a distinct linear factor.

$$\Rightarrow (x - \lambda 1)^1 (x - \lambda 2)^1 (x - \lambda 3)^1 = 0$$

Hence, by above result, the geometric multiplicity of the largest eigen value of A equals 1

14. Given that,

$$W_1 = \{(x_1, x_2, x_3) \in \mathbb{R}^3 : x_1 = x_2 + 2x_3\}$$

$$W_2 = \{(x_1, x_2, x_3) \in \mathbb{R}^3 : x_1 = 3x_2 + 2x_3\}$$

Let $(x_1, x_2, x_3) \in \mathbb{R}^3$, then

$(x_1, x_2, x_3) = (x_2 + 2x_3, x_2, x_3)$

there is two variables x_2 and x_3

So that, dim $W_1 = 2$

Similarly dim $W_2 = 2$

Now, $W_1 \cap W_2 = \{(x_1, x_2, x_3) \in \mathbb{R}^3 : x_1$

$= x_2 + 2x_3,\ x_1 = 3x_2 + 2x_3\}$

$x_2 + 2x_3 = 3x_2 + 2x_3$

$\Rightarrow x_2 = 0$ and $x_1 = 2x_3$

$(x_1, x_2, x_3) \in \mathbb{R}^3$

then $(x_1, x_2, x_3,) = (2x_3, 0, x_3,)$ there is only one variable

So that, dim $(W_1 \cap W_2) = 1$

We know that,

$\dim(W_1 + W_2) = \dim W_1 + \dim W_2 - \dim(W_1 \cap W_2)$

$= 2 + 2 - 1 = 3$

Hence, $\dim(W_1 + W_2) = 3$

15. Let $B = \{1, x, x^2\}$ is a basis for v.

Let $T : V \to v$ be the linear transformation given by $T(P) = 2P + P^1$, for $P \in V$

$T(1) = 2.1 + 0 = 2.1 + 0.x + 0.x^2$

$T(x) = 2.x + 1 = 1.1 + 2.x + 0.x^2$

$T(x^2) = 2.x^2 + 2x = 0.1 + 2.x + 2.x^2$

$$[T]_B = \begin{bmatrix} 2 & 1 & 0 \\ 0 & 2 & 2 \\ 0 & 0 & 2 \end{bmatrix}$$

$\Rightarrow (\lambda - 2)^3 = 0$

$\Rightarrow \lambda = 2, 2, 2$

Here, the number of nonzero entries in the Jordon Canonical from of a matrix T is 5.

16. $I = [2, 3]$

$\Rightarrow$ $m(I) = 3 - 2 = 1$

$J = \mathbb{Q} \cap [4, 6] \Rightarrow m(J) = 0$

$L = \{7 + x : x \in k\}$,

where k is Constant

$\Rightarrow$ $m(L) = 0$

So, $m(I \cup J \cup L) = m(I) + m(J) + m(L)$

$= 1 + 0 + 0 = 1$

Hence, $m(I \cup J \cup L) = 1$

17. Given that,

$u(x, y, z) = x^2 - 2y + 4z^2$

$$\nabla u = \left(\hat{i}\frac{\partial}{\partial x} + \hat{j}\frac{\partial}{\partial y} + \hat{k}\frac{\partial}{\partial z}\right)(x^2 - 2y + 4z^2)$$

$= 2x\hat{i} - 2\hat{j} + \theta z\hat{k}$

Let $\vec{a} = \frac{3}{5}\hat{i} + 0.\hat{j} - \frac{4}{5}\hat{k}$

$|\vec{a}| = \sqrt{\frac{9}{25} + \frac{16}{25}} = 1$

$\vec{a} = \text{Unit Vector} = \frac{\vec{a}}{|\vec{a}|}$

$= \frac{3}{5}\hat{i} + 0.\hat{j} - \frac{4}{5}\hat{k}$

The directional derivative of u in the direction $\frac{3}{5}\hat{i} - \frac{4}{5}\hat{k}$

$= \nabla u \cdot \hat{a}$

$= (2x\hat{i} - 2\hat{j} + 8z\hat{k}) \cdot \left(\frac{3}{5}\hat{i} + 0\hat{j} - \frac{4}{5}\hat{k}\right)$

$= \frac{6x}{5} + 0 - \frac{8 \times 4z}{5}$

$= \frac{6}{5} \times 5 + 0 - \frac{32}{5} \times 0$

$= 6$

18. We know that, $L\{e^{at}\} = \frac{1}{s - a}$ if $S > a$

given that $L\{y(t)\} = \frac{5}{2(s-1)} - \frac{2}{s-2} + \frac{1}{2(s-3)}$

$\Rightarrow y(t) = L^{-1}\left\{\frac{5}{2(s-1)} - \frac{2}{s-2} + \frac{1}{2(s-3)}\right\}$

$\Rightarrow y(t) = L^{-1}\left\{\frac{5}{2(s-1)}\right\} - L^{-1}\left\{\frac{2}{s-2}\right\} + L^{-1}\left\{\frac{1}{2(s-3)}\right\}$

$\Rightarrow y(t) = \frac{5}{2}e^t - 2e^{2t} + \frac{1}{2}e^{3t}$ ...(*i*)

$y'(t) = \frac{5}{2}e^t - 4e^{2t} + \frac{1}{2} \times 3e^{3t}$

$y'(0) = \frac{5}{2} - 4 + \frac{3}{2} = \frac{8}{2} - 4$

$\Rightarrow y'(0) = 4 - 4 = 0$

from Equation (*i*)

$\Rightarrow y(0) = \frac{5}{2} - 2 + \frac{1}{2} = \frac{6}{2} - 2$

$\Rightarrow y(0) = 3 - 2 = 1$

So, $y(0) + y'(0) = 1 + 0 = 1$

Hence, $y(0) + y'(0) = 1$

19. The given differential equation is

$$\left[(x-1)^2 \sin x\right] y'' + \left[\cos x \sin(x-1)\right] y' + (x-1)y = 0$$

$$\Rightarrow y'' + \frac{\cos x \sin(x-1)}{(x-1)^2 \sin x} y' + \frac{x-1}{(x-1)^2 \sin x} y = 0$$

$$\therefore \; P(x) = \frac{\cos x \sin(x-1)}{(x-1)^2 \sin x}$$

$$Q(x) = \frac{x-1}{(x-1)^2 \sin x}$$

Let $(x-1)^2 \sin x = 0$

$\Rightarrow (x-1)^2 = 0$ or $\sin x = 0$

$\Rightarrow x = 1$ or $x = 0$ $\quad \left(\because 0 \le x \le \frac{\pi}{2}\right)$

Now $\lim_{x\to 0} P(x) = \lim_{x\to 0} \frac{\cos x \sin(x-1)}{(x-1)^2 \sin x}$

$= \infty$

but $\lim_{x\to 0} (x-0) P(x)$

$= \lim_{x\to 0} (x-0) \frac{\cos x \sin(x-1)}{(x-1)^2 \sin x}$

$= \sin(-1) = \text{finite}$

and $\underset{x\to 0}{\text{limit}} (x-0) Q(x)$

$= \lim_{x\to 0} (x-0) \frac{(x-1)}{(x-1)^2 \sin x}$

$= 1 = \text{finite}$

$\therefore \; x = 0$ is a regular singular point

Similarly, we can show that $n = 1$ is a regular singular point.

$\therefore$ Number of regular singular point of given differential equation is 2.

20. Let F be a field with 7^6 elements

$\Rightarrow \quad 0(F) = 7^6$ and

let k be a Subfield of F with 49 elements

$\Rightarrow \quad 0(k) = 49 = 7^2$

F is a vector space over k

$$0(\mathbb{F}) = p^n$$

$\Rightarrow$ Base field $\mathbb{F}_p(\mathbb{Z}_p)$

$\mathbb{F}$ is a vector space over $\mathbb{F}_p$

$$[\mathbb{F} : \mathbb{F}_p] = n$$

Now

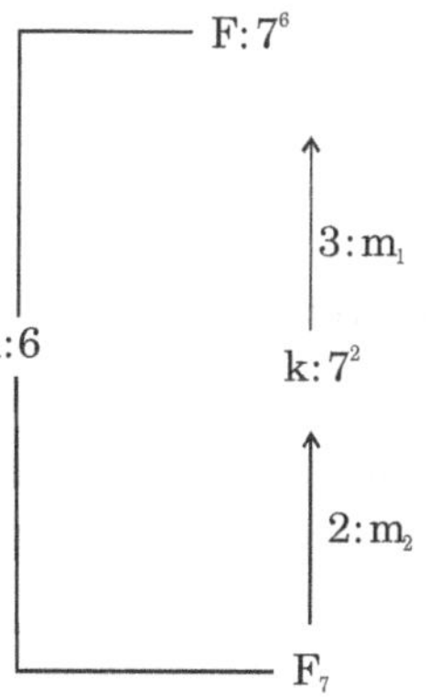

$\Rightarrow n = m_1 m_2$

Then $\dim F = 3$

21. $T : C[0,1] \to C[0,1]$

$$(Tf)(x) = \int_0^1 \sin(x+y) f(y)\,dy, \; x \in [0,1]$$

We know that,

$$\sin(x+y) = \sin x \cos y + \cos x \sin y$$

$$R(T) = \{(Tf)(x) : f \in C[0,1], x \in [0,1]\}$$

$$= \left\{\int_0^1 \sin(x+y) f(y)\,dy : x, y \in [0,1]\right\}$$

$$= \left\{\int_0^1 (\sin x \cos y + \cos x \sin y) f(y)\,dy : x, y \in [0,1]\right\}$$

$$= \left\{\sin x \int_0^1 \cos y\, f(y)\,dy + \cos x \int_0^1 \sin y\, f(y)\,dy : x, y \in [0,1]\right\}$$

$R(T) = \{a \sin x + b \cos x : x \in [0,1]$ where

$$a = \int_0^1 \cos y\, f(y)\,dy$$

$$b = \int_0^1 \sin y\, f(y)\,dy\}$$

$$\Rightarrow \; R(T) = \left\{\begin{matrix} a \sin x + b \cos x : x \in [0,1], \\ a \,\&\, b \text{ are Constant} \end{matrix}\right\}$$

$\Rightarrow \dim R(T) = 2$

22. Given that, $a \in (-1,1)$ if $f(x) = x$

We have, $\int_{-1}^{1} f(x)\,dx \simeq f(-a) + f(a)$

$$\int_{-1}^{1} x\,dx \simeq -a + a$$

$$0 \simeq 0 \text{ (true)}$$

if $f(x) = x^2$, then $\int_{-1}^{1} x^2\,dx \simeq a^2 + a^2$

$$\Rightarrow 2\int_{-1}^{1} x^2 dx \simeq 2a^2$$

$\Rightarrow 2/3 \simeq 2a^2$

$\Rightarrow 1/3 \simeq a^2$

So, $3a^2 = 1$

23. Let X and Y have joint Probability density function given by

$$F_{xy},(x,y) = \begin{cases} 2, 0 \le x \le 1-y, 0 \le y \le 1 \\ 0, \text{otherwise} \end{cases}$$

$F_y(y) = \int_0^{1-y} 2dx = [2x]_0^{1-y}$

$F_y(y) = 2(1-y) - 0$

$F_y(y) = 2(1-y)$

$F_y(1/2) = 2(1-1/2) = 1$

24. Let the Cumulative distribution function of the random variable X be given by

$$F_x(x) = \begin{cases} 0, & x < 0 \\ x, & 0 \le x < 1/2 \\ (1+x)/2, & 1/2 \le x < 1 \\ 1, & x \ge 1 \end{cases}$$

$P[X = 1/2] = F[1/2] - F[1/2^-]$

$= \frac{1}{2}\left(1+\frac{1}{2}\right) - \frac{1}{2}$

$= \frac{1}{2}\left(1 + \frac{1}{2} - 1\right)$

$= \frac{1}{4}$

26. By Cauchy integral Integral theorem,

$$f(Z_0) = \frac{1}{2\pi i}\int \frac{f(Z)dZ}{(Z-Z_0)}$$

$$\int_\Gamma \frac{e^z}{Z^2-2Z} dZ = \int_\Gamma \frac{e^Z/Z}{Z-2} dZ + \int_\Gamma \frac{e^Z/Z-2}{Z} dZ$$

$= 2\pi i f(2) + 2\pi i f(0)$

$= 2\pi i \frac{e^2}{2} + 2\pi i\left(\frac{e^\circ}{0-2}\right)$

$= \pi i e^2 - \pi i$

$= \pi i (e^2 - 1)$

27. Take Z = 1 then Re(Z) = 1, Im (Z) = 0

$\Rightarrow \text{Re}(Z) + \text{Im}(Z) = 1 > 0$

$f(Z) = \frac{Z-1}{Z+i}$

$f(1) = 0$

$\Rightarrow \text{Re}(\omega) = 0, \text{Im}(\omega) = 0$

So, option (*a*), (*b*) & (*c*) are incorrect

Hence, option (*d*) is correct.

28. $\iint_D e^{-(x^2+y^2)} dx\, dy$

$= \int_0^2\int_0^{2\pi} r\, e^{-r^2} dr\, d\theta$

$= \int_0^2 r\, e^{-r^2} 2\pi\, dr$

$= 2\pi\int_0^2 r\, e^{-r^2} dr$

Let $t = r^2 \Rightarrow dt = 2rdr$

$\Rightarrow \quad \frac{dt}{2} = rdr$

$= \frac{2\pi}{2}\int_0^4 e^{-t} dt$

$= -\pi\left[e^{-t}\right]_0^4$

$= -\pi\left[e^{-4} - 1\right]$

$= \pi\left[1 - e^{-4}\right]$

29. We have $P(x) = x^4 + 4$

Let $P(x) = 0$, then

$x^4 + 4 = 0$

$\Rightarrow x^4 = -4$

let $x^2 = t$, then

$t^2 = -4$

$\Rightarrow t = \pm 2i$

Case I : when $t = 2i$, then

$x^2 = 2i$

$\Rightarrow x = \pm\sqrt{2i}$

Case II : When $t = -2i$, then

$x^2 = -2i$

$\Rightarrow x = \pm i\sqrt{2i}$

$\therefore$ roots of $P(x) = x^4 + 4 = 0$ are $\pm 2i, \pm i\sqrt{2i}$

$\therefore P(x) = x^4 + 4$ is irreducible in the ring Q[*x*].

$\therefore$ Option (*b*) is correct.

30. $0(G) = 12 = 2^2 \times 3$

Clearly $2^2 \times 0(G)$

but $\quad 2^{2+1} \times 0(G)$

So, by **Syllow's** theorem (IIIrd)

$1 + 2k/12$ where $k = 0, 1, 2, 3, ...$

if $k = 0$, then 1/12 √

if $k = 1$, then 3/12 √

if $k = 2$, then 5/12 ×

Hence, every group of order 12 has a non trivial Proper normal Subgroup.

31. $|2| \neq 1$, so 2 is not unit

also 2 is not square

Let $\alpha = a + b\sqrt{-p}$ and $\beta = c + d\sqrt{-p}$

take $a = 1, b = -1$ and $p = 5$

So $\alpha = 1 - 1\sqrt{-5} = 1 - i\sqrt{5}$

now taking $c = 1, d = 1, p = 5$

$\beta = 1 + 1\sqrt{-5}$

$\beta = 1 + i\sqrt{5}$

now $\alpha.\beta = (1 - i\sqrt{5})(1 + i\sqrt{5}) = 1 - i^2 \cdot 5$

$= 1 + 5 = 6$

Clearly $2|\alpha \cdot \beta$ but $2|\alpha$ and $2|\beta$

So by the definition of Prime element 2 is not a prime element.

So option (a), (b), (c) are incorrect.

Hence, option (d) is correct.

33. The Partial differential Equation.

$$xu_{xx} + 2x^2u_{xy} = u_x - 1$$

$$\frac{dy}{dx} = \frac{B \pm \sqrt{B^2 - 4AC}}{2A}$$

$$\therefore \quad A = x, B = 2x^2, C = 0$$

$$\frac{dy}{dx} = \frac{2x^2 \pm \sqrt{4x^4}}{2x}$$

$$\Rightarrow \frac{dy}{dx} = x \pm x$$

$$\Rightarrow \frac{dy}{dx} = 2x, \frac{dy}{dx} = 0$$

$y = x^2 + c_1$ and $y = c_2$

Given that, the characteristic curves of the partial differential equation

$$\mu(x, y) = c_1, \upsilon(x, y) = c_2$$

where c_1 and c_2 are constants,

$$y - x^2 = c_1 \Rightarrow \mu(x, y) = x^2 - y$$

$$y = c_2 \Rightarrow \upsilon(x, y) = y$$

Hence option (a) is correct.

34. Let $f : X \to Y$ be a continuous map from a Hausdorff topological Space X to a metric space Y.

P : f is a closed map and

$f^{-1}(y) = \{x \in X : F(x) = y\}$ is compact for each $y \in Y$

Q : $\forall$ Compact Subset $K \subset Y$, $f^{-1}(K)$ is a Compact Subset of X

Clearly P is implies to Q and Q is implies to P

$P \Rightarrow Q$ and $Q \Rightarrow P$

So, that P and Q are equivalent

36. Any two circles are homomorphic to each other

Clearly, $X = \{(x, y) \in \mathbb{R}^2 : x^2 + y^2 = 1\}$ and

$y = \{(x, y) \in \mathbb{R}^2 : x^2 + y^2 \neq 0\}$ are circles

So by the above theorem, option (a) is Correct

39. maximize : $\alpha x_1 + x_2$

Subject to : $2x_1 + x_2 \leq 6$

$-x_1 + x_2 \leq 1$

$x_1 + x_2 \leq 4$

$x_1 \geq 0$, $x_2 \geq 0$

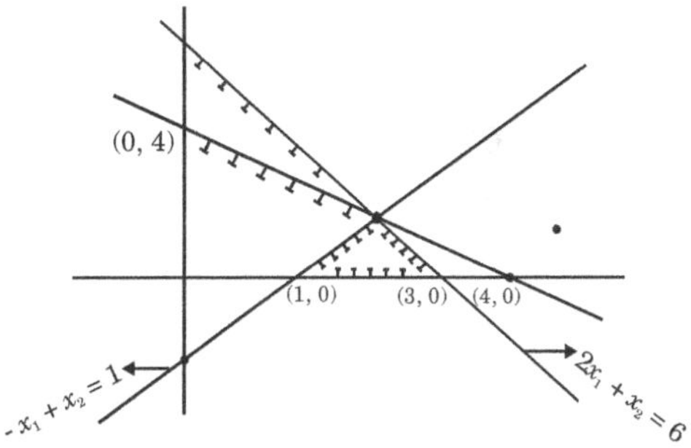

now $\alpha x_1 + x_2 = 3\alpha + 0 = 3\alpha$ is maximum if $\alpha > 2$

So option (d) is correct.

40. Let $M_2(\mathbb{R}) = \begin{pmatrix} a & b \\ c & d \end{pmatrix}_{2\times2}$ where $a, b, c, d \in \mathbb{R}$

Let $B = \left\{\begin{pmatrix} 1 & 0 \\ 0 & 0 \end{pmatrix}, \begin{pmatrix} 0 & 1 \\ 0 & 0 \end{pmatrix}, \begin{pmatrix} 0 & 0 \\ 1 & 0 \end{pmatrix}, \begin{pmatrix} 0 & 0 \\ 0 & 1 \end{pmatrix}\right\}$ is a basis for $M_2(R)$

given that $S : M_2(\mathbb{R}) \to M_2(\mathbb{R})$ by

$S(x) = 2x + x^t$

$$S\begin{pmatrix} 1 & 0 \\ 0 & 0 \end{pmatrix} = \begin{pmatrix} 2 & 0 \\ 0 & 0 \end{pmatrix} + \begin{pmatrix} 1 & 0 \\ 0 & 0 \end{pmatrix} = \begin{pmatrix} 3 & 0 \\ 0 & 0 \end{pmatrix} \quad ...(i)$$

$$S\begin{pmatrix}0&1\\0&0\end{pmatrix}=\begin{pmatrix}0&2\\0&0\end{pmatrix}+\begin{pmatrix}0&0\\1&0\end{pmatrix}=\begin{pmatrix}0&2\\1&0\end{pmatrix} \quad ...(ii)$$

$$S\begin{pmatrix}0&0\\1&0\end{pmatrix}=\begin{pmatrix}0&0\\2&0\end{pmatrix}+\begin{pmatrix}0&1\\0&0\end{pmatrix}=\begin{pmatrix}0&1\\2&0\end{pmatrix} \quad ...(iii)$$

$$S\begin{pmatrix}0&0\\0&1\end{pmatrix}=\begin{pmatrix}0&0\\0&2\end{pmatrix}+\begin{pmatrix}0&0\\0&1\end{pmatrix}=\begin{pmatrix}0&1\\0&3\end{pmatrix} \quad ...(iv)$$

From Equation (*i*)

$$S\begin{pmatrix}1&0\\0&0\end{pmatrix}=\begin{pmatrix}3&0\\0&0\end{pmatrix}$$

$$=3\begin{pmatrix}1&0\\0&0\end{pmatrix}+0\begin{pmatrix}0&1\\0&0\end{pmatrix}+0\begin{pmatrix}0&0\\1&0\end{pmatrix}+0\begin{pmatrix}0&0\\0&1\end{pmatrix}$$

Similarly

$$S\begin{pmatrix}0&1\\0&0\end{pmatrix}=\begin{pmatrix}0&2\\1&0\end{pmatrix}$$

$$=0\begin{pmatrix}1&0\\0&0\end{pmatrix}+2\begin{pmatrix}0&1\\0&0\end{pmatrix}+1\begin{pmatrix}0&0\\1&0\end{pmatrix}+0\begin{pmatrix}0&0\\0&1\end{pmatrix}$$

$$S\begin{pmatrix}0&0\\1&0\end{pmatrix}=\begin{pmatrix}0&1\\2&0\end{pmatrix}$$

$$=0\begin{pmatrix}1&0\\0&0\end{pmatrix}+1\begin{pmatrix}0&1\\0&0\end{pmatrix}+2\begin{pmatrix}0&0\\1&0\end{pmatrix}+0\begin{pmatrix}0&0\\0&1\end{pmatrix}$$

$$S\begin{pmatrix}0&0\\0&1\end{pmatrix}=\begin{pmatrix}0&0\\0&3\end{pmatrix}$$

$$=0\begin{pmatrix}1&0\\0&0\end{pmatrix}+0\begin{pmatrix}0&1\\0&0\end{pmatrix}+0\begin{pmatrix}0&0\\1&0\end{pmatrix}+3\begin{pmatrix}0&0\\0&1\end{pmatrix}$$

$$(S)_B=\begin{pmatrix}3&0&0&0\\0&2&1&0\\0&1&2&0\\0&0&0&3\end{pmatrix}$$

trc(S) = 3 + 2 + 2 + 3 = 10

Hence, trace of S is 10

41. d = dist (x, y)

where $x = (1, 1, 1)$

$y = \text{Span } \{(1,1,0),(0,1,1)\}$

$d = \text{dist}(x, y) = \inf\{\|x-y\| : y \in y\}$

$= \inf\{\|(1,1,1)-(1,1,0)\|, \|(1,1,1)-(0,1,1)\|\}$

$d = \inf\{\|0,0,1\|, \|1,0,0\|\}$

$y \in y \; y = C_1(1,1,0)+C_2(0,1,1)$

$y = (C_1,C_1,0)+(0,C_2,C_2)$

$= \|(1,1,1)-((C_1,C_1,0)+(0,C_2,C_2))\|$

$= \|(1,1,1)-(C_1,C_1+C_2,C_2)\| \qquad C_1,C_2 \in R$

$= \|(1,1,1)\|$

$d = 1/\sqrt{3} \quad d^2 = \frac{1}{3}$

$3d^2 = 1$

42. Let $A = T_9 - 24^T4$

$4 = \frac{1}{3}[1,1,1,1,1,1,1,1,1]$

$$44^T = \frac{1}{3}[1,1,1,1,1,1,1,1,1]\cdot\frac{1}{3}\begin{bmatrix}1\\1\\1\\1\\1\\1\\1\\1\\1\end{bmatrix}$$

$$44^T = \frac{1}{3}\times\frac{1}{3}\times 9 = 1$$

$\Rightarrow 44^T = 1$

$\therefore \quad A = I_9 - 2.1$

$$A=\begin{bmatrix}1&0&0&0&0&0&0&0&0\\0&1&0&0&0&0&0&0&0\\0&0&1&0&0&0&0&0&0\\0&0&0&1&0&0&0&0&0\\0&0&0&0&1&0&0&0&0\\0&0&0&0&0&1&0&0&0\\0&0&0&0&0&0&1&0&0\\0&0&0&0&0&0&0&1&0\\0&0&0&0&0&0&0&0&1\end{bmatrix}-2[1]$$

$$A=\begin{bmatrix}-1&0&0&0&0&0&0&0&0\\0&1&0&0&0&0&0&0&0\\0&0&1&0&0&0&0&0&0\\\cdots&&&&\cdots&&&&\cdots\\0&0&0&0&0&0&0&0&1\end{bmatrix}$$

$\lambda = 1, \; \mu = -1$

$\Rightarrow |\lambda-\mu| = |1-(-1)| = 2$

Hence $|\lambda-\mu| = 2$

44. Let S be the surface of the solid

$V = \{(x,y,z): 0 \le x \le 1, 0 \le y \le 2, 0 \le z \le 3\}$

Let $\vec{F}(x,y,z) = x\hat{i} + y\hat{j} + z\hat{k}$

$$\text{div}\vec{F} = \left(\frac{\partial}{\partial x}\hat{i} + \frac{\partial}{\partial y}\hat{j} + \frac{\partial}{\partial z}\hat{k}\right)\left(x\hat{i} + y\hat{j} + z\hat{k}\right)$$

$= 1 + 1 + 1 = 3$

$$\text{Surface integral} = \iint_S \vec{F}\cdot\hat{n}\,ds = \int \text{div}\vec{F}\,dv$$

$= 3V$

$= 3 \times$ volume of the solid

$= 3 \times 6$

$= 18$

where, V is the volume of the Solid, ie V = 6

46. We have, $y_1 = e^{-x^2}$

$y_1' = -2x \cdot e^{-x^2}$

$y_1'' = -2\left(1 \cdot e^{-x^2} + x \cdot e^{-x^2} \cdot -2x\right)$

$y_1'' = -2\left(e^{-x^2} - 2x^2 e^{-x^2}\right)$

$xy'' + \alpha y' + \beta x^3 = 0$

$-2x\left(e^{-x^2} - 2x^2 e^{-x^2}\right) - 2\alpha x e^{-x^2} + \beta x^3 e^{-x^2} = 0$

$-2x\left(1 - 2x^2\right) - 2\alpha x + \beta x^3 = 0$

$-2x\left(1 + \alpha\right) + x^3\left(4 + \beta\right) = 0$

$1 + \alpha = 0, \quad 4 + \beta = 0$

$\alpha = -1, \quad \beta = -4$

$\Rightarrow \alpha \cdot \beta = 4$

49. Given that,

$p(x) = 2 - (x+1) + x(x+1) - \beta x(x+1)(x-\alpha)$

now $y = 2$ at $x = -1$

$\Rightarrow 2 = 2 - (-1+1) + (-1)(-1+1) - 0$

$\Rightarrow 2 = 2$, True

$y = 1$ at $x = 0$

$1 = 2 - 1 + 0 - 0$

$1 = 1$, True

$y = 2$ at $x = 1$

$2 = 2 - 2 + 2 - 2\beta(1-\alpha)$

$2 = 0 + 2 - 2\beta(1-\alpha)$

$-2\beta(1-\alpha) = 0$

$2\beta(1-\alpha) = 0 \quad \text{....(1)}$

$-7 = 2 - 3 + 2 \times 3 - 2\beta \times 3(2-\alpha)$

$-7 = -1 + 6 - 6\beta(2-\alpha)$

$-7 = 5 - 6\beta(2-\alpha)$

$-12 = -6\beta(2-\alpha)$

$2 = \beta(2-\alpha)$

From equation (1)

$\beta = 0$ or $\alpha = 1$

$\because \beta \neq 0$

So, $\alpha = 1$

$2 = \beta(2-1)$

$\beta = 2$

So, $\alpha + \beta = 1 + 2 = 3$

51. Let $fn(x) = \dfrac{2n\,x^{n-1}}{1+x}$; $x \in [0,1]$

Now $\int_0^1 fn(x)\,dx = \int_0^1 \dfrac{2nx^{n-1}}{1+x}dx$

$$= 2\int_0^1 \frac{d(x^n)}{1+x}dx$$

$$= 2\left[\left(\frac{1}{1+x}\cdot x^n\right)_0^1 + \int_0^1 \frac{1}{(1+x)^2}\cdot x^n\,dx\right]$$

$$= 2\left[\frac{1^n}{1+1} - 0 + \int_0^1 \frac{x^n}{(1+x)^2}dx\right]$$

$$= 2\left[\frac{1}{2} + \int_0^1 \frac{x^n}{(1+x)^2}dx\right]$$

$$= 1 + 2\int_0^1 \frac{x^n}{(1+x)^2}dx$$

$$\Rightarrow \lim_{n\to\infty}\int_0^1 fn(x)\,dx = 1 + 2\lim_{n\to\infty}\int_0^1 \frac{x^n}{(1+x)^2}dx$$

$= 1 + 0$

$= 1$

Since, $\lim_{n\to\infty}\int_0^1 \dfrac{x^n}{(1+x)^2}dx = 0$

Hence, $\lim_{n\to\infty}\int_0^1 fn(x)\,dx = 1$

■■

SOLVED PAPER - 2019

GENERAL APTITUDE

Q. 1 – Q. 5 carry one mark each.

1. The fishermen, _______ the flood victims owed their lives, were rewarded by the government.

(a) whom (b) to which
(c) to whom (d) that

2. Some students were not involved in the strike.

If the above statement is true, which of the following conclusions is/are logically necessary?

1. Some who were involved in the strike were students.
2. No student was involved in the strike.
3. At least one student was involved in the strike.
4. Some who were not involved in the strike were students.

(a) 1 and 2 (b) 3
(c) 4 (d) 2 and 3

3. The radius as well as the height of a circular cone increases by 10%. The percentage increase in its volume is ______.

(a) 17.1 (b) 21.0
(c) 33.1 (d) 72.8

4. Five numbers 10, 7, 5, 4 and 2 are to be arranged in a sequence from left to right following the directions given below:

1. No two odd or even numbers are next to each other.
2. The second number from the left is exactly half of the left-most number.
3. The middle number is exactly twice the right-most number.

Which is the second number from the right?

(a) 2 (b) 4
(c) 7 (d) 10

5. Until Iran came along, India had never been ______________ in kabaddi.

(a) defeated (b) defeating
(c) defeat (d) defeatist

Q. 6 – Q. 10 carry two marks each.

6. Since the last one year, after a 125 basis point reduction in repo rate by the Reserve Bank of India, banking institutions have been making a demand to reduce interest rates on small saving schemes. Finally, the government announced yesterday a reduction in interest rates on small saving schemes to bring them on par with fixed deposit interest rates.

Which one of the following statements can be inferred from the given passage?

(a) Whenever the Reserve Bank of India reduces the repo rate, the interest rates on small saving schemes are also reduced
(b) Interest rates on small saving schemes are always maintained on par with fixed deposit interest rates
(c) The government sometimes takes into consideration the demands of banking institutions before reducing the interest rates on small saving schemes
(d) A reduction in interest rates on small saving schemes follow only after a reduction in repo rate by the Reserve Bank of India

7. In a country of 1400 million population, 70% own mobile phones. Among the mobile phone owners, only 294 million access the Internet. Among these Internet users, only half buy goods from e-commerce portals. What is the percentage of these buyers in the country?

(a) 10.50 (b) 14.70
(c) 15.00 (d) 50.00

8. The nomenclature of Hindustani music has changed over the centuries. Since the medieval period dhrupad styles were identified as baanis. Terms like gayaki and baaj were used to refer to vocal and instrumental styles, respectively. With the institutionalization of music education the term gharana became acceptable. Gharana originally referred to hereditary musicians from a particular lineage, including disciples and grand disciples.

Which one of the following pairings is NOT correct?

(a) dhrupad, baani (b) gayaki, vocal
(c) baaj, institution (d) gharana, lineage

9. Two trains started at 7AM from the same point. The first train travelled north at a speed of 80km/h and the second train travelled south at a speed of 100 km/h. The time at which they were 540 km apart is ______ AM.

(a) 9 (b) 10
(c) 11 (d) 11.30

10. "I read somewhere that in ancient times the prestige of a kingdom depended upon the number of taxes that it was able to levy on its people. It was very much like the prestige of a head- hunter in his own community."

Based on the paragraph above, the prestige of a head-hunter depended upon ________

(a) the prestige of the kingdom

(b) the prestige of the heads

(c) the number of taxes he could levy

(d) the number of heads he could gather

MATHEMATICS

Q. 1 – Q. 25 carry one mark each.

1. For a balanced transportation problem with three sources and three destinations where costs, availabilities and demands are all finite and positive, which one of the following statements is FALSE?

(a) The transportation problem does not have unbounded solution

(b) The number of non-basic variables of the transportation problem is 4

(c) The dual variables of the transportation problem are unrestricted in sign

(d) The transportation problem has at most 5 basic feasible solutions

2. Let $f:[a,b]\to\mathbb{R}$ (the set of all real numbers) be any function which is twice differentiable in (a, b) with only one root a in (a,b). Let f' (x) and f'' (x) denote the first and second order derivatives of f(x) with respect to x . If a is a simple root and is computed by the Newton-Raphson method, then the method converges if

(a) $|f(x)f''(x)|<|f'(x)^2|$, for all $x\in(a,b)$

(b) $|f(x)f'(x)|<|f''(x)|$, for all $x\in(a,b)$

(c) $|f'(x)f''(x)|<|f(x)^2|$, for all $x\in(a,b)$

(d) $|f(x)f''(x)|<|f'(x)|$, for all $x\in(a,b)$

3. Let $f:\mathbb{C}\to\mathbb{C}$ (the set of all complex numbers) be defined by

$$f(x+iy)=x^3+3xy^2+i\left(y^3+3x^2y\right),\ i=\sqrt{-1}$$

Let f'(z) denote the derivative of f with respect to z. Then which one of the following statements is TRUE?

(a) f'(1 + i) exists and $|f'(1+i)|=3\sqrt{5}$

(b) f is analytic at the origin

(c) f is not differentiable at i

(d) f is differentiable at 1

4. The partial differential equation

$$\left(x^2+y^2-1\right)\frac{\partial^2u}{\partial x^2}+2\frac{\partial^2u}{\partial x\partial y}+\left(x^2+y^2-1\right)\frac{\partial^2u}{\partial y^2}=0$$

is

(a) parabolic in the region $x^2 + y^2 > 2$

(b) hyperbolic in the region $x^2 + y^2 > 2$

(c) elliptic in the region $0 < x^2 + y^2 < 2$

(d) hyperbolic in the region $0 < x^2 + y^2 < 2$

5. If $u_n=\int_1^n e^{-t^2}\,dt,\ n=1,2,3,\ldots,$

then which one of the following statements is TRUE?

(a) Both the sequence $\{u_n\}_{n=1}^{\infty}$ and the series $\sum_{n=1}^{\infty}u_n$ are convergent

(b) Both the sequence $\{u_n\}_{n=1}^{\infty}$ and the series $\sum_{n=1}^{\infty}u_n$ are divergent

(c) The sequence $\{u_n\}_{n=1}^{\infty}$ is convergent but the series $\sum_{n=1}^{\infty}u_n$ is divergent

(d) $\lim_{n\to\infty}u_n=\frac{2}{e}$

6. Let

$$\Gamma=\{(x,y,z)\in\mathbb{R}^3:-1<x<1,-1<y<1,-1<z<1\}$$

and $\phi:\Gamma\to\mathbb{R}$ be a function whose all second order partial derivatives exist and are continuous. If ϕ satisfies the Laplace equation $\Delta^2\phi=0$ for all $(x, y, z)\in\Gamma$, then which one of the following statements is TRUE in Γ?

($\mathbb{R}$ is the set of all real numbers, and $\mathbb{R}^3=\{(x,y,z):x,y,z\in\mathbb{R}\}$

(a) $\vec{\Delta}\phi$ is solenoidal but not irrotational

(b) $\vec{\Delta}\phi$ is irrotational but not solenoidal

(c) $\vec{\Delta}\phi$ is both solenoidal and irrotational

(d) $\vec{\Delta}\phi$ is neither solenoidal nor irrotational

7. Let $X = \{(x_1, x_2, ...) : X = \{x_i \in \mathbb{R}\}$ and only finitely many x_i's are non-zero} and $d : X \times X \to \mathbb{R}$ be a metric on X defined by

$$d(x,y) = \sup_{i \in \mathbb{N}} |x_i - y_i|$$

for = $(x_1, x_2, ...)$, y = $(y_1, y_2, ...)$ in X.

($\mathbb{R}$ is the set of all real numbers and $\mathbb{N}$ is the set of all natural numbers)

Consider the following statements:

P : (X, d) is a complete metric space.

Q : The set $\{x \le X : d(\underline{0}, x) \le 1\}$ is compact, where $\underline{0}$ is the zero element of X.

Which of the above statements is/are TRUE?

(a) Both P and Q (b) P only

(c) Q only (d) Neither P nor Q

8. Consider the following statements:

I. The set $\mathbb{Q} \times \mathbb{Z}$ is uncountable.

II. The set {f : f is a function from $\mathbb{N}$ to {0, 1}} is uncountable.

III. The set $\{\sqrt{p} : p$ is a prime number} is uncountable.

IV. For any infinite set, there exists a bijection from the set to one of its proper subsets.

($\mathbb{Q}$ is the set of all rational numbers, $\mathbb{Z}$ is the set of all integers and $\mathbb{N}$ is the set of all natural numbers)

Which of the above statements are TRUE?

(a) I and IV only (b) II and IV only

(c) II and III only (d) I, II and IV only

9. Let $f : \mathbb{R}^2 \to \mathbb{R}$ be defined by

f(x, y) = x6 – $2x^2y - x^4y + 2y^2$.

($\mathbb{R}$ is the set of all real numbers and $\mathbb{R}^2 = \{(x,y) : x, y \in \mathbb{R}\}$)

Which one of the following statements is TRUE?

(a) f has a local maximum at origin

(b) f has a local minimum at origin

(c) f has a saddle point at origin

(d) The origin is not a critical point of f

10. Let $\{a_n\}_{n=0}^{\infty}$ be any sequence of real numbers such that $\sum_{n=0}^{\infty} |a_n|^2 < \infty$. If the radius of convergence of $\sum_{n=0}^{\infty} a_n x^n$ of r, then which one of the following statements is necessarily TRUE?

(a) $r \ge 1$ or r is infinite (b) $r < 1$

(c) $r = \left(\sum_{n=0}^{\infty} |a_n|^2\right)^{\frac{1}{2}}$ (d) $r = \sum_{n=0}^{\infty} |a_n|^2$

11. Let T_1 be the co-countable topology on $\mathbb{R}$ (the set of real numbers) and T_2 be the co-finite topology on $\mathbb{R}$.

Consider the following statements:

I. In $(\mathbb{R}, T_1)$, the sequence $\left\{\frac{1}{n}\right\}_{n=1}^{\infty}$ converges to 0.

II. In $(\mathbb{R}, T_2)$, the sequence $\left\{\frac{1}{n}\right\}_{n=1}^{\infty}$ converges to 0.

III. In $(\mathbb{R}, T_1)$, there is no sequence of rational numbers which converges to $\sqrt{3}$.

IV. In $(\mathbb{R}, T_2)$, there is no sequence of rational numbers which converges to $\sqrt{3}$.

Which of the above statements are TRUE?

(a) I and II only (b) II and III only

(c) III and IV only (d) I and IV only

12. Let X and Y be normed linear spaces, and let T : X → Y be any bijective linear map with closed graph. Then which one of the following statements is TRUE?

(a) The graph of T is equal to X × Y

(b) T^{-1} is continuous

(c) The graph of T^{-1} is closed

(d) T is continuous

13. Let $g : \mathbb{R}^2 \to \mathbb{R}^2$ be a function defined by

$g(x, y) = (e^x \cos y, e^x \sin y)$ and $(a, b) = g\left(1, \frac{\pi}{3}\right)$.

($\mathbb{R}$ is is the set of all real number and $\mathbb{R}^2$ = $\{(x, y) : x, y \in \mathbb{R}\}$

Which one of the following statements is TRUE?

(a) g is injective

(b) If h is the continuous inverse of g, defined in some neighbourhood of $(a, b) \in \mathbb{R}^2$, such that $h(a, b) = \left(1, \frac{\pi}{3}\right)$, then the Jacobian of h at (a, b) is e^2.

(c) If h is the continuous inverse of g, defined in some neighbourhood of $(a, b) \in \mathbb{R}^2$, such that $h(a, b) = \left(1, \frac{\pi}{3}\right)$, then the Jacobian of h at (a, b) is e^{-2}.

(d) g is surjective

14. Let $u_n = \frac{n!}{1.3.5...(2n-1)}, n \in \mathbb{N}$ (the set of all natural numbers). Then $\lim_{x\to\infty} u_n$ is equal to ____.

15. If the differential equation

$$\frac{dy}{dx} = \sqrt{x^2 + y^2}, y(1) = 2$$

is solved using the Euler's method with step-size $h = 0.1$, then $y(1.2)$ is equal to _____ (round off to 2 places of decimal).

16. Let f be any polynomial function of degree at most 2 over $\mathbb{R}$ (the set of all real numbers). If the constants a and b are such that

$\frac{df}{dx} = af(x) + 2f(x+1) + bf(x+2)$, all $x \in \mathbb{R}$, then $4a + 3b$ is equal to _____ (round off to 2 places of decimal).

17. Let L denote the value of the line integral

$$\oint_c (3x - 4x^2y)\,dx + (4xy^2 + 2y)dy,$$

where C, a circle of radius 2 with centre at origin of the xy-plane, is traversed once in the anti-clockwise direction.

Then $\frac{L}{\pi}$ is equal to ______.

18. The temperature $T: \frac{\mathbb{R}^2}{\{(0,0,0)\}} \to \mathbb{R}$ at any point P(x, y, z) is inversely proportional to the square of the distance of P from the origin. If the value of the temperature T at the point R(0, 0, 1) is $\sqrt{3}$, then the rate of change of T at the point Q(1, 1, 2) in the direction of $\overline{QR}$ is equal to ______ (round off to 2 places of decimal).

($\mathbb{R}$ is the set of all real numbers, $\mathbb{R}^2\{(x,y,z): x,y,z \in \mathbb{R}\}$ and $\frac{\mathbb{R}^3}{\{(0,0,0)\}}$ denotes $\mathbb{R}^3$ excluding the origin)

19. Let f be a continuous function defined on [0, 2] such that $f(x) \geq 0$ for all $x \in [0,2]$. If the area bounded by y = f(x), x = 0, y = 0 and x = b is $\sqrt{3+b^2} - \sqrt{3}$, where $b \in (0, 2]$, then f(1) is equal to ______ (round off to 1 place of decimal).

20. If the characteristic polynomial and minimal polynomial of a square matrix A are $(\lambda-1)(\lambda+1)^4(\lambda-2)^5$ and $(\lambda-1)(\lambda+1)(\lambda-2)$, respectively, then the rank of the matrix A + I is ______, where I is the identity matrix of appropriate order.

21. Let ω be a primitive complex cube root of unity and $i = \sqrt{-1}$. Then the degree of the field extension $\mathbb{Q}(i, \sqrt{3}\,\omega)$ over $\mathbb{Q}$ (the field of rational numbers) is ______.

22. Let $\alpha = \int_C \frac{e^{i\pi z}\,dz}{2z^2 - 5z + 2}$,

$C: \cos t + i\sin t, 0 \leq t \leq 2\pi, i = \sqrt{-1}$

Then the greatest integer less than or equal to $|\alpha|$ is ______.

23. Consider the system:

$3x_1 + x_2 + 2x_3 - x_4 = a,$

$x_1 + x_2 + x_3 - 2x_4 = 3,$

$x_1, x_2, x_3, x_4 \geq 0.$

If $x_1 = 1$, $x_2 = b$, $x_3 = 0$, $x_4 = c$ is a basic feasible solution of the above system (where a, b and c are real constants), then a + b + c is equal to ______.

24. Let $f: \mathbb{C} \to \mathbb{C}$ be a function defined by $f(z) = z^6 - 5z^4 + 10$. Then the number of zeros of f in $\{z \in \mathbb{C}: |z| < 2\}$ is ______.

($\mathbb{C}$ is the set of all complex numbers)

25. Let $\ell = \left\{x = (x_1, x_2, ...): x_i \in \mathbb{C}, \sum_{i=1}^{\infty} |x_i|^2 < \infty\right\}$

be a normed linear space with the norm

$$\|x\|_2 = \left(\sum_{i=1}^{\infty} |x_i|^2\right)^{\frac{1}{2}}.$$

Let $g: \ell \to \mathbb{C}$ be the bounded linear functional defined by

$$g(x) = \sum_{n=1}^{\infty} \frac{x_n}{3^n} \text{ for all } x = (x_1, x_2, ...) \in \ell^2.$$

Then $\left(\sup\{|g(x)|: \|x\|_2 \leq 1\}^2\right)$ is equal to _____ (round off to 3 places of decimal).

($\mathbb{C}$ is the set of all complex numbers).

Q. 26 – Q. 55 carry two marks each.

26. For the linear programming problem (LPP):

Maximize $Z = 2x_1 + |4x_2$.

subject to $-x_1 + 2x_2 \leq 4$,

$3x_1 + \beta x_2 \leq 6$,

$3x_1 + \beta x_2 \leq 6$,

$x_1, x_2 \geq 0, \beta \in \mathbb{R}$,

($\mathbb{R}$ is the set of all real numbers)

Consider the following statements :

I. The LPP always has a finite optimal value for any $\beta \ge 0$.

II. The dual of the LPP may be infeasible for some $\beta \ge 0$.

III. If for some β, the point (1,2) is feasible to the dual of the LPP, then for any $Z \le 16$, feasible solution (x_1, x_2) of the LPP.

IV. If for some β, x_1 and x_2 are the basic variables in the optimal table of the LPP with $x_1 = \frac{1}{2}$, then the optimal value of dual of the LPP is 10.

Then which of the above statements are TRUE?

(a) I and III only (b) I, III and IV only

(c) III and IV only (d) II and IV only

27. Let $f : \mathbb{R}^2 \to \mathbb{R}$ be defined by

$$f(x,y)\begin{cases}(x^2+y^2)\sin\left(\dfrac{1}{x^2+y^2}\right), & \text{if } (x,y) \ne (0,0)\\ 0, & \text{if } (x,y) = (0,0)\end{cases}$$

Consider the following statements :

I. The partial derivatives $\frac{\partial f}{\partial x}, \frac{\partial f}{\partial y}$ exist at (0, 0) but are unbounded in any neighbourhood of (0, 0)

II. f is continuous but not differentiable at (0, 0).

III. f is not continuous at (0, 0).

IV. f is differentiable at (0, 0).

($\mathbb{R}$ is the set of all real number and $\mathbb{R}^2 = \{(x,y) : x, y \in \mathbb{R}\}$)

Which of the above statements is/are TRUE?

(a) I and II only (b) I and IV only

(c) IV only (d) III only

28. Let $K = [k_{ij}]_{i,j-1}^{\infty}$ be an infinite matrix over $\mathbb{C}$ (the set of all complex numbers) such that

(i) for each $i \in \mathbb{N}$ (the set of all natural numbers), the ith row $(k_{i.1}, k_{1.2}, \ldots)$ of K is in ℓ^{∞} and

(ii) for every $x = (x_1, x_{2,\ldots}) \in \ell^1$, $\sum_{j=1}^{\infty} k_{i.j}\, x_j$ is summable for all $i \in \mathbb{N}$, and $(y_1, y_2, \ldots) \in \ell^1$, where $y_i = \sum_{j=1}^{\infty} k_{i.j} x_j$.

Let the set of all rows of K be denoted by E. Consider the following statements:

P : E is a bounded set in ℓ^{∞}.

Q : E is a dense set in ℓ^{∞}.

$$\left(\ell^{\infty} = \left\{(x_1, x_2, \ldots) : x_i \in \mathbb{C}, \sum_{i=1}^{\infty}|x_i| < \infty\right\}\right)$$

$$\left(\ell^{\infty} = \left\{(x_1, x_2, \ldots) : x_i \in \mathbb{C}, \sup_{i\in\mathbb{N}}|x_i| < \infty\right\}\right)$$

Which of the above statements is/are TRUE?

(a) Both P and Q (b) P only

(c) Q only (d) Neither P nor Q

29. Consider the following heat conduction problem for a finite rod

$$\frac{\partial u}{\partial t} = \frac{\partial^2 u}{\partial x^2} - xe^t - 2t,\ t > 0,\ 0 < x < \pi$$

with the boundary conditions $u(0, t) = -t^2$, $u(p, t) = -t^2$, $t > 0$ and the initial condition $u(x, 0) = \sin x - \sin^3 x - x$, $0 \le x \le \pi$. If $v(x, t) = u(x, t) + xe^t + t^2$, then which one of the following is CORRECT?

(a) $v(x,t) = \frac{1}{4}(e^{-1}\sin x + e^{-9t}\sin 3x)$

(b) $v(x,t) = \frac{1}{4}(7e^{-1}\sin x + e^{-9t}\sin 3x)$

(c) $v(x,t) = \frac{1}{4}(e^{-1}\sin x + e^{-3t}\sin 3x)$

(d) $v(x,t) = \frac{1}{4}(3e^{-1}\sin x - e^{-3t}\sin 3x)$

30. Let $f : \mathbb{C} \to \mathbb{C}$ be non-zero and analytic at all points in $\mathbb{Z}$.

If $F(z) = \pi f(z)\cot(\pi z)$ for $z \in \frac{\mathbb{C}}{\mathbb{Z}}$, then the residue of F at $n \in \mathbb{Z}$ is ______.

($\mathbb{C}$ s the set of all complex numbers, $\mathbb{Z}$ is the set of all integers and $\frac{\mathbb{C}}{\mathbb{Z}}$ denotes the set of all complex numbers excluding integers)

(a) $\pi f(n)$ (b) $f(n)$

(c) $\frac{f(n)}{\pi}$ (d) $\left(\frac{df}{dz}\right)_{z=n}$

31. Let the general integral of the partial differential equation

$$(2x-1)\frac{\partial z}{\partial x} + (z - 2x^2)\frac{\partial z}{\partial y} = 2(x - yz)$$

be given by $F(u, v) = 0$ where $F : \mathbb{R}^2 \to \mathbb{R}$ is a continuously differentiable function.

($\mathbb{R}$ is the set of all real numbers and $\mathbb{R}^2 = \{(x,y) : x,y \in \mathbb{R}\}$)

Then which one of the following is TRUE?

(a) $u = x^2 + y^2 + z,\ v = xz + y$

(b) $u = x^2 + y^2 - z,\ v = xz - y$

(c) $u = x^2 - y^2 + z,\ v = yz + x$

(d) $u = x^2 + y^2 - z,\ v = yz - x$

32. Consider the following statements:

I. If $\mathbb{Q}$ denotes the additive group of rational numbers and $f : \mathbb{Q} \to \mathbb{Q}$ is a non-trivial homomorphism, then f is an isomorphism.

II. Any quotient group of a cyclic group is cyclic.

III. If every subgroup of a group G is a normal subgroup, then G is abelian.

IV. Every group of order 33 is cyclic.

Which of the above statements are TRUE?

(a) II and IV only (b) II and III only

(c) I, II and IV only (d) I, III and IV only

33. A solution of the Dirichlet problem

$\nabla^2 u(r,\theta) = 0,\ 0 < r < 1,\ -\pi \le \theta \le \pi,$

$u(1,\theta) = |\theta|,\ -\pi \le \theta \le \pi,$

is given by

(a) $u(r,\theta) = \frac{\pi}{2}\sum_{n=1}^{\infty}\left[\frac{(-1)^n - 1}{n^2}\right] r^n \cos(n\theta)$

(b) $u(r,\theta) = \frac{2}{\pi}\sum_{n=1}^{\infty}\left[\frac{(-1)^{n+1}}{n^2}\right] r^n \cos(n\theta)$

(c) $u(r,\theta) = \frac{\pi}{2} + \frac{2}{\pi}\sum_{n=1}^{\infty}\left[\frac{(-1)^n - 1}{n^2}\right] r^n \cos(n\theta)$

(d) $u(r,\theta) = \frac{\pi}{2} - \frac{2}{\pi}\sum_{n=1}^{\infty}\left[\frac{(-1)^n + 1}{n^2}\right] r^n \cos(n\theta)$

34. Consider the subspace $Y = \{(x,x) : x \in \mathbb{C}\}$ of the normed linear space $(\mathbb{C}^2, \|\ \|_\infty)$.

If ϕ is a bounded linear function on Y, defined by $\phi(x, x)$ then which one of the following sets is equal to $\{\psi(1, 0) : \psi$ is a norm preserving extension of ϕ to $(\mathbb{C}^2, \|\ \|_\infty)$.$\}$

($\mathbb{C}$ is the set of all complex numbers,

$$\mathbb{C}^2 = \{(x,y) : x, y \in \mathbb{C}\}$$

and $\|(x_1, x_2)\|_\infty = \sup\{|x_1|, |x_2|\}$)

(a) $\{1\}$ (b) $\left[\frac{1}{2}, \frac{3}{2}\right]$

(c) $[1, \infty)$ (d) $[0, 1]$

35. Consider the following statements:

I. The ring $\mathbb{Z}[\sqrt{-1}]$ is a unique factorization domain.

II. The ring $\mathbb{Z}[\sqrt{-1}]$ is a principal ideal domain.

III In the polynomial ring $\mathbb{Z}_2[x]$, the ideal generated by $x^3 + x + 1$ is a maximal ideal.

IV. In the polynomial ring $\mathbb{Z}_3[x]$, the ideal generated by $x^6 + 1$ is a prime ideal.

($\mathbb{Z}$ denotes the set of all integers, $\mathbb{Z}_n$ denotes the set of all integers modulo n, for any positive integer n

Which of the above statements are TRUE?

(a) I, II and III only (b) I and III only

(c) I, II and IV only (d) II and III only

36. Let M be a 3 × 3 real symmetric matrix with eigenvalues 0, 2 and a with the respective eigenvectors $u = (4, b, c)^T$, $v = (-1, 2, 0)^T$ and $w = (1, 1, 1)^T$.

Consider the following statements:

I. $a + b - c = 10$

II. The vector $x = \left(0, \frac{3}{2}, \frac{1}{2}\right)^T$ satisfies $Mx = v + w$.

III. For any $d \propto$ span {u, v, w}, $Mx = d$ has a solution.

IV. The trace of the matrix $M^2 + 2M$ is 8.

(y^T denotes the transpose of the vector y)

Which of the above statements are TRUE?

(a) I, II and III only (b) I and II only

(c) II and IV only (d) III and IV only

37. Consider the region

$$\Omega = \left\{x + it : 1 \le x \le 2, \frac{-\pi}{3} \le y \le \frac{\pi}{3}\right\},\ i = \sqrt{-1}$$

in the complex plane. The transformation $x + iu \to e^{x+iy}$ maps the Ω onto the region $S \subset \mathbb{C}$ (the set of all complex numbers). Then the area of the region S is equal to

(a) $\frac{\pi}{3}(e^4 - e^2)$ (b) $\frac{\pi}{4}(e^4 + e^2)$

(c) $\frac{2\pi}{3}(e^4 - e^2)$ (d) $\frac{\pi}{6}(e^4 - e^2)$

38. Consider the sequence $\{g_n\}_{n=1}^{\infty}$ of functions, where $g_n(x) = \frac{x}{1 + nx^2}$, $x \in \mathbb{R}, n \in \mathbb{N}$ and $g'_n(x)$ is the derivative of $g_n(x)$ with respect to x.

($\mathbb{R}$ is the set of all real numbers, $\mathbb{N}$ is the set of all natural numbers).

Then which one of the following statements is TRUE?

(a) $\{g'_n\}_{n=1}^{\infty}$ does NOT converge uniformly on $\mathbb{R}$

(b) $\{g'_n\}_{n=1}^{\infty}$ converges uniformly on any closed interval which does NOT contain 1

(c) $\{g'_n\}_{n=1}^{\infty}$ converges point-wise to a continuous function on $\mathbb{R}$

(d) $\{g'_n\}_{n=1}^{\infty}$ converges uniformly on any closed interval which does NOT contain 0

39. Consider the boundary value problem (BVP)

$$\frac{d^2y}{dx^2} + a\,y(x) = 0, a \in \mathbb{R}$$

(the set of all real numbers),

with the boundary conditions $y(0) = 0$, $y(\pi) = k$ (k is a non-zero real number).

Then which one of the following statements is TRUE?

(a) For a = 1, the BVP has infinitely many solutions

(b) For a = 1, the BVP has a unique solution

(c) For a = 1, k < 0, the BVP has a solution y(x) such that y(x) > 0 for all $x \in (0, \pi)$

(d) For a = 1, k > 0, the BVP has a solution y(x) such that y(x) > 0 for all $x \in (0, \pi)$

40. Consider the ordered square I_0^2, the set $[0, 1] \times [0, 1]$ with the dictionary order topology. Let the general element of I_0^2, be denoted by $x \times y$, where $x, y \in [0, 1]$. Then the closure of the subset

$$S = \left\{x \times \frac{3}{4} : 0 < a < x < b < 1\right\} \text{ in } I_0^2 \text{ is}$$

(a) $S \cup ((a, b] \times \{0\} \cup [a, b) \times \{1\})$

(b) $S \cup ([a, b) \times \{0\} \cup (a, b] \times \{1\})$

(c) $S \cup ((a, b) \times \{0\} \cup (a, b) \times \{1\})$

(d) $S \cup ((a, b] \times \{0\})$

41. Let P_2 be the vector space of all polynomials of degree at most 2 over $\mathbb{R}$ (the set of real numbers). Let a linear transformation $T : P_2 \to P_2$ be defined by, $T(a + bx + cx^2) = (a + b) + (b - c)x + (a + c)x^2$.

Consider the following statements:

I. The null space of T is $\{a(-1 + x + x^2) : a \in \mathbb{R}\}$.

II. The range space of T is spanned by the set $\{1 + x^2, 1 + x\}$.

III. $T(T(1 + x)) = 1 + x^2$.

IV. If M is the matrix representation of T with respect to the standard basis $\{1, x, x^2\}$ of P_2, then the trace of the matrix M is 3.

Which of the above statements are TRUE?

(a) I and II only (b) I, III and IV only

(c) I, II and IV only (d) II and IV only

42. Let T_1 and T_2 be two topologies defined on $\mathbb{N}$ (the set of all natural numbers), where T_1 is the topology generated by $B = \{\{2n-1, 2n\} : n \in \mathbb{N}\}$ T_2 is the discrete topology on $\mathbb{N}$. Consider the following statements :

I. In $(\mathbb{N}, T_1)$, every infinite subset has a limit point.

II. The function $f : (\mathbb{N}, T_1) \to (\mathbb{N}, T_2)$ defined by

$$f(n) = \begin{cases} \frac{n}{2}, & \text{if n is even} \\ \frac{n+1}{2}, & \text{if n is odd} \end{cases}$$

is a continuous function.

Which of the above statements is/are TRUE?

(a) Both I and II (b) I only

(c) II only (d) Neither I nor II

43. Let $1 \le p < q < \infty$. Consider the following statements:

I. $\ell^p \subset \ell^q$

II. $L^p(0, 1) \subset L^q[0, 1]$,

where $\ell^p = \left\{(x_1, x_2, ...) : x_i \in \mathbb{R}, \sum_{i=1}^{\infty} |x_i|^p < \infty\right\}$

and $L^p[0, 1] =$

$$\left\{\begin{matrix} f : [0,1] \to \mathbb{R} : f \text{ is } \mu - \text{measurable}, \int_{[0,1]} |f|^p d\mu < \infty, \\ \text{where } \mu \text{ is the Lebesgue measure} \end{matrix}\right\}$$

($\mathbb{R}$ is the set of all real numbers)

Which of the above statements is/are TRUE?

(a) Both I and I (b) I only

(c) II only (d) Neither I nor II

44. Consider the differential equation

$$t\frac{d^2y}{dt^2} + 2\frac{dy}{dt} + ty = 0, t < 0,$$

$$y(0+) = 1, \left(\frac{dy}{dt}\right)_{t=0+} = 0$$

If Y(s) is the Laplace transform of y(t), then the value of (1) Y is _____ (round off to 2 places of decimal).

(Here, the inverse trigonometric functions assume principal values only)

45. Let R be the region in the xy-plane bounded by the curves $y = x^2$, $y = 4x^2$, $xy = 1$ and $xy = 5$.

Then the value of the integral $\iint_R \frac{y^2}{x}\, dy\, dx$ is equal to _______.

46. Let V be the vector space of all 3 × 3 matrices with complex entries over the real field. If

$W_1 = \{A \in V : A = \overline{A}^T\}$ and

$W_2 = \{A \in V : \text{trace of } A = 0\}$

then the dimension of $W_1 + W_2$ is equal to ______.

($\overline{A}^T$ denotes the conjugate transpose of A)

47. The number of elements of order 15 in the additive group $\mathbb{Z}_{60} \times \mathbb{Z}_{50}$ is ______.

($\mathbb{Z}_n$ denotes the group of integers modulo n, under the operation of addition modulo n, for any positive integer n)

48. Consider the following cost matrix of assigning four jobs to four persons:

Persons Jobs

	J_1	J_2	J_3	J_4
P_1	5	8	6	10
P_2	2	5	4	8
P_3	6	7	6	9
P_4	6	9	8	10

Then the minimum cost of the assignment problem subject to the constraint that job J_4 is assigned to person P_2, is _____ .

49. Let $y : [-1,1] \to \mathbb{R}$ with $y(1) = 1$ satisfy the Legendre differential equation

$$(1-x^2)\frac{d^2y}{dx^2} - 2x\frac{dy}{dx} + 6y = 0 \text{ for } |x| < 1$$

Then the value of $\int_{-1}^{1} y(x)(x+x^2)\, dx$ is equal to _____ (round off to 2 places of decimal).

50. Let $\mathbb{Z}_{125}$ be the ring of integers modulo 125 under the operations of addition modulo 125 and multiplication modulo 125. If m is the number of maximal ideals of $\mathbb{Z}_{125}$ and n is the number of non-units of $\mathbb{Z}_{125}$, then m + n is equal to _____.

51. The maximum value of the error term of the composite Trapezoidal rule when it is used to evaluate the definite integral

$$\int_{0.2}^{1.4} (\sin x - \log_e x)\, dx$$

with 12 sub-intervals of equal length, is equal to _____ (round off to 3 places of decimal).

52. By the Simplex method, the optimal table of the linear programming problem:

Maximize $Z = a x_1 + 3x_2$.

subject to $\beta x_1 + x_2 + x_3 = 8$,

$2x_1 + x_2 + x_4 = \gamma$,

$x_1, x_2, x_3, x_5 \geq 0$,

where α, β, γ are real constants, is

$c_j \to$	a	3	0	0	
Basic variable	x_1	x_2	x_3	x_4	Solution
x_2	1	0	2	–1	6
x_1	0	1	–1	1	2
$z_j - c_j$	0	0	2	1	–

Then the value of $\alpha + \beta + \gamma$ is _________.

53. Consider the inner product space P_2 of all polynomials of degree at most 2 over the field of real numbers with the inner product

$$\langle f, g\rangle = \int_0^1 f(t)\, g(t)\, dt \; f, g \in P_2.$$

Let $\{f_0, f_1, f_2\}$ be an orthogonal set in P_2, where $f_0 = 1$, $f_1 = t + c_1$, $f_2 = t_2\ c_2 f_1 + c_3$ and c_1, c_2, c_3 are real constants. Then the value of $2c_1 + c_2 + 3c_3$ is equal to _____.

54. Consider the system of linear differential equations

$$\frac{dx_1}{dt} = 5x_1 - 2x_2,$$

$$\frac{dx_2}{dt} = 4x_1 - x_2,$$

with the initial conditions $x_1(0) = 0$, $x_2(0) = 1$

Then $\log e(x_2(2) - x_1(2))$ is equal to ________.

55. Consider the differential equation

$$x(1+x^2)\frac{d^2y}{dx^2} - 9\frac{dy}{dx} + 7y = 0.$$

The sum of the roots of the indicial equation of the Frobenius series solution for the above differential equation in a neighborhood of x = 0 is equal to _____.

ANSWERS

General Aptitude

1. (c)	**2.** (c)	**3.** (c)	**4.** (c)	**5.** (a)	**6.** (c)	**7.** (a)
8. (c)	**9.** (b)	**10.** (d)				

Mathematics

1. (d)	**2.** (a)	**3.** (d)	**4.** (d)	**5.** (c)	**6.** (c)	**7.** (c)
8. (b)	**9.** (c)	**10.** (a)	**11.** (b)	**12.** (c)	**13.** (c)	**14.** (0 to 0)
15. (2.40 to 2.50)		**16.** (–7.5 to –7.5)		**17.** (31.90 to 32.10)		**18.** (0.21 to 0.23)
19. (0.5 to 0.5)	**20.** (6 to 6)	**21.** (4 to 4)	**22.** (2 to 2)	**23.** (7 to 7)	**24.** (4 to 4)	**25.** (0.125 to 0.125)
26. (b)	**27.** (b)	**28.** (b)	**29.** (a)	**30.** (b)	**31.** (a)	**32.** (c)
33. (c)	**34.** (d)	**35.** (b)	**36.** (b)	**37.** (a)	**38.** (d)	**39.** (d)
40. (a)	**41.** (c)	**42.** (a)	**43.** (b)	**44.** (0.76 to 0.83)		**45.** (12 to 12)
46. (17 to 17)	**47.** (48 to 48)	**48.** (27 to 27)	**49.** (0.25 to 0.30)		**50.** (26 to 26)	**51.** (0.022 to 0.028)
52. (14.5 to 16.5)		**53.** (–3 to –3)	**54.** (1.95 to 2.05)		**55.** (10 to 10)	

EXPLANATIONS

GENERAL APTITUDE

1. "To whom" is used when we don't have a specific person to correspond. In the given case, the subject being corresponded is "The fisherman", So, option (c) is correct.
2. Some student were not involved in the strike also means that some students were also involved in the strike(due the presence of "Some. Thus, option (c) is correct.
3. Let r be the radius and h be the height of a circular cone. Then

$$R = r + \frac{r \times 10}{100} = \frac{11r}{10}$$

$$H = h + \frac{h \times 10}{100} = \frac{11h}{10}$$

∴ Increase percent in volume

$$= \left[\frac{\text{New volume} - \text{old volume}}{\text{old volume}} \times 100\right]\%$$

$$= \frac{\frac{1}{3} \times \pi \times \frac{11r}{10} \times \frac{11r}{10} \times \frac{11h}{10} - \frac{1}{3} \times \pi \times r^2 h}{\frac{1}{3} \times \pi \times r^2 \times h}$$

$$= \frac{\frac{1}{3} \times \pi \times r^2 h\left(\frac{11}{10} \times \frac{11}{10} \times \frac{11}{10} - 1\right)}{\frac{1}{3} \times \pi \times r^2 \times h} \times 100$$

$$= \left(\frac{11 \times 11 \times 11}{1000} - 1\right) \times 100$$

$$= \left[\frac{1331 - 1000}{1000} \times 100\right]\% = \frac{331}{10} = 33.1\%$$

∴ option (c) is correct

4. We have following sequence

10	5	4	7	2

∴ second number from right is 7.

∴ option (c) is correct.

5. The sentence is in passive form and we require the use of "had + been + V3". In the given sentence, third form of "defeat" will be used. So, "defeated" is the correct option.
6. Refer to the line, "Since the last one year, after a 125 basis point reduction in repo rate by the Reserve Bank of India, banking institutions have been making a demand to reduce interest rates on small saving schemes.". So, we can infer from the above lines that the government sometimes takes into consideration the demands of banking institutions before reducing the rates. So, option (c) is correct.
7. The required percentage

$$= \frac{147}{294} \times 100 = \frac{1}{2} \times 100 = 50\%$$

∴ Option (d) is correct.

8. Refer to the lines, "Terms like gayaki and baaf were used to refer to vocal and instrument styles, respectively. So, we can infer from these lines that baaf is a type of vocal and instrument style. Thus baaf is not an institution. Moreover, option (c) is correct.

9. $t_1\,80 + t_2\,100 = 540$

$\Rightarrow t_1 = 3,\ t_2 = 2$

$\therefore$ total time = 3 + 2 = 5h.

= 7 + 5 = 11 A.M.

10. Referring to the above paragraph, we can infer that there is a direct relation between prestige of a kingdom and prestige of a head hunter. As the prestige of a kingdom shows his power by collecting taxes, in the same way, head hunter collects the heads of enemies. Thus, option (d) is correct.

MATHEMATICS

2. Let $f: [a, b] \to \mathbb{R}$ be any function which is twice differentiable in (a, b) with only one root α in (a, b).

Let α be the simple root and is computed by the Newton - Raphson method. We know that method converges if $|\phi'(x)| < 1$.

Newton-Raphson method formula

$$x_{n+1} = x_n - \frac{f(x_n)}{f'(x_n)}$$

Let $\phi(x) = x - \frac{f(x)}{f'(x)}$, then

$$\phi'(x) = 1 - \left[\frac{(f'(x))^2 - f(x)f''(x)}{(f'(x))^2}\right] = \frac{f(x)f''(x)}{(f'(x))^2}$$

Now $|\varphi'(x)| < 1 \Rightarrow \left|\frac{f(x)f''(x)}{(f'(x))^2}\right| < 1$

$\Rightarrow |f(x)f''(x)| < (f'(x))^2\ \forall x \in (a,b)$

$\therefore$ Option (a) is correct.

4. Given partial differential equation is

$$(x^2 + y^2 - 1)\frac{\partial^2 u}{\partial x^2} + 2\frac{\partial^2 u}{\partial x \partial y} + (x^2 + y^2 - 1)\frac{\partial^2 u}{\partial y^2} = 0$$

Here $R = x^2 + y^2 - 1,\ S = 2,\ \tau = x^2 + y^2 - 1$.

$\therefore\ S^2 = 4R\tau = 2^2 - 4(x^2 - y^2 - 1)(x^2 + y^2 - 1)$

$= 4 - 4(x^2 - y^2 - 1)^2$

$= [1 - (x^2 - y^2 - 1)^2]$

For hyperbolic,

$S^2 - 4R\tau > 0$

$\Rightarrow 4[1 - (x^2 + y^2 - 1)2] > 0$

$\Rightarrow (x^2 + y^2 - 1)^2 < 1$

$\Rightarrow (x^2 - y^2 - 1)\ 1$

$\Rightarrow x^2 + y^2$

$\therefore$ Option (b) is incorrect.

For elliphic

$S^2 - 4R\tau < 0$

$\Rightarrow 4[1 - (x^2 + y^2 - 1)^2] < 0$

$1 - (x^2 + y^2 - 1) < 0$

$\Rightarrow (x^2 + y^2 - 1) > 1$

$\Rightarrow x^2 + y^2 > 2$

$\therefore$ Option (c) is incorrect.

For parabolic

$S^2 - 4R\tau = 0$.

$\Rightarrow 4[1 - (x^2 + y^2 - 1)^2] = 1$

$\Rightarrow (x^2 + y^2 - 1)^2 = 1$

$\Rightarrow x^2 + y^2 = 2$.

$\therefore$ Option (a) is incorrect.

9. We have

$f(x, y) = x^6 - 2x^2y - x^4y + 2y^2$

$\therefore\ \frac{\partial f}{\partial x} = 6x^5 - 4xy - 4x^3y, \frac{\partial^2 f}{\partial x^2}$

$= 30x^4 - 4y - 12x^2y$

$\frac{\partial f}{\partial y} = -2x^2 - x^4 + 4y, \frac{\partial^2 f}{\partial y^2} = 4$

$\therefore\ \frac{\partial f}{\partial x} = 0, \frac{\partial f}{\partial y} = 0$

$\Rightarrow 6x^5 - 4xy - 4x^3y = 0$ ...(1)

$-2x^2 - x^4 + 4y = 0$ ...(2)

from (1) and (2), we get

x = 0, y = 0

$\therefore$ (0, 0) is stationary point.

Now $f_{xy} = -4x - 4x^3$.

$\therefore\ (f_{xx})_{(0,0)} = 0, (f_{yy})_{(0,0)} = 4, (f_{xy})_{(0,0)} = 0$.

$\therefore\ f_{xx}f_{yy} - f_{xy}^2 = 0 \times 4 - 0 = 0$

$\therefore$ No conclusion

$\therefore$ all options are incorrect.

14. We have

$$U_n = \frac{n!}{1.2.3...(2n-1)}, n \in \mathbb{N}$$

We know that if $\{U_n\}$ is a sequence of positive real number such that

$\lim_{n\to\infty} \frac{U_{n+1}}{U_n} = l$, then

(i) if $O \le l \le 1$, then $\lim_{n\to\infty} U_n = 0$

(ii) if $l > 1$, then $\lim_{n\to\infty} U_n = 0$

Now, $U_{n+1} = \frac{(n+1)!}{1.3.5...(2n+1)}$

$\therefore \lim_{n\to\infty} \frac{U_{n+1}}{U_n}$

$$= \lim_{n\to\infty}\left[\frac{(n+1)!}{1.3.5...(2n+1)} \cdot \frac{1.3.5..(2n-1)}{n!}\right]$$

$$= \lim_{n\to\infty} \frac{n+1}{2n+1} = \lim_{n\to\infty} \frac{\left(1+\frac{1}{n}\right)}{\left(2+\frac{1}{n}\right)} = \frac{1}{2} = l$$

but here $0 < l < 1$.

Here, $\lim_{n\to\infty} U_n = 0$.

16. Let f(x) = 1, then $\frac{df}{dx} = 0$

$\therefore 0 = a + 2 + b \Rightarrow a + b = -2$ ....(1)

Let f(x) = x, then $\frac{df}{dx} = 1$

$\therefore 1 = ax + 2(x+1) + b(x+2)$

$= (a + 2 + b)\, x + 2 + 2b$

$\therefore\ 2 + 2b = 1 \Rightarrow b = -\frac{1}{2}$

$\therefore$ from (1), we get

$a - \frac{1}{2} = -2$

$\Rightarrow a = -2 + \frac{1}{2} = -\frac{3}{2}$

$\therefore 4a + 3b = 4\left(-\frac{3}{2}\right) + 3\left(-\frac{1}{2}\right)$

$= \frac{-12}{2} - \frac{3}{2} = \frac{-15}{2} = -7.5$

17. We have

$C : x^2 + y^2 = 4$

$\Rightarrow y = \sqrt{4-x^2}$

$dy = \frac{1}{\sqrt{4-x^2}}(-2x)\, dx = \frac{-2x}{\sqrt{4-x^2}}\, dx$

$\therefore\ I = \oint_c \left(3x - 4xy^2\right)dx + \left(4xy^2 + 2y\right) dy$

$\int_0^2 \left(3x - 4x^2\sqrt{4-x^2}\right) dx + \left[4x\left(4 - x^2 + 2\sqrt{4-x^2}\right)\right] \times \left(\frac{-2x}{\sqrt{4-x^2}}\right) dx$

$= \int_0^2 \left[3x - 4x^2\sqrt{4-x^2} - 8x^2\sqrt{4-x^2} - 14x + 4x^2\right] dx$

$= \int_0^2 \left(4x^2 - 13x - 12x^2\sqrt{4-x^2}\right) dx$

$\int_0^2 x\left(4x - 13x - 13x\sqrt{4-x^2}\right) dx$

$2z^2 - 5z + 2$

$2z^2 - 4z - z + 2$

$2z(z-2) - 1(z-2)$

$(2z-1)(z-2)$

$2z^2 - 2 - 4z + z$

18. We have

$T(x,y,z) = \frac{k}{x^2 + y^2 + z^2}$

but $T(0,0,1) = \sqrt{3} = K = \sqrt{3}$

$\therefore\ T(x,y,z) = \frac{\sqrt{3}}{x^2 + y^2 + z^2}$

$\frac{\partial T}{\partial x} = -\frac{2\sqrt{3}x}{\left(x^2 + y^2 + z^2\right)^2}$

$\therefore\ \left(\frac{\partial T}{\partial x}\right)(1,1,2) = -\frac{-2\sqrt{3}}{36} = -0.09$

$\left(\frac{\partial T}{\partial 2}\right)_{(1,1,g)} = \frac{-4\sqrt{3}}{3b} = -0.19$

19. Let f be a continuous function defined $U_n[0, 2]$ such that f(x) ≥ 0 for all x∈[0, 2]. If the area bounded by y = f(x), x = 0, y = 0 and x = b is $\sqrt{3+b^2} - \sqrt{3}$, where b∈(0, 2], then we need to find f(1).

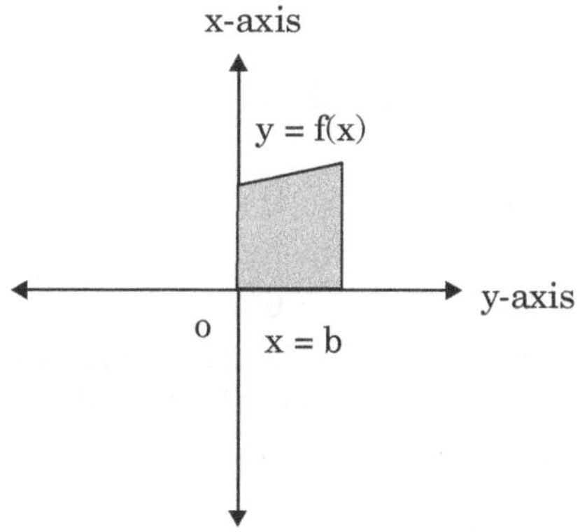

$\therefore$ Area $= \int_a^b f(x)\,dx = \sqrt{3+b^2} - \sqrt{3}$

$\Rightarrow F(b) - F(a) = \sqrt{3+b^2} - \sqrt{3}$

Here a = 0,

$\therefore F(b) - F(10) = \sqrt{3+b^2} - \sqrt{3}$

Comparing on both sides, we get

$F(b) = \sqrt{3+b^2}$, $F(10) = \sqrt{3}$

Therefore, $F(x) = \sqrt{3+x^2}$

$\therefore\ F'(x) = \frac{1}{2\sqrt{3+x^2}}.2x = \frac{x}{\sqrt{3+x^2}} = f(x).$

$\therefore\ f(1) = \frac{1}{\sqrt{3+12}} = \frac{1}{\sqrt{4}} \pm \frac{1}{2}$

but f(x) ≥ 0.

$\therefore\ f(1) = \frac{1}{2} = 0.5$

20. The characteristic polynomial and minimal polynomial of a square matrix A are

$(\lambda - 1)(\lambda + 1)^4(\lambda - 2)^5$

and $(\lambda - 1)(\lambda + 1)(\lambda - 2)$ respectively we need to find rank (A + I). We know that a matrix A is diagonalizable if its minimal polynomial is a product of distinct linear monic factors.

Here, $M_A(x) = (\lambda - 1)(\lambda + 1)(\lambda - 2)$

$\Rightarrow$ J non singular matrix P such that

$$D = PAP^{-1} = P^{-1}AP$$

Now A.M $(\lambda_1 = 1) = 1$, A.M$(\lambda_2 = -1) = 4$, and A.M $(\lambda_3 = 2) = 5$.

G.M $(\lambda_1 = 1) = 1$, G.M $(\lambda_2 = -1) = 4$

and G.M $(\lambda_3 = 2) = 5$

$\therefore$ D looks like

$$D = [1, -1, -1, -1, -1, 2, 2, 2, 2]$$

$\therefore \quad A + I = P^{-1}DP + I = P^{-1}DP + P^{-1}P$

$= P^{-1}(D + I)P$

$\therefore \quad \rho(A + I) = \rho(D + I)$

$= \rho([2, 0, 0, 0, 0, 3, 3, 3, 3, 3)] = 6$

Alternatively :

G.M $(\lambda) = n - \rho(A - \lambda I)$

put $\lambda = -1$, then

G.M $(-1) = 10 - \rho(A + I)$

$\Rightarrow 4 = 10 - \rho(A + I)$

$\Rightarrow \rho(A + I) = 10 - 4 = 6$.

21. Let ω be a primitive complex cube root of unity and $i = \sqrt{-1}$. We need to find the degree of field extension $\left[Q\left(i, \sqrt{3}, \omega\right) : Q\right]$

$$\therefore \quad \omega = \frac{-i + \sqrt{3}i}{2}$$

$$\therefore \left[Q\left(i, \sqrt{3}, \omega\right) : Q\right] = \left[Q\left(i, \sqrt{3}\right) : Q\right]$$

$$\left[Q\left(i, \sqrt{3}\right) : Q(i)\right]\left[Q(i) : Q\right] = 2 \times 2 = 4$$

22. $C : \cos t + i \sin t, \ 0 \le t \le 2\pi,$

$i = \sqrt{-1}$

$C : |z| = 1$

$$\therefore \alpha = \int_c \frac{e^{i\pi z}}{2z^2 - 5z + 2} dz = \int_c \frac{e^{i\pi z}}{(2z - 1)(z - 2)} dz$$

$$= \int_c \frac{\frac{e^{i\pi z}}{(z-2)}}{(2z - 1)} dz = 2\pi i \frac{e^{i\pi\left(\frac{1}{2}\right)}}{\left(\frac{1}{2} - 2\right)}$$

$$= \frac{2\pi i \, e^{\frac{i\pi}{2}}}{\left(\frac{-3}{2}\right)} = -\frac{4}{3}\pi i \, e^{\frac{i\pi}{2}} = 4.18$$

23. The given system is

$3x_1 + x_2 + 2x_3 - x_4 = a$

$x_1 + x_2 + x_3 - 2x_4 = 3$

$x_1 > 0, x_2 > 0, x_3 > 0, x_4 > 0$

Since $x_1 = 1, x_2 = b, x_3 = 0$ and $x_4 = c$ is a basic feasible solution of the system, Therefore

$3 + b - c = a \Rightarrow a - b + c = 3$ ...(1)

$1 + b - 2c = 3 \Rightarrow b - 2c = 2$ ...(2)

from (1) and (2), we get

$$a = 6, b = 4, c = 1$$

$\therefore \quad a + b + c = 6 + 4 + 1 = 11$

24. Let $f : D \to D$ be a function defined by

$f(z) = z^6 - 5z^4 + 10$

we know that if f(x) and g(x) be two analytic function such that

$|g(z)| < |f(z)|$

On, D, then the function f(z) and f(z) + g(z) have some number of zeros.

Let $f(z) = -5z^4$, $g(z) = z^6 + 10$, then f(z) and g(z) are analytic on $\{z \in D \,|\, |z| < 2\}$.

Also $|g(z)| \le |z|^6 + 10 = 2^6 + 10 = 74$

$|f_1(z)| = 5.2^4 = 80$

$\therefore \quad f(z) = f_1(z) + g(z) = z^6 - 5z^4 + 10$

and $f^1(z) = -5z^4$ have same number of zeros.

Hence f(z) has four zeros.

27. Let $f^2 \to \mathbb{R}^2 \to \mathbb{R}$ be defined by

$$f(x,y) = \begin{cases} \left(x^2 + y^2\right)\sin\left(\dfrac{1}{x^2 + y^2}\right), & (x,y) \ne (0,0) \\ 0, & (x,y) = (0,0) \end{cases}$$

$$(I)\left(\frac{\partial f}{\partial x}\right)_{(a,b)} = \lim_{h \to \infty} \frac{f(a+h,b) - f(a,b)}{h}$$

$$\therefore \left(\frac{\partial f}{\partial x}\right)_{(0,0)} = \lim_{h \to \infty} \frac{f(h,0) - f(0,0)}{h}$$

$$= \lim_{h \to \infty} \frac{h^2 \sin \frac{1}{h^2}}{h} = \lim_{h \to \infty} h \sin \frac{1}{h^2}$$

$= 0 \times$ oscillatory number between -1 and $1 = 0$

$\therefore \quad \dfrac{\partial f}{\partial x}, \dfrac{\partial f}{\partial x}$ exist at $(0,0)$.

Let $y = mx$, then

$\lim\limits_{h \to 0}\left(x^2 + m^2x^2\right)\sin\left(\dfrac{1}{x^2 + m^2x^2}\right)$ does not exist.

$\therefore$ Unbounded in any neighbourhood of (0, 0).

$\therefore$ true.

$$(II) \ f'(z) = \lim_{z \to \sigma} \frac{f(z) - f(0)}{z}$$

$$f'(0) = \lim_{z\to 0} \frac{(x^2+y^2)\sin\left(\frac{1}{x^2+y^2}\right)}{x+iy}$$

$$= \lim_{(x,y)\to(0,0)} \frac{(x+iy)(x-iy)\sin\left(\frac{1}{x^2+y^2}\right)}{(x+iy)}$$

Let y = mx, then

$$= \lim_{x\to\infty} x(1-im)\sin\left(\frac{1}{x^2+m^2x^2}\right)$$

= 0 × oscillatory number between –1 and 1 = 0

∴ f(x,y) is differentiable at (0,0) and hence it is continuous at (0, 0) because every differentiable function is continuous.

∴ true.

(III) Not true (IV) true.

∴ Option (b) is correct.

31. The given partial differentiable equation is

$$(2xy-1)\frac{\partial z}{\partial x} + (Z-2x^2)\frac{\partial z}{\partial y} = 2(x-yz)$$

Lagrange equation is

$$\frac{dx}{2xy-1} = \frac{dy}{z-2x^2} = \frac{dz}{2(x-yz)}$$

$$= \frac{xdx + ydy + \frac{dz}{2}}{2x^2y - x + yz - 2x^2y + x - yz}$$

$$\therefore xdx + ydy + \frac{dz}{2} = 0$$

$$\Rightarrow \frac{x^2}{2} + \frac{y^2}{2} + \frac{z}{2} = c_1$$

⇒ $x^2 + y^2 + z = c1$

∴ $u = x^2 + y^2 + z$

$$\text{Now, } \frac{dx}{2xy-1} = \frac{dy}{z-2x^2} = \frac{dz}{2(x-yz)}$$

∴ zdx + xdz + dy = 0

⇒ d(zx) + dy = 0

⇒ $zx + y = c^2$

∴ x = xz + y

∴ F(u, v) = 0,

where $u = x^2 + y^2 + z$ and u = xz + y.

∴ Option (a) is correct.

32. (I). Let $f: Q \to Q$ defined by f(x) = 0 $\forall n \in Q$. then f is a homomorphism but it is not an isomorphism.

∴ Not true.

(II). Let G = <a> and $N \leq G$

Then $\frac{G}{N} = \langle aN \rangle$

which is cyclic.

∴ true

(III). We know that all subgroup of Q_2 are normal subgroup but Q_8 is not abclian group.

∴ Not true.

(IV). O(G) = 33 = 3 × 11

Also $\frac{3}{11-1}$

∴ G is cyclic group.

∴ true.

∴ Option (c) is correct.

33. The Dirichlet problem

$$\nabla^2 u(r,\theta) = 0, 0 < r < 1, -\pi \leq \theta \leq \pi$$

$$u(1,\theta) = |\theta|, -\pi \leq \theta \leq \pi$$

We know that the solution of

$$\nabla^2 u = 0$$

$u(a, \theta) = f(\theta)$, $0 \leq \theta \leq 2\pi$ is

$$u(r,\theta) = \frac{a_0}{2} + \sum_{n=1}^{\infty}\left(\frac{r}{a}\right)^n [a_n \cos n\theta + b_n \sin n\theta]$$

where a_0, a_n, b_n, are constants and r < a.

$$a_0 = \frac{1}{\pi}\int_0^{2\pi} f(\theta)d\theta, \quad a_n = \frac{1}{\pi}\int_0^{2\pi} f(\theta)\cos\theta d\theta$$

$$b_n = \frac{1}{\pi}\int_0^{2\pi} f(\theta)\sin x d\nu$$

Here a = 1, f(θ)= |θ|

Now $f(-\theta) = \nu = |\theta| = f(\nu)$

⇒ f is an even function.

∴ $b_n = 0$.

$$a_0 = \frac{2}{\pi}\int_0^{\pi} f(\theta)d\theta = \frac{2}{\pi}\int_0^{\pi} \nu d\nu = \frac{2}{\pi}\left(\frac{\nu^2}{2}\right)_0^{\pi}$$

$$= \frac{2}{\pi}.\frac{\pi^2}{2} = \pi.$$

$$a_n = \frac{2}{\pi}\int_0^{\pi} f(\nu)\cos n\theta d\theta = \frac{2}{\pi}\int_0^{\pi} \nu\cos n\theta d\theta$$

$$= \frac{2}{\pi}\left[\left(\frac{\sin n\nu}{n}\right), \nu - \frac{-\cos n\theta}{n^2}\right]_0^{\pi} = \frac{2}{\pi}\left[\frac{(-1)^n - 1}{n^2}\right]$$

$$\therefore u(r,v) = \frac{\pi}{2} + \sum_{n=1}^{\infty} \frac{2}{\pi}\left[\frac{(-1)^n - 1}{n^2}\right] r^n \cos n\theta$$

∴ Option (c) is correct.

36. Let M be a 3 × 3 real symmetric matrix with eigenvalues 0, 2 and a with the respective eigentvectors $u = (4, b, c)^T$, $v = (-1, 2, 0)^T$ and $\omega = (1, 1, 1)^T$

clearly $a \in \mathbb{R}$.

Also we know that the eigen vector corresponding to different eigen values of real symmetric matrix are orthogonal.

$\therefore$ u,v, ω are orthogonal.

$\Rightarrow <u, v> = 0$

$\Rightarrow -4 + 2b + 0 = 0 \Rightarrow 2b = 4 \Rightarrow b = 2.$

if $a \neq 2$, then

$<v, \omega> = -1 + 2 + 0 = 1 \neq 0$

$\therefore <v, \omega> = 0 < v, \omega > \Rightarrow a = 2.$

$<v, \omega> = 0 \Rightarrow 4 + b + c = 0$

$\Rightarrow 4 + 3 + c = 0$

$\Rightarrow c = -6$

(i) $a + b - c = 2 + 2 - (-6) = 10$

$\therefore$ true.

(ii) $v+\omega = \begin{bmatrix} -1 \\ 2 \\ 0 \end{bmatrix} + \begin{bmatrix} 1 \\ 1 \\ 1 \end{bmatrix} = \begin{bmatrix} 0 \\ 3 \\ 1 \end{bmatrix} = (0,3,1)^a$

$$\therefore M \begin{bmatrix} 0 \\ \frac{3}{2} \\ \frac{1}{2} \end{bmatrix} = \begin{bmatrix} 0 \\ 3 \\ 1 \end{bmatrix} \Rightarrow \begin{bmatrix} 0 \\ \frac{3}{2} \\ \frac{1}{2} \end{bmatrix} = 2 \begin{bmatrix} 0 \\ \frac{3}{2} \\ \frac{1}{2} \end{bmatrix}$$

$\Rightarrow My = \lambda x$ for $\lambda = 2$.

$\therefore$ true.

(iii) $d \in$ span {u, v,ω}

$\therefore Mx = d$, where $d \neq 0$.

$\therefore \rho(M) = 2$.

$$\text{Let } M = \begin{bmatrix} a_1 & a_2 & a_3 \\ a_2 & a_4 & a_5 \\ a_3 & a_5 & a_6 \end{bmatrix} \sim \begin{bmatrix} b_1 & b_2 & b_3 \\ b_2 & b_4 & b_5 \\ 0 & 0 & r \end{bmatrix}$$

$\therefore$ Not true

(iv) $M^2 + 2M = 02 + 2.0 + 22 + 2.2 + 22 + 2.2 = 16$

$\therefore$ Not true.

$\therefore$ Option (b) is correct.

38. (a) We have

$$I_n(x) \frac{x}{1+nx^2}, x \in \mathbb{R}, n \in \mathbb{N}$$

$$\therefore I_n'(x) \frac{(1+nx^2)1. - 2nx.x}{(1+nx^2)}$$

$$= \frac{1+nx^2 - 2nx^2}{(1+nx^2)} = \frac{1 = nx^2}{(1+nx^2)}$$

$$\lim_{n\to\infty} I_n'(n) = \begin{cases} 1, & x \\ 0, & x \neq 0 \end{cases}$$

which is a discontinuous function.

$\therefore$ Option (c) is incorrect.

Also $\lim_{n\to\infty} I_n'(x)$ discontinuous in interval $\left[-\frac{1}{2}, \frac{1}{2}\right]$ which does not contain I.

$\therefore$ Option (b) is incorrect.

Also $\lim_{n\to\infty} I_n'(x)$ is discontinuous in $\left[\frac{1}{2}, \frac{3}{2}\right]$ which does not contain 0.

$\therefore$ Option (d) is incorrect.

$$\text{Now, } \lim_{n\to\pi} g_n(x) \begin{cases} \frac{1}{2\sqrt{n}}, & -1 \leq x \leq 1 \\ \frac{1}{n}, & \text{otherwise} \end{cases}$$

which is discontinuous in $\mathbb{R}$.

$\therefore I_n(x)$ does not converge uniformly on $\mathbb{R}$.

$\therefore$ Option (a) is correct.

39. The given boundary value problem is

$$\frac{d^2y}{dx^2} + ay(x) = 0, \ a \in R$$

with $y(0) = 0, y(\pi) = k, k \neq 0$

Let a = 1, then

$$\frac{d^2y}{dx^2} + y(x) = 0$$

Auxiliary equation is

$\lambda^2 + 1 = 0 \Rightarrow \lambda = \pm i$

$\therefore y(x) = c_1 \cos x + c_2 \sin x$

But $y(0) = 0$

$\Rightarrow 0 = c_1$

$\therefore y(x) = c_2 \sin x$

$y(\pi) = k \Rightarrow k = c_2 \sin \pi$

Here we cannot determined c_2.

$\therefore$ No solution exists.

Let a = –1, then

$$\frac{d^2y}{dx^2} - y(x) = 0$$

Auxiliary equation is

$\lambda^2 - 1 = 0 \Rightarrow \lambda = \pm 1$

$\therefore y(x) = c_1e^{-x} + c_2 e^{-x}$

but $y(0) = 0 \Rightarrow c_1 + c_2 = 0$ ...(2)

$y(\pi) = k \Rightarrow c_1 e^{\pi} + c_2 e^{-\pi} = k$ ...(2)

$$\Rightarrow c_1 = \frac{k}{e^{\pi} - e^{-\pi}}, c_2 = \frac{k}{e^{\pi} - e^{-\pi}}$$

$$\therefore y(x) = \frac{k}{e^{\pi} - e^{-\pi}}[e^x - e^{-x}]$$

$\therefore$ for $k > 0, y(x) > 0 \ \forall x \in (0,\pi)$

$\therefore$ option (c) is correct.

41. Let p_2 be the vector space of all polynomials of degree at most 2 over, R.

Let $T : P_2 \to P_2$ be defined by

$$T(a + bx + cx^2) = (a + b) + (b - c)x + (a + c)x^2$$

Let $p_2 = \{ 1, x , x^2\}$.

$\therefore$ $T(1) = 1 + x^2 = 1.1 + 0.x + 1.x^2$

$T(x) = 1 + x = 1.1 + 1.x + 0.x^2$

$T(x^2) = -x + x^2 = 0.1 - 1.x + 1.x^2$.

$$\therefore\ [M]_{p2}^{T} = \begin{bmatrix} 1 & 1 & 0 \\ 0 & 1 & -1 \\ 1 & 0 & 1 \end{bmatrix}$$

$\therefore$ trace $M = 1 + 1 + 1 = 3$.

$\therefore$ IV is correct.

$T(1 + x) = 2 + x + x^2$

$\therefore$ $T(T(1 + x)) = T(2 + x + x^2)$

$= 3 + 3x^2 = 3(1 + x^2) \neq 1 + x^2$

$\therefore$ III is incorrect

Let $a + bx + cx^2 \in$ Null space of T, then

$T(a + bx + cx^2) = 0$

$\Rightarrow (a + b) + (b - c)x + (a + c)x^2 = 0$

$\Rightarrow a + b = 0, b - c = 0, a + c = 0$

$\Rightarrow a + b = 0, b = c, a + c = 0$

$b = \alpha$, and $a = -\alpha$.

$\therefore$ Null space of

$T = \{a + bx + cx^2 : a = -\alpha, b = \alpha, c = 2\ \alpha \in R\}$

$= \{-\alpha + \alpha x + \alpha x^2 : \propto c -1R\}$

$= \{\propto(-1 + x + x^2) : \alpha \in R\}$

$\therefore$ I is true.

Hence option (c) is correct.

46. Let v be the vector space of all 3 × 3 matrix with complex entries over the real filed. Let

$W_1 = \{A \in V : A = A^{-T}\}$

$W_2 = \{A \in V : \text{trace}(A)\}$

We need to find the dim $(W_1 + W_2)$.

$$\text{Let, } A = \begin{bmatrix} a_{11} + ib_{11} & a_{12} + ib_{12} & a_{13} + ib_{13} \\ a_{21} + ib_{21} & a_{22} + ib_{22} & a_{23} + ib_{23} \\ a_{31} + ib_{31} & a_{32} + ib_{32} & a_{33} + ib_{33} \end{bmatrix}$$

$a_{ij} - b_{ij} \in \mathbb{R} \forall i, j = 1,2,3$

Now $A = A^{-T}$

$\Rightarrow a_{ij} + ib_{ij} = a_{ji} - ib_{ji}$

$\Rightarrow a_{ij} = a_{ji}$ and $b_{ij} = -b_{ji}$

Thus A will be

$$A = \begin{bmatrix} A_{11} & a_{12} + ib_{12} & a_{13} + ib_{13} \\ a_{12} - ib_{12} & a_{22} & a_{23} + ib_{23} \\ a_{13} - ib_{13} & a_{23} - ib_{23} & a_{33} \end{bmatrix}$$

$\therefore$ dim(w1) = 9

Now trac(A) $= a_{11} + ib_{11} + a_{22} + ib_{22} + a_{33} + ib_{33} = 0$

$\Rightarrow a_{11} + a_{22} + a_{33} + i(b_{11} + b_{22} + b_{33}) = 0$

$\Rightarrow$ $a_{11} + a_{22} + a_{33} = 0, b_{11} + b_{22} + b_{33} = 0$

$\therefore$ $\dim(w_2) = 18 - 2 = 16$

Now Let $A \in W_1 \cap W_2$, then

$A = A^{-T}$ and Trace $(A) = 0$.

$\Rightarrow$ $a_{ij} = a_{ji}$, $b_{ij} = -b_{ji}$ and $a_{11} + a_{22} - a_{33} = 0$.

$\therefore$ $\dim(W_1 \cap W_2) = 9 - 1 = 8$

$\therefore$ $\dim(W_1 + W_2) = \text{dinw}_1 + \text{dimw}_2 - \dim(W_1 + W_2)$

$= 9 + 16 - 8 = 17$

50. We have

$(\mathbb{Z}_{125}, +_{125}, \bullet_{125})$ is ring of integers modulo 125.

m = Now of maximal ideals of $\mathbb{Z}_{125}$

n = No. of non unites of $\mathbb{Z}_{125}$.

we need to find m + n.

Now = $\mathbb{Z}_{125} = \mathbb{Z}_5 3$

m = No. of maximal ideals of $\mathbb{Z}_5 3$

= No. of primes of $\mathbb{Z}_5 3 = 1$.

$n = 125 - \phi(125) = 125 - \phi(5^3)$

$= 125 - (5^3 - 5^2) = 125 - 100 = 25$

Therefore, m + n = 1+ 25 = 25

53. Let $P_2 = \{1, x, x^2\}$

$\therefore$ $u_1 = 1, u_2 = x, u_3 = x^2$.

Then $f_0 = u_1 = 1$

$f_1 = u_2 - < u_2 f_0 > f_0$.

$$= x - \left(\int_0^1 t.\,dt\right).1 = x - \left[\frac{t^2}{2}\right]_0^1 = x - \frac{1}{2}$$

$$\therefore\ c_1 = -\frac{1}{2}.$$

$$f_2 = u_3 - < u_3, f_0 > - < u_3, f_1 > f_1$$

$$= x^2 - \int_{0-}^{1} t^2\,dt - \left(x - \frac{1}{2}\right)\int^1 t^2\left(t - \frac{1}{2}\right)dt$$

$$= x^2 - \left[\frac{t^3}{3}\right]_0^1 - \left(x - \frac{1}{2}\right)\left[\frac{t^4}{4} - \frac{t^3}{6}\right]_0^1$$

$$= x^2 - \frac{1}{12}x - \frac{7}{24}$$

$$x^2 - \frac{1}{12}x + \frac{1}{24} - \frac{8}{24}$$

$$x^2 - \frac{1}{12}\left(x - \frac{1}{2}\right) - \frac{1}{3} = x^2 - \frac{1}{12}f_1 - \frac{1}{3}$$

$$\therefore\ c_2 = -\frac{1}{12}, c_3 = -\frac{1}{3}.$$

Thus, $2c_1 + c_2 + 3c_3 = 2\times\left(-\frac{1}{2}\right) - \frac{1}{12} - 1$

$= -1 - \frac{1}{12} - 1 = -2 - \frac{1}{12}$

$= \frac{-25}{12} = -2.08$

54. The given system of equation is

$$\frac{dx_1}{dt} = 5x_1 - 2x_2$$

$$\frac{dx_2}{dt} = 4x_1 = x_2$$

with the initial condition $x_1(0) = 0$, $x_2(0) = 1$.

which can be written as

$$\frac{dx}{dt} = Ax, \text{where } A = \begin{pmatrix} 5 & -2 \\ 4 & -1 \end{pmatrix}, x = \begin{pmatrix} x_1 \\ x_2 \end{pmatrix}$$

Now $|A - \lambda I| = 0$

$$\Rightarrow \begin{vmatrix} 5-\lambda & -2 \\ 4 & -1-\lambda \end{vmatrix} = 0$$

$\Rightarrow (5-\lambda)(-1-\lambda) + 8 = 0$

$\Rightarrow \lambda^2 - 4\lambda + 3 = 0 \Rightarrow \lambda_2 = 1, \lambda_2 = 3$

$\therefore$ eigen vector corresponding to eigen value $\lambda_1 = 1$ is

$$\begin{pmatrix} 5-1 & -2 \\ 4 & -1-1 \end{pmatrix}\begin{pmatrix} x_1 \\ x_2 \end{pmatrix} = \begin{pmatrix} 0 \\ 0 \end{pmatrix}$$

$$\Rightarrow \begin{pmatrix} 4 & -2 \\ 4 & -2 \end{pmatrix}\begin{pmatrix} x_1 \\ x_2 \end{pmatrix} = \begin{pmatrix} 0 \\ 0 \end{pmatrix}$$

$\Rightarrow 4x - 2y = 0$

$\Rightarrow 2x = y$

take $x = 1$,

then $y = 2$.

$$\therefore X_1\begin{pmatrix} x_1 \\ x_2 \end{pmatrix} = \begin{pmatrix} 1 \\ 2 \end{pmatrix}$$

is the eigen vector corresponding to $\lambda_1 = 1$.

Let $X_2\begin{pmatrix} x_1 \\ x_2 \end{pmatrix}$ be the eigen vector corresponding to $\lambda_2 = 3$. Then

$$\begin{pmatrix} 5-3 & -2 \\ 4 & -1-3 \end{pmatrix}\begin{pmatrix} x_1 \\ x_2 \end{pmatrix} = \begin{pmatrix} 0 \\ 0 \end{pmatrix}$$

$$\Rightarrow \begin{pmatrix} 2 & -2 \\ 4 & -2 \end{pmatrix}\begin{pmatrix} x_1 \\ x_2 \end{pmatrix} = \begin{pmatrix} 0 \\ 0 \end{pmatrix}$$

$\Rightarrow 2x_1 - 2x_2 = 0$

$\Rightarrow x_1 = x_2$

take $n_1 = 1$,

then $x_2 = 1$.

$\therefore X_2 = \begin{pmatrix} x_1 \\ x_2 \end{pmatrix} = \begin{pmatrix} 1 \\ 1 \end{pmatrix}$ is the eigen vector corresponding to $\lambda_3 = 3$.

$\therefore$ Solution is

$$\begin{pmatrix} x_1(t) \\ x_2(t) \end{pmatrix} = c_1\begin{pmatrix} 1 \\ 2 \end{pmatrix}e^t + c_2\begin{pmatrix} 1 \\ 1 \end{pmatrix}e^{3t}$$

$\Rightarrow x_1(t) = c_1e^t + c_2c^{3t}$

$x_2(t) = 2c_1e^t + c_2c^{3t}$

But $x_1(0) = 0 \Rightarrow c_1 + c_2 = 0$ ...(1)

$x_2(0) = 1 \Rightarrow 2c_1 + c_2 = 1$ ...(2)

from (1) and (2), we get

$c_1 = 1, c_2 = -1$

$\therefore x_1(t) = e^t - e^{3t}$

$x_2(t) = 2e^t - e^{3t}$

$\therefore x_2(2) - x_1(2) = 2c^2 - e^6 - e^2 + e^6 = e^6$

$\therefore \log_e(x_2(2) - x_1(2)) = \log_e(e^2) = 2.$

55. The given differential equation is

$$x(1+x^2)\frac{d^2y}{dx^2} - 9\frac{dy}{dx} + 7y = 0$$

Let $y = \sum_{\mathbb{R}}^{n} a_{\mathbb{R}}x^{\mathbb{R}+m}$

$$\therefore \frac{dy}{dx} = \sum a_{\mathbb{R}}(\mathbb{R}+m)x^{\mathbb{R}+m-1}$$

$$\therefore \frac{d^2y}{dx^2} = \sum a_{\mathbb{R}}(\mathbb{R}+m)(m+\mathbb{R}-1)x^{m+\mathbb{R}-2}$$

$\therefore$ from equation (1), we get

$$(x^3+x)\sum a_{\mathbb{R}}(m+\mathbb{R})(m+\mathbb{R}-1)x^{m+\mathbb{R}-2}$$
$$-9\sum a_{\mathbb{R}}(m+\mathbb{R})x^{m+\mathbb{R}-2} + 7\sum a_{\mathbb{R}}x^{m+\mathbb{R}} = 0$$

$$\Rightarrow \sum a_{\mathbb{R}}(m+\mathbb{R})(m+\mathbb{R}-1)x^{m+\mathbb{R}-1}$$
$$+\sum a_{\mathbb{R}}(m+\mathbb{R})(m+\mathbb{R}-1)x^{m+\mathbb{R}-1}$$
$$-9\sum a_{\mathbb{R}}(m+\mathbb{R})x^{m+\mathbb{R}-1} + \sum a_{\mathbb{R}}x^{m+\mathbb{R}}$$

$\therefore$ indicial equation is

$A_0 M(m-1) - a_0 m = 0, a_0 \neq 0.$

$\therefore m^2 - m - 9m = 0$

$\Rightarrow m^2 = 0, 10$

$\therefore$ Sum of roots of indicial equation, $0 + 10 - 10$.

SOLVED PAPER - 2020

GENERAL APTITUDE

Q. 1 – Q. 5 carry one mark each.

1. Rajiv Gandhi Khel Ratna Award was conferred _____ Mary Kom, a six-time world champion in boxing, recently in a ceremony _____ the Rashtrapati Bhawan (the President's official residence) in New Delhi.

(a) with, at (b) on, in

(c) on, at (d) to, at

2. Despite a string of poor performances, the chances of K.L. Rahul's selection in the team are ______.

(a) slim (b) bright

(c) obvious (d) uncertain

3. Select the word that fits the analogy:

Cover : Uncover :: Associate : _____

(a) Unassociate (b) Inassociate

(c) Misassociate (d) Dissociate

4. Hit by floods, the kharif (summer sown) crops in various parts of the country have been affected. Officials believe that the loss in production of the kharif crops can be recovered in the output of the rabi (winter sown) crops so that the country can achieve its food-grain production target of 291 million tons in the crop year 2019-20 (July-June). They are hopeful that good rains in July-August will help the soil retain moisture for a longer period, helping winter sown crops such as wheat and pulses during the November-February period. Which of the following statements can be inferred from the given passage?

(a) Officials declared that the food-grain production target will be met due to good rains.

(b) Officials want the food-grain production target to be met by the November-February period.

(c) Officials feel that the food-grain production target cannot be met due to floods.

(d) Officials hope that the food-grain production target will be met due to a good rabi produce.

5. The difference between the sum of the first 2n natural numbers and the sum of the first n odd natural numbers is _____.

(a) $n^2 - n$ (b) $n^2 + n$

(c) $2n^2 - n$ (d) $2n^2 + n$

Q. 6 – Q. 10 carry two marks each.

6. Repo rate is the rate at which Reserve Bank of India (RBI) lends commercial banks, and reverse repo rate is the rate at which RBI borrows money from commercial banks.

Which of the following statements can be inferred from the above passage?

(a) Decrease in repo rate will increase cost of borrowing and decrease lending by commercial banks.

(b) Increase in repo rate will decrease cost of borrowing and increase lending by commercial banks.

(c) Increase in repo rate will decrease cost of borrowing and decrease lending by commercial banks.

(d) Decrease in repo rate will decrease cost of borrowing and increase lending by commercial banks.

7. P, Q, R, S, T, U, V, and W are seated around a circular table.

1. S is seated opposite to W.
2. U is seated at the second place to the right of R.
3. T is seated at the third place to the left of R.
4. V is a neighbour of S.

Which of the following must be true?

(a) P is a neighbour of R.

(b) Q is a neighbour of R.

(c) P is not seated opposite to Q.

(d) R is the left neighbour of S.

8. The distance between Delhi and Agra is 233 km. A car P seated travelling from Delhi to Agra and another car Q seated from Agra to Delhi along the same road 1 hour after the car P started. The two cars crossed each other 75 minutes after the car Q started. Both cars were travelling at constant speed. The speed of car P was 10 km/hr more than the speed of car Q. How many kilometers the car Q had travelled when the cars crossed each other?

(a) 66.6 (b) 75.2

(c) 88.2 (d) 116.5

9. For a matrix $M = [m_{ij}]$; $i, j = 1, 2, 3, 4$, the diagonal elements are all zero and $m_{ij} = -m_{ji}$. The minimum number of elements required to fully specify the matrix is _____.

(a) 0 (b) 6

(c) 12 (d) 16

10. The profit shares of two companies P and Q are shown in the figure. If the two companies have invested a fixed and equal amount every year, then the ratio of the total revenue of company P to the total revenue of company Q, during 2013-2018 is _____.

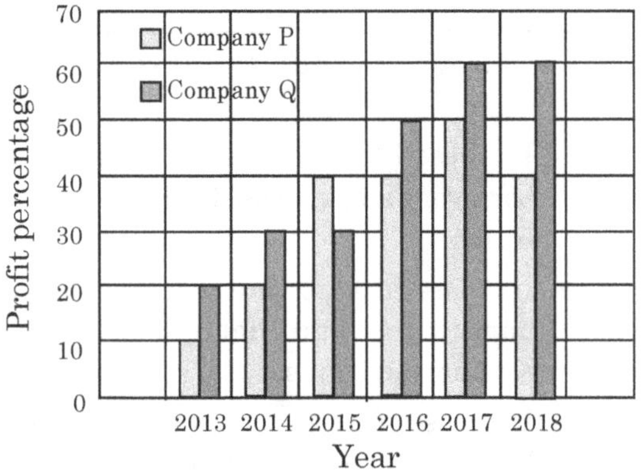

(a) 15 : 17 (b) 16 : 17

(c) 17 : 15 (d) 17 : 16

MATHEMATICS

Q. 1 – Q. 25 carry one mark each.

1. Suppose that $\Im_1$ and $\Im_2$ are topologies on X induced by metrics d_1 and d_2, respectively, such that $\Im_1 \subseteq \Im_2$. Then which of the following statements is TRUE?

(a) If a sequence converges in (X, d_2) then it converges in (X, d_1)

(b) If a sequence converges in (X, d_1) then it converges in (X, d_2)

(c) Every open ball in (X, d_1) is an open ball in (X, d_2)

(d) The map $x \to x$ from (X, d_1) to (X, d_2) is continuous

2. Let $D = [-1, 1] \times [-1, 1]$. If the function $f : D \to \mathbb{R}$ is defined by

$$f(x,y) = \begin{cases} \dfrac{x^2 - y^2}{\left(x^2 + y^2\right)^2}, & (x,y) \neq (0,0) \\ 0, & (x,y) = (0,0) \end{cases}$$

then

(a) f is continuous at (0, 0)

(b) both the first order partial derivatives of f exist at (0, 0)

(c) $\iint_D |f(x,y)|^{\frac{1}{2}}\, dx\, dy$ is finite

(d) $\iint_D |f(x,y)|\, dx\, dy$ is finite

3. The initial value problem

$y' = y^{\frac{3}{5}}$, $y(0) = b$ has

(a) a unique solution if $b = 0$

(b) no solution if $b = 1$

(c) infinitely many solutions if $b = 2$

(d) a unique solution if $b = 1$

4. Consider the following statements:

I. $\log(|z|)$ is harmonic on $\mathbb{C} \setminus \{0\}$

II. $\log(|z|)$ has a harmonic conjugate on $\mathbb{C} \setminus \{0\}$

Then

(a) both I and II are true

(b) I is true but II is false

(c) I is false but II is false

(d) both I and II are false

5. Let G and H be defined by

$G = \mathbb{C} \setminus \{z = x + iy \in \mathbb{C} : x \le 0, y = 0\}$,

$H = \mathbb{C} \setminus \{z = x + iy \in \mathbb{C} : x \in \mathbb{Z}, x \le 0, y = 0\}$.

Suppose $f : G \to \mathbb{C}$ and $g : H \to \mathbb{C}$ are analytic functions. Consider the following statements:

I. $\int_\gamma f\,dz$ is independent of paths γ in G joining $-i$ and i

II. $\int_\gamma g\,dz$ is independent of paths γ in H joining $-i$ and i

Then

(a) both I and II are true

(b) I is true but II is false

(c) I is false but II is true

(d) both I and II are false

6. Let $f(z) = e^{\frac{1}{z}}, z \in \mathbb{C} \setminus \{0\}$ and let, for $n \in \mathbb{N}$,

$R_n = \left\{z = x + iy \in \mathbb{C} : |x| < \frac{1}{n}, |y| < \frac{1}{n}\right\} \setminus \{0\}$. If for a subset S of $\mathbb{C}$, $\overline{s}$ denotes the closure of S in $\mathbb{C}$, then

(a) $\overline{f(R_{n+1})} \neq \overline{f(R_n)}$

(b) $\dfrac{\overline{f(R_n)}}{\overline{f(R_{n+1})}} = \overline{f\left(\dfrac{R_n}{R_{n+1}}\right)}$

(c) $\overline{f\left(\cap_{n=1}^{\infty} R_n\right)} = \cap_{n=1}^{\infty}\overline{f(R_n)}$

(d) $\overline{f(R_n)} = \overline{f(R_{n+1})}$

7. Suppose that

$$U = \mathbb{R}^2 \setminus \{(x,y) \in \mathbb{R}^2 : x, y \in \mathbb{Q}\},$$

$$V = \mathbb{R}^2 \setminus \left\{(x,y) \in \mathbb{R}^2 : x > 0, y = \frac{1}{x}\right\}.$$

Then, with respect to the Euclidean metric on $\mathbb{R}^2$,

(a) both U and V are disconnected

(b) U is disconnected but V is connected

(c) U is connected but V is disconnected

(d) both U and V are connected

8. If (D1) and (D2) denote the dual problems of the linear programming problems (P1) and (P2), respectively, where

(P1) : minimize $x_1 - 2x_2$ subject to $-x_1 + x_2 = 10$, x_1, $x_2 \geq 0$,

(P2) : minimize $x_1 - 2x_2$ subject to $-x_1 + x_2 = 10$, $x_1 - x_2 = 10$, x_1, $x_2 \geq 0$, then

(a) both (D1) and (D2) are infeasible

(b) (P2) is infeasible and (D2) is feasible

(c) (D1) is infeasible and (D2) is feasible but unbounded

(d) (P1) is feasible but unbounded and (D1) is feasible

9. If (4, 0) and $\left(0, -\frac{1}{2}\right)$ are critical points of the function

$f(x, y) = 5 - (\alpha + \beta)x^2 + \beta y^2 + (\alpha + 1)y^3 + x^3$, where $\alpha, \beta \in \mathbb{R}$, then

(a) $\left(4, -\frac{1}{2}\right)$ is a point of local maxima of f

(b) $\left(4, -\frac{1}{2}\right)$ is a saddle point of f

(c) $\alpha = 4$, $\beta = 2$

(d) $\left(4, -\frac{1}{2}\right)$ is a point of local minima of f

10. Consider the iterative scheme

$$x_n = \frac{x_{n-1}}{2} + \frac{3}{x_{n-1}}, n \geq 1, \text{ with initial point } x_0 > 0.$$

Then the sequence $\{x_n\}$

(a) converges only if $x_0 > 1$

(b) converges only if $x_0 < 3$

(c) converges for any x_0

(d) does not converges for any x_0

11. Let C[0, 1] denote the space of all real-valued continuous functions on [0, 1] equipped with the supremum norm $\|.\|_\infty$. Let $T : C[0, 1] \to C[0, 1]$ be the linear operator defined by

$$T(f)(x) = \int_0^x e^{-y} f(y)\,dy. \text{ Then}$$

(a) $\|T\| = 1$

(b) I – T is not invertible

(c) T is surjective

(d) $\|I + T\| = 1 + \|T\|$

12. Suppose that M is a 5 × 5 matrix with real entries and p(x) = det(xI – M). Then

(a) p(0) = det(M)

(b) every eigenvalue of M is real if p(1) + p(2) = 0 = p(2) + p(3)

(c) M^{-1} is necessarily a polynomial in M of degree 4 if M is invertible

(d) M is not invertible if $M^2 - 2M = 0$

13. Let C[0, 1] denote the space of all real-valued continuous functions on [0, 1] equipped with the supremum norm $\|.\|_\infty$. Let $f \in C[0, 1]$ be such that

$|f(x) - f(y)| \leq M|x - y|$, for all $x, y \in [0, 1]$ and for some M > 0

For $n \in \mathbb{N}$, let $f_n(x) = f\left(x^{1+\frac{1}{n}}\right)$. If $S = \{f_n : n \in \mathbb{N}\}$, then

(a) the closure of S is compact

(b) S is closed and bounded

(c) S is bounded but not totally bounded

(d) S is compact

14. Let $K : \mathbb{R} \times (0, \infty) \to \mathbb{R}$ be a function such that the solution of the initial value problem

$$\frac{\partial u}{\partial t} = \frac{\partial^2 u}{\partial x^2}, u(x,0) = f(x), x \in \mathbb{R}, t > 0, \text{ is given by}$$

$$u(x,t) = \int_{\mathbb{R}} K(x-y,t)\, f(y)\, dy$$

for all bounded continuous function f. Then the value of $\int_R K(x,t)dx$ is _____

15. The number of cyclic subgroups of the quaternion group $Q_8 = \langle a, b \mid a^4 = 1, a^2 = b^2, ba = a^3 b \rangle$ is _____

16. The number of elements of order 3 in the symmetric group S_6 is _____

17. Let F be the field with 4096 elements. The number of proper subfields of F is _____

18. If (x_1^*, x_2^*) is an optional solution of the linear programming problem,

minimize $x_1 + 2x_2$

subject to

$4x_1 - x_2 \geq 8$

$2x_1 + x_2 \geq 10$

$-x_1 + x_2 \leq 7$

$x_1, x_2 \geq 0$

and $(\lambda_1^*, \lambda_2^*, \lambda_3^*)$ is an optimal solution of its dual problem, then $\sum_{i=1}^{2} x_i^* + \sum_{j=1}^{3} \lambda_j^*$ is equal to _____ (correct up to one decimal place)

19. Let a, b, c $\in \mathbb{R}$ be such that the quadrature rule

$$\int_{-1}^{1} f(x)dx \approx af(-1) + bf(0) + cf'(1)$$ is exact for all polynomials of degree less than or equal to 2. Then b is equal to _____ (rounded off to two decimal places)

20. Let $f(x) = x^4$ and let p(x) be the interpolating polynomial of f at nodes 1, 2 and 3. Then p(0) is equal to _____

21. For $n \geq 2$, define the sequence $\{x_n\}$ by

$$x_n = \frac{1}{2\pi} \int_0^{\frac{\pi}{2}} \tan^{\frac{1}{n}} t\, dt.$$

Then the sequence $\{x_n\}$ converges to _____ (correct up to two decimal places)

22. Let

$L^2[0, 10] = \{f : [0, 10] \to \mathbb{R} : f$ is Lebesgue measurable and $\int_0^{10} f^2 dx < \infty\}$ equipped with the norm $\| f \| = \left(\int_0^{10} f^2 dx\right)^{\frac{1}{2}}$ and T be the linear functional on $L^2[0, 10]$ given by

$$T(f) = \int_0^2 f(x)dx - \int_3^{10} f(x)dx.$$ Then $\| T \|$ is equal to _____

23. If $(x_{13}, x_{22}, x_{23} = 10, x_{31}, x_{32}, x_{34}\}$ is the set of basic variables of a balanced transportation problem seeking to minimize cost of transportation from origins to destinations, where the cost matrix is,

	D_1	D_2	D_3	D_4	Availability
O_1	6	2	−1	0	10
O_2	4	2	2	3	$\lambda + 5$
O_3	3	1	2	1	3λ
Demand	10	$\mu - 5$	$\mu + 5$	15	

and $\lambda, \mu \in \mathbb{R}$, then x_{32} is equal to _____

24. Let $\mathbb{Z}_{225}$ be the ring of integers modulo 225. If x is the number of prime ideals and y is the number of nontrivial units is $\mathbb{Z}_{225}$, then x + y is equal to _____

25. Let u(x, t) be the solution of

$$\frac{\partial^2 u}{\partial t^2} - \frac{\partial^2 u}{\partial x^2} = 0,\ u(x,0) = f(x),\ \frac{\partial u}{\partial t}(x,0) = 0, x \in \mathbb{R}, t > 0,$$

where f is a twice continuously differentiable function. If $f(-2) = 4$, $f(0) = 0$, and $u(2, 2) = 8$, then the value of u(1, 3) is _____

Q. 26 – Q. 55 carry two marks each.

26. Let $\{e_n\}_{n=1}^{\infty}$ be an orthonormal basis for a separable Hilbert space H with the inner product $\langle .,. \rangle$. Define

$$f_n = e_n - \frac{1}{n+1} e_{n+1} \text{ for } n \in \mathbb{N}. \text{ Then}$$

(a) the closure of the span $\{f_n : n \in \mathbb{N})$ equals H

(b) $f = 0$ if $\langle f, f_n \rangle = \langle f, e_n \rangle$ for all $n \in \mathbb{N}$

(c) $\{f_n\}_{n=1}^{\infty}$ is an orthogonal subset of H

(d) there does ot exist nonzero $f \in H$ such that $\langle f, e_2 \rangle = \langle f, f_2 \rangle$

27. Suppose V is a finite dimensional non-zero vector space over $\mathbb{C}$ and $T : V \to V$ is a linear transformation such that Range(T) = Nullspace(T). Then which of the following statements is FALSE?

(a) The dimension of V is even

(b) 0 is the only eigenvalue of T

(c) Both 0 and 1 are eigenvalues of T

(d) $T^2 = 0$

28. Let $P \in M_{m\times n}(\mathbb{R})$. Consider the following statements:

(I) If $XPY = 0$ for all $X \in M_{1\times m}(\mathbb{R})$ and $Y \in M_{n\times 1}(\mathbb{R})$, then $P = 0$.

(II) If $m = n$, P is symmetric and $P^2 = 0$, then $P = 0$.

Then

(a) Both I and II are true

(b) I is true but II is false

(c) I is false but II is true

(d) both I and II are false

29. For $n \in \mathbb{N}$, let $T_n : (l^1, \|\cdot\|_1) \to (l^\infty, \|\cdot\|_\infty)$ and $T : (l^1, \|\cdot\|_1) \to (l^\infty, \|\cdot\|_\infty)$ be the bounded linear operators defined by

$T_n(x_1, x_2, \ldots) = (y_1, y_2, \ldots)$ where $y_j = \begin{cases} x_j, & j \le n \\ x_n, & j > n \end{cases}$

and $T(x_1, x_2, \ldots) = (x_1, x_2, \ldots)$. Then

(a) $\|T_n\|$ does not converge to $\|T\|$ as $n \to \infty$

(b) $\|T_n - T\|$ converges to zero as $n \to \infty$

(c) for all $x \in l^1$, $\|T_n(x) - T(x)\|$ converges to zero as $n \to \infty$

(d) for each non-zero $x \in l^1$, there exists a continuous linear functional g on l^∞ such that $g(T_n(x))$ does not converges to $g(T(x))$ as $n \to \infty$

30. Let $P(\mathbb{R})$ denote the power set of $\mathbb{R}$, equipped with the metric

$d(U,V) = \sup_{x\in\mathbb{R}} |\chi_U(x) - \chi_V(x)|$, where χ_U and χ_V denote the characteristic functions of the subsets U and V, respectively, of $\mathbb{R}$. The set $\{\{m\} : m \in \mathbb{Z}\}$ in the metric space $(P(\mathbb{R}), d)$ is

(a) bounded but not totally bounded

(b) totally bounded but not compact

(c) compact

(d) not bounded

31. Let $f : \mathbb{R} \to \mathbb{R}$ be defined by

$f(x) = \sum_{n=0}^{\infty} \frac{1}{2^n} \chi(n, n+1](x)$, where $\chi(n, n+1]$ is the characteristic function of the interval (n, n+1].

For $\alpha \in \mathbb{R}$, let $S_\alpha = \{x \in \mathbb{R} : f(x) > \alpha\}$. Then

(a) $S_{\frac{1}{2}}$ is open

(b) $S_{\frac{\sqrt{5}}{2}}$ is not measurable

(c) S_0 is closed

(d) $S_{\frac{1}{\sqrt{2}}}$ is measurable

32. For $n \in \mathbb{N}$, let $f_n, g_n : (0, 1) \to \mathbb{R}$ be functions defined by

$f_n(x) = x^n$ and $g_n(x) = x^n(1 - x)$. Then

(a) $\{f_n\}$ converges uniformly but $\{g_n\}$ does not converge uniformly

(b) $\{g_n\}$ converges uniformly but $\{f_n\}$ does not converge uniformly

(c) both $\{f_n\}$ and $\{g_n\}$ converge uniformly

(d) neither $\{f_n\}$ nor $\{g_n\}$ converge uniformly

33. Let u be a solution of the differential equation $y' + xy = 0$ and let $\phi = u\Psi$ be a solution of the differential equation $y'' + 2xy' + (x^2 + 2)y = 0$ satisfying $\phi(0) = 1$ and $\phi'(0)$. Then $\phi(x)$ is

(a) $(\cos^2 x)e^{-\frac{x^2}{2}}$ (b) $(\cos x)e^{-\frac{x^2}{2}}$

(c) $(1 + x^2)e^{-\frac{x^2}{2}}$ (d) $(\cos x)e^{-x^2}$

34. For $n \in \mathbb{N} \cup \{0\}$, let y_n be a solution of the differential equation

$xy'' + (1 - x)y' + n y = 0$

satisfying $y_n(0) = 1$. For which of the following functions w(x), the integral

$\int_0^\infty y_p(x) y_q(x) w(x)\,dx$, $(p \ne q)$ is equal to zero?

(a) e^{-x^2} (b) e^{-x}

(c) xe^{-x^2} (d) xe^{-x}

35. Suppose that

$X = \{(0,0)\} \cup \left\{\left(x, \sin\frac{1}{x}\right) : x \in \mathbb{R} \setminus \{0\}\right\}$ and

$Y = \{(0,0)\} \cup \left\{\left(x, x\sin\frac{1}{x}\right) : x \in \mathbb{R} \setminus \{0\}\right\}$ are

metric spaces with metrics induced by the

Euclidean metric of $\mathbb{R}^2$. Let B_X and B_Y be unit balls around (0, 0) in X and Y, respectively. Consider the following statements:

I. The closure of B_X in X is compact.

II. The closure of B_Y in Y is compact.

Then

(a) both I and II are true

(b) I is true but II is false

(c) I is false but II is true

(d) both I and II are false

36. If $f:\mathbb{C}\setminus\{0\}\to\mathbb{C}$ is a function such that $f(z)=\left(\frac{z}{|z|}\right)$ and its restriction to be unit circle is continuous, then

(a) f is continuous but not necessarily analytic

(b) f is analytic but not necessarily a constant function

(c) f is a constant function

(d) $\lim_{z\to 0} f(z)$ exists

37. For a subset S of a topological space, let Int(S) and $\bar{S}$ denote the interior and closure of S, respectively. Then which of the following statements is TRUE?

(a) If S is open, then $S=\text{Int}(\bar{S})$

(b) If the boundary of S is empty, then S is open

(c) If the boundary of S is empty, then S is not closed

(d) If $\frac{\bar{S}}{S}$ is a proper subset of the boundary of S, then S is open

38. Suppose $\Im_1, \Im_2$ and $\Im_3$ are the smallest topologies on $\mathbb{R}$ containing S_1, S_2 and S_3, respectively, where

$$S_1=\left\{\left(a, a+\frac{\pi}{n}\right): a\in\mathbb{Q}, n\in\mathbb{N}\right\},$$

$$S_2=\{(a,b): a<b, \quad a,b\in\mathbb{Q}\}$$

$$S_3=\{(a,b): a<b, \quad a,b\in\mathbb{R}\}.$$ Then

(a) $\Im_3\supseteq\Im_1$

(b) $\Im_3\supseteq\Im_2$

(c) $\Im_1=\Im_2$

(d) $\Im_1\supseteq\Im_2$

39. Let $M=\begin{bmatrix}\alpha & 3 & 0\\ \beta & 3 & 1\\ 0 & 1 & 2\end{bmatrix}$. Consider the following statements:

I. The exists a lower triangular matrix L such that $M = LL^t$, where L^t denotes transpose of L.

II. Gauss-seidel method for $Mx=b\left(b\in\mathbb{R}^3\right)$ converges for any initial choice $x_0\in\mathbb{R}^3$. Then

(a) I is not true when $\alpha>\frac{9}{2}, \beta=3$

(b) II is not true when $\alpha>\frac{9}{2}, \beta=-1$

(c) II is not true when $\alpha=4, \beta=\frac{3}{2}$

(d) I is true when $\alpha = 5$, $\beta = 3$

40. Let I and J be the ideals generated by $\{5,\sqrt{10}\}$ and $\{4,\sqrt{10}\}$ in the ring

$\mathbb{Z}\left[\sqrt{10}\right]=\left\{a+b\sqrt{10}\,\middle|\,a,b\in\mathbb{Z}\right\}$, respectively. Then

(a) Both I and J are maximal ideals

(b) I is a maximal ideal but J is not a prime ideal

(c) I is not a maximal ideal but J is a prime ideal

(d) neither I nor J is a maximal ideal

41. Suppose V is a finite dimensional vector space over $\mathbb{R}$. If W_1, W_2 and W_3 are subspaces of V, then which of the following statements is TRUE?

(a) If W1 + W2 + W3 = V then

$\text{span}(W_1\cup W_2)\cup\text{span}(W_2\cup W_3)$
$\cup\,\text{span}(W_3\cup W_1)=V$

(b) If $W_1\cap W_2=\{0\}$ and $W_1\cap W_3=\{0\}$, then $W_1\cap(W_2+W_3)=\{0\}$

(c) If $W_1 + W_2 = W_1 + W_3$, then $W_2 = W_3$

(d) If $W_1 \neq V$, then span $\left(\frac{V}{W_1}\right)=V$

42. Let $\alpha,\beta\in\mathbb{R}, \alpha\neq 0$. The system

$x_1-2x_2+\alpha x_3=8$
$x_1-x_2+x_4=\beta$
$x_1, x_2, x_3, x_4\geq 0$

has NO basic feasible solution if

(a) $\alpha<0, \beta>8$ (b) $\alpha>0, 0<\beta<8$

(c) $\alpha>0, \beta<0$ (d) $\alpha<0, \beta<8$

43. Let $0 < p < 1$ and let

$$X = \left\{ f : \mathbb{R} \to \mathbb{R} \text{ is continuous and} \int_{\mathbb{R}} |f(x)|^p \, dx < \infty \right\}$$

For $f \in X$, define $|f|_p = \left(\int_{\mathbb{R}} |f(x)|^p \, dx \right)^{\frac{1}{p}}$. Then

(a) $|.|_p$ defines a norm on X

(b) $|f + g|_p \le |f|_p + |g|_p$ for all f, g $\in$ X

(c) $|f + g|_p^p \le |f|_p^p + |g|_p^p$ for all f, g $\in$ X

(d) if fn converges to f pointwise on $\mathbb{R}$, then $\lim_{n\to\infty} |f_n|_p = |f|_p$

44. Suppose the ϕ_1 and ϕ_2 are linearly independent solutions of the differential equation $2x^2y'' - (x + x^2)y' + (x^2 - 2)y = 0$, and $\phi_1(0) = 0$. Then the smallest positive integer n such that

$$\lim_{x\to 0} x^n \frac{\phi_2(x)}{\phi_1(x)} = 0 \text{ is } \_\_\_\_\_\_$$

45. Suppose that $f(z) = \prod_{n=1}^{17} \left(z - \frac{\pi}{n} \right), z \in \mathbb{C}$ and $\gamma(t) = e^{zit}$, $t \in [0, 2\pi]$. If $\int_\gamma \frac{f'(z)}{f(z)} dz = \alpha\pi i$, then the value of α is equal to ______

46. If $\gamma(t) = \frac{1}{2} e^{3\pi i t}, t \in [0, 2]$ and

$\int_\gamma \frac{1}{z^2(e^z - 1)} dz = \beta \pi i$, then β is equal to ______ (correct up to one decimal place)

47. Let $K = \mathbb{Q}\left(\sqrt{3 + 2\sqrt{2}}, \omega\right)$, where ω is a primitive cube root of unity. Then the degree of extension of K over $\mathbb{Q}$ is ______

48. Let $\alpha \in \mathbb{R}$. If $(3, 0, 0, \beta)$ is an optimal solution of the linear programming problem

minimize $x_1 + x_2 + x_3 - \alpha x_4$

subject to

$2x_1 - x_2 + x_3 = 6$

$-x_1 + x_2 + x_4 = 3$

$x_1, x_2, x_3, x_4 \ge 0$

then the maximum value of $\beta - \alpha$ is ______

49. Suppose that $T : \mathbb{R}^4 \to \mathbb{R}[x]$ is a linear transformation over $\mathbb{R}$ satisfying $T(-1, 1, 1, 1) = x^2 + 2x^4$, $T(1, 2, 3, 4) = 1 - x^2$, $T(2, -1, -1, 0) = x^3 - x^4$.

Then the coefficient of x^4 in $T(-3, 5, 6, 6)$ is ______

50. Let $\vec{F}(x, y, z) = (2x - 2y\cos x)\hat{\imath} + (2y - y^2 \sin x)\hat{\jmath} + 4z\,\hat{k}$ and let S be the surface of the tetrahedron bounded by the planes $x = 0, y = 0, z = 0$ and $x + y + z = 1$. If $\hat{n}$ is the unit outward normal to the tetrahedron, then the value of $\iint_S \vec{F}.\hat{n}\, dS$ is ______ (rounded off to two decimal places)

51. Let $\vec{F} = (x + 2y)e^z\hat{\imath} + (ye^z + x^2)\hat{\jmath} + y^2 z\hat{k}$ and let S be the surface $x^2 + y^2 + z = 1$, $z \ge 0$. If $\hat{n}$ is a unit normal to S and $\left| \iint_S (\nabla \times \vec{F}).\hat{n}\, dS \right| = \alpha\pi$. Then α is equal to ______

52. Let G be a non-cyclic group of order 57. Then the number of elements of order 3 in G is ______

53. The coefficient of $(x - 1)^5$ in the Taylor expansion about $x = 1$ of the function

$$F(x) = \int_1^x \frac{\log_e t}{t - 1} dt, \quad 0 < x < 2 \text{ is } \_\_\_\_\_\_ \text{ (correct}$$

up to two decimal places)

54. Let u(x, y) be the solution of the initial value problem $\frac{\partial u}{\partial x} + \left(\sqrt{u}\right)\frac{\partial u}{\partial y} = 0$, $u(x,0) = 1 + x^2$. Then the value of u(0, 1) is ______ (rounded off to three decimal places)

55. The value of

$$\lim_{n\to\infty} \int_0^1 nx^n e^{x^2} dx \text{ is } \_\_\_\_\_\_ \text{ (rounded off to three}$$

decimal places)

ANSWERS

General Aptitude

1. (*c*)	**2.** (*b*)	**3.** (*d*)	**4.** (*d*)	**5.** (*b*)	**6.** (*d*)	**7.** (*c*)	**8.** (*b*)	**9.** (*b*)	**10.** (*b*)

Mathematics

1. (*a*)	**2.** (*c*)	**3.** (*d*)	**4.** (*b*)	**5.** (*b*)	**6.** (*a* or *d*)
7. (*c*)	**8.** (*a*)	**9.** (*b*)	**10.** (*c*)	**11.** (*d*)	**12.** (*c*)
13. (*a*)	**14.** (1 to 1)	**15.** (5 to 5)	**16.** (80 to 80)	**17.** (5 to 5)	**18.** (5.5 to 5.5)
19. (1.70 to 1.80)	**20.** (36 to 36)	**21.** (0.25 to 0.25)	**22.** (3 to 3)	**23.** (5 to 5)	**24.** (121 to 121)
25. (10 to 10)	**26.** (*a*)	**27.** (*c*)	**28.** (*a*)	**29.** (*c*)	**30.** (*a*)
31. (*d*)	**32.** (*b*)	**33.** (*b*)	**34.** (*b*)	**35.** (*c*)	**36.** (*a*)
37. (*b*)	**38.** (*c*)	**39.** (*d*)	**40.** (*b*)	**41.** (*d*)	**42.** (*d*)
43. (*c*)	**44.** (3 to 3)	**45.** (56 to 56)	**46.** (0.5 to 0.5)	**47.** (4 to 4)	**48.** (7 to 7)
49. (5 to 5)	**50.** (1.30 to 1.40)	**51.** (2 to 2)	**52.** (38 to 38)	**53.** (0.04 to 0.04)	
54. (1.610 to 1.625)		**55.** (2.710 to 2.725)			

EXPLANATIONS

GENERAL APTITUDE

1. Rajiv Gandhi Khel Ratna Award was conferred on Mary Kom, a six time world champion in boxing, recently in ceremony at the Rashtrapati Bhawan (the President's official residence) in New Delhi.
2. Despite means without being affected by something.
3. Dissociate is the opposite of Associate.
4. Officials hope that the food grain production target will be met due to a good rabi produce.
5. Sum of first n natural numbers

$$= \frac{[n(n+1)]}{2}$$

Sum of first 2n natural numbers

$$= \frac{[2n(2n+1)]}{2} \quad ....(1)$$

Sum of first n odd numbers $= n^2$ ...(2)

Difference of (1) and (2)

$D = 2n^2 + n - n^2 = n^2 + n$

6. Decrease in repo-rate will decrease cost of borrowing and increase lending by commercial banks is the correct inference.

7.

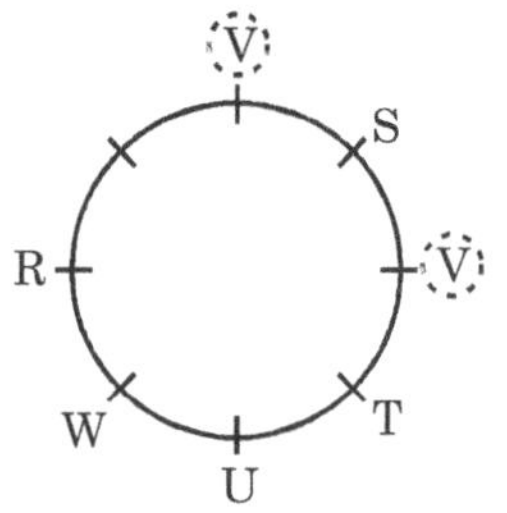

V can take any of the two positions.

In above diagram, P can not be seated opposite to Q.

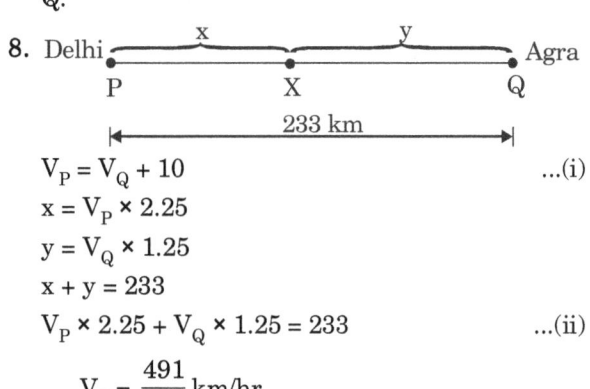

8.

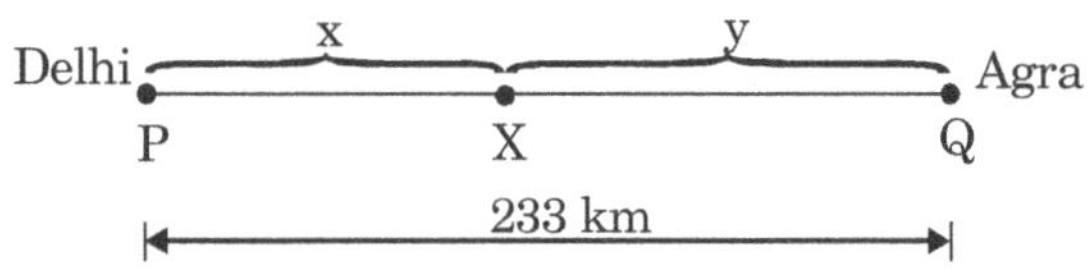

$V_P = V_Q + 10$ ...(i)

$x = V_P \times 2.25$

$y = V_Q \times 1.25$

$x + y = 233$

$V_P \times 2.25 + V_Q \times 1.25 = 233$ ...(ii)

$$V_P = \frac{491}{7} \text{ km/hr}$$

$$V_Q = \frac{421}{7} \text{ km/hr}$$

Distance travelled by Q

$\Rightarrow y = V_Q \times 1.25$

$= \frac{421}{7} \times 1.25$

$y = 75.17$ km

9. Total no. of elements in in 4×4 matrix is 16; of which four diagonal elements are zero. Remaining 12 elements can be divided in to two equal groups of 6 elements each. Both groups are opposite signed elements to meet the given condition.

10. Let the fixed investment annually be 'A'.

Total revenue of company P (2013 to 2018) = 1.1A + 1.2A + 1.4A + 1.4A + 1.5A + 1.4A = 8A

Total revenue of Company Q (2013 to 2018) = 1.2A + 1.3A + 1.3A + 1.5A + 1.6A + 1.6A = 8.5 A

MATHEMATICS

1. If $X = \{0\}$, then there is nothing to show. Thus, assume that there exists some $v \in X \setminus \{0\}$.

Let T_1, T_2 denote the topologies induced by d_1, d_2, respectively. First, assume (1.49) holds, i.e. the norms are equivalent.

If $A \in T_1$ and $x \in A$, then there exists $\varepsilon > 0$ such that $B_{\in,d_1}(x) \subseteq A$.

Thus, for each $y \in B_{\delta,d_2}(x)$ satisfying $\delta := a \in$, one obtains

$$d_1(x,y) \le \frac{1}{\alpha}\|x-y\|_2 < \frac{\delta}{\alpha} = \in,$$

showing $B_{\delta,d_2}(x) \subseteq B_{\in,d_1}(x) \subseteq A$ and that $A \in T_2$.

Now assume $A \in T_2$.

If $x \in A$, then there exists $\in > 0$ such that $B_{\in,d_2}(x) \subseteq A$.

Then, for each $y \in B_{\delta,d_1}(x)$ with $d : \in/\beta$, it holds that

$$d_2(x,y) \le \beta\|x-y\|_1 < \beta\delta = \in,$$

showing $B_{\in,d_1}(x) \subseteq B_{\in,d_2}(x) \subseteq A$.

Hence, $\quad A \in T_1$.

So, far we have proved that the validity of (1.49) impulies $T_1 = T_2$ (i.e. d_1 and d_2 are equivalent).

Thus, if the sequence (X, d_2) converges, then $x(d_1)$ also converges.

2. (c) $$f_{(x,y)} = \begin{cases} \frac{x^2-y^2}{\left(x^2+y^2\right)^2}, & (x,y) \ne (0,0) \\ 0, & (x,y) = (0,0) \end{cases}$$

$$\lim_{x\to 0}\Big|_{y=0} f(x,y) = \lim_{x\to 0}\Big|_{y=0} \frac{x^2-0}{\left(x^2+0\right)^2} = \frac{1}{x^2} = \infty$$

Again,

$$\lim_{y\to 0}\Big|_{x=0} f(x,y) = \lim_{x\to 0}\Big|_{y=0} \frac{0-y^2}{\left(0+y^2\right)^2} = -\frac{1}{y^2} = \infty$$

$\therefore$ f is not continuous at (0, 0)

and both the first order partial alleviative of f does not exist at (0, 0)

Now, $\iint\limits_D |f(x,y)|^{\frac{1}{2}}.\, dx.dy$

$$\int_{-1}^{1}\int_{-1}^{1}\left(\frac{\sqrt{x^2-y^2}}{x^2+y^2}\right).dx.dy.$$

This is finite

3. (d) $y^1 = (y)^{\frac{3}{5}}$

$$\frac{dy}{dx} = (y)^{\frac{3}{5}}$$

$$\frac{dy}{y^{\frac{3}{5}}} = dx$$

Integrating both sides, we have.

$$\int \frac{dy}{(y)^{\frac{3}{5}}} = \int dx$$

$$\frac{y^{\left(\frac{-3}{5}+1\right)}}{\left(\frac{-3}{5}+1\right)} = x + c, \text{ where C = constant.}$$

$$\frac{5}{2}(y)^{\frac{2}{5}} = x + c$$

From given condition, at x = 0, y = b.

$$\frac{5}{2}(b)^{\frac{2}{5}} = 0 + c \Rightarrow c = \frac{5}{2}(b)^{\frac{2}{5}}$$

$$\therefore \frac{5}{2}(y)^{\frac{2}{5}} = x + \frac{5}{2}(b)^{\frac{2}{5}}$$

For b = 1,

$$\frac{5}{2}(y)^{\frac{2}{5}} = x + \frac{5}{2}$$

This gives a unique solution.

4. log |z| log |z| has no harmonic conjugate in C\{0}C\{0}

If f is a branch of logarithm we require that for all $z \in G$,

$$e^{f(z)} = e^{a+ib} = e^{a(z)}e^{ib(z)} = z = |z|e^{i\theta}$$

where $a(z), b(z) \in R$ and $\theta = \arg z$.

Now, $e^{a(z)} = |z|$ and $e^{ib(z)} = e^{i\theta}$.

So we must have $a(z) = \log |z|$, and $b|z| = \theta + 2\pi k\,(z) \in (-\pi, \pi]$ for some $k(z) \in N$.

So we obtain that

$$f(z) = \log|z| + i[\theta + 2\pi k(z)]$$

where $k : G \to Z$.

But since f is continuous (we assume f is a branch) and that G is connected set.

Hence, k is constant function. We now show that there exists a sequence, $z_n \to z$ such that $f(z_n) \to f(z)$ so f is not continuous.

Consider $z = e^{i\pi}$, and the sequence of points,

$z_n = e^{i^{(-1)^n\left(\pi - \frac{1}{\pi}\right)}}$. Then

$$|f(z) - f(z_n)| = |\log 1 - \log z_n + i(\theta - \theta_n)|$$

$$= \left|\log\left|\cos\left(\pi - \frac{1}{n}\right)\right| + i\left(\pi - (1)^n\left(\pi - \frac{1}{n}\right)\right)\right|$$

$$\geq \left|\pi - (-1)^n\left(\pi - \frac{1}{n}\right)\right|$$

which does not converge.

7. Suppose that X is not connected. Thus, there exists two disjoint non-empty open subsets of X, U and V such that $X = U \cup V$.

Then $q(U) \cap q(V) = \theta$.

For otherwise, let $y \in q(U) \cap q(V)$.

Therefore,

$$q^{-1}(y) = (q^{-1}(y) \cap U) \cup (q^{-1}(y) \cap V),$$

and it is obvious that $q^{-1}(y) \cap U$ and $q^{-1}(y) \cap V$ are both nonempty open subsets of $q^{-1}(y)$, which contradicts the connectedness of $q^{-1}(y)$.

Since q is a quotient mapping,

$V = q^{-1}(q(V))$ and $U = q^{-1}(q(V))$, $q(U)$ and $q(V)$ are disjoint nonempty open subsets such that

$Y = q(U) \cup q(V)$, which contradicts the connectedness of Y.

Thus X must be connected.

Thus, U is connected but V is disconnected.

9. (b) $f(x, y) = 5 - (\alpha + \beta)x^2 + \beta y^2 + (\alpha + 1)y^3 + x^3$.

We know that for $r.s - t^2 < 0$, then we get a siddle point.

Now, $f_x(x,y) = -2(\alpha + \beta)x + 3x^2$ ...(i)

and $f_y(x,y) = +2\beta.y + 3(\alpha + 1)y^2$ ...(ii)

Point (4, 0) are critical point.

$\therefore f_x(4,0) = -2 \times 4(\alpha + \beta) + 3(4)^2 = 0$

$-8(\alpha + \beta) + 48 = 0$

$\boxed{(\alpha + \beta) = 6}$ ...(iii)

Again, Point $\left(0, \frac{-1}{2}\right)$ are critical point

$\therefore f_y\left(0, -\frac{1}{2}\right) = 2\beta\left(-\frac{1}{2}\right) + 3(\alpha + 1)\left(-\frac{1}{2}\right)^2 = 0$

$-\beta + \frac{3}{4}(\alpha + 1) = 0$

$\boxed{-4\beta + 3\alpha = -3}$ ...(iv)

From equation (iii) and (iv), we have.

$7\alpha + 21 \Rightarrow \alpha = 3$, and $\beta = 3$

Now, Putting α, β in equation (i) and (ii), we get

$f(x, y) = -2(6)x + 3x^2 \Rightarrow 3x^2 - 12x$.

$f_y(x, y) = 6y + 2y^2$

On double differentiation.

$f_{xx}(x, y) = 6x - 12$

$f_{yy}(x, y) = 24y + 6$

and . $f_{xy}(x, y) = 0$

Check at point $\left(4, -\frac{1}{2}\right)$;

$f_{xx}(x, y) = -12 + 24$

$= 12 > 0$

$f_{yy}(x,y) = 24\left(-\frac{1}{2}\right) + 6 = -6 < 0$

$f_{xy} = 0$

Now, $f_{xx} . f_{yy} - f_{xy}$

$= 12(-6) = -72 < 0$

Hence, point $\left(4, -\frac{1}{2}\right)$ is a siddle point.

10. (c) $x_n = \frac{x_{n-1}}{2} + \frac{3}{x_{n-1}}, n \geq 1.$

Let $x_n \to l$ {x_n converges to l}

then $x_n \to l$.

$\therefore l = \frac{l}{2} + \frac{3}{l} \Rightarrow l = \frac{l^2 + 6}{2l}$

$2l^2 = l^2 + 6 \Rightarrow l^2 = 6$

$l = \pm\sqrt{6}$

As $x_0 \geq 0$, so, l can not be negative.

$\therefore l = \sqrt{6}$

$\therefore x_n$ converges to $\sqrt{6}$. i.e. independent to any x.

Hence, x_n converges for any x_0.

12. (c) P(x) = let (xI – M)

Ad M = 5 × 5 matrix

dog P(x) = 5

Let $P(x) = x^5 + a_4x^4 + a_3x^3 + a_2x^2 + a_1x + a_0$--- (i)

Now, As M is invertible ⇒ det (M) ≠ 0.

$\therefore a_0 = (-1)^n$. det (M) ≠ 0.

$m^5 + a_4m^4 + a_3m^3 + a_2m^2 + a_1m + a_0I$ ---- 0

$M(m^4 + a_4 + a_3m^2 + a_2m + a_1) = -a_0I$

$$M\left[-\frac{1}{a_0}\left(m^4 + a_4m^3 + a_3m^2 + a_2m + a_1\right)\right] = 1$$

We know that $A.A^{-1} = I$

$$\therefore M^{-1} = -\frac{1}{a_0}\left(M^4 + a_4m^3 + a_3m^2 + a_2m + a_1\right)$$

Hence, M^{-1} is necessarily a polynomial in M of degree 4.

14. (a) From heat equation,

$$\frac{\partial u}{\partial t} = k.\frac{\partial_y^2}{\partial x^2}, x \in R, t > 0$$

and u (x, 0) = f(x)

Then the solution is.

$$u_{(x,t)} = \frac{1}{\sqrt{4\pi kt}}\int_{-\infty}^{\infty} e^{-\frac{(x-y)^2}{4kt}}.f(y).dy$$

On equating this solution will given solution, we get.

$$u(x,t) = \int_{-\infty}^{\infty} k(x-y,t)f(y).dy =$$

$$\int_{-\infty}^{\infty}\frac{1}{\sqrt{4\pi kt}}.e^{\frac{-(x-y)^2}{rkt}}.f(y)dy$$

$$\therefore k(x-y,t) = \frac{e^{\frac{-(x-y)^2}{rkt}}}{\sqrt{4\pi kt}}$$

here k = 1,

$$\therefore k(x-y,t) = \frac{e^{\frac{-(x-y)^2}{4t}}}{\sqrt{4\pi kt}}$$

$$k(x,t) = \frac{e^{-\frac{x^2}{4t}}}{\sqrt{4\pi t}}$$

$$\text{Now, } \int_R k(x,t).dt = \int_{-\infty}^{\infty}\frac{e^{-\frac{x^2}{4t}}}{\sqrt{4\pi t}}dx$$

$$= \frac{1}{\sqrt{4\pi t}}\int_{-\infty}^{\infty} e^{-\frac{x^2}{4t}}.dx = \frac{1}{\sqrt{4\pi t}}.\sqrt{4\pi t}$$

= 1.

15. 5 Quaternion group Q_8

$$= \langle a, b \mid a^4 = 1, a^2 = b^2, ba = a^3b\rangle$$

Q_8 have cardinality 8

$Q_8 = \{\pm 1, \pm i, \pm j, \pm k\}$

∴ each element have 4 elements

Subgroups are

$H_1 = \{1\}$, $H_2 = \{\pm1\}$, $H_3 = \{\pm1, \pm j\}$, $H_4 = \{\pm1, \pm j\}$, $H_5 = \{\pm1, \pm k\}$, and $H_6 = Q_8$.

Cyclic subgroup have same element order as group order.

Here, In H_1, H_2, H_3, H_4 and H_5, element order is equal to group order.

Hence Number of cyclic subgroup = 5

16. (80) Here

Here 6 → 1, 1, 1, 3
→ 3,3

On partition of 6, we get 6 in two ways

Now, we get element 1, 1, 1, 3 in $\frac{6!}{1^3 \times 3^1.3!} = 40$

We get element 3, 3, in $\frac{6!}{3^2.2!} = 40$.

∴ total number of elements of order 3 in the symmetric group $8_6 = 40 + 40 = 80$.

17. 5 $4096 = 2^{12}$ – This is field of order 2 raises to 12.

In general, if F_{p^n} then F_{p^m} is a subfield of F_{p^n} iff m divide n.

Now n = 12, m = Number of division of 12.

$12 = 2^2 \times 3^1$

Number of division = (2 + 1) (1 + 1) = 6

∴ Number of proper subfields of F = 6 – 1 = 5.

19. (1.70) $\int_{-1}^{1} f(x).dx = af(-1) + bf(0) + cf'(1)$

Let $f(x) = x^0 = 1$

$\Rightarrow \int_{-1}^{1} 1.dx = 2 = a + b \quad ...(i)$

$f(x) = x^1 = x$

$\Rightarrow \int_{-1}^{1} x.dx = 0 = -a + c \quad ...(ii)$

$f(x) = x^2 = x^2$

$\Rightarrow \int_{-1}^{1} x^2.dx = \frac{2}{3} = -a + c \quad ...(iii)$

From equation (ii) and (iii), we get

$2a = \frac{2}{3} \Rightarrow a = \frac{1}{3}.$

Putting in equation (i), we get

$\frac{1}{3} + b = 2$

$b = 2 - \frac{1}{3} = \frac{5}{3} \approx 1.7$

20. 36 $f(x) = x^4$ ...Given function

x	$x_1 = 1$	$x_2 = 2$	$x_3 = 3$
f(x)	f(1) = 1	f(2) = 16	f(3) = 81

$L_1(x) = \frac{(x - x_2)(x - x_3)}{(x_1 - x_2)(x_1 - x_3)}$

$= \frac{(x-2)(x-3)}{(1-2)(1-3)} = \frac{1}{2}(x^2 - 5x + 6)$

$L_2(x) = \frac{(x - x_1)(x - x_3)}{(x_2 - x_1)(x_2 - x_3)}$

$= \frac{(x-1)(x-3)}{(2-1)(2-3)} = -1(x^2 - 4x + 3)$

$L_3(x) = \frac{(x - x_1)(x - x_2)}{(x_3 - x_1)(x_3 - x_2)}$

$= \frac{(x-1)(x-2)}{(3-1)(3-2)} = \frac{1}{2}(x^2 - 3x + 2)$

Now, $P(x) = L_1(x).f_1(x) + L_2(x)f_2(x) + L_3(x).f_3(x)$

$= \frac{1}{2}(x^2 - 5x + 6) - (x^2 - 4x + 3)(16) +$

$\frac{1}{2}(x^2 - 3x + 2).81$

$= \frac{6}{2} - 48 + \frac{2 \times 81}{2}$

$= 3 - 48 + 81 = 36$

21. (0.25) $x_n = \frac{1}{2\pi}\int_0^{\frac{\pi}{2}} \tan^{\frac{1}{n}} t..dt$

$\{x_n\} = \frac{1}{2\pi}\int_0^{\frac{\pi}{2}} \left[\tan^{\frac{1}{2}} t + \tan^{\frac{1}{3}} t + \tan^{\frac{1}{4}} ...\infty\right] dt$

for $n \geq 2$

Now, Let tan (t) = k (constant)

Now, $(k)^{\frac{1}{2}} + (k)^{\frac{1}{3}} + (k)^{\frac{1}{4}} + ...\infty \approx 1.$

$\therefore \tan^{\frac{1}{2}} t + \tan^{\frac{1}{3}} t + \tan^{\frac{1}{4}} t + ...\infty = 1$

$\therefore \{S_n\} = \frac{1}{2\pi}\int_0^{\frac{\pi}{2}} \left[\tan^{\frac{1}{2}} t + \tan^{\frac{1}{3}} t + \tan^{\frac{1}{4}} t + ...\infty\right] dt$

$= \frac{1}{2\pi}\int_0^{\frac{\pi}{2}} .1.dt$

$= \frac{1}{2\pi}.\left[\frac{\pi}{2}\right] = \frac{1}{4} = 0.25$

22. (3) $L^2 [0, 10] = \{f : [0, 10] \rightarrow R : f$ is lebesgue measurable and $\int_0^{10} f^2.dx < \infty\}$

If $T \in L^2(x)$, then $\exists\, ! g \in L^2(x)$,

where $\frac{1}{p} + \frac{1}{q} = 1$

Such that $T(f) = \int_x fgdx$

and $\|T\|_{L^{px}} = \|g\|_{L^2}$

For P = 2, q = 2, x = [0, 10]

$$g(x) = \begin{cases} -1, & 3 \le x \le 10 \\ 0, & 2 < x < 3 \\ 1, & 0 \le x \le 2 \end{cases}$$

$$\therefore T(f) = \int_0^2 f(x).dx + \int_2^3 0.dx + (-1)\int_3^{10} f(x).dx$$

$$= \int_0^{10} f.g.dx$$

Now $\|g\|_2 = \left(\int_0^{10} g^2(x).dx\right)^{\frac{1}{2}}$

$$\|T = \|g\|_2 = \left[\int_0^2 (1)^2 .dx + \int_2^3 0.dx + \int_3^{10} (-1)^2 .dx\right]^{\frac{1}{2}}$$

$$= \left[2 + (10-3)\right]^{\frac{1}{2}} = (9)^{\frac{1}{2}} = 3$$

23. Hint

Let us assume in general that there are m- sources S_1, S_2, ..., S_m with capacities a_1, a_2, ..., a_m and n-destinations (sink) with requirements b_1, b_2, ..., b_n respectively. The transportation cost from i_{th} - source to the j_{th} - sink is c_{ij} and the amount shipped is x_{ij}. If the total capacity of all sources is equal to the total requirement of all destinations, what must be values of x_{ij} with i = 1, 2, ..., m and j = 1, 2, ..., n for the total transportation cost be minimum

		Sink (Destination)					Availability
		D_1	D_2			D_n	a_i
Source	S_1	c_{11}	c_{12}			c_{1n}	a_1
	S_2	c_{21}	c_{22}			c_{2n}	a_2
	:	:	:			:	:
	:	:	:			:	:
	S_m	c_{m1}	c_{m2}			c_{mn}	a_m
Demand (b_j)		b_1	b_2			b_n	$\Sigma a_i = \Sigma b_j$

Upon examining the above statement of the problem, we realize that it has an objective function which is

$$f(x) = c_{11}x_{11} + ... + c_{21}x_{21} + ... + c_{2n}x_{2n} + ... + c_{m1}x_{m1} + ... + c_{mn}x_{mn}$$

$$= \sum_{i=1}^{m}\sum_{j=1}^{n} c_{ij}x_{ij}$$

Secondary, in view of the condition that the total capacity is equal to the total requirement, i.e.,

$\sum a_j = \sum b_j$, the individual capacity of each source must be fully utilized and the individual requirement of each destination must likewise be fully satisfied.

Hence we have m capacity constraints and n requirements constraints. The capacity constraints impose on the solution the condition that the total shipments of all destinations from any source must be equal to the capacity of that source. Thus,

$X_{i1} + X_{i2} + ... + X_{in} = a_i$,

$i = 1, 2, ..., m$.

On the other hand, the requirement constraints require that the demand of every destination be fully satisfied by the total shipments from all sources. Thus,

$X_{1j} + X_{2j} + ... + x_{mj} = b_j$, $j = 1, 2, ... , n$.

Thirdly, there are the usual non-negativity costraints, i.e. $X_{ij} \ge 0$ for all i and j. They are based on the practical aspect that either we shall send some positive quantity or no quantity from any source to any sink.

To sum up, we have the following mathematical formulation of the transportation problem :

Minimize, $z = \sum_{i=1}^{m}\sum_{j=1}^{n} c_{ij}x_{ij}$ (i)

Subject to $\sum_{i=1}^{n} x_{ij} = a_i$ $i = 1, 2, ... m$ (ii)

$\sum_{i=1}^{m} x_{ij} = bj$ $j = 1, 2, ... n$ (iii)

and x_{ij} ³ for all i and j (iv)

The above formulation looks like an LLP. This special LPP will be called a transportation problem (T.P.).

Matrix form a TP: We can see write (i) – (iv) in matrix form as

Minimize $z = cx$, c, $x^T \in R^{mn}$

subject to $Ax = b$, $x \ge 0$, $b^T \in R^{m+n}$

where $x = [x_{11} ... x_{1n}\ x_{21} ... x_{2n}\ x_{m1} ... x_{mn}]$

$b = [a_1, a_2 .... a_m\ b_1\ b_2 .... b_n]$

and A is a (m + n) × (mn) real matrix containing the coefficients of constraints and c is the cost vector. The elements of A are either 0 or 1. Thus, a LPP can be reduced to a TP if

1. the a_{ij}'s are restricted to the values 0 and 1.
2. The units among the constraints are homogeneous.

Based on given that we can find the values of x32 = 5

24. (121) z^{225} be the ring of integers modulo 225.

x = Number of prime ideals.

y = Number of non-trivial units.

We know that, $\frac{J}{I}$ is a prime ideal of $\frac{R}{I}$

(Where R is a ring and I, J are ideals)

if J is a prime ideal of R if J $\geqslant$ I.

there, $\frac{R}{I} = \frac{\mathbb{Z}}{225\mathbb{Z}}$ and $\frac{J}{I} = \frac{J}{225\,\mathbb{Z}}$

Let J = P $\mathbb{Z}$, where P = Prime number

$<P> = J = P\mathbb{Z} \geq 225\mathbb{Z} = <225>$

$225 \in <225> \leq <P> > 225 \in <P>$

$\Rightarrow 225 = P^k$, for $k \in \mathbb{Z}$

$\Rightarrow P/225$

On prime factorization of 225.

$225 = 3^2 . 5^2$

Prime factors are 3 and 5.

Now, $\frac{J}{225\mathbb{Z}} = \frac{3\mathbb{Z}}{225\mathbb{Z}}, \frac{5\mathbb{Z}}{225\mathbb{Z}} \Rightarrow x = 2$

Again, We know that u is a unit in Z_{225}.
if gcd (u, 225) = 1

$y + 1 = Q(225) = 225\left(1-\frac{1}{3}\right)\left(1-\frac{1}{5}\right)$

$= 225 \times \frac{2}{3} \times \frac{4}{5} = 120$

$\therefore y = 120 - 1 = 119.$

Hence, $x + y = 2 \times 119 = 121.$

25. (10) From wave equation, we know that if the wave equation

$\frac{\partial^2 u}{\partial t^2} = \frac{c^2 \partial^4 u}{\partial x^2}$ is satisfied by

$u(x, 0) = f(x)$

$\frac{\partial u}{\partial t}(x,0) = g(x)$

Then its solution is given by

$$u(x,t) = \frac{1}{2}[f(x+ct) + f(x-ct)] + \frac{1}{2c}\int_{x+ct}^{x+ct} g(x).dx$$

On comparing given equation with above equation we get c = 1, g(x) = 0 and u(2, 2) = 8

$\therefore$ Solution is $u(x,t) = \frac{1}{2}[f(x+ct) + f(x-ct)] + 0$

$u(2,2) = \frac{1}{2}[f(2+2) + f(2-2)]$

$8 = \frac{1}{2}[f(4) + f(0)]$

$\therefore f(4) = 16.$

Now $u(1, 3) = \frac{1}{2}[f(1+3) + f(1-3)]$

$= \frac{1}{2}[f(4) + f(-2)]$

$= \frac{1}{2}[16 + 4] = 10$

27. (c) By Rank – Nullity Theorem

dim (v) = Rank (T) + Nullity (T)

From question, Rank (T) = Null space (T)

$\therefore$ dim (v) = Rank (T) + Rank (T)

= 2 Rank (T).

(i) Now, for any Rank (T), dim (v) will be even

(ii) Let $x \in V$, T (x) $\therefore$ Rang (T)

$T^2(x) = T(T(x))$

Again as Rang (T) = Null space (T)

$\therefore$ Range of T(x) is Null space (T).

$\therefore T^2(x) = T(T(x)) = 0;\ \forall\ x \in V$

(iii)$T^2(x) = 0$ is a Nillopotent operation because, if $T^k = 0$ for some $K \in N$

Then operation T is only Nillopotent operator and Nillopotent operator have eigenvalue as 'O' only not 1.

28. (a) From student I

XPY = 0 for all $X \in M_{1\times m}(R)$

and $Y \in M_{n\times 1}(R)$

Let e_i and e_j two row matrix met column matrix, such that

$e_i = [0,0,0...1,0....,0,0]$

$$e_j = \begin{bmatrix} 0 \\ 0 \\ 0 \\ \vdots \\ 1 \\ . \\ . \\ . \\ 0 \\ 0 \\ 0 \end{bmatrix}$$

Now, XPY = 0 $\forall$ x, y

$\therefore e_i P e_j = 0\ \forall i, j$

$\Rightarrow P_{ij} = 0$

$\therefore P = 0$

Hence, statement I is true

Statement-II : From spectral theorem, if P is symmetric matrix, then it is diagonalisable.

Again, If $p^k = 0$, then p is miloptent matrix.

Here K = 2, P2 = 0, P is niloptent.

and Non-zero miloptent matrix is never diagonalization.

But P is diagonalisable {given}.

Hence P have zero miloptent matrix.

$\therefore P = 0.$

31 (d) $f(x)=\sum_{n=0}^{\infty}\frac{1}{2^n}\chi(n,n+1]^{(x)}$,

$$f(x)=\frac{1}{20}\chi_{(0,1)}(x)+\frac{1}{2^1}\chi_{(1,2)}x+\ldots\frac{1}{2^n}\chi_{(n,n+1)}x$$

and $\chi_E(x)=\begin{cases}1 & x\in E\\ 0 & x\notin E\end{cases}$

$$\therefore f(x)=\begin{cases}0, x\le 0\\ \left(\frac{1}{2}\right)^0, 0<x\le 1\\ \frac{1}{2}, 01<x\le 2\\ \left(\frac{1}{2}\right)^2, 2<x\le 3\\ \text{---------------}\\ \left(\frac{1}{2}\right)^n, x<x\le x+1\end{cases}$$

$S_\propto = \{\propto \in R, f(x) \propto$

$$S_{\frac{1}{2}}=\left\{\propto\in R, f(x)>\frac{1}{2}\text{ for}\left[0,\frac{1}{2}\right]\right.$$

Hence, $S_{\frac{1}{2}}$ is close, $\therefore$ option (a) is false

Again $S_{\frac{\sqrt{5}}{2}}$ = d is measurable, $\therefore$ option (b) is false

Again, $S_0 = \{x \in R ; f(x) \ge 0.$ for $(0, \infty)$

This is open interval. $\therefore$ option (c) is false option

(d) $S_{\frac{1}{\sqrt{2}}}$ is obtained for $0 < x \le 1$

This is measurable, Hence, correct option.

32. Since uniform covergence is equivalent to convergence in the uniform metric, we can answer this question by computing $d_u(f_n, f)$ and checking if $d_u(f_n, f)\to 0$.

We have, by definition

$$d_u(f_n, f)=\sup_{0\le x\le 1}\left|x^n-0\right|=\sup_{0\le x\le 1}x^n=1$$

Therefore, $\lim_{n\to\infty} d_u\left(x^n,0\right)=\lim_{n\to\infty}1=1\neq 0.$

The sequence of functions xn does not converage uniformly on the interval [0, 1].

$$g_n(r) = x^n(1-x) \;\forall\; x\in(0,1)$$

Let $\quad y = |f_n(x) - f(x)| = x^n(1-x)$

Now, y is maximum or minimum when

$$\frac{dy}{dx} = n.x^{n-1} - (n+1)x^n = 0$$

$$x^{n-1}(n-(n-1)x)=0$$

or $x = 0$ or $\dfrac{n}{(n-1)}$

Now $\quad \dfrac{d^2y}{dx^2} = n(n-1)x^{n-2} - (n+1)nx^{n-1}$

At $\quad x = \dfrac{n}{(n-1)}, \dfrac{d^2y}{dx^2} = -\text{ve}$

$$\therefore \quad y_{\max} = \left(\frac{n}{n-1}\right)^n\left(1-\frac{n}{n-1}\right)\to\frac{1}{e}\times 0$$

$$= 0 \text{ as } n\to\infty$$

Hence, sequence is uniformly convergent on (0, 1) by M-Test.

33.
$$y' + xy = 0$$
$$\frac{dy}{dx} = -xy$$
$$\Rightarrow \quad \frac{dy}{y} = -x.dx$$
$$\text{In } y = -\frac{x^2}{2}$$
$$\Rightarrow \quad y = e^{-\frac{x^2}{2}}$$

Now, $\quad$ Let $\phi(x) = e^{-\frac{x^2}{2}}.\Psi(x)$

$$\phi(0) = e^{-(0)}.\phi(0)$$
$$= \phi(0) = 1$$

and $\quad \phi'(x) = e^{-\frac{x^2}{2}}.(-x).\Psi(x) + e^{-\frac{x^2}{2}}\Psi'(x)$

$$= e^{-\frac{x^2}{2}}[\Psi'(x) = x.\Psi(x)]$$
$$\phi'(0) = e^{-(0)}[\Psi'(0) - 0] = 0$$
$$\therefore \quad \Psi'(0) = 0$$

Here we got that $\Psi(0) = 1$ and $\Psi'(0) = 0$

For $\quad \Psi(x) = \cos x,$

$$\Psi(0) = \cos(0) = 1$$

and $\quad \Psi'(x) = -\sin x$

$$\Psi'(0) = -\sin(0) = 0$$

$$\therefore \quad \phi(x) = e^{-\frac{x^2}{2}}.\cos x$$

Now, $\quad \phi'(x) = e^{-\left(\frac{x^2}{2}\right)}[x.\cos x + \sin x]$

$$\phi''(x) = e^{-\left(\frac{x^2}{2}\right)}[x(x\cos x + \sin x) - (2\cos x - \sin x)]$$

Now, $y'' + 2xy' + (x^2 + 2)y = 0$

$$e^{-\frac{x^2}{2}}\left[x(x\cos x + \sin x) - (2\cos x - x\sin x)\right]$$

$$+ 2x\left[-e^{-\left(\frac{x^2}{2}\right)}(x\cos x + \sin x)\right] + (x^2+2)e^{-\left(\frac{x^2}{2}\right)}\cos x$$

$= 0$

Hence, $\boxed{\phi(x) = \cos x . e^{-\left(\frac{x^2}{2}\right)}}$

34. Ths solutions $L_n(x)$ of the general Laguerre differential equation

$$xy'' + (a + 1 - x)y' + ny = 0$$

are known as generalized Laguerre polynomials.

Their orthogonality is given by the weighted inner product:

$$\int_0^\infty L_n(x)L_m(x)x^a e^{-x}dx = 0,\ m \neq n.$$

Laguerre Polynomials

The solutions of the Laguerre differential equation

$$x''y + (1 - x)y' + ny = 0$$

are known as Laguerre polynomials. This is the particular case $a = 0$ of the generalized Laguerre polynomials.

To put the equation into the Sturm-Liouville form, let us first divide the equation by x.

$$y'' + \frac{1-x}{x}y' + n\frac{1}{x}y = 0$$

and then calculate the integrating factor

$$p(x) = e^{\int^x \frac{1-z'}{x'}dx'} = e^{\ln x - x} = xe^{-x}$$

Multiplying the last equation by this integrating factor, we have

$$x\,e^{-x}y'' + (1-x)e^{-x}y' + n\,e^{-x}y = 0$$

Since, $\left[x\,e^{-x}y'\right]' = x\,e^{-x}y'' + (1-x)e^{-x}y'$,

the equation can be written as

$$\left[x\,e^{-x}y'\right]' + n\,e^{-x}y' = 0.$$

This is in the form of a Sturm-Liouville equation with $p(x) = x\,e^{-x}$, $q = 0$, $w(x) = e^{-x}$.

Since $p(0) = p(\infty) = 0$, this is a singular Sturm-Liouville problem.

Therefore, if $L_n(x)$ and $L_m(x)$ are two solutions of this problem, then they must be orthogonal with respect to the weight function $w(x) = e^{-x}$, that is

$$\int_{-\infty}^{\infty} L_n(x)L_m(x)e^{-x}dx = 0 \quad \text{for } n \neq m.$$

36. $f(x) = f\left(\frac{z}{|z|}\right)$ and its restriction to the unit circle is continuous.

$\therefore\ |z| < 1 \Rightarrow -1 < z < z.$

Now, for $z < 0$,

$$f(z) = -\frac{z}{z} = -1$$

and for $z > 0, f(z) = \frac{z}{z} = 1$

Hence $f(z)$ is continuous but not analytic as,

$$f(z)\big|_{z<0} \neq f(z)\big|_{z>0} \text{ in the region.}$$

39. The cholesky decomposition of a hermition positive definite. Matrix A is a decomposition of are from

$$A = L.L^T$$

then,
$$\begin{bmatrix} A_{00} & A_{01} & A_{02} \\ A_{10} & A_{11} & A_{12} \\ A_{20} & A_{21} & A_{22} \end{bmatrix}$$
$$= \begin{bmatrix} L_{00} & 0 & 0 \\ L_{10} & L_{11} & 0 \\ L_{20} & L_{21} & L_{22} \end{bmatrix}\begin{bmatrix} L_{00} & L_{10} & L_{20} \\ 0 & L_{11} & L_{21} \\ 0 & 0 & L_{22} \end{bmatrix}$$

Basis of cholesky decomposition algorithm are.

$$L_{j.j} = \sqrt{A_{j.j} - \sum_{K=0}^{J-1}(L_{J,K})^2}$$

and
$$L_{j.j} = \frac{1}{L_{j.j}}\left(A_{j.j} - \sum_{K=0}^{j-1} L_{S,K}.L_{j,K}\right)$$

Based on above algorithm, we get

$\alpha = 5$ and $\beta = 3$.

40. (b) Let $R = \mathbb{Z}\left[a + b\sqrt{10}\right]$

and $I\langle 5, \sqrt{10}\rangle$, $J = \langle 4, \sqrt{10}\rangle$

Now, $J = \langle 4, \sqrt{10}\rangle \subset \langle 2, \sqrt{10}\rangle \neq \mathbb{Z}\left[\sqrt{10}\right]$

Here, ideal generated by $\langle 2, \sqrt{10}\rangle$ are maximal ideal

$\therefore$ J is not maximal

Let $\phi : \mathbb{Z}\left[a + b\sqrt{10}\right] \to \mathbb{Z}_5$

Homomorphism

$a + b\sqrt{10} \to a \bmod (5)$

$\Rightarrow \phi(1) = \bar{1}, \phi(2) = \bar{2}$

$\therefore$ ϕ is subjective ring. homomorphism.

Now $\text{Ker}\phi = \{a + b\sqrt{10} \in R \mid \text{and}(5) = \bar{0}\}$

ideal $I = \langle 5, \sqrt{10}\rangle = \left\{a + b\sqrt{10} \in R \mid \frac{5}{a}\right\}$

{Here 5 divide a}

$$\Rightarrow \frac{\mathbb{Z}\left[a + b\sqrt{10}\right]}{\langle 5, \sqrt{10}\rangle} \cong \mathbb{Z}_5$$

$\Rightarrow$ I is maximal

42. Le the equation is AX = B.

Where $A = \begin{bmatrix} 1 & -2 & \alpha & 0 \\ 1 & -1 & 0 & 1 \end{bmatrix}\begin{bmatrix} x_1 \\ x_2 \\ x_3 \\ x_4 \end{bmatrix} = \begin{bmatrix} 8 \\ \beta \end{bmatrix}$

$$\begin{bmatrix} 1 & -2 \\ 1 & -1 \end{bmatrix}\begin{bmatrix} x_1 \\ x_2 \end{bmatrix} = \begin{bmatrix} 8 \\ \beta \end{bmatrix}$$

$$\begin{bmatrix} -2 & \alpha \\ -1 & 0 \end{bmatrix}\begin{bmatrix} x_2 \\ x_3 \end{bmatrix} = \begin{bmatrix} 8 \\ \beta \end{bmatrix}$$

and $\begin{bmatrix} \alpha & 0 \\ 0 & 1 \end{bmatrix}\begin{bmatrix} x_3 \\ x_4 \end{bmatrix} = \begin{bmatrix} 8 \\ \beta \end{bmatrix}$

The solution is not feasible for $\alpha < 0$ and $\beta < 8$.

45. $f(z) = \left(z - \frac{\pi}{1}\right)\left(z - \frac{\pi}{2}\right)\left(z - \frac{\pi}{3}\right) \text{---} \left(z - \frac{\pi}{17}\right) = 0$

Then number of roots of f(z) = 17

Now, from given equation $y(t) = e^{2.it}$, $t = \in(0, 2\pi)$

This is a circle of unit radius.

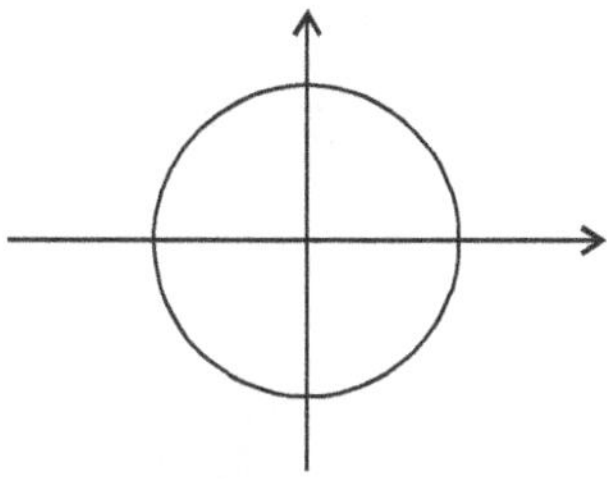

Now, we see that three roots

$z = \pi, \frac{\pi}{2}$ and $\frac{\pi}{3}$ lies outside the circle, so, number of roots lies inside the circle

= 17 – 3 = 14

As circle varies 2 times,

So, Number of roots inside it = 2 × 14 = 28.

From Argument principal theorem.

$$\int_y \frac{f'(z)}{f(z)} = 2\pi i(N - P)$$

Where N is number of roots in region y and P is number of pole.

Here from given function, Number of pole (P) = 0

$$\int_y \frac{f'(z)}{f(z)} = 2\pi i(28 - 0)$$

$= 56\pi i$

$\therefore$ a = 56

49. (5) $T(-1, 1, 1, 1) = x^2 + 2x^4$

$T(1, 2, 3, 4) = 1 - x^2$

$T(2, -1, -1, 0) = x^3 - x^4$

Now, T (–3, 5, 6, 6) = a (–1, 1, 1, 1) + b (1, 2, 3, 4) + c (2, –1, –1, 0)

T (–3, 5, 6, 6) = (–a + b + 2c, + 2b – c, a + 3b – c, a + 4b)

Making the form equal

–a + b + 2c = –3 ...(i)

a + 2b – c = 5 ...(ii)

a + 3b – c = 6 ...(iii)

a + 4b = 6 ...(iv)

On solving equation (i) to (iv), we get

a = 2, b = 1, c = –1

Now, We know that, $T(\alpha a) = \alpha T(a)$

$\therefore$ On transformation

$T(-3, 5, 6, 6) = 2(x^2 + 2x^4) + (1 - x^2) - (x^3 - x^4)$

$= 1 + x^2 - x^3 + 5x^4$

Hence, coefficient of x^4 = 5

51. (2) $\vec{F} = (x + 2y)e^z\hat{i} + \left(y.e^z + x^2\right)\hat{j} + y^2z\hat{k}$

Surface $S : x^2 + y^2 + z = 1, z \geq 0$

$z = 1 - x^2 - y^2$

By stroke's theorem,

$$\left|\iint_S \left(\nabla \times \vec{F}\right).\hat{n}ds\right| = \oint_S \vec{F}.\vec{dS}$$

Now on x-y-plane, z = 0

$\therefore x^2 + y^2 = 1$

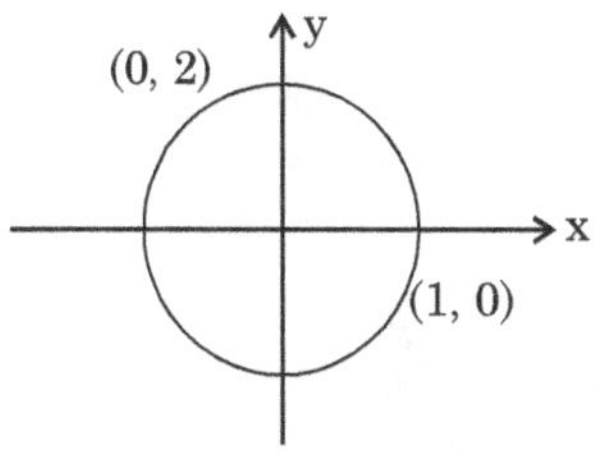

$$\therefore \left| \iint_S (\nabla \times \vec{F}).\hat{n}ds \right|$$

$$= \oint_C \left\{ (x+2y)e^z dx + (y.e^z + x^2).dy + y^2 z.dz \right\}$$

$$= \oint_C (x+2y)dx + (y+x^2).dy + 0$$

Here, C is region enclosed by circle of unit

Now, By Green's theorem.

$$\oint_C (x+2y)dx + (y+x^2).dy = \iint_R (2x-2)dx.dy$$

Taking $x = r \cos\theta$, $y = r \cos\theta$

$r \to (0, 1)$, $\theta \Rightarrow (0, 2\pi)$

$$\therefore \iint_R (2x-2)dxdy = 2\int_0^{2\pi}\int_0^1 (r\cos\theta - 1).rdx.d\theta$$

$= 2\pi = \propto\pi$

$\therefore \boxed{\propto = 2}$

52. (38) G is a non-cyclic group of order 57

$57 = 3 \times 19$

By Sylow's theorem

n_{19} = no. of Sylow 19 – Subgroup

then $n_{19} = 1 \pmod{19}$

$\Rightarrow n_{19} = 1$

Thus, there is only are Sylow 19-Subgroup of order 19.

As 19 is a prime number, then this is a cyclic subgroup.

Let $g \in G$,

$0(g) = 1$ or $0(g) = 3 = 57 - 19 = 38$.

53. From Taylor series expansion

$$f(x) = f(a) + \frac{f'(a)}{11}(x-a) + \frac{f''(a)}{21}(x-a)^2 + \frac{f'''(a)}{31}(x-a)^3 + \ldots +$$

Now, cofficient of $(x-1)^5$ is

$$\frac{f'''''(a)}{5!} = \frac{24}{5\times4\times3\times2\times1\times5}$$

$$= \boxed{0.04}$$

SOLVED PAPER - 2021

GENERAL APTITUDE

Q. 1 – 5 carry one mark each.

1. The ratio of boys to girls in a class is 7 to 3.

   Among the options below, an acceptable value for the total number of students in the class is:

   (A) 21 (B) 37

   (C) 50 (D) 73

2. A polygon is convex if, for every pair of points, P and Q belonging to the polygon, the line segment PQ lies completely inside or on the polygon.

   Which one of the following is <u>NOT</u> a convex polygon?

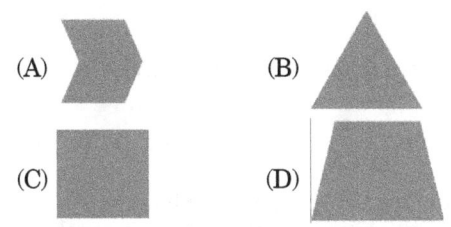

   (A)  (B) 

   (C)  (D) 

3. Consider the following sentences:

   (i) Everybody in the class is prepared for the exam.

   (ii) Babu invited Danish to his home because he enjoys playing chess.

   Which of the following is the CORRECT observation about the above two sentences?

   (A) (i) is grammatically correct and (ii) is unambiguous

   (B) (i) is grammatically incorrect and (ii) is unambiguous

   (C) (i) is grammatically correct and (ii) is ambiguous

   (D) (i) is grammatically incorrect and (ii) is ambiguous

4. A circular sheet of paper is folded along the lines in the directions shown. The paper, after being punched in the final folded state as shown and unfolded in the reverse order of folding, will look like ___________ .

   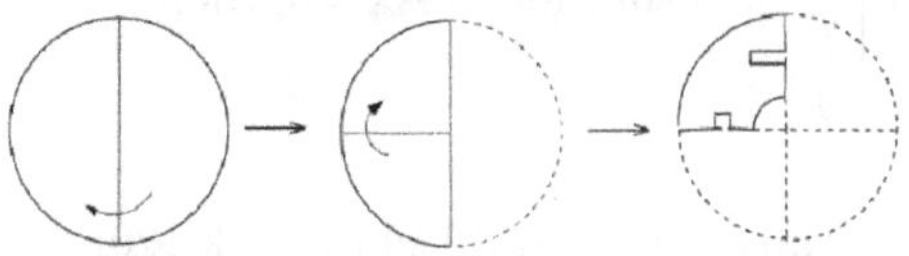

   (A) 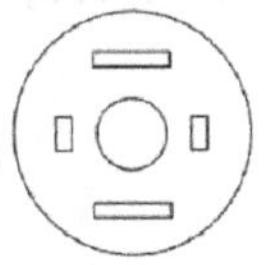 (B) 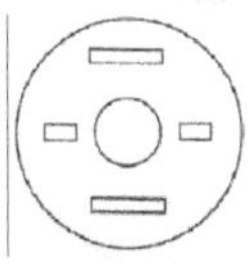

   (C) 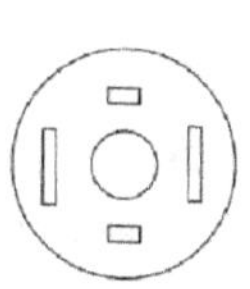 (D) 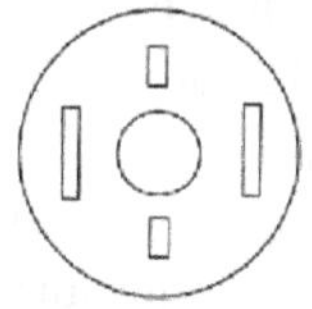

5. _______ is to surgery as writer is to _______

   Which one of the following options maintains a similar logical relation in the above sentence?

   (A) Plan, outline

   (B) Hospital, library

   (C) Doctor, book

   (D) Medicine, grammar

Q. 6 - 10 Multiple Choice Question (MCQ), carry TWO marks each

6. We have 2 rectangular sheets of paper, M and N, of dimensions 6 cm × 1 cm each. Sheet M is rolled to form an open cylinder by bringing the short edges of the sheet together. Sheet N is cut into equal square patches and assembled to form the largest possible closed cube. Assuming the ends of the cylinder are closed, the ratio of the volume of the cylinder to that of the cube is ___________

   (A) $\frac{\pi}{2}$ (B) $\frac{3}{\pi}$

   (C) $\frac{9}{\pi}$ (D) 3π

7.

Items	Cost (Rs.)	Profit %	Marked Price(Rs.)
P	5,400	-	5,860
Q	-	25	10,000

   Details of prices of two items P and Q are presented in the above table. The ratio of cost of item P to cost of item Q is 3:4. Discount is calculated as the difference between the marked price and the selling price. The profit percentage is calculated as the ratio of the difference between selling price and cost, to the cost (Profit % = $\frac{\text{Selling price} - \text{Cost}}{\text{Cost}} \times 100$).

   The discount on item Q, as a percentage of its marked price, is __________

   (A) 25 (B) 12.5

   (C) 10 (D) 5

8. There are five bags each containing identical sets of ten distinct chocolates. One chocolate is picked from each bag.

   The probability that at least two chocolates are identical is ____________

   (A) 0.3024 (B) 0.4235
   (C) 0.6976 (D) 0.8125

9. Given below are two statements 1 and 2, and two conclusions I and II.

   Statement 1: All bacteria are microorganisms.

   Statement 2: All pathogens are microorganisms.

   Conclusion I: Some pathogens are bacteria.

   Conclusion II: All pathogens are not bacteria.

   Based on the above statements and conclusions, which one of the following options is logically CORRECT?

   (A) Only conclusion I is correct
   (B) Only conclusion II is correct
   (C) Either conclusion I or II is correct.
   (D) Neither conclusion I nor II is correct.

10. Some people suggest anti-obesity measures (AOM) such as displaying calorie information in restaurant menus. Such measures sidestep addressing the core problems that cause obesity: poverty and income inequality.

    Which one of the following statements summarizes the passage?

    (A) The proposed AOM addresses the core problems that cause obesity.
    (B) If obesity reduces, poverty will naturally reduce, since obesity causes poverty.
    (C) AOM are addressing the core problems and are likely to succeed.
    (D) AOM are addressing the problem superficially.

MATHEMATICS

Q.1 - 14 Multiple Choice Question (MCQ), carry ONE mark each

1. Let A be a 3×4 matrix and B be a 4×3 matrix with real entries such that AB is non-singular. Consider the following statements:

   P: Nullity of A is 0.

   Q: BA is a non-singular matrix.

   Then

   (A) both P and Q are TRUE
   (B) P is TRUE and Q is FALSE
   (C) P is FALSE and Q is TRUE
   (D) both P and Q are FALSE

2. Let $f(z) = u(x, y) + i\,v(x, y)$ for $z = x + iy \in \mathbb{C}$, where x and y are real numbers, be a non-constant analytic function on the complex plane C. Let u_x, v_x and u_y, v_y denote the first order partial derivatives of $u(x, y) = \text{Re}(f(z))$ and $v(x, y) = \text{Im}(f(z))$ with respect to real variables x and y, respectively. Consider the following two functions defined on $\mathbb{C}$:

   $g_1(z) = u_x(x, y) - iu_y(x, y)$ for $z = x + iy \in \mathbb{C}$,

   $g_2(z) = v_x(x, y) + i\,v_y(x, y)$ for $z = x + iy \in \mathbb{C}$,

   Then

   (A) both $g_1(z)$ and $g_2(z)$ are analytic in $\mathbb{C}$
   (B) $g_1(z)$ is analytic in $\mathbb{C}$ and $g_2(z)$ is NOT analytic in $\mathbb{C}$
   (C) $g_1(z)$ is NOT analytic in $\mathbb{C}$ and $g_2(z)$ is analytic in $\mathbb{C}$
   (D) neither $g_1(z)$ nor $g_2(z)$ is analytic in $\mathbb{C}$

3. Let $T(z) = \dfrac{az+b}{cz+d}$, $ad - bc \neq 0$, be the Möbius transformation which maps the points $z_1 = 0$, $z_2 = -i$, $z_3 = \infty$ in the z-plane onto the points $w_1 = 10$, $w_2 = 5 - 5i$, $w_3 = 5 + 5i$ in the w-plane, respectively. Then the image of the set $S = \{z \in \mathbb{C} : \text{Re}(z) < 0\}$ under the map $w = T(z)$ is

   (A) $\{w \in \mathbb{C} : |w| < 5\}$
   (B) $\{w \in \mathbb{C} : |w| > 5\}$
   (C) $\{w \in \mathbb{C} : |w - 5| < 5\}$
   (D) $\{w \in \mathbb{C} : |w - 5| > 5\}$

4. Let R be the row reduced echelon form of a 4×4 real matrix A and let the third column of R be $\begin{bmatrix} 0 \\ 1 \\ 0 \\ 0 \end{bmatrix}$. Consider the following statements:

   P: If $\begin{bmatrix} \alpha \\ \beta \\ \gamma \\ 0 \end{bmatrix}$ is a solution of $Ax = 0$, then $\gamma = 0$.

   Q: For all $b \in \mathbb{R}^4$, $\text{rank}[A/b] = \text{rank}[R/0]$.

Then

(A) both P and Q are TRUE

(B) P is TRUE and Q is FALSE

(C) P is FALSE and Q is TRUE

(D) both P and Q are FALSE

5. The eigenvalues of the boundary value problem

$$\frac{d^2y}{dx^2} + \lambda y = 0, x \in (0, \pi), \lambda > 0,$$

$$y(0) = 0,\ y(\pi) - \frac{dy}{dx}(\pi) = 0,$$

are given by

(A) $\lambda = (n\pi)^2$, n = 1,2,3,...

(B) $\lambda = n^2$, n = 1,2,3,...

(C) $\lambda = k_n^2$, where k_n, n = 1,2,3,... are the roots of $k - \tan(k\pi) = 0$

(D) $\lambda = k_n^2$, where k_n, n = 1,2,3,... are the roots of $k + \tan(k\pi) = 0$

6. The family of surfaces given by $u = xy + f(x^2 - y^2)$, where f: $\mathbb{R} \to \mathbb{R}$ is a differentiable function, satisfies

(A) $y\frac{\partial u}{\partial x} + x\frac{\partial u}{\partial y} = x^2 + y^2$

(B) $x\frac{\partial u}{\partial x} + y\frac{\partial u}{\partial y} = x^2 + y^2$

(C) $y\frac{\partial u}{\partial x} + x\frac{\partial u}{\partial y} = x^2 - y^2$

(D) $x\frac{\partial u}{\partial x} + y\frac{\partial u}{\partial y} = x^2 - y^2$

7. The function u(x, t) satisfies the initial value problem

$$\frac{\partial^2 u}{\partial t^2} = \frac{\partial^2 u}{\partial x^2}, x \in \mathbb{R}, t > 0,$$

$$u(x, 0) = 0,\ \frac{\partial u}{\partial t}(x, 0) = 4xe^{-x^2}.$$

Then u(5, 5) is

(A) $1 - \frac{1}{e^{100}}$

(B) $1 - e^{100}$

(C) $1 - \frac{1}{e^{10}}$

(D) $1 - e^{10}$

8. Consider the fixed-point iteration

$x_{n+1} = \varphi(x_n)$, $n \geq 0$,

with $\varphi(x) = 3 + (x - 3)^3$, $x \in (2.5, 3.5)$, and the initial approximation $x_0 = 3.25$.

Then, the order of convergence of the fixed-point iteration method is

(A) 1 (B) 2

(C) 3 (D) 4

9. Let $\{e_n : n = 1, 2, 3,...\}$ be an orthonormal basis of a complex Hilbert space

H. Consider the following statements:

P: There exists a bounded linear functional $f : H \to \mathbb{C}$ such that $f(e_n) = \frac{1}{n}$ for n = 1,2,3,... .

Q: There exists a bounded linear functional $g : H \to \mathbb{C}$ such that $g(e_n) = \frac{1}{\sqrt{n}}$ for n = 1,2,3, ...

Then

(A) both P and Q are TRUE

(B) P is TRUE and Q is FALSE

(C) P is FALSE and Q is TRUE

(D) both P and Q are FALSE

10. Let f: $\left(\frac{-\pi}{2}, \frac{\pi}{2}\right) \to \mathbb{R}$ be given by $f(x) = \frac{\pi}{2} + x - \tan^{-1}x$. Consider the following statements:

P: $|f(x) - f(y)| < |x - y|$ for all $x, y \in \left(\frac{-\pi}{2}, \frac{\pi}{2}\right)$.

Q: f has a fixed point.

Then

(A) both P and Q are TRUE

(B) P is TRUE and Q is FALSE

(C) P is FALSE and Q is TRUE

(D) both P and Q are FALSE

11. Consider the following statements:

P: $d_1(x, y) = \left|\log\left(\frac{x}{y}\right)\right|$ is a metric on (0,1).

Q: $d_2(x, y) = \begin{cases} |x| + |y|, & \text{if } x \neq y, \\ 0, & \text{if } x = y, \end{cases}$ is a metric on (0,1).

Then

(A) both P and Q are TRUE

(B) P is TRUE and Q is FALSE

(C) P is FALSE and Q is TRUE

(D) both P and Q are FALSE

12. Let $f : \mathbb{R}^3 \to \mathbb{R}$ be a twice continuously differentiable scalar field such that $\operatorname{div}(\nabla f) = 6$.

Let S be the surface $x^2 + y^2 + z^2 = 1$ and $\hat{n}$ be unit outward normal to S. Then the value of

$\iint_S (\nabla f \cdot \hat{n})\, dS$ is

(A) 2π (B) 4π

(C) 6π (D) 8π

13. Consider the following statements:

P: Every compact metrizable topological space is separable.

Q: Every Hausdorff topology on a finite set is metrizable. Then

(A) both P and Q are TRUE

(B) P is TRUE and Q is FALSE

(C) P is FALSE and Q is TRUE

(D) both P and Q are FALSE

14. Consider the following topologies on the set $\mathbb{R}$ of all real numbers:

$T_1 = \{U \subset \mathbb{R} : 0 \notin U \text{ or } U = \mathbb{R}\}$,

$T_2 = \{U \subset \mathbb{R} : 0 \in U \text{ or } U = \varnothing\}$,

$T_3 = T_1 \cap T_2$.

Then the closure of the set $\{1\}$ in $(\mathbb{R}, T_3)$ is

(A) $\{1\}$

(B) $\{0,1\}$

(C) $\mathbb{R}$

(D) $\mathbb{R} \setminus \{0\}$

Q.15 - 25 Numerical Answer Type (NAT), carry ONE mark each.

15. Let $f : \mathbb{R}^2 \to \mathbb{R}$ be differentiable. Let $D_u f(0,0)$ and $D_v f(0,0)$ be the directional derivatives of f at (0,0) in the directions of the unit vectors $u = \left(\frac{1}{\sqrt{5}}, \frac{2}{\sqrt{5}}\right)$ and $v = \left(\frac{1}{\sqrt{2}}, \frac{-1}{\sqrt{2}}\right)$, respectively. If $D_u f(0,0) = \sqrt{5}$ and $D_v f(0,0) = \sqrt{2}$, then $\frac{\partial f}{\partial x}(0,0) + \frac{\partial f}{\partial y}(0,0)$ = ____________.

16. Let π denote the boundary of the square region R with vertices (0, 0), (2, 0), (2, 2) and (0, 2) oriented in the counter-clockwise direction. Then

$\oint_r (1 - y^2)\, dx + x\, dy =$ ____________.

17. The number of 5-Sylow subgroups in the symmetric group S_5 of degree 5 is ______.

18. Let I be the ideal generated by $x^2 + x + 1$ in the polynomial ring $R = \mathbb{Z}_3[x]$, where $\mathbb{Z}_3$ denotes the ring of integers modulo 3. Then the number of units in the quotient ring R/I is ____________.

19. Let $T: \mathbb{R}^3 \to \mathbb{R}^3$ be a linear transformation such that

$$T\left(\begin{bmatrix}1\\1\\1\end{bmatrix}\right) = \begin{bmatrix}1\\-1\\1\end{bmatrix}, T^2\left(\begin{bmatrix}1\\1\\1\end{bmatrix}\right) = \begin{bmatrix}1\\1\\1\end{bmatrix}, \text{ and } T^2\left(\begin{bmatrix}1\\1\\2\end{bmatrix}\right) = \begin{bmatrix}1\\1\\1\end{bmatrix}.$$

Then the rank of T is _________.

20. Let y(x) be the solution of the following initial value problem

$$x^2\frac{d^2y}{dx^2} - 4x\frac{dy}{dx} + 6y = 0,\ x > 0,$$

$$y(2) = 0,\ \frac{dy}{dx}(2) = 4.$$

Then y(4) = ____________.

21. Let

$f(x) = x^4 + 2x^3 - 11x^2 - 12x + 36$ for $x \in \mathbb{R}$.

The order of convergence of the Newton-Raphson method

$$x_{n+1} = x_n - \frac{f(x_n)}{f'(x_n)}, \quad n \geq 0,$$

with $x_0 = 2.1$, for finding the root $\alpha = 2$ of the equation f(x) = 0 is __________.

22. If the polynomial

$p(x) = \alpha + \beta(x+2) + \gamma(x+2)(x+1) + \delta(x+2)(x+1)x$ interpolates the data

x	-2	-1	0	1	2
f(x)	2	-1	8	5	-34

then $\alpha + \beta + \gamma + \delta =$ ___________.

23. Consider the Linear Programming Problem P:

Maximize $2x_1 + 3x_2$

subject to

$2x_1 + x_2 \leq 6,$

$-x_1 + x_2 \leq 1,$

$x_1 + x_2 \leq 3,$

$x_1 \geq 0$ and $x_2 \geq 0$.

Then the optimal value of the dual of P is equal to __________.

24. Consider the Linear Programming Problem P:

Minimize $2x_1 - 5x_2$

subject to

$2x_1 + 3x_2 + s_1 = 12,$

$-x_1 + x_2 + s_2 = 1,$

$-x_1 + 2x_2 + s_3 = 3,$

$x_1 \geq 0, x_2 \geq 0, s_1 \geq 0, s_2 \geq 0,$ and $s_3 \geq 0.$

If $\begin{bmatrix} x_1 \\ 2 \\ s_1 \\ s_2 \\ s_3 \end{bmatrix}$ is a basic feasible solution of P, then $x_1 + s_1 + s_2 + s_3 =$ ________.

25. Let H be a complex Hilbert space. Let $u, v \in H$ be such that $\langle u, v \rangle = 2$. Then

$$\frac{1}{2\pi}\int_0^{2\pi} \left\| u + e^{it}v \right\|^2 e^{it}\, dt = \_\_\_\_\_\_\_\_.$$

Q.26 - 43 Multiple Choice Question (MCQ), carry TWO mark each

26. Let $\mathbb{Z}$ denote the ring of integers. Consider the subring $R = \{a + b\sqrt{-17} : a, b \in \mathbb{Z}\}$ of the field $\mathbb{C}$ of complex numbers.

Consider the following statements:

P: $2 + \sqrt{-17}$ is an irreducible element.

Q: $2 + \sqrt{-17}$ is a prime element.

Then

(A) both P and Q are TRUE

(B) P is TRUE and Q is FALSE

(C) P is FALSE and Q is TRUE

(D) both P and Q are FALSE

27. Consider the second-order partial differential equation (PDE)

$$\frac{\partial^2 u}{\partial x^2} + 4\frac{\partial^2 u}{\partial x \partial y} + \left(x^2 + 4y^2\right)\frac{\partial^2 u}{\partial y^2} = \sin(x + y)$$

Consider the following statements:

P: The PDE is parabolic on the ellipse $\frac{x^2}{4} + y^2 = 1$.

Q: The PDE is hyperbolic inside the ellipse $\frac{x^2}{4} + y^2 = 1$.

Then

(A) both P and Q are TRUE

(B) P is TRUE and Q is FALSE

(C) P is FALSE and Q is TRUE

(D) both P and Q are FALSE

28. If u(x, y) is the solution of the Cauchy problem

$$x\frac{\partial u}{\partial x} + \frac{\partial u}{\partial y} = 1, \quad u(x, 0) = -x^2, x > 0,$$

then u(2,1) is equal to

(A) $1 - 2e^{-2}$ (B) $1 + 4e^{-2}$

(C) $1 - 4e^{-2}$ (D) $1 + 2e^{-2}$

29. Let y(t) be the solution of the initial value problem

$$\frac{d^2y}{dt^2} + a\frac{dy}{dt} + by = f(t), \; a > 0, b > 0, a \neq b,$$

$a^2 - 4b = 0,$

$$y(0) = 0, \; \frac{dy}{dt}(0) = 0,$$

obtained by the method of Laplace transform. Then

(A) $y(t) = \int_0^t \tau e^{\frac{-a\tau}{2}} f(t - \tau)\, d\tau$

(B) $y(t) = \int_0^t e^{\frac{-a\tau}{2}} f(t - \tau)\, d\tau$

(C) $y(t) = \int_0^t \tau e^{\frac{-b\tau}{2}} f(t - \tau)\, d\tau$

(D) $y(t) = \int_0^t e^{\frac{-b\tau}{2}} f(t - \tau)\, d\tau$

30. The critical point of the differential equation

$$\frac{d^2y}{dt^2} + 2\alpha\frac{dy}{dt} + \beta^2 y = 0, \alpha > \beta > 0, \text{ is a}$$

(A) node and is asymptotically stable

(B) spiral point and is asymptotically stable

(C) node and is unstable

(D) saddle point and is unstable

31. The initial value problem

$$\frac{dy}{dt} = f(t,y), \; t > 0, \; y(0) = 1,$$

where $f(t, y) = -10y$, is solved by the following Euler method

$y_{n+1} = y_n + h f(t_n, y_n), n \geq 0,$

with step-size h. Then $y_n \to 0$ as $n \to \infty$, provided

(A) $0 < h < 0.2$ (B) $0.3 < h < 0.4$

(C) $0.4 < h < 0.5$ (D) $0.5 < h < 0.55$

32. Consider the Linear Programming Problem P:

Maximize $c_1x_1 + c_2x_2$

subject to

$a_{11}x_1 + a_{12}x_2 \leq b_1$,

$a_{21}x_1 + a_{22}x_2 \leq b_2$,

$a_{31}x_1 + a_{32}x_2 \leq b_3$,

$x_1 \geq 0$ and $x_2 \geq 0$, where a_{ij}, b_i and c_j are real numbers (i = 1, 2, 3; j = 1, 2).

Let $\begin{bmatrix} p \\ q \end{bmatrix}$ be a feasible solution of P such that $p\,c_1 + q\,c_2 = 6$ and let all feasible solutions $\begin{bmatrix} x_1 \\ x_2 \end{bmatrix}$ of P satisfy $-5 \leq c_1x_1 + c_2x_2 \leq 12$.

Then, which one of the following statements is NOT true?

(A) P has an optimal solution

(B) The feasible region of P is a bounded set

(C) If $\begin{bmatrix} y_1 \\ y_2 \\ y_3 \end{bmatrix}$ is a feasible solution of the dual of P, then $b_1y_1 + b_2y_2 + b_3y_3 \geq 6$

(D) The dual of P has at least one feasible solution

33. Let $L^2[-1, 1]$ be the Hilbert space of real valued square integrable functions on $[-1, 1]$ equipped with the norm $\|f\| = \left(\int_{-1}^{1} |f(x)|^2\, dx\right)^{1/2}$.

Consider the subspace $M = \{f \in L^2[-1, 1] : \int_{-1}^{1} f(x)dx = 0\}$.

For $f(x) = x^2$, define $d = \inf\{\|f - g\| : g \in M\}$. Then

(A) $d = \frac{\sqrt{2}}{3}$ (B) $d = \frac{2}{3}$

(C) $d = \frac{3}{\sqrt{2}}$ (D) $d = \frac{3}{2}$

34. Let C[0,1] be the Banach space of real valued continuous functions on [0,1] equipped with the supremum norm. Define T: C[0,1] → C[0,1] by

$$(Tf)(x) = \int_0^x x f(t)\, dt.$$

Let R(T) denote the range space of T. Consider the following statements:

P: T is a bounded linear operator.

Q: T^{-1}: R(T) → C[0,1] exists and is bounded.

Then

(A) both P and Q are TRUE

(B) P is TRUE and Q is FALSE

(C) P is FALSE and Q is TRUE

(D) both P and Q are FALSE

35. Let $\ell^1 = \{x = (x(1), x(2), \ldots, x(n), \ldots) \mid \sum_{n=1}^{\infty} |x(n)| < \infty\}$ be the sequence space equipped with the norm $\|x\| = \sum_{n=1}^{\infty} |x(n)|$. Consider the subspace

$$X = \left\{x \in \ell^1 : \sum_{n=1}^{\infty} n|x(n)| < \infty\right\},$$

and the linear transformation $T: X \to \ell^1$ given by $(Tx)(n) = n\,x(n)$ for n = 1, 2, 3,... . Then

(A) T is closed but NOT bounded

(B) T is bounded

(C) T is neither closed nor bounded

(D) T^{-1} exists and is an open map

36. Let $f_n: [0,10] \to \mathbb{R}$ be given by $f_n(x) = nx^3 e^{-nx}$ for n = 1,2,3,... . Consider the following statements:

P: (f_n) is equicontinuous on [0,10].

Q: $\sum_{n=1}^{\infty} f_n$ does NOT converge uniformly on [0,10].

Then

(A) both P and Q are TRUE

(B) P is TRUE and Q is FALSE

(C) P is FALSE and Q is TRUE

(D) both P and Q are FALSE

37. Let f: $\mathbb{R}^2 \to \mathbb{R}$ be given by

$$f(x, y) = \begin{cases} \sqrt{x^2 + y^2}\, \sin(y^2/x) & \text{if } x \neq 0, \\ 0 & \text{if } x = 0. \end{cases}$$

Consider the following statements:

P: f is continuous at (0, 0) but f is NOT differentiable at (0, 0).

Q: The directional derivative $D_u f(0, 0)$ of f at (0, 0) exists in the direction of every unit vector $u \in \mathbb{R}^2$.

Then

(A) both P and Q are TRUE

(B) P is TRUE and Q is FALSE

(C) P is FALSE and Q is TRUE

(D) both P and Q are FALSE

38. Let V be the solid region in $\mathbb{R}^3$ bounded by the paraboloid $y = (x^2 + z^2)$ and the plane $y = 4$. Then the value of $\iiint_V 15\sqrt{x^2+z^2}\,dV$ is

(A) 128π (B) 64π
(C) 28π (D) 256π

39. Let $f: \mathbb{R}^2 \to \mathbb{R}$ be given by $f(x,y) = 4xy - 2x^2 - y^4$. Then f has
(A) a point of local maximum and a saddle point
(B) a point of local minimum and a saddle point
(C) a point of local maximum and a point of local minimum
(D) two saddle points

40. The equation $xy - z\log y + e^{xz} = 1$ can be solved in a neighborhood of the point (0,1,1) as $y = f(x,z)$ for some continuously differentiable function f. Then

(A) $\nabla f(0,1) = (2, 0)$ (B) $\nabla f(0,1) = (0, 2)$
(C) $\nabla f(0,1) = (0,1)$ (D) $\nabla f(0,1) = (1, 0)$

41. Consider the following topologies on the set $\mathbb{R}$ of all real numbers.

T_1 is the upper limit topology having all sets (a, b] as basis.

$T_2 = \{U \subset \mathbb{R} : \mathbb{R} \setminus U \text{ is finite}) \cup \{\phi\}$.

T_3 is the standard topology having all sets (a, b) as basis.

Then
(A) $T_2 \subset T_3 \subset T_1$
(B) $T_1 \subset T_2 \subset T_3$
(C) $T_3 \subset T_2 \subset T_1$
(D) $T_2 \subset T_1 \subset T_3$

42. Let $\mathbb{R}$ denote the set of all real numbers. Consider the following topological spaces.

$X_1 = (\mathbb{R}, T_1)$, where T_1 is the upper limit topology having all sets (a, b] as basis.

$X_2 = (\mathbb{R}, T_2)$, where $T_2 = \{U \subset \mathbb{R} : \mathbb{R} \setminus U \text{ is finite}\} \cup \{\phi\}$.

Then
(A) both X_1 and X_2 are connected
(B) X_1 is connected and X_2 is NOT connected
(C) X_1 is NOT connected and X_2 is connected
(D) neither X_1 nor X_2 is connected

43. Let $\langle \cdot,\cdot \rangle : \mathbb{R}^n \times \mathbb{R}^n \to \mathbb{R}$ be an inner product on the vector space $\mathbb{R}^n$ over $\mathbb{R}$. Consider the following statements:

P: $|\langle u,v\rangle| \le \frac{1}{2}(\langle u,u\rangle + \langle v,v\rangle)$ for all $u,v \in \mathbb{R}^n$.

Q: If $\langle u,v\rangle = \langle 2u,-v\rangle$ for all $v \in \mathbb{R}^n$, then $u = 0$.

Then
(A) both P and Q are TRUE
(B) P is TRUE and Q is FALSE
(C) P is FALSE and Q is TRUE
(D) both P and Q are FALSE

Q.44 - 55 Numerical Answer Type (NAT), carry TWO mark each

44. Let G be a group of order 5^4 with center having 5^2 elements. Then the number of conjugacy classes in G is _______.

45. Let F be a finite field and $F^\times$ be the group of all nonzero elements of F under multiplication. If $F^\times$ has a subgroup of order 17, then the smallest possible order of the field F is _______.

46. Let $R = \{z = x + iy \in \mathbb{C} : 0 < x < 1 \text{ and } -11\pi < y < 11\pi\}$ and π be the positively oriented boundary of R. Then the value of the integral $\frac{1}{2\pi i}\int_\pi \frac{e^z dz}{e^z - 2}$ is _________.

47. Let $D = \{z \in \mathbb{C} : |z| < 2\pi\}$ and $f: D \to \mathbb{C}$ be the function defined by

$$f(z) = \begin{cases} \dfrac{3z^2}{(1-\cos z)} & \text{if } z \neq 0 \\ 6 & \text{if } z = 0 \end{cases}$$

If $f(z) = \sum_{n=0}^{\infty} a_n z^n$ for $z \in D$, then $6a_2 =$ _______.

48. The number of zeroes (counting multiplicity) of $P(z) = 3z^5 + 2iz^2 + 7iz + 1$ in the annular region $\{z \in \mathbb{C} : 1 < |z| < 7\}$ is _______.

49. Let A be a square matrix such that $\det(xI - A) = x^4(x-1)^2(x-2)^3$, where det(M) denotes the determinant of a square matrix M.

If $\text{rank}(A^2) < \text{rank}(A^3) = \text{rank}(A^4)$, then the geometric multiplicity of the eigenvalue 0 of A is ___________.

50. If $y = \sum_{k=0}^{\infty} a_k x^k, (a_0 \neq 0)$ is the power series solution of the differential equation $\frac{d^2y}{dx^2} - 24x^2y = 0$, then $\frac{a_4}{a_0} =$ ________.

51. If $u(x, t) = Ae^{-t}\sin x$ solves the following initial boundary value problem

$$\frac{\partial u}{\partial t} = \frac{\partial^2 u}{\partial x^2}, 0 < x < \pi, t > 0,$$

$$u(0, t) = u(\pi, t) = 0, t > 0,$$

$$u(x, 0) = \begin{cases} 60, & 0 < x \le \frac{\pi}{2}, \\ 40, & \frac{\pi}{2} < x < \pi, \end{cases}$$

then $\pi A =$ ___________.

52. Let $V = \{p : p(x) = a_0 + a_1x + a_2x^2, a_0, a_1, a_2 \in \mathbb{R}\}$ be the vector space of all polynomials of degree at most 2 over the real field $\mathbb{R}$. Let $T : V \to V$ be the linear operator given by

$T(p) = (p(0) - p(1)) + (p(0) + p(1))\,x + p(0)\,x^2.$

Then the sum of the eigenvalues of T is__________.

53. The quadrature formula

$$\int_0^2 x f(x)\,dx \approx \alpha f(0) + \beta f(1) + \gamma f(2)$$

is exact for all polynomials of degree ≤ 2. Then $2\beta - \gamma$ = __________.

54. For each $x \in (0,1]$, consider the decimal representation $x = \cdot d_1d_2d_3 \ldots d_n \ldots$. Define $f: [0,1] \to \mathbb{R}$ by $f(x) = 0$ if x is rational and $f(x) = 18n$ if x is irrational, where n is the number of zeroes immediately after the decimal point up to the first nonzero digit in the decimal representation of x.

Then the Lebesgue integral $\int_0^1 f(x)\,dx$ = _____.

55. Let $\tilde{x} = \begin{bmatrix} 11/3 \\ 2/3 \\ 0 \end{bmatrix}$ be an optimal solution of the following Linear Programming Problem P:

Maximize $4x_1 + x_2 - 3x_3$

subject to

$2x_1 + 4x_2 + ax_3 \le 10,$

$x_1 - x_2 + bx_3 \le 3,$

$2x_1 + 3x_2 + 5x_3 \le 11,$

$x_1 \ge 0$, $x_2 \ge 0$ and $x_3 \ge 0$, where a, b are real numbers.

If $\tilde{y} = \begin{bmatrix} p \\ q \\ r \end{bmatrix}$ is an optimal solution of the dual of P, then $p + q + r$ = __________

(round off to two decimal places).

ANSWERS

General Aptitude

1. (C)	**2.** (A)	**3.** (C)	**4.** (A)	**5.** (C)	**6.** (C)	**7.** (C)	**8.** (C)	**9.** (D)	**10.** (D)

MATHEMATICS

1. (D)	**2.** (B)	**3.** (C)	**4.** (D)	**5.** (C)	**6.** (A)
7. (A)	**8.** (C)	**9.** (B)	**10.** (D)	**11.** (A)	**12.** (D)
13. (A)	**14.** (C)	**15.** 4 to 4	**16.** 12 to 12	**17.** 6 to 6	**18.** 6 to 6
19. 2 to 2	**20.** 32 to 32	**21.** 1 to 1	**22.** 1 to 1	**23.** 8 to 8	**24.** 5 to 5
25. 2 to 2	**26.** (B)	**27.** (A)	**28.** (C)	**29.** (A)	**30.** (A)
31. (A)	**32.** (B)	**33.** (A)	**34.** (B)	**35.** (A)	**36.** (B)
37. (A)	**38.** (A)	**39.** (A)	**40.** (A)	**41.** (A)	**42.** (C)
43. (A)	**44.** 145 to 145	**45.** 103 to 103	**46.** 11 to 11	**47.** 3 to 3	**48.** 4 to 4
49. 2 to 2	**50.** 2 to 2	**51.** 200 to 200	**52.** 1 to 1	**53.** 2 to 2	**54.** 2 to 2
55. 3.14 to 3.18					

EXPLANATIONS

GENERAL APTITUDE

1. Let us consider the number of boys = B
And total number of students = S
So, we have

$$\frac{B}{(S-B)} = \frac{7}{3}$$

$$B = \frac{7S}{10}$$

Thus, S must be multiple of 10. Hence, answer is 50.

2. If we choose two points P, Q such that P is the top-left corner and Q is the bottom left corner then the line joining P, Q will not lie on the polygon. Hence, option (a) is the correct answer.

3. Every body is prepared means they are ready for the exam, the second sentence does not clearly state whether babu will play with Danish or not.

Babu loves playing chess the does not means danish knows how to play chess. So statement

(i) is grammatically correct and

(ii) is ambiguous.

Statement (ii) is ambiguous because we do not know who enjoys playing chees, Babu or Danish.

So, statement (i) is grammatically correct.

Hence, option (c) is the correct answer.

4. Unforhed in reverse order of folding, it's look like option (a)

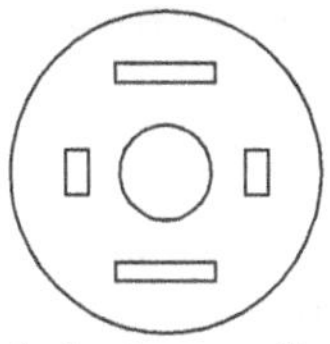

5. A doctor performs surgery just as a writer writes a book. It is the relation of person and skill.

6.

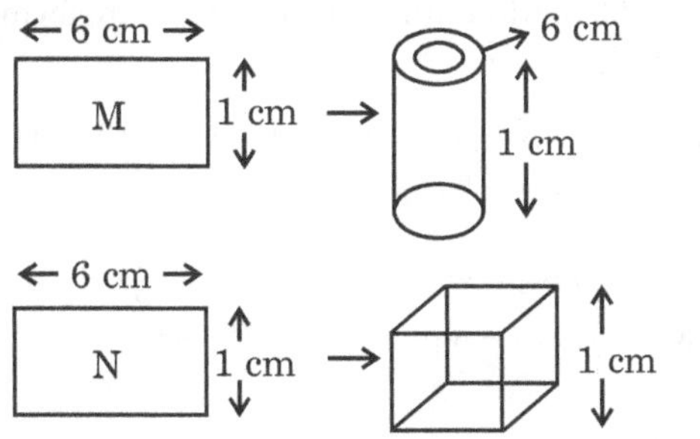

The circumference of lower circle $2\pi r = 6$

$$\Rightarrow r = \frac{3}{\pi}$$

Volume of a cylinder $= \pi r^2 h = \pi \times \frac{3}{\pi} \times \frac{3}{\pi} \times 1 = \frac{9}{\pi}$

Volume of a cube = $(1)^3$
So, request ratio

$$= \frac{\left(\frac{9}{\pi}\right)}{1} = \frac{9}{\pi}$$

Hence, option (c) is the correct answer.

7. As given that
$CP_p = 5400$
$MP_P = 5860$

Cost of Q$(CP_q) = \left(\frac{4}{3}\right) * CP_p = 7200$

Let, selling price (S.P) of Q = S

$$25 = \left(SP_q - 7200\right) * \frac{100}{7200}$$

$SP_q = 9000$
Discount on Q = $MP_q - SP_q = 10000 - 9000 = 1000$

$$\text{Discount\%} = \frac{1000}{10000} \times 100 = 10\%$$

Discount on SPq i.e. 1000 is 10% of marked price (MP_q) of Q i.e. 10, 000.
So, answer is 10%.
Hence, option (c) is the correct answer.

8. P (exactly 1 =) Probability that all the picked chocolates are different:

$$= \frac{(10 * 9 * 8 * 7 * 6)}{10^5} = 0.3024$$

Probability that at least two of the picked chocolates are identical:

$\Rightarrow 1 -$ (Probability that all the picked chocolates are different)

$\Rightarrow 1 - 0.3024 = 0.6976$

9.

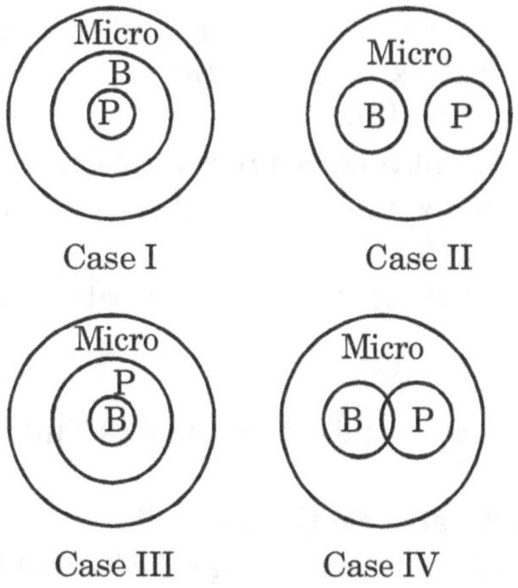

So, none of the two conclusions will satisfy all the 4 case. Hence, option (d) is the correct answer.

10. Superficially is the deciding key word which means apparently or seemingly.

As AOM are not addressing the core problems, they are superficial.

Superficial means shallow, cursory mean lacking in depth or solidity. Superficial implies a concern only with surface aspects or obvious features. A superficial analysis of the problem shallow is more generally derogatory in implying lack of depth in knowledge, reasoning, emotions, or character.

Hence, option (d) is the correct answer.

TECHNICAL APTITUDE

1. The following results are very essential to learn, in order to solve the question.

Result–1

Let A and B are two matrices such that product of matrices AB is defined, then $\rho(AB) \le \min\{\rho(A), \rho(B)\}$ i.e., $\rho(AB) \le \rho(A)$ and $\rho(AB) \le \rho(B)$.

Result–2

Let A be $n \times n$ matrix then

(i) $\rho(A) = n$ if and only if A is non-singular matrix.

(ii) $\rho(A) < n$ if and only if A is singular matrix.

Result–3

Let A be $m \times n$ matrix and B is $n \times p$ matrix then

$$\rho(AB) = \begin{cases} \rho(A) & \text{If } \rho(B) = n \\ \rho(B) & \text{If } \rho(A) = n \end{cases}$$

Result–4

If A is $m \times n$ matrix then $\rho(A) \le \min\{m, n\}$.

Result–5

Let $T : U \to V$ be a linear transformation and A is the matrix representation of linear transformation T then

rank (A) + Nullity (A) = number of columns of A.

Given A is 3×4 matrix and B is 4×3 matrix implies AB is 3×3 matrix.

Also given that AB is non-singular matrix implies $\rho(AB) = 3$.

So,

A is 3×4 matrix and $\rho(A) = 3$ implies Nullity (A) $= 4 - 3 = 1$.

Therefore, statement (P) is FALSE.

Since B is 4×3 matrix having rank 3 and A is 3×4 matrix having rank 3 implies BA is 4×4 matrix and $\rho(BA) = 3 < 4$.

$\Rightarrow$ BA is singular matrix.

Therefore, statement (Q) is also FALSE.

Hence, equation (3) is correct.

2. As given that

$g_1 = u_x - iu_y$

$U = u_x$, $V = -u_y$

$U_x = u_{xx}$, $V_y = -u_{yy}$

$$\begin{array}{l|l} U_x = V_y & U_y = u_{xy} \\ = u_{xx} = -u_{yy} & V_x = -u_{yx} \\ = u_{xx} + u_{yy} = 0 & -V_x = u_{yx} \end{array}$$

$U_y = -V_x \Leftrightarrow u_{xy} = u_{yx}$

$g_2 = V_x + iV_y$

$U = V_x$ $V = V_y$

$U_x = V_{xx}$ $V_y = V_{yy}$

$U_x \ne V_y$

$= V_{xx} = V_{yy}$

$= V_{xx} - V_{yy} = 0$

Hence, $g_1(z)$ is analytic in C and $g_2(z)$ is NOT analytic in C.

3. In order to solve the question it is essential to learn the following results.

Result–1: The linear fractional transformation $w = f(z)$ maps three distinct points z_1, z_2, z_3 uniquely into three distinct point w_1, w_2, w_3.

The map is determined by the equation

$$\frac{(w - w_1)(w_2 - w_3)}{(w - w_3)(w_2 - w_1)} = \frac{(z - z_1)(z_2 - z_3)}{(z - z_3)(z_2 - z_1)}$$

Result–2: Under linear fractional transformation $w = f(z)$, cross-ratio is invariant.

Given $T(z) = \dfrac{az + b}{cz + d}$, $ad - bc \ne 0$ be the mobius transformation (linear fractional transformation) such that

$$T\underbrace{(0)}_{z_1} = \underbrace{(10)}_{w_1},\ T\underbrace{(-i)}_{z_2} = \underbrace{(5 - 5i)}_{w_2},\ T\underbrace{(\infty)}_{w_3} = \underbrace{(5 - 5i)}_{w_3}$$

$$\frac{(w - w_1)(w_2 - w_3)}{(w - w_3)(w_2 - w_1)} = \frac{(z - z_1)(z_2 - z_3)}{(z - z_3)(z_2 - z_1)}$$

$$\frac{(w - 10)(5 - 5i - 5 - 5i)}{(w - 5 - 5i)(5 - 5i - 10)} = \frac{(z - 0)z_3\left(\dfrac{z_2}{z_3} - 1\right)}{z_3\left(\dfrac{z}{z_3} - 1\right)(-i - 0)}$$

$$\frac{(w-10)(-10i)}{(w-5-5i)(-5-5i)} = \frac{z(-1)}{(-1)(-i)}$$

$$\frac{(w-10)(-10i)}{(w-5-5i)(-5)(1+i)} = \frac{z}{(-i)} \times \frac{i}{i}$$

$$\frac{(2w-20)}{w-5-5i+wi-5i+5} = z$$

$$\frac{(2w-20)}{w-+wi-10i} = z$$

Now, take the set $\{w \in C : |w-5| < 5\}$.

It is a circle with center (5, 0) with radius 5.

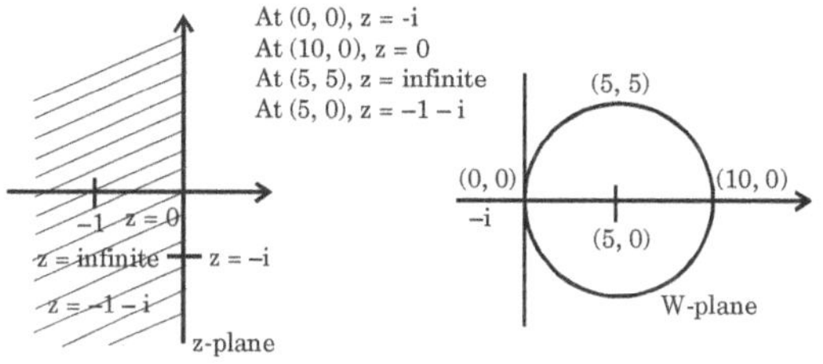

$\Rightarrow$ The image of the set $s = \{z \in C : Re(z) < 0\}$

under the map w = f(z) is $\{w \in C : |w-5| < 5\}$.

Hence, option (c) is true.

4. Let R be the row reduced echelon form of a 4 × 4 real matrix A and let the third column of

R be $\begin{bmatrix} 0 \\ 1 \\ 0 \\ 0 \end{bmatrix}$. Then which is true?

P) : If $\begin{bmatrix} \alpha \\ \beta \\ \gamma \\ 0 \end{bmatrix}$ is a so solution of Ax = 0, then $\gamma = 0$.

Q) : For all $b \in R^4$, rank [A | b] = rank [R | b].

For P

$$\begin{bmatrix} a & b & 0 & 0 \\ 0 & 0 & 1 & 0 \\ 0 & 0 & 0 & \phi \\ 0 & 0 & 0 & 0 \end{bmatrix} \begin{bmatrix} \alpha \\ \beta \\ \gamma \\ 0 \end{bmatrix} = \begin{bmatrix} 0 \\ 0 \\ 0 \\ 0 \end{bmatrix}$$

$a\alpha + b\beta + 0 + 0 = 0$

$0 + 0 + \gamma + 0 = 0$

$\Rightarrow \gamma = 0$

For Q

Rank of a matrix and rank of Row echelon matrix is same. So Q is also correct. So both the statements are true.

5. According to the Question,

$\lambda \neq 0$

$\lambda \neq -n^2$

$\lambda = -n^2$

$(D^2 + n^2)\, y = 0$

$\Rightarrow m^2 + n^2 = 0$

$\Rightarrow m = \pm ni$

$y = c_1 \cos nx + c_2 \sin nx$

$y(0) = 0 \Rightarrow c_1 = 0 \Rightarrow y = c_2 \sin nx$

$y'(x) = nc_2 \cos nx$

$y(\pi) - y'(\pi) = c_2 (\sin n\pi - n\cos n\pi) = 0$

$\therefore C_2 \neq 0,$

$\Rightarrow \sin n\pi - n \cos n\pi = 0$

$\Rightarrow \tan n\pi - n = 0$

$\Rightarrow n - \tan n\pi = 0$

Hence, when $\lambda = k_n^2$, where k_n, n = 1, 2, 3, ... are the roots of $k - \tan(k\pi) = 0$.

6. $u_x = y + f'(x^2 - y^2).2x \times y$

$u_y = x + f'(x^2 - y^2)(-2y) \times x$

$$\begin{aligned} yu_x &= y^2 + 2xyf'(x^2 - y^2) \\ + \quad xu_y &= x^2 - 2xyf'(x^2 - y^2) \\ \hline yu_x + xu_y &= x^2 + y^2 \end{aligned}$$

Hence, option (a) is the correct answer.

7. As given that,

$$\frac{\partial^2 u}{\partial t^2} = \frac{\partial^2 u}{\partial x^2}, \ x \in \mathbb{R}, \ t > 0,$$

$$\frac{\partial^2 u}{\partial t^2} = c^2 \frac{\partial^2 u}{\partial x^2} - c = 1$$

$$= u(x, 0) = f(x), \text{ and } \frac{\partial u}{\partial t} = g(x)$$

$$u(x,t) = \frac{1}{2}[f(x-ct) + f(x+ct)] + \frac{1}{2c}\int_{x-ct}^{x+ct} g(s)ds$$

$$= 0 + \frac{1}{2}\int 4xe^{-x^2} dx$$

$-x^2 = p$

$-2xdx = dp$

$2xdx = -dp$

$$= \int 2xe^{-x^2} dx = \left[-e^{-x^2}\right]_{x-t}^{(x+t)}$$

$$= -e^{(x+t)^2} + e^{(x-t)^2}$$

$= e^{-(x-t)^2} + e^{-(x+t)^2}$

$u(5,5) = e^0 - e^{-100} = 1 - \frac{1}{e^{100}}$

Hence, option (a) is correct answer.

8. As given that

$\phi(x) = x$

$3 + (x-3)^3 = x$

$x = 3$

$\phi(r) = r, \phi'(r) \neq 0$ (1)

$\phi'(r) = 0, \phi''(r) \neq 0$ (2)

$\phi'(r) = \phi''(r) \neq 0, \quad \phi'''(r) \neq 0$ (3)

$\phi(x) = 3 + (x-3)^3, \phi'(x) = 3(x-3)^2, \phi'(3) = 0$

$\phi''(x) = 6(x-3), \phi''(3) = 0,$

$\phi'''(x) = 6, \phi'''(3) \neq 0$

Hence, the order of convergence of the fixed-point iteration method is 3.

9. Bessel's inequality:

Let H be a Hilbert space, and suppose that $e_1, e_2 \ldots$ is an orthonormal sequence in H, then for any x in H, we have

$$\sum_{k=1}^{\infty} |(x, e_k)| \leq \|x\|^2 \qquad \ldots(1)$$

Riesz Representation Theorem:

Let H be a Hilbert space and f be continuous linear functional on H, then $\exists$ a unique vector v in H such that

$$f(x) = (x, v), \ \forall x \in x$$

$$\text{and } \|f\| = \|v\| \qquad \ldots.(2)$$

$$= g : H \frac{\text{Cont}}{\text{bdd}} C$$

$$g(e_n) = \frac{1}{\sqrt{n}}, \ n = 1, 2 \ldots$$

RRT: $\exists$ i v s.t

$g(x) = (x, v). \forall x$

$$\sum_{n=1}^{\infty} |(v, e_n)|^2 \leq \|v\|^2$$

$$\sum_{n=1}^{\infty} |(e_n, v)|^2 \leq \|v\|^2$$

$$\Rightarrow \sum_{n=1}^{\infty} |g(en)|^2 \leq \|v\|^2$$

$$\Rightarrow \sum_{n=1}^{\infty} \left(\frac{1}{\sqrt{n}}\right)^2 \leq \|v\|^2 \text{ (finite)}$$

$$\Rightarrow \sum_{n=1}^{\infty} \frac{1}{n} \leq \|v\|^2$$

$\Rightarrow Q \to$ false

$P \to g : H \quad$ bdd C

$$g(e_n) = \frac{1}{n}\left(\frac{1}{\sqrt{n}}\right)$$

$$g(x) = \sum_{n=1}^{\infty} (x, e_n) \frac{1}{n}$$

$g(e_n)$

$$= (e_n, e_n) \frac{1}{n}$$

$$g(e_n) = \frac{1}{n}$$

$\|g(x)\| \leq k\|n\|$

$$\|g(x)\| = \left\| \sum_{n=1}^{\infty} (x, e_n) \frac{1}{n} \right\|$$

$$\left| \sum_{n=1} \underset{a}{(x, e_n)} \underset{b}{\frac{1}{n}} \right|$$

$$\leq \sqrt{\underbrace{\sum_{n=1}^{\infty} |(x, en)|^2}_{\leq \|x\|^2} \underbrace{\sum_{n=1}^{\infty} \frac{1}{n^2}}_{R}}$$

$\leq A\|x\|$

$\|g(x)\| \leq A\|x\|$

$$g(e_n) = \frac{1}{n}$$

$g \to f'$.

Hence, option (b) is the correct answer.

11. For any $x.y \in (0, 1)$, $\left|\log\left(\frac{x}{y}\right)\right| \geq 0$

If $x = y \Rightarrow d(x, y) = \log\left[\frac{x}{y}\right) = \log(1) = 0$

$$\Rightarrow d_1(x, y) = \left|\log\left(\frac{x}{y}\right)\right| = \left|\log\left(\frac{y}{x}\right)^{-1}\right|$$

$$= \left|-\log\left(\frac{y}{x}\right)\right| = \left|\log\left(\frac{y}{x}\right)\right|$$

$$d_1(x, z) = \left|\log\left(\frac{x}{z}\right)\right| = |\log(x) - \log(z)$$

$$+ \log(y) - \log(y)|$$

$$= \left|\log\left(\frac{x}{y}\right) + \log\left(\frac{y}{z}\right)\right|$$

$$\therefore,\ d(x,y) = \begin{cases} |x|+|y|, & (x,y)=(0,0) \\ 0 & x = y \\ \geq 0 & (x,y)=(0,0) \end{cases}$$

$$\therefore\ d(y,x) = \begin{cases} (y)+(x), & (y,x)\neq(0,0) \\ 0, & y = x \end{cases}$$

$$= \begin{cases} |x(+|y|, & (x,y)\neq(0,0) \\ 0, & x = y \end{cases} = d(x,y)$$

$$d(x,y) = \begin{cases} \underbrace{|x|+|z|}, & x+2 \\ 0, & x = 2 \end{cases}$$

$$d(x,y) = \begin{cases} |x|+|y|, & x\neq y \\ 0, & x = y \end{cases}$$

$$d(y,z) = \begin{cases} |y|+|z|, & y\neq z \\ 0, & y = z \end{cases}$$

$d(x, z) < d(x, y) + d(y, z)$

$y = x = z$

$y \neq x = z \qquad y = x \neq z$

$y \neq x \neq z \qquad x = 4$

$|y| = |x|$

12. As we know that,

$$\iint_S F\ nds = \iiint_V \operatorname{div} f\, dv$$

$$\iint_S \nabla f\ n\ ds =$$

G.DT

$$\iiint_V \operatorname{div}(\nabla f)dv$$

$$= \iiint_V 6\,dv = 6\iiint_V 1dv$$

$$= 6\left\{\frac{4}{3}\pi(r)^3\right\} = 6\times\frac{4}{3}\pi = 8\pi$$

Then the value of $\iint(\nabla f.\hat{n})SdS$ is 8π

13. P: Compact + metrizable ⇒ seprable

Q: Finite + Hausdorff ⇒ metrizable

Every finite set compact & compact + Hausdroff ⇒ metrizable

Hence, both P and Q are True.

14. $\tau_1=\{USR\,|\,\underbrace{\{O\notin dU},\ U = IR\}$

$\tau_2=\{USR\,|\,\underbrace{\{O\}\in U}$ or $U = \phi\}$

If $U \leftarrow \tau_1 \cap \tau_2$

either $D\in U$ or $O\notin U$

Find closure of {1} in $\tau_1\cap\tau_2$

$\tau_3 = \tau_1\cap\tau_2 = \{\phi, IR\}$ indiscrete topology

$\overline{\{1\}} = \{1\}\cup(\{1\})$

$(U\cap A) - \{x\} \neq \phi \qquad \cup$ open set

$\cup \leftarrow \tau$

In topology, x is limit of {1}, if every open set (u) in $\tau\,\rho_1$

$x\in U$ intersect {1} in some point other that x itself

$x = 2$, $U = IR$

$U\cap\{1\} = \{IR\cap\{1\}\} - \{2\} = \{1\} \neq \phi$

$1R\cap\{0\} = \{0\} - |z\} \neq \{0\} + \phi$

$x = 1$

$\{IR\cap\{1\}\} - \{1\} = \{1\} - \{1\} = \phi$

$\Rightarrow (\{1\}) = 1R - \{1\}$

$\Rightarrow \overline{(\{1\})} = \{1\}\cup\{IR - \{1\}\}$

$= IR$

Hence, the closure of the set {1} in $\mathbb{R}$, T3 is $\mathbb{R}$.

15. $\vec{u} = \left(\frac{1}{\sqrt{5}}, \frac{2}{\sqrt{5}}\right)$, $\vec{v} = \left(\frac{1}{\sqrt{2}}, \frac{-1}{\sqrt{2}}\right)$, Let $f{:}IR^2 \to IR.f.1$

$D_u f(0, 0) = \sqrt{5}$, $D_v f(0, 0) = \sqrt{2}$ then find $f_x(0, 0) + f_y(0, 0)$

Let $a = f_x(0, 0)$, $b = f_y(0, 0)$

By deti of DD

$D_y f(0, 0) = \nabla f\vec{u}$ $D_v f(0, 0) = \nabla f.\vec{v}$

$D_u f(0, 0) < f_x(0, 0), f_y(0, 0) >$

$$< \frac{1}{\sqrt{5}}, \frac{2}{\sqrt{5}} > D_v f(0, 0)$$

$$= < f_x(0, 0)$$

$$\sqrt{5} =< a, b >< \frac{1}{\sqrt{5}}, \frac{2}{\sqrt{5}} >, D_v f(0, 0) < a, b) < \frac{1}{\sqrt{2}}, \frac{-1}{\sqrt{2}}$$

$$\sqrt{5} = \frac{a}{\sqrt{5}} + \frac{2b}{\sqrt{5}}, \qquad \sqrt{2} = \frac{a}{\sqrt{2}} - \frac{b}{\sqrt{2}}$$

$5 = a + 2b$ ...(i)$2 = (a - b) \times 2$

$4 = 2a - 2b$ ...(ii)

$5 = a + 2b$ ...(i)

$+4 = 2a - 2b$ ...(ii)

$9 = 3a$

$\Rightarrow a = 3$

$2 = 3 - b \Rightarrow b = 3 - 2 = 1$

$f(x)(0, 0) + fy(0, 0) = a + b = 3 + 1 = 4$

16. According to the question:

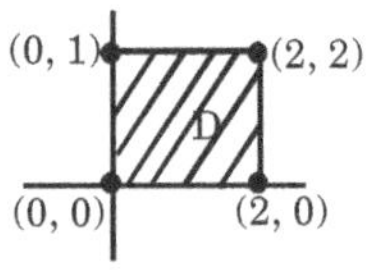

As we know that,

$$\int_C Mdx + Ndy = \iint_D \left(\frac{\partial N}{\partial x} - \frac{\partial M}{\partial y}\right)dxdy$$

$$= \iint_D 1-(0-2y)dxdy$$

$$= \int_0^2\int_0^2 (1+2y)dxdy = \int_0^2 (1+2y)(x)_0^2 dy$$

$$= \int_0^2 (1+2y)2dy$$

$$= 2\int_0^2 (1+2y)dy$$

$$= 2\left[y+y^2\right]_0^2$$

$= 2[2 + 4] = 2(6) = 12$

17. We look at the 5-Sylow subgroups of S_5. They will be of order 5 each as S_5 is of order 120 and 5 is the highest power of 5 dividing it. Hence, the only possibility for the 5-Sylow subgroups is to contain 5 cycles. Now, the number of r cycles of S_n is $\binom{n}{r}(r-1)!$. Hence there are 24 5-cycles. As each 5-Sylow subgroup consists of 4 cycles and as any two 5-Sylow subgroups has only identity in their intersection so number of 5-Sylow subgroups is $\frac{24}{4} = 6$.

19. Let T is a L.T

$T:1R^3$, such that

$T(1, 1, 1) = (1, -1, 1)$, $T^2(1, -1, 1) = (1, 1, 1)$,

$T^2(1, 1, 2) = (1, 1, 1)$

Then $\rho(T) = ?$

$T^2(1, 1, 1) = (1, 1, 1)$ $\left\{\begin{matrix}\lambda \text{ is e.value of A} \\ f(\lambda) \text{ is e.value } f(A)\end{matrix}\right\}$

$T^2(1, 1, 2) = (1, 1, 1)$

$\Rightarrow T^2$ is not 1 – 1

$\Rightarrow$ '0' is an e.value of T^2

$\Rightarrow$ '0' is an e.value of T

$\rho(T) < 3$ ...(1)

$T^2(1, 1, 1) = T(T(1, 1, 1))$

$= T(1, -1, 1) = (1, 1, 1)$

$T(1, 1, 1) = (1, -1, 1)$

$\rho(T) \leq 2 < 3$

$\rho(T) = 2$

Hence, then the rank of T is 2.

20. $\frac{x^2d^2y}{dx^2} - 4x\frac{dy}{dx} + 6y = 0 \qquad x > 0$

$y(2) = 0, \frac{dy}{dx}(2) = 4$

$[D(D - 1) - 4D + 6]y = 0$

$m^2 - 5m + 6 = 0$

$m^2 - 3m - 2m + 6 = 0$

$(m - 3)(m - 2) = 0 \qquad \Rightarrow m = 2, 3$

$y = C_1e^{2z} + C_2e^{3z} = C_1x^2 + C_2x^3$

$y(2) = 0, \quad 4C_1 + 8C_2 = 0$ ...(1)

$y'(2) = 4, \quad y' = 2C_1x + 3C_2x^2$

$y(2) = 4C_1 = 12C_2 = 4$ ...(2)

Solving (1) & (2)

$4C_2 = 4 \qquad \Rightarrow \boxed{C_2 = 1}$

$4C_1 + 8 = 0$

$\boxed{C_1 = -2}$

$\Rightarrow y = -2x^2 + x^3$

$y(4) = -2 \times 4^2 + 4^3 = 64 - 32 = 32$

21. $f(z) = 0$

$f'(x) = 4x^3 + 6x^2 - 22x - 12$

$f'(2) = 0$

$f''(x) = 12x^2 + 12x - 22$

$f''(2) = 50 \neq 0$

$\boxed{\text{2 is of multiplicity 2}}$ of f(x)

it is not simple root

so order of convergence = 1

so to change order of convergence multiply by multiplicty.

$$x_{n+1} = x_n - \frac{mf(x_n)}{f'(x_n)}$$

$$x_{n+1} = x_n - \frac{2f(x_n)}{f'(x_n)}$$

but in question multiplicty if (1) = (m)

so

$\boxed{\text{order of convergence} = 1}$

22. Here equipaced value of x

so use Newton's forward Interpolation formula

$y = y_0 + P\Delta y_0 +$

$$\frac{P(P-1)}{2!}\Delta^2 y_0 + \frac{P(P-1)(P-2)}{3!}\Delta^3 y_0 P + \ldots.. \quad ...(1)$$

Given polynomial:

x	f(x)	Δf(x)	$\Delta^2 f(x)$	$\Delta^3 f(x)$	$\Delta^4 f(x)$
–2	2	–3	12	–24	
–1	–1	9	–12	–24	0
0	8	–3	36		
1	5	–39			
2	–34				

$x_0 = -2, h = 1 \qquad P = \frac{x - x_0}{h} = x + 2$

From (1)

$$P(x) = 2 + (x + 2)(-3) + \frac{(x+2)(x+1)}{2!} \times 12 + \frac{(x+2)(x+1)x}{3!}(-24)$$

$P(x) = 2 + (-3)(x + 2) + 6(x + 2)(x + 1) + (-4)(x + 2)(x + 1)x$ by comparing

$\alpha = 2, \beta = -3, \gamma = 6, \delta = -4$

$\boxed{\alpha + \beta + \gamma + \delta = 1}$

23.

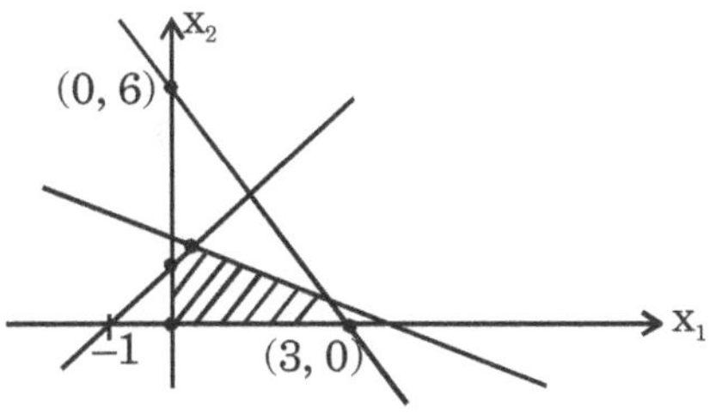

	$z = 2x_1 + 3x_2$
(1,2)	z = 8 (Max)
(0,0)	z = 0
(0,1)	z = 3
(3,0)	z = 6

Hence, max of Primal = 8

So, dual's max = 8

24. Here in objective function we have 2 variable and

we have 3 equation and $\text{B.F.S} = \begin{bmatrix} x_1 \\ x_2 \\ S_1 \\ S_2 \\ S_3 \end{bmatrix}$

here $x_2 = 2$

then the equations becomes

$2x_1 + S_1 = 6 \quad ...(1)$

$-x_1 + S_2 = -1 \quad ...(2)$

$-x_1 + S_3 = -1 \quad ...(3)$

from (2) and (3) $\boxed{S_2 = S_3}$

4 variables 3 equations

$n - m = 1$

One variable need to be zero

If w take $S_1 = 0$

then $\boxed{x_1 = 3}, \boxed{S_2 = S_3 = 2}$

then min z = 6

If we take $S_2 = 0$

then $x_1 = 1, S_3 = 0, S_1 = 4$

then min z = 2

$$\begin{bmatrix} x_1 \\ 2 \\ S_1 \\ S_2 \\ S_3 \end{bmatrix} = \begin{bmatrix} 1 \\ 2 \\ 4 \\ 0 \\ 0 \end{bmatrix} = \begin{bmatrix} 3 \\ 2 \\ 0 \\ 2 \\ 2 \end{bmatrix}$$

↑

B.F.S

$x_1 + S_1 + S_2 + S_3 = 1 + 4 + 0 + 0 = 5$

25. In order to solve the question, we have to learn the following results.

Result – 1:

Let V be a vector space over $\mathbb{C}$. Suppose to each pair of vectors, u, v ∈ V there is assigned a complex number, denoted by $\langle u, v \rangle$. This function si called a complex inner product on V if it satisfies the following axioms:

I. $\langle au_1 + bu_2, v\rangle = a\langle u_1, v\rangle + b\langle u_2, v\rangle$ (Linear property)

II. $\langle u, v\rangle = \overline{\langle u, v\rangle}$ (Conjugate symmetric property)

III. $\langle u, v\rangle \geq 0$ and $\langle u, v\rangle = 0$ if and only if u = 0. (Positive Definite Property)

Result – 2:

The non-negative number $\sqrt{\langle u, v\rangle} = \|u\|$ or $\langle u, v\rangle = \|u\|^2$ is called norm or length of u.

Result – 3:

An inner product space which is complete with respect to the norm induced by the inner product is called a Hilbert space.

Given H be a complex Hilbert space. Let, u, v $\in$ H be such that $\langle u, v\rangle = 2$.

Now, $\|u + e^{it}v\|^2 = \langle u + e^{it}v,\ u + e^{it}v\rangle$

$= \langle u, v\rangle + \overline{e^{it}}\langle u, v\rangle + e^{it}\langle u, v\rangle + e^{it}\overline{e^{it}}\langle u, v\rangle$

$= \|u\|^2 + 2e^{-it} + e^{it}\overline{\langle u, v\rangle} + \|v\|^2 \ \left(\because \langle u, v\rangle = \overline{\langle u, v\rangle}\right)$

$= \|u\|^2 + 2e^{-it} + 2e^{it} + \|v\|^2 \ \left(\because \langle v, u\rangle = \overline{\langle u, v\rangle} = 2\right)$

Therefore, $\frac{1}{2\pi}\int_0^{2\pi} \|u + e^{it}v\|^2 e^{it}dt$

$= \frac{1}{2\pi}\int_0^{2\pi}\left(\|u\|^2 + 2e^{-it} + 2e^{it} + \|v\|^2\right)e^{it}dt$

$= \frac{1}{2\pi}\left[\|u\|^2 \frac{e^{it}}{i}\Big|_0^{2\pi} + 2t\big|_0^{2\pi} + 2\frac{e^{i2t}}{2i}\Big|_0^{2\pi} + \|v\|^2\frac{e^{it}}{i}\Big|_0^{2\pi}\right]$

$= \frac{1}{2\pi}\left[\frac{\|u\|^2}{i}(e^{2\pi i} - e^0) + 2(2\pi - 0) + \frac{1}{i}(e^{4\pi i} - e^0) + \frac{\|v\|^2}{i}(e^{2\pi i} - e^0)\right]$

$= \frac{1}{2\pi}\cdot 4\pi = 2$. $\left(\because e^{2\pi i} = e^{4\pi i} = 1\right)$

Therefore, $\frac{1}{2\pi}\int_0^{2\pi} \|u + e^{it}v\|^2 e^{it}dt = 2$.

26. Defer-

Irreducible element:

Let R be an integral domain. A non-zero non-unit element $a \in R$ is said to be irreducible element of R if:

a = b·c, $b \in R$ and $c \in R$

Then either b is unit or c is unit.

Prime element: Let R be an integral domain. A non-zero non-unit element $c \in R$ is said to be prime element of R if:

c/a·b

Then, c/a or c/b

As per given question,

$R = \{a + b\sqrt{-17},\ a, b \in Z\}$ where Z = set of integers

$= \left\{a + \sqrt{17}ib,\ a, b \in Z\right\}$

Statement P: $2 + \sqrt{-17}$ is an irreducible element.

Let $\alpha = 2 + \sqrt{-17}$

$= 2 + \sqrt{17}i$

Then, $\alpha = \left(a + \sqrt{17}ib\right)\left(c + \sqrt{17}id\right)$ ... (1)

Taking conjugate on b/s, we get

$2 - \sqrt{17}i = \left(a - \sqrt{17}ib\right)\left(c - \sqrt{17}id\right)$ ... (2)

Multiply eq. (1) and (2), we get

$21 = (a^2 + 17b^2)(c^2 + 17d^2)$ ... (3)

Case I: If $a^2 + 17b^2 = 21$, then $c^2 + 17d^2 = 1$

$\Rightarrow c + \sqrt{-17}d$ is unit i.e. $c + \sqrt{17}id$ is unit.

Case II: If $c^2 + 17d^2 = 21$, then $a^2 + 17b^2 = 1$

$\Rightarrow a + \sqrt{17}id$ is unit.

Case III: If $a^2 + 17b^2 = 3$, then $c^2 + 17d^2 = 7$

Since a, b, c, d $\in Z$, then the case III is not possible.

From Case I and Case III, we get,

$\alpha = 2 + \sqrt{-17}$ is an irreducible element.

$\therefore$ Statement (P) is true.

Statement Q: $2 + \sqrt{-17}$ is a prime element.

Now, $(2 + \sqrt{-17})(2 - \sqrt{-17}) = 4 + 17 = 21 = 3 \times 7$

$\Rightarrow \frac{(2 + \sqrt{-17})}{21}$

$\Rightarrow \frac{2 + \sqrt{-17}}{3 \times 7}$ [But $2 + \sqrt{-17}$ not divide by 3 and 7]

If division is possible, suppose $\frac{2 + \sqrt{-17}}{3}$

$\Rightarrow \exists \in Z\left[\sqrt{-17}\right] = R$ s.t.

$3 = (2 + \sqrt{-17})\cdot c$

$= (2 + \sqrt{-17})(a + \sqrt{-17}b)$

$c = a + \sqrt{-17}\ b \in R$, where $a, b \in Z$

$= 2a + 2\sqrt{-17}b + \sqrt{-17}a - 17b$

$= (2a - 17b) + i\left(2\sqrt{17}b + \sqrt{17}a\right)$

$3 + i \times 0\sqrt{17} = (2a - 17b) + i\sqrt{17}(2b + a)$

Comparing real and imaginary values:

$3 + 2a - 17b$

and $2b + a = 0$

$2b = -a$

$2b = -a \Rightarrow a = -2b$

Now $3 = 2a - 17b$

$= -2 \times 2b - 17b$

$= -4b - 17b$

$= -21b$

$$b = -\frac{3}{21} = -\frac{1}{7} \notin Z$$

$$\text{and } a = -2b = -2 \times -\frac{1}{7} = \frac{2}{7} \notin Z$$

$2+\sqrt{-17}$ is not divisible by 3

So, our supposition is wrong.

Case II: $2+\sqrt{-17}/7$:

If possible, suppose $2+\sqrt{-17}/7$

Then $\exists$ $c = a+\sqrt{-17}\cdot b \in R,\ a, b \in Z$ s.t.

$7 = (2+\sqrt{-17})\cdot c$

$= (2+\sqrt{-17})(a+\sqrt{-17}b)$

$= (2a-17b)+i(2\sqrt{17}b+\sqrt{17}a)$

$7+i\times 0\sqrt{17} = (2a-17b)+i\sqrt{17}(2b+a)$

Comparing real and imaginary parts

$2a - 17b = 7$ ↓ $2(-2b) - 17b = 7$, $-4b - 17b = 7$, $-21b = 7$

$2b + a = 0$, $2b = -a$, $a = -2b$ ↓

$$b = -\frac{7}{21} = -\frac{1}{3} \notin Z \qquad a = -2\left(-\frac{1}{3}\right) = \frac{2}{3} \notin Z$$

$\boxed{2+\sqrt{-17}}$ is not divisible by 7.

So, our supposition is wrong.

So, $2+\sqrt{-17}$ is not divisible by 3 and 7.

$\therefore 2+\sqrt{-17}$ is not prime element.

Statement (Q) is false.

So, option (b) is correct.

27. It is required to learn the following result in order to solve the question.

Result:

Consider 2nd order linear partial differential equation $Au_{xx} + Bu_{xy} + Cu_{yy} + Du_x + Eu_y + Fu = G$, where A, B, C, D, E, F and G are in general functions of the independent variables x, y and constant. We can classify the 2nd order linear partial differential equation with the help of sign of $B^2 - 4AC$ i.e.,

$$B^2 - 4AC \begin{cases} > 0, & \text{then equation is hyperbolic.} \\ = 0, & \text{then equation is parabolic.} \\ < 0, & \text{then equation is elliptic.} \end{cases}$$

The given partial differential equation is

$$\frac{\partial^2 u}{\partial x^2} + 4\frac{\partial^2 u}{\partial x \partial y} + (x^2 + 4y^2)\frac{\partial^2 y}{\partial y^2} = \sin(x+y)$$

Here, $A = 1$, $B = 4$ and $C = (x^2 + 4y^2)$.

Now, $B^2 - 4AC = 16 - 4(x^2 + 4y^2)$

$= 16 - 4x^2 - 16y^2$.

Case 1: For Parabolic –

$B^2 - 4AC = 0, \Rightarrow 16 - 4x^2 - 16y^2 = 0,$

$$\Rightarrow 4x^2 + 16y^2 = 16, \Rightarrow x^2 + \frac{y^2}{4} = 0$$

Case 2: For Hyperbolic :–

$B^2 - 4AC > 0, \Rightarrow 16 - 4x^2 - 16y^2 > 0,$

$$\Rightarrow 4x^2 + 16y^2 < 16, \Rightarrow x^2 + \frac{y^2}{4} < 1.$$

Therefore, statement (Q) is TRUE.

Both the statements (P) and (Q) are TRUE.

Hence, option (a) is correct.

28. As given that

$$x\frac{\partial u}{\partial x} + \frac{\partial u}{\partial y} = 1, \quad u(x, 0) = x^2, x > 0$$

then $u(2, 1) = ?$

29. Applying L.T on (A)

$(s^2y(s) - sy(0) - y'(0)) + a[sy(s) - y(0)] + b\,y(s) = F(s)$

$(s^2 + as + b)\,y(s) - (a + s) \times 0 = F(s)$

$$y(s) = \frac{F(s)}{s^2 + as + b}; \qquad s = \frac{-a + \sqrt{a^2 - 4b}}{2}$$

$$= \frac{F(s)}{\left(s + \frac{a}{2}\right)^2}$$

Applying inverse L.T. = (Convolution theorem)

$$\boxed{y(t) = \int_0^1 e^{-\frac{a}{2}(\tau)} f(t-\tau)d\tau}$$

37. Given $f(x, y) = \sqrt{x^2+y^2}\sin\left(\frac{y^2}{x}\right)$

$$|f(x, y)-0| = \left|\sqrt{x^2+y^2}\cdot\sin\left(\frac{y^2}{x}\right)\right| \le \left|\sqrt{x^2+y^2}\right| < \epsilon$$

By definition of continuity, choose $\delta = \epsilon$

$\therefore$ For this $\delta(=\epsilon)$, we have

$|f(x, y) - f(0, 0)| < \epsilon$,

whenever $\sqrt{x^2+y^2} < \delta$.

$|f(x, y) - f(a, b)| < \epsilon$ where $\boxed{|x|, |y| < \delta}$

$\boxed{\sqrt{x^2+y^2}} < \delta$

f is differentiable at (a, b) if

$f(a + h, b + k) - f(a, b) = A\cdot h + B\cdot k + h\cdot\phi(h,k) + k\psi(h, k)$, where

$A = f_x(a, b), B = f_y(a, b)$, tis$(x, y) \to (0, 0), \phi, \Psi \to 0$

$f(a+h, b+k) - f(a,b) = A\cdot h + B\cdot k$

$$+ \sqrt{h^2+k^2}\cdot\phi(h,k),$$

where $\lim\limits_{(h,k)\to(0,0)} \phi(h,k) = 0$

$f(h,k) - f(0,0) = f_x(0, 0)\cdot h + f_y(0, 0)\cdot k$

$$+ \sqrt{h^2+k^2}\cdot\phi(h, k)$$

$$f_x(0,0) = \lim_{h\to 0}\frac{f(0+h,0)-f(0,0)}{h}$$

$$= \lim_{h\to 0}\frac{\sqrt{h^2+0}\cdot\sin\left(\frac{\partial}{h}\right)}{h} = 0$$

$$f_y(0,0) = \lim_{k\to 0}\frac{f(0,0+k)-f(0,0)}{k} = \lim_{k\to 0}\frac{0-0}{k} = 0$$

$$\therefore f(h,k) - f(0,0) = 0\cdot h + 0\cdot k + \sqrt{h^2+k^2}\cdot\phi(h,k)$$

$$\sqrt{h^2+k^2}\cdot\sin\left(\frac{k^2}{h}\right) = \sqrt{h^2+k^2}\cdot\phi(h, k)$$

$$\phi(h, k) = \sin\left(\frac{k^2}{h}\right)$$

$$\lim_{(h,k)\to(0,0)}\phi(h,k) = \lim_{(h,k)\to(0,0)}\sin\left(\frac{k^2}{h}\right)$$

Put $h = mk^2$

$$\Rightarrow \lim_{(h,k)\to(0,0)}\phi(h,k) = \lim_{(h,k)\to(0,0)}\sin\left(\frac{k^2}{h}\right)$$

$$= \lim_{k\to 0}\sin\left(\frac{k^2}{mk^2}\right)$$

$$= \sin\left(\frac{1}{m}\right) \ne 0 \text{ for each m.}$$

For directional derivative, in the direction $\bar{a} = (a_1, a_2)$

$$DF_a(x,y) = \lim_{h\to 0}\frac{f(x+ha_1, y+ha_2) - f(x,y)}{h}$$

$$DF_a(0,0) = \lim_{h\to 0}\frac{f(ha_1, ha_2) - f(0,0)}{h}$$

$$= \lim_{h\to 0}\frac{\sqrt{h^2a_1^2 + h^2a_2^2}\cdot\sin\left(\frac{h^2a_2^2}{ha_1}\right) - 0}{h}$$

$$= \lim_{h\to 0}\frac{h\sqrt{a_1^2 + a_2^2}\cdot\sin\left(\frac{ha_2^2}{a_1}\right)}{h}$$

$$= \lim_{h\to 0} 1\sin\left(\frac{ha_2^2}{a_1}\right) = 0$$

Hence, both P and Q are TRUE.

39. $f(xy) = 4xy - 2x^2 - y^4 + 1$

$f_x = 0 = 4y - 4x$

$f_y = 0 = 4x - 4y^3$

$f_{xx} = -4$

$f_{yy} = 12y^2$

$y = x$

$x = y^3$

$y = y^3$

$y - y^3 = 0$

$y(1 - y^2) = 0$

$y(1 + y)(1 - y) = 0$

$y = 0, 1, -1$

So, the coordinates are

(0, 0)(1, 1)(–1, 1)

Hence, a point of local maximum and only one saddle point.

41. As given that

τ_1 = upper limit topology

τ_2 = finite compliment top

τ_3 = standard topology

$\tau_1 \le \tau_3 \le \tau_3$

$= \{(a, b) \mid a, b, \in IR\}$

$= \{\cap \leq IR \mid \upsilon$ is either finite or ϕ, or $IR\}$

$= \{(a, b)/ a, b \in IR\}$

$U^c = (-\infty, 0) \cup (0, \infty)$

τ_1 τ_2

$A = [0, \infty]$ $B = [-2, \infty]$

Every finite set is closed in IR

If U^c is finite $\Rightarrow$ U is open in IR under u – f

$\Rightarrow$ every open set τ_2 is open in τ_1

Hence, $T2 \subset T3 \subset T1$

44. As per given question,

G = Group of order $(5)^4$

Then, $O(G) = (5)^4$

Z(G) = Center of group G of order $(5)^2$

i.e. $O(Z(G)) = (5)^2$

Now, $O(G) = (5)^4$ and $O(Z(G)) = (5)^2$

$\Rightarrow O(Z(G)) \neq O(G)$

$\Rightarrow$ G is non-abelian

($\because$ G is abelian iff $G = Z(G)$)

By dass equation, $O(G) = \sum_{a \in G} \frac{O(G)}{O(N(a))}$,

$$O(G) = \sum_{a \in Z(G)} \frac{O(G)}{O(N(a))} + \sum_{a \in Z(G)} \frac{O(G)}{O(N(a))}$$

Result- If G is a finite group and $a \in G$

Then $O(d(a)) = \frac{O(G)}{O(N(a))}$

$N(a) = \{x \in G \mid xa = ax\}$ = Normaliser of $a \in G$

$$\therefore O(d(a)) = \frac{OG}{O(N(a))} = \frac{(5)^4}{(5)^3} = 5, \text{ where } a \notin Z(G)$$

Now, $O(G) = (5)^2 + \sum_{a \notin Z(G)} \frac{O(G)}{O(N(a))}$

$$(5)^4 = (5)^2 + \underbrace{5 + 5 + \cdots + 5}_{k\text{-times}}$$

$(5)^4 - (5)^2 = 5k$

$$R = \frac{(5)^4 - (5)^2}{5} = 5^3 - 5 = 125 - 5 = 120$$

Also,

$$O(G) = \sum_{a \in Z(G)} \frac{O(G)}{O(N(a))} + \sum_{a \notin Z(G)} \frac{O(G)}{O(N(a))}$$

$$= \sum_{a \in Z(G)} O(l(a)) + \sum_{a \notin Z(G)} O(d(a))$$

$$= \underbrace{1 + 1 + 1 + \cdots + 1}_{25\text{-times}} + \underbrace{5 + 5 + \cdots + 5}_{120\text{-times}}$$

($\because$ If G is a group and $a \in Z(G)$)

Then $l(a) = \{a\}$ i.e. $O(l(a) = 1)$

Total number of conjugacy classes in G

$= 25 + 120 = \boxed{145}$

45. We have to remember the following results, in order to solve the question.

Result – 1

IF F is a finite field of order p^n, where p is prime number and n is positive integer then

$F \simeq GF(p^n)$.

Result – 2

If F is a finite field then $(F^{\times}, .)$ is a cyclic group of order $|F| - 1$.

i.e., $(F^{\times}, .) \simeq Z\ |F| - 1$.

Result – 3

If G be a finite group and H be a subgroup of G then $|H|\ |G|$.

It is known as Lagrange's theorem.

Given F is a finite field implies

$F \simeq GF(p^n)$ implies $|F| = p^n$.

Also, $(F^{\times}, .) \simeq Z_{|F|-1}$ implies $|F^{\times}| = |F| - 1$

$= p^n - 1$.

Since $F^{\times}$ has a subgroup of order 17 implies 17 $|F^{\times}|$ implies $17 \mid p^n - 1$.

Now, $17\ |p^n - 1| \Rightarrow p^n - 1 = 17k$, where $k \in Z$.

$\Rightarrow p^n = 17k + 1$, where $k \in Z$.

If we take k = 15, we have $p^n = 256 = 2^8$.

Therefore, smallest possible order of the filed F $= 2^8 = 256$.

46.

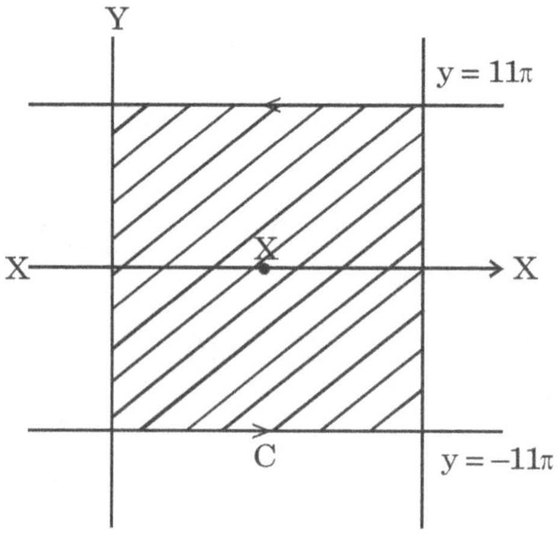

$e^z - 2 = 0$

$e^z = 2$

$\Rightarrow z = \log 2$

$z = \log 2 + 2n \;\forall\; n$

$\int \frac{f(z)}{(z-z_0)} dz = 2\pi i f(z_0)$

$\int f(z) dv = 2\pi i \sum \text{Res}$

$$\left[\begin{array}{l} \because \frac{1}{2\pi i}\int_s \frac{e^z}{e^e - 2} dz \\ = \frac{1}{2\pi i}\{2\pi i\{\text{Res}(f, \log 2)\}\} \end{array}\right]$$

$$\lim_{z\to\log 2} \frac{(z-\log 2)}{e^z - 2}\left(\frac{0}{0}\right)$$

$$= \lim_{z\to\log 2} \frac{(z-\log 2)e^z + e^z(1)}{e^z}$$

$$= \lim \frac{e^{10g^2}}{e^{\log 2}} = 1$$

47. Let $D = \{z \in \mathbb{C} \mid |z| < 2\pi\}$

$f: D \to \mathbb{C}$ be function

$$f(z) = \begin{cases} \frac{3z^2}{1-\cos z} & z \neq 0 \\ 6 & z = 0 \end{cases}$$

$$\text{if } (z) = \sum_{n=0}^{\infty} a_n z^n \text{ for } z \in 0$$

Then $6a_2 = ?$

for $z \neq D$, $f(z) = \frac{3z^2}{1-\cos z}$

$$= \frac{3z^2}{1-\left(1-\frac{z^2}{2!}+\frac{z^4}{4!}+\ldots\right)}$$

$$= \frac{3z^2}{\frac{z^2}{2!}-\frac{z^4}{4!}+\ldots}$$

$$= \frac{3}{\frac{1}{2!}-\frac{z^2}{4!}+\ldots}$$

$$= \left[\frac{3}{1-\frac{z^2}{12}+\ldots}\right]$$

$$= \frac{2\times 3}{\left(1-\frac{z^2}{12}+\ldots\right)}$$

$$= 6\left(1-\frac{z^2}{12}+\ldots\right)^{-1}$$

$$= 6\left[1-\frac{z^2}{12}+\ldots\right]$$

$$= 6 + \frac{1}{2}z^2 + \ldots$$

Hence,

$$6a_2 = 6 \times \frac{1}{2} = 3$$

48.

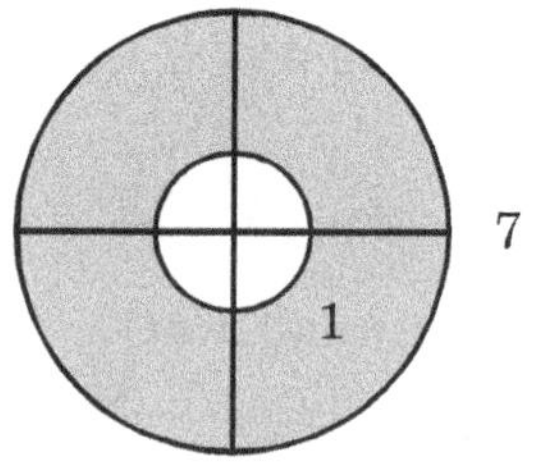

Rouche's theorem

f, g anlytic function D

st $|f(z)| \leq |g(z)| \;\forall\; z \in D$

Then $N_g = N_{f+g}$

Let $g(z) = 7iz$, $f(z) = 3z^5 + iz^2 + 1$

$|f(z)| = |3z^5 + iz^2 + 1| \leq 3|z|^5 + |z|^2 + 1$

$= 3 + 1 + 1 = 5 < 7 = |g(z)|$

$|f(z)| \leq |g(z)| \;\forall z \in D$

So, P(z) has 1 root in $|z| = 1$

On $|z| = 7$, $P(z) = 3z^5 + iz^2 + 7iz + 1$

$g(z) = 3z^5$, $f(z) = iz^2 + 7; z + 1$

$|f(z)| = |iz^2 + 7i + 1| \leq |z|^2 + 7|z| + 1$

$= 49 + 49 + 1 = 99$

$|g(z)| = |3z^5|$

$= 3|z|^5$

$= 3|z|^5$

$= 3(7)^5$

$|f(z)| = |iz^2 + 7iz + 1| \le |z|^2 + 7|z| + 1$

$= 49 + 49 + 1 = 99 \le 3(7)^5$

$|f(z)| \le |g(z)| \ \forall\ z \in 0 = \{z \,|\, |z| = 7\}$

P(z) has 5 root's $|z| = 7$

Hence, the number of zeroes is $5 - 1 = 4$.

52. Let $V = \{P(n) \,|\, a_1 + a_1x + a_2n^2 \,|$ be a vector space of polynomial of degree at most 2.

T is L.T. defined by $T(P(x)) = P((0) - P(1)) + (P(n)n + P(0)n^2$

Then sum of e values of matrix of transformation T__

$B = \{1, x, x^2\}$

$T(1) = 0 + (1 + 1)x + x^2 = \underline{2x + x^2}$

$T(x) = (-1) + x$

$T(x^2) = -1 + x$

$$T = \begin{bmatrix} 0 & -1 & -1 \\ 2 & 1 & 1 \\ 1 & 0 & 0 \end{bmatrix}$$

Sum of e. value = tr(T) = 1

53. $\int_0^2 x.xdx = \alpha(0) + \beta(1) + \gamma(2)$

$$\Rightarrow \left[\frac{x^3}{3}\right]_0^2 = \beta + 2\gamma$$

$$\Rightarrow \frac{8}{3} = \beta + 2\gamma$$

$\Rightarrow 3\beta + 6\gamma = 8 \qquad ...(1)$

$$\left[\frac{x^4}{4}\right]_0^2 = \alpha(0) + \beta(1) + \gamma(4)$$

$$\Rightarrow \frac{4 \times \cancel{4}}{\cancel{4}} = \beta + 4\gamma \Rightarrow \beta + 4\gamma + 4 \ ...(2)$$

$3\beta + 6\gamma = 8$

$3\beta + 12\gamma = 12$

$$\begin{array}{r} \cancel{3}\beta + 6\gamma = 8 \\ 3\cancel{\beta} + 12\gamma = 12 \\ \hline -6\gamma = -4 \end{array} \qquad \Rightarrow \beta + \frac{8}{3} = 4$$

$$\boxed{\gamma = \frac{2}{3}} \qquad \Rightarrow \beta = 4 - \frac{8}{3} = \frac{4}{3}$$

$$\beta = \frac{4}{3}, \ \gamma = \frac{2}{3}$$

So, $\frac{\text{Boys}}{\text{Girls}} = \frac{7}{3}$

Boys are in multiple of 7

Girls are in multiple of 3.

Total Boys + Girls should be in multiple of 10.

Hence, ans. 50

CPSIA information can be obtained
at www.ICGtesting.com
Printed in the USA
BVHW011757281022
650563BV00012B/892

9 789391 061227